GREENWICH

*An Architectural History of
the Royal Hospital for Seamen
and the Queen's House*

JOHN BOLD

with contributions by

PETER GUILLERY, PAUL PATTISON, ANN ROBEY AND JOANNA SMITH

architectural graphics by

ANDREW DONALD

photographs by

DEREK KENDALL

Published for

THE PAUL MELLON CENTRE
FOR STUDIES IN BRITISH ART

by

YALE UNIVERSITY PRESS
NEW HAVEN AND LONDON

in association with

ENGLISH HERITAGE

Designed by Gillian Malpass

Printed in Singapore

Library of Congress Cataloging-in-Publication Data

Bold, John.
Greenwich: an architectural history of the Royal Hospital for Seamen
and the Queen's House /
John Bold with contributions by Peter Guillery . . . [et al.];
architectural graphics by Andrew Donald;
photographs by Derek Kendall.
p. cm.
Includes bibliographical references and index.
ISBN 0-300-08397-1 (cloth : alk. paper)
1. Greenwich (London, England) – Buildings, structures, etc.
2. Greenwich (London, England.) Queen's House.
3. Royal Hospital for Seamen at Greenwich.
4. Architecture – England – London.
I. Title.
DA690.G83 B65 2000   942.1′62 – dc21   00-42880

A catalogue record for this book is available from
The British Library

Frontispiece The King William Building of the Royal Hospital for Seamen
viewed from the colonnade of the Queen Mary Building

Contents

Acknowledgements

The survey on which this book is based was begun in 1995 for the Royal Commission on the Historical Monuments of England, when the future of the Royal Naval College, formerly the Royal Hospital for Seamen, was in doubt. I am grateful to the Secretary of the Royal Commission, Tom Hassall, and the Chairman, Lord Faringdon, for encouraging the project. I am grateful also to English Heritage for its support of the publication, following merger with the Royal Commission in 1999.

A venture of this nature is collaborative, and I am greatly indebted to the following former colleagues at the Commission for their major contributions to research and writing: Paul Pattison (the landscape and the archaeology of the site), Ann Robey (the Queen's House), Joanna Smith (nineteenth-century improvements, the Infirmary and the buildings of the Seamen's Hospital Society), Peter Guillery (the Royal Naval Asylum, Greenwich Hospital School and the National Maritime Museum). I am grateful also to Charlotte Bradbeer for her early research into the Royal Observatory, to Tara Draper for work on statues and for a very great deal of bureaucratic and word-processing assistance, aided and abetted by Nick Seal, and to June Warrington for her very assiduous guidance with illustrations. I am indebted to the photographic staff of the Commission, particularly to Derek Kendall for most of the new photography, to Mike Seaforth for printing it, and also to Sid Barker and Amanda Polito. Many other current and former colleagues have contributed information, illustrations and insights: David Birks, Roger Bowdler, Wayne Cocroft, Stephen Croad, Lesley Fraser, John Greenacombe, Gordon Higgott, Ian Leith, Kathryn Morrison, Stephen Porter, Treve Rosoman, Colin Thom, Mike Turner, the staff of the National Monuments Record and of the former English Heritage drawings collection. A particular debt is owed to Andrew Donald, whose development drawings of the main buildings on the site have not only made the complex architectural history so much easier to understand but have also, as a result of his difficult questions, contributed significantly to improving the clarity of the text.

During the period of investigation and research we have worked closely with the staff of the Royal Naval College who kindly facilitated access. Our thanks go in particular to Commander I. R. Wellesley-Harding RN and to Commander J. M. C. Maugham RN, and to the property managers Chris Andrews and John Snipe. At the National Maritime Museum we have received invaluable help from Tina Chambers, Geraldine Charles, Marilla Fletcher, Alan Giddings, Gillian Hutchinson, Roger Quarm, David Taylor and Pieter van der Merwe, and from the authors of the history of the institution, Beverley Butler and Kevin Littlewood. In Greenwich Park we have been assisted by the current and former superintendents Joseph Woodcock and Jim Buttress, and by the staff of the Royal Parks Agency. We wish to thank also the owners and occupiers of houses on the site for their generosity in allowing access: Mr and Mrs Browne-Clayton, Don and Janet Gott, the Revd Canon Giles Harcourt, Sue and Peter McNeil, James Plummer, Nick and Pat Roberts and Arthur and Joan Wilkes. We have profited from advice and information provided by architects who have worked on the site: Gordon Bowyer, Clive England of Thomas Ford and Partners, Diane Haigh of Allies and Morrison, Harold Yexley and particularly Trevor Dannatt and David Johnson, who are the architects for the continuing restoration of the buildings of the former Royal Hospital. We wish to thank those archaeologists and consultants who have worked on the history of the landscape and buildings and have freely contributed information: Julian Bowsher, Gustav Milne, Julian Munby, Geoffrey Parnell, Harvey van Sickle and Land Use Consultants. We are grateful also, for diverse contributions, to Kerry Bristol, Libby Brooks, Edward Chaney, Monique Chatenet, Bridget Cherry, Anthony Cross, Erica Davies, Alice Dugdale, Gabriele Finaldi, Simon Grant, George Knox, Mary Mills, Benjamin Mouton, Charles Newton, Alan Pearsall, Adam Perkins, Andrew Saint, Jeff Saward, Christine Stevenson and Lady Susan Sykes. We thank Tom Hiney, Chaplain of the Royal Hospital at Chelsea, for permitting photography of the altarpiece in the chapel.

In addition to the institutions mentioned above and those noted in the acknowledgements for illustrations, we should like to thank Greenwich Hospital, the University of Greenwich and the Greenwich Foundation for the Royal Naval College for their continuing encouragement, and the staff of the following libraries and collections for enabling a prolonged programme of research: the British Architectural Library, the British Library, Greenwich Local History Library (particularly Frances Ward and Julian Watson), the London Library, the National Library of Wales, the Public Record Office, the Library of the Royal Greenwich Observatory, Cambridge, the Library of the Royal Society of Medicine, the Wellcome Institute Library and the libraries of the Courtauld and Warburg Institutes.

All historians of the architecture of the seventeenth and eighteenth centuries in England are indebted to Howard Colvin, John Harris and John Newman. My thanks to them may be classed as general rather than specific, for helpful remarks and important texts. Kerry Downes has been both general and specific, and I am grateful to him for his insights, his example, his critical reading of this text and his continuing, invaluable guidance.

The publication of this book has been made possible by a fruitful collaboration between English Heritage, Yale University Press and the Paul Mellon Centre for Studies in British Art: I am very grateful for all their efforts to Robin Taylor of English Heritage, to Gillian Malpass and Elizabeth McWilliams of Yale University Press and to Yale's text editor, Ruth Thackeray.

My final thanks go to my former colleague at the Royal Commission on the Historical Monuments of England, Nicholas Cooper, who was the first person I spoke to on my first day of employment at the Commission and ever after has shared his knowledge and provided constructive criticism and encouragement, on sites and in the office, teaching me more than I thought I needed to know. It is a pleasure to thank him here for his support.

John Bold
London, June 2000

Author's Note

Chapter 1 sketches the context of the site: the development of the landscape and the shift from the private to the public use of Greenwich Park, with its associated water conduits, buildings and monuments, and the building of Wren's Flamsteed House. In order to make the chapters on the significant individual buildings as self-contained as possible, with the aim of achieving a balance between a thematic and a chronological account, there is some minor repetition of some aspects of the building history. The nomenclature of the few specified rooms in the former Royal Hospital follows that used during the final years of the Royal Naval College.

All the architectural plans made for this book are oriented with north (the River Thames) at the bottom of the page, as this is the direction from which the buildings customarily have been depicted. The scale bars on the plans are given in both imperial and metric measurements; the text cites measurements in imperial only.

The numbering of storeys follows the British convention: the first floor is the one above the ground floor.

The fundamental documentary sources for the history of the Hospital and the Queen's House are the papers in the Public Record Office (PRO) and the drawings in the National Maritime Museum (NMM) and in the British Architectural Library (BAL). Transcripts of documents and fuller building accounts and plans are available in the project archive in the National Monuments Record (NMR).

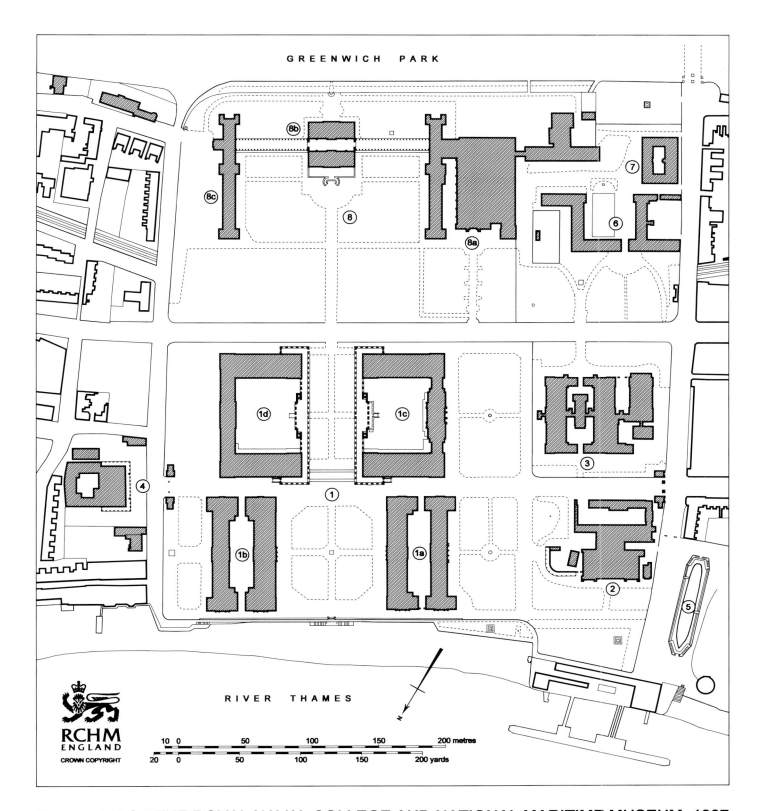

SITE PLAN OF THE ROYAL NAVAL COLLEGE AND NATIONAL MARITIME MUSEUM, 1997

1 The Royal Naval College: 1a King Charles Building
                                       1b Queen Anne Building
                                       1c King William Building
                                       1d Queen Mary Building

2 Pepys Building

3 Dreadnought Seamen's Hospital

4 Trafalgar Quarters

5 The *Cutty Sark*

6 Devonport House (former Nurses' Home)

7 Devonport Pathological Laboratory

8 The National Maritime Museum: 8a West Wings, with Neptune Hall
                                                8b The Queen's House
                                                8c East Wing

1   Site plan of the Royal Naval College and the National Maritime Museum, 1997.

2 Aerial view of Greenwich from the north, 1996.

Introduction

The Royal Hospital for Seamen . . . ; the park, the queen's house, the Observatory on the hill . . . are all things so well known, they need no particular description.

Daniel Defoe[1]

The former Royal Hospital for Seamen, the Queen's House and the buildings of the National Maritime Museum comprise one of the most important and inspiring ensembles in European architecture, fit to stand comparison with the masterworks of Renaissance Paris or Baroque Rome, yet quintessentially English. Set within a picturesque landscape which marries art with contrived nature as it stretches from the River Thames to the top of the hill in Greenwich Park (fig. 2), a view memorably rendered by Canaletto, the buildings include work of European importance by architects of the highest quality at the height of their powers – Inigo Jones, John Webb, Sir Christopher Wren and Nicholas Hawksmoor – and in Sir James Thornhill's Painted Hall the most effective piece of Baroque decorative painting in England.

The Hospital, founded in 1694, ceased to function as such in 1869, serving from 1873 as the Royal Naval College. A government decision in 1995 to move service training facilities elsewhere gave rise to uncertainty about the long-term future of the site and prompted the Royal Commission on the Historical Monuments of England to ignore Daniel Defoe and begin its investigation into the buildings and their history. Following an earlier, analytical survey of the archaeology of Greenwich Park, which had enabled the RCHME to contribute in 1994 to the Royal Parks Review, there was an opportunity to participate in a discussion, addressing the evolution of buildings within a landscape, at a time of considerable public concern about their future.

The granting of World Heritage Site status to historic 'Maritime Greenwich' in December 1997 alleviated that concern and gave an international imprimatur to a site of enormous architectural, archaeological and historical significance. This formal acknowledgement of heritage value set the seal on a process which arguably had begun with the establishment of the National Maritime Museum over sixty years earlier and with the associated construction of the idea of 'Maritime Greenwich'.[2] In 1998 the future of the buildings of the former Naval College was secured when responsibility for them was passed to the Greenwich Foundation, a charitable management trust specifically formed to ensure that they and their surroundings are cared for and used appropriately and that public access is maintained. The principal buildings are now being occupied by the University of Greenwich, with the exception of the King Charles Building, next to the river, which will be home to Trinity College of Music from 2001.

Although the RCHME survey began with the park and the College, it rapidly became apparent that the Queen's House, which sits mid-way between the two and forms the centrepiece of the National Maritime Museum, could not be excluded. Not only is this a building which fully exposes the fallacy that everything that there is to be known about well-known buildings has been discovered already; the Queen's House also was fundamental to the development of the buildings and landscape as a whole, with a significance far in excess of its modest size. It was built as an adjunct to a royal palace which does not survive, the Hospital being built over much of its site. The existence of the palace is acknowledged here but no attempt has been made to re-create the demolished and superseded. It has anyway been well described by others.[3] The buildings of the Royal Observatory on top of the hill are mentioned only in passing. They present a long and complex story, much of which, together with that of the development of the instruments they housed, has been described elsewhere.[4]

In the seventeenth century, Greenwich and neighbouring Deptford together formed the largest urban centre in England after London itself, Norwich and Bristol, with about 15,000 inhabitants: 'a centre of population, of naval construction, and of royal influence, commanding the most important waterway in England and the nation's main highways to Europe'.[5] This book, based on physical investigation and documentary research, attempts to describe the evolution of a remarkable ensemble within that larger settlement, the surviving buildings and landscape of one of the finest and best-loved prospects in Europe which has been a place of resort for Londoners for over 200 years: the former Royal Hospital for Seamen, the Queen's House and National Maritime Museum, and Greenwich Park (fig. 1).

3   The view from Island Gardens.

Chapter 1

GREENWICH PARK: LANDSCAPE AND BUILDINGS

The View from Island Gardens

There are two views of Greenwich: the one from the top of the hill, looking towards the River Thames and the City of London, exploited by landscape painters since the seventeenth century; and the one from the Isle of Dogs on the north bank of the river which in the early eighteenth century became the recognised point from which to depict Sir Christopher Wren's Royal Hospital for Seamen (fig. 3). This is where Canaletto stood in the early 1750s to sketch (and later paint in his studio) the just-completed buildings, the riverscape before and the landscape beyond. As a result of the creation of Island Gardens as a municipal park in 1895, protecting the site directly opposite the Hospital from future development,[1] it is still possible to stand close to where Canaletto stood and to see much of what he saw. In so doing one is able to recognise both the magnificence of the prospect and the genius of the artist.

In order to see London it is necessary either to climb a hill or a building, or to go to the waterside where the river affords wide panoramas.[2] With a sensibility attuned to the view of the Bacino di San Marco, Canaletto sought its equivalent in London, finding in the broad sweep of the Thames an opportunity to look from east to west and north to south, and back again, in paintings of St Paul's, Westminster and Whitehall, from the terrace of Somerset House, and in views of Chelsea and Greenwich.[3] Of his two views of Greenwich, it is the slightly larger one in the National Maritime Museum – *Greenwich Hospital from the North Bank of the Thames* – painted around 1752–3, which is the better known and the more artful in its deceptions (fig. 4).[4]

The Isle of Dogs is a tongue of reclaimed land, protected from flooding for several centuries by a bank or wall, of earth and chalk.[5] Rising up to 15 feet high, this broad, flat-topped wall would have provided Canaletto with an ideal point from which to depict the Hospital. Later visitors had the benefit of a viewing platform (fig. 5).[6] The elevated viewpoint, which would have put the horizon at eye-level, contrasts strongly with the view which is possible today. From our lower position, the river appears to be wider and the buildings further away, the breadth of the river accentuated by its emptiness in contrast with an almost Venetian level of activity depicted by Canaletto; this was a river where Celia Fiennes in 1697 had seen '100 saile of shipps pass by in a morning which is one of the finest sights that is' (fig. 6).[7] The concentra-

tion of this riverine activity towards the centre of the painting, together with the framing masts to left and right, leads the eye directly into the grand courtyard of the Hospital, towards the twin drums and domes of the Queen Mary and King William blocks, which Canaletto made relatively slimmer and taller in order to frame the view of the landscape to the south. He made the central openings of the river fronts of the Queen Anne and King Charles Buildings identical, which no doubt ideally they should be, but are not; yet he masterfully succeeded in having the best of both worlds by casting one into the deep shadow which renders it realistic. The angle of the King Charles Building to the right of the painting has been shifted by some 10 degrees in order to open up the central space, giving a wide-angle view and accentuating the funnelling effect of the avenue leading to Inigo Jones's Queen's House which the artist pushed back and reduced in size, possibly the consequence of using an optical instrument. Beyond are trees, the hill and the Observatory: the omnipresent backdrop of Greenwich Park. The subtle shifts in the angles of view and in the architectural elements transform this painting from being a static record of things seen into an evocation of a landscape of feelings. Canaletto here transformed a well-known and much admired scene into a landscape which mingles objective observation with memory and desire. There could be no finer advertisement than this painting for the delights of the buildings and landscape at Greenwich, which in their broad particulars have not substantially changed since Canaletto created this memorable image of the Royal Hospital for Seamen, the Queen's House, the Royal Observatory and the park. Visitors now may still feel at one with Horace Walpole who, writing in 1755, observed: 'Would you believe I had never been in Greenwich Park? I never had, and am transported. Even the glories of Richmond and Twickenham hide their diminished rays'.[8]

Early Remains

In the mid-eighteenth century, the park had long been a royal preserve, with restricted access, but it had a much longer history of occupation and use. In the first century AD, a small shrine was constructed on a prominent mound on the edge of the escarpment overlooking the Thames, mid-way between the two major trade routes to and from London, the most important city of a

4   Canaletto, *Greenwich Hospital from the North Bank of the Thames*, c.1752–3 (NMM).

5   J. W. Carmichael, *Greenwich from the North-east*, 19 October 1848 (NMM).

Roman province – the river itself and to the south the major road (the present A2) which links London with Canterbury and Dover (fig. 7). This shrine, possibly built in two phases, was in all probability a temple of Romano-Celtic type. A tiny fragment, in a railed enclosure, is all that remains. Such temples were simply built, comprising a small shrine or *cella*, of square, round or polygonal form, of two-storey height but open to the roof, rising above a surrounding ambulatory. Many are known in England, often asso-ciated with native deities to which Roman attributes might also be assigned. The portable finds from the shrine included pottery, a remarkable number of coins, part of a near life-size statue, window glass, some rare fragments of decorative ivory and parts of monumental inscriptions, including one which may have been to Aesculapius, the god of healing (fig. 8). The coins covered all four centuries of the Romano-British period and there were also some older, Republican issues.[9]

The next evidence for the occupation and use of what was to become the park is the survival of a radially planned group of thirty-one Anglo-Saxon burial mounds, from an original total of about forty, dating from the sixth century (fig. 9). Positioned on a small natural rise, a short distance south-west of the Royal Observatory, this barrow cemetery shares with other surviving examples of the type in south-eastern England a siting which is locally prominent but not visible from a great distance. Whereas prehistoric barrows tended to dominate the skyline, the Greenwich mounds were set back over 320 feet from the edge of the escarpment and so were not visible from the river. Roughly circular, the mounds are up to 33 feet in diameter and 2 feet 3 inches high, with the appearance of inverted saucers, although originally they might have had rather steeper sides and flatter tops than their current rounded profiles suggest (fig. 10).[10] Almost all of the barrows show signs of disturbance from the excavations carried out in the early eighteenth century by a park keeper named Hearne and then in 1784 by James Douglas.[11] Each of the

barrows opened by Douglas covered a single, primary inhumation burial. The bones had decomposed almost completely because of the acid subsoil, but grave goods were present in several, confirming that the burials were pagan rather than Christian. The finds, customary in Anglo-Saxon burials, included spearheads, knives, a shield boss, glass beads, woollen textiles and linen, as well as fragments of iron and decayed wood which could have been the remains of wooden coffins.[12]

The Medieval Park

The Roman and Anglo-Saxon monuments are isolated survivals from land-use patterns which are largely unknown. The park itself is a late medieval creation and today it comprises 190 acres of landscape, most of which has been carefully manicured since the early fifteenth century. It may have formed part of a recognisable estate as far back as the eighth century, when it was said to have

6   The Royal Naval College, formerly Greenwich Hospital, and the Queen's House from the north, 1996.

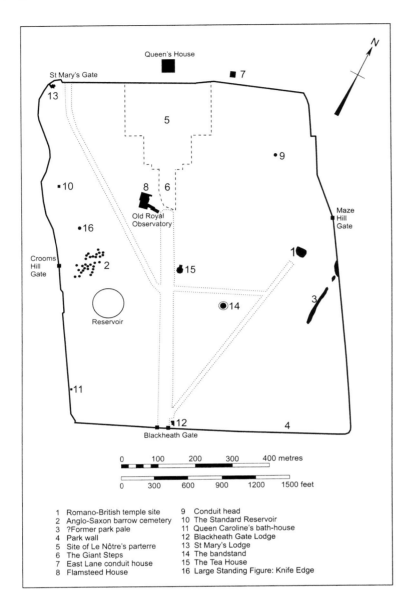

9 One of the burial mounds in the Anglo-Saxon cemetery in Greenwich Park.

10 Barrows in Greenwich Park (*Illustrated London News*, 29 June 1844).

1 Romano-British temple site
2 Anglo-Saxon barrow cemetery
3 ?Former park pale
4 Park wall
5 Site of Le Nôtre's parterre
6 The Giant Steps
7 East Lane conduit house
8 Flamsteed House
9 Conduit head
10 The Standard Reservoir
11 Queen Caroline's bath-house
12 Blackheath Gate Lodge
13 St Mary's Lodge
14 The bandstand
15 The Tea House
16 Large Standing Figure: Knife Edge

7 (*above*) Plan of Greenwich Park, showing the locations of the principal archaeological features.

8 A decorated ivory from the site of a Roman temple in Greenwich Park (BM).

been a royal possession of King Alfred, granted before the Conquest to the Abbot of Ghent.[13] It remained with the Abbey as the manor of East Greenwich until 1414, when it was returned to the Crown, and then passed in 1426 to Humphrey, Duke of Gloucester. In 1433 he obtained a licence to enclose the land as a park, to build in it a tower of stone and mortar (see chapter 2), and to crenellate his new riverside house.[14] The latter structure was partly revealed during excavations as a substantial brick building almost 70 feet long and 28 feet wide and at least two storeys high.[15] It stood close to the Thames, within its own enclosure and courts, possibly with a garden to the south which certainly was there by 1447.[16] Duke Humphrey's house subsequently was engulfed by the north, riverside range of the Tudor palace of Placentia, the remains

11 Anon., *Greenwich from the Park showing the Tudor Palace, c.*1615 (NMM).

of which lie underneath the north side of the Grand Square of the Royal Hospital.[17]

The park was created from land of mixed value. The grant of 1433 referred to 'pasture, wood, heath, virses and gorse'.[18] It is probable that the most useful land lay at the foot of the escarpment, near the river, while the remainder, open heathland with pockets of scrub, gorse and bracken, was taken from the plateau of Blackheath. The nature of the terrain – the east-west escarpment, with two combes, each with plentiful water from springs, cutting into the scarp edge – and the variety of vegetation made this an ideal park for hunting, offering good cover for deer and other game. As originally enclosed, the park was surrounded by a pale, a close timber fence crowning an earthen bank, probably with a ditch, carefully maintained to prevent the egress of deer. A short length of the fence is shown on an anonymous painting of around 1615,[19] not long before it was replaced by a brick wall, and a low earthwork bank might still be detected in the south-eastern part of the park, north of the Flower Garden (fig. 11).[20]

The Park Wall

The first part of the seventeenth century saw considerable activity in the park and royal palace with the creation of new gardens and the building of the Queen's House. In order to reinforce the privacy of the royal domain, between 1619 and 1624 the park pale was levelled and replaced with a brick wall, 12 feet high and over 2 miles long, at a cost of £2001.[21] It has been assumed that the wall was built along the line of the earlier pale but there may have been some changes. Defoe, writing in about 1724, noted that the park was enlarged before being 'wall'd about',[22] and there is some primary evidence of dispossession: 'a field of arable ground, 10 acres, in the occupation of John Morten otherwise John Gardener,

upon the King's Majesty enclosing with a brick wall his Park, he took a great portion of these 10 acres and of the common towards the River, whereupon I petitioned him but never got anything for the loss. God turne his Harte'.[23]

The wall survives as a bold and striking feature, largely on its original course, albeit extensively rebuilt and patched in innumerable phases of repair and replacement up to the present day, resulting in great variation in bricks, bonds and mortars. Early brickwork survives in places, notably between the sites of Chesterfield Lodge and Montague House, east of Park Hall on Croom's Hill, and south of Maze Hill Gate. Elsewhere the wall has suffered the normal depredations of nature and the vagaries of fashion; from Croom's Hill to the north-west corner of the park, the original wall was replaced with iron railings on stone-coped brick dwarf walls in several early nineteenth-century phases, when the prosperous took the opportunity to provide themselves with a view into the park while at the same time putting a stop to 'nuisances of the most offensive nature' for which the wall provided a screen.[24] Comparable replacement on the Maze Hill side occurred in 1905.[25] The wall at the south-east corner of the park was rebuilt in 1922 as a classical war memorial in Portland stone, a concave quadrant set well back from the former line of the wall. Designed by Charles P. Courtenay, the Borough Engineer and Surveyor, this was put in place by Greenwich Borough Council to commemorate the more than 1600 local men who died in the First World War.[26]

Part of the north wall of the park, originally constructed with a parallel wall to run along both sides of the road straddled by the Queen's House (fig. 12), was removed for the building of the Royal Naval Asylum in 1807–12, now part of the National Maritime Museum, and for George Basevi's fine neo-classical church of St Mary to the west, now demolished, which opened in 1825 (fig. 13).[27] Following the re-siting of the road to the north

12 Hendrik Danckerts, *Greenwich from the Park showing the Queen's House*, c.1670 (NMM). The walls along the sides of the road are clearly shown. John Webb's King Charles Building is depicted next to the river.

in 1697–9, the walls abutting the Queen's House became redundant for all but the containment of the deer within the park and appear to have been superseded by the construction in the eighteenth century of a ha-ha to the south of the house, later augmented by the present low brick wall, with stone coping, which probably was built with the move of the Royal Naval Asylum to Greenwich. In the centre of the wall, concentric stone steps lead down from the garden of the house to a doorway into the park, possibly inserted for Greenwich Hospital around 1860.[28]

The Park following the Restoration

Charles II's plans for a new palace at Greenwich included extensive works in the park, where he intended to create a formal landscape to complement the new palace for which John Webb provided designs. Only one of Webb's proposed ranges, the King Charles Building, was built, later to become part of the Royal Hospital for Seamen.[29] Very little is known about the origins of the landscape design and the evidence for its implementation is

scant. Greenwich was not the only park where works were commissioned by the king; there was extensive commissioned work at St James's Park and Hampton Court, the former certainly with the help of the Frenchmen André and Gabriel Mollet. These brothers came from a family of eminent gardeners and André had written the influential manual *Jardin de plaisir* (1651), in which he set out the guiding principles of French formal garden design. The principal concept was the unification of house and garden about a single extended axis, the ideal plan being a rectangle divided by *allées* and forming a succession of features at successive points away from the house.

The Mollet brothers had been in England previously, André designing a garden for Henrietta Maria at Wimbledon before the Civil War.[30] Although there is no direct evidence for the involvement of the brothers in the Greenwich design, some of the typical devices which they promoted are visible: the single axis, the *patte d'oie*, the long *allées* and *bosquets* (coppices) of Charles II's park are first shown on a plan of around 1675–80 which reveals a grand design encompassing the entire area within James I's lofty brick wall (fig. 14).[31] However, this was not a tightly formal and symmetrical arrangement. The idiosyncrasies of the topography con-

13   George Basevi, church of St Mary, Greenwich, photographed by
A. R. Martin shortly before demolition in 1936.

tributed to an irregular layout which is immediately apparent. The
design could not be wholly symmetrical because the precise
geometry of a flat site was not possible without enormous earth
movement and complex engineering. Nevertheless, a formal,
geometric design was achieved, with a principal axis and an
extensive series of straight tree-lined avenues which focused on
the Queen's House and the emerging new palace (fig. 16). This
attempt to link the house with its park on such a grand scale was
new to England at this date. The principal axis extended south-
wards from the Queen's House up the escarpment by way of a
series of grass terraces or 'ascents' (later called the 'Giant Steps'),
and on towards Blackheath. This axis divided the park into two
unequal strips with two cross-walks, one close to and along the
edge of the escarpment, the other along its foot. At the southern
end near the Blackheath Gate, planting of the central walk was
carried into four concentric semicircles, called 'The Rounds', from
which two more walks ran diagonally north and north-west,
forming a *patte d'oie*, with further diagonal walks dividing the area
between the two cross-walks. On each side of The Rounds, fourteen rectangular blocks of coppice woodland, The Wildernesses,
divided by *allées*, extended to the park boundaries. Small pockets

of informal planting survived from earlier times, notably on the
slope north-east of the Royal Observatory.

Little is known about the sequence of events by which this
design was implemented in the park and even this evidence is
confined to the period 1661–5, although work on the palace trick-
led on until 1669. The practical implementation of the work in
the park was assigned initially to Sir William Boreman, who had
been made Clerk Comptroller of the King's Household as a
reward for help he had afforded to Henrietta Maria in more trou-
bled times. Between September 1661 and June 1662 he supervised
the planting of seven avenues, The Wilderness coppices, the establishment of a dwarf orchard and the cutting of the twelve ascents.
The avenue trees were mainly elm and chestnut but other trees
planted included birch, holly, hawthorn, ivy, privet and ash.[32]
Samuel Pepys recorded progress in April 1662 when he went
'to Greenwich by water; and there . . . Sir Wm [Sir William Penn]
and I walked into the Parke, where the King hath planted trees
and made steps in the hill up to the Castle, which is very
magnificent'.[33]

The ascents carried the main axis in a gradual climb up the
escarpment. Each step comprised a sloping riser and a very gently
sloping tread: engravings by Francis Place of about 1676–80 show
that the risers had central ramps for easier pedestrian access (figs
15 and 17).[34] Today, although there has been considerable erosion
and disturbance, slight traces of the ascents remain as earthworks.
They are contained between two eastward-facing scarps which cut
straight up the hill: the western one is now partly overlaid by spoil
from construction of the Observatory path, built probably by
1790, which also partly overlies the upper steps. Single lines of
Scots fir trees originally lined the containing scarps. Between
them, only three treads and four risers survive of the ascents, probably recut in the early eighteenth century. The last riser is much
steeper than the others and the original intended gentle ascent is
lost (fig. 18).[35]

While the work under Boreman's direction continued, Charles
II sought further advice from France, enlisting the help of another
even more celebrated French garden designer, André Le Nôtre. In
May 1662 a letter was written to the French Foreign Secretary:
'The King of England, walking two days ago in St. James's Park,
and talking of the alterations he hoped to make in his gardens,
especially at Greenwich, notified that he would require the help
of Le Nôtre who was in charge of the [French] King's gardens
and he begged me to write to his Majesty to ask that he would
allow him to make the journey to England'.[36] Louis XIV granted
permission for such a visit and although there is no evidence that
it took place, Le Nôtre did provide detailed advice. One of his
working drawings survives, annotated largely in his own hand. This
'Plan de la maison de Grenuche', designed for the dowager Queen
Henrietta Maria, shows both the earthworks and internal detail
for a large parterre which was to be established immediately south
of the Queen's House and which would have extended to the
foot of the ascents (fig. 19).[37] The notes on the plan give instructions for laying out the parterre – the heights, widths and regularity of the slopes as well as basic surveying instructions to ensure
the maintenance of right angles. One comment concerns the
laying out of an *allée* where it joined the parterre. More impor-
tantly, there is a note making it clear that this was not the first
working sketch; 'the terrace' had already been formed under his
instructions. Another note mentions that the gardeners should seek
further advice at certain stages of the work.

14 A plan of Greenwich Park, *c*.1675–80 (Pepys Library, Magdalene College, Cambridge).

15 (*below*) Francis Place, *The Royal Observatory and the Giant Steps*, *c*.1676–80 (NMM).

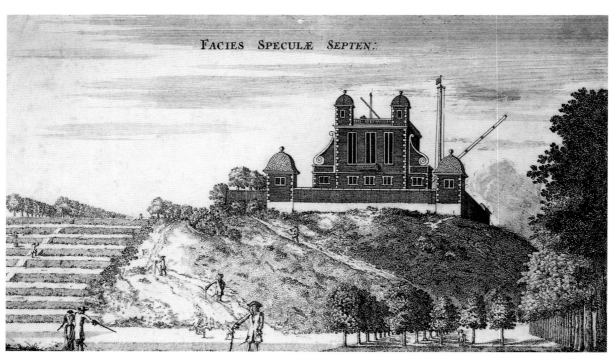

FACIES SPECULÆ SEPTEN:

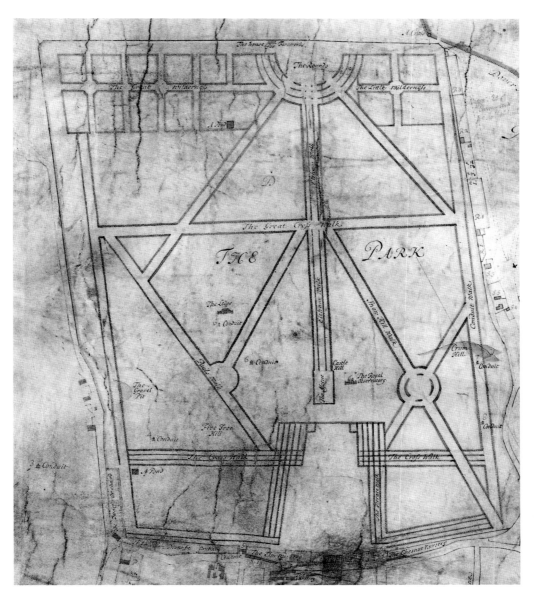

16 Samuel Travers, plan of Greenwich Park, c.1695, showing the principal features of the Restoration design (PRO MR 253).

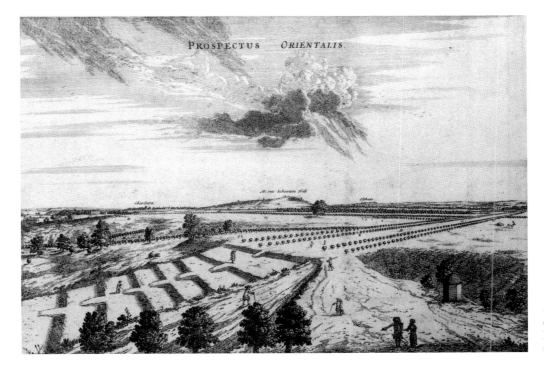

17 Francis Place, *The Giant Steps and Blackheath Avenue*, c.1676–80 (Pepys Library, Magdalene College, Cambridge).

18   The Royal Observatory with the remains of the Giant Steps and the parterre earthworks by André Le Nôtre, revealed by low sunlight in November 1993.

Le Nôtre's parterre design was grand but simple. Referred to later by Nicholas Hawksmoor as 'The Grand Esplanade by monsr Le Notre', which he dated 1666,[38] it comprised a broad central walk leading south from the Queen's House towards and then around a large circular basin and fountain. The walk was flanked by two smaller octagonal basins, also with fountains, and fairly simple *parterre de broderie* work. The plan also includes several pedestal bases for statuary or other garden ornaments and a perimeter walk, while the Queen's House is shown with the corner pavilions which were planned but never built, although foundations were dug in 1663. The sketch also depicts, centrally at the southern end of the parterre before the ascents, an arcade of seven arches, to which notes in another hand refer: 'vos arches'. Le Nôtre had created a similar eye-catcher at Vaux-le-Vicomte, where an arrangement of seven arches, forming a grotto, occupies a position at the foot of rising ground.[39] At Greenwich his arcade would have formed an architectural link with the 'Grott & ascent', designed by John Webb as part of his palace design, to close the view at the top of the hill (fig. 20).[40]

Although Webb's grand multi-terraced structure was not built, it is apparent that Charles II wished to elaborate the design of the park, contemplating the addition of a cascade falling down the ascents, like those in contemporary French gardens at Rueil, St Cloud, Fontainebleau, Liancourt and Vaux-le-Vicomte.[41] He wrote in October 1664 to his sister Henriette at St Cloud: 'Pray lett Le Nostre goe on with the modell and only tell him this addition that I can bring water to the top of the hill, so that he may add much to the beauty of the desente by a cascade of watter'. It was possibly in this connection that payments were made in 1665 for 'the making of a modell for ye Fountaine in the Parke and making of stakes setting out the Ground &c'.[42] This must have been for one of the fountains planned for the parterre and it suggests that some work was undertaken. There is no evidence of any further progress, however, and the earliest surviving plans and illustrations of the park, dating from the 1670s, show the parterre as a lawned area. The extensive disturbance by Second World War allotments probably precludes the survival of any archaeological evidence for the internal detail of the parterre.

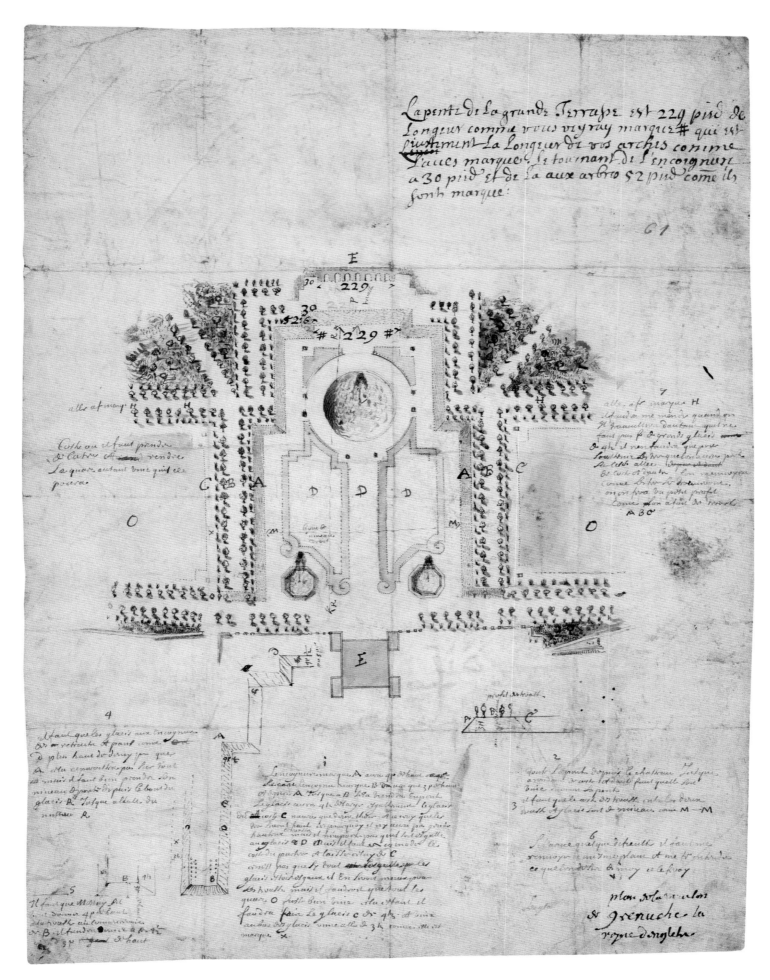

19   André Le Nôtre, design for a parterre in Greenwich Park, *c.*1666 (Bibliothèque de l'Institut de France, Paris). The Queen's House, with proposed corner pavilions, is shown at the bottom of the plan.

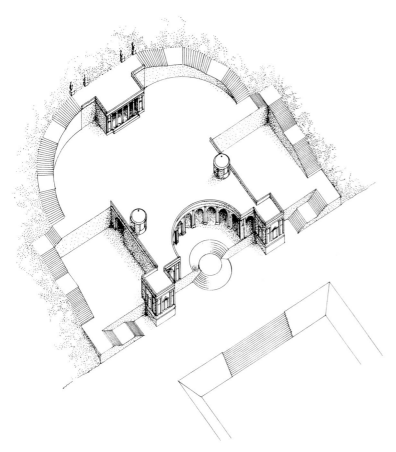

20   Reconstruction of John Webb's proposed 'Grott & ascent', *c.*1665 (based on drawings in the BAL).

Today the large, carefully cut earthworks forming the framework for the parterre remain, very much as they were abandoned in the later 1660s and of almost exactly the dimensions noted by Le Nôtre. This is a very large and empty area of some 8½ acres, with maximum internal dimensions of 721 feet (north-west to south-east) by 518 feet (north-east to south-west). The northern half of the parterre is open to the Queen's House: the southern end closed by the earthworks which take two inward double right-angled turns, the first just over halfway from the northern end and the second close to the southern end. The parterre is remarkably level across its short axis and the slope from south to north is gentle and even, produced mainly by limited grading work; but in its southern third, where it comes onto rising ground at the foot of the escarpment, it is cut deeply into the natural slope, producing a massive north-facing scarp up to 11½ feet high at the foot of the terrace before the ascents. This terrace would have supported the arcade in Le Nôtre's sketch and its construction required considerable effort, particularly on the eastern side where it impinges on the mouth of the natural combe between One Tree Hill and Observatory Hill. This may imply that the entire south-eastern corner of the parterre and the terrace behind it is the result of very careful landscaping of made-up ground, a considerable undertaking: perhaps this is the 'great pitt' referred to in Sir William Boreman's accounts in 1662 as being partly infilled.[43] The terrace is carried round onto the flanks of the parterre on massive, flat-topped earthen banks constructed to provide raised walks, originally lined by multiple rows of English elms. From these walks the parterre could be viewed and admired.

After 1665 there are no more specific details about work on the park layout although it has been suggested that in about 1698 William III invited a further design from André Le Nôtre, who in turn recommended his nephew Claude Desgotz. A drawing which has been attributed to Desgotz and assigned to Greenwich shows a design which not only misrepresents the alignment of the Queen's House but also shows no understanding of the topography of the site in proposing an oblong strip of water which would have required earthworks on an impossibly ambitious and destructive scale.[44] It is moreover highly improbable at this time in the history of the Queen's House, as work was beginning on the nearby Hospital, that William would have wished to make a further investment in the landscape of Greenwich Park, where major work had in fact ceased with the abandonment of the whole palace project in 1669. After this date the programme was confined to one of maintenance: in 1670 Hugh May was appointed inspector of the French gardeners at Whitehall, St James's, Greenwich and Hampton Court.[45]

From the plan of around 1675–80 it appears that the park works were substantially completed with only the internal details of the parterre missing, but the whole design lacks the carefully orchestrated overall unity, symmetry and intricate detail of such contemporary French gardens as those at Vaux-le-Vicomte. In contrast, Greenwich has an awkward plan, with such peculiarities as the misalignment of an *allée* of the Great Wilderness with the eastern perimeter walk, the manner in which the *patte d'oie* appears to truncate the coppices of The Wildernesses, and the asymmetry of many of the walks (fig. 21). This is partly because of the constraints imposed by the shape of the park and its awkward combes and changes in level, but it may also be a result of poor implementation. It has been suggested that Boreman's work, up to June 1662, concentrated on the plateau, where most of the asymmetry is apparent, and that Le Nôtre was involved with the parterre design and the avenues immediately adjoining, where symmetry is achieved, between the summer of 1662 and the spring of 1664.[46] In the end, Charles II overstretched his resources on several palace projects and Greenwich suffered. Had the plan been completed, the intimate relationship of the axis, palace and parterre would have been distinctly French: looking from the Queen's House, the eye would have been led over the parterre along the axis to the ascents. From the top of the ascents in the park the parterre would have been inseparable from the palace, forming a natural arena, framed by tree-lined *allées*, drawing the viewer into the palace buildings: a carefully contrived setting for the court, its politics and its entertainments.

Although incomplete, the layout of the park did represent a single design which was to endure, largely unchanged, until the early nineteenth century (fig. 22). Even today, several of the avenues remain and the overall imprint is still apparent. Although Charles II did not finish his palace, the park found its focus in the early eighteenth century on the magnificent array of buildings of the Royal Hospital: the intimate relationship between the Hospital and the park is shown admirably in the perspective produced by Johannes Kip in the early eighteenth century (fig. 24). The Restoration planting proved to be handsome and durable, with formal coppices and avenues of elm, oak and chestnut. Their rigid lines complemented rather than tamed the dramatic, natural topography of the escarpment and the park retained a hint of its medieval parkland essence. The unfinished parterre took on the appearance of an immense lawn, framed by raised walks and mul-

21   Jules Arnout, view of Greenwich Park, (?)mid-1860s, published in Paris and London as an 'excursion aérienne'. Ostensibly drawn 'après nature', from a balloon, some of the architectural and topographical inconsistencies indicate that the artist augmented his own observations by reference to illustrations of various dates. Despite the inaccuracies, this is an excellent evocation of the overall landscape of Greenwich.

tiple avenues of trees, to become a striking feature of many late seventeenth- and eighteenth-century landscape paintings. These capture a landscape which is peculiarly English, one in which even dramatic change is integrated rapidly, so that the old blends with the new in a way that yields an idiosyncratic atmosphere about which it is easy to feel sentimental (fig. 25).

The Water Conduits

There were several natural sources of water within the park and its environs. Filtered by gravels in the Blackheath Beds which form the cap of the escarpment, water issued beneath the scarp edge as a series of springs at the junction of this stratum with the underlying impervious clays of the Woolwich Beds. The channelling of this fresh water was of great importance and is of considerable antiquity, although the precise origin of a conduit system is open to speculation. As part of Duke Humphrey's extensive works, an

aqueduct was built in 1434 between his manor house and 'a certain fount in Greenwich, called Stockwell', at the junction of modern Stockwell and Nevada Streets.[47] In the following century, the needs of the Tudor court were even greater and water supply determined how long it could remain in one place. Desiring longer periods of residence for his enlarged court, Henry VIII had the water supply systems of all his greater houses remade, to provide running water for up to 1500 people for two months or more at a time. The water supply at Greenwich, which had been improved initially under Henry VII, was again improved under Henry VIII who ordered the construction of a new system in 1515.[48]

To this date can probably be attributed the East Lane Conduit House, which survives against the north-eastern margin of the park, the last upstanding structure from the Tudor palace. It is towards the east end of a group which also incorporates fragments of late Stuart stables, and extensions of 1807 by Daniel Alexander and of 1829 by Joseph Kay to accommodate officials of the Royal

22   Henry Sayer, plan
of Greenwich Park,
1840, oriented with
north at the top
(PRO WORK 32/23).

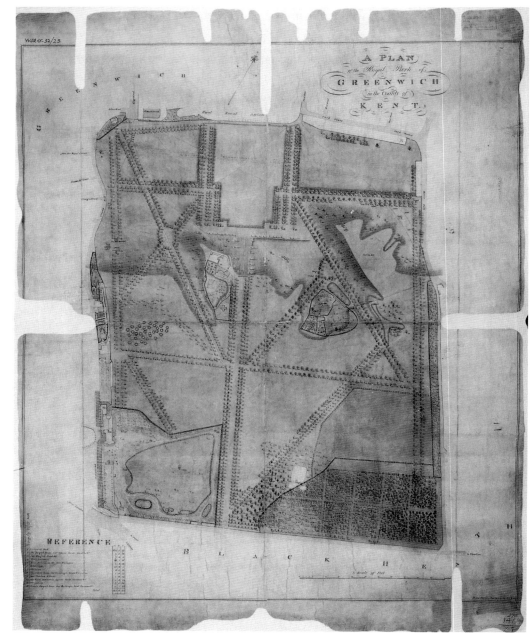

23 (*below*)   St Alfege's
Vicarage, Park Place
(now Park Vista),
Greenwich, 1934. The
early sixteenth-
century conduit house
is to the left, behind
the early seventeenth-
century park wall.
Joseph Kay's extension
of 1829 is to the
right, beyond Daniel
Alexander's Auditor's
House of 1807
(LMA).

Naval Asylum and Greenwich Hospital respectively. The whole
group was converted by Samuel Sanders Teulon in 1866 to be the
Vicarage to St Alfege (fig. 23). It was subdivided and altered in
1965–75 to create four private houses – The Vicarage, 34 Park
Vista, The Chantry and 36 Park Vista – with a new house, 37 Park
Vista, added to the east, all to the designs of Raymond Smith.[49]

Tudor conduit houses were secure structures built to ensure
both water purity and safety from poisoning. The Greenwich
example was originally close to the boundary of the park, a free-
standing building with a high-level tank, collecting water from
conduits and overlooking the Woolwich Road at the head of East
Lane.[50] It is shown in the anonymous painting of about 1615[51]
and in the view of about 1670 by Hendrik Danckerts:[52] both show
a square building with gables. The later painting also shows a door
to the park, round windows within the gables, and the park wall
which had been built up to it. The basic structure of this conduit
house survives, although the building has been made two storeyed
under a pyramidal tiled roof. It is a very solid red-brick block

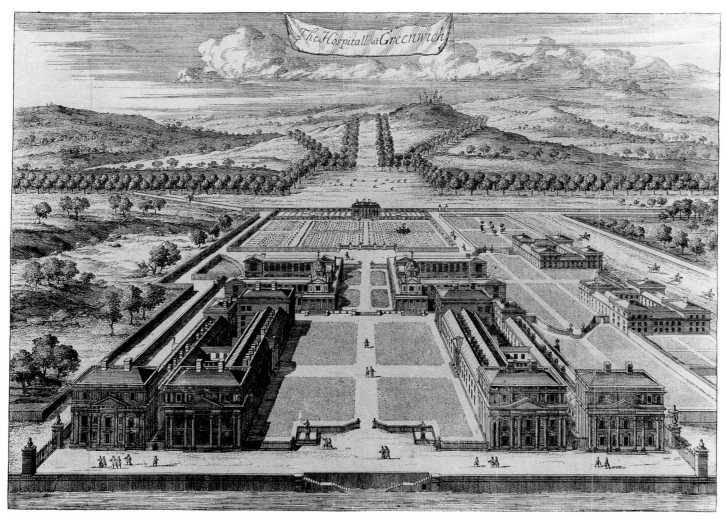

24 Johannes Kip, *The Hospitall at Greenwich* (GLHL). The general layout of the site is shown correctly, but in combining the built with the proposed, there are substantial inaccuracies in the architectural detail, most notably in the inclusion to the right of Hawksmoor's unexecuted proposals for the out-offices and Infirmary buildings.

25 Johannes Vorsterman, *Greenwich from One-Tree Hill*, c.1680 (NMM).

about 18 feet 4 inches square, with walls 2 feet thick. Some original brickwork survives among much refacing. On the north wall, a replica limestone panel, based on a 'greatly perished' original and installed in 1977, displays the arms of Henry VIII with lion and dragon supporters.[53] Below it is an early moulded string course, echoed to the south. The structure has a splayed plinth, stone dressed to the south, where it steps down to the centre for an entrance.

26   Hyde Vale Conduit, Greenwich Park.

27   The Standard Reservoir of 1710–11, Greenwich Park.

Towards the end of the seventeenth century, with plans being made for the Royal Hospital, a commission was established in 1695 to report, among other things, on the water supply. It noted the existence of eight conduits supplying the palace and these are marked on Samuel Travers's map of the same year; five conduit heads lay within the park.[54] Subsequently, around 1707, control of the water supply in the park was granted to the Royal Hospital by Queen Anne's consort, Prince George of Denmark, and it is from this time that there is evidence that the system was comprehensively rebuilt. Hawksmoor, who was assisting Wren in the designing and building of the Hospital, received instructions to enlarge and vault the conduits so that they could be cleaned by someone going in. There was a financial interest to be served since the Hospital wished to satisfy not only its own needs and those of the deserving poor, but also to raise revenue by providing a water supply to private homes.[55] Masons were at work in 1707–8, paving the conduits and building aqueducts on the eastern side of the park adjacent to the original Hospital burial ground.[56] Extensive work is recorded on the western side of the park in 1710 and 1711,[57] involving the construction of what is now known as Hyde Vale Conduit and the Standard Reservoir. There was further masons' work on conduits in 1713.[58]

It appears likely that the Admiralty's engineers replaced the existing conduits rather than creating entirely new ones, although there is no brickwork in the surviving investigated tunnels to suggest an origin earlier than the late seventeenth century or the early eighteenth. Remains of at least three conduit systems survive in the park: the Little Conduit under One Tree Hill, Croomhill Conduit (now Hyde Vale Conduit) and the Park Conduit, just west of Lovers Walk. The Little Conduit is sealed and inaccessible, but the other two are broadly similar in construction, both being brick-built, vaulted tunnels large enough, or nearly so, for a person to walk along them upright (fig. 26). Their large size and elaborate construction, necessary to facilitate maintenance, has caused some to doubt whether they were used simply to channel water; a series of bizarre alternative interpretations, such as secret escape routes for the Tudor monarchy, have been proposed.[59]

Each conduit was designed to collect and channel water from the springs in the gravels both in the park and on Blackheath to the foot of the Greenwich escarpment; hence, each system runs from south to north. The pattern of each conduit is similar, with several capillary tunnels at the top of the system channelling water downwards into a main artery. In the basal courses of the capillary tunnels, open brickwork allowed water to percolate through from the surrounding subsoil, collecting in narrow, lead-lined channels recessed into the floor on one side of the tunnel. Since this water contained quantities of silt, there were occasional small dams which allowed the water to form ponds and thus enable the settlement of sediment. The conduits fed small reservoirs and cisterns at the conduit heads, from which water was piped to the Hospital.

The Admiralty's conduit heads, put up under the direction of Hawksmoor, were robust, simple and picturesquely varied in form and scale. They comprised both free-standing buildings and hillside revetments, many of them recorded on eighteenth-century drawings and maps. As a group they formed a delightful, Romantic complement to the blend of Baroque formality and natural irregularity which characterised the park. Many of these structures were taken down in the later nineteenth century. In 1891 the

Admiralty abandoned the park springs as a water supply to the Royal Naval College, but the Board of Works was persuaded to maintain rather than remove the surviving redundant buildings.[60]

The principal standing conduit building is the Standard Reservoir, constructed in 1710–11 by bricklayer Richard Billinghurst (fig. 27).[61] This is a rectangular structure set into the slope near the base of Croom's Hill, of stock brick with red-brick dressings and a low slate roof. The north elevation has a screen front with a round-headed doorway in a broad and deep apsidal niche, with inscribed panels above: 'Greenwich Hospital' and 'Standard Reservoir'. Inside there is a 'bell-shaped chamber', 80 feet in diameter.[62] All the conduits on the west side of the park drained into a large cistern here, fed by an underground cistern to the south. The water was then piped to the Hospital.[63]

Another conduit head, probably one of those remade in 1708, survives as a small hillside revetment on the eastern side of the park, in the lee of One Tree Hill near Maze Hill House Gate.[64] Probably the head of Little Conduit, this is a rectangular block with a simple stone-dressed polychrome brick arch, with a weathered stone panel above, the inscription now illegible. The ramped flanking walls appear to be nineteenth-century additions (fig. 28).

The Hospital's early eighteenth-century system of water supply was improved after 1831 when Joseph Kay gained permission to make three new underground reservoirs,[65] but more improvements were deemed necessary. The Admiralty wished not only to supply water to the Royal Hospital but also to provide fire mains leading there and to the Naval Dockyard and Victualling Yards in Deptford. The site chosen for a large, open reservoir, with the agreement of the Commissioners of Woods and Forests, was close to Great Cross Avenue, threatening the destruction of several of the Anglo-Saxon burial mounds. Excavations were begun in 1844, and some barrows were flattened before vigorous opposition to this 'invasion of the sylvan shades of Greenwich, that most favourite resort of the smoke-dried Londoners' and 'the last place that ought to be profaned by the axe and trowel', caused works temporarily to be abandoned.[66] The triumph was short-lived. The Admiralty resumed the works in 1845, some feet to the south, and the reservoir was built at a cost of £3069 to plans drawn up by Sir William Thomas Denison, Superintendent at Portsmouth Dockyard, under the overall direction of Captain Henry Roland Brandreth, Director of the Admiralty Works Department. In the words of 'Simon Sensitive', 'the crowning outrage is now being effected. I am ashamed, I am grieved, I am indescribably distressed as I record the fact'.[67] The opposition had, however, succeeded in saving the burial mounds.

Capable of holding 1,125,000 gallons, the new reservoir, which survives, although empty and disused, was originally a simple construction comprising a large, circular bank of earth, part excavated and part made-up, about 160 feet across its base. The raised banks were and remain encircled by spearhead cast-iron railings on a stone-coped brick wall. Following the closure of the Hospital, the reservoir was covered over in 1871 by the Kent Water Works Company, to comply with the provisions of the Metropolis Water Supply Act of 1852. This was achieved by the construction of five concentric circles of brick piers 8 feet tall supporting iron girders carrying brick vaults, the whole covered with turf and screened by shrubbery.[68]

★   ★   ★

28   Screen at conduit head in Greenwich Park, probably of 1708, shown on an undated postcard (GLHL).

Flamsteed House

The most remarkable building within the park is not properly speaking a park building at all, although it has the picturesque qualities associated with the type. In view of its date, Flamsteed House of 1675–6, the earliest building of the Royal Observatory, might be regarded as a precursor, in form if not in function, of a host of spectacularly sited park buildings – eye-catchers and follies – throughout the country. The complex evolution of the numerous buildings which have made up the Observatory and the relationship of their architecture to observational requirements and methods has been well told elsewhere.[69] Here it is desirable only to review the circumstances of the construction and use of Flamsteed House, the best known and most prominently sited of the buildings of the Royal Observatory, noting later buildings in passing.

The late seventeenth century was one of the most fertile periods in the history of English science, with a palpable excitement of discovery on a range of topics. Joseph Glanvill, Rector of Bath and a polemicist on behalf of the new science, had noted in 1668 'the inexhaustible variety of Treasure which Providence hath lodged in Things'.[70] In the biological and physical sciences, enormous advances were made at this time, based on the precise observation of phenomena and on conducting experiments. It is within this broader context of scientific investigation and discovery that the contributions made by Robert Hooke, John Flamsteed and Edmond Halley to astronomical observation and to the recording and understanding of the movements of heavenly bodies should be seen.

A priority for a maritime, trading nation lay in mapping the stars in order to find a means whereby sailors could identify their position at sea. Once out of sight of land they had no accurate way of knowing exactly where they were, a point given tragic emphasis in 1707 when Admiral Sir Clowdisley Shovell and nearly 2000 men were lost and his squadron was wrecked on the Isles of Scilly. Position on earth can be determined by the two

29 *The Rake's Progress*, scene VIII, *The Madhouse* (in Bethlem Hospital – see fig. 131), engraved by H. Fernell after William Hogarth's painting of *c*.1733–4 (in Sir John Soane's Museum, London), in which the search for longitude is lampooned.

co-ordinates, latitude (distance north or south of the equator) and longitude (distance east or west of a given point or 'prime meridian'). Latitude may be determined by observation of the midday sun or certain stars, but the calculation of longitude was rather more difficult since it is a function of time (fig. 29). Since one complete revolution of the earth (360 degrees) takes twenty-four hours, each hour is equivalent to fifteen degrees of rotation. To find longitude at sea, therefore, knowledge of local time as well as what time it is at some other known location – a home port, for example – is required. The time difference is then translatable into longitude, a difference of four hours, for example, being a difference in longitude of 60 degrees. The problem which navigators had until the late eighteenth century was how to discover what time it was at their home port, or some other point of departure, when they were far away from it. The alternatives, which bore fruit at almost exactly the same time, were to perfect a marine timekeeper which would remain accurate and unaffected

by the motion of the ship and by temperature changes (eventually achieved by John Harrison), or by using the lunar-distance method, to use the predictable movement of the moon against the fixed stars as a kind of clock. With the positions of the moon at different times listed on tables, longitude could be calculated by observation. The Observatory at Greenwich was founded with the express purposes of making charts of the skies and recording the position of the moon throughout the year, its most significant early achievement as an institution being the annual publication, from 1766, of the *Nautical Almanac*.[71]

John Flamsteed, the son of a Derby maltster, was encouraged locally in his interest in astronomy and later found it necessary to apologise for adapting his observations 'to the meridian of a place no more famous than Derby'.[72] He became acquainted with Sir Jonas Moore, Surveyor-General of the Ordnance, through their common interest in astronomy and the mathematician proved himself staunch in the younger man's support, writing in 1674:

'And I am resolved God willing further to assist you with either books or instruments, as you will please to call for them. . . . I rejoice much that I may again hope to see you and do with all earnestness beg from you, that whilst you stay in London you will make my house your abode'.[73] It was early in the following year that Moore, along with Christopher Wren, Robert Hooke and others, attended, at Charles II's request, a meeting with the Sieur de St Pierre, a French astronomer introduced to the court by Louise de Kerouaille, initially maid of honour to the king's sister, Henrietta, and subsequently a favourite of the monarch himself. St Pierre claimed that he could provide a solution to the longitude problem, by using knowledge of the positions of the stars. These remarks proved to be a catalyst for further investigations. Moore consulted Flamsteed who dismissed the claims but pointed out that it would be possible to find longitude by lunar observations only after accurate star catalogues and lunar tables had been completed, after years of observation with large instruments. His remarks found favour and as a result of the support of Moore, Flamsteed was appointed 'Astronomical Observator' to the king on 4 March 1675, with a salary of £100 per year, and Charles decreed the building of an observatory, the expenses to be borne by the office of Ordnance.[74] Flamsteed was charged, in the words of the royal warrant, 'forthwith to apply himself with the most exact Care and Diligence to . . . rectifying the Tables of the Motions of the Heavens, and the places of the fixed Stars, so as to find out the so much desired Longitude of Places for perfecting the art of Navigation'.[75]

The choice of Greenwich as the site for the Observatory followed the recommendation of Wren, who was charged with its design. It was deemed suitable since it was an available royal site, on high ground, away from the smoke of London, but easily accessible. The king, in the words of the warrant issued in June 1675 to Sir Thomas Chicheley, Master-General of the Ordnance,

> resolved to build a small observatory within Our Park at Greenwich upon the highest ground at or near the Place where the Castle stood, with lodging rooms for our Astronomical Observator and Assistant. Our Will and Pleasure is that according to such plot and design as shall be given you by Our Trusty and well-beloved Sir Christopher Wren Knight, Our Surveyor General, of the place and scite of the said Observatory, you cause the same to be fenced in, built and finished.[76]

The king provided £500 towards the cost of building the Observatory which Wren, assisted by Hooke, erected on the foundations of the 'Castle'; Hooke visited the site to 'set out' the building (fig. 30).[77] Slighted during the Interregnum, the 'Castle', Duke Humphrey's Tower, was still standing at the Restoration, but in a state of decay (see chapter 2). Flamsteed House sits on the very broad basement walls (3⅓–4 feet thick) of the tower, an economy which Flamsteed was soon to regret, writing in 1676 to his friend Richard Towneley: 'It were much to be wished our walls might have been meridional but for saving of Charges it was thought fit to build upon the old ones which are some 13½ degrees false and wide of the true meridian' (fig. 31).[78] Much of the Observatory was built with re-used materials: the total cost of £520 9s 1d was only about 4 per cent over budget.

The Observatory is a quintessential folly, albeit one that shares with all the best jokes a high seriousness of intent. There is in Wren's design an element of knowing fantasy that predates the

30   *The Royal Observatory, Greenwich*, lithograph after T. H. Shepherd, 1824 (Hertford Museum, Hertfordshire).

'castle air' to which Sir John Vanbrugh was later to aspire: the central octagon room is framed by domed turrets above italianate scrolls in a Jacobean revival style which recalls also the turrets of the Tower of London, the headquarters of the Board of Ordnance for which the Observatory was built. This is a very English precursor of arch postmodernism, made the more remarkable by the contrast that it offered to Inigo Jones's purist masterpiece at the bottom of the hill.

During the building of the Observatory, Flamsteed had lodged, kept equipment and made observations from the Queen's House. He moved into the new building in July 1676, occupying the living accommodation on the ground and basement floors, and began observations in September (fig. 32). The walls of the Observatory were not aligned north–south and the timber floor of the octagonal Great or Star Room was susceptible to jarring by movements as light as a footfall. Its generous space and tall windows enabled the use of long telescopes and the pendulum clocks required for timekeeping, but this was not a building from which all observational requirements could be met (fig. 34). Rather, as Wren recalled in a letter of 1681, the Observatory was built 'for the Observator's habitation & a little for Pompe'. Fundamental astronomical observations were made from instruments fixed to a wall, 'trewly built in the meridian', in the adjacent open court (fig. 35).[79] Although Wren the scientist was sensitive to the functional requirements of an observatory, and sympathetic to the idea of using astronomical methods in order to find longitude at sea,[80] like Claude Perrault at the contemporary Paris Observatory he had to achieve a compromise between observational and presentational requirements: meetings of the scientific community taking place in some state, inside, with observations taking place on firm surfaces outside.

From 1689 Flamsteed provided himself with additional structures in the grounds of the Observatory to the south – the Sextant House and the Quadrant House – where he built two meridian walls and installed his instruments. When he died in 1719, his widow removed the instruments on the grounds that they had all been purchased by Flamsteed himself. Government funding in Britain, particularly for research, is notoriously parsimonious, and in a manner which was to be repeated at the bottom of Greenwich Hill at the Hospital for Seamen, the early years of the

32 (right) The Royal
Observatory, Greenwich, plans
of ground and first floors
(RCHM, London, v, East
London, 1930).

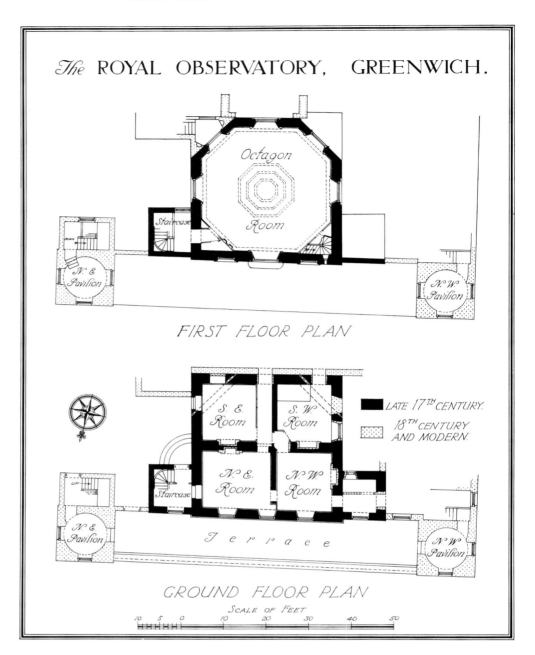

31   The Royal Observatory,
Greenwich, plan of the
north-east part of the basement,
1996, showing the thick walls
of Duke Humphrey's Tower on
which the Observatory was
constructed.

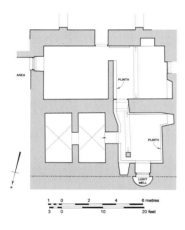

Observatory 'show a half-heartedness on the part of the government that is almost as striking as the original foundation'.[81]

Notwithstanding the difficulties of funding, Flamsteed made an
enormous contribution to astronomical observation. He was also,
belying his reputation for peevishness of behaviour and despite his
gout, able to discuss his findings with visitors, 'with uncommon
civility (which is in England most unusual)'.[82] He shared with
many an English academic a reluctance to publish, but following
the pirating of his work by Edmond Halley in a publication in
1712, he resolved to produce a catalogue of star positions, which
eventually was posthumously achieved in 1725 in the Historia
Coelestis Britannica, followed in 1729 by the Atlas Coelestis – 'monuments to fifty years' labour by a great astronomer',[83] and a tribute
also to the strength of a Greenwich friendship. Sir James Thornhill had included portraits of Flamsteed and his assistant Thomas
Weston in the ceiling of the Painted Hall at the Hospital, with
the rather bold, but, as it transpired, accurate predictive dating of
an eclipse in 1715, prominently painted (fig. 33).[84] After the

PROSPECTUS INTRA CAMERAM STELLATAM.

34 *The Octagon Room of the Royal Observatory*, engraved by Francis Place, 1676 (NMM).

33 (*facing page bottom*) John Flamsteed with his assistant Thomas Weston to his right, depicted by Sir James Thornhill in the south-east corner of the ceiling of the Painted Hall of the Royal Hospital for Seamen. The date of the eclipse – 'Apr: 22 1715' – is painted on the parchment held by Flamsteed.

35 Anon., *The Royal Observatory from Croom's Hill*, c.1680. The painting shows Flamsteed's open court to the rear of the Observatory with the 80 foot mast holding his 60 foot long refracting telescope (NMM).

Astronomer Royal's death (1719), Thornhill 'out of gratitude for favors formerly received from Mr. Flamsteed', drew the images of the constellations for publication and arranged for them to be engraved.[85]

Flamsteed House continued to be the official residence of the Astronomer Royal until 1948, when the Royal Observatory began an extended move to Herstmonceux in Sussex. Since 1960 it has been open to the public as part of the National Maritime Museum. It was the first of many buildings on the site, most of which survive. The buildings and their functions were accretive since there was a need to maintain constant readings, avoiding the interruptions which rebuilding and the removal of instruments would have caused. Although, as a result of atmospheric pollution, no more positional observations were made at Greenwich after 1954, the site remains rich in the history of astronomical observation. Edmond Halley, the second Astronomer Royal, built a new Quadrant House next to Flamsteed's about 1724, and his successor, James Bradley, built a third one onto that in 1749, to utilitarian designs by Board of Ordnance engineers. In this way, the present Meridian Building (a modern name) extended eastward over the period of a century, a process culminating in 1857 with the construction of the Great Equatorial Building during the regime of the seventh Astronomer Royal, Sir George Biddell Airy. Under the next Astronomer Royal, William Christie, there was a return to ornamental architecture with the building in 1894–9 of two structures by Christie and the Admiralty architect William Crisp – the Altazimuth Pavilion and the South Building. Of red brick and terracotta, these shapely buildings resemble nothing so much as jelly moulds. By the time of their construction, Greenwich had gained international recognition as marking the Prime Meridian in one of the earliest global agreements on the standardisation of practice, the acceptance of Greenwich Mean Time at the International Meridian Conference held in Washington, D.C., in 1884.

The higher profile of the Observatory under Christie also drew unwanted attention. French anarchists plotted to bomb it, but the scheme went disastrously wrong and the bomb exploded as a M. Bourdin carried it across Greenwich Park,[86] an absurd scene immortalised in fiction by Joseph Conrad in *The Secret Agent*: 'Bomb in Greenwich Park. . . . Half past eleven. Foggy morning. Effects of explosion felt as far as Romney Road and Park Place. Enormous hole in the ground . . . All round fragments of a man's body blown to pieces. . . . No doubt a wicked attempt to blow up the Observatory'. As Mr Verloc, the fictional perpetrator of the dynamic outrage was later to observe with feeling, 'I wish to goodness . . . I had never seen Greenwich Park or anything belonging to it'.[87] Greenwich in fiction is perhaps more accurately represented in Giuseppe Tomasi di Lampedusa's *The Leopard* than in Conrad. The mid-nineteenth-century hero, concerned to escape the quotidian by taking refuge in the starry regions, 'plunged into reading the latest number of the *Journal des savants*. "Les dernières observations de l'Observatoire de Greenwich présentent un intérêt tout particulier "'.[88] The contemplation of the stars afforded scope for both intellect and reverie and Greenwich provided the ideal locus for the indulgence of both. Long vacated now by the original Royal Observatory organisation (which was itself abolished in 1998), the buildings, as part of the National Maritime Museum, continue to play an important public educational role in telling the story of longitude, Greenwich time and modern astronomy, as well as allowing the young and flexible to maintain the illusion of being in both the Eastern and Western hemispheres when they straddle the imaginary line of longitude 0 degrees which runs through the Observatory and joins the North and South poles.

Public Access to the Park

The Hospital pensioners and their relatives, as well as a small number of local residents, had been granted access to the park in 1705, when the first group of seamen were admitted to Wren's new building. At about the same time, the park was opened to the general public during holidays, but it did not become a fully public amenity until the 1830s.[89] Even though the park was not open at all times, the keeper in 1718 was given seven assistants, each paid £2 per year, following the report of 'frequent disturbances . . . committed in the Park by loose disorderly persons, as well as abusing the trees and annoying the Deer, as offering incivilities to women who walk there'.[90] The park was a popular venue at Easter and Whitsuntide when the famous Greenwich Fair, the earliest reference to which was in 1709, was held in the town. By 1730 the fairs and their associated less organised amusements in the park had become notorious for revelry and excess:

> great numbers of people from London and the adjacent Parts diverted themselves, as is common on public Holidays, with running down the Hill (formerly called the Giant's Steps) . . . but some others more venturesome would run down the steeper part of the said Hill under the Terrace of the Royal Observatory; one of them, a young woman, broke her Neck, another ran against one of the Trees with such Violence that she broke her Jaw-bone and a third broke her leg.[91]

By 1761 as many as 15,000 people were visiting Greenwich at holiday times, a number which increased tenfold with the introduction of river steamers in 1836. After the coming of the world's first suburban railway line, which reached Greenwich two years later, the number of visitors rose to about 250,000. The young Charles Dickens recorded his impressions in 1835 of this 'periodical breaking out . . . a sort of spring-rash; a three day's fever, which cools the blood for six months afterwards, and at the expiration of which, London is restored to its old habits of plodding industry'. The principal day-time amusement recorded by Dickens had not changed in a century: 'to drag young ladies up the steep hill which leads to the observatory, and then drag them down again, at the very top of their speed, greatly to the derangement of their curls and bonnet-caps, and much to the edification of lookers-on from below' (fig. 36).[92] When night fell, the action moved to the adjacent fair in the town where itinerant theatres, travelling menageries, dwarfs and giantesses, and a temporary ballroom competed for the attention of the enormous crowds. All in this 'artificial Eden' was 'primitive, unreserved and unstudied'.[93] Such rowdy delights could not be allowed to continue, particularly since it was 'the profligate part of the lower orders' which made up most of the numbers and they tended to squander their money in the 'Booths and Shows' rather than spending it wisely in the town to the benefit of the tradesmen of Greenwich. A campaign to close the fair began in 1825 and in 1857 the *Greenwich*

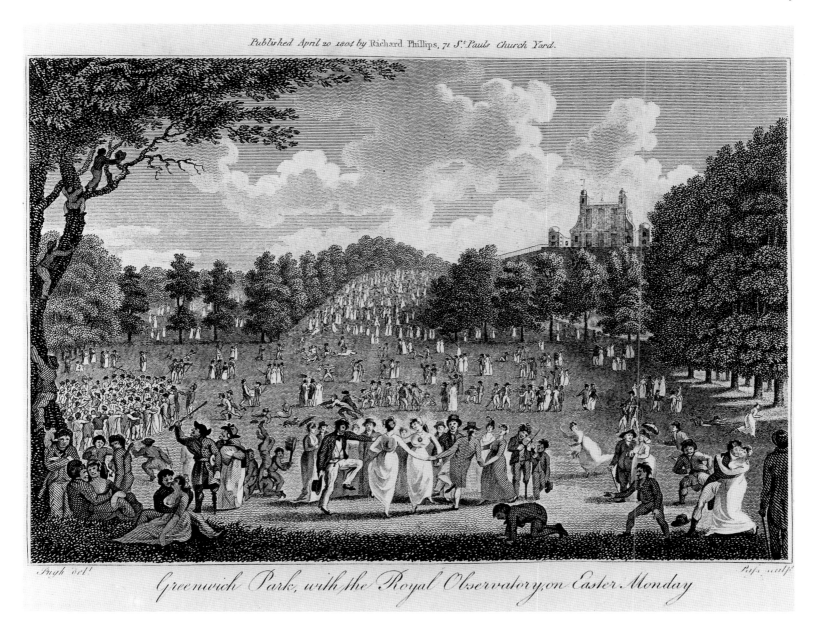

Published April 20 1804 by Richard Phillips, 71 St Pauls Church Yard.

Greenwich Park, with the Royal Observatory, on Easter Monday

36 *Greenwich Park with the Royal Observatory on Easter Monday*, engraved by Pugh, 1804.

Free Press was able to report the abolition of 'that old market of vice and debauchery'.[94]

The park itself was hugely popular in the nineteenth century, used by all classes, 'from the unwashed sweep, to the clean confectioner; the mealy baker, to the fan-tailed coalheaver'.[95] It became public at approximately the same time as the Select Committee on Public Walks in 1833 recommended an increase in the number of open spaces for poorer Londoners. Such a provision, it was argued, 'would assist to wean them from low and debasing pleasures. Great complaint is made of drinking houses, dog fights, and boxing matches, yet unless some opportunity for other recreation is afforded to workmen they are driven to such pursuits'.[96] In circumstances in which suburban building expansion was taking over hitherto open country, it was recognised that parks fulfilled an essential public need. At Greenwich this recognition went beyond merely allowing admission, to pressing for the reinstatement of the space lost to such encroachments as the grounds of the Keeper's Lodge and other private enclosures, such as the 15

acres of Wilderness which Princess Caroline had appropriated for use as a private garden (see chapter 3). Following a petition to Parliament in 1850, agreement to a campaign of improvements was secured.[97] These were to include the provision of more gates and in time resulted in the building of a number of new public facilities.

Access into the park in the sixteenth century had been through the Blackheath Gate on its south side, just off the old London to Dover road, and on its north side by way of the gatehouse which bridged the road which divided the park from the Tudor palace of Placentia. This was demolished to make way for the Queen's House and a new gate was constructed in 1623–4 to the design of Inigo Jones (fig. 37).[98] The Blackheath Gate was rebuilt in 1855 following the substantial widening of Blackheath Avenue, the road within the park, two years earlier. A pair of wrought-iron carriage gates, and two side gates for pedestrians, separated and flanked by spearhead railings, were put up by W. Marshall with eight white brick piers dressed in Portland stone, for £396. Two more pairs of gates,

37 Inigo Jones, elevation for a Tuscan carriage gateway, possibly for Greenwich Park (BAL).

for cyclists, were added in 1900–01 by L. Faulkner and Sons, for £142.[99] The Inigo Jones gateway was lost with the building of the Royal Naval Asylum in the early nineteenth century, replaced c.1820 by St Mary's Gate to the west, the only vehicular entrance to the park on its north side. The current, much wider gates (installed in 1929), are the most ornate in the park, a fine essay in wrought iron with elaborate scrolled cresting and intricately detailed leafwork (fig. 38). Made in 1919 by the Morris-Singer Company of London and Frome for £920, to the design of G. K. Myers in the Office of Works, they were intended originally for the top of the stairs at the St James's Park end of King Charles Street, Westminster. A change of plan rendered them redundant until they were brought to Greenwich, with the addition of matching outer footway gates and further railings by the Morris-Singer Company at a cost of £462.[100] Following the opening of the park to the public there was a significant increase in the number of gates, both public and private. Many of them originally had heavy timber doors which were replaced in about 1900 by the park superintendent A. D. Webster, with ornamental wrought-iron gates made by Faulkner and Sons.[101] The most imposing of the surviving foot gates is Maze Hill Gate, opposite Vanbrugh Castle which it antedates (fig. 39). Constructed originally c.1710, it was rebuilt with much new brick in a slightly more southerly position in 1905. A handsome entrance, with a tall gauged-brick arch and a moulded-brick, pedimented head, it is reminiscent in form of Inigo Jones's seventeenth-century gateway.[102]

The deer, said by a visitor in 1710 to be 'uncommonly tame',[103] had been introduced in 1515 by Henry VIII and roamed throughout the park until increasing traffic and dogs caused them to be confined (in 1927), first at weekends, the busiest times, then all the time in their own paddock in the Great Wilderness at the

38 St Mary's Gate at the north-west corner of Greenwich Park.

39 Maze Hill Gate, Greenwich Park, with Vanbrugh Castle beyond.

40   A late nineteenth-century view northwards in Greenwich Park, down The Avenue (formerly Snow Hill Walk) towards St Mary's Lodge, with unfenced deer to the right.

south-east corner of the park.[104] By the end of the nineteenth century this no longer existed as a formal feature but had been transformed by felling and thinning of the trees into a small tract of wood pasture. Confinement here protected the deer from indiscriminate feeding. It was noted in 1876 that 'the deer . . . are so tame and fearless that they will not only feed from visitors' hands, but even steal cakes from unwary children'.[105] In order to protect his daughter from the attentions of one of the more ebullient deer, Mr Howe of Gray's Inn, visiting in 1872 with his family, proffered biscuits on behalf of the child: belying its reputation for tameness, the deer charged and plunged its antlers into 'the thick part of my thigh'. In public-spirited vein the victim wrote to *The Times*, wishing to warn others of such cervine dangers since his doctor had told him that had the antlers gone one inch either way, he would not have been leaving Greenwich that night.[106]

The public works in the park were mainly on a small scale, designed to provide attractive facilities for visitors, bringing to Greenwich the trappings of an urban park. The new buildings included shelters, drinking fountains, lavatories and, around the turn of the century, two indispensable amenities which, although modest, are of some architectural merit: the Bandstand and the Tea House. The Bandstand, an open octagon with ornamental cast iron and a well-proportioned, tented, iron-framed roof, was designed and constructed by the Coalbrookdale Company Ltd in 1891 at a cost of £282 (fig. 42).[107] The Tea House, a successor to a refreshment pavilion and to various tents, was built in 1906–7 for £1066

as a neat, two-storey, octagonal, rustic kiosk to the designs of Sir Henry Tanner of the Board of Works (fig. 43).[108] The open veranda which ran round the circumference was enclosed *c.*1967, with small-pane glazing making the whole appear bulkier. Its centre of gravity has been further lowered by the removal of balustrading on top of the veranda.[109] Specific facilities for children were provided *c.*1900 near the north-east corner of the park with the creation of 'Seaside in Greenwich Park', a large sandpit for them to use 'without fear of molestation'.[110] A generation later an anonymous benefaction of £5000 funded the construction in 1929–30 of the concrete-lined and kidney-shaped Children's Boating Pond to the west.[111] The sandpit subsequently became the Children's Playground with an octagonal gazebo shelter of 1934 that has been adapted to be a first-aid hut, then a supervisor's kiosk, reflecting developing attitudes towards the protection of children.[112]

As well as the removal of such decaying features as the old lodge in the middle of the park, which had gone by 1852, stagnant ponds and old gravel workings were filled and landscaped.[113] The irregular nature of the escarpment within the park had been accentuated by the exploitation of the layered gravels which lay just beneath the surface. Great bites were taken, all now carefully landscaped into graded slopes which add to the sinuous character of the terrain. There is no direct evidence of the beginning of gravel extraction at Greenwich. It may have begun during the late medieval period but the earliest depiction comes on the maps of *c.*1675–80 and 1695, both of which show the large pit just below

Maze Hill Gate.[114] Small-scale extraction was still taking place in the nineteenth century, much to the chagrin of one observer: 'These privileged spirits . . . needed gravel, forsooth, for their gardens – and gravel they must have, and gratis, too, torn from the bowels of Greenwich Park. A pit was opened at the back of the Observatory, and a fair hillside permanently disfigured'.[115] By 1899 several small gravel pits at the southern end of the park had been transformed into 'a picturesque little lakelet', surrounded by sunken paths, shrubberies and rockeries, shaped from the unsightly and neglected old workings.[116]

New lodges replaced old ones. A 'damp, smoky and unwholesome' house of around 1700, near the north-west entrance to the park, was replaced in 1807–8 by a new house for the park underkeeper, a restrained italianate version of the Picturesque lodge, latterly known as St Mary's Lodge. Designed by John Nash, as one of his earliest works in the Office of Woods and Forests,[117] the lodge was intended to be an ornamental eye-catcher at the end of a long downhill vista, obscured by the deviation in the road towards St Mary's Gate (figs 40 and 41). It is now a tea house

42   The Bandstand, Greenwich Park.

41   St Mary's Lodge, Greenwich Park, designed by John Nash and built in 1807–8.

and information centre. At the other end of the park, the Blackheath Gate Lodge was built in 1851–2 to a design by John Phipps for the head keeper who had been housed in the lodge in the middle of the park (fig. 44). The new lodge was built at the edge of the park in response to the criticism of encroachments. Phipps was an obscure official architect within the Office of Works who here produced a robust building remarkable for its date. The design stands so far out from the run of mid-nineteenth-century park lodges in its debt to vernacular Tudor models that it has generally been assumed to have been of thirty to fifty years later. Excepting sympathetic additions to the rear, it has scarcely been altered and it retains its original use (fig. 45).[118]

The Monuments

There are notable monuments in the park and in the grounds of the former Naval College. The oldest is John Michael Rysbrack's statue of George II portrayed in the guise of a Roman emperor and carved in 1735 from a block of marble prudently purchased in 1714. This was set up at the expense of the Hospital's longest serving Governor, Sir John Jennings, in the Grand Square between the King Charles and Queen Anne Buildings, looking towards the river (fig. 47). To the west of the King Charles Building are two commemorative obelisks. Philip Hardwick's memorial to Joseph René Bellot (1855), a monument to fruitless, heroic endeavour, is dedicated to the French naval lieutenant who lost his life in the

43 Plan and elevations of the Tea House, Greenwich Park, 1906, designed by Sir Henry Tanner (PRO WORK 38/360).

44   Blackheath Gate Lodge, Greenwich Park, depicted in 1855 (GLHL).

45   The Blackheath Gate and Gate Lodge.

46   Philip Hardwick, memorial to Joseph René Bellot, 1855, with the King Charles Building of the Royal Hospital for Seamen.

Arctic while conveying dispatches for Sir Edward Belcher, who was searching for the lost explorer Sir John Franklin (fig. 46). Close by, the New Zealand war memorial, a granite obelisk, possibly by C. Raymond Smith, which was approved for erection in 1872, commemorates the naval dead of the Maori Wars of 1863–4, a conflict which reduced Maori numbers by half and rendered the survivors 'a most peaceful race . . . among the most loyal subjects of King George'.[119] To the east of the Queen Anne Building, another obelisk, set in a round basin on a square plinth, was designed by Sir Edwin Lutyens in 1925 as a memorial of the tenth anniversary of the Gallipoli landing. First installed on Horse Guards Parade, it was moved to Greenwich in 1951. Among the many monuments in the former Hospital burial ground to the south of Romney Road is *Britannia*, sculpted by C. Raymond

47 (*facing page*) John Michael Rysbrack, statue of George II, Grand Square of the Royal Hospital for Seamen, in front of John Webb's King Charles Building. The reclining figures of Fortitude and Dominion of the Sea, supporting the cartouche of the royal Stuart arms, were carved by Joshua Marshall in 1665–8.

Smith in 1892 and unveiled the following year as a memorial to the 'gallant officers and men of the Royal Navy and Marines' who were there interred (fig. 257).[120]

Within the park, the potentially most striking of statues was happily never constructed. John Flaxman's *Britannia* (by Divine Providence Triumphant; celebrating victory at the Battle of the Nile) of 1799–1801, more than 200 feet high, was to be placed on top of the hill where the 10 foot figure of General James Wolfe now stands, next to the Observatory.[121] Wolfe, brought up at Macartney House in Greenwich, died in 1759 in capturing Quebec for Britain: he is commemorated by the bronze statue by Robert Tait McKenzie, a gift of the Canadian people in 1930 which was unveiled by the Marquis de Montcalm, a direct descendant of Wolfe's principal opponent on the Fields of Abraham overlooking Quebec (fig. 48). Wolfe is buried in the church of St Alfege. At the foot of the hill, near St Mary's Gate, stands Samuel Nixon's monumental granite figure of the 'Sailor King', William IV. Originally erected in King William Street in the City of London in 1844, the statue was moved to its present location in 1936, the former site of George Basevi's church of St Mary, demolished that year (fig. 49).

Near the crest of the hill, on the west side of the park, is Henry Moore's masterpiece of abstract figuration, *Large Standing Figure: Knife Edge* (fig. 50). A bronze sculpture, 12 feet high, it is one of an edition of six, said to have been 'worked up from a fragment of bone' and cast in Berlin in 1976.[122] Placed here in 1979, it is a wonderfully apposite piece of public art for a justly celebrated public place, a fine complement to a natural landscape which has been shaped by centuries of human occupation.

48 (*facing page top left*)   Robert Tait McKenzie, statue of General James Wolfe, to the east of the Royal Observatory, Greenwich Park.

49 (*facing page top right*)   Samuel Nixon, statue of King William IV, next to the north-west entrance to Greenwich Park.

50 (*facing page bottom*)   Henry Moore, *Large Standing Figure: Knife Edge*, to the west of the Royal Observatory, Greenwich Park.

51 The north front of the Queen's House, Greenwich, photographed in 1983. The creation of a ramped entrance to the basement door in 1999 involved the lowering of the ground level and the addition of three extra steps to each flight of the stair.

Chapter 2

THE QUEEN'S HOUSE: BUILDING AND FUNCTION

Introduction

The Queen's House is one of the best known and least understood of great English buildings. Handsome, perfectly proportioned, refined and stately, it is the *locus classicus* of the
seventeenth-century villa, the epitome of the taste and aspirations
of the Stuart court. Designed by Inigo Jones soon after the last of
his study tours to the most advanced buildings and gardens of
Europe, it holds the distinction of being regarded as the first truly
classical Renaissance building to be erected in England (fig. 51).

Inigo Jones first visited Italy in 1601; he then went to Denmark
in 1604 at the request of Christian IV of Denmark, brother of
Queen Anne (the queen of James I of England), and travelled in
France in 1609. But his most extensive and important visit to Italy
began in July 1613, when he accompanied the Earl and Countess
of Arundel, who were escorting the newly married Princess Elizabeth and her husband, Frederick, the Elector Palatine, to their
court at Heidelberg. The party proceeded to Milan, from whence
Jones, already well schooled in the literature of architecture, took
the opportunity to compare theory with practice and toured
throughout the major cities of Italy until August 1614, when he
returned home through France. As well as visiting many buildings
which were to be of fundamental importance in his future practice, he met the aged Vincenzo Scamozzi and, along with Arundel,
acquired an extensive collection of architectural drawings.[1] The
experience gained was formative. Jones has been aptly described
as the first English architect to move away from 'the pursuit of
variety and turn to the classical tradition' (fig. 52).[2]

But to the early seventeenth-century observer, even to one with
advanced taste, within the inner court circle, the design of the
Queen's House was truly odd and probably misunderstood. In
1617 it was described as a 'curious device' – an interesting conceit
– a usage indicating the retention into the Stuart era of the Elizabethan predilection for witty, formal inventiveness in poetry, art
and architecture.[3] The Queen's House, planned to form an H, may
have been perceived as belonging to the tradition of the device
as visual symbol, to be seen in the same context as Sir Thomas
Tresham's Triangular Lodge at Rushden, Northamptonshire
(1593–7) or his Lyveden New Bield in the same county
(1594–1605), although an H for Queen Anne would have been a
rather anachronistic conceit. The most important characteristic of
the device was an ingenuity of form or plan, and as such they

were often built as lodges or retreats. But although 'curious', the
Queen's House did not belong within this tradition. Rather, it
represented architecture at a turning-point, marking both an
ending and the beginning of something new in English architecture, the emergence of a pure classicism – albeit, in this case, one
with singular planning requirements.

Acceptance of the Jonesian style within court circles was rapid.
By 1642, when writing of Lord Arundel's contribution to English
architecture, James Howell noted that although uniform and

52   William Dobson, portrait of Inigo Jones, possibly a study from the
life for the portrait at Chiswick House (NMM).

53 View of the Queen's House from the north-east. The later colonnades follow the line of the original road which divided the house into two halves.

regular italianate building was 'distasteful at first, as all innovations are, yet they find now the commodity, firmness and beauty thereof, three main principles of Architecture'.[4] He was following Sir Henry Wotton, who had earlier paraphrased the Vitruvian triumvirate for an English audience: 'Well building hath three Conditions. Commoditie, Firmenes, and Delight'.[5] The Queen's House was perhaps the first major English building to embrace these three elements in an appropriately classical manner.

Architectural historians have recounted the building history of the house and the role of Inigo Jones, and have made significant contributions to our understanding of the evolution of the fabric and the place of the building in Jones's oeuvre.[6] But design and construction are just one part of the story, and besides, it is of the essence of great architecture that there is always more to be explored and more questions to be asked. Why was such a building designed by Jones and built at Greenwich for the Stuart queens, Anne and Henrietta Maria, and what was its intended purpose?

With eyes conditioned by the engraved plates of Colen Campbell's *Vitruvius Britannicus*, which depict buildings in splendid isolation, and with sensibilities coloured by the Palladian propaganda

that encourages us to see purity and simplicity of built form within a bland and limitless rural vista, we have tended to look at a Queen's House divorced from both its original and later contexts. It should not be viewed in isolation. The natural landscape and setting, the formal gardens and the relationship with the adjacent palace and the lodge in the park need to be explored before the meaning of the house can be understood. The principal difficulty in reaching such an understanding lies in the fact that its intended purpose changed during the course of the very long period of construction and decoration, and once built, it was not in this use for very long. The needs and desires of Queen Anne, who commissioned the building in 1616 (when she was forty-two), were very different to those of the young Henrietta Maria, for whom it was finished and decorated during the 1630s. Inigo Jones played a central role throughout the twenty-four years of building, but his ideas inevitably evolved over that period. The changes in fashion and taste at a vibrant court, open to new ideas and influences, and the different personalities of those at its heart – Anne of Denmark and Henrietta Maria – are of more significance than has been recognised.

Externally, the façade of the Queen's House projected decorum

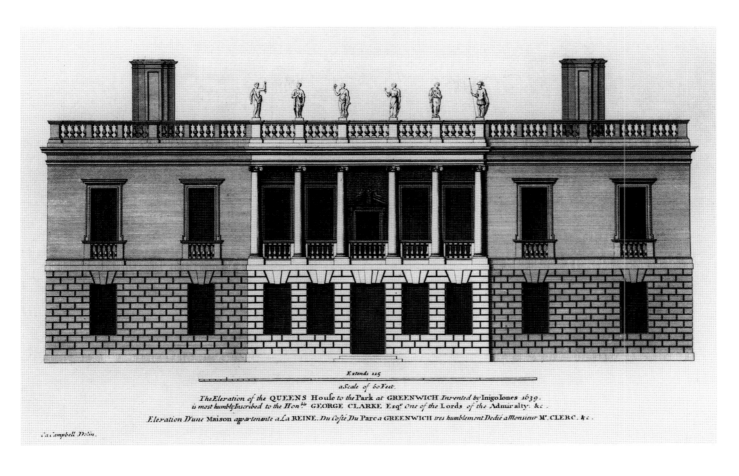

Extends 115

a Scale of 60 Feet.

The Elevation of the QUEENS House to the Park at GREENWICH Invented by Inigo Iones 1639.
is most humbly Inscribed to the Honble GEORGE CLARKE Esqr One of the Lords of the Admiralty. &c.

Elevation D'une Maison appartenante a La REINE. Du Costé Du Parc a GREENWICH tres humblement Dedié a Monsieur Mr. CLERC. &c.

C. Campbell Delin.

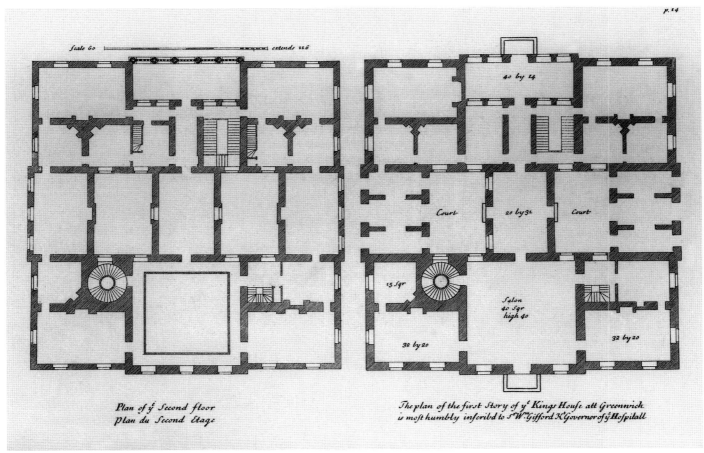

p. 14

scale 60   extends 116

40 by 14

Court   20 by 32   Court

15 Sqr   Salon
                                        40 Sqr
                                        high 40

32 by 20   32 by 20

Plan of ye Second floor
Plan du Second Etage

The plan of the first Story of ye Kings House att Greenwich
is most humbly inscribd to Sr Wm Gifford Kt Governor of ye Hospitall

54   The south elevation and floor plans of the Queen's House after the addition of the outer Bridge Rooms. The plans are arranged with the ground floor to the right and the first floor to the left. They are oriented with north at the bottom (Colen Campbell, *Vitruvius Britannicus*, I, 1715).

and restraint – a flat, stone and rendered-brick backdrop to orna-mental gardens and the variegated red-brick buildings of the old palace. To the world outside it showed the refined and educated taste of the most powerful in the land. The interior decoration was lavish and sumptuous, but it was not intended to be seen except by very few. The note which Inigo Jones made in his Roman Sketchbook in January 1613/14 is highly pertinent:

> all thes Composed ornamentes the wch Proceed out of ye aboundance of dessignes . . . in my oppignion do not well in sollid Architecture and ye facciati of houses, but in gardens loggis, stucco or ornamentes of chimnie pieccies . . . for as out-wardly euery wyse ma[n] carrieth a grauiti in Publicke Places, whear ther is nothing els looked for, & yt inwardly hath his Immaginacy set free, and sumetimes licenciously flying out, as nature hirsealf doeth often tymes Strauagantly. . . . So in archi-tecture ye outward ornamentes oft to be Sollid, proporsionable according to the rulles, masculine and unaffected.[7]

For historians, the Queen's House has become the pre-eminent representation in bricks and mortar, of the aesthetic aspirations, philosophical beliefs, courtly behaviour and fantastic dreamworld of those of advanced thought and taste within the Stuart court. To Henrietta Maria, the building arguably was to be even more, a statement at once domestic, national and cosmic: an affirmation of marital love and fidelity, an expression of divinely ordered royal supremacy and glory, and a Neoplatonic encapsulation of the harmony between man and nature. But it was a house which was delivering a message to those who were already converted and, in this respect, it might serve as a symbol for a monarchy which was out of touch with its subjects. For Henrietta Maria, the Queen's House was a private space. No written accounts of the interior in her time or descriptions of events inside have been discovered.

The Queen's House as it is today comprises two buildings linked by three bridges at first-floor level which span a former road (fig. 53). The north building is of three storeys, with a terrace in front which obscures the original basement. The south build-ing, as a consequence of the slope of the land, was of two storeys, without an original basement, although cellars were dug out in the nineteenth century. The building arrived at this form after three main building campaigns (fig. 72): between 1617 and 1619 the north building, comprising ground floor and basement, and the south building with just a ground floor were erected; between 1629 and 1638 an upper storey was added to each building, the central Bridge Room was built and the north side terrace was added; between 1661 and 1663 two further Bridge Rooms were created at the east and west sides, turning the first-floor plan of the house from an H into a square (fig. 54). Subsequent institu-tional usage, with associated alterations, and a number of exten-sive restorations and refurbishments, most notably during the 1930s and 1980s, have made it difficult to see clearly what was intended by architect and patrons. The twentieth-century restorations, in their pursuit of elusive and romantic ideals, have in fact obscured as much as they have elucidated the history, and in the manner of many retrospectively questionable performances, say more about the singer than the song.

★　　★　　★

Early Greenwich

Throughout the Tudor period the royal palace at Greenwich was a popular residence for the monarch, especially during the summer months when it served as a rural retreat away from the heat and stench of central London. Henry VII extended the brick-built riverside range and renamed the palace Placentia. During the reign of Henry VIII Greenwich was a favoured location for hunting and martial sports of all kinds: jousting, tilting, archery and falconry. Most construction undertaken during the reign was associated with these pastimes. Several new stable blocks were built, as well as two tilt-yard towers, linked by a gallery from which the court could watch the tournament below.[8] During 1537–8 elaborate revels took place at Greenwich within specially commissioned temporary structures, comprising a banqueting house and theatre. Many members of the Painter-Stainers' Company were involved in the decoration of these buildings, including Hans Holbein, who painted a canvas depicting the Siege of Therouanne of 1513 and an elaborate astronomical design for the ceiling of the theatre.[9] Anthonis van den Wyngaerde completed two views of Greenwich in 1558, one looking north and the other south, which give some idea of the size and layout of the Tudor palace and show the rela-tionship of the riverside buildings to the gardens, tilt yard and park (figs 55 and 56).[10] In the centre of the view looking north the old gatehouse is depicted, spanning the road which ran between the royal garden and the park, later to be replaced by the Queen's House which was built almost on the same spot.

On the hill in the park, now the site of the Observatory, was a lodge or tower, clearly shown in one of Wyngaerde's views and in paintings of about 1615 (fig. 11) and 1626–8 (fig. 57).[11] The original building on the site, a tall park lodge, was constructed during the 1430s by Humphrey, Duke of Gloucester, who was at the same time building the original palace by the riverside at Greenwich, later called Bella Court. In 1433 Humphrey and his wife Eleanor were given permission by the Crown 'to enclose two hundred acres of their land pasture, wood, heath, virses, and gorse thereof to make a park in Greenwich: and by the same authority to make towers there of stone and lime'.[12] The resulting lodge, known as 'Duke Humphrey's Tower', was a building which was sufficiently solidly built and prominently sited to proclaim the power of its owner. It would have functioned as a perfect obser-vation platform for the appreciation of the magnificent prospect of palace, river and countryside to the north and for the con-templation of the contrived landscape of the park. Its situation was such that the entire perimeter of the park would have been visible from its upper storey, so it was ideally placed to function also as a standing from which to watch the progress of the hunt.

Although depictions of the building are consistent in showing that it had a crenellated tower, this was more ornamental than functional: often known as Greenwich Castle (the hill on which it stood was still referred to as Castle Hill even after the building of the Observatory[13]), this was not a defensible building. During the reign of Henry VIII, in 1525–6, it was rebuilt or substantially altered: 'newly repaired and builded'.[14] Here the monarch indulged in romantic dalliance, the building being described by George Put-tenham in his *Arte of English Poesie* as the place where Henry VIII lodged 'a fayre lady whom [he] loved'.[15] On one occasion when Henry was arriving by barge with his standard-bearer, he was so

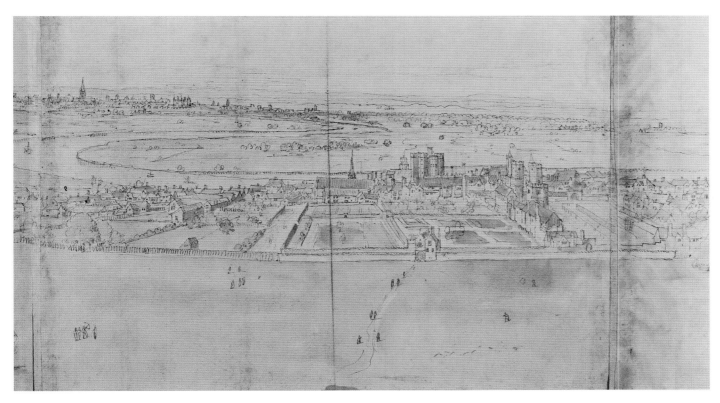

55 Anthonis van den Wyngaerde, *Greenwich Palace*, 1558, looking north from the park. The Queen's House was built approximately on the site of the gatehouse which spans the road (Ashmolean Museum, Oxford).

56 Anthonis van den Wyngaerde, *Greenwich Palace*, 1558, looking south from the river. Duke Humphrey's Tower is on top of the hill on the site later occupied by the Royal Observatory (Ashmolean Museum, Oxford).

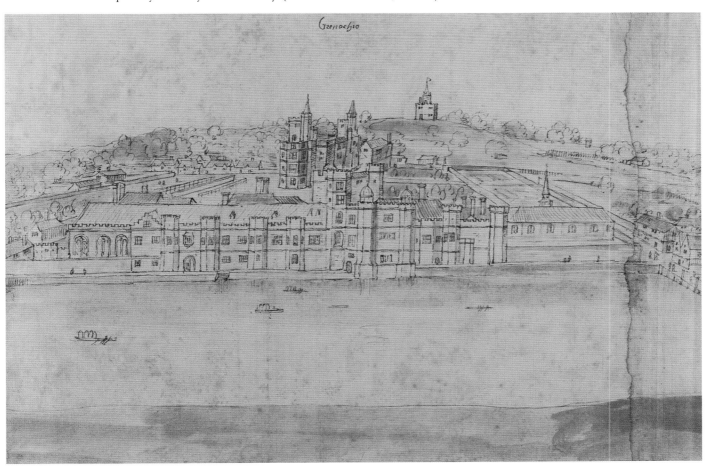

57   Flemish School, *View of Greenwich*, *c*.1626–8. The Earl of Northampton's Lodge, formerly Duke Humphrey's Tower, is on the far right of the painting – see also fig. 68 (Museum of London).

merry that he encouraged his servant to participate in a rhyming game. The king began the rhyme:

> Within this towre
> There lieth a flowre
> That hath my hart.

Flamock replied, 'within this bower, she will, etc with the rest in so vncleanly terms, as might not now become me by the rule of Decorum to vtter writing to so great a Maistie, but the King tooke them in so euill part, as he bid Flamock, auaunt varlet'.[16]

From 1605 the lodge or tower was granted to Henry Howard, Lord Northampton. An educated and cultured man, he operated as an unprincipled and unscrupulous politician, becoming an important member of the court of James I, especially after the succession, which he helped to secure. For much of his life, Northampton had been dependent on the financial support of the monarchy, as a result of the political and religious troubles which had embroiled members of his family during the reign of Elizabeth I, which had cost them most of their wealth and some of their heads. But by the time of his death in 1614 Northampton was an exceedingly wealthy man, despite the declaration in his will that he had 'nothing to present worthie his Majestie but the straynes and prayers from a loyal harte that his dayes be long and happie and his seede endure to the worldes end'.[17] Not only did he hold the lodge and the keepership of Greenwich Park, in 1613 becoming involved in a dispute with Queen Anne over the stewardship of the park which she desired for herself, but also a house near modern Greenwich Pier, west of the royal palace, which he had purchased in 1605 from Robert Dudley, Earl of Leicester, for £500.[18] Northampton's 'lower house' at Greenwich was inherited by his kinsman Thomas Howard, 2nd Earl of Arundel, in 1616. Soon after Arundel's return from Italy, where he had travelled with Inigo Jones, extensive alterations were made at the house, possibly under the supervision of the architect. Said to have been one of the best houses of the new century, it was destroyed by fire in 1617.[19]

Around 1613–14, shortly before he died, improvements to the hilltop lodge were initiated by Northampton, possibly assisted by Simon Basil who lived near Northampton's lower house near the Thames and was working for Queen Anne on the palace.[20] In an inventory made at the time of his death, the three-storey 'Lodge in the Parke' is fully described. On the upper floor were the 'pallatte chamber, bedchamber, closset and gallery'. The bedchamber was furnished with leather hangings of azure and gold and contained an ornate 'half headed bedstead with a canopie of crimson damaske laced and frindged with golde 7 guilte cuppes with the traine or two curtens of crimson damaske with loopes of golde and crimson silke unlaced'.[21] The middle floor contained the great and the withdrawing chambers and wardrobe, and on the 'lowest floor' were a hall and four chambers for servants.[22] In 1617–18 it was decorated by John de Critz, Sergeant Painter to the King from 1605 until his death in 1642, who painted the weathervane and gilded the fleurs-de-lis, the serpent's head and the crowns that decorated it.[23]

The crenellated building, ornamented by a round turret, was bounded by a private garden. A visitor in 1640 referred to it as the castle of 'Millefleur' and stated that, although small, it had three floors, a kitchen and a wine-cellar and that its apartments were well proportioned and prettily furnished, although the whole building was only nineteen paces long and twelve wide. Despite its size, this was a self-contained lodge, capable of sustaining periods of residence. From the flat, lead-covered roof, the visitor had a magnificent prospect over London.[24] The building was largely destroyed during the Interregnum, when it was 'razed to the ground by the parliamentarians',[25] and in 1675 Charles II granted the site for the building of an observatory, 'at Greenwich upon the highest ground at or near the Place where the Castle stood'.[26] Wren's Royal Observatory was built on the original footings of Duke Humphrey's Tower (see chapter 1).

During the reign of Elizabeth I (who, like her sister Mary, had been born there), little structural work was carried out on the fabric of Greenwich Palace, which as a result was somewhat decayed. In contrast, there had been much expenditure on the gardens, including the installation of at least two magnificent marble fountains during the latter part of the reign; one of these cost over £500, perhaps indicating that in her declining years Greenwich was a favoured retreat for rest and relaxation.[27] The cult of Elizabeth as Flora or the Tudor Rose gave rise to much contemporary horticultural imagery in both the visual arts and the written word – 'the Queen, the kingdom, the spring, the garden and flowers became inextricably intertwined'.[28] Indeed, the poet John Davies in his *Hymnes to Astraea*, published in 1600, specifically mentions Greenwich in the first stanza of Hymn IX, 'To Flora':

> E mpresse of flowers, tell where away
> L ies your sweet Court this merry May
> I n Greenewich garden allies?
> S ince there the heauenly powers do play
> A nd haunt no other vallies.[29]

Queen Anne and the 'Curious Device'

Soon after James I and his consort Queen Anne came to the throne, work on modernising the palace and refurbishing the gardens was being undertaken at Greenwich, during a period of political and economic stability: 'Gardening goes hand in hand with architecture and both are the products of peace and prosperity'.[30] In 1607–9 new lodgings were built for the queen and during 1611 the gardens were receiving attention as 'Salomon de Caus, gardener to the Queen' was paid £60 for works.[31] In the following year he received a further £205.[32]

Salomon de Caus was the principal exponent of Mannerist gardening in Europe. He had studied the writings of the ancients Hero of Alexandria and Archimedes on engineering, hydraulics and automata, and was also fully aware of the work carried out in Renaissance Italy by such men as Filippo Brunelleschi and Leonardo da Vinci, whose schemes and automata had been incorporated into many Italian celebrations. But it was the garden at Pratolino, just north of Florence, probably visited by Inigo Jones in 1601, that was for de Caus perhaps the most influential and which he attempted to emulate in his own garden designs. Pratolino was created by Bernardo Buontalenti for Grand Duke Francesco I de' Medici in 1569–84 as an enclosed artificial environment where hydraulic effect and surprise were the main elements.

Salomon de Caus spent the first decade of the seventeenth century employed in the Low Countries, at Mariemont and Brussels, constructing fountains and grottoes for Albert, Archduke of Austria, and his wife Isabella. From 1610 until 1612 he lived in England as a member of the court of Henry, Prince of Wales, and designed a number of royal gardens, including those at Denmark (Somerset) House and Richmond Palace.[33] At Greenwich he was engaged in extensive replanning and by 1612 the gardens there not only comprised the new orchard and lodge and the old great garden, but also 'the new garden'.[34] Later known as the Queen's Garden, this is shown on a plan of about 1694–5, lying to the north-west of the Queen's House and to the east of Friars Road (fig. 58). Under de Caus's instruction, the roof of the bird house at Greenwich was raised by adding another storey with an arcade of five arches, each 10 feet wide, and sixteen niches for nests.[35] The Greenwich aviary was possibly depicted by him as 'problesme VII et VIII' in the second book of *Les raisons des forces mouvantes*, published in 1624 (figs 59 and 60). He might have been responsible also for the water maze or labyrinth which existed from at least 1614 in the Conduit Court of the old palace.[36] Repairs to the lead channels, stopcocks and paving that surrounded the maze were carried out regularly between 1614 and 1640.[37] De Caus also laid out the gardens at the royal residence at Heidelberg in 1616–19 for Anne of Denmark's daughter, the Princess Elizabeth, who had recently moved there with her husband, Frederick, the Elector Palatine.

De Caus's real genius lay in the invention of automata, often associated with waterworks, and these phenomena were at the heart of the gardens he designed for the Stuarts (fig. 61). In 1616, when James I and his favourite, George Villiers, later Duke of Buckingham, were walking through the gardens at Greenwich, the young Prince Charles turned on a fountain hidden in a statue of Bacchus, soaking Villiers, for which his father boxed his ears.[38] In 1629 Abram Booth, a Dutch visitor, described Greenwich as 'having lovely gardens adjacent in which are several beautiful fountains decorated with marble statues. Likewise, several sculptured things which appear to have been very nice, yet now mostly are beginning to decay'.[39] The visitor in 1640 more fully described the completed gardens, some of which were the work of de Caus:

> The garden of this palace is very beautiful, and it has in the middle a fine fountain in which a marble statue pours water from a cornucopia into a great basin. The grotto is one of the prettiest that I have ever seen. It is in a little house which is closed in front by an iron grille, and the walls are dressed in mother-of-pearl, mussels and all sorts of shells, in such a manner however that the moss and grasses are not allowed to be separated in the regularly proportioned spaces, so it seems that art had hardly any part in the construction of this little building. At the bottom of the grotto there was a woman representing a centaur, made of shells. who was bringing forth a great quantity of water, just like the two other figures to either side of her.[40]

The early seventeenth century was perhaps one of the most important and innovative periods of garden design in Europe, although generally imperfectly acknowledged as such since so few of the great gardens constructed at that date survive. It is in the nature of planting that change will occur, growth and decay being abetted by shifts in taste. Any intended 'rapprochement' between architecture and its artfully natural setting will in time be lost,[41] making it difficult to recapture the original idea of the house and garden as an ensemble. This difficulty of re-creation is compounded when the garden is designed not merely as a static setting but as a place for participation and fantasy – a waking dream. For this idea, however, there is a retrievable literary source which allows some of the flavour of the fantasy garden to be captured: Francesco Colonna's *Hypnerotomachia Poliphili*. First published in Venice in 1499 and reprinted in 1545, this was partly translated into English by R. D., believed to be Robert Dallington, in 1592, as *The Strife of Love in a Dreame*.[42] Like de Caus, Dallington was a member of the court of Prince Henry and had travelled extensively in Italy, including one visit with Inigo Jones at the beginning of the century. The *Hypnerotomachia* is the story of Poliphilo and his search for his true love Polia. His journey takes him through a humanist dreamworld, where fantastic architecture, classical ruins, amazing fountains, a water maze, exotic topiary and garden structures are minutely described, allying antiquity to sexuality and romance: 'the sustained sense of erotic longing in the narrative . . . is mirrored by wonderment at the visual splendour

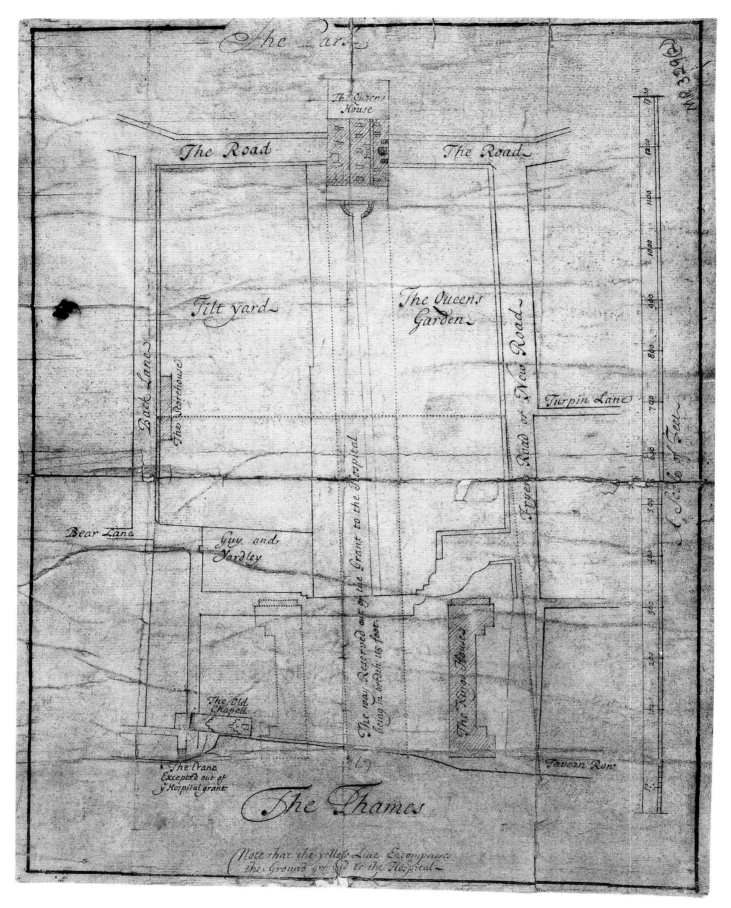

The following labels appear within the survey plan:

- The Park
- The Queen's House
- The Road
- The Road
- Tilt yard
- The Queen's Garden
- Back Lane
- The Storehouse
- Freyers Road or New Road
- Turpin Lane
- A Scale of Feet
- The way Reserved out of the Grant to the Hospital being in breadth 115 foot
- Bear Lane
- Guy and Yardley
- The Kings House
- The Old Chapell
- Tavern Row:
- The Crane Excepted out of y Hospital grant
- The Thames
- Note that the yellow Line Encompasses the Ground granted to the Hospital

58   Survey plan of Greenwich Palace, *c.*1694–5, showing the Queen's Garden and the tilt yard of the palace to the north of the Queen's House. The side elevation of the Queen's House is depicted, together with the avenue leading to the river which was excluded from the grant of land to Greenwich Hospital. John Webb's 'Kings House' is shown with the proposed pendant range indicated opposite (PRO MR1/329 (2)).

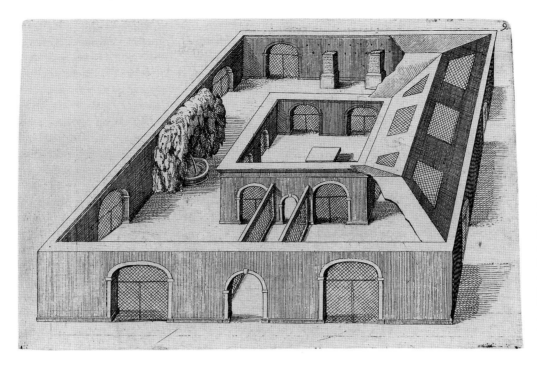

59 Salomon de Caus, aviary, Problesme VIII, *Les raisons des forces mouvantes*, 1624. The aviary, roofed with copper wire, with iron grilles in the arches of the walls, is disposed around a rectangular viewing area (BL, Hirsch I 108 (1–2)).

60 Salomon de Caus, grotto and aviary, Problesme VII, *Les raisons des forces mouvantes*, 1624. The grotto is seen through the arcaded wall which divides the internal viewing area from the aviary. The iron grilles are omitted in this illustration (BL, Hirsch I 108 (1–2)).

61 Salomon de Caus, a fountain statue, Problesme V, *Les raisons des forces mouvantes*, 1624 (BL, Hirsch I 108 (1–2)).

of ancient civilization'.[43] Dallington's text captures Colonna's dualism in proclaiming a fundamental message of the Renaissance: 'take away order and rule, and what thing can any man make, eyther beautifull to the eye, or of commendable proportion and durable', while taking great pleasure in pointing out the risks of failing to heed the lesson of order and constancy in the face of amorous provocation. Beset by alluring nymphs and advised to eschew the 'slypperie and transitorie', which can bring only brief pleasure, the hero finds himself 'provoked by their perswasive alluring intisements, to unlawfull concupiscence'.[44]

The direct influence of the *Hypnerotomachia* on architecture has been questioned, but its importance in providing a rich collection of images for painters, sculptors and engravers has been demonstrated,[45] together with its literary significance in England both for Ovidian romances and for the court masque. Indeed, Ben Jonson's ownership of a copy of the 1545 edition 'confirms the impression conveyed by his masques and some of his poems that he knew the work'.[46] Parallels between the *Hypnerotomachia*'s evocations and real gardens are also apparent, particularly in Italy, while north of the Alps, in England and France, the woodcuts showed how antique detail could be grafted onto a native tradition.[47] The gardens created by de Caus at Greenwich lie firmly within this tradition of incorporating formal structures within a contrivedly natural world, fulfilling the desire to strike a balance between the permanent and the transitory. In their elusive combination of classical form with a temporarily tamed nature, in which the users play a fully participatory role, they may be read as the *Hypnerotomachia* realised.

In 1613 James I formally granted the manor and palace of Greenwich to Queen Anne, adding them to her jointure 'by her late pacification'. This phrase reputedly refers to the reconciliation of the couple after the deep dismay that she had felt after killing her husband's favourite hound when hunting at Theobalds, their house in Hertfordshire. The king, although angered at first, soon forgave her, and the next day sent her a diamond worth £2000 as a legacy from the dog, as well as adding Greenwich to her possessions.[48]

Very soon afterwards she began to plan improvements to her apartments there in association with the Surveyor of the King's Works, Simon Basil. Brought up in the Danish court of Frederik

62   Paul van Somer, *Anne of Denmark*, 1617, with the palace of Oatlands in the background (The Royal Collection © 2000, HM Queen Elizabeth II).

II, during a northern flowering of Renaissance culture, and brother to Christian IV, 'the most ardent building-enthusiast of all the kings of Denmark', Queen Anne was both knowledgeable and enthusiastic about architecture.[49] This manifested itself early in her marriage to James when as queen in Scotland she commissioned a new lodging at Dunfermline Abbey,[50] and later in the work she initiated at Somerset House. In her reconstruction of the apartments at Greenwich she showed an interest in the most up-to-date architectural ideas from the continent. In 1615–16 a three-arched loggia was constructed: 'setting of three arches of canestone at the end of the Queens lodging in the garden with ashlar in the spandrels . . . for setting of architrave frieze and cornise over the same arches and over the two great windows standing upon the same arches'.[51] In the following year the floor of the loggia was completed, when workmen were paid 'for rubbing, squaring and laying with black and white stones Arras wayes the square place under the Arches'.[52] The resulting building has been likened to the loggia built at Somerset House by Simon Basil in 1609–11, but with only a single storey above.[53]

When Basil died in September 1615, Inigo Jones was appointed Surveyor of the King's Works, having already been surveyor to Henry, Prince of Wales, who had died in 1612. With Jones's arrival, Anne found herself in a position to realise more fully her architectural aspirations. Jones was to retain his position as arbiter of artistic taste within the court until the outbreak of the Civil War in 1642. As the principal designer of court masques and revels, he already was well respected and trusted by the queen herself, who had worked closely with him on these productions from the start of the reign. Her knowledge of sets and scenery, which over the years had become more and more classically influenced, would have helped in her relationship with the architect: Jones did not think of architecture and masques as discontinuous, but as two forms, both inspired by nature and by past works of art.[54] Queen Anne was a worthy and enlightened patron in the Renaissance manner for the architect, who more than anyone in England before him sought to imbue native building with the spirit, light and intellectual rigour of the south. If she had lived longer and had enjoyed greater resources, her importance as an influential patron of the arts might have been more fully appreciated. She took her pleasures seriously, being a noted horsewoman and a great collector of jewellery as well as 'devoting herself . . . to dancing, court entertainments and the design and decoration of her houses and gardens'.[55] She was also a conscientious woman of fashion who went so far in the presentation of her image as to have her official portraits retouched in order to bring her hairstyle up to date.[56] Paul van Somer's famous full-length portrait, now at Windsor Castle, bears eloquent witness to the queen's self-image (fig. 62). The painter, introduced to the English court by Anne's brother Christian IV,[57] shows her fashionably dressed for the hunt, with rakish hat, accompanied by her groom and her horse and dogs, in front of her palace of Oatlands with its prominent Tuscan gateway erected by Inigo Jones in 1616,[58] the year before the painting of the portrait. The picture represents a 'court aesthetic revolution'.[59]

When Anne determined on her new building at Greenwich, she again turned to Inigo Jones. The success of the revolutionary Queen's House has always been attributed to his artistic genius, but however great the architect and however much he may be a dictatorial 'Dominus Do-all',[60] the practice of architecture is

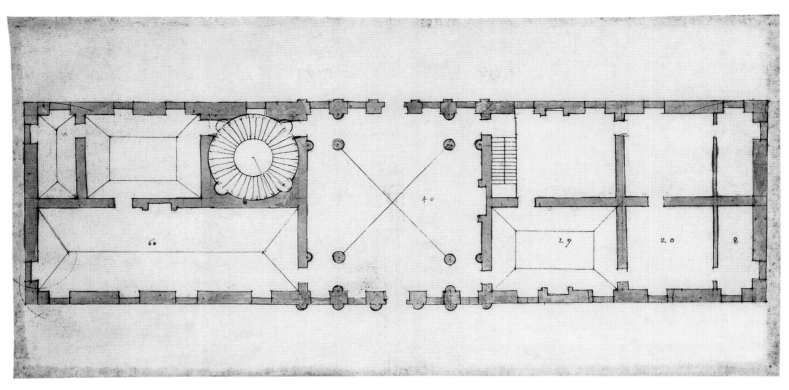

63 Inigo Jones, preliminary ground plan for the Queen's House, Greenwich (BAL).

essentially collaborative. The project was initiated by Anne, and owes more to her ideas and desires than has been adequately acknowledged; one of these was to effect a crossing over the public road which separated the palace garden from the park, 'in privacy and without muddying her feet'.[61]

The idea of building above or over a road was unusual but not unique. The Holbein Gate at Whitehall provided a route over King Street into St James's Park. Christian IV was building over water at Frederiksborg at this time and also, more significantly, Anne of Denmark herself had built over a road at her palace at Dunfermline Abbey.[62] The new building at Greenwich had to fulfil the same function as the Tudor gatehouse which it replaced, spanning the public right-of-way. There seems never to have been any question of permanently diverting the road until the 1690s, when the construction of Greenwich Hospital began.

In 1616 Inigo Jones prepared at least two prototypes for the queen, charging £10 'in making the first module of the new building at Grenewich' and a further £16 'in making and perfecting the second module for the same buildings at Grenewich in the forme the same was to be builded and finished'.[63] Whether these were plans or models is unclear, the words being interchangeable at this date, but models were not commonly made in this period. Their usefulness in solving planning difficulties and showing a completed work to a patron, rather than working things out as the building proceeded, was just being realised in England, rather later than on the continent. It might therefore be assumed that Jones completed drawings for two schemes for the queen. The final plan appears not to have survived; what does survive is perhaps the rejected first design, showing a long rectangular building incorporating a large spiral staircase placed adjacent to a 40 foot square central hall. It is a much larger building than that which was constructed, being 188 feet long and 50 feet wide and

in this design the hall was to have been single-storey, with its vaulted ceiling supported by four free-standing columns (fig. 63).[64] It is perhaps significant that the accounts refer firstly to 'a new building' and then to 'the same buildings'. A single range would not have performed the required crossing function. Two buildings joined in the middle would fulfil the requirement.

This is what Jones seems to have drawn next in a side elevation which shows the road passing under the centre of the house (fig. 64).[65] He ingeniously used the unusual site to design a building which was in essence an H-plan house: one half in the garden, the other in the park, linked by a central covered bridge. The plan-shape was loosely based on the villa at Poggio a Caiano, near Florence, where an H plan comprising two wings of double-pile depth, linked by a central salone, had been created by Giuliano da Sangallo the elder for Lorenzo de' Medici in the 1480s (figs 65

64 Inigo Jones, preliminary elevation of the east or west side of the Queen's House, Greenwich (Worcester College, Oxford).

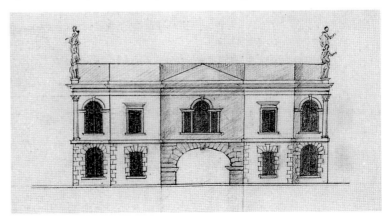

65   The south, entrance front of the Medici villa at Poggio a Caiano, near Florence. The original straight flights of steps up to the terrace were replaced in the early nineteenth century by the semicircular staircase.

66   The west, side elevation of the Medici villa at Poggio a Caiano, near Florence, showing the two wings linked by the central salone.

and 66). For the spectacular circular staircase, present in the design from the beginning, Jones would have been familiar with precedents at Andrea Palladio's Convento della Carità in Venice (now the Accademia), where the stair is oval, and at Giacomo Barozzi da Vignola's Palazzo Farnese at Caprarola.

Work on the Queen's House began in the early summer of 1617, first in 'taking downe the olde house over the park gate there, as in digging the foundation of the newe building, making of sellers [the vaulted basement], and bringing up the brick walls of the said new building'.[66] In June it was stated that 'The Queen is building at Greenwich, after a plan of Inigo Jones'.[67] When commenting on the new building, a member of the court remarked somewhat optimistically that it 'must be finished this summer' and would cost 'above' £4000. What was actually paid by the queen in total is unclear, although in October 1616 Jones received £200 to be 'imployed on her m[ajestie]s buildings at Grenewich and Otelands', a further £200 the following February and in May 1617, another £1000.[68]

The building as planned was not finished (fig. 71). At the end of the summer of 1618 Anne became ill, dying in March the following year. In 1619 workmen were 'laying a floor at the bottom

of the wall in the park, with a roof for the same, setting up postes and rails and paling the same'.[69] By the time of her death, work already had ceased and what had been erected remained incomplete until the 1630s.

It appears that what was actually built in this first phase were two separate buildings, one on the park side of the road and one on the garden side (fig. 72). The park side building was one storey high, without a basement. On the garden side, the slope of the land towards the river necessitated the construction of a vaulted basement beneath the ground floor. The two separate buildings were unconnected, without a bridge at this stage, although it was evidently intended, its footings being embedded in the walls. In the Flemish School *View of Greenwich* of 1626–8,[70] the two separate blocks can be discerned, individually but fully roofed, with the road running between them (fig. 68).

It has been suggested that the complex sequence of unheated brick-vaulted spaces in the basement (fig. 67) may have been intended as a grotto, perhaps similar to the one designed by Isaac de Caus (the son or nephew of Salomon) beneath the Banqueting House, Whitehall, which was used by the king as a private cellar (he could retire there with friends for drinking sessions), or like the surviving de Caus grotto at Woburn, or that constructed at Wilton but now demolished.[71] Grottoes occasionally were built in Italy within the structure of the house, rather than as discrete garden features, as for example at Caprarola. The ground-floor grotto constructed for Isabella d'Este within the Castello di San Giorgio at the Palazzo Ducale, Mantua, may also have provided a precedent. But there is no architectural evidence at the Queen's House for a grotto: there are no decorative traces and the drainage channels (necessary for watery diversions), which were discovered during investigations in the 1980s, were no older than the eighteenth century. Anne, moreover, although no stranger to excess, surely is unlikely to have required two such structures in such close proximity. She already had the exquisite grotto constructed by Salomon de Caus in a separate building in the garden which survived until the 1640s. It remains unclear what function the base-

67   The central passage room in the basement of the Queen's House, viewed from the east in 1996. The brick-vaulted basement was rendered in 1999.

68 Flemish School, *View of Greenwich*, *c.*1626–8; detail of fig. 57 (Museum of London). The two low blocks of the Queen's House are shown to the left, next to the buildings of the Tudor palace.

ment was intended to have. During the 1980s restoration, the nineteenth-century rendering was removed and the rough brick of the basement left uncovered. More recent archaeological investigation has revealed traces of seventeenth-century rendering on the walls below the level of the inserted eighteenth-century floor.[72] It remains uncertain when this rendering was applied, but it might not have been added until the 1660s, when the introduction of a staircase between basement and ground floor caused the lower storey to become more fully incorporated into the circulation system of the house. It is possible that the basement initially was left unfinished and then was relegated to being a storage area when building recommenced in the 1630s, or, given the lack of heating and internal access, that it was always intended to be a storage area. It is implausible to suppose that Jones would have been party to leaving the crudely finished brickwork in its naked state if any sort of polite usage had been planned either by Anne or by Henrietta Maria. Anne might have intended such usage, but died before the work could be completed. Certainly, the entrance to the basement is framed by a handsome, rusticated stone doorway which survives at the rear of the passage that runs beneath the later (1630s) terrace (fig. 69). This originally was the outside door, comparable in style with a design by Jones for a door surround datable to around 1616.[73] After going through the door, one might have expected to go into a modestly finished room giving onto a staircase, but this does not appear to have been the case. Originally the basement would have been well lit, with three

69 The entrance to the basement, originally an outside door, on the north side of the Queen's House. The passage underneath the terrace was rendered in 1999.

70   The windows on the west side of the north front of the Queen's House, designed to light the basement but later obscured by the terrace, revealed during works of restoration in 1934–5.

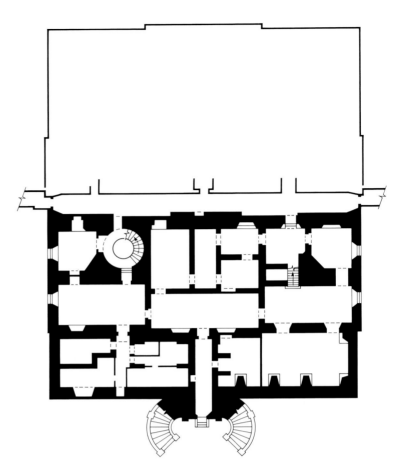

round-headed windows to each side of the door on the north, garden side (fig. 70),[74] and the upper parts of a further six windows receiving a light from the road. There is, however, no sign of an original internal staircase from the basement to the ground floor. The grand circular 'Tulip' stair began at ground-floor level and was not extended downwards until the nineteenth century: the springing of the supporting brick vaulting for the stair was discovered at basement level during the 1980s restoration.[75] The back stair on the west side of the basement is also a later insertion, possibly added at this level in 1662, when new 'pairs of stairs' were being installed: 'inclosing the back stairs and making a door to go in the cellar that way'.[76] Although there appears to have been an original secondary stair at this point from ground- to first-floor level, it is unclear how one moved from the basement to the ground floor. If indeed there was no connection between the two floors, the possibility that the basement was always intended only for storage becomes more likely. In such circumstances, it is may be hypothesised that entry to the ground floor was intended by way of stone or wooden external staircases, rising from the garden in straight flights to either side of the entrance door, up to a projecting balcony, in the manner of certain Italian villas (fig. 72).[77] There does not appear to be any sign of the remains of such stairs in the existing fabric, so, if built at all, they were perhaps in wood rather than stone, leaving no traces of their passing. The greater likelihood is that they were never built. It is customary in the building trade to leave the finishing of stairs until near the end of the works in order to limit the potential damage caused by workmen using them.

Since the Queen's House was left unfinished when Anne died, its intended purpose can only be conjectural. It is possible that it was designed to perform a dual function, as a place of reflection for the queen, and also to serve a ceremonial rather than

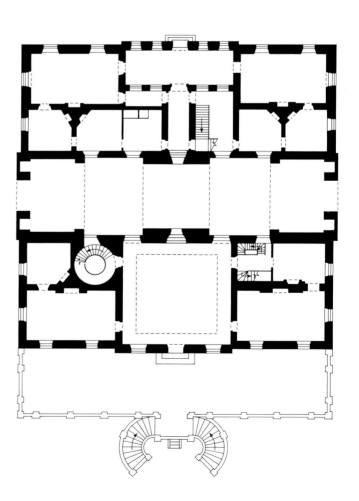

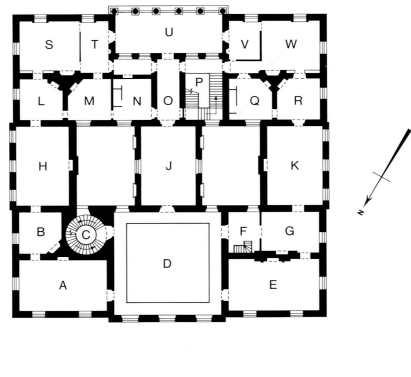

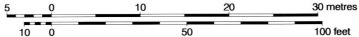

71 (*above and facing page top right and bottom right*)   The basement, ground and first-floor plans of the Queen's House, Greenwich. The basement plan (facing page top right) shows the cellars beneath the terrace and north range of the building; the nineteenth-century cellars of the south range are not shown. The lettering on the first-floor plan (above) follows G. H. Chettle's denotation of the rooms on the ground and first floors, identical for each floor, for the works of 1934–5 which are detailed in Appendix 8. The names given to the rooms have changed periodically. The following key gives the names known to have been used for the first-floor rooms during four periods:

	1630s	1660s	After the 1930s' restoration	After the 1980s' restoration
A	Queen's Cabinet or Withdrawing Room	King's Presence Chamber	Queen's Drawing Room	King's Presence Chamber
B	Cabinet Room	King's Ante-Room	North-East Cabinet	King's Ante-Room
C	Round Stairs	Round Stairs	Round Staircase	Round Staircase
D	Hall or Great Room	Hall or Great Room or Great Hall	Great Hall and Gallery	Great Hall and Gallery
E	Queen's Bedchamber	Queen's Presence Chamber	Queen's Bedroom	Queen's Presence Chamber
F	Back Stairs	—	Back Stairs	—
G	Queen's Ante-Room	Queen's Ante-Room	North-West Cabinet	Queen's Ante-Room
H	[not yet built]	King's Privy Chamber	East Bridge Room	King's Privy Chamber
J	—	—	Central Bridge Room	Centre Bridge Room
K	[not yet built]	Queen's Privy Chamber	West Bridge Room	Queen's Privy Chamber
L	—	King's Antechamber	South-East Cabinet	King's Antechamber
M	—	Closet	South-East Room	Writing Closet
N	—	Closet	South-East Room	Closet
O	—	—	South Corridor	—
P	—	—	South Staircase	South Staircase
Q	—	Closet	South-West Room	Closet
R	—	Queen's Antechamber	South-West Room	Queen's Antechamber
S	—	King's Bedchamber (with partition to T)	King's Bedroom (without partition)	King's Bedchamber (with partition reinstated)
T	—	King's Closet (with partition to S)	King's Bedroom (without partition)	King's Closet (with partition reinstated)
U	—	Portico	Loggia	Loggia
V	—	Queen's Closet (with partition to W)	South-West Room (without partition)	Queen's Closet (with partition reinstated)
W	—	Queen's Bedchamber (with partition to V)	South-West Room (without partition)	Queen's Bedchamber (with partition reinstated)

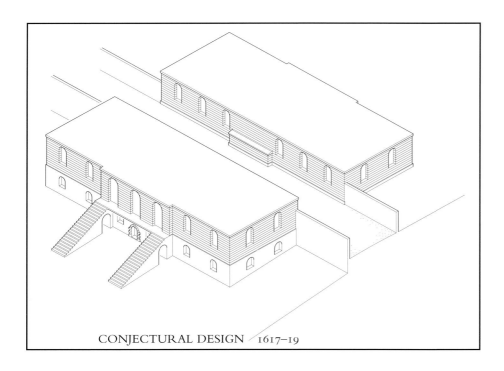

CONJECTURAL DESIGN 1617–19

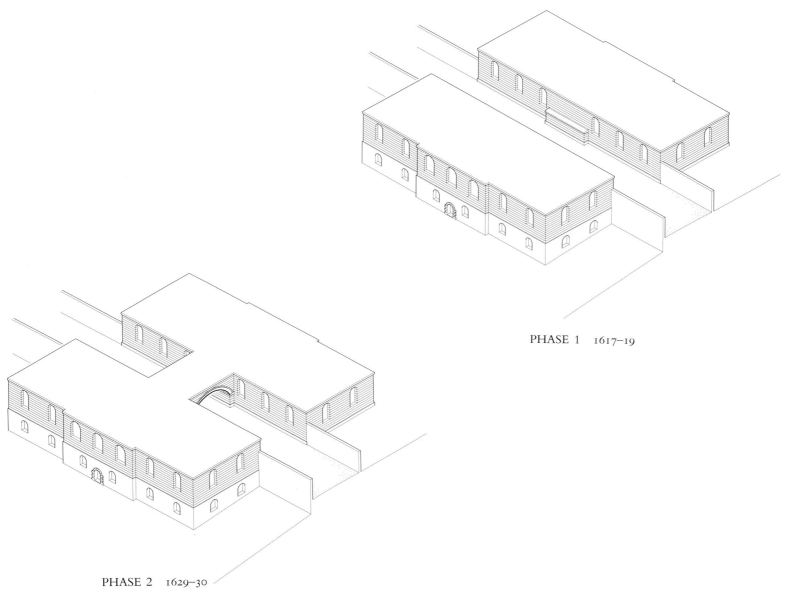

PHASE 1 1617–19

PHASE 2 1629–30

72 The building phases of the Queen's House, Greenwich. The phased development drawings are based on structural and documentary analysis. The conjectural design showing straight flights of steps represents a hypothesis based on inference and possibility.

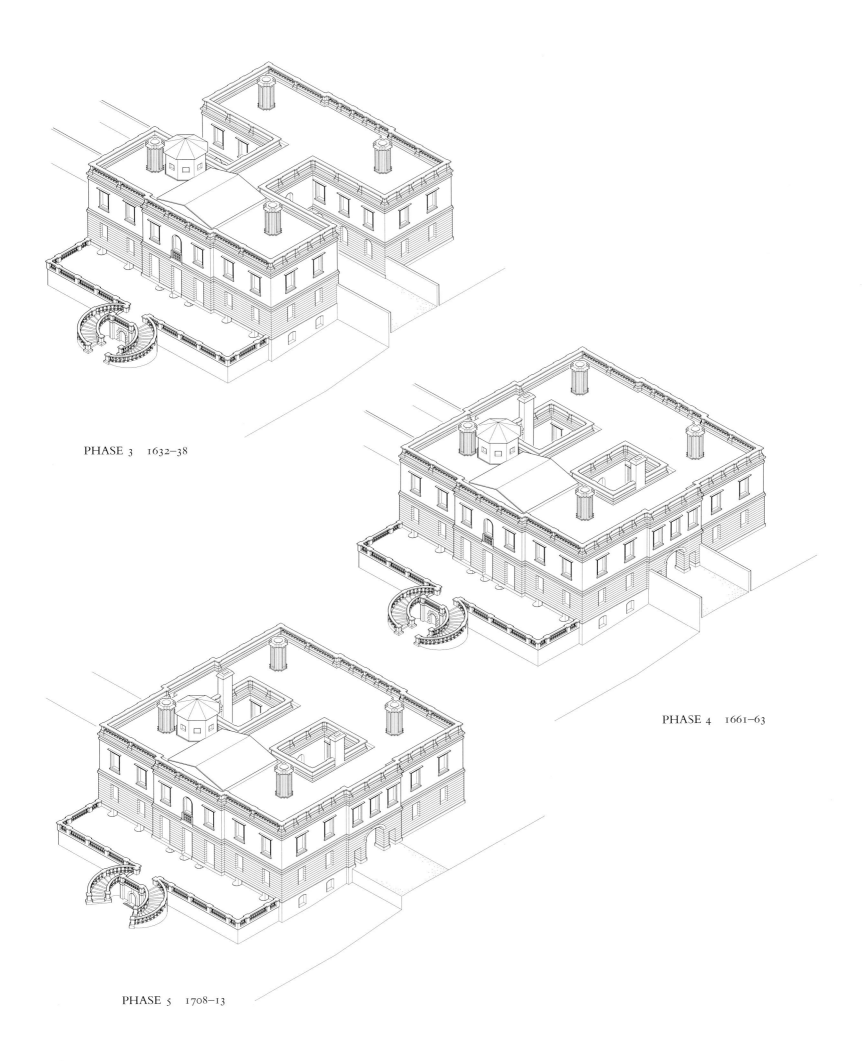

PHASE 3   1632–38

PHASE 4   1661–63

PHASE 5   1708–13

household role as an entertainment suite. Greenwich was the first palatial port of call for ambassadors coming to the court. Charles I in 1627 reminded John Finet, his Master of Ceremonies, of the sequence of three 'welcomes' to new ambassadors at specified locations, the first at Gravesend, the second at either Greenwich or Tower Wharf (depending upon the status of the ambassador[78]) and the third at his official residence.[79] The old palace also supplied the setting for ceremony. In May 1629 the peace with France was proclaimed 'by sound of trumpet and four heralds at Greenwiche in the conduyt court, the Kyng and Queene in a window of the gallery there privately beholding the manner of yt'.[80] It was used also as a point of departure. The ambassador of the Duke of Savoy in 1631 'took his leave of both theyr majestyes together in the kyngs Presence Chamber at Greenwich'.[81] Arrival and departure were moments of great formality; routes were prescribed and proscribed. In 1629 the French ambassador 'passed by the way of the garden (an irregularity) to the Councell Chamber, thence to the Presence where both the Kyng and Queen together receyved him'.[82] It may have been Queen Anne's intention to include the Queen's House in the official route, bringing guests to the new building to receive refreshments and to cross from the garden side to the park side, where they could stand in the loggia and watch hunting and other pursuits taking place to the south. The adventurous might then have braved the deer and gone to the top of the hill to view the house and palace and the river and countryside beyond.

The building was also likely to have been intended as a retreat for the queen, possibly as a separate, occasional residence away from the old palace; her relationship with the king was, by 1616, distant. In the first phase of construction the Queen's House would not necessarily have needed a kitchen and service areas since these were in separate, adjacent buildings to the north-east, originally used to serve the old palace and the banqueting house near the tilt yard.[83]

If the ensemble of house and garden had been completed, it might well have functioned for the queen as if it were the backdrop to a permanent court entertainment in which she took the leading role, moving as in a masque from the Tudor royal palace through the contrived disorder of the artfully created gardens in the latest style, a nature tamed and cultivated, to the well-ordered, most modern house in England.[84] Such a conceit would have been consistent with what is known of Anne's character and interests. In Thomas Campion's *The Caversham Entertainment*, given for the queen in 1613 at Caversham, near Reading, on her way to Bath, Anne, a non-speaking participant in the masque, as the subject of its praises, was so well pleased by the performers that 'she vouchsafed to make her self the head of their revels, and graciously to adorn the place with her personal dancing'. The conventional expression of the harmony between the house, garden and park, to which a new route had been created at Caversham for the celebration of the queen's visit by the 'forcing' of a 'new passage . . . through arable land', is gracefully expressed in terms which might equally have been applied at Greenwich:

> Welcome, O welcome, ever-honoured Queen,
> To this now-blessed place,
> That grove, that bower, that house is happy
> Which you vouchsafe to grace.[85]

After Anne's death, the palace of Greenwich, including the nascent Queen's House, was granted to Prince Charles, retained by him after his accession in 1625, and in 1629 granted to his wife, Henrietta Maria. She commissioned Inigo Jones to complete the masterpiece which he had begun and turned it into an altogether more private building. There is no evidence to suggest that the house was added to the public, ceremonial route at the palace during her period of occupation. The older buildings continued to be the ones used for the rituals of entertainment, arrival and departure: in 1637 'the lords of the councell then at Greenwich, having concluded the state affayrs . . . went altogether to his highnes lodging in the Tylt Yard or garden, there to take their leaves of him and his brother. . . . That night theyr highnesses farewelled all the great ladyes in the Queens privy gallery'.[86]

Little is known about what was done inside the house between 1619 and 1629, not even whether it was used and just how finished any of the rooms were. There certainly were some habitable rooms on the ground floor as in 1623/4 money was spent on 'mending two chimney peeces in the new building'.[87] There is no evidence that any part of the building was dismantled. In 1627–8 payment was made for 'new paling and mending the pales blown down at the new building in the parke, and putting in new postes, rayles and shoares'.[88] This perhaps indicates that the unfinished Queen's House was surrounded by a fence to prevent unauthorised entry and that supports were needed to shore up some of the structure.

Although work on the house may have ceased with the death of Anne, the grounds continued to be embellished. In 1619–24 the palace gardens and the park were newly walled in brick, replacing the earlier picket fence and shielding the royal household from the public road which crossed the site.[89] In 1623–4 a fine gateway was built by Jones between the road and the park, the work being described as 'a fayre great gate', 'arched over with a rustick arche and rustick pillasters with architrave freeze and parte of the cornish round about and a peryment overhead together with a skeame [segmental] arche over the gate' (fig. 37).[90] The house, the gateway and the wall are all clearly visible in the *View of Greenwich* of *c*.1632 by Adriaen van Stalbemt and Jan van Belcamp. This picture, apparently topographically accurate and thus a key document in the consideration of the evolution of the Queen's House, was on display in Greenwich Palace until the Interregnum.[91]

Henrietta Maria and the 'House of Delight'

Work was resumed on the Queen's House in 1629–30 when workmen were paid 'in framing and setting up a newe Roofe over the Arch of the new building' in thatch, and for 'Thatching the Roofe of the Arch of the new buildings'.[92] It was customary to thatch unfinished brickwork to protect it from rain and frost; since this is the first entry in the accounts for such a practice at the Queen's House, it suggests that new building must have taken place in that year, perhaps in preparation for the construction of an upper floor.

The painting by van Stalbemt and van Belcamp shows a single-storey house, nine bays wide at the bottom of the hill (fig. 73). Covering the house is a flat raft which spans both the park and palace sides of the building, as well as the road in between. In the

73 Adriaen van Stalbemt and Jan van Belcamp, *View of Greenwich*, *c*.1632 (The Royal Collection © 2000, HM Queen Elizabeth II). King Charles I and Queen Henrietta Maria are depicted in the centre of the group in the foreground.

centre is the thatched 'Toblerone-shaped' covering (triangular in section) of the arch designed to carry the central Bridge Room. In the past the raft has been interpreted as a roof, implausibly covering both buildings and so regarded as doubtful evidence for the appearance of the house at this time. It may be explained, not as a roof, but as a large platform from which to construct the upper floor in a situation in which it was not possible, because of the road, to erect scaffolding on the inner sides of the two blocks. No mention is made in the building accounts in the early 1630s of the closure or diversion of the road to allow work to take place. This contrasts with the works carried out in 1661–4 when the two additional Bridge Rooms were constructed. The road was temporarily diverted and gates were used to control the movement of carts and carriages while building was taking place.[93]

At the time of the painting, work was just about to restart on the building, which had been granted to Henrietta Maria in 1629. In June 1632, following an apparent hiatus in the construction programme, Henry Wickes, Master of Her Majesty's Works, was paid

£500 'by way of advance for the finishing of some buildings at Greenwich' which the queen 'gave order unto Mr Inego Jones, Surveyor general of her highness' works to go on withall'.[94] The phrasing offers a powerful argument against the view that the Queen's House was razed to the ground and completely rebuilt for Henrietta Maria. It also shows that at this time the house was still regarded as two buildings, one on each side of the road. Building continued into 1633: unusually the queen was not in residence at Greenwich Palace during April, May and June of that year, her usual practice, which might suggest that extensive works were being undertaken at the time. Wickes was paid a further £500 in September 1633 'for and towards the charges of the New buildings at Greenwich'.[95] By March 1634 Henrietta Maria was evidently pleased with progress, for Inigo Jones, as well as receiving his annual £20 pension in his role of Surveyor of Her Majesty's Works, was granted £100 'out of her free bounty'.[96]

By 1635 the building works were almost complete; in that year Wickes received a total of £1000 from the Queen's Treasurer 'for and towards the going on and full finishing of the Queens Majesties buildings at Greenwich'.[97] In May 1635 the king and queen went to stay at Greenwich, he to hunt and she 'to see the completion of a special erection of hers, which is already far advanced';[98] it was not until 1638 that the final payment of £1500 was made to Wickes for 'advancement' of the construction of the Queen's House.[99] The datestone on the north front confirms both the ownership and the date of completion of the building, if not of the fitting-out:

HENRICA MARIA REGINA
1635

Work was also done outside the house. In 1635 the old walls in the tilt yard to the north-east were pulled down and rebuilt, and new walls built in the park and the privy garden to the west of the new building.[100] In 1637–8 posts were set up in the highway 'neare the new building to preserve the cellar windows from the carts'.[101] In 1637 Wickes was paid £4000 for 'her Majesties buildings at Greenwich', and a further £1500 was paid to Vere Babington, underkeeper of her Majesty's house and gardens at Greenwich, for extensive garden works, including 'the perfecting of the gardens there which her Majesty heretofore caused to be altered' and 'for the performing of the reformation of her majesties gardens'.[102] A further £200 was paid to Babington in the first half of 1637.[103]

The Mannerist garden, created for Queen Anne, inevitably was not fashionable enough twenty years later for Henrietta Maria. She was highly influenced by French garden design and even dispatched a servant to France 'to get some fruit-trees and some flowers'.[104] At least one anonymous French designer submitted a design for the queen for 'a ffountaine in a wall at Greenwich' in 1637. This was redrawn by John Webb, Jones's pupil and assistant at that time, who changed the order from Tuscan to Ionic (fig. 74).[105] Through Henrietta Maria's connection with the French court, the garden designers André and Gabriel Mollet were brought over to England to work at St James's Palace, where her mother Marie de' Medici was to live in exile for several years from October 1638. They possibly worked at Greenwich as well (see chapter 1). In 1629 Marie de' Medici had employed the French gardener Jacques Boiceau at the Palais du Luxembourg, where he had designed and planted giant *parterres de broderie*, a feature designed to be viewed from an elevated position on the double terrace that surrounded three sides of the garden. It is possible that the 'reformation' carried out at Greenwich may have involved the planting of similar elaborate flower-filled parterres in the gardens to the north of the Queen's House.

A suitable viewing point would have been provided by the newly built north-side terrace, reached by a grand pair of curving steps, and indeed the need for such an elevated platform may have been an important factor in its construction. Before the 1630s the gardens to the north of the Queen's House, which separated the building from the old palace, had been places in which to wander and marvel – an artifice of masonry, planting, grotto and water-jets. There was no need to view the garden from above ground level until it was planted in such a way that a raised viewpoint was necessary in order to appreciate the intricate beauty of the positioning of flowers and the integrity of the design. The addition of two iron balconies on the north side of the building at this time, one outside the Queen's Bedchamber and one

adjoining the Queen's Cabinet would have provided similar viewing points, and a still broader view would have been possible from the flat roof. At this time, it was only on the north side that access to the leads could be achieved without indecorous clambering, since the belvedere over the Tulip staircase was flush with the parapet walling, preventing ready access to the central bridge. Easy access to the park side roof was not possible until after the building of the east bridge at the Restoration. This underlines the relative significance of the two sides of the house and the views from them during the 1630s.

The building of the terrace, paved in 1636, but begun in 1635, the date of Jones's drawing 'for ye doure in to ye volte under ye tarras',[106] signalled a significant shift in emphasis in the use of the house (fig. 75). The sketch, for a rusticated door surround, differs from the present door (which appears to be early eighteenth century in style), but its dating confirms that it was the new outside door which gave onto the vaulted passage under the terrace which led to the now internal door of about 1617 which provided access to the basement. The new terrace provided an area

74   A redrawing by John Webb of a design by an anonymous French designer for a fountain at Greenwich Palace, 1637 (Worcester College, Oxford).

75 Inigo Jones, drawing for the door leading into the vaulted entrance passage under the new terrace at the Queen's House, 1635 (BAL).

on which to stand, to view the garden, and a grand route into the building. That the terrace had not been planned by Queen Anne is made fully apparent by the surviving windows and outside door which it covers. On the south side of the building, van Stalbemt and van Belcamp depict round-headed windows, similar to those which light the central Bridge Room and to the one which survives at the centre of the north front on the first floor. More pertinently, they are comparable with the round window-heads which preceded the segmental window-heads at basement level and to the segmental heads which survive, blocked, behind the supporting structures of the east and west Bridge Rooms. The introduction of straight architraves to the outer-facing windows was a change presumably made by Inigo Jones in the work for Henrietta Maria. Originally, the terrace was cut back at the windows to provide lightwells in order to light the basement. In 1662 some of these windows were barred in order to prevent illicit entry,[107] and in 1708 further security was provided by the addition of seven 'sinkgrates' which would have covered the lightwells over each window and over the original door.[108] These might have been replacements for earlier grates, necessary in the centre at least to allow entry through the front door without risk of falling down a hole. One of these grated lightwells survives.

The new grandeur of the route into the building via steps and terrace is paradoxical since whereas the evidence points towards Queen Anne's desire to combine both public and private uses in her house, Henrietta Maria's intention appears to have been to use it only as a private retreat for herself and her husband. The house was not described by visitors who were in fact taken on a route which entirely avoided it. When he visited in 1640, the Sieur de Mandelslo was shown the latest parts of the old palace and was then conducted through the garden and into the park, where he visited the pleasure house on top of the hill and admired the view, a prescribed route which precisely mimicked that followed by Neumayr von Ramssla, the escort of the Duke of Saxony, who had visited in 1613. For Mandelslo, who was not an unobservant man, it was as if the Queen's House, now considered to be one of the most remarkable domestic buildings of its time in England, did not exist any more than it had for his predecessor who was

there before it was built.[109] Notwithstanding Inigo Jones's intention to effect 'a total revolution in British architectural expression', it was at the Whitehall Banqueting House that he was able to make a more visible impact. The Queen's House was 'obscurely situated between the garden and the deer-park' of an 'out-of-London palace' and appears to have been so regarded even by those who made the journey to the east.[110]

Although the new terrace and the handsome ascent may suggest display, the original conformation of the steps militates against such a reading. Now, the steps and the terrace appear to be directly imitative of the arrangement at Pratolino,[111] but when first built, the steps curved round further than they do today, so that the twin flights were not horseshoe-shaped but were turned to face each other directly, unlike Pratolino, and framed the new door into the basement, just as those by Philibert de l'Orme did at the crypto-porticus on the garden side at Anet, and those by Vignola, on a far larger scale, did at Caprarola, both of which are likely to have been visited by Jones (fig. 76).[112] In so doing the steps represented an internalising, enclosing sensibility, rather than one which was outward looking or seeking to draw attention to itself. Later, probably around 1713, the two flights were cut back, a process that involved some reconstruction, in order symbolically to embrace the view towards the Thames (figs 77 and 78).[113] This cutting back and the consequent raising of the ground level at the foot of the steps, rendering them at least three steps shorter than they were originally, had the effect of obscuring the view of the lower part of the door into the basement, an unhappy visual truncation which marred Inigo Jones's design and was as disturbing in its effect on appearance as an *acqua alta* on the *palazzi* of the Grand Canal (fig. 51). G. H. Chettle intended to take the ground back to its original level in the 1930s but nothing was done (see Appendix 8); the scheme to improve access, under way in 1999, has created a longer, gentler slope, going some way towards reinstating the view of the basement door.

Those considering the evolution of the Queen's House are greatly hampered by the absence of depictions from the north in the seventeenth century. There was only one known drawing of it at this time (fig. 79).[114] The drawing, which has been dated to

76   An eighteenth-century engraving by Giuseppe Vasi of the south front of Vignola's Palazzo Farnese, Caprarola.

*c.*1640, is now lost but photographs of it provide valuable information by showing the projecting balconies on the first floor and, most surprisingly for a house which has come to be considered a restrained, purist masterpiece, by indicating areas of wall painting. Unfortunately, the unidentified draughtsman treated the terrace as ground level and omitted it from the drawing. Whereas the north front was regarded as the private side of the house, seen only by

77   The footings of the original steps at the Queen's House, revealed during restoration work in the 1980s.

those in the old palace and the palace gardens, the south front was the relatively more public face. It was depicted frequently from the seventeenth century onwards by the numerous painters of the magnificent view from the hill. Whether Jones intended originally to provide the north front with an order at first-floor level, as well as the south, has been the subject of some speculation, although a north-facing loggia in England would have been a dubious benefit. An elevation drawing, datable to 1616–17, which is so clearly Palladian that for a long time it was assigned to Palladio himself, shows a façade with an upper-floor order which might have been for either front (fig. 80). The more experienced architect of the 1630s had moved away from such direct dependence.[115]

The elegant first-floor Ionic loggia of the Queen's House was almost certainly one of the first to appear in England (fig. 81), although loggias were a common feature of Italian and French houses and had been used in England at ground-floor level. As noted above, Anne had added a ground-floor loggia to the palace and it may be that she originally intended a ground-floor loggia on the south front of her new house as well, in the position of the room which became the orangery (fig. 82).[116] In 1615 Jones noted in the margin of his copy of Palladio that a central loggia, forming 'a frontispice in the midest', was the greatest ornament that a house could have.[117] Built in order to allow the royal family to view the park from a sheltered position of eminence, the first-floor loggia was completed between 1632 and 1635 (fig. 83). As a feature which linked private to public and inner to outer, it served a symbolic as well as an architectural function, effecting a link between the queen and her entourage in the house and those who were privileged to use the park, which at that time was still a royal preserve. Jones was building a similar loggia at Hyde Park Lodge

78   The western flight of the horseshoe steps of the Queen's House in 1983.

79 The north front of the Queen's House, drawn *c.*1640 (BAL).

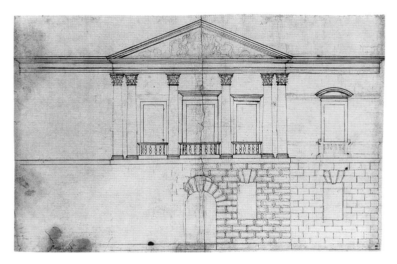

80 Inigo Jones, preliminary design for the north or south front of the Queen's House, *c.*1616–17 (BAL).

81 The south front of the Queen's House.

in 1634–5[118] and his enthusiasm for the form was fundamental to its adoption in England as a favoured Palladian device. Although desirable, loggias were expensive to maintain in the English climate and extensive restoration was required at Greenwich in 1662 when a new channel for rainwater was introduced and the floor was relaid with 400 feet of black and white marble.[119] Roger North, writing in the 1690s, although 'a great freind to portico walks abroad' in drier climates, was critical:

> It hath bin the use of the Italians, and ill imitated in England, by some fond surveyors, to set the portico into the house, as wee find at Greenwich, the Queen's house, which looks towards the Observatory, and Sir John Maynard's house in Gunnersbury, which looks upon Braintford road. This robbs the house of principall room, and interrupts the file of rooms, which is a prime beauty, and which is worse it darkens the best rooms.

In view of the singular plan of the Queen's House, this last point was hardly relevant. But even North had to concede that a loggia was 'most agreable to view, and, at many times of the year, use'.[120]

Between 1632 and 1638 Henrietta Maria paid from her own income a total of at least £7500 towards the building of the Queen's House and over £1700 towards the redesigning of the gardens. In addition payments were made by the king for work that was in some way connected with the park or road going through the house. However these costs do not include any payments for the works of art or decoration that were to adorn the building. In 1637–8, more than twenty years after the project began, workmen were paid for 'putting up the Queen's canvases'. The Queen's House as 'House of Delight' and royal art gallery began to take shape.[121] Some information can be gleaned from the building accounts about the interior design of individual rooms, usually in connection with the extensive decorative schemes and specially commissioned works of art, but the detailed accounts that would enable the fully finished house to be re-created do not survive.

The completed Queen's House represents the perfect embodiment of a change in fashion: a move away from the medieval palace of the past, where privacy was often difficult to achieve, towards the provision of intimate, secluded spaces. The Queen's House stood in the same relation to the nearby palace as Giacomo del Duca's private Palazzina del Piacere of the 1580s did to the Farnese palace at Caprarola. It was to be Henrietta Maria's secret house where she could retire comfortably for extended periods of time, the 'culmination of an already existing tradition of elaborate, architectually precocious garden lodges, created – like miniatures, sonnets and villas – for intimacy and pleasure'.[122] But it was much more than that; because of the symbolic significance of the Queen's House to Henrietta Maria, the building was more than simply a place for escape: it epitomised the quasi-mythical status of her marriage to Charles I (fig. 84).

Life in the Caroline court was remarkably decorous: in striking contrast to the court of James I, it was temperate, chaste, serious and very formal: 'the fools, and bawds, mimics and catamites of the former Court grew out of fashion'.[123] The court masque, full of human uncertainty during the Jacobean period, became during the reign of Charles I and Henrietta Maria a far more confident assertion of public virtue and political will. While all passion, 'controlled and idealised', revolved around the queen, the king, in the time-honoured manner of those governors who persistently and wilfully confuse private morality with public virtue, insisted 'on the perfections of marriage as the central element in a harmonious commonwealth'.[124]

Henrietta Maria played a central role in the cultural life of the court, but she also had a gift for frivolity and fantasy, and a strong natural inclination to believe in the allegories which ultimately were to prove so deceptive. In 1625 it was reported that she was 'much delighted with the River of Thames and doth love to walk in the meadows and look upon the haymakers and will sometimes take a rake and fork and sportingly make hay with them'.[125] By nature playful and gay, she enjoyed singing, dancing and such pastimes as 'ducking upon the Thames',[126] and shared with Robert Herrick's Corinna the bittersweet 'harmlesse follie' of 'Maying' in springtime:

> Then, while time serves, and we are but decaying;
> Come, my Corinna, come, let's goe a Maying.[127]

As well as the usual royal perquisites, the ownership of dogs and horses, Henrietta Maria indulged a taste for the earthy, keeping not only parrots (at Greenwich) and monkeys, but watching bear-baiting with the king and the Swedish ambassador at Greenwich in 1634.[128] She also enjoyed the company of dwarfs: Jeffrey and Sarah were usually in attendance. But although apparently frivolous and whimsical, she developed around herself a strict moral code of conduct. The household and personal behaviour of the queen was based on the French practice of 'préciosité' or courtly and platonic love; as the courtier James Howell noted, 'there is a love called Platonic Love that much sways there . . . it is a love abstracted from all corporal, gross impressions and ideas of mind, not in any carnal fruction'.[129]

The Neoplatonic qualities of beauty, love and virtue were harnessed by the women of the court (Henrietta Maria, her friends and members of her household including the maids-of-honour) in the cause of engendering cordial relations between the sexes. These qualities, allied with the deep religious beliefs of the queen and those who surrounded her, combined to promote social harmony in a court which was pious and chaste, but none the less adept in its pursuit of pleasure. In the masque *The Temple of Love* by Inigo Jones and William Davenant, performed by Henrietta Maria and her ladies at Whitehall in 1635, and repeated three times, this miraculous court is further explained:

> Certain young lords at first disliked the philosophy,
> As most uncomfortable, sad, and new,
> But soon inclined to a superior vote,
> And are grown as good Platonical lovers
> As are to be found in an hermitage.[130]

The Queen's House may be read as the embodiment of these beliefs, particularly through the symbolism of the paintings displayed and intended within the building. The story of Cupid and Psyche was especially pertinent and a sequence of paintings on the theme was commissioned. The dramatist Shackerley Marmion, whose plays were performed for the royal family during the 1630s, wrote an important poem based on the legend told by Apuleius in *The Golden Ass*. His *Cupid and Psyche; or an Epic Poem of Cupid and his Mistress* was first published in London in 1637; a second edition appeared in the following year, evidence of its popularity, while a third was published after the Restoration, in 1666.[131]

82 The ground-floor orangery at the centre of the south front of the Queen's House.

83 The first-floor loggia of the Queen's House, completed 1632–5, offering views into the park.

Psyche, the personification of beauty, represents the human soul, which, purified by passions and misfortunes, achieves immortality. Cupid represents love and desire and together their union is the mingling of the divine with the earthly. The idea of the king and queen rather hubristically representing Cupid and Psyche appears

84 Daniel Mytens, *Charles I and Henrietta Maria departing for the Chase* (The Royal Collection © 2000, HM Queen Elizabeth II).

to have started right at the beginning of their marriage when in 1625 the Duke of Buckingham was sent to escort the future queen to London. While in Paris, Buckingham formed a friendship with Peter Paul Rubens, and seems to have suggested that a commemorative painting be commissioned recording his trip to Paris and the Anglo-French alliance. A sketch survives depicting Mercury (Buckingham) conducting Psyche (Henrietta Maria) to Olympus. Thus Psyche is brought to Cupid (Charles), who is kneeling before James, receiving his posthumous approval of the union. The sketch was never developed into a painting, but shows how from the very beginning of the reign the marriage of Charles and Henrietta Maria was thought of in legendary terms, which were to be more fully developed in the decoration of the Queen's House.[132]

The magical royal palace at the heart of the story of Cupid and Psyche, described by Apuleius as a 'worthy mansion for the powers of heaven', may have encouraged Henrietta Maria to create an earthly equivalent for herself: 'For the embowings above were of Citron and Ivory, propped and undermined with pillars of gold, the walls covered and seeled with silver, divers sorts of beasts were graven and carved that seemed to encounter with such as entered in. All things were so curiously and finely wrought, that it seemed either to be the worke of some Demy god, or God himselfe'.[133]

It was the general idea of the legendary palace which was more important than specific details: 'Every part and angle of the house was so well adorned, that by reason of the pretious stones and inestimable treasure there, it glittered and shone in such sort, that the chambers, porches, and doores gave light as it had beene the Sunne',[134] a topos which not only recalls the fantastic architecture of the *Hypnerotomachian* dream, but also shares a strong similarity of tone with the description of the Temple of Chaste Love in *The Temple of Love*. This had been hidden by mists and clouds, but later stood revealed: 'the further part of the temple running far from the eye . . . with pilasters, niches and statues, and in the midst a stately gate adorned with columns and their ornaments, and a frontispiece on the top, all which seemed to be of burnished gold'.[135]

In the legend the beautiful princess Psyche is visited nightly by Cupid in her magical palace, a sequence of events which culminated after many tribulations in the heroine's immortality, her marriage to the god and the birth of a child whose name was Pleasure. The king and queen, obsessively in love with each other throughout the 1630s, used this story in the fictions of the court masques and appear to have sought to turn it into reality in the Queen's House. In *The Temple of Love*, Blind Cupid, the symbol of illicit sensual love, is replaced by Seeing Cupid, the emblem of a higher and purer spiritual love, which Indamora, the Queen of Love, played by Henrietta Maria, brings to the fortunate isle. At the end of the masque the king and queen contemplate a vision of the Temple of Chaste Love and Chaste Cupid sings:

> Whilst by a mixture thus made one,
> Y'are th'emblem of my Deity,
> And now you may, in yonder throne,
> The pattern of your union see.

As Roy Strong observed, 'While the queen reigns as the subject of a love cult, the blissful royal marriage and her ever fruitful womb are exalted almost to the level of a state philosophy'.[136]

The complete sequence of Cupid and Psyche paintings intended for the Queen's House was not finished (see chapter 3). Nevertheless, in commissioning paintings from Jacob Jordaens, Charles and Henrietta Maria perhaps were seeking to emulate two great decorative schemes of the sixteenth century: Raphael's Loggia di Psiche at the Villa Farnesina, Rome,[137] and the extraordinary Sala di Amore e Psiche at the Palazzo Te, Mantua, by 'that rare Italian Master', Giulio Romano.[138] In so doing, they were situating themselves firmly in the tradition of courtly patronage, but were adding their own moralising twist to the story by laying stress on the purification of the passions, rather than on their unrestrained indulgence. It would be a rare visitor who left Mantua musing on the benefits of chastity.[139]

This was not the first instance during the reign of Charles I that he had sought directly to emulate the Renaissance courts of Europe. Since his visit, when Prince of Wales, to the Spanish court in 1623, he had begun to build up a comparable collection of paintings and also had attempted unsuccessfully to recruit Philip IV's Surveyor of the Royal Works, Giovanni Battista Crescenzi, to his service.[140] His most splendid achievement in this field, transforming the royal collection, was to secure by 1631, after prolonged negotiations, a large part of the Gonzaga collection of paintings and sculptures from Mantua for a little over £30,000. He could not buy the Gonzaga buildings as well, but they were known in court circles. The Earl of Arundel in 1623 had requested from Ferdinando, Duke of Mantua 'a model of the courtyard of the Palazzo in Mantua that was built not long ago with a rustic order' – probably the Cortile della Cavallerizza of the Palazzo Ducale, which was begun by Giulio Romano, continued by Giovanni Battista Bertani, but not completed until around 1600 – as well as a model of the Palazzo Te.[141] As a semi-rural pleasure retreat, just outside the city, sumptuously decorated, the Queen's House may be interpreted as a modest imitation, in concept if not in style, of the Palazzo Te, a place for restorative leisure, and Inigo Jones as the Stuart court's paler equivalent to Mantua's great 'Court Architect, Painter and Impresario', Giulio Romano.[142]

The cultural impact made by Charles and Henrietta Maria was such that it successfully drew praise from those political opponents who might have regretted many aspects of the monarchical mode of governance. Lucy Hutchinson, the widow of a Parliamentary colonel, writing in the mid-century, was generous in her comments on the Caroline court: 'Men of learning and ingenuity in all the arts were in esteeme, and receiv'd encouragement from the King, who was a most excellent judge and a great lover of paintings, carvings, gravings, and many other ingenuities less offensive than the bawdy and prophane abusive witt which was the only exercise of the other court'.[143] But cultivation, connoisseurship and the enactment of obscure hermetic allegories were not enough:

> Viewed from outside the Banqueting House, the masque could be seen to provide the monarchy chiefly with an impenetrable insulation against the attitudes of the governed. Year after year designer and poet recreated an ideal commonwealth, all its forces under rational control, its people uniquely happy and endlessly grateful. . . . The vision was a perfectly accurate projection of the way Charles saw his realm.[144]

Chapter 3

THE QUEEN'S HOUSE:
DECORATION AND LATER HISTORY

Art and Decoration of the Principal Rooms

It is not easy now to recapture the flavour of the Queen's House during the occupancy of Henrietta Maria in that brief efflorescence of the arts which preceded the fracturing of the Stuart idyll in 1642. As it stands, the house, substantially reconstructed in the 1930s and redecorated fifty years later, bears only a loose relationship with the ensemble intended by the queen and her architect. The paintings were dispersed during the Commonwealth and years of institutional usage have taken a heavy toll. It must also be acknowledged that most historical and critical attitudes are coloured by the perception of the Queen's House as a Palladian building, a view promulgated through the neo-Palladian propaganda of Colen Campbell in *Vitruvius Britannicus* and by Richard Boyle, 3rd Earl of Burlington, and his circle in the early eighteenth century. Campbell regarded Palladio as having exceeded all who had gone before him, arriving at a 'Ne plus ultra of his Art', yet notwithstanding this mastery, Jones had gone still further, having all the regularity of Palladio, 'with an Addition of Beauty and Majesty'.[1] Jones was far too good an architect either to rely on one source or to fail to make something new from a number of sources. As noted, there are reminiscences of Palladio at the Queen's House, but equally the architect was indebted to Sangallo and Vignola. This was intended to be a building in the Renaissance tradition rather than a Palladian tradition, but in a culture which requires heroes, it is simpler to find one and look no further, than it is to acknowledge a diversity of influences. The ideas and intentions of the patrons – Queen Anne and Queen Henrietta Maria – were of the greatest importance in the evolution of the design of the Queen's House.

Seventeenth-century French design was particularly evident in the chimneypieces and overmantels of Henrietta Maria's house. For the adornment of the fireplaces necessary in northern climates there were few Italian examples to imitate. Of greatest importance was the work of Jean Barbet, whose *Livre d'architecture, d'autels, et de cheminées* was published in 1633. Two designs for the Queen's House, one dated 1637 'for the room next the bakstaiers' and another described 'for Greenwich' come almost literally from Barbet (figs 86 and 87).[2] Another, for the Bedchamber, has draped herms from Barbet (fig. 88) and a fourth for the Cabinet Room

(fig. 89), behind the Tulip stair, was taken in the same year from an anonymous French designer, perhaps at the behest of the queen, whose name is inscribed beneath the pediment of the overmantel.[3] None of these survives, but a further Jonesian chimneypiece, inspired by Barbet, is now at nearby Charlton House, possibly having been taken there from the Queen's House.[4] A replica was installed in the Queen's Bedchamber in the 1980s.

★　★　★

86　Inigo Jones, elevation for a chimneypiece in the room next to the backstairs in the Queen's House (the Queen's Ante-Room – room G, first floor) (BAL).

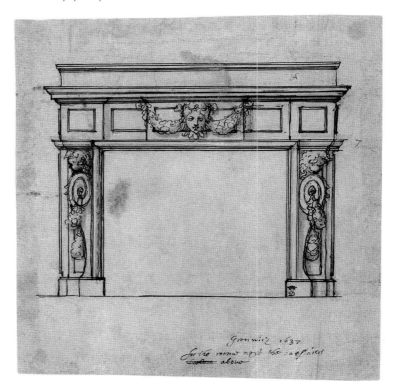

　The marble floor of the Great Hall of the Queen's House, laid 1636–7.

87 Inigo Jones, design for a chimneypiece in the Queen's House, inscribed 'HMR' (for Henrietta Maria) (BAL).

88 (*below left*) Inigo Jones, elevations of *c.*1637 for the chimneypiece in the Bedchamber of the Queen's House (room E, first floor) (BAL).

89 (*below right*) Inigo Jones, elevation dated 1637 for the chimneypiece and overmantel of the Cabinet Room of the Queen's House, inscribed HENRIETTA MARIA REGNA beneath the pediment (room B, first floor) (BAL).

THE GREAT HALL

The two-storey Great Hall is the centrepiece of the Queen's House. Along with the other principal state rooms, the Queen's Bedchamber and Queen's Cabinet on the first floor, it is on the north side of the building and comprises a 40 foot single cube (fig. 90). An equivalently grand single-storey hall appears to have been intended by Anne of Denmark. The change to a two-storey hall, perhaps the one major change in plan between the work for Anne and the work for Henrietta Maria, reflects Jones's notable enthusiasm for cube and double-cube rooms. Its main purpose was to serve as a grand reception area for those entering the house, a place to assemble before climbing the Tulip stairs to the *piano nobile*; but it also functioned as a place for display, a sculpture gallery for the queen, similar in concept to the one depicted by Daniel Mytens in his famous portrait of the Earl of Arundel.[5]

In 1638–9 workmen were preparing the settings for the antique statues, 'working and making ten carved pedestals to set marble statues on and setting those stages on them in the gr[ea]t room'. Zachary Taylor carved 'ten pedestal of timber for marble statues to stand on with bullheads festoons fruits leaves and flowers at 60s the peece'. At the same time John Hooker, a turner, was paid for 'turning 15 great pedestals of olive timber with their bases and capitals at 12s the peece'.[6] The statues had been brought to Greenwich from other palaces, some coming from Oatlands: 'to Philip Winds for his paines in helping of the purveyor to lode and unload the kings effigies sent from Oatlands'.[7] Some repairs were necessary, perhaps following damage in transit; Nicholas Stone was paid 'for altering and new carving the thighs legs and feet of a marble statue of a young man'. The works eventually were set up and payment was made 'To Robert Peeke and other masons for raising of statues and setting them on pedestals at the new building'.[8]

Some of the statues were part of the former Gonzaga collection from Mantua. It is not known exactly which of these were placed in the Hall of the Queen's House, although the inventory of the king's goods, made at the time of the Commonwealth sale, indicates that some of the finest works were at Greenwich, including studies of Bacchus and Sabena both valued at £150, and others representing Adonis, Apollo, Perseus, Diana, Jupiter and Venus.[9] Statues from the collection were also displayed at St James's and Whitehall, while others filled the galleries and terraces of Denmark (Somerset) House.[10] These were no doubt among the 'broken-nosed marbles', upon which, together with 'old rotton pictures', Charles was said by a later pejorative commentator to have squandered millions of pounds.[11]

The niche in the south wall of the Great Hall was likely to have been the setting for the most important piece of contemporary sculpture at Greenwich, Gianlorenzo Bernini's bust of King Charles I, based on a triple portrait by Anthony Van Dyck, but transforming the painter's series of melancholic images into the bust of a visionary and majestic leader.[12] The queen, who had commissioned the bust through her papal envoy, Gregorio Panzani, was so delighted with the likeness when it arrived in mid-1637, that she sent Bernini a diamond worth 4000 *scudi* (£800) and planned to have a comparable work sculpted of herself. Indeed, Van Dyck painted three portraits of Henrietta Maria to be sent to Rome in 1638, but after an order to proceed in 1639, no more was heard of the commission.[13] The Bernini was the most valuable item sold from Greenwich at the Commonwealth sale,

90   The Great Hall of the Queen's House, view from the south-east.

fetching £800. At the Restoration it was recovered by Charles II but was destroyed in the fire at Whitehall in 1698. There is a strikingly Berninesque copy, now at Windsor Castle, possibly by Francis Bird, which is based on a plaster cast of the original (fig. 91). This fully conforms to the conventions of the three-quarter political portrait identified by Roland Barthes: 'the gaze is lost nobly in the future, it does not confront, it soars, and fertilizes some other domain, which is chastely left undefined . . . the face is lifted towards a supernatural light which draws it up and elevates it to the realm of a higher humanity', reaching 'the Olympus of elevated feelings, where all political contradictions are solved'.[14]

It is possible to interpret the single cube of the Queen's House as Jones incorporating the great hall into Renaissance architecture. The gallery, essential for circulation at first-floor level, so comparable with Venetian villa architecture, has aspects also of the minstrels' galleries of earlier times. The wooden brackets supporting it are simply carved, appearing almost identical with a design for exterior brackets shown in sketches for the stage sets for the masque *Britannia Triumphans* dating from 1638.[15] The design of the brackets at the Banqueting House, Whitehall, is by contrast much

91   Copy after the bust by Gianlorenzo Bernini of King Charles I (The Royal Collection © 2000, HM Queen Elizabeth II). The original, initially displayed in the Great Hall of the Queen's House, was destroyed in the fire at Whitehall in 1698.

a further £400 by the king 'in reward of service done by him unto his majesty without accompt'.[19]

The Queen's House paintings demonstrated how, under the patronage of Charles I, the arts in England had enjoyed a renaissance: Peace, assured through Victory, achieved by Strength and Concord, provided the climate in which the liberal arts could flourish (fig. 93).[20] In the context of the Queen's House, the paintings sought to reinforce and idealise the idea of an English Utopia, flourishing under the benign rule of the perfect royal couple: Charles and Henrietta Maria. Inigo Jones may have had a part to play in the development of the iconographic scheme of the ceiling. Certainly, he was responsible for the basic architectural setting, the Venetian compartment system, which he appears to have derived from the vault of the Sala dell'Olympo in Palladio's Villa Barbaro at Maser, frescoed by Paolo Veronese, which he had visited. The central roundel, 20 feet in diameter, on the flat ceiling of the Queen's House, with eight separate panels around it, closely follows Palladio's arrangement, although at Maser the central field is octagonal. Around the base of the vault of the ceiling, in the absence of an upper floor, Veronese created a fictive balustrade, with figures looking down into the room. The Queen's House gallery, suitably animated, would have made a comparable theatrical impression, the real figures on the gallery combining with the painted representations on the ceiling to create an equivalent to Veronese's sublime scenography at Maser.[21]

During 1633–4 the painters Matthew Gooderick and Benjamin

92   Orazio Gentileschi, *Architecture*, one of the four roundels at the corners of *The Allegory of Peace and Arts under the English Crown*, painted for the Queen's House and later moved to Marlborough House, London (The Royal Collection © 2000, HM Queen Elizabeth II).

more sophisticated and precise. When finished in the 1630s, the Queen's House ceiling and gallery were painted white with gilded enrichments.[16] Within this magnificent space were set Orazio Gentileschi's nine canvases, *The Allegory of Peace and Arts under the English Crown*, celebrating Charles I's reign. The ceiling decoration of around 1636–8 is 'the most comprehensive illustration of the relationship between the subject matter of Gentileschi's works and the ideals of the court', well understood by this time by the artist who had been in residence in London since 1626, and had been working for the Crown since before that date.[17] Gentileschi had been introduced from Paris into the royal service by the Duke of Buckingham, leaving the employment of Marie de' Medici at the Palais du Luxembourg, where he perhaps felt himself to be in the shadow of Rubens, to work for a Catholic queen. Ironically the judgement of history has placed him in that same shadow in England where he showed himself to be a very effective but rather conservative painter of static scenes at Greenwich, in comparison with the dramatic foreshortening and vigorous movement achieved by Rubens at the Whitehall Banqueting House; following the later removal and adaptation of the Queen's House ceiling paintings, however, to fit a new location, their quality is not easy to assess (fig. 93). Gentileschi had evidently been working for the English Crown before arriving in London: a payment to him for £100 in arrears of an annuity of £100 for three years up to Christmas 1627 was not made until 1630.[18] In 1632 he was paid

93   Orazio Gentileschi, *The Allegory of Peace and Arts under the English Crown*, painted c.1636–8 for the ceiling of the Great Hall of the Queen's House and later installed in the saloon at Marlborough House, Pall Mall, London (The Royal Collection © 2000, HM Queen Elizabeth II).

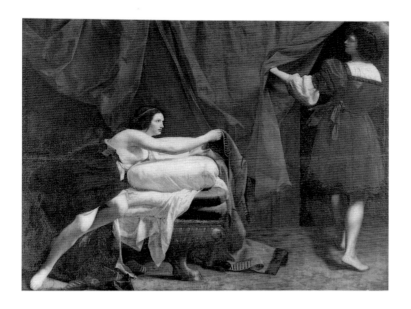

Dawson were preparing three frames for pictures to go into the Queen's House. The subjects were described as 'Pharoes Daughter', 'Joseph and Pottifers wife' and 'the Muses'. At the same time they were painting, varnishing and gilding 'one frame of a lesser moulding' for a 'Tarquin and Lucretia'.[22] *Joseph and Potiphar's Wife* (fig. 94), *Apollo and the Muses* (location unknown) and *The Finding of Moses* (fig. 95) were all by Orazio Gentileschi, and the *Tarquin and Lucretia* (location unknown) by his daughter

94   Orazio Gentileschi, *Joseph and Potiphar's Wife*, painted *c.*1632 and originally displayed at the Queen's House (The Royal Collection © 2000, HM Queen Elizabeth II).

95 (*below*)   Orazio Gentileschi, *The Finding of Moses*, the earlier of the artist's two versions of the subject, mentioned in 1633–4 as being at Greenwich and probably hung in the Great Hall of the Queen's House (private collection).

Artemisia.[23] *The Finding of Moses* was recorded at Greenwich in the lists drawn up in 1649 for the Commonwealth sale of the late king's property: 'A Peece. wth pharoagh Daughter findeing Moses. done by Gentelisco' and valued at £80.[24] It has been argued that Gentileschi here 'introduced a river landscape which is unmistakably English in character', towards which the pharaoh's daughter's maidens point, to indicate where the child had been found. If the painting had been hung on the west wall of the Hall, as suggested, their gestures would have led the eye not only to the landscape within the picture but also towards the river outside, beyond the buildings of the Tudor palace. The pharaoh's daughter points towards the child's genitals and this combination of gestures permits the conclusion that the painting was intended as a programmatic piece of royal propaganda, following the birth of the Prince of Wales (later Charles II) in 1630: 'a parallel could conveniently have been drawn between the salvation [on the Isle of Dogs, opposite the Queen's House] of the infant Moses, the future redeemer of the people of Israel, and the birth of a male heir to perpetuate the royal line', enabling the continuation of the happy situation enjoyed under the Stuart dynasty which was depicted in the ceiling.[25]

Listed next to *The Finding of Moses* in the valuation inventory, Gentileschi's *Lot and his Daughters* (fig. 96)[26] also was valued at £80. Its placing in the inventory implies physical proximity and it may well have hung opposite, on the east wall of the Great Hall, although it was not intended as a pendant painting from the start, being hung first at Whitehall, then, by 1639, in the Queen's Withdrawing (Cabinet) Room on the first floor of the Queen's House.[27] It probably was moved into the Great Hall when the Jordaens *Cupid and Psyche* paintings arrived in 1641 and displaced it. It may be viewed as a private picture in terms of subject matter, although this is a painting of considerable monumentality and luxurious restraint, lacking the lubricious qualities which tend to distinguish paintings on this theme, and it does, furthermore, have

96 Orazio Gentileschi, *Lot and his Daughters*, painted by 1628, hung originally at Whitehall Palace, then in an upper room at the Queen's House and later moved probably into the Great Hall (Museo de Bellas Artes, Bilbao).

the appropriate dynastic theme for the Hall of the continuation of the race.[28] The two canvases are slightly different in size, the *Moses* being the larger, but both are about 8 feet high by 10 feet wide. They could have been accommodated at gallery level, but it is more likely, given the narrowness of the gallery and the difficulty of viewing, that they occupied the large blank wall surfaces between the doors on the east and west walls, with the sculptures along the south wall and in the corners. Before the hanging of *Lot and his Daughters*, unless there was an earlier pendant painting, it is possible that the east wall was devoted entirely to sculptures. The harmonious balance of full-length sculpture and over life-size figure painting was a short-lived moment of equilibrium. The Hall and the works of art within it were intended to be seen as a unified whole: the pattern of the marble floor (fig. 85), laid by Nicholas Stone in 1636–7, reflects the compartments of the ceiling (in a manner reminiscent of Philibert de l'Orme's chapel at Anet, albeit in a less geometrically complex manner), and the sculpture and paintings relieve the formality of the architecture. Without that synergy, the Hall is an undeniably handsome but austere space, rather at odds with the idea of a 'House of Delight'. Following their sale during the Commonwealth, Henrietta Maria recovered both *The Finding of Moses* and *Joseph and Potiphar's Wife*, taking them back to France to her residence at Colombes, so underlining her role as patron of the artist and owner of these pictures which, among others, she had commissioned or purchased for her house.[29]

During the Commonwealth period the Gentileschi ceiling, reserved at the sale and valued at £600,[30] may have been taken down and put into temporary storage. The house was said by a Dutch visitor in 1661, William Schellinks, himself a painter of note, to be 'without furniture and pictures' at that time,[31] and in 1662 both the Great Hall and the Queen's Bedchamber were scaffolded for the installation of pictures. The designation of the latter is ambiguous since by that time there were two such Bedchambers.[32] The intention does, however, signify a conscious attempt after the Restoration to re-establish the artistic integrity of the Queen's House.

Whether or not they had been taken down earlier, then reinstalled, the Gentileschi paintings appear to have been removed finally from the Hall by 1708, when the Queen's House became the designated residence of the Greenwich Hospital Governor Sir William Gifford, and the ceiling was mended and painted. They were granted by Queen Anne to her favourite, Sarah, Duchess of Marlborough, and installed at Marlborough House, probably in 1711, when building work on the new house was completed. The paintings were cut down to fit the available space and remain *in situ*.[33] From the beginning of the eighteenth century until 1969, it appears that the ceiling of the Great Hall remained unadorned, simply plastered in a plain manner, with the preposterous addition during the nineteenth century of a plaster ceiling rose.

In 1969 the National Maritime Museum purchased a picture by Louis Cheron for the centre roundel for just £200 (fig. 97).[34] Cheron had left France for England in 1695 and as a Protestant, decided to stay. His most significant work was carried out for Ralph, 1st Duke of Montagu at Boughton House.[35] The painting installed at the Queen's House, originally thought to be by James Thornhill, was painted for Halnaker House, near Chichester, but later was moved to The Grange, Chichester, from whence it was acquired by the National Maritime Museum. This Poussinist

97   Louis Cheron, *The Triumph of Peace*, acquired for the ceiling of the Great Hall in the Queen's House in 1969.

98   A 'Scanochrome' reproduction of Gentileschi's original ceiling paintings for the Queen's House, installed during the restoration work in the 1980s.

Triumph of Peace shows Minerva, Goddess of Wisdom, receiving the kneeling figure of Peace, who is being crowned by Fame.[36] This was an appropriate subject for the Queen's House ceiling, but only twenty years later, when the decision was made to install a replica of the Gentileschi ceiling (fig. 98), the Cheron was sold at auction.[37]

THE ROUND (TULIP) STAIRS

Access to the most important rooms on the *piano nobile*, from the Hall, was by way of the so-called 'Tulip' stairs, which rose from the ground floor to the roof, the extension to the basement being a nineteenth-century alteration (fig. 99).[38] These round stairs have gained this name because of the floral motif on the wrought-iron balustrade. It is likely that the design was intended to represent a stylised fleur-de-lis, the emblem of the Bourbon family of which Henrietta Maria was a member (fig. 100). Rose and lily symbolism were commented upon in a letter from Balthazar Gerbier to Rubens in 1625: 'It was evident God had made known to the King of Great Britain that he made the lilies to unite with the roses'.[39] Constructed during the 1630s, although planned as early as 1616, this was the first geometrical, self-supporting stair to be built in England. Above the staircase originally stood a polygonal turret or roof pavilion for obtaining access to the leads. It is shown clearly on the view by Wenceslaus Hollar of 1637 (and later edi-

tions), a grand, panoramic demonstration piece; his first important work in England following his arrival at the end of 1636 under the sponsorship of Lord Arundel (fig. 101).[40] During the restoration work of the 1980s the base of the turret was found above the stairs. However, there were no similar footings on the northwest part of the roof, confirming that the two turrets shown on the elevation drawing of about 1640 were just a dream of symmetry.[41] The turret was removed in the early nineteenth century, during the occupation of the house by the Royal Naval Asylum.

THE QUEEN'S BEDCHAMBER (FIRST FLOOR, WEST SIDE, NORTH FRONT – ROOM E)

John de Critz painted the Royal Closet at Somerset House with grotesque work on a white ceiling. The ceiling cove of the Queen's Bedchamber at Greenwich was similarly painted, either by de Critz or Matthew Gooderick, and is a fine example of a form of italianate decoration which distinguishes many of the interiors both at Caprarola and the Palazzo Te (fig. 102). In England, only the ceiling of the Single Cube Room at Wilton House, executed by Gooderick, displays work to a higher degree of skill. The mottoes at the angles of the ceiling spell out an appropriately idealistic message for a Stuart bedchamber: MUTUA FECUNDITAS: SPES REIPUBLICAE/ARDET AETERNUM: CUM ODORE CANDORE

99   The Round stairs in the north range of the Queen's House.

100   The fleur-de-lis balustrade of Inigo Jones's Round stairs in the Queen's House.

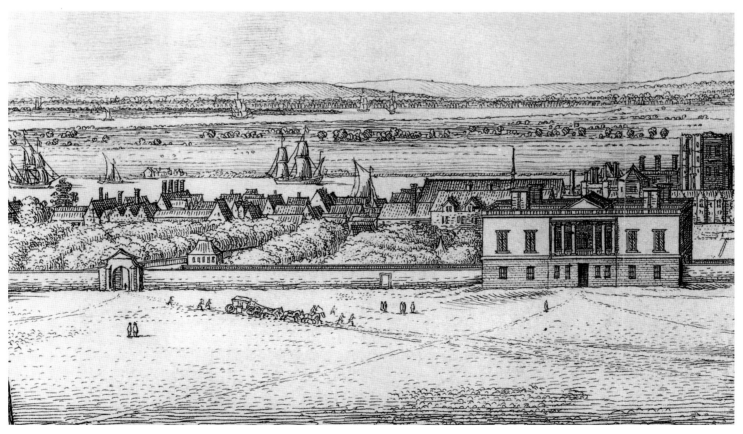

101   A detail of Wenceslaus Hollar's panorama of Greenwich, 1637, showing the Queen's House from the south. The single polygonal turret above the Round stairs is shown on the north-east side of the house, with the buildings of the palace visible beyond. The walls alongside the road and Inigo Jones's gateway are clearly delineated.

102   The Queen's Bedchamber on the first floor of the Queen's House. The chimneypiece is a resin cast of the chimneypiece now at Charlton House, Greenwich, which has been attributed to Inigo Jones. The tapestries, formerly at Eltham
Lodge, Kent, were installed after the restoration in the 1980s. Woven in Brussels in the seventeenth century, they illustrate
the appropriately chaste story of Theodosius II (of Byzantium) and the Apple.

103   G. B. Bolognini, etching of *Bacchus and Ariadne*, after Guido Reni (BM).

104 The ceiling of the Queen's Bedchamber at the Queen's House. The central field, which was to have been filled by Guido Reni's *Bacchus and Ariadne*, now contains an *Aurora*, the authorship of which is uncertain.

('Mutual fruitfulness, the hope of the state, burns forever with pure fragrance').[42]

The Bedchamber retains all of its ceiling painting except the main, central canvas, which was to have been by Guido Reni, one of the queen's favourite artists. In March 1637 she asked the papal agent to the Stuart court, George Con, to mediate with Cardinal Francesco Barberini to commission Guido to paint a mythological work for the ceiling of her Bedchamber. His first choice of subject, *Cephalus and Aurora*, depicting a rape, was considered unsuitable and was soon abandoned for a *Bacchus and Ariadne*. By August 1640 Con's successor, Conte Carlo Rossetti, reported the work to be finished and arranged for it to be sent to England. However, it became evident that the picture, although of high quality, included several undraped figures, so in view of the changing political climate in England, Barberini recommended that the painting should not be sent, especially 'in these Parliamentary times'. The queen did not seem unduly concerned and requested that the picture be despatched. But it did not arrive and was apparently destroyed in France in 1650.[43] The frieze-like picture is known through the existence of an etching by G. B. Bolognini (fig. 103) and of copies, one of which (now destroyed) was sent as a gift to Charles II together with another version of the subject, intended as a replacement for the Guido (also destroyed) by Giovanni Francesco Romanelli; both were recorded at Hampton Court in 1681.[44] It was indeed unfortunate that this important late painting, which had cost the artist much labour, should have fallen into the hands of someone who regarded its nudity as excessive.

Notwithstanding the conservative views of Cardinal Barberini, this was a far from lascivious painting, praised in a panegyric written in 1640 for its grace and restraint.[45]

Instead of the Guido, Giulio Romano's *Daedalus and Icarus* was inserted into the empty space in the Bedchamber. This was at St James's Palace in 1631–2.[46] Recorded as measuring 14 feet by 7 feet, framed, it was put up in the Queen's House soon after 1639–40, when Richard Dirgin carved three frames for the Queen's Bedroom, one measuring 29 feet 'run', which was probably intended for the central ceiling painting.[47] In 1649 it was described in the appraisal of the pictures at Greenwich as 'One peece in ye seeleing, being Deadulus Aicorus done by Julio Romano', valued at £500.[48] Apart from the Gentileschi ceiling in the Hall, this was the most valuable painting in the Queen's House, an indication of the high regard in which Giulio Romano was held.

After the Restoration, in anticipation of occupation by Charles II's queen, Catherine of Braganza, the room was refurbished as the Queen's Presence Chamber. The Giulio Romano painting, despite being 'reserved' in the Commonwealth inventory, appears to have been sold during the Interregnum, leaving a gap to be filled, but when this happened is not known. If the Romanelli, intended as a replacement for the Guido, was at Hampton Court in 1681, any time which it spent at Greenwich would have been short. The room may have been scaffolded for the installation of a painting in 1662,[49] which probably was about the time that the picture would have arrived from Italy, but measuring approximately 10 feet by 20 feet, it was rather larger than the available space.[50] The date of the installation and the authorship of the current painting in the Bedchamber ceiling are unknown. The depiction, of Aurora dispersing the shades of night, clearly appropriate for a bedchamber, inevitably has been attributed to Thornhill, given its location at Greenwich, and indeed payments were made to him for unspecified works in 1731–2,[51] but it has also been suggested that it may be by a late seventeenth-century follower of Nicolas Poussin (fig. 104).[52]

THE QUEEN'S ANTE-ROOM (FIRST FLOOR, WEST SIDE, SOUTH-WEST ROOM – ROOM G)

As a devout Catholic, Henrietta Maria would certainly have desired a place of private devotion within the Queen's House. No provision for a private chapel was made by Inigo Jones in the original plans and no evidence survives to show where her private oratory was, but it is likely to have been in the small room to the rear of the Queen's Bedchamber. This room is placed next to a back staircase, replaced in the nineteenth century, rising from the ground to the first floor, which would have allowed the priest easy and discreet access. In 1637, during the main decorative phase when Jones produced his design for a chimneypiece for this room, the queen in a letter to Monsieur de Chavigny sent him 'the measure of a picture, which her majesty wishes to have executed by Guido, for her chapel at Greenwich'.[53] This was the same year that she commissioned Reni to paint the large mythological scene for the ceiling of her Bedchamber. The existence of a chapel at the Queen's House was mentioned during the 1680s, when the Marquis de Ruvigny was in occupation.

105   The Queen's Cabinet or Withdrawing Room, on the first floor of the Queen's House, which was to have been the setting for Jacob Jordaens's series of paintings of the legend of Cupid and Psyche.

THE QUEEN'S CABINET OR WITHDRAWING ROOM (FIRST FLOOR, EAST SIDE, NORTH FRONT – ROOM A)

The Cabinet Room, if completed as intended, would have been distinguished by the most magnificent of the decorative schemes devised by Inigo Jones and Henrietta Maria. It would have embodied in permanent form the legend of choice of the Caroline court, Cupid and Psyche, a theme central to the element of fantasy within the royal marriage and to the self-perceptions of the king and queen as divinely ordained rulers of a perfect state. The richly carved and gilded mouldings of the beams and entablature would have framed Jacob Jordaens's cycle of twenty-two paintings which were intended to cover the ceiling and walls of the room. The sequence, closely based on Apuleius' *The Golden Ass*, was never completed and only eight panels were installed during the early 1640s.

All that survives are the richly decorated cornice, frieze and ceiling beams, constructed in pine (fig. 105). The acanthus scrolls of the frieze link the fleur-de-lis of France with cartouches with the crowned monogram of Charles and Henrietta Maria, the soffits of the beams bearing festoons of fruit and flowers in high relief, intersected by masks. The original design incorporated balconies on both the north and east walls onto which the windows opened.

Negotiations for the Cupid and Psyche sequence were begun in 1639, when the room was already richly hung with large paintings, at least one of which, Gentileschi's *Lot and his Daughters*, subsequently was moved into the Hall to make way for the new pictures. The other paintings in the 'quins Witdrauwing chamr' (or Cabinet), identified in Abraham van der Doort's inventory, were Artemisia's *Tarquin and Lucretia*, a Van Dyck portrait, *The Archduchess Isabella*, a large *Flora*, a Giulio Romano, *The Emperor Otho on his Funeral Pyre*, one of the group of eleven Emperors from the Mantua collection, and the magnificent Tintoretto, *The Muses* – 'nijn neckit mussis so big als te lijff', which also seems to have been moved to make way for Jordaens, being appraised at Denmark House in 1649 at £80 (fig. 106).[54]

Sir Balthazar Gerbier, who had been born in Holland but became a British citizen and 'esquire of his Majesty's body extraordinary', was one of Charles's most important agents, notwithstanding a 'disastrous diplomatic career'.[55] Based in Brussels in 1639, he was requested to approach Jacob Jordaens through L'Abbé de Scaglia, Cesare Alessandro Scaglia di Verrua, a retired diplomat living in Antwerp and well connected within the artistic community of the city, to commission a cycle of paintings for the Queen's Cabinet depicting the story of Cupid and Psyche. Inigo Jones provided Gerbier with instructions for commissioning the paintings and a copy by John Webb of this remarkable document makes it possible to picture the lost and unfinished room, described as 'ye Queenes room with glasses' (mirrors) (see Appendix 7). The instructions were accompanied by drawings (a plan of the compartmented ceiling, with scale) and elevations, to 'show which way the lights doe come to strike on ye payntings, so as the shadowes may bee given accordingly'. In order to avoid the sort of confusion which had occurred on other occasions with measurements, the scale was to be accompanied by more tangible measures in 'lines in pack thread'.[56] This shows the great care and attention to detail that the architect paid to the decoration of the interior of the house. Not only did Jones require 'the greatest

106 (*above*) Jacopo Tintoretto, *The Muses*. Recorded in Mantua in 1627, this allegory of the harmony of the universe was acquired by Charles I and displayed at the Queen's House. After being sold at the Commonwealth sale, it returned to the Royal Collection at the Restoration (The Royal Collection © 2000, HM Queen Elizabeth II).

107 Jacob Jordaens, drawing for *Psyche Consoled by Pan*, the first of the paintings sent by the artist in 1640 for the decoration of the Queen's Cabinet at the Queen's House (Stedelijk Prentenkabinet, Antwerp).

peece in ye middle of the ceeling to bee of Cupid and Psyche in Heaven, and Jove setting presenting a cupp of Nectar unto her' (thereby assuring her immortality), but he also instructed the artist to choose and depict 'as many of the Gods as may bee without confusion', suggesting Juno, Pallas, Hebe, Bacchus, Apollo and 'other Robustious Gods' such as Mars, Hermes, Neptune, Pluto and Vulcan, 'and of these to choose such as ye paynter shall like best'.

Jordaens, whose work was less expensive than that of either Rubens or Van Dyck at this time, was not to know the intended destination of the pictures, presumably to maintain the price at a low level; in fact Gerbier sent papers to Jordaens in French to confuse him, reporting to Jones that 'it will be well he remayns (as long as possible) in that thrifty ignorance for these men know that a pound sterling is more than a patacon' (a silver coin worth about 4s 8d). Confusion certainly seems to have occurred, since when Jordaens wrote to Scaglia concerning the pictures, it was in 'un francais impossible, une orthographe fantaisiste et une écriture souvent indéchiffrable'.[57] Jordaens requested £680 to complete the pictures and stated that he could finish them within two years, sending them, as requested by Jones, 'as they are finished', in instalments of two or three pieces.[58]

Soon after the initial negotiations, Gerbier wrote to Jones suggesting that Rubens might undertake the work 'as of the two most certain Sir Peter Reubens is the gentilest in his representations'.[59] It appears that for some time Jones considered that both men might work on the scheme and Rubens even presented ideas for the design of the ceiling, but his death in May 1640 prevented any collaboration. The first picture was completed by Jordaens during the same month and was despatched to London.

By May 1641 seven more canvases had been finished, but after Gerbier left Brussels in August, it is unclear whether further work was undertaken. At the time of the Parliamentary inventory, the eight completed pictures by Jordaens were installed in the Queen's Cabinet and valued at £200.[60] Since the Gentileschi and Giulio Romano paintings listed on the same page of the inventory are specified as 'seeleing' paintings, while the Jordaens is simply 'eight peeces in one room', it seems unlikely that the ceiling canvases, of which nine were required to fill the compartments, were ever completed, despite having been asked for first. The arrival of eight new pictures to go on the walls clearly would have prompted the re-hang which sent *Lot and his Daughters* into the Hall. It is not known what became of Jordaens's paintings, but they were surely in a style well suited to the portrayal of 'Robustious Gods'. Seven other paintings for the sequence, four of which were for the ceiling, were said to be in the course of execution when negotiations between London and Antwerp broke down following the death of Scaglia in 1641. There were problems with payment; there had been no formal contract and a legal dispute followed.[61] One drawing by Jordaens survives for the Queen's House *Cupid and Psyche* sequence, at the Stedelijk Prentenkabinet, Antwerp (fig. 107). Closely following Apuleius' text, this shows Pan with his arm around Echo, whom he has been teaching to tune her songs and pipes, comforting Psyche, who stands damply distraught after being saved by a sympathetic river from drowning herself for love: 'goe not about to slay your selfe, nor weepe not at all, but rather adore and worship the great god Cupid'.[62] In February 1640 Jordaens submitted a *modello* of this subject to Charles I, and the finished painting of *Psyche Consoled by Pan* was the first of the cycle to be sent to England in May of the same year.[63]

We might also gain an idea of Jordaens's approach to the subject from the surviving paintings on the Cupid and Psyche theme, one of which is dated 1652, which he carried out for his house in Antwerp. The central ceiling painting in this sequence is squarer in format than the rectangle required for Greenwich, but the subject is the same as the one specified by Jones: *Cupid and Psyche in Heaven*, with Jove presenting a cup of nectar to her.[64] These paintings are distinguished by a dramatic foreshortening which recalls the work of Giulio Romano at the Palazzo Te, a technique which Jordaens either learned directly or through the mediation of Rubens. The appearance of his third Cupid and Psyche sequence, carried out with great speed and presumably therefore involving a lot of workshop assistance, is entirely unknown since it was destroyed by fire in 1697. This was carried out in the late 1640s for Queen Christina of Sweden.[65] It is conceivable that for both of these decorative schemes, Jordaens may have re-used some of the paintings begun, but not sent, earlier in the decade for Henrietta Maria.[66]

It has been noted that Jordaens's figures of the years around 1640 have a healthily earthy quality which may not have accorded with Charles's expressed wishes for the Queen's Cabinet, that the faces of the women were to be as beautiful as possible and the figures 'gracious and svelta'. In view of this preference, it is surprising that Van Dyck, who was resident in London, was not invited to paint the required poesie. In the one very beautiful canvas on this theme which he did complete, *Cupid and Psyche* (now in the Royal Collection), the king's requirements are fully met in a Titianesque masterpiece which fuses sensual desire and idealised love. The artist shows Cupid rescuing Psyche from the 'infernall and deadly sleepe' into which she had fallen after 'over-much curiositie' had caused her once more to ignore wiser counsels and to open the box filled by Proserpine with the 'mysticall secret' of divine beauty.[67] In 1638 Van Dyck had requested payment of £100 for a painting which he had done for Greenwich but if the later dating of *c*.1639–40 for *Cupid and Psyche* is correct, then this painting may have been intended for somewhere else. It remained unframed in the King's Gallery at Whitehall.[68]

The Queen's House may never have been all that Henrietta Maria and her architect had envisaged, as its decoration, although outstanding, remained incomplete, and its occupation by the royal couple was brief. Charles paid his last visit to Greenwich in 1642; Henrietta Maria left England in 1644 and when she briefly returned to the building after the Restoration, it was as queen dowager. As a widow in France, she recalled the 1630s, the time when the Queen's House was under construction, as the best years of her life: 'I was the happiest and most fortunate of queens, for not only had I every pleasure the heart could desire, I had a husband who adored me'.[69] In 1659 Thomas Phillipot, a Kent antiquarian, praised the work of the Stuart queens and their palatial vision: 'Queen Anne . . . builded that new Brick-work towards the Garden, and laid the foundation of the House of Delight, towards the Park, which Queen Mary [by which name Henrietta Maria frequently was known], hath so finished and furnished, that it far surpasseth all other of that kind in England'.[70] The phrase 'of that kind' begs the question of what other buildings Phillipot had in mind. So far as can be gathered at this distance in time, its architecture, contents and mode of occupation made the Queen's House a short-lived, unique ensemble, albeit one which had a place in the broad class of houses of retreat and retirement. Recently the view has been expressed that the house was disliked because it appeared cold and naked, crisply built in lime-washed brick and stone, but lacking the traditional 'comforts and adornments of the sixteenth-century English house', but there is little evidence to support this endorsement of old-fashioned cosiness.[71] Indeed, as noted above, there was almost no comment on the house itself at all. This proves the success of the whole project: the house was personal and private, a celebration of the marital harmony and dynastic ambition of God's divine representatives on earth. As the political climate of the country worsened, and Charles withdrew more and more from public view, we might imagine that the make-believe world of the Queen's House and all that it symbolised became increasingly important to the royal couple in circumstances where fantasy was easier to contemplate than reality.[72]

Later History

THE INTERREGNUM

In 1642 the outbreak of the Civil War temporarily brought an end to court life in London. Inigo Jones left the capital, leaving John Webb as his deputy, a short-lived role which was ended for Webb the following year (for political reasons) when he was replaced by Edward Carter.[73] In September 1643, when an order was given 'for seizing . . . all His majesty's, the Queen's and Prince's Houses, Manors, lands etc', the Queen's House fell into Parliamentary hands. The house was reserved for the use of the state and in 1651 was prepared for the ambassador from the United Provinces.[74] In 1652, according to John Evelyn, the Queen's House was 'given by the Rebells to Bolstrood Whittlock one of their unhappy Counselors, keeper of pretended Liberties', who reputedly occupied the house for a short period.[75] Bulstrode Whitelocke was a member of the Council of State who had been created High Steward and Keeper of Greenwich Park in February 1649, a position from which he resigned just four months later.[76]

Although the Queen's House suffered less physical damage than many of the other royal residences during the years of Parliamentary rule, its interior did not survive unscathed. On 10 May 1650 the Trustees appointed to value the king's goods were admonished for selling 'diverse necessary things' from Greenwich, despite the fact that the house along with the fixtures and fittings had been reserved for the use of the state.[77] This included the use of the Great Hall for laying out the bodies of high-ranking officers. In July 1653 the body of General-at-Sea Richard Deane, after the victory of the Gabbard,[78] was brought from Greenwich to Westminster for a state funeral and in 1657 Admiral Robert Blake, the greatest English commander of his age, also lay there before his burial.[79] The revival of the state funeral was strongly promoted during the Commonwealth, and the use of the Queen's House as a suitable resting place for the bodies of its most eminent officers is significant, showing that notwithstanding its royal origins and associations, the building and in particular Inigo Jones's Hall were considered a proper and dignified place for the greatest Parliamentarians in the land, as well as being suitably positioned for a journey by state funeral barge to Westminster. During the same period, the house (or perhaps the palace) may also have suffered inappropriate usage. Vere Babington, formerly the underkeeper of Henrietta Maria's house and gardens and now 'keeper of Greenwich House', reported in October 1654 to the Council of State that several persons were lodging without authority, to the prejudice of the property.[80]

THE RESTORATION

In January 1660 Greenwich was the scene of civil unrest in support of the monarchy: 'On Sunday night in some parishes in this city and at Greenwich four miles away, armed supporters of the King came out, but they had no time to unite together and the scattered bodies were too feeble, so the soldiers had no difficulty in dispersing them in confusion instantly'.[81] It was not long, however, before the return of the royal family to Greenwich.

In 1661 work began on repairing and enlarging the Queen's House, in anticipation of its becoming a royal residence for occupation by Charles II and Catherine of Braganza, whose marriage treaty was signed in June of that year. Catherine arrived in England from Portugal and married Charles in May 1662, but in fact it was Charles's mother, the dowager Queen Henrietta Maria, who briefly re-occupied the house while her larger palace, Somerset House, was being restored. Arthur Haughton, Purveyor to the King's Works, was paid for 'taking the plott of Greenwich house' and Willem de Keyser was paid for 'draughts with the upwrights for the intended Building at Greenwich'.[82] In August 1661, when William Schellinks visited Greenwich, he took the opportunity to visit the Queen's House, possibly while the builders were at work in the building:

A little inland is the Queen's House or palace, a fine, stately building with many large and small rooms and nice stone spiral stairs with iron banisters leading to the upper rooms and to the flat roof, which is lead-covered and railed in, from where one has beautiful views all round. This building too has suffered some damage in the recent war and is at present without furniture and pictures, but is now on the King's orders being repaired.[83]

In October of the following year he returned, describing the building as 'now in somewhat better order than when we saw it anno 1661'. He noted that the old palace buildings had been demolished to create 'a large level area', but in fact demolition had been begun rather than completed by this time.[84] As well as repairing damage incurred during the Interregnum, the king wished to enlarge the accommodation of the Queen's House in order to make it fully appointed and habitable as a house, rather than merely the temporary retreat which it had been for his mother. He added two new first-floor Bridge Rooms across the public road, obscuring the original H plan, and creating a 'King's side' on the east and a 'Queen's side' to the west (fig. 108). In October 1661 keystones were set in great arches (the Bridge Rooms) and by January 1662 the rooms were so advanced that doorcases were being formed on both sides. In April 'boarding two final floors over the foot passages in the highway' was undertaken and the public road was re-opened, workmen 'taking down the fences in the highway on each side of the buildings'.[85] The mullion and transom windows (renewed in the 1980s) which face the road were made square-headed at this time with the cutting of 'straight arches', replacing the original segmental heads which can be seen on the blocked windows beneath the new Bridge Rooms.[86]

Between 1661 and 1663 the plasterer John Grove completed four 'fret' ceilings: two of them were in the newly created Bedchambers at the corners of the park side of the house, where Inigo Jones's original rooms were partitioned to form apartments; the other two, much grander and more exuberant in their modelling, were in the new Bridge Rooms (figs 109 and 110).[87] Very soon afterwards, marble chimneypieces were being set in the King's and Queen's Bedchambers.[88] The principal accommodation now was divided between the King's side and the Queen's side, which largely mirrored each other in function. After the alterations, the *piano nobile* of the house comprised a pair of uninterrupted state apartments designed for the daily routine of the court: Presence Chambers (north-east and north-west corner rooms), Ante-rooms, Privy Chambers (east and west Bridge Rooms), Antechambers, Bedchambers (south-east and south-west corner rooms), and Inner and Outer Closets (fig. 71).

Other internal alterations were also carried out: a marble chimneypiece from a lower room was dismantled and moved up to the 'new room above stairs'; further accommodation was provided by the partitioning of the two south-side corner rooms on the ground floor; two ornamental balconies were made by the smith George Drew at a cost of £30 12s; three of the rooms in the cellars were ceiled, and two doors were hung; new 'pairs of stairs' were inserted, probably providing direct access for the first time between the basement and the ground floor.[89] In 1661–2 Robert Streeter, Sergeant-Painter to Charles II from 1660, was paid for

108   The central and west bridges over the road at the Queen's House.

'mending the Ceeling peice wch. came from St. Jameses house'. This painting, 11 feet in diameter, would have fitted the central oval field of the King's Bedchamber, for which carpenters made a 'streyning frame' in 1662.[90] Together with the Hall, the Queen's Bedchamber was scaffolded for the installation of pictures, but whether this was for the original or new Bedchamber is unclear.[91] Extensive repairs, including the laying of a new marble floor, were carried out on the loggia but these did not long withstand the weather and at the end of the decade the new gutter had to be removed where the boards had rotted and the marble paving partly taken up and reset. The problems were so serious that a 40 foot wooden shed had to be constructed 'upon the marble pavement of the Porticoe . . . to secure it from the weather', while the workmen undertook the extensive repairs.[92]

The refitting of the Queen's House was not taking place in isolation. Charles II had grander intentions, perhaps, it has been suggested, in order to reinstate Greenwich as the major reception centre for ambassadors which the old palace had been earlier in the century.[93] It was certainly once again in use for embassies, William Schellinks noting in December 1662 that one of the visiting Russian ambassadors, 'unwell from the hardships of the journey, . . . had for this reason remained at Greenwich'.[94] In October 1661 John Evelyn had discussed the siting of a new palace with the Surveyor of the Works, Sir John Denham, 'which I would have had built betweene the River & the Queenes house, so as a large Square Cutt, should have let in the Thames like a Baye'. Sir John did not agree, favouring 'seting it on Piles at the very brink of the water, . . . & so I came away, knowing Sir John to be a better Poet than Architect, though he had Mr. Webb (Inigo Jone's Man) to assist him'.[95] But it was not until 1663, when Webb was by his own account called 'to react for yor Majestie at Greenwich', that decisions were made on the construction of a new palace, even though parts of the old one were being dismantled from 1662.[96]

On 28 July 1662 John Evelyn 'went to Greenewich to waite on the Queene now landed'. She returned the compliment by visit-

ing him in August at his 'poore Villa', Sayes Court in nearby Deptford.[97] Henrietta Maria had returned to the house which she had
planned throughout the 1630s, but barely saw finished before
fleeing from England. She stayed in the Queen's House very
briefly, although it appears to have been the intention that she
would stay longer while Somerset House was being renovated. Sir
Edward Nicholas reported to Heneage Finch, 2nd Earl of
Winchilsea, the Queen Mother 'remains att Greenwich till Som-
ersett house be ready to receive her'.[98] But as early as September
1662, long before the renovations (1661–5) at Somerset House
were completed, it was reported that 'the Queen Mother . . . proceeded to London, from Greenwich, to her Palace of Somerset
where she will spend the rest of her life, as she does not propose
to leave England or London any more'.[99] Wherever she lived in
England she seems to have been doomed to live on a building
site. In fact she did not end her life there. It is generally accepted
that bad health forced her back to France in June 1665, to
Colombes, where she died in 1669, although she may have delayed
her journey and attempted to find a cure in England. Henry
Howard reported in a letter to the Earl of Winchilsea in July or
August 1665: 'Our Queen Mother allsoe is ill and goes nott for
France butt to the Spaw i heare'.[100]

After the addition of the Bridge Rooms, while contemplating
the building of a new palace, Charles II first agreed to an enlargement of the Queen's House. In 1663 John Webb produced drawings for the addition of four corner pavilions, each containing
bedchambers and associated suites of accommodation,[101] a design
somewhat reminiscent in plan of Poggia Reale, near Naples, which
had been praised by Sebastiano Serlio as 'very well compartitioned'
since 'a nobleman and his entourage could be lodged in each of
the corners'.[102] Work began on the foundations at the south-east
and south-west corners and later the ground was marked out to
the north as well, where the pavilions would have abutted the
terrace. Progress was desultory, however, and Webb's attention
shifted to the design of a three-range palace next to the Thames.
Only one of the blocks, the King Charles Building, the 'King's
side' of the palace, was built and even this was left boarded up
with an unfinished interior when work, latterly spasmodic, finally
stopped in 1672. It seems to have become apparent to the architect
that the most that he could hope for was the building of two
ranges, facing each other across a courtyard, without the central
linking range which would have obscured the view of the Queen's
House from the river. He proposed the addition of a dome and
porticoes to the Queen's House and raising it one storey higher
in order to give it the greater emphasis which it needed in order
to serve as a strong central accent. These aggrandisements,
together with the pavilions, would have altered entirely the character and scale of the Queen's House, but apart from marking out
the ground and the underpinning of the quoins at the corners,
nothing really was achieved and by 1670 the foundations for the
pavilions had been filled in and the scheme abandoned (figs 111
and 112).[103]

109 (*right top*)   The east Bridge Room of the Queen's House, seen from
the south.

110 (*right bottom*)   The west Bridge Room of the Queen's House, seen
from the north.

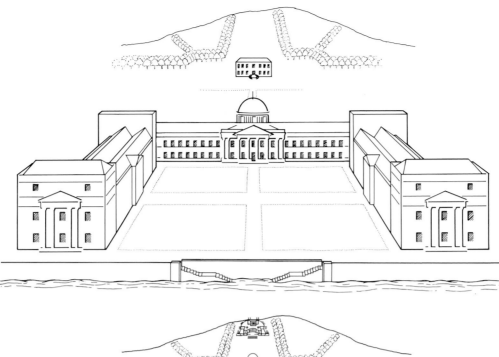

III(a) Reconstruction of John Webb's proposal for a three-range royal palace next to the River Thames at Greenwich, with the Queen's House in the background (based on drawings at All Souls College, Oxford).

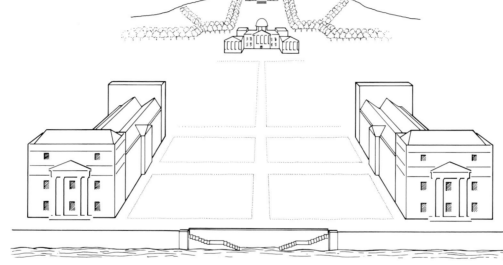

III(b) Reconstruction of John Webb's proposal for a palace of two ranges at Greenwich, with an enlarged Queen's House and a grotto towards the top of the hill (based on drawings at BAL). The King Charles Building, the only part of this proposal to be realised, is on the right.

To complement the building works, Charles II employed Sir William Boreman in planting avenues of trees and in 1662 expressed a wish for André Le Nôtre, creator of the parks at Vaux-le-Vicomte and Versailles, to design an extensive formal landscaping scheme for Greenwich (see chapter 1). The focus of this was to be a giant parterre with fountains under the hill, south of the Queen's House. The commission probably had been directed through Henrietta Maria, to whom reference is made on the plan of 'Grenuche', made by Le Nôtre for 'la reyne' (fig. 19).[104] Schellinks reported in October of 1662 that two avenues of trees had been planted, and 'near the top of the hill, where it was too steep to climb up, steps had been cut into the ground to walk up in comfort'.[105] By June 1664 terracing had been completed and '500 great Elme Trees for the Terrace Walks' had been planted.[106] In May 1665 Bulstrode Whitelocke accompanied Adrian May, brother of the architect Hugh May, Paymaster of the Works, to see 'his plantations att Greenwich Parke'.[107] As part of the overall landscaping scheme, and mindful of the need to create an adequate termination of the view from the river, Webb proposed around

1665 a grand 'Grott & ascent', a multi-terraced, italianate complex of garden buildings and steps designed to regularise the ascent of the hill (fig. 20).[108] This scheme, together with many of Le Nôtre's proposals, was abandoned, but 7600 trees were planted.[109]

Work continued throughout the decade on improvements to the Queen's House. In 1667 the floors which had been disturbed for the underpinning of the quoins were repaired and 'ledges for hangings' were set up. Some ceilings were mended, along with 'washing and whiting some stains' on the ceilings and walls.[110] In 1669 the lower-storey windows were repaired and in 1671 a painter was paid 15s for 'colouring the iron rail at round stairs' in the Queen's Building.[111] Other repairs were still required. In May 1674 a Dutch embassy visited Greenwich and one of its members, the minister Joannes Vollenhove, described the Queen's House:

builded in this manner that we could drive under it; a curious stone winding stairs brought us to a square gallery, looking out on the floor and beautiful pictures of arts and sciences [the Gentileschi ceiling paintings]; spacious rooms with marble chimneys, but the marble leaf-work mutilated: the noses of all the faces cut off from love of mischief, committed in the times of Cromwell.[112]

By the 1670s and 1680s the Queen's House was little used by the monarch, even though it was granted by Charles II to Cather-ine of Braganza in 1670, and later to James II's queen, Mary of Modena. At times the house was used to accommodate royal ser-vants. During the mid-1670s John Flamsteed lodged there, noting that 'whilst the Observatory was building and fitting up for my

well received by the king, who 'has given me Greenwich for a home, believing the air there will be good for my health'.[118] Another Frenchman, the great traveller Sir John Chardin, also appears to have fled from France in 1681, becoming jeweller to the English court and residing for some time at Greenwich with

112 View from the north of the Royal Hospital for Seamen and the Queen's House (based on survey and reconstruction drawings, omitting the Observatory buildings on top of the hill).

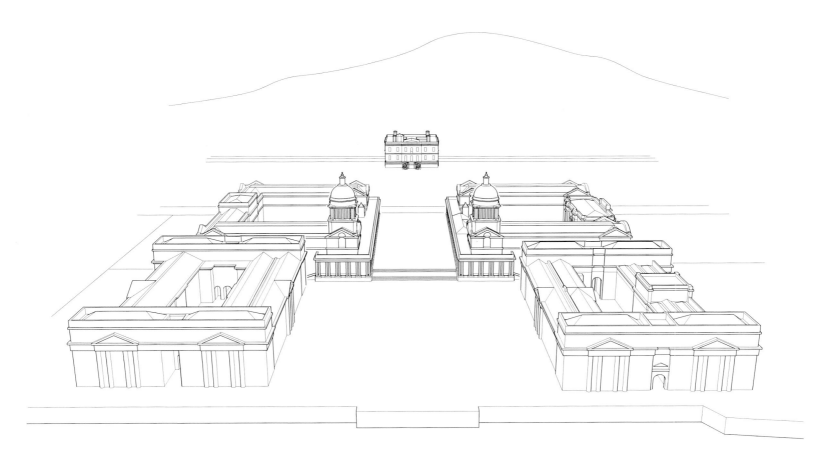

habitation, my quadrant and telescope were kept at the Queen's house, where with them I observed her [the moon's] appulses to the planets and the fixed stars, as often as convenient opportuni-ties offered themselves'.[113] He moved some of his equipment from the Queen's House to the Observatory in May 1676 in prepara-tion for the observation of a partial solar eclipse.[114] At about the same time the south-west room on the ground floor of the build-ing was used as a studio by one or both of the Dutch marine artists Willem van de Velde, father and son, painters of sea battles to both Charles II and James II.[115] In March 1675 the southern light obviously presented a problem, so carpenters were 'imployed in making and hanging of three pairs of shutters of slit deale for three windows in a lower room att the Queens building next the park (where the Dutch painter works)'.[116]

By 1686 the Queen's House had become the home of the exiled Frenchman Henri de Massue, Marquis de Ruvigny, deputy-general of the Protestant churches of France between 1653 and 1679, and according to his neighbour, John Evelyn, 'a Person of great Learning & experience'.[117] Ruvigny stated that he had been

Ruvigny.[119] For several years the chapel 'in a Rome of the Queenes house' became a regularly used place of worship for Ruvigny and other exiled Huguenots, with services performed there in French.[120] The main parish church of Greenwich was also the venue for services for the exiled French community, which may have numbered over a hundred in 1687.[121]

William and Mary rarely visited Greenwich, preferring Kens-ington Palace and Hampton Court. Thus, when Charles Sackville, Earl of Dorset was created the first ranger of Greenwich Park during the 1690s, there was little objection to the Queen's House becoming the official residence of the ranger. When he took over the house it is evident that a great deal of repair work was needed on the building, especially, once again, to the loggia, described in the accounts as 'the gallery at the Queen's house Park side that is decayed'. Here the marble paving was taken up in 1689 and new black and white tiles laid in 1693 (fig. 113). Some tiles were also replaced and the gallery repaired in the Great Hall in 1693 and Robert Streeter was paid for gilding a ceiling, possibly that of the Hall, in 1695. The two iron balconies on the north side of the

113   The black and white paving of the loggia of the Queen's House was again relaid in 1934–5, on a reinforced concrete floor.

building were renewed in 1694 and '10 new Scrowles for ye round stayres' were prepared in the same year by the smith William Pache.[122] In 1697–9 the removal northwards of the Romney Road[123] enabled the later construction of a room at ground level, underneath the central Bridge Room, shown on John James's eighteenth-century plan.

★   ★   ★

THE EIGHTEENTH CENTURY

In his *Remarks on the Founding and Carrying on the Buildings of the Royal Hospital at Greenwich*, published in 1728, Nicholas Hawksmoor explained the circumstances of Queen Mary's grant of land for the Hospital in 1694, which determined 'the Disposition of the Buildings, as they are now placed and situated':

Her Majesty, ever sollicitous for the Prosecution of the Design, had several times honour'd Greenwich with her personal Views

114   A view along the enclosed roadway, separating the two ranges of the Queen's House, taken from underneath the east Bridge Room during the restoration of 1934–5. By this time, rooms had been constructed under all the Bridge Rooms and the lightwells roofed and glazed at first-floor level.

of the Building erected by King Charles II., as Part of his Palace, and that built by Mr. Inigo Jones, called the Queen's House, etc. On which Views, she was unwilling to demolish either, as was propos'd by some. This occasioned the keeping of an Approach from the Thames quite up to the Queen's House, of 115 Feet broad, out of the Grant that was made to the Hospital, that her Majesty might have an Access to that House by Water as well as by Land; and she retained a Desire to add the Four Pavilions to that Palace, according to Inigo Jones's Design [*sic*], that she might make that little Palace compleat, as a Royal Villa for her own Retirement, or from whence Embassadors, or publick Ministers might make their Entry into London. She also proposed (as it was then advised) that the Governors of the Hospital might be her House-Keepers, Rangers of her Park, and Stewards of her Mannor and Honour of Greenwich; and that the said House and Mannor should not be alienated, unless to the Royal Hospital. . . . Afterwards Queen Anne determined to settle the Park, Queen's House, Mannor and Honour of Green-

wich, upon the Hospital; and Prince George purchased the Lease of My Lord Romney, in order to Compleat this Settlement; but something intervened, and the Prince dying, the said Premises remain'd in the Crown.[124]

In 1708 the Queen's House became the designated residence of the Governor of the Royal Hospital, who also was made keeper of the park, although he did not move in until 1710. Hawksmoor estimated that it would cost almost £400 to make the Queen's House habitable for the new governor, Sir William Gifford.[125] Numerous works, individually minor but cumulatively considerable, were carried out between 1708 and 1713 in the house and garden: sinkgrates were installed on the terrace; walls were papered for the first time; wainscot and chimneypieces and the Hall paving were repaired; the basement was levelled for paving; and the central Bridge Room was adorned with bucks' heads. In the kitchen, which by this time had been moved inside the house into the south-east corner room on the ground floor (possibly in the

115   The jealously guarded view north towards the river from the terrace of the Queen's House.

1660s), a new range was installed. The most far-reaching alteration was the removal in 1708 of the ground-floor mullion and transom windows on all four of the outer sides of the house (and on the inner wall of the south-side vestibule, later the orangery), the lowering of their sills and the installation of sashes. Apparently at the same time, the Gentileschi ceiling paintings were removed, later to be installed at Marlborough House, and the ceiling was mended and painted. The alteration to the windows and ceiling had a profound and lasting impact on the appearance of the house, significantly altering the Jonesian proportions and removing the one work of art which still survived at the Queen's House to symbolise its brief, halcyon period of royal occupation.[126] It was probably during this period, following the removal of the roadway in 1697–9, that doorways were inserted for the first time from the north and south ranges into the new room created underneath the central Bridge Room (fig. 114).

On the west side of the house, various old buildings were replaced by a barn, coachhouse and stables built by John James with 'most frugality'.[127] The gardens, too, were altered: a fountain in the north garden was repaired in lead and the walk leading to it paved. The old Tudor tilt yard was ploughed and planted with strawberries. A melon garden was fenced to the south-east of the house and cucumber frames were erected.[128] Both the gardens and

the house had become more domestic in appearance and function: in 1713 a weeding woman was employed at 8d per day.[129]

It was in October 1711 that the view envisaged by Queen Mary, from the Queen's House to the river, was again fully opened up when the master mason Edward Strong was paid for 'making a clear vista through the works on the middle line of the Queen's House';[130] some of the old palace buildings were still present when work began on building Greenwich Hospital and once those works had begun, their associated materials obscured the view (fig. 115). In March 1713 it is likely that the alignment of the foot of the steps down from the terrace was altered to the now familiar horseshoe shape, becoming more open and outward-looking towards the newly created view to the Thames. Strong was paid for 'Purbeck Mitchel paving in ye circular stair-case of the north front'; the doorcase appears (on stylistic grounds) to have been reconstructed at the same time. Strong also repaired the two other flights of steps up to the terrace which were next to the house: 'coping the half paces and ye steps at ye east and west ends of ye north terrace'.[131] One of these is shown on an eighteenth-century view of the north front (fig. 116).[132]

For many years the Hospital evidently hoped that a formal grant of the Queen's House and the park would be made by the Crown in its favour, but none was forthcoming. In 1713 the Lord Trea-

116   John Charnock, view of the Queen's House from the north-east, mid- to late eighteenth century (NMM).

surer Robert Harley, 1st Earl of Oxford, was requested to make a decision on the building since the Hospital had spent a great deal of money in the expectation of a grant. Despite the expenditure by the Hospital of almost £3000 to 'keep the House, Park and Gardens from Ruine', the house was said to be 'very much out of repair'; it was estimated by John James that a further £750 was needed 'to put the outside of the house and Lead Covering into tolerable good Repair'.[133] Although no decision was forthcoming, the fabric was at risk and in 1718 James prepared new estimates for repairs, recommending the expenditure of £210 on re-leading and a further £400 on replacing the existing lime-rendering and 'new casing' it in hardstone lime. James's survey plan and elevation of the south front probably date from this period, during which he appears to have had prime responsibility for the works

(fig. 118).[134] This was very appropriate in view of his respect for the work of Inigo Jones, which he noted in a letter of 1711 to the Duke of Buckingham,[135] and which culminated in his design of around 1724–7 for Wricklemarsh in nearby Blackheath. Although this fine house was demolished in 1787–1800, illustrations confirm the clear indebtedness of the architect, not only to Jones in the adaptation of loggia and curving steps, but also to John Webb's King Charles Building.[136]

The works proposed by James at the Queen's House were undertaken, and shortly afterwards, in 1723, the kitchen (which he indicated on the plan) was reconverted into a parlour and an external kitchen built to the east, to reduce the odours in the house.[137] The new service building is shown in eighteenth-century views of the house from the south (fig. 117).[138] It was during this period that the timbers of the roof over the Hall, already repaired after Hawksmoor's report in 1708, again needed attention.[139] In the present roof, three of Inigo Jones's original tie-beams survive (fig. 119). These retain mortices for king and queen posts and a stub of a principal rafter rising at a very shallow angle. Two timbers were required for each tie-beam in order to span the 40 foot wide Hall, with the original scarf joints of the 1630s timbers held together by iron straps, all but one of which are original. The beams now are stabilised by inserted supporting beams. The early eighteenth-century repairs, which seem to be unspecified in the building accounts, involved the bolting of the original rafters to the beams. A re-roofing in 1822 has been followed by the addition in the 1930s of a steel frame reinforcement. The original north gable end of the roof was frequently incorrectly depicted in engravings of the Hospital from the river as a pediment. Only 6 to 7 feet high, this was in fact a more modest termination, substantially hidden behind the balustrade.[140]

Between 1708 and 1726 repairs to the Queen's House, as well as the maintenance of the park (including attending the deer) and the associated gardens, had cost the Hospital over £7846. In 1729 it was resolved by the General Court of Greenwich Hospital that since there was still no expectation that the Hospital would be

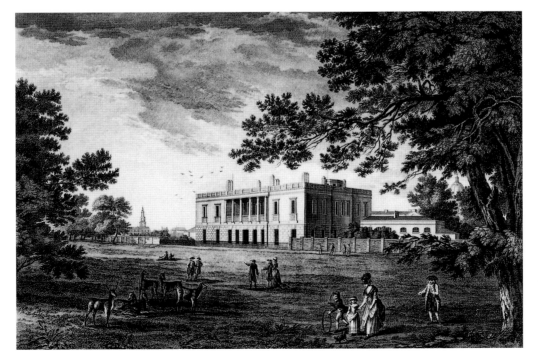

117   Thomas Morris (after a painting by George Robertson), engraved view of the Queen's House from the south-east, c.1781, showing the service building added by John James. James's recasing of the medieval tower of St Alfege, carried out in 1730, is visible in the distance (NMM).

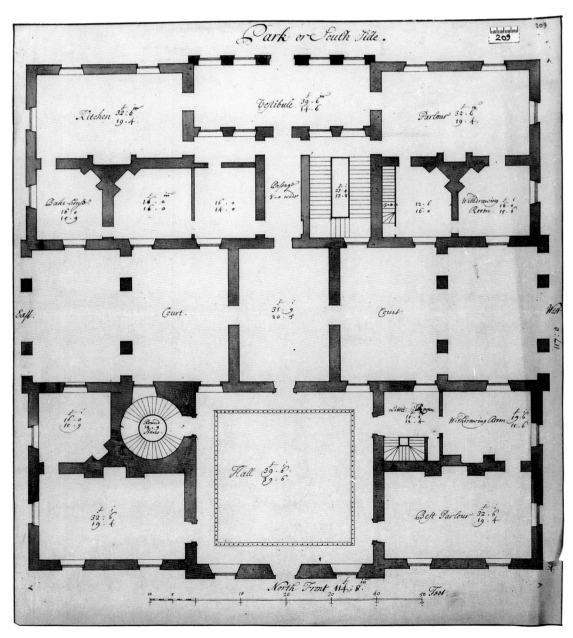

118   John James, south elevation and ground plan of the Queen's House (Worcester College, Oxford).

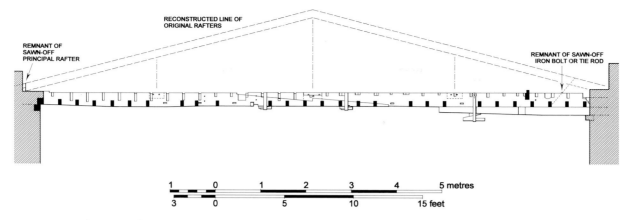

119 Survey drawing of an original tie-beam in the roof over the Great Hall of the Queen's House. The later roof truss and steel reinforcement are omitted.

formally granted the Queen's House, no further expenditure should be undertaken.[141] In fact it was granted to Queen Caroline in 1730, although it continued for the time being to be occupied by the Governor of the Hospital, Sir John Jennings, in his capacity as ranger of the park.[142] In April 1736 it was the scene of a royal wedding and an almost ritualistic 'putting to bed' of the royal couple, Frederick, Prince of Wales, and Augusta, Princess of Saxe-Gotha. After the wedding ceremony, the party returned to the Queen's House and the couple received a formal blessing from the king 'in the drawing-room'. Later,

> Their Majesties retiring to the apartments of the Prince of Wales, the bride was conducted to her bedchamber, and the bridegroom to his dressing-room, where the Duke undressed him, and his Majesty did his Royal Highness the honour to put on his shirt. The bride was undressed by the Princesses, and, being in bed in a rich dress, his Majesty came into the room, and the Prince followed soon after in a night gown of silver stuff and a cap of the finest lace: afterwards the quality were admitted to see the bride and bridegroom sitting up in the bed, surrounded by all the Royal family.[143]

In the middle of the eighteenth century the Queen's House was more commonly known as the Ranger's Lodge or Pelham House, being an occasional place of residence of the Prime Minister, Henry Pelham, whose wife, Lady Catherine, was ranger of the park.[144] It was also a period of extensive, but unfortunately unspecified works. In 1745 over £3000 was spent on the house, with a further £1700 spent during the next two years.[145] After Lady Catherine Pelham's death in 1780 the house was unoccupied (ill managed by stewards, who reputedly used it as a centre for smuggling) until it was suggested that Caroline, Princess of Wales, appointed ranger in 1805, might live there, rather than at Montague House, Blackheath, where she had lived since 1798. A survey undertaken in 1806 by another interested party, the Royal Naval Asylum, described the property:

> The Premises are of great extent as will appear by the plan. The House consists of a vaulted basement story and two lofty stories above it. The Building is very substantial and with common repairs is capable of standing a century or more. The external walls are partly built with stone and partly brick, the whole face whereof is covered with plaster, except the window dressings,

cornices and balustrades. . . . The Roof is substantial except some of the principal timbers supporting the ceiling of the Great Hall which ceiling we find to be out of its proper level and therefore requires examination. The whole building is covered in strong lead in good condition: The Kitchen Offices, Laundry, Brewhouse building and Stable offices together with the boundary walls are substantial requiring only ordinary repairs.[146]

It was estimated that to repair the house in a 'plain manner' would cost £3000, but to repair it for Princess Caroline 'by regilding the ornamental ceilings in the State Rooms, cleaning retouching and varnishing the paintings and in other fashionable fittings up and finishings' would increase the cost to £6000.[147] The princess and her advisers in October 1806 were persuaded to convey the 'House of the Ranger of Greenwich Park' to the Commissioners of the Naval Asylum for the sum of £7875.[148] There were clear grounds for separating Caroline from the Queen's House at a time when she was seen as a threat to the throne, but the prosaic financial concerns expressed by John Fordyce, the Surveyor General, provided reasons enough, without recourse to arguments rooted in symbolism:

> The Rangers House, from its situation between the Park and the Hospital does not seem to be a fit object of Sale to Individuals and it is not perhaps improbable that it may continue, as it has already done for many years unoccupied, and of no profit whatever to the Crown or the Public – while its situation near to the Hospital seems to point it out as naturally adapted to the purposes to which it is to be appropriated by the Commissioners and it is not likely that any buildings affording equal conveniences for the asylum could be purchased for the sum found to be necessary for providing the accommodation desired by the Princess.[149]

Caroline remained at Montague House until 1813, a sojourn which is well described elsewhere.[150] She had begun already in 1805 to enclose the Little Wilderness at the south-west corner of the park, in order to create a private garden of 15 acres, and from 1806 she altered and extended the house.[151]

★   ★   ★

120   The eastern colonnade, looking west, one of two designed by Daniel Alexander in 1809–11 in order to provide covered play areas along the former road, linking the new buildings of the Royal Naval Asylum to the former Queen's House.

THE NINETEENTH CENTURY

The early nineteenth century was one of the most damaging phases in the history of the form and fabric of the Queen's House. In 1807–11 it became the central component of the linked buildings that formed the Royal Naval Asylum, which was amalgamated in 1821 with the Greenwich Hospital School (see chapter 8). The building was divided into residences for the officers of the Asylum between 1807 and 1816. Space was provided also for schoolrooms, a refectory and a dormitory for up to 200 girls. By the 1930s only the Great Hall, the Queen's Drawing Room and the east Bridge Room had been left unpartitioned and without additional doorways and fireplaces. In November 1806 Daniel Asher Alexander, the Royal Naval Asylum's architect, drew up plans and a report for the 'disposition and arrangement' of the buildings for the school.[152] He stated later that he had obtained the commission because he had recommended that the architect be directed to

form his plan in strict accordance with the style of Inigo Jones, and indeed his long colonnades were a sympathetic addition to the house. Constructed in 1809–11 along the line of the former road, these linked the Queen's House with the new east and west wings and provided covered play areas for the pupils (fig. 120).

Inside, work was carried out throughout the house. Attics were inserted into the roof space and into the upper-floor rooms, evidence for which survives above the north-west Cabinet Room, where there appear to have been two top-lit rooms, both wallpapered. An underground passage was constructed, running beneath the colonnade, linking the east and west wings. In 1810 Alexander commissioned Sir Francis Chantrey to make four portrait busts of British admirals for display in the Hall – Duncan, Howe, St Vincent and Nelson – for each of which the sculptor was paid £10.[153] In May 1822, after Greenwich Hospital had taken over, investigations were undertaken into the 'sinking of the roof' and it was concluded that it had occurred largely before the insertion of the attics in 1807. Reinstatement was required, with new trusses,[154] and in June 1822 the central attic storey was removed 'in consequence of the ceiling beneath having sunk considerably'.[155] Work was carried out throughout the summer under the supervision of H. H. Seward in taking down the stonework, presumably including the belvedere, removing the old timbers, fixing the new rafters and erecting a new roof.[156] In 1824 some chimney-pieces were removed from the Board Room of the school and taken to St James's Palace.[157]

The girls' school closed in 1841 and by mid-century the Queen's House had been subdivided to accommodate at least thirteen people, including schoolmasters, matrons, the chaplain and the headmaster of the upper school, in separate apartments.[158] The west Bridge Room was in use as the Officers' Library, while the central Bridge Room was converted for lavatories. The former roadway, partly enclosed in the centre in the early eighteenth century, now was enclosed fully to form classrooms.[159] By this time it is likely that the cellars on the south side of the house had been excavated to increase the accommodation (fig. 121).[160]

In 1860 some thought was given to the Queen's House by the Commissioners appointed to look into the administration of Greenwich Hospital. They recommended that 'in dealing with the building in the centre of the colonnade [The Queen's House], care should be taken to preserve the architectural features of the rooms, many of which are of great beauty and interest'.[161] As late as 1911 mock seventeenth-century panelling was installed in the Great Hall (fig. 122).[162]

THE TWENTIETH CENTURY: 1930S' RECONSTRUCTION AND 1980S' REDECORATION

The likely removal from Greenwich of the Royal Hospital School during the 1920s and the need to find a new use for the Queen's House led to influential members of the Society for Nautical Research launching a campaign for a National Naval Museum. In 1927 the intention to use the building for a national museum was made public. During the 1930s the Office of Works was given the task of restoring and renovating the Queen's House, 'coincident with, but not dependent on the establishing of a museum'.[163] The representatives who visited in 1933 were not only sympathetic to the museum project but also very critical of Greenwich Hospital for allowing the building to fall into disrepair. In work which took

121   Ground- and first-floor plans of the Queen's House, 1900, showing the subdivision of rooms and, on the first-floor plan, the rooflights over the formerly open spaces between the Bridge Rooms (PRO WORK 31/413).

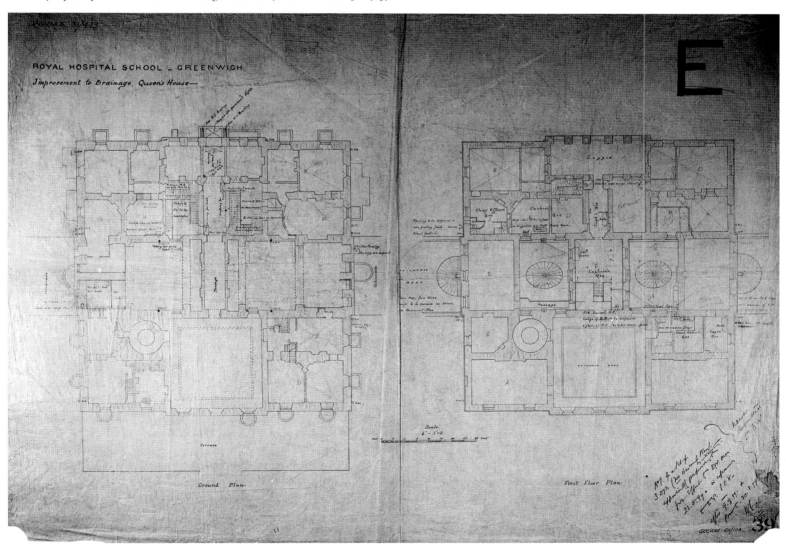

122   The Great Hall of the Queen's House with panelling, seen from the north before restoration in the 1930s. The door into the room underneath the central Bridge Room obscured the niche in which Bernini's bust of Charles I probably had been originally displayed.

place between 1934 and 1936, the house was largely reconstructed under the direction of the architect and Inspector of Ancient Monuments, George H. Chettle, author of the monograph on the house published with the support of the new National Maritime Museum in 1937. Both the book and the reconstruction of the house were exemplary in concentrating on the idea of Inigo Jones. Although it was stated before work began that 'the object of all work is to make the house into a series of rooms suitable for the purpose of the Maritime Museum',[164] Chettle, possibly under pressure from Professor Geoffrey Callender, the prime mover in the establishment of the National Maritime Museum and its first director from 1934, was as concerned to take the house back as far as possible, to the essentially irrecoverable 1630s. He could not remove the 1660s Bridge Rooms, but by removing the partitions added to the south side and altering the Bedchamber ceilings to allow them to sit rather uncomfortably over larger rooms, he reinstated, so far as it was possible, the plan of the building as it

was before Charles II's introduction of the King's and Queen's Bedchambers and Closets.

In 1934 an Ancient Monuments Inspector stated that 'all modern work ought to be cleared away – but the 1730s alterations are in a different category; they must be judged on their merits'.[165] A schedule of work to be undertaken was drawn up in October 1934, and a progress report produced in February 1935 (see Appendix 8). These detail the truly extensive nature of the refurbishment, which is referred to in the later document as a 'reconstruction'.[166] The balustrading of the loggia was reinstated, doors and windows were unblocked, fireplaces removed and new chimneypieces imported, many floors were replaced with reinforced concrete, modern partitions were removed and the roadway cleared of structures and lowered to the original level.[167] The remarkable result of Chettle's efforts to return the Queen's House to a putative Jonesian state was his creation, in essence, of a proto-modernist villa whose undecorated surfaces display a clear synchronicity with the flat white planes of neo-Palladianism.[168] In view of his background as an articled pupil of C. R. Ashbee and a member of the Art Workers' Guild, this tells us a great deal about the underlying spirit of the age, which will tend to influence responses to the past, as well as about the strength of will of those who would seek to reinterpret the past in the light of an ideal. Chettle's architectural sympathies apparently lay with the Arts and Crafts movement rather than with Le Corbusier, but he apparently was pressed towards the re-creation of a Jonesian plan by Callender and 'a small coterie of architects'.[169] When the National Maritime Museum was opened by King George VI and Queen Elizabeth in April 1937, it was noted in a letter from St James's that the restoration of the Queen's House 'will be of inestimable historical interest to the public'.[170]

The opportunity was taken during the restoration to refurbish the south-side staircase (figs 123 and 124). Although in the position designated by Inigo Jones, with its original barrel-vaulted ceiling, the treads of the stairs belonged to a later reconstruction and the balustrading dated from the nineteenth century. Following criticism of the stair from Sir Edwin Lutyens, the 1730s wrought-iron balustrading from Pembroke House, Whitehall, under demolition in preparation for the erection of new government offices, was installed at the Queen's House in 1936.[171] In an early design for Greenwich Hospital, in which he incorporated the Queen's House, Wren had proposed to add a second south-side staircase, leading from the central Bridge Room and Loggia to the ground, and to widen the corridor between the two staircases.[172] This was not carried out and the corridor remains improbably tall and narrow, with its barrel vault reinstated by Chettle.

In view of its location next to the Royal Naval College and not far from the docks, the Queen's House was fortunate to survive the Second World War largely intact. From 1939 the northeast basement was used as an air-raid shelter, capable of accommodating fifty-four people.[173] Precautionary steps were taken to minimise the effect of bomb blasts – criss-crossing windows with tape, sand-bagging basement openings and shoring of some ceilings to prevent collapse if hit – but some bomb damage nevertheless was sustained, especially during the raids of October 1940 and March to April 1941. Incendiary bombs caused damage to the roof and to the plaster in the Loggia and many windows were broken by blasts. There was serious damage to the balustrades on

123 The south-side staircase of the Queen's House, balustrading installed 1936.

124 The vaulted ceiling over the south-side staircase of the Queen's House.

the terrace and part of the painting in the Queen's Bedchamber was lost.[174] In 1945 minor repairs were undertaken on the shrapnel-damaged roof and on the plaster and glazing, and in 1947–8 the ceilings were made safe and the repairs completed.[175] The interior was painted a yellowish off-white.[176] During the postwar period, changes were minor. The papering of some rooms in flock wallpaper in the mid-1960s escaped the criticism even of Sir John Summerson,[177] and in 1967 an unsatisfactory version of Van Dyck's full-length portrait of Charles I, in the east Bridge Room, was covered up. In 1975 the Queen's House was redecorated, but tastes and fashions were by that date beginning to change and the house was considered too cluttered; a suggestion was made that there should be 'less wallpaper'.[178]

For almost forty years the Queen's House posed an interesting problem for the National Maritime Museum to solve: should it continue to be a series of galleries used to display the Museum's collections or should it be presented as an architecturally important house in its own right? During the late 1970s some attempt was made to add colour to the interior of the building through the addition of more seventeenth-century furnishings to the principal state rooms, but none was of the right quality or period because of a lack of resources. The dilemma of the presentation of the Queen's House was not addressed fully until the following decade, when it was decided to restore it as an important royal residence, rather than simply another gallery of the Museum. A working party was set up in 1984 to decide on its future and to

re-evaluate the way in which the building was to be presented to the public. Paint analysis, documentary research and archaeological investigation took place, before over £3.5 million was spent on the restoration, carried out by the Property Services Agency and the architects Thomas Ford and Partners between 1984 and 1989. The stated aim of the restoration was 'to make the House itself the exhibit, rather than as a place to exhibit unrelated items, and to present the House in a form in which it had actually existed historically',[179] notwithstanding the fact that 'much that is now [1989] taken for Inigo Jones's work is in fact no more than fifty years old'.[180]

The first phase of renovation was undertaken in 1984 and involved re-leading the roof, timber treatment and climate control. The second phase, which began in 1987, comprised the partial reinstatement and refurbishment of the seventeenth-century state apartments and the restoration of the brick vaults.[181] The decision was made to present the house as a building of the 1660s, the first date at which the east and west Bridge Rooms existed. The plans by Wren and James provided a firm basis for the re-establishment of the proportions of the two royal bedrooms and adjacent closets. The majority of joinery features surviving or copied by Chettle were from this period and information was available on his removal of the partitions. The choice of date did not gain unanimous approval; Peter Thornton argued for the need to keep one of the bedchambers in a style typical of the 1630s.

For presentational reasons, the reinstatement of the Hall was

125 A reproduction of Inigo Jones's chimneypiece and overmantel in the original first-floor Cabinet Room (room B), based on Jones's drawing (fig. 89).

regarded as one of the most important tasks in the restoration. Initially, it was hoped that the original Gentileschi ceiling could be returned from Marlborough House, the canvases altered once more to fit the ceiling of the Great Hall for which they had been designed, but in view of the expense and difficulty this entailed, other possibilities were explored. The options included the retention of the painting by Louis Cheron (fig. 97); a photograph of the original Gentileschi in sepia or colour; a plain plaster ceiling; a reproduction based on photogrammetric photography, or commissioning a reconstruction by an artist.[182] Cheron's painting, which at the time was thought to be by or after Thornhill, was considered to be the wrong scale and too Baroque in style. By February 1987 it had been removed[183] and a decision made to reproduce the original ceiling by the 'Scanochrome' process, using the new techniques of laser analysis and computer reconstruction of the missing areas (fig. 98). Although the resulting copy is graphically accurate and gives some idea of the scale of Gentileschi's originals, the pictures are without the depth and vitality which is

still apparent, despite all their trials, in the works at Marlborough House.

In an attempt to reinstate the original statuary, plaster casts were commissioned to replace those sold during the Commonwealth sale: five from France (*Diane Chasseresse*, *Boy with Goose*, *Crouching Aphrodite*, *Dancing Satyr* and a *Venus*) and two from Germany (including an *Aphrodite*) arrived in 1990. An interest had been shown by the City of Liverpool Museums in making a large-scale loan of statues, busts and urns formerly at Ince Blundell Hall, which might have resulted in more authentic statuary being placed in the Great Hall, but the proposal does not seem to have been pursued.[184]

Throughout the house, the attempt to return to the mid-seventeenth century was thorough-going: the bedchambers and associated closets were partitioned and a state bed installed; Inigo Jones's chimneypieces were reproduced in modern materials on the basis of his drawings (fig. 125); doors and shutters were renewed; the paintwork was cleaned and restored; silk hangings of authentic pattern were introduced into the rooms; the four windows which had been inserted into the original Bridge Room in the nineteenth century were filled in, leaving the original two (middle) windows; servants' stairs were reinstated and the vaults were restored.[185] In order to reveal the original floor of the basement, about 3¼ feet of waste material was removed, thereby uncovering eighteenth-century drainage channels, and the nineteenth-century cement rendering was stripped to reveal the damaged facing of the naked brickwork.

The intention throughout the 1980s renovation works was to respect and preserve the surviving historic fabric of the Queen's House, not only from the time of Inigo Jones, but also from later alterations and restorations, including Chettle's work of the 1930s. The decision to furnish and present the house as it might have been at the time of the Restoration of Charles II was in view of the existence of the Bridge Rooms, made for logical reasons, but the work inevitably was compromised by the decline in funding for public works in the 1980s and by the need to balance two fundamental requirements. The desire for archaeological accuracy and integrity, which saw the vaulted basement left in a raw brick state, as left incomplete by Jones, sat uneasily with the desire to present a lived-in house, an aim made newly fashionable by the enormous impact of Mark Girouard's *Life in the English Country House*, which pioneered the consideration of historic houses in terms of 'how they operated or what was expected of them when they were first built', rather than merely in terms of architects, craftsmen and owners.[186] The particular problem with this approach at the Queen's House is that it was occupied as an occasional retreat, rather than as a fully lived-in house, for only a very brief period by Henrietta Maria and Charles I, and after the Restoration, the queen dowager stayed for only two months in 1662. So to base re-created furnishings on the inventory of her possessions made in 1669 upon her death in France was to pursue an idea of Stuart decoration and possessions rather than one which was specific to Greenwich.

Although it was inauthentic to attempt to present the Queen's House as a 'lived-in' palace of the early 1660s, some criticism has been unnecessarily extreme. To characterise the result of the restoration as a Disneyland, notwithstanding the reproduction furniture and chimneypieces, is unfair both to Disney and the National Maritime Museum.[187] The work represented an honourable, although misguided, attempt to capture a period of occupation which in truth never existed: the restorers were bent on the pursuit of a chimera. Ten years on from the restoration it is time to look at the presentation of the Queen's House again. The building has been disguised and hidden by half-truths, especially in the supposed use and decoration of rooms. Like Chettle's restoration in the 1930s, the work reflects the climate of the times in which it was carried out more than it does life in the seventeenth-century royal retreat. Throughout an existence of over 350 years, the Queen's House has been used for its intended purpose for only seven, from 1635 until 1642. Even then, what the house represented to architect and patron was fleeting, ephemeral, incomplete, and accessible, physically and conceptually, only to the few. The building performed a unique role for a specific and transitory moment. The glory of the interior of the house cannot be recaptured, neither can the beauty of the garden setting. Although the Queen's House may be acknowledged as one of the first and finest classical buildings in England by one of the greatest of British architects, it was essentially a secret house which to this day remains an enigma.

126   The domes and colonnades of the Queen Mary and King William Buildings, framing the view of the distant Queen's House.

Chapter 4

THE ROYAL HOSPITAL FOR SEAMEN: A BENEVOLENT FOUNDATION

There is nothing which reflects greater honour upon human nature, than those Institutions which owe their rise to motives of Benevolence.

J. Cooke and J. Maule[1]

The building of the Royal Hospital for Seamen at Greenwich, in fulfilment of the wishes of Queen Mary, took place in four principal phases over a period of fifty-five years. The initiative had begun with James II in 1687, when it was reported that the king had given his house at Greenwich 'to be fitted for the service of impotent sea commanders and others', but it was Mary who was to be the prime mover (fig. 127).[2] In 1691 she 'signified her pleasure to the Treasury Lords that the house at Greenwich shall be converted and employed as a hospital for seamen',[3] but it was the severe casualties sustained against the French at the victorious naval engagement at La Hogue in May 1692 which gave a spur to the endeavour. In October that year the Commissioners of the Treasury were advised of 'Their Majesties having granted the "house" at Greenwich to be a hospital for wounded seamen',[4] initially in a temporary arrangement to house the sick and injured.[5] In January 1693 Sir Christopher Wren visited the 'King's House' with a view to converting the John Webb building, left incomplete when the funds and impetus for a new royal palace had dried up in 1672, the year of the architect's death (figs 128 and 129). The King Charles Building had been in use as a gunpowder store and in 1694, following the expression of the queen's pleasure that 'so much ground should be set out at Greenwich adjoining the new unfinished house there as shall be necessary for the convenience of an Hospital to be founded for the relief of seamen',[6] £500 was granted to the Treasurer of the Ordnance 'towards the charge of building a storehouse and removing the gunpowder' (fig. 130).[7] The Hospital petitioned in 1715 and again in 1760 to have it taken away from Greenwich altogether because of the risk to the town and to the security of the Hospital.[8] It was the intention of Queen Mary, as stated in the Royal Warrant of 1694, to grant the land on which to build a hospital

> for the reliefe and support of Seamen serving on board the Shipps or Vessells belonging to the Navy Royall who by reason of Age, Wounds or other disabilities shall be uncapable of further Service at Sea and be unable to maintain themselves. And

> for the sustentation of the Widows and the Maintenance and Education of the Children of Seamen happening to be slain or disabled in such service and also for the further reliefe and Encouragement of Seamen and Improvement of Navigation.[9]

Mary died, 'full of Spotts', in the 'very mortal' smallpox epidemic in December 1694.[10] Her husband, respecting her wishes, then issued the warrant in both their names, backdating it to 25 October, the last quarter-day of the legal year.

Queen Mary had reserved to the Crown 'the ground, 115 feet long, now staked out for a way or passage through the premises to and from the Thames and to and from their Majesties' house called the Queen's House' (fig. 58).[11] This was a recently created vista, since the old palace buildings had obstructed the view from the Queen's House to the river until well after the Restoration.[12]

127 Queen Mary and King William, the founders of the Royal Hospital for Seamen, depicted by Sir James Thornhill in the ceiling of the Painted Hall of the Hospital.

128 The 'King's House', depicted in an 'actual survey' of Greenwich, dated June 1693 (detail of fig. 130) (PRO MR 1/329 (1)).

The view was to be obstructed again by the building works on the Hospital until 1711, when the mason Edward Strong was instructed to clear a way through the works.[13] The queen's intention, according to Nicholas Hawksmoor, was to 'have an Access to that House by water as well as by Land'. The first beneficiary of the reinstated view to the river was the Hospital governor, Sir William Gifford, who during his occupancy of the Queen's House ordered two large oak seats for the terrace in 1712, in order to enjoy it (fig. 115).[14] The retention of the Queen's House and the avenue leading to it was to prove highly inconvenient in design terms, prohibiting the grand central accent which a building on this scale might have been expected to have. Hawksmoor recorded

that 'Queen Anne determined to settle the Park, Queen's House, Mannor and Honour of Greenwich, upon the Hospital; and Prince George purchased the Lease of my Lord Romney [which had been granted in 1697, excluding the new way 'lately set out' on the north side of the Queen's garden], in order to Compleat this Settlement; but something intervened, and the Prince dying, the said Premises remain'd in the Crown'. Despite frequent attempts to re-open this matter, there they remained. It was not until 1730 that the financial burden of maintaining the Queen's House was removed from the Hospital, when the house was granted by George II to Queen Caroline.[15]

The restriction on the design of the Hospital imposed by the Queen's House inspired invention – forced, in response to the constraint, to forgo the obvious, Wren produced a design of genius. The Hospital is bilaterally symmetrical without any hierarchical centrepiece save for the distant Queen's House, which is too small to perform the function. Instead of a towering central dome, there is a quintessentially English compromise between the planned and the accidental, resulting in two domes and a long view in which a degree of formality has been grafted onto a picturesque landscape. While the compromise may be English, the inspiration may well have been Roman: the twin domes recall Carlo Rainaldi's Piazza del Popolo and the colonnades, Gianlorenzo Bernini's Piazza in front of St Peter's (fig. 126).[16] Taking into account the pediments of the King William and Queen Mary courts, there may also be a debt to Palladio's unbuilt design for

129 John Webb's King Charles Building – the 'King's House' – granted in 1692 to be a hospital for wounded seamen.

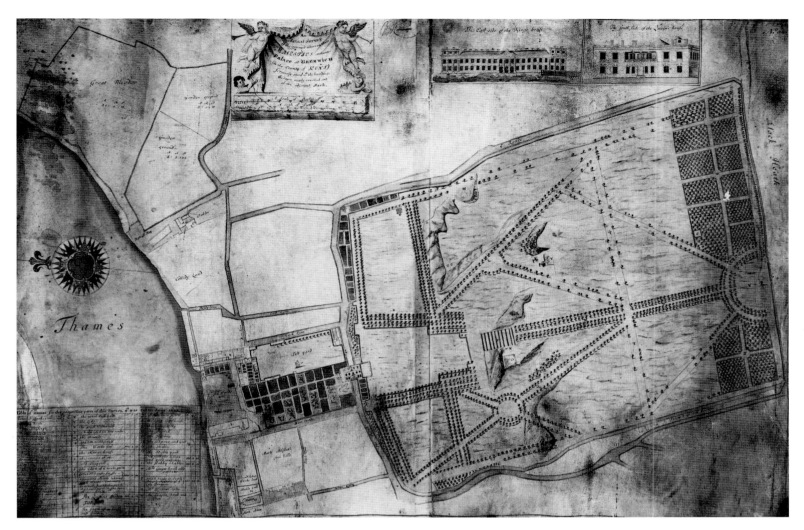

130 'An actual survey of the ground whereon their Majesties ancient Palace at Greenwich formerly stood', dated June 1693. The plan is oriented with north to the left. The avenue between the Queen's House and the river, reserved to the Crown, is not marked on this plan (see fig. 58). The King Charles Building and the Queen's House are shown in elevation at the top of the drawing; the west side of the Queen's House is depicted next to the Queen's Garden. The area next to the river, in front of the King Charles Building, is designated 'The Works' (PRO MR 1/329 (1)).

the Rialto bridge in Venice.[17] It is perhaps ironic that Greenwich Hospital, the most fully achieved Baroque ensemble in England, should have a void at its heart,[18] but it is an irony which Inigo Jones himself might have appreciated. The result is akin to those perspective scenes in the court masques which lead the eye into the empty distance: one merely awaits the arrival of the players.

After Queen Mary's death the impetus was maintained by King William, who issued a further warrant in February 1695, appointing as Commissioners 'George, Prince of Denmark, the Archbishop of Canterbury and 175 others', with the task of considering 'how far the present buildings will be unfit for the Hospital hereby intended to be erected and how far to alter such as shall be thought fit to stand: to prepare plans for the erection of the said intended Hospital for the King's approbation: to prepare a charter of foundation for it and statutes, constitutions, orders and ordinances for its perpetual management, order and good government'.[19] He promised an endowment of £2000 per year which rapidly fell into arrears. Frequent petitions over the years failed to produce results. Others who had promised money also defaulted. The king's payment was four years in arrears by Christmas 1701 and shortly afterwards there was more than £19,000 owing for

the works, with many of the workforce and contractors having to be paid in tallies – promises to pay.[20] The revenue of sixpence per month which was due from deductions from both Royal Navy and merchant seamen's wages was inconsiderable during the War of the Spanish Succession (1702–13). The merchant fleet, hampered by the war, was sailing less, and the men of the Royal Navy were not being paid: 'deductions from her Majesty's seamen cannot be collected till they are paid off'. Queen Anne in 1703 'does not think fit to give the allowance so long as the war lasts'.[21] In 1719 the opinion of the former Attorney-General Sir Edward Northey was that King William's grant was of no validity, 'nor any benefit to be hop'd for from it'.[22] Fortunately, the same year, the 'considerable estate' of Robert Osboldston of Greenwich, which included property valued at £20,000 and his grant of dues of £1400 per year from ships which passed the North and South Foreland lighthouses, was left in part to the Hospital, but the most important asset, ensuring completion of the fabric, came in 1735 with the granting of the rents and profits of the Derwentwater estate, following the execution of Sir James Radcliffe, the eponymous 3rd Earl in 1716 for his part in the Jacobite rising.

The uncertainty of funding and the constant indebtedness of

the works not only resulted in a protracted building campaign, but one which was carried out in a fractured manner in four major phases, in most of which work was going on all over the site; this was not only inconvenient but dangerous for those pensioners who arrived to find themselves living on a building site. Wren, appointed Surveyor in 1696, in charitable spirit 'chearfully engag'd in the Work'[23] free of charge, assisted by Hawksmoor, who became Clerk of Works in 1698, a post he held through various vicissitudes until 1735 (the year before he died) and by John James, assistant Clerk of Works from 1705 and joint Clerk of Works from 1718 at first with Hawksmoor, continuing until his own death in 1746. Sir John Vanbrugh was a member of the Board of Directors of the Hospital from 1703 and became Surveyor in succession to Wren in 1716. He was followed first by Colen Campbell in 1726, then by Thomas Ripley in 1729. It is ironic that the weakest designer among these architects should have presided over the building of the Hospital at precisely the time when funding became more assured. But Ripley, thanks in part to Vanbrugh's scorn, expressed in a letter in 1721 – 'When I met with his Name, (and Esquire to it) in the News paper; such a Laugh came upon me, I had like to have Beshit my Self. Poor Hawksmoor, What a Barbarous Age, have his fine, ingenious Parts fallen into',[24] – and to historians' justifiable feelings of outrage on behalf of the passed-over Hawksmoor, has had an unduly bad press. Certainly, Hawksmoor himself was less than content, mourning 'the decay of a great vision'. As he wrote in 1734: 'There is imperiall Mischief . . . don to Greenwich Hospitall since Sr John dy'd; and I need not say by who. . . . I once thought it wou'd have been a public Building but it will sink into a deformed Barrac'.[25] Ripley was not an inspired designer – so much is obvious from the Queen Mary Building and from his earlier, ill-proportioned Admiralty on Whitehall – but he was competent and he would gain credit nowadays for being a good manager. He appears to have been supportive of Hawksmoor and James, paying them at some stages out of his own pocket and acting as a buffer between Hawksmoor and a sometimes vindictive and ungracious Board to which he was not always as biddable as might have been expected. It did not fall to Ripley to be creative. Rather, it was his job to complete the Hospital in accordance with Wren's overall plan.

The Evolution of the Plan

Edward Hatton in *A New View of London*, published in 1708, had recourse to a familiar trope when describing the royal hospitals at Chelsea and Greenwich. At Chelsea he found 'a Situation and Building that would be taken by Strangers rather for the Palace of a Prince than a Habitation for Pensioners',[26] and at Greenwich 'there is now building one of the most sumptuous Hospitals in the World, much liker the Palace of a Prince than a Harbour for the Indigent'.[27] It was with these two buildings and with Bethlem Hospital that England began to rival the provision of charitable institutions already established in Italy and France, and nearer home, the contemporary foundation of the Royal Hospital, Kilmainham, Dublin, begun in 1680. In Paris in 1644 John Evelyn found the Hôtel-Dieu built to a 'Princly, pious and prodigious expense' and at the Hôpital de la Charité, 'I have taken great satisfaction to see how decently and Christianly the sick People are tended, yea even to delicacy'.[28] An earlier visitor to the Hôtel-

131 A contemporary engraving of Bethlem Hospital, Moorfields, London, built in 1674–6 'for the releife and cure of persons distracted' (see also fig. 29).

Dieu had described in 1626 a long gallery of four ranks of beds in which 'it is sweeter walking . . . than in the best streets of Paris'.[29] Visiting the Ospedale di San Spirito in Rome in 1645, Evelyn found 'one of the most pious and worthy Foundations that ever I saw', not only for its ample provision of well-planned and ventilated spaces, but also for the opportunity which it afforded for 'divers Young Physitians & Chirurgions, [to] reape by the experience they learne here amongst the sick, to whom those students have universal accesse'.[30] The admiration of English visitors for continental hospitals continued well into the eighteenth century, when the products of a golden age of hospital foundation in London prompted a change in direction; Dr Jacques Tenon visited England on a fact-finding mission in 1787 in the course of drawing up proposals for improving the hospitals of Paris.

Bethlem, Chelsea and Greenwich were not primarily institutions designed for the care of the physically sick. Bethlem (1674–6) was 'a palace for pauper lunatics' (fig. 131),[31] while Chelsea and Greenwich, as royal foundations for military personnel, were almshouses, primarily for the long-term care of those who had survived the rigours of active service. However they were recognisably within a tradition of hospital planning and in their turn influenced future developments. The arrangement of long galleries at Bethlem, with cells to one side, was doubled at Chelsea in 1682 to provide galleries and cabins to either side of a spine wall (figs 132 and 133). This provision of privacy was in the line of development from English monastic infirmaries in which first partitions and then cubicles were installed,[32] and such continental hospitals as the Hôtel-Dieu in Paris and the Ospedale Maggiore in Milan in which the beds were curtained, or, in the case of the Annunziata in Naples, set into alcoves. As Gilbert Burnet, later Bishop of Salisbury, noted on his visit in 1685–6: 'The riches of the Annunciata are prodigious: it is the greatest Hospital in the World. . . . one convenience for their sick I observed in their Galleries, which was considerable, that every Bed stood as in an Alcove, and had a Wall on both sides separating it from the Beds on both hands, and as much void space of both sides of the Bed that the Bed it self

132   Chelsea Pensioners photographed outside their cabins in 1922. The plan of the wings allowed for heated, well-lit galleries to either side of a spine wall.

took up but half the Room'.[33] Burnet also visited the Lazaretto in Milan, described earlier in the century by Fynes Moryson: 'a Gallery runs all along before the Chambers, so that as the service is convenient, the sick have a covered walk before their Doors'.[34]

Greenwich, as an almshouse rather than a medical treatment centre, did not get its own dedicated infirmary until the mid-eighteenth century. Disease took a far higher toll of seamen than did enemy action, and the Navy was pioneering in the use of hospital ships from the Protectorate onwards, but there were no permanent naval hospitals on shore. The Admiralty, in the Tudor and Stuart periods, hired temporary sick quarters in taverns and private houses and requisitioned beds in such hospitals as St Bartholomew's. John Evelyn, as a member of the Sick and Hurt Board, during the reign of Charles II, pressed for permanent accommodation, proposing a hospital at Chatham, but although having an important part to play in the establishment of

133   Chelsea Hospital for Soldiers, begun in 1682 to the design of Christopher Wren, viewed from the south-east.

134 Plan and elevations of the north and west wings of St Bartholomew's Hospital, London, published in John Stow's *Survey of the Cities of London and Westminster*, 1754 (St Bartholomew's Hospital Archives and Museum).

envisaging a comparable institution in London and struck by the accounts of the building he had received from 'Seigneurs Anglois' returning from France, requested details.[36] Drawings arrived in 1678.[37] L'Abbé Perau's large folio volume on Les Invalides, published in 1756, followed three previous accounts, the first of which, published in 1683, a *Description générale*, by Le Jeune de Boulencourt, inspired an anonymous English translation in 1695: *A Pattern of a Well-Constituted and Well-Governed Hospital: or, a Brief Description of the Building, and Full Relation of the Establishment, Constitution, Discipline, Oeconomy and Administration of the Government of the Royal Hospital of the Invalids.* This volume was dedicated to William III, the stated intention of the author being to encourage and support the King's 'Noble Resolution . . . of providing an Habitation and Relief for Your Disabled and Distressed Seamen'. Although, as might be expected, Les Invalides is described as 'not much inferior to the Louvre itself',[38] it is not the architecture which has inspired the author, but the 'admirable Order, Discipline, and good Oeconomy that is established and practised there'.[39] He hoped to see at Greenwich that same 'good Order and Discipline, those methods of Oeconomy and Police established and faithfully observed, that we have been admiring and commending in our Neighbour Nation'.[40]

The rules for behaviour at Greenwich and Les Invalides were very similar, although Greenwich did not acknowledge any indebtedness for either the conduct of the institution or for the architecture. Drawing on the example of Chelsea, in order to emulate or to surpass, was to be encouraged, but openly to look across the English Channel for inspiration from a country with which relations were often tempestuous was perhaps inadvisable. Nevertheless, it is very likely that Wren did draw lessons from the architecture of Les Invalides in developing his plans and in emulating its dome. A clear reference was made during the building of the King William block to adding 'necessary places (as it is at the Invalides at Paris) on each floor at the west end of the south dormitory'.[41] Wren had visited France in 1665–6, intending to return with 'almost all France in Paper, which I found by some or others ready design'd to my Hand'.[42] French inspiration would not have been new in his architecture. Furthermore, when Les Invalides was threatened with closure in 1791, by a proposal for its replacement with a number of separate hospitals, its significance as an example for neighbouring nations was recalled: 'several neighbouring peoples, struck by such a great example, were eager to follow it. The English built the Hospital at Greenwich, which yields nothing in magnificence to the Hôtel, and that at Chelsea intended for the pensioners of the army'. The author, 'M.L.T.', stressed the importance of such buildings in national life, a point he felt was understood in England where on the terrace at Greenwich the sailor towards the end of his life could contemplate the element which brought him glory.[43] Seats were provided on the river front of the Hospital in 1794 with such contemplation in mind.[44]

The principal ranges of Les Invalides are disposed to either side of a grand central court, to the north of the central church and Jules Hardouin Mansart's commanding dome, which was completed in 1690.[45] The two long north–south wings to each side of the central court are each linked in the centre by an east–west wing, which creates subsidiary courtyards (fig. 136). In the four two-storey-high refectories, which frame the central court, paintings of successful campaigns and conquests enabled the soldiers to recall their moments in the pursuit of national glory. Beneath the

Greenwich, he failed to convince the Admiralty of the desirability of investing in a modern naval medical hospital. The Commission for Sick, Wounded and Prisoners, appointed in 1702, recommended building hospitals for the exclusive use of the Navy, but although permanent hospitals were established overseas in the early eighteenth century in Jamaica, Lisbon and Minorca for the sick and wounded of the armed forces, it was not until the building of Haslar at Portsmouth (1746–61) and Stonehouse, near Plymouth (1758–62), that this long-standing need was met at home.[35] Both of these, in their internal planning, together with James Gibbs's rebuilding of St Bartholomew's, begun in 1730, are indebted to the example of Greenwich (fig. 134).

The direct inspirations for Wren's Greenwich design were his own Chelsea Hospital for Soldiers, founded by Charles II in 1682 and completed four years before work had begun at Greenwich, and the Hôtel des Invalides in Paris, founded by Louis XIV in 1670 for the accommodation of disabled veterans, a function it continues to fulfil (fig. 135). According to l'Abbé Perau, Charles II,

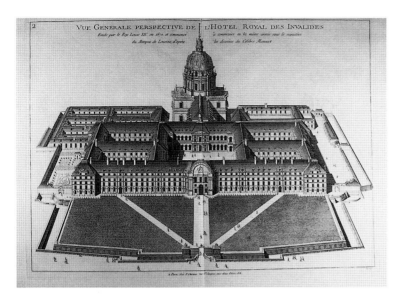

135 Perspective view of the Hôtel des Invalides, Paris, from the north, published in L'Abbé Perau's *Déscription historique de l'Hôtel Royal des Invalides*, 1756.

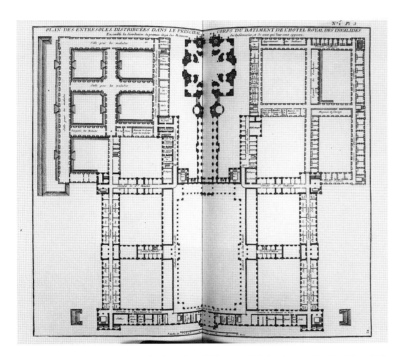

136 Plan of the Hôtel des Invalides, published in J. F. Blondel's *L'architecture françoise*, 1752–3.

refectories were wine cellars, and above, one floor of rooms for soldiers, a floor for the manufacturing by pensioners of clothing for the army (to encourage the industrious and enable them to earn money) and, in the roof, granaries and rooms for drying linen (which at Greenwich was dried outside, in courts to both the east and west). The outer wings had rooms for soldiers on all four floors, arranged to either side of central corridors. Officers, two per room, had curtained beds and a fireplace. Ordinary soldiers inevitably were granted less privacy and comfort. Although they had their own beds, which was an improvement on the bed-sharing arrangements which pertained in such French hospitals as the Hôtel-Dieu,[46] these were uncurtained, in unheated rooms

which accommodated either four or six men. For warmth, the men had access to eight heated halls, two of which were designated for smokers.[47]

Chelsea Hospital was not only influential in the evolution of Wren's ideas in planning Greenwich, it was to be a precedent and comparator for the governors of the Naval Hospital throughout the eighteenth century: comparison of constitution; the nature of diet and clothing; the raising of money (the institutions combined forces in 1708 to raise money through the coal tax); the salaries of staff; whether the nurses were entitled to feather beds; whether there was an exemption from paying duty on beer; whether precautionary measures were being taken against the plague. While both had an almshouse function, the overall massing and the internal layout differed. At Chelsea, Wren was able to provide a modest equivalent of the commanding central dome of Les Invalides. Positioned above the entrance vestibule, between the great hall and the chapel, it provided the central focus which Greenwich always lacked, although Wren and later Hawksmoor, in several speculative proposals,[48] tried to remedy the defect by proposing a 'great Church' on the central axis.[49]

In his *Remarks on the Founding and Carrying on the Buildings of the Royal Hospital at Greenwich*,[50] published in 1728, Hawksmoor recorded the view of 'sundry Workmen' that Webb's King Charles Building of the 1660s could be demolished:

They, as it is indifferent to all Workmen whether they get Money by destroying or erecting Fabricks. gave their Opinion that it was nothing but a Heap of Stones, and that it might

137 Wren's proposal of *c.*1695 for a hospital to the east of the avenue from the Queen's House to the river (All Souls College, Oxford, IV, 19).

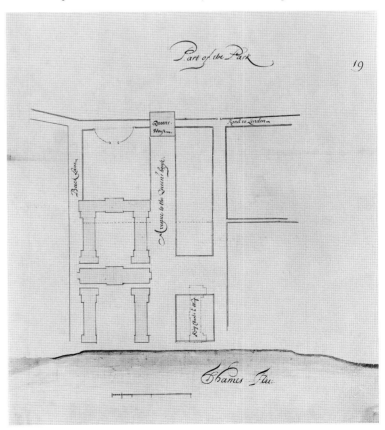

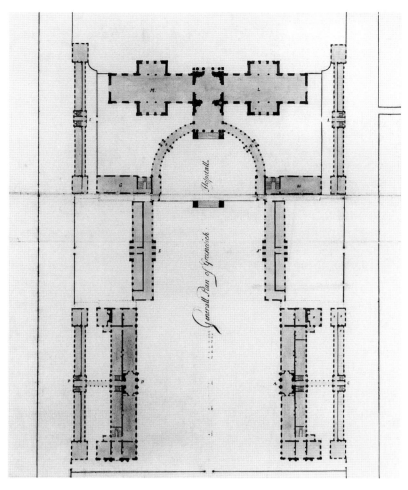

138 Plan of Wren's proposal for a hospital with a central domed cross-wing (Sir John Soane's Museum, II/6).

139 Perspective of Wren's proposal for a hospital with a central dome (Sir John Soane's Museum, II/5).

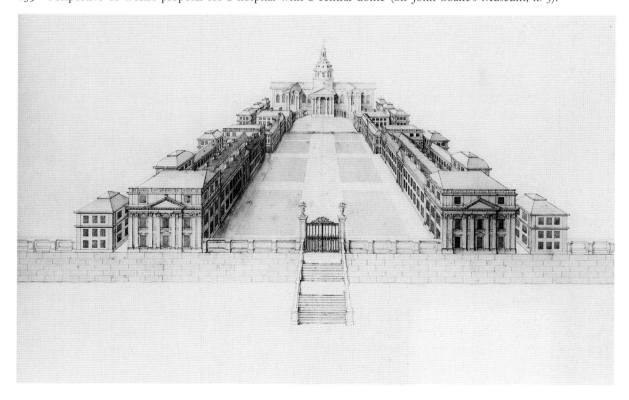

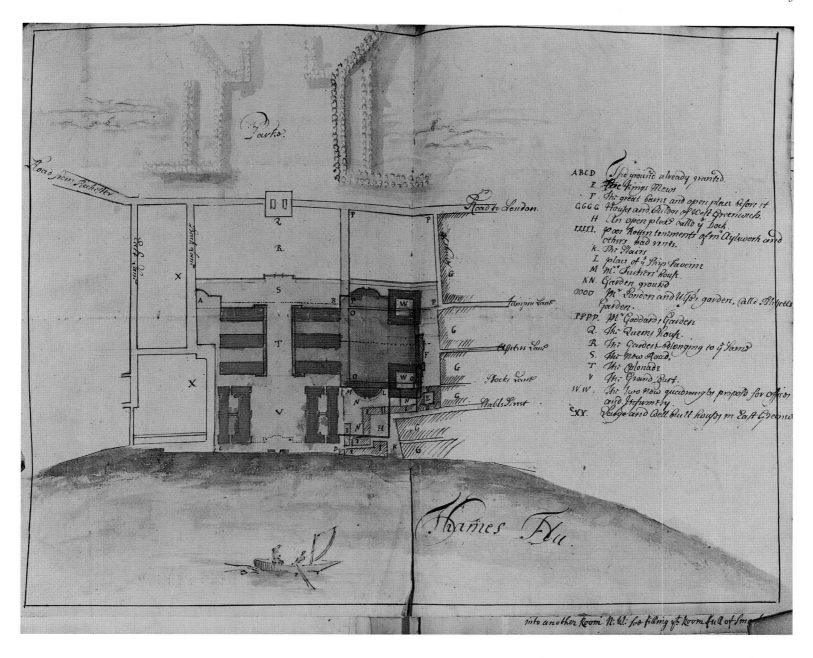

140 Plan of Wren's proposal for a hospital with ranges of lateral blocks to the south, drawn by Hawksmoor (Lambeth Palace Library, MS 933/99).

141 An unofficial engraving of the proposal for Greenwich Hospital, based on the plan with lateral blocks to the south.

lawfully and reasonably be destroyed. . . . But her Majesty received the Proposal of pulling down that Wing, with as much Indignation as her excellent good Temper would suffer her, order'd it should remain, and the other Side of the Royal Court made answerable to it, in a proper Time.[51]

Notwithstanding the queen's wishes, Wren's first thought appears to have been to attempt to avoid altogether the problem posed by the existence of the King Charles Building and the Queen's House in a design for a building with four north–south ranges, linked by two east–west cross-wings, sited immediately to the east of the avenue from the Queen's House to the River Thames (fig. 137).[52] Since it had always been the intention of the founders to include the King Charles Building, he next proposed a scheme in which a wing would be built opposite it, with further wings to the south,

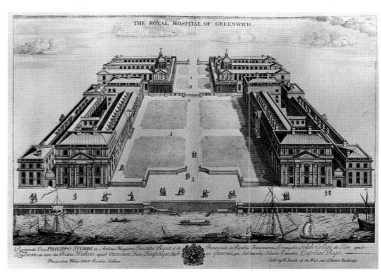

flanking a narrower court, ending in quadrant colonnades and a domed cross-wing (figs 138 and 139).[53] This, like Webb's designs for a palace (1660s),[54] would have cut across the axis from the Queen's House to the river, so further schemes, introducing the idea of two domes, were considered. These included a proposal for the Charles Building and a pendant range opposite, both with narrower outer, base blocks, and two ranges of three blocks, each arranged laterally to the south, in a layout recalling Les Invalides, the first of each of these accommodating the hall and chapel (figs 140 and 141).[55] A further scheme, repeating the twin domes over a hall and chapel, but with seven lateral blocks, entirely disregarded the area of land granted for the Hospital by crossing the Romney Road and going right up to the Queen's House, with a central avenue framed by colonnades in echelon. This plan has been recognised as remarkably predictive of the later colonnaded, pavilion plan of the Royal Naval Hospital, Stonehouse, of 1765.[56] Although the plan with three lateral blocks had a popular currency which survived long enough for it to be engraved in about 1707,[57] the wooden model of around 1699, now in the National Maritime Museum,[58] shows that by this time the plan had assumed its current form, with the King Charles Building and a pendant range, both with base blocks; a hall and chapel, each with domes; and, instead of the central lateral blocks to the south, two north-south ranges facing the colonnades across open courts (fig. 142).

142   Wooden model of Greenwich Hospital, c.1699 (NMM).

Thus did Wren develop the architecture of Greenwich towards ever greater articulation and magnificence, producing a far grander performance than he had essayed at Chelsea, forced by the circumstances of the site and the existing buildings to find an alternative to the obvious Baroque solution of the central commanding dome. The greater grandeur of Greenwich was entirely appropriate in view of the pre-eminence of the Navy within the armed forces and given that it was in the eighteenth century the largest and most complex of all government services. Wren's open-centre plan, with Charles facing Anne to the north, William facing Mary to the south, and the domes and colonnades leading the eye to the Queen's House and the park, presents a vista of grandeur unparalleled in English architecture, a view immortalised by Canaletto in about 1752–3 (fig. 4).[59] The terrace and river wall

next to the Thames, which serve as a visual plinth for the whole composition, were Wren's invention, although not completed until the Surveyorship of Ripley in the 1730s and further extended in 1777, with the embankment enlarged in 1781, a regularisation of the river frontage between Crane's Stairs to the east and the old palace landing stage to the west, the remains of which were identified in the inter-tidal zone in 1996.[60] The King Charles Building had been constructed at the water's edge and the north pavilions of Queen Anne built on land reclaimed from the river.[61]

The *Penny Magazine*, on 9 June 1832, in its item 'Holiday Walks', recognised the grandeur of the view, recommending arrival by water: 'the domes and colonnades . . . will rise from the shore, and impress your mind with a magnificence of which the architecture of England presents few examples'. It was this magnificence in what he perceived merely as a charitable institution, which Samuel Johnson was famously to condemn when he visited in 1763, disregarding the deeper impulses which lay behind the form and appearance of the building: the desire to demonstrate in a very public manner, on the main route into London from continental Europe, the political and naval power of the state, and the duty felt by the monarch to shelter those who had spent their lives in its service. Wren himself was aware of architecture's wider significance: 'Architecture has its political Use; publick Buildings being the Ornament of a Country; it establishes a Nation, draws People and Commerce, makes the People love their native Country, which Passion is the Original of all great Actions in a Commonwealth'.[62] But as James Boswell recorded, Johnson took a narrower view:

> I was much pleased to find myself with Johnson at Greenwich, which he celebrates in his 'London' as a favourite scene. I had the poem in my pocket, and read the lines aloud with enthusiasm:
>
> > On Thames's banks in silent thought we stood,
> > Where Greenwich smiles upon the silver flood:
> > Pleas'd with the seat which gave ELIZA birth,
> > We kneel, and kiss the consecrated earth.
>
> He remarked that the structure of Greenwich hospital was too magnificent for a place of charity, and that its parts were too much detached to make one great whole.[63]

Elsewhere in *The Life*, Boswell records Johnson's more qualified, later view that charity 'is not definable by limits. It is a duty to give to the poor, but no man can say how much another should give to the poor'.[64]

Johnson may not have been alone in censuring the magnificent, which he defined in his *Dictionary* as 'grand in appearance; splendid; pompous':[65] this was not Renaissance Paris or Baroque Rome. But his was perhaps the first century in which censure might be expected – against which defences had to be erected. In his *Remarks* on Greenwich Hospital, Hawksmoor twice made the point that magnificence was part of the architect's brief, as if he were defending a position, noting Queen Mary's desire to have Greenwich built 'with great Magnificence and Order' and later, after an historical account, 'We mention this to shew her Majesty's fixt Intention for Magnificence'.[66]

Two years after the publication of Hawksmoor's *Remarks*, William Mildmay of Essex visited Les Invalides in the course of his Grand Tour. He found it 'large, regular and noble', with 'the

Air of a Palace', and he reflected on attitudes to charitable institutions which were current in England:

> I have often heard it observed that in acts of Charity of this publick nature for the encouragement of souldiers or sea men, the money which is thus thrown away as it were on building and outward ornament had better have been spared towards makeing a more ample supply of Provisions and necessaries, and that more beef and worse beds would give greater contentment to these wretches[.] however true this may be as to the English, tis not wholly so as to the french, who are generally more taken with outside show and appearance; and I believe tis with chearfulness these men abate a pound of meat in a week, for the sake of being so magnificently lodged.[67]

But magnificent lodgings and the idea of charity might not always be at odds. A further definition of 'magnificent', not offered by Johnson, is provided by the *Oxford English Dictionary*: 'characterised by expenditure or munificence [i.e. 'splendid liberality in giving'] on a great scale'. With this definition, we might infer that it was charitable to be magnificent in circumstances in which magnificence was an indicator of a noble liberality. In a brilliant essay on 'Robert Hooke's Bethlem', Christine Stevenson has pointed out that 'Architectural writers since Alberti had been concerned to draw the distinction between luxury and magnificence. . . . Generally speaking, luxury was self-regarding ostentation; magnificence the reverse, a noble liberality that scorned to calculate personal return'. In this persuasive reading, Bethlem 'was meant to evoke different but simultaneous appreciations in the way in which great houses could: magnificent beauty, charitable hospitality, good and healthful order'. The designs of both Chelsea and Greenwich, Hatton's 'Palaces of Princes', arguably were informed by that same impulse: it was charitable to be magnificent, 'as long as this magnificence could be seen to be God's, operating through the knowing governors . . . each and every one [of whom] will find his reward in Heaven'.[68] This appears to have been understood by John Gwynn. Like Johnson he criticised the composition of the Hospital, which 'wants a proper center', but he was able to acknowledge magnificence while condemning the absurdity of bestowing 'such extraordinary expences on a building designed for charitable purposes'. He advocated the creation of a *cordon sanitaire* around this, 'the grandest building in England', which was 'encumbered with brick walls and a great number of miserable houses, all of which should be immediately destroyed and not be permitted to deform and disgrace a work so truly magnificent' (fig. 143).[69]

Notwithstanding the later changes to the buildings, the original layout of the Hospital established by Wren is readily recoverable. The plan of the King Charles Building which was agreed in 1696 originally provided for the accommodation of up to 350 seamen in large wards. In the main block, the east side of the ground floor of Webb's range was opened out to form two large dining rooms between the entrance vestibule and the pavilions, with tables to each side of a central aisle.[70] This space would later be converted into accommodation when the dining areas beneath the Chapel and Painted Hall were completed. Above, Webb's long gallery was retained, although reduced in height, and the partitions in his state suite to the south were removed. The spaces have subsequently been re-partitioned but the Cormorant Hall, a lecture theatre, occupies approximately half the length of

143 The town, pressing against the walls of Greenwich Hospital, shown in a watercolour of 1848 by Clarkson Stanfield. This is a nostalgic representation since Fisher's Alley, here depicted, was demolished during the programme of improvements to the environs of the Hospital during the 1840s (NMM).

the original gallery and retains a bolection moulded chimney-piece of the 1690s. A new floor was inserted above, ceilings removed and subdivisions inserted, to provide a single, long, heated ward with cabins placed to each side. In the base wing, the cabins were arranged in the manner of Chelsea, to either side of the spine wall, giving onto heated, well-lit open galleries.[71] The system of wards and cabins, with each cabin containing a bed and a chest for possessions, was adopted from the start.[72]

Since the King Charles was for many years the only building which was completed, it fell short of its proposed capacity, since it had to accommodate a council chamber, a kitchen, scullery and barber's shop as well as rooms for officers, nurses and cooks. Records for the numbers of pensioners accommodated at any one time tend to be conflicting, poised between hope and expectation. A document in the Greenwich Hospital Album (in Sir John Soane's Museum, London), which might have been drawn up by John James, details the officers and numbers of men in the Royal Hospital and what it will contain when finished, 'according to the present plan', dated November 1728. This offers what seems to be a reliable guide, although the figures differ from those given on Hawksmoor's plan of the same year (fig. 144).[73] The Album states

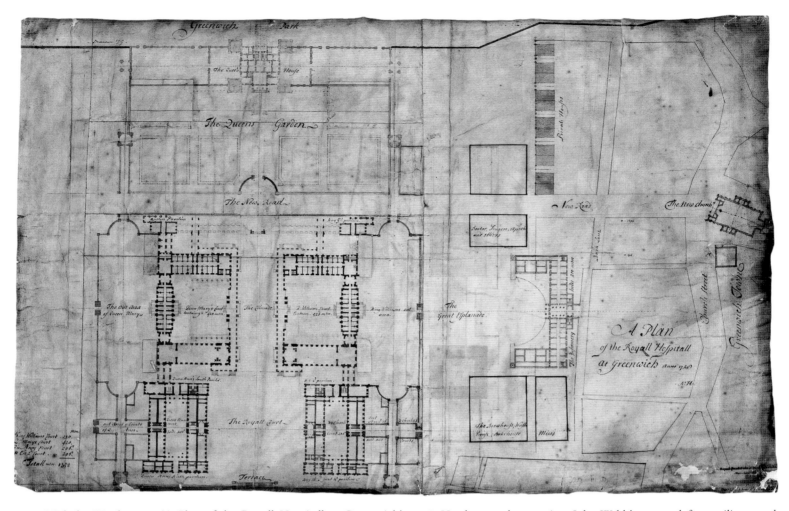

144   Nicholas Hawksmoor, 'A Plan of the Royall Hospitall at Greenwich', 1728. Hawksmoor here revives John Webb's proposal for pavilions at the corners of the Queen's House and includes, on the west side of the Hospital, his design for the Infirmary (BAL E5/11).

that the King Charles Building will accommodate 192 men, the administrative naval officers (Lieutenant-Governor, Captain, three Lieutenants and chaplains), the civilian staff (steward, cooks, scullery man and mates, porter and barber) and thirty nurses. Hawksmoor's plan provides for 206 men.

The pendant range to King Charles, Queen Anne, initially known as the Princess Anne Building, was planned with four large open wards to each floor of its main and base ranges, giving a total for the two blocks of eight wards per floor: twenty-four in all. Later subdivisions of all but the heavily restored Collingwood Room, the former ground-floor south-west ward, have not obscured this basic arrangement of large wards to either side of a spine wall (fig. 145). According to the Album, 300 men were to be accommodated (206 according to Hawksmoor), with lodgings in the pavilions for the secretary, treasurer and four other officers next to the river, with a kitchen and lodgings for three officers,

145   The Collingwood Room, the ground-floor south-west room of the Queen Anne Building, seen from the south. This undivided space was one of the very few rooms before the restoration of the building in 1999 to give an indication of the size of the original wards. The arched opening is an insertion made after the removal of the Naval Museum to the new National Maritime Museum in 1936–7.

cooks, scullery men and their mates in the south pavilions. The architecture of the north pavilions reflects this usage with higher status fittings – vaulted upper rooms and handsome stone doorcases.

The open wards of the Queen Anne Building may be proposed as a precedent for James Gibbs's rebuilding of St Bartholomew's, which had precisely the same arrangement of four large wards to each floor (fig. 134)[74] and for the early designs of back-to-back wards for the naval hospital at Haslar, subsequently abandoned in favour of paired single-pile ranges with central open areas in between.[75]

In a plan of about 1701, made when the 'sustentation of the widows . . . and education of the children of seamen' was beginning to be explored, Hawksmoor proposed to have navigation and writing schools in the Princess Anne Building (fig. 146). The 'sustentation' was never achieved but the educational role was later developed. The Anne and Charles Buildings at this early stage were to have narrow base blocks, with small pavilions, and the William and Mary Buildings were to have circular vestibules framing the centres of their west and east ranges and forming links to the north and south wings. The plan is of more than usual interest in representing a detailed scheme with a list of proposed names of wards and numbers of occupants: up to seventy-two men in each ward of William and Mary, and up to twenty-five in each of Charles and Anne, with extra accommodation for women and children – an overall complement of 2044.[76] Some of these original ward names remained constant throughout the Hospital's history, honouring ships and admirals; others changed according to the desire to commemorate significant persons or events or, in the case of Ormonde (later Orford) Ward to remove the name of one who had fallen from grace (see Appendix 1).

For the planning of the King William and Queen Mary ranges, Wren stayed with his original proposal of rooms disposed to either side of vaulted corridors which barrel dramatically through the centre of the blocks in the manner of Les Invalides. In the Greenwich Hospital Album it was proposed that 544 men would be accommodated in each of the buildings; Hawksmoor's drawing of 1728 noted that there would be 520 in William and 420 in Mary, with no explanation for the difference. The accommodation in William was to include lodgings for the matron and butler, rooms for the physicians and dispenser, and a beer cellar. In both William and Mary, between four and six pensioners were anticipated in each of the predominantly unheated rooms. A further 200 men would be capable of being accommodated in an infirmary, giving an overall total complement of 1780 pensioners.[77] According to Hawksmoor's plan of 1728, there would be 1352 men (excluding those who might be in an infirmary which would bring the total to 1552), considerably less than his earlier estimated complement of 2044 persons, excluding officers and staff. In the earlier drawing of about 1701, he proposed pavilions for officers at the centre of the east and west colonnades.[78] Later, in 1728, these pavilions have been moved south to the Romney Road and designated King's and Queen's Pavilions. They were never built. A variation of up to 25 per cent in the estimated number of men who could be accommodated may be considered a very significant indicator of evolving positions and divergences in viewpoint of the officers involved in the building of the Hospital. Such a variation must have made difficult the overall planning and the computation of income and expenditure. The figures changed again during the surveyorship of Thomas Ripley, who by increasing the number of rooms in the east range of Queen Mary and by narrowing the central corridor on each floor of the south range, thus

146   Nicholas Hawksmoor, plan of the Hospital, c.1701 (BAL E5/2).

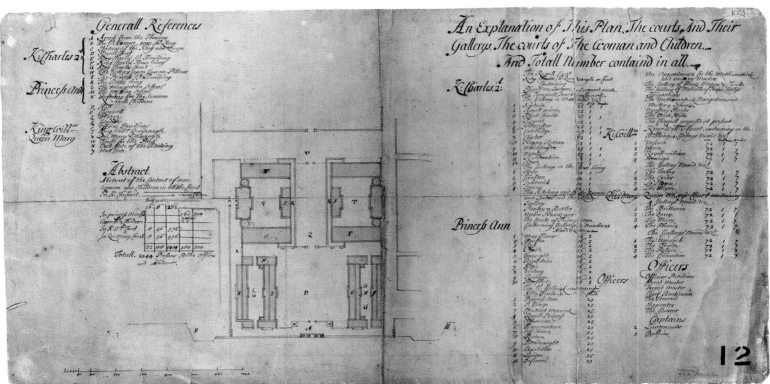

increasing the size of the rooms, was able to accommodate a total of 905 within the building, with room for 200 boys in the garrets.[79]

After Ripley's increases in accommodation and the building of the Infirmary, the total complement of the Hospital by the 1760s was in the region of 2000, five times the capacity of Chelsea. Before his surveyorship, growth had been slow, the capacity not reaching 1000 until 1738. Thereafter, it speeded up, reaching 2381 by 1793 (see Appendix 5), 2447 by 1803; at the peak of occupation in 1814 it approached the 3000 complement of Les Invalides (which was far larger), accommodating 2710, of whom 290 were in the Infirmary. Even with the lower numbers envisaged by Ripley, the pressure to squeeze the men into more confined spaces led to such strategies as reducing the width of dining tables (with the exception of those used by officers) in order to accommodate an extra row, and substituting curtains for wainscot around beds in order to increase the capacity of the wards. Such reductions must have reminded the men of the social and physical pressures of the intensely communal life which they had experienced on board ship.

Before the building of the Infirmary by Ripley's successor, James Stuart, the infirmary wards were placed in William, although this was a compromise born of necessity. There was insufficient funding to embark on a separate infirmary building for which first Hawksmoor and then Ripley provided designs. The infirmary wards in William followed Hawksmoor's proposals for the planning of a dedicated infirmary in having a small number of beds in each room, perhaps in order to achieve a separation of cases; this would not have been possible in the large wards which had become a feature of the English general hospitals of the time. Nevertheless, the inadequacy of the accommodation was such as to make difficult the containment of contagious disease.

Progress of the Works

PHASE 1: 1696–1710

Site laid out; foundations dug.

King Charles Building remodelled; narrower base wing and pavilions built; linking gallery erected between the two blocks.

Queen Anne Building and base block built, without pavilions; the main building brick-fronted; temporary chapel erected between the two blocks.

King William Building: all ranges erected; colonnade begun but not roofed.

Queen Mary Building: foundations only.

A report on the land granted by King William in October 1694 for 'erecting and establishing a hospital at Greenwich for disabled seamen' was made after a site visit the following May by a group which included Wren. They agreed that 'the said unfinished house, called the Kings house (part whereof is still made use of by the officers of the ordnance for keeping powder), may be fitted up and made capable of receiving conveniently between three and four hundred seamen, provided there be an additional building erected to form a base court on the west side therof'. Referring to a plan produced by Wren, the report noted the difficulty caused by the 'avenue or visto from the Queen's house' which separated the King's house from the other part of the land 'whereon any

additionall building must be erected to render it uniform with the present'. A request was made that the king might reconsider the exception to the grant of land, and that the Lords Commissioners of the Treasury might enquire into the restitution of the water springs and conduits belonging to the former Greenwich Palace and now needed for the Hospital, 'which of late have been very much diverted or obstructed by private persons, on various pretences'. Following a further site visit, it was noted that the ground granted 'will be very scanty and narrow for a design so generall as the entertainment of aged and disabled seamen their widows and children', so a request was made to the Hospital Commissioners not only to ask for the avenue for the Hospital's use but also the Queen's House, the former tilt yard, covering 2 acres to the south of the Hospital site, and the park of 206 acres, 'for this good and publick use'.[80] Such requests were made in vain. Following the appointment of a committee of sixty in December 1695, charged to form out of their number three standing sub-committees of twenty each for the fabric, revenue and constitution of the Hospital, work began in earnest in the following month with the approval of Wren's design and the recommendation that it should be put before the king for his agreement. Craftsmen were then appointed following invitations to tender (Master Bricklayer Richard Stacey's comment is representative: 'I am able to performe the said Work as well and as Cheap as any other person whatsoever');[81] workmen were hired and a Clerk of Works, the short-lived John Scarborough, who was succeeded in November 1696 by Henry Symmonds (who had spent ten years as Clerk of Works at Hampton Court), appointed at the rate of 5 s per day. On 30 June 1696 the foundations were begun and a cornerstone laid; a gratuity was given to the workmen by each person present.[82]

The responsibility of the Fabric Committee was to oversee and direct the design (fig. 147), to prepare estimates, to issue contracts and to make recommendations to the Grand Committee, quorate if a mere seven attended, which in turn put them forward for approval at the general meeting of Commissioners. Initially, five members of the Fabric Committee constituted a quorum but this was soon reduced to three, meeting monthly, usually at Scotland Yard. Members did not stint themselves – four ribs of beef, a leg of mutton, six chickens, two loaves of bread and ten half-flasks of wine were required to aid deliberations at a meeting in August 1697.[83] Rooms had been fitted up in the north pavilion of Charles in 1696, furnished with two tables and twenty-four Russian leather chairs, for the holding of Commissioners' meetings.[84] In the first months of building work, effective bureaucratic procedures were established and such loyal and long-serving men as Edward Strong the mason (later partnered on the site by his son, Edward the younger), Richard Billinghurst the bricklayer and Robert Jones the carver were appointed; the project was thus put onto a sound footing, almost immediately undermined, however, by financial concerns. John Evelyn (fig. 148), as treasurer from 1696 until 1703, was with Christopher Wren (fig. 149) one of the heroes of the building of the Hospital. He was straightaway faced with the problem of extracting the king's promised £2000 from the Treasury and found that notwithstanding the beginning of work on the foundations in June, by the end of July the project was already at risk. A warrant for the money was issued in October, but only part payment – £800 – had been received by November, to set against expenses which had already reached £5000: a pattern was

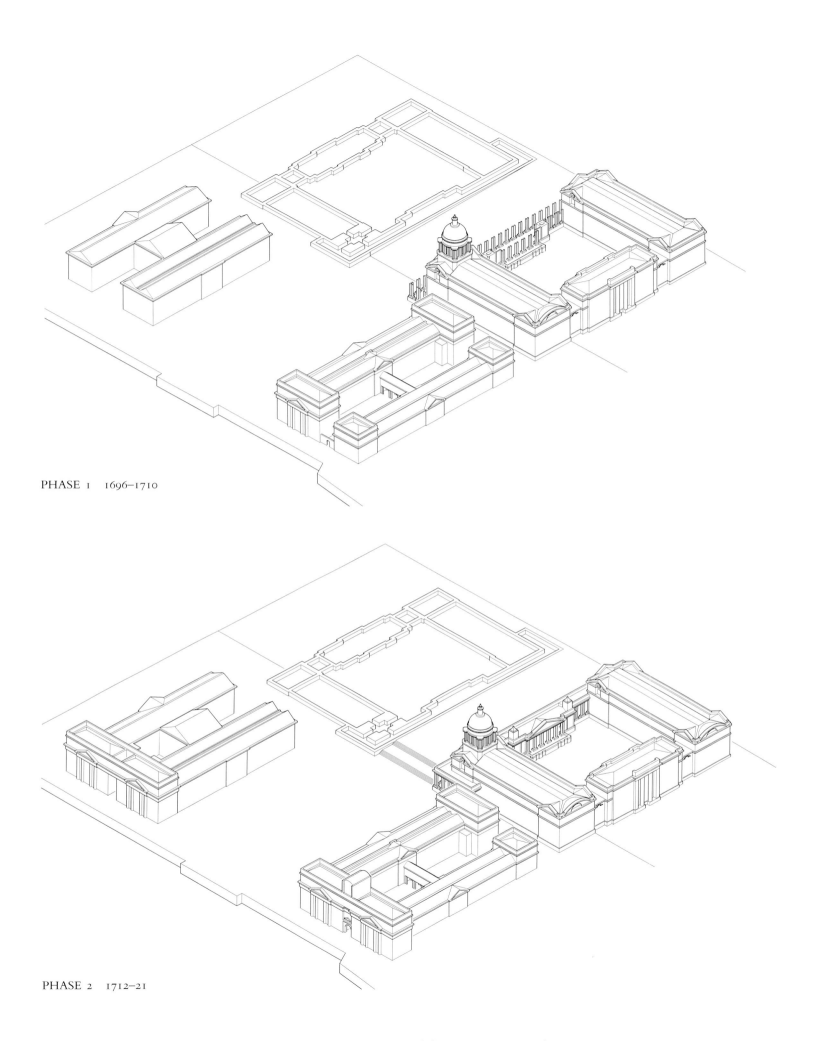

PHASE 1   1696–1710

PHASE 2   1712–21

147 (*above and following pages*)   The building phases of the Royal Hospital for Seamen, Greenwich.

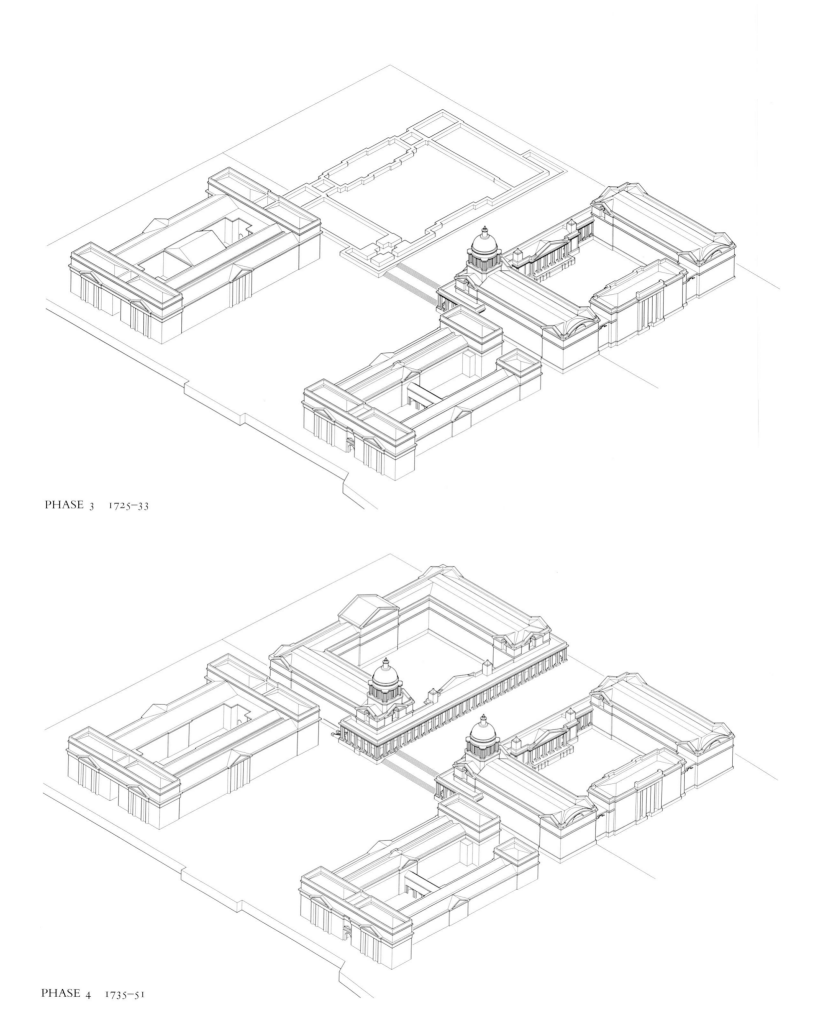

PHASE 3 1725–33

PHASE 4 1735–51

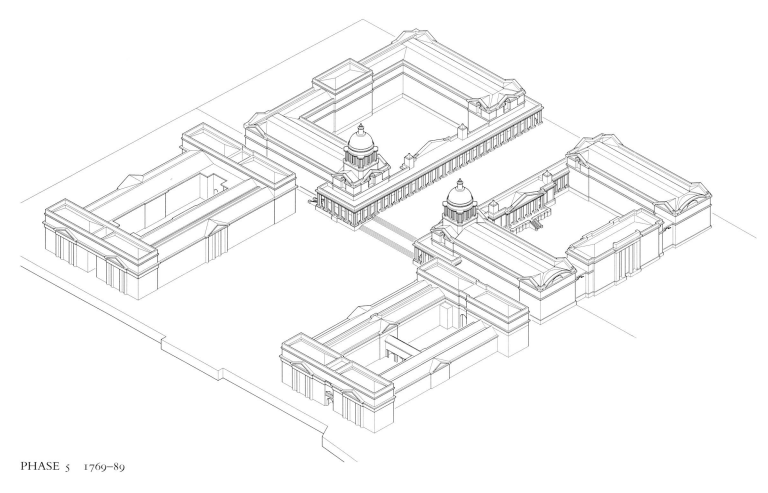

PHASE 5   1769–89

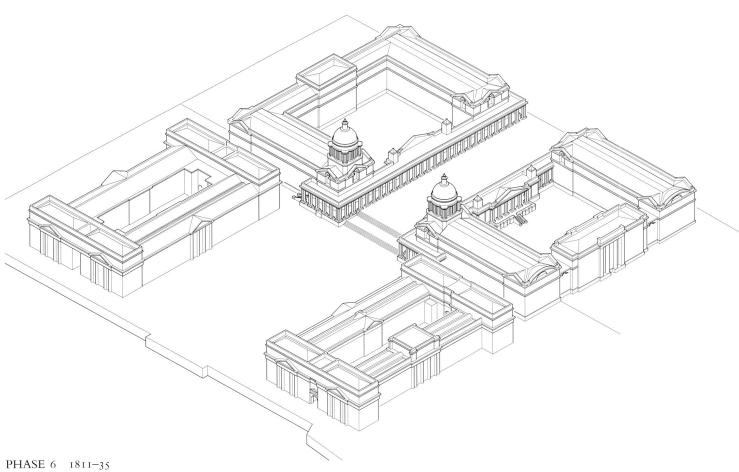

PHASE 6   1811–35

148 Robert Walker, *John Evelyn*, 1648 (NPG).

149 Sir Godfrey Kneller, *Sir Christopher Wren*, 1711 (NPG).

150 Sir Henry Cheere, *Nicholas Hawksmoor*, 1730s (All Souls College, Oxford).

set. It was clear that a 'speedy and effectual means' of providing money was required if the work was to proceed efficiently, and contractors and labourers were not to be discouraged by non-payment. In order to maintain control, the treasurer was required to provide weekly accounts to the Fabric Committee, which would determine spending according to what they considered to be most pressing.[85] The Grand Committee agreed a general brief for funding: 'collecting the benevolence of all persons in England'; a proportion of merchant seamen's wages, in addition to the monthly sixpences of the Royal Navy's seamen; a duty on all getting a livelihood by water; forfeits on deserters; the power to run lotteries; and a payment from the poor rate of every parish.[86] By such measures, £36,352 had been raised by November 1699 and the project was £133 in credit. This included £12,518 from the royal and £10,033 from the mercantile navies, and two payments of the 'King's Benevolence': £2000 in 1696 and 1697, but nothing in 1698 and 1699.[87]

The foundations for all four blocks of the Hospital were laid between 1696 and 1701. Hawksmoor (fig. 150), as Wren's clerk, was involved from the beginning, preparing all the drawings on the Surveyor's instructions and examining the works carried out. As Clerk of Works from 1698, he was paid £50 per year for 'drawing and designing'. By this time, work was going on all over the site. Although Wren had needed to compromise in terms of plan, he was not prepared to do so in extent. His desire to pre-empt any curtailment of the scheme by establishing it in its totality from the start was no doubt due to experience of the uncertainty of funding which throughout history has bedevilled grand projects. It is thanks to his foresight that the Hospital was ultimately completed.

By 1699 the narrow base block of Charles had been built, its west front ornamented with festoons of drapery and flowers and a large pediment, 30 feet long and 7 feet 9 inches high, with the king's arms in bas relief 'held up by two Genii, with Trophys and ornaments relating to Marine affairs', carved by Robert Jones in 1697–8.[88] Wren's initial thoughts appear to have been French in inspiration, but as built the west pediment was triangular rather than segmental and the small pavilions were terminated with para-pets rather than the mansard roofs originally proposed (fig. 151). Within, the great kitchen occupied two floors of the south-west pavilion, and the whole of the first floor of the base wing was occupied by one long ward capable of accommodating eighty-nine men.[89] Charles itself was remodelled in 1696, with a new deal floor inserted, cross-walls removed and sash windows installed on the east front (figs 152–5).[90] A first-floor bridge across the internal court, linking the two buildings, was completed in 1699.[91]

Work began in April 1698 on the erection of the north (Hall) and south ranges of the William Building, to plans provided by Wren.[92]

Hawksmoor was appointed Clerk of Works in 1698 following the death of Henry Symmonds, receiving nine of thirteen votes cast after a process involving both references and interview. John James, the runner-up, was advised that he would be preferred as opportunity arose. In view of his continuing to receive £50 per year as clerk to the Surveyor, Hawksmoor was appointed to his new post at 4s per day, 1s less than the previous incumbent. He was told also that he would be expected to live on site. His first (less than glamorous) task was to make an inventory of the stores,[93] but he was shortly able in January 1699 to supplement his salary in a more appropriate manner, being paid £57 for three models, in cases, of the Hospital, Infirmary, Church and Queen's House, according to the proposals of Wren.[94] The approved design was engraved in 1699 and made available for sale to subscribers in an issue of one hundred, twenty-four of which were pasted onto cloth and framed. In April 1700 Evelyn accompanied Wren to Kensington, where, in the presence of Evelyn's 'dear & worthy Reverend ffriend'[95] Thomas Tenison, Archbishop of Canterbury, the king was presented 'with the Model & several drafts ingraved,

151   Attributed to Jan Griffier the elder, *Royal Yachts on the Thames with Greenwich beyond, c.*1712. This shows Wren's red brick pavilion to the west of John Webb's King Charles Building, with an archway between. Demolition of the pavilion and rebuilding in stone began towards the end of 1712 (cf. fig. 141) (Phillips International Fine Art Auctioneers).

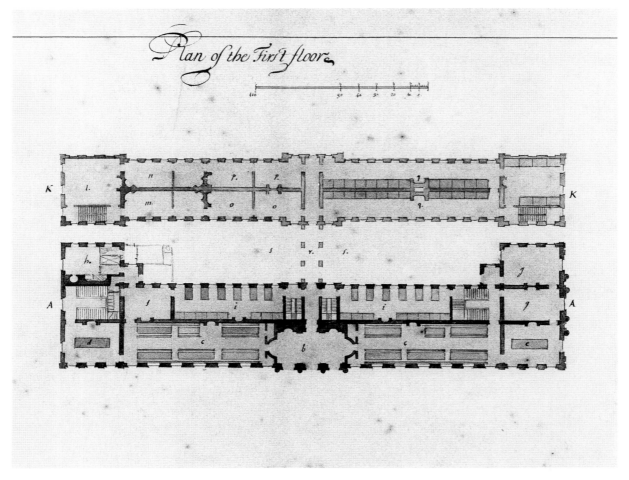

152 Plan of the ground ('first') floor of the King Charles Building (showing its conversion to Hospital use) and the narrower base wing to the west (NMM ART 4/1).

153 Cross-section of the King Charles Building and the base wing. The upper floor, on the east front of the King Charles Building, is an insertion carried out as part of the conversion of the building to Hospital use (NMM ART 4/7).

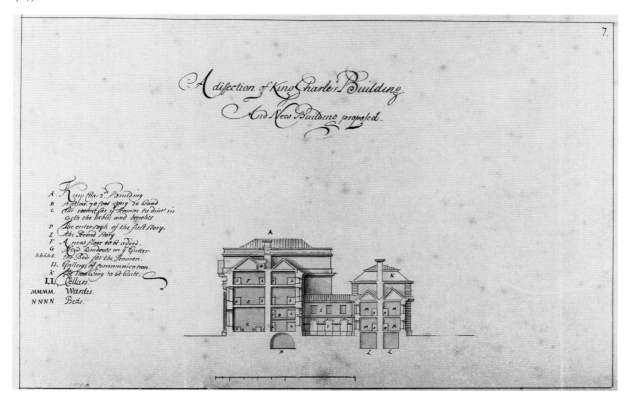

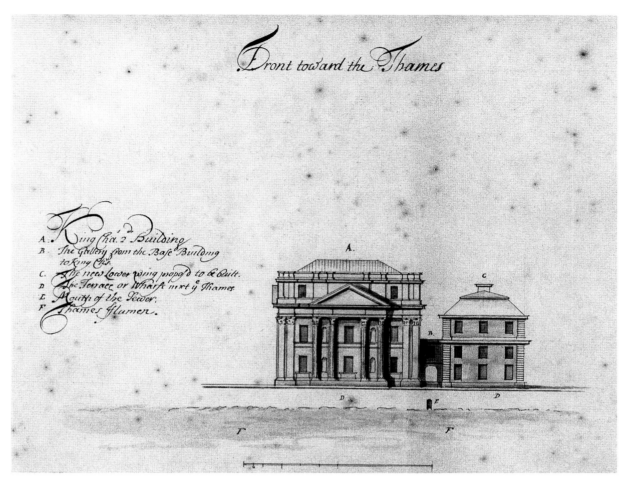

A. King Cha. 2 Building
B. The Gallery from the Base Building to King C.
C. The new Lower wing propo'd to be Built.
D. The Terrace or Wharfe next y Thames
E. Mouth of the Sewer.
F. Thames Flumen.

154   North elevation of the King Charles Building and the base wing, as proposed, towards the river (NMM ART 4/6).

155   The west front of the base wing of the King Charles Building (NMM ART 4/8).

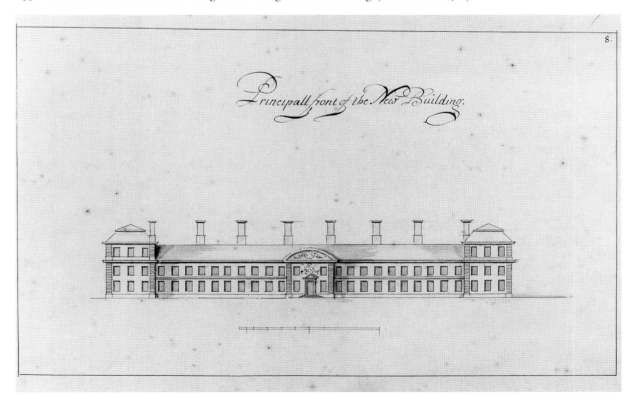

Principall front of the New Building.

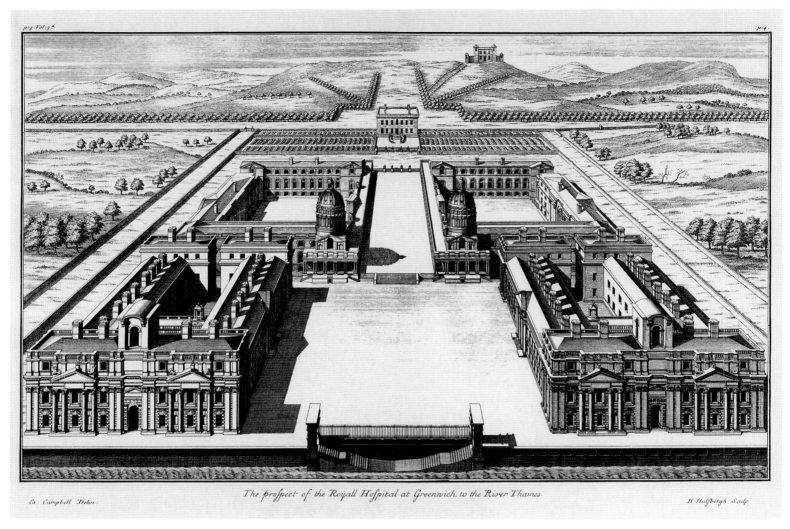

Ca: Campbell Delin:

The prospect of the Royall Hospital at Greenwich, to the River Thames

H Hulsbergh Sculp

156   The broadly accurate perspective of the Royal Hospital for Seamen, published by Colen Campbell in *Vitruvius Britannicus*, 1725, by which time the design had been established.

of the Hospital now erecting at Greenewich . . . His Majestie receiving us with greate satisfaction, & incouraging the prosecution of the Work' (fig. 156).[96]

Models had been firmly recommended by both Henry Wotton and Sir Roger Pratt, based on their Italian experience. Wren was cautious in commending them since 'a model is seen from other Stations and Distances than the Eye sees the Building', but Pratt, in 1660, wrote in terms which Wren would no doubt have approved: 'the model being often well considered and examined as it ought, it will not only prevent all future alteration in the building, a thing of a most vast expense, but will likewise avoid all complaint of the master, and abuse of the contriver, being that this will ever remain a justification of the invention of the one, and a most plain conviction of the consent of the other'.[97] The model continued in use on the site, being mended in 1707, 'glueing the parts that were unglued'.[98] This is not to say that the design did not change in detail during the building programme; it did, but within the parameters defined by Wren which were respected by all who followed. A comparably protective attitude was extended to the definition of the site as a whole. In 1697 the acquisition of the Queen's House by Henry Sidney, Earl of Romney, caused the committee to wish to make it clear to him

where his stewardship ended and that of the Hospital began. They went so far as to send Henry Symmonds in 1697 to the discussions concerning the moving of what was to become the Romney Road to ensure that there was no encroachment on the Hospital land, following this by fencing the site and putting a rail alongside the avenue from the Queen's House to the river.[99] A fence was an adequate marker of the site, but was not a defence against encroachment. On a site as large as this, theft was inevitable. Following the loss of a great quantity of lead, the committee required the Clerk of Works in February 1697 to provide two labourers, for whom he was made accountable, to act as night watchmen, supported in their endeavours by a dog and a horn 'to give notice'.[100]

The committee also was responsible for regulating behaviour. The Hospital Secretary, William Vanbrugh, cousin of Sir John, in June 1697 lodged a complaint against Daniell Sheppard, 'Messenger and Sollicitor', 'a person of scandalous behaviour, and disorderly in the said imployment, to the prejudice of the business of the said Commission'. The alleged behaviour included 'courting of a woman at Greenwich, being a married man', but more significant no doubt from Vanbrugh's point of view was that he had used 'scurrilous language at all times to the Secretary' and had been given to self-promotion in styling himself Deputy Treasurer. He was said also to have displayed 'impudent carriage' not only to the Earl of Romney's steward, Mr Watson, but also to the Archbishop of Canterbury, who was one of the Commissioners. This was the crucial charge and after due consideration the committee found that Sheppard had 'misbehaved himselfe in his carriage to his Grace the Arch:Bishop of Canterbury; and that some other articles of misdemeanor are proved against him'. He was suspended and required to apologise to Vanbrugh, which he did. Evelyn was charged with the delicate task of appeasing his friend the archbishop. Unfortunately his *Diary* is mute on the matter – pages are missing from the manuscript[101] – but the minutes report that, on being told about the manner in which Sheppard had been dealt with, his grace was 'pleased to remit', 'but still felt he is not fit for that service'. In a display of admirable pragmatism, this caveat subsequently was heavily deleted from the minutes (although now discernible in a good light) and two weeks later Sheppard's

suspension was removed. He was reprimanded, reinstated and told that a further offence would lead to dismissal.[102] His lesson learned, Sheppard did not trouble the committee again. He is next documented in 1699, when it was ordered that he should have an escritoire in which to keep his papers,[103] then again in January 1704, when his widow petitioned for the pay which he had not received for a year before his death.[104]

It was intended that pensioners would arrive as soon as possible. Cabins for one hundred were being prepared in the base block of Charles in the new year of 1700, with rooms fitted out for the serving women at the north end, with the services themselves at the south end of the new base wing.[105] Although it had been agreed that the cabins should be 'finished with wainscoat, and as near the manner, as may be, as Chelsea colledge is', approval subsequently was given for finishing the cabins in the wards with curtains in front of the beds, reserving wainscot for the sides.[106] Five deal tables and benches were ordered in February 1700 for

157 The courtyard of the King William Building. The Painted Hall, to the left, was intended initially to be stone-clad, with carvings of Neptune, Galatea and Tritons under the upper windows.

the Hospital's first dining room, on the ground floor of Charles, which was linked to the kitchen by a covered way.[107] There was, however, much work still to be done and the first galleries and cabins, wainscoted and fitted with beds and chests on rollers, for the occupation of a hundred men, were not completed until April 1701.[108] The masons were meanwhile urged to proceed with all speed to finish the Hall in the King William Building so that it could be roofed in the summer. Progress on the stonework had been hampered by the defectiveness of the supplies. There were complaints about saltpetre in the stone, and later (in 1707) there were attempts to lower the duty payable on Portland stone, which stood at 12s per ton for all except royal palaces and royal excep-

158 (*above*) Heads of Neptune, Galatea and lions, carved by Robert Jones for the decoration of the exterior of the Painted Hall.

159 Two of Robert Jones's carved heads set into a chimneypiece in the basement dining room of the Queen Mary Building, underneath the Chapel.

tions. St Paul's Cathedral was charged only 6s per ton and a request was made that the duty for the building of Greenwich should be dropped on the grounds that it was a royal foundation and a public work.[109] Hawksmoor was deputed to send a suitable person to Portland to investigate and meanwhile recommended the use of Roche Abbey stone.[110] Five hundred tons of Roche Abbey, together with 500 tons of Ketton stone were brought in April 1700, with a further 1000 tons of each in February 1701. Problems were also caused by the non-payment of Edward Strong who in June 1700 was owed £1680 and as a result could not pay his men who went on strike – £500 was provided to enable work to continue.

Initially it was intended that the Painted Hall would be stone-clad, with appropriate decoration. This was still the intention at the end of the eighteenth century (fig. 157).[111] Robert Jones put in a bill in January 1700 for sixteen large lions' heads to go under the windows of the Hall[112] and in 1704 carved a further thirty-eight heads of Neptune, Galatea and Tritons in Ketton stone with triglyphs underneath, together with three more lions' heads, to go under the upper window cills of the north and south sides (fig. 158).[113] For reasons of cost, the Painted Hall received its stone cladding only on the north side; on the south side there are merely stone dressings to the brickwork. As a result, these carved heads were not required. Two of the Neptunes and Galateas subsequently were set into a chimneypiece which survives in the dining room underneath the Chapel (fig. 159); a further twenty-nine heads, marked N[orth] and S[outh], including five lions, survive in store in the sole intact survival from the royal palace, the Jacobean undercroft beneath the Queen Anne Building (figs 160 and 161). Rediscovered during the war by Helmut Gernsheim during his photographic campaign and published as 'Lost Baroque Keystones',[114] they represent a rather free interpretation of their subjects, yet they are remarkably accomplished, naturalistic pieces for a little known sculptor who spent twenty-four years of his working life at the Hospital until his death in 1722.[115] Jones was responsible also in 1701 for the carving of the capitals of the Hall, the heads which adorn the outside of the King William cupola, and the keystones with heads of Neptune on the west front of William. Some of Jones's details appear to have been carved before they were needed – the final designs of the fronts of the west range of King William were not determined until 1707 – but that of the north pavilion, the west end of the Painted Hall, was certainly completed to the extent that Jones could submit his bill for £170 in September 1701 for the 26 foot long segmental pediment, which displays four large heads representing the four winds, with a sea-lion, a unicorn, several sorts of large fish and two large groups of trophies 'proper to Sea affairs'.[116] He also carved the two groups of three entwined large fish in Portland stone, in 1706, flanking the trophy on the east pediment of Queen Anne.[117]

The Hall was ready for covering in June 1700, when James Grove the carpenter erected the splendid surviving roof composed of nineteen 58 foot trusses.[118] Although there has been substantial piecemeal re-roofing at the Hospital, most notably in 1830–44 and in 1906–8 at the King Charles and Queen Anne Buildings,[119] and again in 1957 and in the early 1990s in the north pavilions and main ranges of King Charles,[120] several early king post roofs survive: in the south-west pavilion and southern half of the east range of Queen Anne, in the north-west pavilion (and in the later south-west pavilion) of King Charles and, remarkably, in the east

160 The central octagonal pier of the Jacobean undercroft beneath the Queen Anne Building.

range of King Charles, where the trusses of the 1660s remain (fig. 162). The Hall roof is, with that of the post-fire Chapel, the most important of the surviving eighteenth-century roofs. It has an exceptionally wide span for its date, with tie-beams which appear to be composed of laminated members of triple thickness. This is unlike Wren's solutions to similar problems at Chelsea, but directly comparable with Hawksmoor's roofing of Beverley Minster.[121] The roof was surveyed by William Newton around 1782 and depicted by him in a drawing which includes the roof of Hawksmoor's St Alfege, executed by John James, Inigo Jones's St Paul's, Covent Garden, and 'Mr Mylne's design for Greenwich Chapel' (fig. 163).[122] Together with the adjoining dome, it was reinforced with steel trusses in 1906–10.[123]

In 1701 James Grove produced a model and prices for the roof over the south range of King William next to the Romney Road, which was completed the following year (the eastern half survives), 'according to the [very detailed] manner given him by Mr Hawksmoor'.[124] The more detailed the costings, the greater is the scope for reduction. The committee was not slow to appreciate this and asked Hawksmoor to examine the model and reduce the estimate. This he did, but the following year presented them with a paper which demonstrated that the prices at Greenwich were much lower than those of other public works in London[125] and,

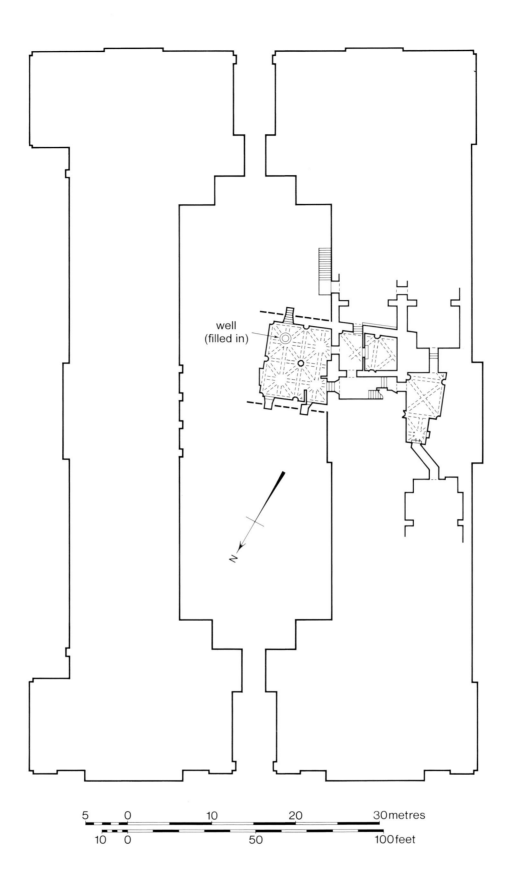

well
(filled in)

5　　0　　　　10　　　　20　　　　30 metres
10　0　　　　　　50　　　　　　100 feet

161　Plan of the undercroft in the basement of the Queen Anne Building.

after receiving a petition from Grove regarding his 'extraordinary performance in the roofe of the hall', the committee repented of its parsimony and in May 1702 granted the carpenter a bonus of £130.[126] Models of details provided a basis for both costing and approval of works, and now also provide a broad basis for an attribution of designs. Hawksmoor in 1700 requested £27 'For making a Moddle for ye Great hall . . . shewing all the Vaulting of the lower hall and the Tables & Formes in the upper Halls and the Cupola'.[127] This splendid groin-vaulted, lower-ground-floor space, later used as a dining hall, has the clarity and simplicity of design of great Renaissance architecture in the Albertian tradition (figs 223 and 224).[128] After the model had been completed, the ground was dug for the foundations for the columns and by January 1701 Edward Strong the mason and Thomas Hughes the bricklayer were at work, the latter submitting his bill for £43 9s in March for 'Brickwork done in the Vaulting and Groining of the Great Hall Elliptically extraordinarily done'.[129]

Although there was significant progress on the works in these early years, funding remained a problem. In July 1702 a debt of £19,000 was estimated, so great that without some extraordinary supply it was expected that the works would not be able to proceed. The new queen was petitioned in vain for £8000, in payment of the late king's overdue subscription,[130] but nevertheless work did continue, a tribute to Evelyn's skills as treasurer, to the officers involved for their management of resources and an indication long before the example of modern debt-based economies of how much can be achieved without direct payment, particularly if workers are somehow able to survive without financial remuneration for months and in some cases, years. Greenwich was not unique in public works of the time in this respect, and not all workers could survive, but it is nevertheless remarkable from a modern viewpoint that so much was achieved in such circumstances. Nevertheless, work did slow down in 1703: the retirement of Evelyn as treasurer in that year, at the age of eighty-three, to be succeeded by his son-in-law William Draper,[131] who had married his daughter Susanna in 1693,[132] prompted a review of the accounts. With the building regarded as half-built, £84,908 having been spent between 1696 and 1701, according to Evelyn when he closed his account, it was estimated that a further £128,384 would be needed, principally for the Queen Anne (£44,052) and Queen Mary (£49,251) Buildings. The dormitories of King William also awaited completion and £15,200 was included in the estimate for the infirmary, the out-offices and a market.[133] The grant of the right to run a market in Greenwich had been assigned to the Hospital by Lord Romney and Hawksmoor had been instructed in 1700 to survey the ground proposed, in the High Street, to consider any other places he might think appropriate, and to prepare a scheme and estimate.[134] Evelyn had almost balanced the books, passing on a credit of £1574 to his son-in-law. As treasurer from 17 June 1696 to 10 August 1703, he had received £89,879, which included £26,457 from merchant seamen's sixpences per man per month and £43,444 from the seamen of the royal ships. He had spent £88,305.[135]

Work on the Queen Anne Building was in hand by May 1699, when Edward Strong was carrying out masonry work and making good the vaulting of the Jacobean undercroft under the west range of what at this stage was occasionally referred to, confusingly, as the King William Building, sometimes as 'the great Corinthian

Building opposite to that of K:Charles'[136] and, from 1701, the court of the Princess Anne.[137] Initially of brick, without pavilions, the two main ranges of the building were being floored in March 1703;[138] later that year work was begun on the masonry of the east front of the base wing and its roof was leaded.[139] The main building was leaded in 1704.[140] The vaulted undercroft had been constructed in 1604–5 under a timber hall. The reason for its building is unclear although it has been suggested that it may have been partly to counteract the settlement inevitable on land next to the river. The reasons for its retention when the Hospital was being erected are similarly elusive, but possibly it was easier to retain than to remove and, connecting with the cellars, it did provide extra storage space and, in recent years, a cellar-bar for off-duty naval officers attending the College.[141]

At the south end of the King Charles Building, the portico built by John Webb, which had been designed to provide the link to the cross-wing of his proposed palace – and is clearly depicted in the topographical views of Hendrik Danckerts (fig. 12),[142] Johannes Vorsterman (fig. 25)[143] and Jan Griffier the elder [144] – was no longer required. An undercover link between Charles and William was to be provided later by an underground kitchen to dining-room passage between their respective basements. In March 1702 the portico was pulled down.[145] The following month John Kip was paid £20 for engraving the general perspective of the Hospital, an official riposte to unauthorised depictions.[146] In 1706 Edward Strong submitted his account for the newly repaired south front (fig. 164).[147]

When the King Charles Building was left boarded up in 1672, it was unfinished. Of its major interior spaces designed by John Webb, only the apsidally ended entrance vestibule survives, although even this has been partly rebuilt following bomb damage in the Second World War (fig. 167). The two main staircases at each end both date from the early eighteenth century, although they are in the positions designated by Webb. The materials for the north stair were accounted for in November 1704: 267 square feet of oak was needed for the trusses, strings and half-paces and eighty-four oak plank steps throughout all three storeys, 19 cubic feet of fir in the old half-paces, 142 square feet of wainscot and three large semicircular steps at the stair foot.[148] Edward Strong submitted his account the following month for the masonry of chimneypieces, doorcases, washing places and paving in King Charles. The doors adjacent to the north stairs and elsewhere have the handsome unequivocally Office of Works character which might be expected of a mason working under the direction of Hawksmoor (figs 165 and 166).

During this period of relatively limited activity, effort was put into the completion of the King William cupola, Edward Strong submitting an account in December 1702 for the stonework, which included letting in 726 feet of iron chain to tie it together[149] and James Grove providing models in the spring of 1703 for its roof and lantern.[150] The cupola was leaded in September,[151] although interior carving of cornice and capitals continued, under the direction of Robert Jones. The brazier John Smith submitted his account in November 1704 for the $7\frac{1}{2}$ feet high copper vase and ball on top of the cupola (£84) and the copper sea-lion, after the design of Robert Jones,[152] 'to show the wind' on top of the vase (£36).[153] This proved to be too large to be sufficiently mobile and was replaced in 1726[154] with a view to selling the original. It was still in Hawksmoor's possession in 1731, a lapse of memory

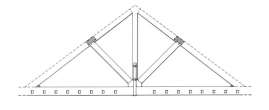

KING CHARLES BLOCK EAST RANGE
1664-1669

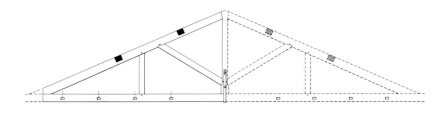

QUEEN ANNE BLOCK EAST RANGE
1701-1705

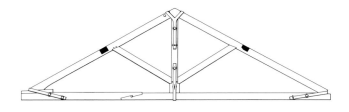

KING CHARLES BLOCK NORTH-WEST PAVILION
1712-1715

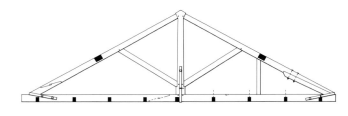

QUEEN ANNE BLOCK SOUTH-WEST PAVILION
c. 1730

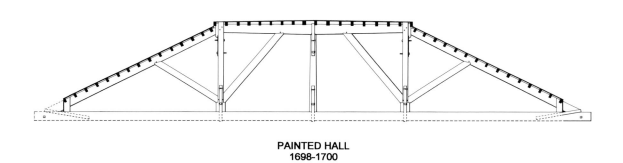

PAINTED HALL
1698-1700

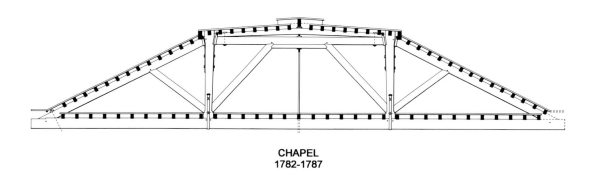

CHAPEL
1782-1787

162   Survey drawings of surviving, original roof trusses in the Royal Hospital for Seamen.

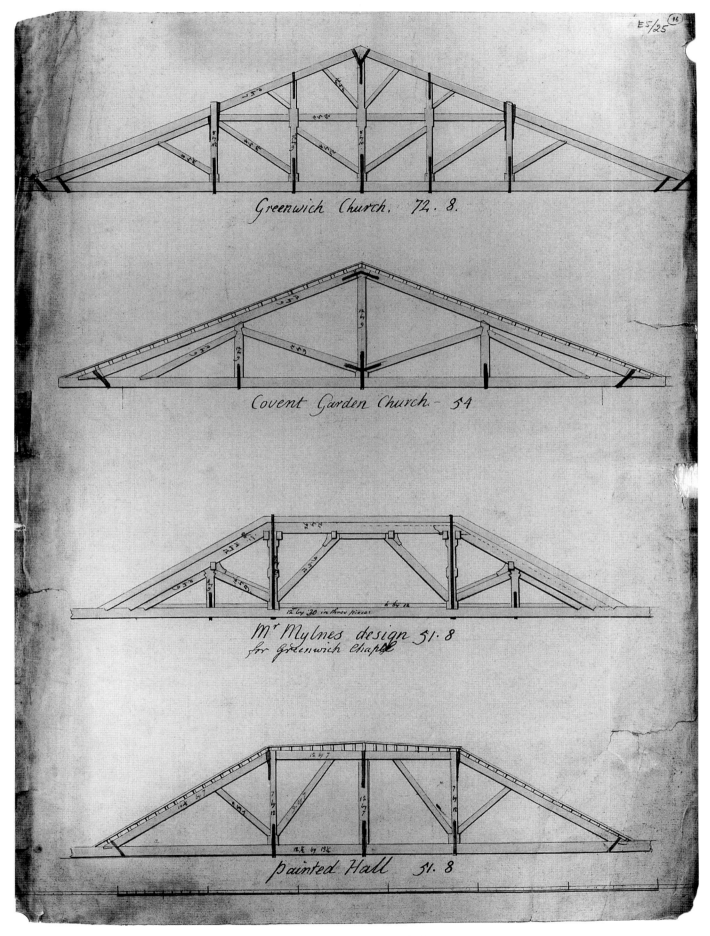

Greenwich Church. 72.8.

Covent Garden Church. — 54

Mr Mylnes design 51.8
for Greenwich Chapel

Painted Hall 51.8

163   William Newton, survey drawings of roof trusses, c.1782 (BAL E5/25 (16)).

164 (*above left*)   The south front of the King Charles Building. The right-hand pavilion was repaired by Edward Strong after the removal of John Webb's portico in 1702; the left-hand pavilion was rebuilt to match in 1769–74.

166 (*above right*)   The north staircase of the King Charles Building, looking upwards towards the first-floor landing.

165 (*left*)   The ground-floor stair hall looking towards the north-east pavilion of the King Charles Building.

167 (*facing page*)   The entrance vestibule on the east side of the King Charles Building, seen from the north. The soffits of the originally open arcade were carved by Joshua Marshall and John Young in 1666. The south wall was rebuilt after bomb damage in the Second World War.

which he could only put down to his difficulties with gout – Ripley was told to decide what to do with it.[155]

The domes are the literal and metaphorical high points of the architecture of the Hospital. The idea of twin domes over the King William and Queen Mary Buildings was certainly Wren's (fig. 169).[156] As built, they are 'higher and richer in execution' than in the first drawings.[157] An expressive plan and elevation in Hawksmoor's hand, dated 1702, indicates his responsibility for working out the King William design under Wren's overall direction (fig. 168).[158] This shows the dome, 29 feet in diameter, almost as built, but it was slightly modified in the execution, the consoles being omitted, the upper oculi being reduced in number and the footprint of the columns adjusted.[159] The strongly projecting paired, coupled columns that quarter the drum, which occur also at Mansart's Les Invalides (fig. 171), and derive ultimately from Michelangelo's St Peter's, here serve as buttresses on the diagonals to support the thrust of the weight above (fig. 170). At Les Invalides, the columns are set on square plinths with two at the front and two behind. At Greenwich, the geometry is more

complex and a visually more arresting result is achieved. The rear columns are brought forward in order to provide pairs at the front corners of the plinths, which then lead the eye to the set-back columns which frame the drum. A survey drawing, made after the Chapel fire which damaged the identical Queen Mary cupola in 1779, compares the built structure with Hawksmoor's proposal (fig. 172).[160] This confirms that his original intention had been to bring the rear columns still further forward, narrowing the recessed angle at the front of the plinths in the pursuit of still greater Baroque expression. We are on the way here to the west towers of St Paul's Cathedral (fig. 173).[161]

The twin domes may be appreciated as outstanding pieces of architecture in their own right, but they are more than that since they are integral to the design of the whole. Viewed from the Isle of Dogs, the repetition of coupled columns from the riverside to the north front of the colonnades, a theme adumbrated by John Webb, is continued in the rhythms of the drums of the domes. Beneath the domes, the interpenetration of architectural elements through the subtle employment of triangular and segmental

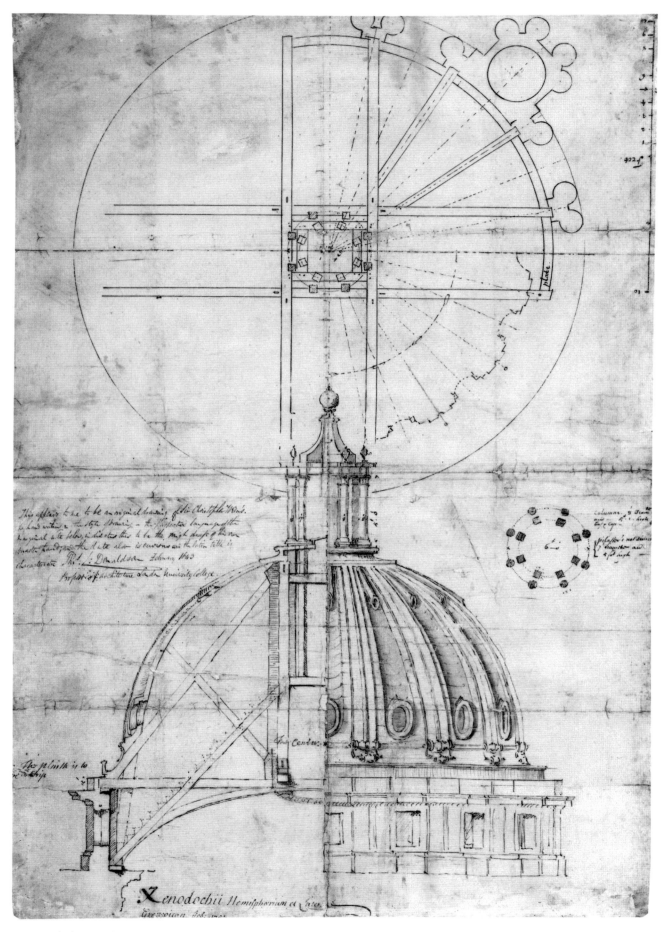

168　Nicholas Hawksmoor, plan and elevation of the cupola of the King William Building (BAL E5/5).

169 (*facing page*)　The twin domes of the King William and Queen Mary Buildings, seen from the east range of Queen Mary.

171   Jules Hardouin Mansart, dome of the Hôtel des Invalides, Paris.

173   Sir Christopher Wren, the west towers of St Paul's Cathedral, London, photographed by Helmut Gernsheim.

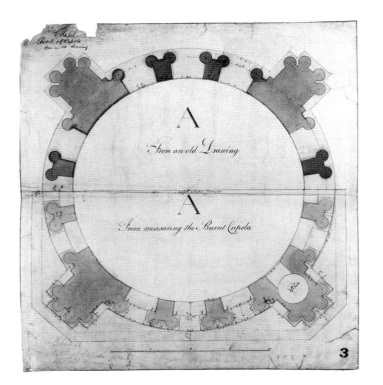

pediments, unites the structures from ground level to lanterns. It is the resolution and sense of contained movement achieved by Wren and Hawksmoor in balancing the horizontal and vertical axes and tying the building to the landscape which places Greenwich Hospital among the highest achievements of European architecture.

Prince George of Denmark, Lord High Admiral and now chairman of the Commissioners, in August 1703[162] urged the directors of the Hospital, under the chairmanship of Wren, to get on with putting the completed parts of the building into a condition for receiving pensioners. The following June it was reported that for an expenditure of £4000, the outstanding joinery and paving work on King Charles and its base wing could be completed by Michaelmas (29 September), and in August it was reported that fifty men could be accommodated with a further 150 by the end of November. There was room for another hundred by April 1705 and a further hundred by Christmas 1706.[163]

172 (*left*)   A plan of the dome of the Chapel, divided into two halves, which compares a survey drawing of the cupola burned in the fire of 1779 (below) with a design drawing (above), probably made after an original by Hawksmoor for the identical dome of the King William Building (BAL E5/17 (5)).

170 (*facing page*)   The colonnade and dome of the King William Building, Greenwich.

The imminent arrival of occupants prompted rapid action in accommodation, supplies and regulations. Hawksmoor was responsible for fitting up quarters for the officers – the captain and lieutenant were accommodated in the south pavilion of King Charles and the deputy-governor, for whom a new kitchen chimney and back stairs were required, in the north, although this was to prove too close to the water and injurious to his health in the winter, so he was allocated a small winter apartment on the west side of King William in 1709.[164] Agreements were struck with suppliers of pewter, locks and leather shoes and with a butcher, brewer and baker. A matron, four nurses (soon increased to six per hundred men), a surgeon and physician were appointed, although it was not anticipated that major surgery or mental care would be carried out: an agreement was made in 1706 that those who needed limbs removing would be sent to St Bartholomew's and the mad would go to Bethlem.[165] In view of the absence of a general infirmary, ten beds were made available at the west end of the south wing of King William, with the provision expanding in early 1706 on the lines indicated by Hawksmoor for his dedicated Infirmary building with three or four beds per room (with flock rather than feather mattresses), and the provision of a bathing tub. The temporary nature of this location was underlined in 1707 by the recognition that shutters were needed to prevent passers-by from looking in through the inconveniently low windows.[166] A further ad hoc improvement in 1709 was the provision of ropes to enable the helpless men to turn themselves in bed.[167] Even by 1730 the sanitation had not been satisfactorily sorted out. There were insufficient 'necessary houses' for the number of users. The inconvenience of the use of tubs for the pensioners 'to ease themselves', in the absence of 'a proper place', was compounded on Sundays when, in the absence of staff, two of the abler pensioners had to be paid to carry out the task on behalf of their less active colleagues.[168] Further washhouses and 'necessary places' eventually were erected in 1749 in detached blocks to the east and west of the principal Hospital buildings.[169] When they were removed one hundred years later, they were described as '24 open seats in privies over a sewer house . . . and 20 water closets and 14 urinals'.[170]

Wren had requested a copy of Chelsea's guidelines for food and clothing in December 1703, and the following October it was confirmed that Greenwich would follow suit, although the clothes would be different colours – dark grey coats (later changed to brown and then to blue) with a blue lining, and grey serge gowns for the women (see Appendix 3).[171] Several pages of rules for the government of the house were prepared, in a manner reminiscent of Les Invalides, with penalties for transgressions: missing daily chapel (a temporary chapel had been fitted up in King Charles), swearing or drunkenness – lose one day's diet; frequenting whores or houses of ill repute – a diet of bread and water for a week; defilement, defacing or lying – the offender to be exposed in the hall with a broom and shovel tied to him for three meals. In the 1720s yellow coats were introduced for miscreant pensioners who were known as 'canaries' and were assigned menial tasks. The advantages of good government had been well attested by the anonymous author of the account of Les Invalides published in 1695: 'What is more surprising than to see so great a Number of Men, of different Countries and Humours, used to all the Licenciousness and Dissoluteness of a Military Life, so Reformed in their Behaviour and Morals, as to become the soberest, civillest, modestest and the most Industrious men in the whole Nation?'.[172]

The punishments for misbehaviour at Les Invalides were more severe than those at Greenwich: swearing or blasphemy – three days in the pillory; drunkenness – eight days in prison on bread and water, followed by twenty-two days without wine at meals; bringing 'Naughty Women' into the house – the woman and the offender were tied back-to-back on the wooden horse in the sight of all for several hours.[173] But it was perhaps not the risk of punishment for misdemeanours which motivated the French towards good behaviour, but that they were able to earn money through manufacturing (of uniforms, silk hangings etc.) so were less likely to be as bored and mischievous as their English equivalents became, a point which was noted when the future of Greenwich Hospital was under consideration in the mid-nineteenth century.

Since the risk of fire was a constant concern in large institutions, smoking was regulated through the provision of designated rooms at both Greenwich Hospital and Les Invalides. At Greenwich a brick-enclosed smoking room was provided in December 1705 between the Upper Painted Hall and the west ward of King William, later known as the Nelson Room.[174] A great deal of thought was given to firewalls, cut through the roof of King Charles in 1706,[175] an arrangement upon which the Hospital was congratulated in the 1840s. Hawksmoor was pleased with the results, noting in 1728 that if a part of the building should take fire, 'the Whole is so guarded and separated with Stop-Fires, Turrets, and Party Walls, that the Fire . . . could not make a total Devastation'.[176] The water supply also was well considered. There were lead cisterns and stone troughs for washing, stone urinals, a 'wast well' and 'boghouse' with a leather-lined sluice door[177] in the inner courtyard of King Charles, conduits to pipe water up into washing places in the wards and specifically in the event of fire, a 'worm engine' and one hundred buckets.[178] A large hand-powered engine was installed in the courtyard of King Charles in 1706 to raise water from a well to a cistern at the top of the building.[179]

The haste with which completion was being carried out resulted in some bureaucratic confusion: the directors, in the manner of directors throughout institutional history, were surprised by being given only one day's notice for a meeting of the general court, asking for one week in future 'in order to lay their Papers relating to the hospitall before the Generall Court with such decency as they desire'.[180] Also in the manner of all directors who must strive to maintain a balance between strategic direction and operational management, they began to involve themselves in the more tangible issues of detail which offered the appearance and consolation of rapid results. They instructed Hawksmoor, who by this time was referred to as Deputy Surveyor, as Wren began to disengage from the detailed management of the project, to inform them in writing if workmen did not immediately act upon his orders, and ordered him to keep a book in which he was to enter all decisions sent from the board. In June 1707 they also asked for the separation of accounts so that they could see what each part of the building was costing, rather than just being presented with an overall total. Such close involvement was understandable, given the nature of their responsibility, given that meetings were frequent – monthly, at Greenwich – and given that they were unpaid and therefore in the perverse manner of volunteer overseers everywhere, the more predisposed to making their time count. But the increasing bureaucracy, required

174 Hawksmoor's staircase in the south-east pavilion of the King Charles Building, with ironwork by Jean Tijou.

175 The back stair in the south-east pavilion of the King Charles Building, which originally received natural light through the round-headed openings, now blocked, which gave onto the main stair hall.

not just in order to keep control of the works and the end in view, but to keep close tabs on the process as well, cannot have been other than irritating to Hawksmoor and James. In this respect, Greenwich Hospital follows the pattern of many institutions, beginning with a clear vision and purpose, but rapidly losing sight of it as the quotidian round of practicalities emphasises processes rather than ends. The directors were themselves aware of this and occasionally found it necessary to remind themselves of their higher purpose.[181]

By 1706 this purpose was the completion of the King William and King Charles Buildings. Hawksmoor made a model for the 'peristylium' at the east end of the Hall, a design for the chimneypiece in the Upper Hall, where at this time, the servants dined, and directed the fitting-up of wards in the first floor of the south wing of William in order to accommodate the next hundred men, with an adjacent apartment for an overseeing lieutenant. All of the floors in this wing originally were partitioned, but with the exception of some surviving original panelling on the second floor, all of the present partitions are modern. The joiners were directed to fit as many cabins into each room as possible.[182]

Hawksmoor also prepared an estimate and design for the great stone stairs at the south end of Webb's range to replace the temporary 'rough stairs'.[183] Webb had provided for a single grand stair compartment, but Hawksmoor's design, approved by the directors in January 1707, occupied the same space but had a grand stone

stair, rising from a paving of Swedish marble to the first floor,[184] with an inserted Ketton stone wall 'with ye Overtures according to the modell' dividing it from a stone backstair rising to the top of the building (fig. 174). Originally there was central access at ground level directly from the backstair to the main range through a doorway (now blocked) (fig. 175). The three 'Overtures' per storey – round-headed openings in the wall, with Portland stone cills, to light the secondary stair, have been filled in, but can still be seen on the back of the wall, and on the front in a raking light. They would have given this room something of the grandeur, albeit on a smaller scale, which Hawksmoor and Vanbrugh were to achieve in the arcaded hall at Blenheim. On those stairs visible from the hall through the openings in the wall, the soffits are decoratively carved; those unseen are plain. The 17 yards of ironwork in the balustrade of the main stair were provided by Jean Tijou at £5 per yard, to his own design, approved by Hawksmoor and reduced by £1 per yard from Tijou's quote.[185]

Soon after the pensioners began to arrive in June 1705, there was a need for somewhere to bury them other than in the parish churchyard, for which there was a charge of 6s 8d per burial as well as its being 'a grievance to the parishioners'.[186] An average mortality rate of 200 men per year in the period 1777–88 meant that the number of deaths in the twelve-year period was equal to the total Hospital complement at that time.[187] Prince George gave a warrant in 1707 for a site for burials at the north-east corner of

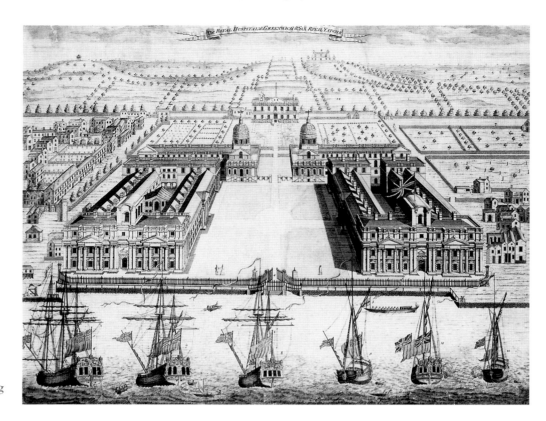

176 Engraved
perspective of the
Royal Hospital for
Seamen, which
includes the
temporary chapel in
the courtyard of the
Queen Anne Building
(NMM).

the park walled in by John James (see chapter 6). There was also a need for a dedicated chapel, as the numbers of men had risen to 300, beyond the limits of temporary provision in an existing room. Consideration was given to using the Hall for this purpose (as indeed had happened at Les Invalides), but the preferred solution was a brick and tile 'tabernacle' in the courtyard of Queen Anne, to be built as cheaply as possible and to be ready within two months – by the summer of 1707 (fig. 176). By May part of the parapet of Queen Anne was being taken down in order to accommodate the Chapel roof – 61 feet wide, with trusses 16 feet high and 440 feet of fir for six beams. In July the floor was paved, the sash windows glazed and the fittings installed. In August it was painted.[188] A vestry was created in Queen Anne, near the entrance

177 Carving by Robert Jones above the arch at the upper end of the Painted Hall: Mars and Pallas frame the arms of William and Mary.

to the Chapel and a pathway laid across the centre of the court from King Charles.[189]

Although some stone carving appears to have been carried out in advance of the time when it was required, no doubt as a result of the availability of large stocks of stone ready to be worked, the Hospital, in common with other institutions, tended to react to circumstances when prompted. So, for example, it was not until the nurses were installed and had presumably raised the matter that the quality of their beds was considered: the steward was asked in February 1705 to find out how they managed these affairs at Chelsea 'and if they have feather beds the like is to be provided for them at Greenwich'; a week later the directors were wondering how Chelsea arranged its laundry.[190] The Infirmary initially was to be fitted with feather beds, screened by green curtains with brown stripes. Early in 1709, by which time there were 350 pensioners, the precedent of Chelsea was again sought in order to determine the appropriate allowance of salaries to servants and whether officers were entitled to servants – they were not.[191] There was no need to refer to Chelsea when it was discovered that eight of the pensioners had been officers – it was agreed immediately that they should be distinguished from the men by having gold edging round their hats, by being placed at the upper end of tables and in the principal cabins of wards and by receiving an extra sixpence per week.[192]

In 1705 it was resolved that the Great Hall should be finished, with the ceiling plastered by Mr Dogood (probably Henry Doogood) 'after the best manner fit for painting, with kids hair, well trowelled and floted', at 2s 4d per yard,[193] but it was not until two years later that plans were made in earnest for the decoration of the room which came to be known as the Painted Hall (fig. 178; see also chapter 5). In June 1707 several of the directors agreed to contribute to the cost of painting and scaffolding was erected. James Thornhill was asked in July to proceed as soon as the

178   The Painted Hall, viewed from the east, looking towards the Upper Hall.

179   Jan Griffier the elder, *A Panorama of Greenwich and the River Thames*, detail showing work in progress at Greenwich Hospital *c.*1705–7. The colonnade of the King William Building is not yet roofed and the two blocks of the Queen Anne Building are both without their pavilions and their stone cladding (Lane Fine Art).

180 The east front of the west range of the King William Building.

scaffolding and priming had been completed, 'and that he make such Alterations in his design by inserting what more he can relating to maritime affaires till the same shall be approved by this board'.[194] Despite the apparent urgency, priming was not begun for another year, after Thornhill had been asked to proceed 'with all expedition: and he left it to the Board to pay him for the same, as they shall judge he deserves'.[195] Tarpaulin was tacked over the windows in 1709 to eliminate reflections on the ceiling.[196] Robert Jones charged £70 in December 1707 for carving the arms of William and Mary in stone, with two large figures of Mars and Pallas, over the arch at the upper end of the Hall (fig. 177).[197]

Hawksmoor meanwhile was giving his attention to completing all the outstanding building work on the west side of the Hospital, including the colonnade, which in this first phase of building

was left unroofed, with a view to completing work by the summer of 1708. An important view by Jan Griffier the elder, on the London art market in 1997, shows work in progress c.1705–7 (fig. 179).[198] Edward Strong was asked in 1707 for his 'proposition' for the upper masonry of the two façades of the west range of King William. The authorship of these extraordinary and idiosyncratic, over-scale frontispieces has been the subject of considerable critical analysis (figs 180 and 181).[199] In a critical tradition which privileges naming and attribution, uncertainty of authorship leads us to doubt our perceptions and conclusions. At Greenwich we are not in the realms of a challenging anonymity, but are engaged in the assessment of a project which was essentially collaborative.[200] For its realisation, architecture is never solely dependent upon the architect, and in the construction of the façades of King William

181　The west front of the west range of the King William Building, with the King Charles Building beyond.

there were at least three significant creative contributors: the architect, the clerk of works/assistant surveyor, and the mason. Work on the façades had begun in 1701 and the design certainly had been established in its broad principles by 1702, but some of the detail, including the entablature, remained to be imagined and constructed. Strong's 'proposition' denotes his responsibility for realisation rather than for design. Hawksmoor's 'draughts' imply design, while, most instructively, a decision by the Board was deferred in the absence of Wren, who by this time was an infrequent attender. Vanbrugh was present but evidently not in a position of authority sufficient to give approval. This had to wait until the next meeting when Wren corrected and marked up Strong's propositions. Towards the end of the year Hawksmoor was requested to 'lay his designs for finishing' before Wren for his consideration: this appears to be a Hawksmoor design prepared under the aegis of Wren.

Scaffolding was erected in March 1708 to enable Robert Jones to carve the architraves and ornament on the east front of King William and precautionary rails were erected in the courtyard around the vaults to 'prevent ye old men's falling in'.[201] At the same time as he was engaged upon the completion of one of the most dramatic pieces of architecture in England, Hawksmoor was carrying out a survey of the conduits which provided the Hospital's water supply (see chapter 1).

Finances were again proving to be uncertain: the £10,000 per year deducted from the pay of seamen was paid irregularly and anyway was insufficient to maintain both the building programme and the resident pensioners.[202] By the end of 1707 the debt was

estimated at £24,690; in March 1708 the sum of £3100 was required to prepare the King William Building for occupation. On the east side, the greater part of Queen Anne had been erected and covered, but to finish and to build Queen Mary on its completed foundations would require a further £120,000. An Act of 1708 granted shares to the Hospital of forfeited and unclaimed naval prizes and bounty money, and following a proposal from Chelsea it was agreed that the two institutions should join forces to raise money from a coal tax.[203] This bore fruit in 1710 with the granting of £6000 per year to Greenwich from a duty on coal, an arrangement which was to continue until 1728. Financial uncertainty probably lay behind the sensitivity with which the Board reacted to unauthorised depictions of the Hospital which might not only make money for others, but also might mislead potential subscribers. By this time, the layout of the building was established in all its major particulars and a true and proper design was ordered in November 1708 to combat the potentially adverse effects of another unauthorised print which was 'notoriously false and much to the discredit of that noble structure'. Hawksmoor was requested to correct existing plates and have them issued as the accurate design.[204]

Work by 1709 had slowed almost to a standstill – Wren and Vanbrugh attended a meeting for the first time in a year that April[205] and almost exactly a year later the General Court questioned whether a Surveyor of the Works was needed at all.[206] The post survived this crisis, as it was to do on every subsequent occasion because of the need for 'constant and needful repairs', for preserving the unfinished parts and for carrying out those incidental works which are 'unavoidable in the first fixing a Family'.[207] There was, moreover, a continuing need for a Clerk of Works and assistant.[208] During this year of relative inactivity, Hawksmoor had spent most of his time on the site in moving conduits and securing the water supply with such effectiveness that a surplus was available for sale. This and his continuing work on drawing all designs and producing surveys of the park saved his salary which had been threatened in December 1710. The General Court acknowledged that if they had commissioned someone new to investigate and restore the conduits, then that alone would have cost them more than Hawksmoor's £50 per year.[209] Discussions at meetings during this moribund period were not conducive to dedicated attendance: the steward was ordered to visit the laundry, repeatedly and unexpectedly, to see 'whether any ways are prac-

tised that may be the means of ye shirts being so extraordinarily worn out in the lower parts'.[210]

At the end of this first phase in 1710, the King Charles Building and its narrower base wing, with a linking gallery, had been completed; King William had been erected, although the southwest pediment remained to be installed and work on the interior and the roof of the colonnade was outstanding, and work had begun on the painting of the Painted Hall; the main block of Queen Anne had been erected in brick, with its base block in stone, both roofed, without pavilions, with a temporary chapel between the two ranges; Queen Mary had progressed no further than its foundations. Fifteen years of building work had produced half a Hospital – Les Invalides had been substantially completed in four.

Chapter 5

THE ROYAL HOSPITAL FOR SEAMEN:
BUILDING AN INSTITUTION

Progress of the Works

PHASE 2: 1712–21

King Charles Building: north-west pavilion taken down and rebuilt in stone; archway built between the two pavilions; turret for a flag erected.

Queen Anne Building: north pavilions built.

King William colonnade roofed; south-west pediment installed; steps between King William and Queen Mary built.

The parishioners of St Alfege's church in the centre of Greenwich petitioned successfully for a new church after the roof of the old one collapsed in 1710. The body of the building, by Hawksmoor, was erected between 1711 and 1714, paid for by money granted by the Fifty New Churches Act of 1711 (fig. 182).[1] The directors of the Hospital were quick to react, petitioning the House of Commons for a new church and for funds to continue the Hospital buildings (fig. 183). They had just cause to press, since while St Alfege was being rebuilt, the parishioners used the Hospital Chapel. This went on for longer than anticipated, continuing to be a 'great hindrance' in 1716.[2] The directors also, to demonstrate that matters had not been forgotten, again determined to petition the queen for the annexation of the park and of the Queen's House, now occupied by the Governor of the Hospital, Sir William Gifford, who was also keeper of the park, and asked Wren to investigate how the queen's warrant might be obtained to free the Hospital from paying duty on Portland stone. Hawksmoor's new perspective and ground plan of the 'whole design', underlining the directors' determination to complete, was approved for engraving and consideration was given to the possible expansion of the site by purchasing property to the west. Towards the end of 1711 it was agreed that the first task when money became available, as it was to do in 1712 when the Exchequer released funds from 'prizes', would be the rebuilding in stone of the riverside pavilion of the King Charles base block, at an estimated cost of £11,518, to match Webb's design.[3] In view of the incomplete state of the Hospital, the decision to rebuild the very recently erected pavilion appears quite extraordinary. It perhaps reflects the preoccupation with magnificence and the desire to present an imposing front to the world.

Completion of the interior of the west range of the King William Building was proposed at a cost of £1473, paid for out of revenue, Hawksmoor being asked in 1712 to produce a design for the stone stairs. Part of the range was to be occupied by up to one hundred 'wholsome' boys, 'with no distempers about them', aged between fourteen and eighteen, for instruction in writing, arithmetic and navigation, justifying the new title of the institution: 'The Royall Hospitall at Greenwich for the encrease of Seamen and improvement of Navigation'.[4] In fact only between three and thirty boys were accommodated at any one time between 1715 and 1730. They were not above being mischievous – in 1727 a rainwater pipe had to be encased in stone in the west dormitory 'to prevent the Boys throwing Nastiness down behind the Wainscot at the Matron's Lodgings'.[5]

182 St Alfege's church, Greenwich, rebuilt by Nicholas Hawksmoor, 1711–14, with its medieval tower encased by John James in 1730.

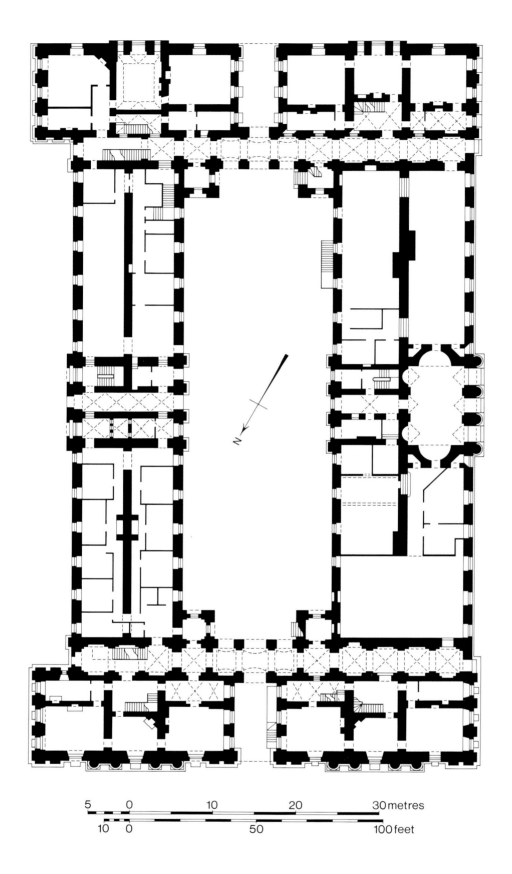

5   0   10   20   30 metres

10   0   50   100 feet

QUEEN ANNE BUILDING

183 (*this and following pages*)   Ground plans of the four principal blocks of the Royal Hospital for Seamen.

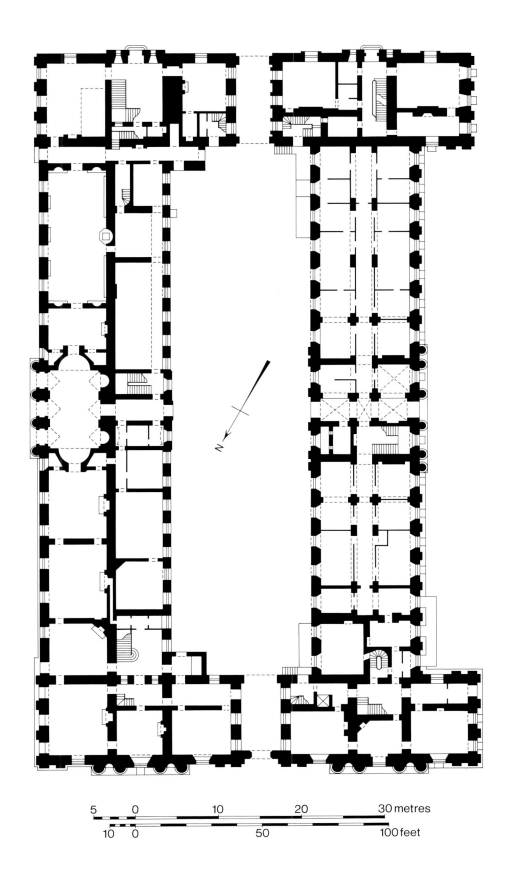

5   0   10   20   30 metres
10   0   50   100 feet

KING CHARLES BUILDING

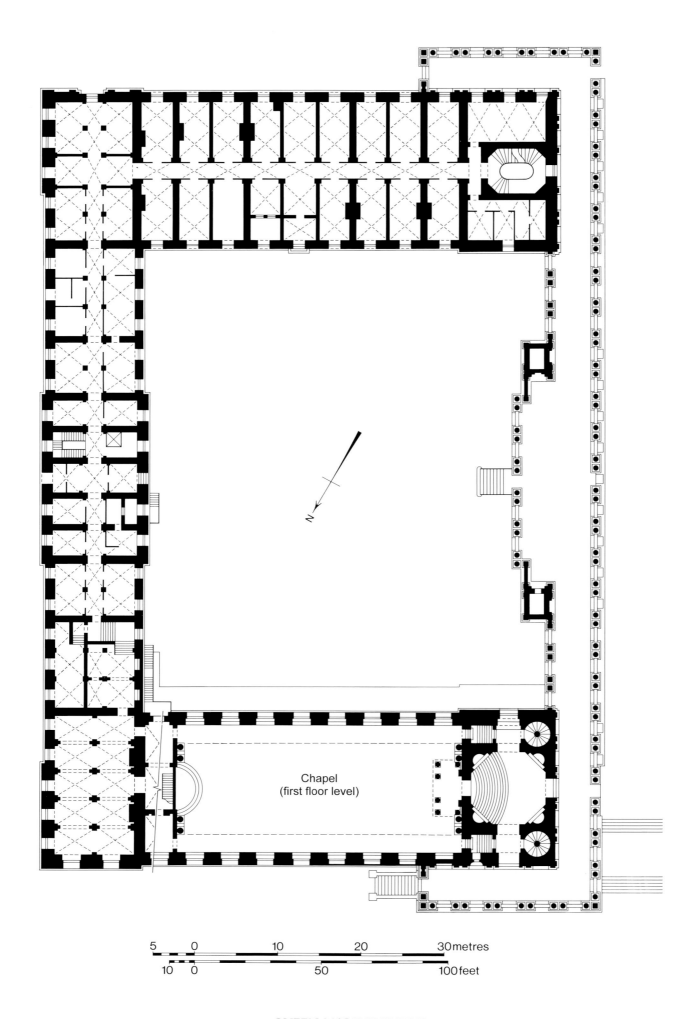

Chapel
(first floor level)

5 0   10   20   30 metres
10 0   50   100 feet

QUEEN MARY BUILDING

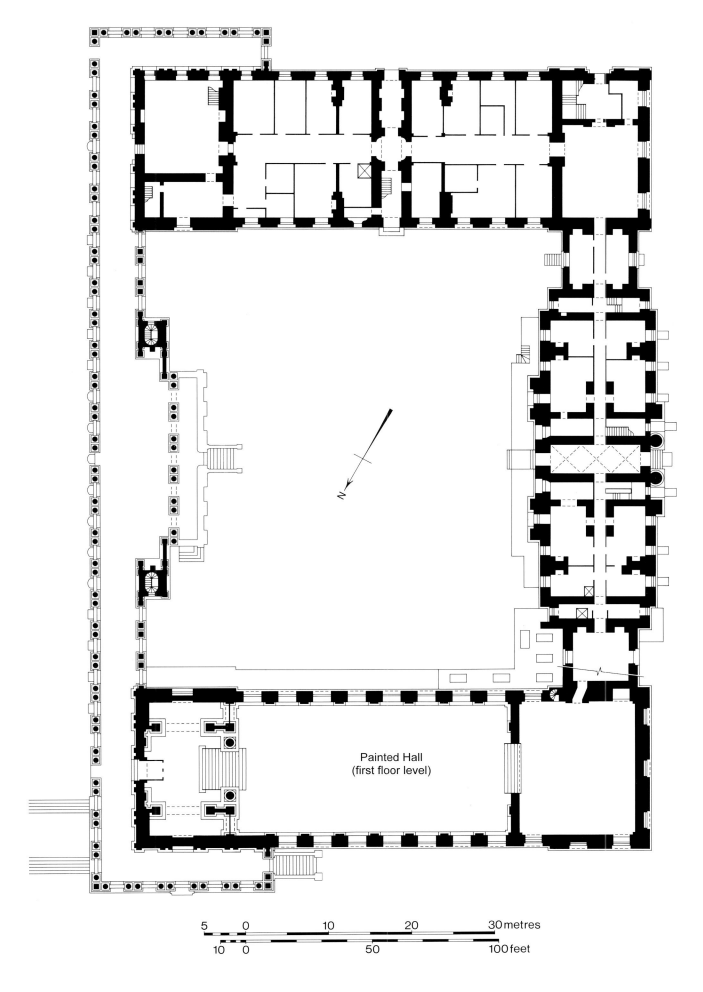

Painted Hall
(first floor level)

5   0   10   20   30 metres

10 0   50   100 feet

KING WILLIAM BUILDING

Preparations for restarting building began in earnest in August 1712 with the advertising in the *Gazette* of the need for masons, bricklayers and carpenters and the beginning of the demolition of the King Charles brick pavilion.[6] More cabins were created in both Charles and William[7] and the directors, recognising that distinctions must be preserved even in death, agreed that part of the south end of the burial ground should be set aside for a vault for the remains of officers, which survives (see chapter 6).[8] Interments continued here until 1749, although the queen had requested the removal of the burial ground from 'her Park' in 1733 and there was also public, local opposition to the continuation of burials.[9] The directors continued to mix issues of principle and practice in their discussions – in 1713 they ordered cheaper beds with coarser linen for the 'ward of slovenly men'.[10]

James Thornhill's painting of the ceiling of the Painted Hall was completed in 1712, but he did not begin the Upper Hall until six years later. The decision to paint the Upper Hall appears to have been an afterthought, since the west wall, at the end, had been built with windows, the central one of which Edward Strong blocked on the inside, taking down the cornice in 1713 before the plastering (on a wooden frame which stands proud of the wall) preparatory to painting: four tons of lime at £5 per ton were obtained from Derbyshire, brought by ship from Gainsborough in Lincolnshire to Porters Key, next to the Customs House, and thence by lighter to Greenwich.[11] The plasterer himself, Mr Hurst, charged £33 13s 6d for his efforts. Later, in 1718, two more windows at the west end were blocked internally and turned into niches.[12]

When building started again, it followed the earlier established pattern and did so at several points. Strong was in 1713 also directing work in the north part of Queen Anne, to create a ward and space for fourteen cabins for very helpless and disabled men for whom there was no room in the Infirmary; the west end pediment of the south range and the steps of the east and west central entrances to King William were about to be erected; work continued on the masonry of the conduits and on miscellaneous works at the Queen's House; and, in a separately accounted activity, work by Strong on the north pavilion of the King Charles base block was under way.[13]

Wren, by 1713, was almost wholly disengaged from the building of the Hospital. His attendance had been infrequent for some years but in May 1713 it was agreed that since he was too busy elsewhere on the queen's business, Hawksmoor and James would take responsibility for drawing up contracts with the masons and preparing the account books for the Board.[14] In 1716 Wren was asked directly whether he was prepared to continue his 'constant inspection' – he excused himself in August on grounds of age, being by this time eighty-three. He ought to have been succeeded by Hawksmoor, but it was Vanbrugh who was appointed Surveyor at a salary of £200 per year.[15] By this time the overall design was established. Hawksmoor was later to claim that he had seen no need for the continuation of the office of Surveyor. Writing to Charles Howard, Lord Carlisle, in 1726, after Vanbrugh in his turn had been succeeded by Colen Campbell, he recalled:

> Sr John Vanb- had obtaind, of Mr Dorrington (when in ye Admiralty), to be Surveyour of Greenwich hospitall, and an allowance of 200 £ p annm,
>
> This place I desired the Lords of ye Admiralty to sink, (as useless) and soe did all that were concernd for they all knew

184   The King William colonnade, looking south.

that I had carryed on, and finished so much as was done of that fabrick; for little more than one hundred pds p annm.

> But Mr Colin Campell Author of a book calld Vitruius Britanicus. Smelling this out, in spite of all ye Lords of ye Admiralty could doe; got ye place Sr John, had made at Greenwich hotell. with all ye allowances therof.
>
> So that in that place we are hansomly saddled – however thank God and yr Lp, for what we have got.[16]

The change in Surveyor prompted a review of procedures. After checking the instructions given to Wren by the Commissioners for building St Paul's Cathedral, the directors agreed that since the general design of the Hospital was already formed and that the Board met fortnightly, there was no need to give general instructions to the Surveyor; rather, he should point out what was needed and then take directions. They required that fortnightly written reports on the works should be provided by the Clerk of Works.[17]

Hawksmoor continued to act in effect as Deputy Surveyor, producing an estimate in 1713 for the finishing of the west side colonnade and the steps leading up to it from the north, and a design for a west wall with gates to replace the wooden fence which stood between the Painted Hall and the kitchen in King Charles. In 1714 Strong worked on the 'grand ascent' from the river, building steps and the 'rustick piers' of a new watergate; on the architrave and frieze of the King William colonnade (fig. 184);[18] and on 'Cleaning ye stonework of the west gate daub'd by ye Painters leting their Pot fall'.[19] Masonry work on the new pavilion progressed rapidly. In the second half of the year the entablature was

185   The archway between the two riverside pavilions of the King Charles Building.

186   The entrance to the Palazzo Farnese at Caprarola, published by G. B. da Vignola, *Regola delli cinque ordini d'architettura*, 1635 (BAL).

set up over the arch of Roche Abbey stone between the two pavilions (fig. 185).[20] The Mannerist arch, for which Robert Jones carved the mouldings in 1715,[21] is taken from Vignola – the entrance to the Palazzo Farnese at Caprarola, a borrowing noted by Fritz Saxl and Rudolf Wittkower, who also recognised that this prominent feature of the palace façade, in its translation to the cramped circumstances at Greenwich, acquired a wholly different character.[22] The portal could have been known to the architect through one of the many editions of Vignola's text (fig. 186)[23] or through the version published by Joseph Moxon in his popular English edition, published in London with a dedication to Wren.[24] The overall responsibility for the design of the new pavilion lay with Hawksmoor, who was asked to produce proposals for its completion in 1715 (fig. 187).[25] The design of the paired pavilions was then copied by John James for the Queen Anne Building (fig. 188).[26]

James's close professional association with Hawksmoor over thirty-five years, not only at Greenwich but also on the Queen Anne churches, has been discussed by Sally Jeffery, who concluded that they were 'partners but not collaborators'.[27] In addition to his work on the river front of the Hospital and his probable design of the vaulted kitchen in the south-east pavilion of the Queen Anne Building,[28] James probably did little original designing at Greenwich until after Hawksmoor's departure when he became sole Clerk of Works (1735–46), assisting Ripley. He probably was responsible for the works on the Queen's House carried out for

Sir William Gifford, but he seems to have regarded himself as over-looked, responsible for the smooth running of the works but not having an opportunity to make significant designs until after the form of the building had been fixed. In his letter of 1711 to the incoming head of the Tory administration, Lord Treasurer Robert Harley, 1st Earl of Oxford, he sounds a note of irritation, and without naming Hawksmoor seeks to advance his superior claims:

> perhaps no person pretending to Architecture among us, Sr Chr Wren excepted, has had ye Advantage of a better Education in ye Latin Italian and French Tongues, a competent Share of Mathematicks and Ten years Instruction in all the practical parts of Building, by Mr Banks, who was well known in their Majestys works in ye late Reign, and yet wthall the Friends I could make, I have never been able to obtain any office in ye publick works that would be a comfortable support, tho' I don't think I ever did anything to disoblige Sr Chr Wren or those that have had ye greatest influence on him.[29]

In 1716 the directors urged the completion of the new King Charles pavilion with all convenient speed: the stairs, doorcases and chimneypieces (one of which was decorated in 1718 by Robert Jones with scrolls and flowers)[30] to be stone and the rooms wainscoted, as neater and more durable than tapestry.[31] At the same time work began on the north pavilions of Queen Anne and continued on the west colonnade[32] and Vanbrugh was asked to fit up

187   The inner courtyard of the King Charles Building, showing the west front of the east range and the south side of the river-front pavilions.

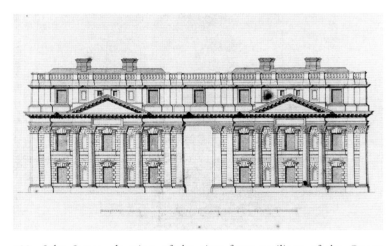

188   John James, elevation of the river-front pavilions of the Queen Anne Building (NMM ART 3/8).

a library-cum-exhibition room at the south end of Charles, replacing the dining room, with desks and bookcases and provision for displays of globes, maps, models and 'marine rarities'. This room, fitted up for the reception of 'persons of quality' who visited the Hospital, was completed in 1718.[33] It reverted to being a dining hall in 1772 but, following the nineteenth-century refitting, was again used as a library during the tenure of the Royal Naval College.

Although work was going on continuously on the site during this period, shortage of money was cited by the directors as disabling them from a more vigorous approach. In 1717 they petitioned for arrears of £23,000 due from the government.[34] A

feeling of irritability surfaces in the meetings because of this slow progress. In 1718 the managers of the works were warned that those who executed designs without the approval of the Board would find themselves defraying the costs themselves, and there were repeated warnings issued to the carpenters in particular for being neglectful. It was difficult to maintain momentum and enthusiasm for the task in hand.[35] The necessary pragmatism of the approach to building the Hospital in financially constrained circumstances is shown not only by the directors' desire to keep a close watch on costs and to beat down the estimates of the craftsmen, but (ironically, given their later reputation for architectural excess) by the eye for a bargain displayed by both Hawksmoor and Vanbrugh. Hawksmoor reported seeing a block of marble suitable for a statue in September 1714; he was asked to survey and price it in October; it was obtained for £125 and brought by barge in November in order to be made into a statue of Queen Anne.[36] Four years later it was determined that this should become a King William instead and James was deputed to approach Francis Bird for a design.[37] Nothing came of this and eventually Governor Sir John Jennings in 1735 paid £400 for the marble to be carved by John Michael Rysbrack into a likeness of King George II in imperial Roman guise. The statue stands, rather eroded, in the central courtyard between the King Charles and Queen Anne Buildings (fig. 47).[38]

Vanbrugh was to act similarly in the provision of a pulpit when, being asked by James in 1716 to supply a design, he recommended the purchase of a pulpit from Hampton Court for £10. This seemed less of a bargain to the directors when they received a bill from the joiner for £8 9s for altering it, but James approved the charge.[39] Cost cutting, although sensible in principle, often appears in retrospect to have been a false economy or a matter of giving with one hand and taking away with the other. In 1718, when concern about security was such that James was being instructed to build a wall along the Romney Road, 8 feet high and 695 feet long at a cost of £180, to replace the paling, with a gate in the centre opposite the gate to the gardens of the Queen's House, the services of the watchman's dog were dispensed with at a saving of a mere £3 per year. James himself, elevated in December 1718 to the post of joint Clerk of Works with Hawksmoor at 5s per day, and put in charge of the stores, found his income reduced one week later, when both men had their standing travelling charges stopped in favour of a system which paid only when they actually travelled, losing their respective annual allowances of £12 (Hawksmoor) and £10 (James).

In 1718 the finishing by John Cleave, the smith, of the iron balustrade of the staircase, and the cleaning of chimneypieces and doorcases 'injured' in the works, signalled the completion of the new King Charles pavilion, at a cost of £13,268, i.e. £1750 above the estimate. A flagstaff on a turret was placed between the two pavilions. This survived only until 1733, but its appearance may be conjectured. Colen Campbell depicted substantial barrel-vaulted turrets on both the King Charles and Queen Anne Buildings (fig. 156)[40] and the likelihood is, given Hawksmoor's stylistic preferences elsewhere, that these were based on the turret as built, being broadly comparable with the upper stage of his unbuilt design for the central tower of the street front of Queen's College, Oxford.[41]

The exterior of the Queen Anne north pavilions, worked on by both Edward Strong senior and junior, was completed by 1720 and rooms for confining disorderly pensioners had been fitted up

189 The south-west staircase in the south range of the King William Building.

in the Queen Anne base wing. In King William, where work had been particularly spasmodic, the upper dormitories of the west range, in which a dramatically over-scale stepped chimneypiece survives, had been paved in 1714, but the main south-west stair, which boasts a magnificently assertive doorway on its upper landing, was not begun until 1719 when Vanbrugh presented a design; whether by himself or by Hawksmoor is not clear – the latter had been asked to produce one seven years earlier (fig. 189).[42] The stair is at an inconvenient distance from the present central entrance to the building, but originally the room to the north, which links the south pavilion with the west range, was a vaulted entrance hall with doors on both east and west sides.

By this time work was again grinding to a halt for lack of funds. The estate of Robert Osboldston was to be divided between the charities of Greenwich Hospital and the 'late Queens Bounty to Poor Clergy', but no money would be forthcoming until after the payment of annuities and legacies.[43] In January 1720 the directors recorded the 'great distress' which the Hospital was suffering. Owed £31,499 and owing £14,066, they found that far from prosecuting the works with vigour, they were at a loss to know how to maintain the standing charge of keeping the pensioners.[44] Edward Strong (father or son) alone was owed £8461, yet in 1721 when James was ordered to stop him working on the King William staircase because of the great debt, Strong preferred to finish it because all the stonework was prepared already. He 'would expect no interest' and wait for the money in the usual way. It

was agreed that no new work would be undertaken until further notice.[45]

THE PAINTED HALL

Sir James Thornhill was paid £2810 in May 1724, four years after submitting his account and twelve years after completing the main ceiling, for the 'Painting done in the great Hall of the Royal Hospital at Greenwich': '540 yards of History with Figures etc: on the Ceiling of the great Hall at £3 p.yard'; '1341 yards of Painting on the Sides with Trophies Flutings etc: at 20sh p.yard'.[46] The directors followed their usual practice of looking for precedents for costs. Thornhill had requested £5 per yard and asked the Board to appoint inspectors who could judge the value of his work. Hawksmoor and James were asked to find out what had been paid elsewhere for comparable painting – Windsor, Hampton Court, Blenheim, Burlington House, Montague House and Oxford – and to consult other ceiling painters. They reported back the costs (not listed in the minutes) and the view of Thornhill's peers that the Hall was 'equall to any in England, of the like kind, and Superiour in the Number of figures and Ornaments'. Thornhill himself sent a note on charges for comparable work: £10 per yard for Rubens at the Banqueting House; £3 12s per yard for Verrio at Hampton Court and Windsor, plus wine, lodgings and a pension of £200 per year; and £700 for Sebastiano Ricci for the staircase at Burlington House. The directors clearly did not doubt the merit of Thornhill's work since they were keen for him to prepare designs for the Upper Hall, 'to make the whole appear Uniform'.[47]

Although the main Hall ceiling was completed in 1712, the scaffolding was still standing in 1713 when Edward Strong opened it to allow the Duke of Ormonde (who was to fall from grace two years later; see Appendix 1) to see the painting, and then unavailingly submitted a bill for £131 'for the wast and consumption of scaffold in ye Great Hall, having stood near four years longer than was first intended and the mason obliged to buy more for want of this'.[48] It was to stand another year before Thornhill, prompted by the promise of a further payment of £200, moved it in order to prime the Upper Hall.[49] But it was not until 1717 that a payment was approved to Strong for the continuing use of his scaffolding and not until the following year that the walls and ceiling were painted a plain colour in preparation.[50] Thornhill's price was cut to £3 per square yard (£1 per square yard more than he was paid for his grisaille paintings of scenes from the Acts of the Apostles in the dome of St Paul's Cathedral)[51] on the grounds that this was his first great work in England, which had 'served as an Introduction to bring him into reputation'. The directors were in a strong bargaining position, since the work was done, and the implication is that he would not have got even £3 if he had not agreed to complete the Upper Hall at the same price. Thornhill is said to have declared himself satisfied, probably to be paid at all, and following acceptance of his sketches he was granted an imprest of £500 in December 1717 to enable him to carry on the work. In 1719 he applied again for the arrears owing and was promised a further £1000.[52]

One thousand copies of Thornhill's undated *An Explanation of the Painting in the Royal-Hospital at Greenwich* were published in English and French around 1726/7,[53] by which time the Hall was already a tourist attraction, with a further 1000 in 1730.[54] A description of the main ceiling – 'a great and noble Design' and

190   James Thornhill, ceiling of the Painted Hall.

191 James Thornhill, ceiling of the Painted Hall: King William and Queen Mary attended by the Virtues. William presents Peace and Liberty to Europe and tramples on Tyranny and Arbitrary Power. Below, the figure of Architecture holds up a drawing of the King William Building.

192 (*above*)   The upper (west) end of the ceiling of the Painted Hall, showing the stern of a British man-of-war being filled by Victory with spoils and trophies taken from the enemy.

193 (*left*)   The upper end of the ceiling of the Painted Hall: detail showing the personification of London sitting on the great rivers, including the Thames and the Tyne, which bring treasures to the city.

194 (*facing page*)   The lower (east) end of the ceiling of the Painted Hall: a captured Spanish galley filled with trophies, with personifications of the River Severn and the River Humber beneath.

'an Honour to our Nation' – had been published already by Richard Steele (fig. 190).[55] There had been a charge for entry since at least December 1720.[56] This is one of the finest pieces of Baroque decorative painting in England. It is the culmination of the phase inaugurated by Rubens at the Banqueting House, but represents a decisive movement away from the rigidly compartmented ceilings of the Venetian Renaissance such as Inigo Jones had designed for both the Banqueting House and the Queen's House, in the direction of the *quadratura* masterpiece painted by

and a final £500, as agreed, for the ceiling and sides of the cupola and vestibule.[72] In all, Thornhill was paid £6685,[73] a sum deemed 'insuffisante' by the writer of an appreciative French guide which was sold at the Hospital.[74] Thornhill was knighted in 1720. By the time that he received his final payment for the work at Greenwich, the public career of 'the greatest History Painter this Kingdom ever produced' was over. His later years 'were employ'd in copying the rich Cartoons of Raphael in the Gallery of Hampton Court, which tho' in Decay, will be reviv'd by his curious Pencil'.[75]

Notwithstanding the conventional praise which he received in his obituary, Thornhill has been unfortunate in his critical reception. Since he was not a specialist in either of the two genres beloved by the English, the recognisable portrait or the identifiable landscape, he has been faintly praised as a decorative painter who was not as good as his Italian contemporaries who were working in England, Sebastiano Ricci and Antonio Pellegrini. Since few artists of the early eighteenth century anywhere were as accomplished as the two Venetians, this is a criticism which is hardly fair. On the evidence presented in the main ceiling of the Painted Hall, Thornhill was not just the finest native-born decorative painter, he was one of the best English painters there has been, and as such has been remarkably neglected in the literature of English art. This is an exceptionally well-organised work of art with a sophisticated iconographical programme which achieves a balance between the specific – the beneficent power and authority of the monarchy, supported by Virtue and Wisdom – and the generic – the seasons, the signs of the zodiac and the elements. Programmatically, in its celebration of the triumph of the Protestant monarchy under the later Stuarts, and the ordered Hanoverian Succession, all sustained by maritime power and mercantile prosperity, it is also a narrative *tour de force*. Stylistically, while the depictions of William and Mary are stiffly formal, in the tradition of court portraiture, there is a strikingly Raphaelesque quality to the kneeling figures in front of them, and elsewhere, particularly in the personifications of the English rivers at each end of the ceiling, a delightfully Venetian fluidity of form. Hawksmoor was not exaggerating when he referred to 'the excellent Sir James Thornhill'.[76]

The atmospheric pollution and lack of adequate ventilation in the Painted Hall, notwithstanding its only occasional ceremonial use for dining, must have been considerable, since within a relatively short time the mildew was such as to require the cleaning and 'refreshing' of the paintings in 1733–5, then again in 1743 by 'Mr Bouttats'.[77] It was 'restored' again in 1752 and in 1777 a further cleaning and reparation was carried out by Mr Devis (probably the fashionable portraitist Arthur, rather than his half-brother, the landscape painter Anthony) for £1000 on the recommendation of the Surveyor, James Stuart.[78] Most of these interventions, and those which followed in 1797, 1807, 1824, 1845 and 1937, involved varnishing, so by the time of the restoration (completed in 1960 after over two years of work by the Ministry of Works team) there were over fifteen layers on the ceiling. These were removed in stages, a procedure rendered the more difficult by Thornhill's tendency to add varnish to his oil medium in order to achieve a glazed effect.[79]

★   ★   ★

202   The north pavilions of the Queen Anne Building, with the 'Five-Foot Walk' next to the river.

Work on the Hospital during the early 1720s was confined to general maintenance and to the completion of parts begun. The grand stone staircase in King William was completed in 1721; the wooden fittings in the Infirmary were dismantled and then reassembled in 1722 to enable 'a Man to kill the Bugs';[80] the capitals on the north pavilions of Queen Anne were carved in 1723 (fig. 202).[81] In 1721 Hawksmoor was sufficiently underemployed to make improvements to his own house on site, raising the eaves, at his own expense, in order to accommodate another bed.[82] Robert Jones, the long-serving carver, who was to die the following year, had, unlike Edward Strong, been fully paid for his work to date, but in acknowledgement of the forced inactivity which was ruining him, he was paid an imprest of £50 in 1721 by a Board 'sensible of his necessities'. The members had just received the encouraging news that the Treasury was to supply £10,000, although, given the sums owing (£15,000 in 1722), this in itself was not sufficient to enable a start on significant works. Earlier in the building programme, progress had been hampered during the War of the Spanish Succession when the seamen who

203   Nicholas Hawksmoor, east front of the Queen Anne Building.

had not been paid could not be expected to contribute their six-pences; now that the nation was at peace, there were fewer ships at sea so the revenue was less. Maintenance alone of pensioners and buildings was exceeding income by £3000 per year. A pro-posal for a lottery was put to the House of Commons with the aim of raising £50,000 and endowing the Hospital as William had intended, in order to 'render that noble Charity more extensive, by taking a greater Number of Pensioners and encourage men to love a Seafaring life, at the Prospect of such a Provision for them when they are worn out in their Countries Service'. As the first of its kind, the Board was concerned to make sure that the pro-posed lottery would not be 'too much crowded with tickets'.[83]

During this period of relative inactivity in building, the direc-tors were confined largely to matters of housekeeping. They approved the expenditure of £40 on green serge curtains for the north and south windows of the chapel; the making of a new suit for a new pensioner, Richard Jewell, who 'is too bigg for any of the new Cloathes in Stores'; and the purchase of £60 worth of

medicines as a precaution against the spread of plague from France, an expenditure which was in part prompted in a spirit of com-petition since Chelsea was ignoring the threat. The Hospital was by 1721 an established institution with a public role beyond the terms of its foundation. The appointment of a porter, memorable if for no other reason because of his name – John Webb – was in direct response to this circumstance. Webb, gowned and carrying a staff at all times when on duty, was to take care of the gates, to keep out children and vagabonds, to wind the clock, to take care of visitors, treating with respect any visiting gentleman or lady, and in a manner akin to Samuel Beckett's Watt, to serve the consid-erable quantity of surplus broth or soup to the poor and to the families of pensioners at the outer gate. He also took on the responsibility for showing the Painted Hall[84] and in 1730, fol-lowing the death of the sluice man, his duties were extended, presumably laying aside his gown and staff, to 'opening and shut-ting the sluices of the common boghouses at £5 per annum'.[85] Webb proved to be a good and faithful servant to the Hospital

204 The courtyard of the Queen Anne Building, looking south.

and when he died in 1742, leaving his wife Sarah with four small children in 'necessitous circumstances', she was given a position as a nurse.[86]

In 1724 the directors anticipated an improvement in financial fortunes when the king mentioned Greenwich in his speech to Parliament. The clerks of works were asked to draw up an abstract of works completed and, with the Surveyor, to work out the costs of completion. The overall estimate of £150,000 included Vanbrugh's costing of the stone facing of the west front of the Queen Anne Building at £6500 and the paving of the west colonnade at £598. Stone was reserved for the outer faces of Queen Anne (fig. 203), the interior court being finished in brick, with stone frontispieces, in overall appearance very similar in its quintessential late seventeenth- to early eighteenth-century sobriety to such understated buildings as Chelsea Hospital and James Gibbs's church of St Peter's, Vere Street, Marylebone (1721–4) (fig. 204).

PHASE 3: 1725–33

King Charles Building: flag turret removed.

Queen Anne Building: north pavilions fitted out; south pavilions erected; west front of the main block faced in stone.

In May 1725 approval was given to proceed with the Queen Anne front at a cost not exceeding £7000, on the basis of estimates provided by James (fig. 206).[87] In addition to the principal masonry work, carried out by Edward Strong the younger (whose father had died the year before) and Christopher Cass in 1725–6, decorative flowers and husks were carved in the soffits of the open arches of the west entrance by Richard Chicheley, who had succeeded Robert Jones (fig. 205), the roof was constructed and the windows sashed, rather belatedly – the absence of windows prompted Vanbrugh in the last meeting he attended before he died

to report floor damage caused by water penetration.[88] The pediment was to remain empty although Ripley in 1753 proposed it as the site for a 'New Clock and Carving'.[89] The General Court preferred to put the clock in the tower above the Chapel, with wind dials above the Painted Hall.[90] Vanbrugh was succeeded as Surveyor in May 1726 by Colen Campbell, who held the post for only three years – long enough to preside over works of completion, but not to make any significant contribution to the design, much though he might have wished to do so. In 1728 he joined Hawksmoor and James in arguing strongly at a public meeting of the Hospital governors against the potential false economy of using the coarsely textured and badly coloured Bath stone in London, which had been suggested as a cheap solution to the recurring problems of supply from Portland.[91]

As work proceeded, the directors again periodically found it necessary to issue reminders about the purpose of the enterprise. In 1726 the Governor Sir John Jennings, finding that there was a new plan for a state room in Queen Anne, possibly by Campbell, warned officers not to presume to change the agreed design, but notwithstanding Jennings's desire to get on with building wards for seamen, the works again slowed down and in 1727 the windows and doors of the north pavilion were boarded up and work on the wards themselves was desultory.[92] It was not until September 1728 that the accounts were submitted for the oak roofing and the carving of the west front and south pavilion of Queen Anne; the completing of the west and south dormitories of King William, 'in Order to the Receiving The Pensioners'; and the creation of fourteen additional cabins in King Charles, by narrowing those already there in order to increase the accommodation.[93]

205 The entrance vestibule of the Queen Anne Building, looking north, which mirrors the vestibule of King Charles. The glazing of the arcade was removed in 1999.

206   The west front of the Queen Anne Building, photographed by Helmut Gernsheim. The facing of this façade in stone was probably carried out under the direction of John James.

By September 1727 the sum of £210,741 had been spent on the building with a further £41,856 spent on 'contingent works', which included the Queen's House, the park and gardens, the temporary chapel, the cemetery and salaries.[94] In January 1728 Campbell, Hawksmoor and James estimated that a further £131,750 would be needed in order to complete the whole building for the accommodation of 1200 seamen (with a further 200 in an infirmary). It was clear to the directors that a secure fund was required for both completion and running costs, which when the full complement was accommodated would be £25,053 per annum. Since the current income was only £12,517, with only 450 men accommodated, they determined with irrepressible optimism to try once again to wrest King William's promised £2000 per year from the Crown and embarked on further cost-cutting measures. These included the reduction by half of the salaries of the Governor (to £500 per year) and the naval officers (Lieutenant-Governor, four captains and one lieutenant), the reduction of the number of Clerks of Works to one as soon as one of them died, and the loss of the £50 allowance to Hawksmoor for 'drawing and designing'. The Surveyor's £200 per

year was temporarily at risk but it was acknowledged yet again that while works continued, so should his salary. By completing seven wards in the base wing of Queen Anne, at an estimated cost of £3500, and the King William dormitories, a further 220 men could be housed, with another eighty if the sick and infirm on the lower floor of King William could be moved to an infirmary, but this, costing £15,000, was in the realms of hope rather than expectation. The costings, accompanied by a plan of the buildings drawn by Hawksmoor, were submitted to the Admiralty in May 1728.[95] The results were positive, Parliament agreeing an annual grant of £10,000. One year later, the General Court, at its quarterly meeting, expressed confidence that the finances were on a sounder footing and ordered the prosecution of the stalled works:[96] in Queen Anne, flooring the ground floor and plastering the upper floors of the base wing; painting cabins and installing sash windows in the main block; wainscoting the rooms, plastering the ceilings, fitting up kitchens, carving mouldings, chimneypieces and doorcases in the north pavilions; flooring the interior and dressing the stonework of the south pavilions.[97]

By January 1730 almost £5000 had been spent on these works

of completion and the new Surveyor, the much maligned Thomas Ripley, was in charge. It fell to this lesser Palladian architect, appointed following the death of Colen Campbell in September 1729, to ensure the completion of one of the greatest of Baroque buildings. Hawksmoor, passed over again for a post which ought to have been his by right, quickly tried to circumvent his new boss but was told by the directors not to bring forward propositions without showing them first to the Surveyor. His first task in the new regime was to estimate the cost of a turret over the Queen Anne north pavilions to match the one on King Charles, 'if the erecting thereof shall be found necessary'.[98] Ripley proceeded with some vigour, in 1730 producing a scheme for fitting 300 more men into Queen Anne and in the same year overseeing the completion of the north-east pavilion for the occupation of the physician, captain, lieutenant, secretary and treasurer.[99] The south pavilions were roofed and the attic balustrade erected, and in both the main building and the base block, doorcases and staircases were installed, walls were rendered, ceilings plastered and sash windows installed and glazed.[100] Work was continuing throughout the Queen Anne Building in 1731: panelling was installed in the wards of the main range; cabins were set up in the base block; a bathing cistern installed in one of the north pavilions; capitals cut for the piers of the vaulted room underneath the kitchen which was being completed in the south-east pavilion; and the roofs of both blocks were cut in order to join them to the south pavilions.[101] The ground-floor south-west ward, now the Collingwood Room, was fitted up as a dining hall and, in acknowledgement of overcrowding, pews were removed from the temporary chapel in order to accommodate a further 200 pensioners, taking the overall total to 900.[102] The use of the Painted Hall for dining appears during this period to have been reserved for special occasions: the anniversary of the king's accession (11 June) being one such, and the birthday of William III (4 November) another, when pensioners dined in the body of the Hall, and officers in the Upper Hall.[103]

The prosecution of the works under Ripley in the early 1730s, with a view to completing the accommodation in Queen Anne and to generally tidying up the site, by clearing and paving the Great Court and erecting a statue of the king, initially was rapid, but continued to be tempered by the need for restraint. Rather than erecting a turret on Anne, it was decided that symmetry could be more simply achieved by removing the one on Charles, which had cost £800 to erect and would cost a further £150 to dismantle, and substituting 'ornaments'. The turret had besides caused problems by causing the chimneys to smoke. In 1731 Ripley produced proposals for completing the Hospital and for enclosing it next to the river in order to provide a footpath – the 'Five Foot Walk' – for the local residents.[104] Hawksmoor, having lost his annual fee of £50 for drawing and designing, continued to cause alarm by producing unsolicited schemes, submitting a bill for £137 which was referred to the Surveyor for ratification. Ripley pragmatically delayed for a year before recommending a payment of £60 in May 1732, which was not approved by the General Court until December. The directors determined that the Hospital should be completed 'according to the Original Design, and in the most frugal manner', but completion had to wait because with the account books balanced between revenue and expenses at £22,767, there was no scope for further works, despite good intentions. In July 1733 payments to the Clerks of Works

were suspended.[105] Hawksmoor petitioned on the grounds of hardship and long service, with the result that both he and James continued in post, paid for by Ripley himself, whose offer to do so was readily accepted by the shameless General Court in 1734.[106]

The minutes of meetings inevitably offer only a partial view of the attitudes of those involved, but in principle the directors appear to have been motivated, in their desire to finish the task in hand, by a paternalism which worked in favour of the well-behaved, but consistently caused problems whenever cost-saving was allowed to get in the way of common sense. In endeavouring to fulfil the overall requirements of the magnificent charitable foundation, they tended to lose sight of how their actions might affect individuals, and in the manner of institutions everywhere, the hardest task for the directors of the Hospital was the achievement of consistency. In 1717 they took the admirable step of ensuring that the lower officers of the house 'worn out by age, or by any other Casualty' should be superannuated on half-pay and maintained by the Hospital.[107] By 1742 the number of superannuated nurses was such that the Hospital had to review its generosity, limiting a reduced payment to those who had served at least seven years.[108] In 1735 they allowed the lunatic pensioner Edward Hill, who was deemed unfit to wear the Hospital clothing, to be given money in lieu, but 'this is not to be a precedent', and the following year the 'weak and infirm' pensioner John Simpson was given money in lieu of provisions since he was unable to eat the Hospital food.[109] In 1738 Robert Webb, a labourer on the site for twenty years, had laboured his last upon falling into a well, which is now filled in, in the Jacobean undercroft under the temporary chapel while cleaning a drain, and breaking his shoulder: the Hospital continued to pay him, at least 'for the time being'.[110] In matters of cleanliness, the directors also reacted appropriately at a time when this was a relative concept. As Georges Vigarello has shown, while it had long been the case that it was the washing of linen rather than the bathing of the body which was an indicator of cleanliness, by the eighteenth century the number of such washes was changing: 'standards long the norm amongst the elite began to be adopted by institutions designed for the masses'. There was an increase in both the number of shirts supplied to the sick and the frequency with which they were changed.[111] In 1741 the directors, in keeping with this trend, finding that many pensioners were 'dirty and lousy', especially in the summer, approved a doubling of the allowance to two shirts per week in June, July and August.[112] In 1756 they put a stop to the common practice of the nurses of obtaining wills in their favour from the sick and helpless, 'by irregular methods'.[113]

In the matter of Samuel Clarke however, they proved to be far less sympathetic. When the directors decided in 1728 that two watchmen were no longer required, Clarke, the longer-serving of the two, was allowed to continue for a short period but the General Court resolved that having got rid of the watchmen's dog and one of the watchmen, they could readily save more money by sacking the other and assigning duties to volunteer pensioners. A similar ploy had failed in the past when the pensioners had refused in 1705 to sweep up, so labourers were employed.[114] Clarke, losing his job at the end of 1728, found himself eight months later in Maidstone Gaol for stealing lead from the site. He and his wife Mary both petitioned the directors in vain for bail, and in September 1729 his family was given one month's notice to quit their tied house. Mary, equipped with a letter of attorney from her unfortunate husband, at least was able to claim his pay, but the Hospital failed to show further mercy and Clarke and his accomplice, pensioner Walter Shaw, were prosecuted for theft in 1730.[115] The constables of Greenwich were paid 2 guineas for holding the miscreants and conveying them to Maidstone. The following year Alexander Blakely was discharged from the Hospital's service following his trial at Maidstone for buggery, despite having been acquitted for lack of evidence.[116] Such proceedings show the institution in a poor and petty light. It was not until 1851, when large numbers of people were expected to visit Greenwich during the Great Exhibition, that the Metropolitan Police were formally introduced to maintain order at the Hospital. For over a century this job, which required some tact and diplomacy, was assigned to pensioners who through the very act of volunteering for a thankless and meddling task ought to have disqualified themselves. They were frequently insulted and assaulted by watermen. In July 1733 pensioner Adam Friendship, acting on orders not to let anyone through the gate with a lighted pipe, was abused and thrown against a stone by pipe-smoking waterman John Mitchell with such force that he broke his thigh. The Hospital prosecuted, but following a petition from Mitchell's wife Jane, agreed to relent if Mitchell apologised and agreed to paying the costs of the action. Regrettably, it was reported, he 'continues insolent', so the prosecution went ahead.[117]

In 1739 it was again reported that several boatswains and pensioners were abused and insulted in the execution of their duties. A recent incident was recounted as typical: the Boatswain of the Guard, 'acquainting one of the Labourers of the Works, that was Pissing in the Publick way, that that was not a proper place for so doing, the Person spoke to, without any further Provocation, first struck him with his Fist in the Face, and then beat him with a Stick he had in his hand'. The directors agreed to take measures, including the employment of a solicitor who would prosecute on behalf of the Hospital, preserving its rules and orders, and doing justice to those on guard, 'or any other who endeavour to hinder people from those irregular practices'.[118] So the reduction of short-term costs by sacking efficient watchmen (the silence in the minutes concerning their activities suggests that they were indeed efficient), replacing them with men predisposed to being irritatingly officious, in the long run probably resulted in greater expense and certainly occasioned the need for a disproportionate amount of discussion.

The police, although at first regarded with jealousy and suspicion, 'disarmed opposition by the conciliatory and effective manner in which they discharge their duties'. They had the advantage not only of being above suspicion of favouritism or prejudice, but were also fitter than the pensioners, able to deal with the drunken or insubordinate, although most were of 'generally good and docile disposition', and less likely to suffer from the periodic fatal epidemics of colds and flu to which ninety-nine pensioners succumbed in January 1837.[119]

*   *   *

PHASE 4: 1735–51

Queen Anne Building: interior of south pavilions fitted out; temporary chapel removed.

Queen Mary Building erected; corridor to King William constructed.

In March 1735 Ripley estimated that the buildings could be completed at a cost of £80,444 and in April laid his plans before the Board. The estimates included £340 for the still incomplete King William, £6000 for the interior of the south pavilions of Queen Anne, £3000 for walls and gates, and £1500 for fitting up an apartment for the Governor in the south-east pavilion of King Charles, including new marble fireplaces, and later, at additional cost, the conversion of the old brewhouse into a stable and coach-house capable of accommodating eight horses and two coaches, subsequently increased to respectively twelve and three.[120] But the principal cost was an estimated £62,829 for Queen Mary, considerably less than the estimate of 1708 for a rather grander building, with a further £2750 for fitting up a chapel. Carrying out this final phase of the main works was made possible through the passing in Parliament in 1735 of

> An Act for the Application of the Rents & Profits of the Estates forfeited by the attainders of James late Earl of Derwentwater & Chas Radcliffe, [by which] it is enacted that the Rents & Profits of the said Estates shall, during his Mat.'s Estate & interest therein (subject to the payment of the Debts) be apply'd towards the finishing the Building of the Royal Hospital for Seamen at Greenwich, & afterwards towards the Maintainance of the Decrepit Seamen.

The sums involved were not such as to permit excess: Ripley's Queen Mary Building is the least magnificent of all, and he had to struggle with the Board to achieve even as much as he did. The annual rents from the forfeited estates amounted to a little less than £6000, with encumbrances of over £2000, bringing an annual profit of £3705. Many of the estates however were out of lease or were ill-managed, and it was considered that if the lead mines and collieries were 'Lett to proper Adventurers', they would realise a further £2000 per year. The governors of the Hospital were empowered to appoint stewards, receivers and bailiffs to ensure proper management and to maximise revenue.[121]

In July 1735 Ripley's full salary of £200 per year was restored, with James again paid officially, at £60 per year, initially as Clerk to the Surveyor, then as Clerk of Works and Storekeeper. Hawksmoor, who was to die in March 1736, was no longer involved.[122] Following the opening-up of the foundations of the Queen Mary Building and an estimate of the brickwork required (97,400 place bricks at 12s per thousand, and 29,000 grey stocks at 17s per thousand), costings were estimated for the stonework of the dining room under the Chapel, and for that of the adjacent kitchen, and workmen invited to tender.[123] As work got under way on the building, and one of the last of the old houses on the site of the Queen Mary court (lived in by the Governor's secretary) was demolished,[124] the directors, inspired by progress and the possibility of still more income, revived the idea of a twice-weekly market at the west side of the Hospital. Ripley's proposal for a building costing £800 was rejected in 1737 in favour of spending £300 on sheds and booths, with a further £150 for paving.[125]

The plan for Queen Mary established by Hawksmoor in 1728[126] was a mirror image of King William, with rooms to each side of central corridors in the east and south wings, and powerfully articulated façades. Ripley's first proposal, possibly drawn by John James, was greatly to simplify the façades and to provide a mixture of small cells in the south wing and large rooms in the east (fig. 207).[127] His subsequent plan, prepared in the 1730s, shows a further simplification towards the 'deformed Barrac' feared by Hawksmoor, with corridors giving access to uniform rows of cells, and with remarkably restrained staircase provision (fig. 208).[128] The east-wing corridors are vaulted to the north (fig. 209), but not to the south, which suggests either a hierarchy of occupation, or simply cost-cutting. Although Queen Mary and King William had been intended to be alike, in Queen Mary 'more regard has been paid to convenience than to ornament, and the whole front of it is of Portland stone and in a plain style'.[129] Ironically, although

Queen Mary was designed to be cheaper and 'more convenient' than King William, it proved to be much less flexible. Its stone and brick partition walls, erected in order to inhibit the spread of fires, proved less capable of adaptation than William's wooden partitions, since they could not be moved without threatening the structure (fig. 210). Towards the time of the Hospital's closure, when consideration was being given to using Queen Mary as a hospital for the sick, the cabins were characterised as 'retired fire-proof safes' in which disease would lodge, encouraged by poor ventilation and lively vermin.[130]

The grand stair proposed by Hawksmoor at the south-east corner of Queen Mary, reflecting the King William stair, was abandoned in favour of an elegant geometrical stair at the west end of the south range (fig. 211), with two secondary stairs, recorded in a drawing, near the centre of the east range (one of which has been removed for the installation of a lift).[131] For the building with

207 Ground plan of the Royal Hospital prepared under the direction of Thomas Ripley, showing his simplification of the plan of the Queen Mary Building (NMM ART 3/4).

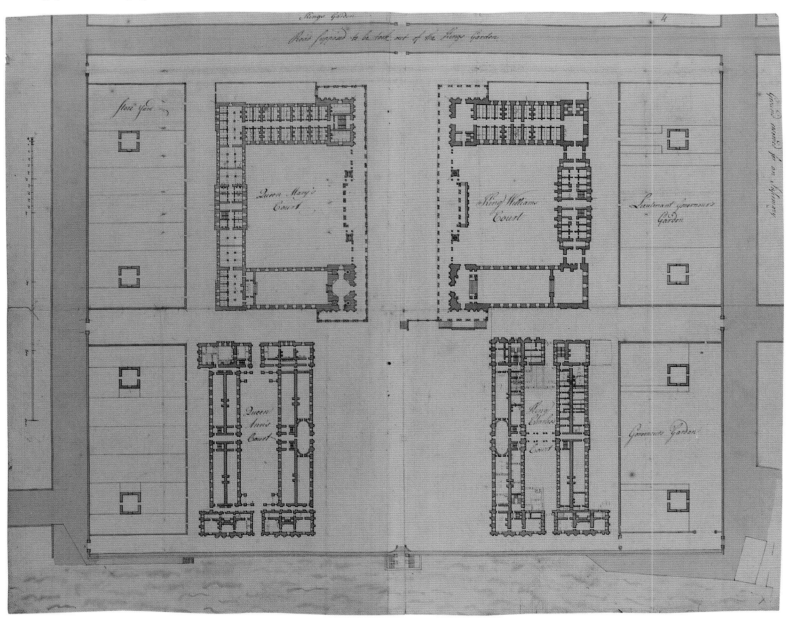

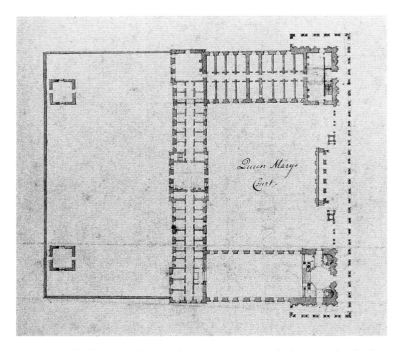

208   Detail of a ground plan of the Royal Hospital, showing the further simplifications by Thomas Ripley to the plan of the Queen Mary Building (NMM ART 3/5B).

the highest occupancy, this modest arrangement cannot have been other than a serious impediment to circulation. This same drawing, and a variant from the same period, proposes further (unbuilt) utilitarian blocks to the west of William and Charles.[132]

Towards the end of 1736 the Queen Mary Building had risen as far as the cills of the ground-floor windows and a further 524,520 bricks were ordered the following year (figs 212–15).[133] Minor works had continued in this period in the south pavilions of Queen Anne but greater impetus was given to that part of the site by the death of a pensioner who was killed instantly in January 1738 by falling down the stone stairs at the south end of the building which had been left unfinished (fig. 216).[134] It was anticipated that by the end of 1739 the walls of the Chapel would be up to 25 feet above the plinth and the tower beneath the dome would have reached the base of the columns.[135] In the south-east pavilion of Queen Anne, the vaulting of the cellars and the kitchen and the building of partition walls was carried out throughout the building,[136] while on the ground floor of the main block, the wainscoting of cabins continued in both west wards.[137]

In 1731, in an attempt to achieve more precise accounting, at the inevitable cost of greater bureaucracy, the directors had effected a division in the accounts between new works and works of maintenance which did not require immediate authorisation.[138] It is a truth which ought to be universally acknowledged, that directors of organisations tend to interest themselves with the controllable minutiae of processes, to the detriment of the achieve-

209   A vaulted, central corridor in the east range of the Queen Mary Building.

210   The third-floor corridor in the west range of the King William Building.

211 (*facing page*)   The geometrical stair at the west end of the south range of the Queen Mary Building.

212 The courtyard of the Queen Mary Building. The south wall of the Chapel is on the right. The steps up to the colonnade were added by Joseph Kay in 1835.

213 The west front of the east range of the Queen Mary Building.

214 The east side of the east range of the Queen Mary Building.

215 The south side of the south range of the Queen Mary Building.

216   The staircase at the south end of the east range of the Queen Anne Building.

217   The underground corridor between the King William and Queen Mary Buildings, looking east.

ment of the larger ends for which they were appointed. The steady growth in bureaucratic procedures at the Hospital, throughout its life, was strongly criticised in 1860 by the investigator who reported to the Commission of Enquiry into the running of the institution that the minutely detailed accounting system involved 'an immense amount of labour, without, it appears to me, any commensurate return'.[139] The directors had always been at some pains to ensure that works did not proceed without their approval; now, with tighter accounting in mind, they had provided a loophole which enabled enterprising officers to take executive action. This they did immediately, getting retrospective approval in December for the 'necessary houses' built in the summer at the Queen Anne Building, without which, the directors agreed, life for the new pensioners would have been 'very inconvenient':[140] even with the new facilities, a journey of some distance was still entailed. A more significant exploitation of the loophole occurred in 1741 when Ripley built the underground communication corridor between the King William and Queen Mary blocks (now known anachronistically as the Chalk Walk, having been given the name of the long chalk-groined basement room at right angles to it which runs underneath the east colonnade) (figs 217, 218 and 231).[141] Ripley apologised to the directors for his 'mistake' in believing that the corridor had been marked on the original plan. The directors approved payment for this essential improvement to the circulation, but saved face by reiterating their order that no building should be carried on without their prior approval of plans and estimates,[142] and ordered that all plans and elevations of the Hospital delivered to Parliament should be bound in a book for their future reference.[143]

By 1742 work on the Queen Anne south pavilions was complete and work on Queen Mary had advanced as far as leading the dome and carrying out the carpentry of the lantern,[144] which was leaded the following year.[145] By 1740 the accommodation in the King William temporary infirmary was insufficient for the numbers of sick and helpless pensioners, so extra space was arranged in the Council Ward on the ground floor of Queen Mary. In 1743, following serious complaints to the directors, a more generous replacement space was arranged elsewhere in the south range of Queen Mary, utilising the two lower storeys.[146] It was clear that the complaints could not properly be answered until a dedicated building had been erected. In King William, the deficiencies were numerous: there was nowhere to prepare the specific diets required, so cures were greatly retarded; there was no laboratory for medicines; the wards were too small and inconvenient, so the sick could not adequately be grouped according to the nature of their afflictions; the wards were not secure, so liquor could easily and improperly be brought in; there were delays in providing sufficient beds; and many enfeebled and disabled men who were not sick had to be housed on upper floors, to their great inconvenience, because the ground floor was occupied by infirmary cases – 'the sick, hurt and helpless'. In short, without a detached infirmary, the whole Hospital was inconvenienced and, moreover, put at risk in 'epidemical and contagious' situations. But there was still insufficient money to build the long-planned new Infirmary; indeed there was now a brief hiatus in all building work, with the principal part of it finished. The precedent of suspending the post of Clerk of Works having been set a decade earlier, it was again invoked in 1743 and Ripley unfortunately again found himself responsible for John James's salary once James had, with good reason after forty years' service, registered regret.[147] In fact, James had little more to do with the works on which he had spent the best part of his working life. The house which he had occupied, next to the Queen Mary Building, was demolished in October 1745 as part of a general tidying of the site as the Hospital approached completion.[148] James died seven months later,[149] as work began again under Ripley's direction on fitting up apartments and completing the Chapel. An attempt by Ripley to build the planned pavilions at the south-east and south-west corners of the site to house respectively the Surveyor and the Clerk of the Works, and the Clerk of the Cheque, was foiled by the directors who considered that there was room enough for offices for officers on the ground floor of Queen Mary.[150]

The Surveyor had more success with the Chapel (fig. 219). In 1746 the holes for the trusses supporting the gallery were cut and George Worrall submitted his account for the enriched plaster cornice.[151] The directors had approved the drawing for the ceiling,

218 The Chalk Walk, in use as a Smoking Gallery in 1865 (*Illustrated London News*, 22 April 1865).

219 T. Malton and G. Bickham, engraving of Ripley's Chapel in the Queen Mary Building.

The Inside of the New Chapel in the Royal Hospital at Greenwich.

220   Sebastiano Ricci, *Resurrection*, Chapel of the Royal Hospital, Chelsea.

but when its finishing was put in hand in 1747, they slyly questioned the need for gilding since it would cost £850 and had not been estimated. Furthermore, gilding had not of course been shown on the (black and white) drawing.[152] Wiser counsels prevailed and the directors came to the view that 'as the Hospital is a Magnificent National Building . . . [the Chapel] should be finished in an Elegant manner suitable to the other Parts of the Building'.[153] The gilding, and the carving of cherubims' heads (by William Barlow) over the arch at the east end, was carried out in 1747.[154] Decorative plasterwork and marble paving followed in 1748,[155] the great doors and the organ case[156] in 1749[157] and the wainscot and altar rail in 1750.[158] For the consecration of the Chapel, the precedent of Chelsea was again considered, Queen Mary's directions to the Lord Bishop of London being reviewed. In one further respect, the governors of Greenwich appear to have tried to emulate Chelsea, without success. Although Robert Pope was paid £45 in 1749 for four paintings in the Chapel, a grander gesture had been contemplated. At Chelsea around 1715, during the great age of Italian decorative painting in England, Sebastiano Ricci had produced the magnificent *Resurrection* for the apse of the Chapel (fig. 220).[159] There is a reference of 1738 to a painting proposed for Greenwich by the 'famous Signor Amaconi', the Venetian Jacopo Amigoni.[160] During his ten years in England, he was responsible among other things for the splendid *Return of the Prodigal Son*, presented in 1734 to Emmanuel College, Cam-

bridge, and for the sumptuous decoration of around 1732 of Moor Park, Hertfordshire, with scenes from the story of Jupiter and Io, replacing Thornhill's paintings of the heroic virtues. He left England in 1739, having painted 'several historical great works masterly and well approved of but in that kind of painting finding not full employment'.[161] Any sadness at the missed opportunity of such a commission for Greenwich should be tempered by the fact that the painting would not have survived the fire which gutted the Chapel on 2 January 1779.

The governors, by 1747 determined to finish the building at last, invited Ripley to produce plans and estimates for a detached infirmary, and to suggest ways of accommodating more pensioners. There was still no unanimity on the need for a separate infirmary. Ripley's estimate for a building costing £40,000 was deemed too high, so he produced a plainer design to be built at half the cost. Even this did not receive approval since some considered still that part of Queen Mary would serve.[162] It was not until after James Stuart had taken over the Surveyorship on Ripley's death in 1758 that the Infirmary for 200 sick, with apartments for a physician, a surgeon and a dispenser, 'as plain and inexpensive as possible', was agreed (see chapter 7). Stuart's design, 'a very proper one for the purpose', was approved in 1763.[163] Following its erection, the conversion of the old infirmaries to cabins in Queen Mary allowed for the accommodation of a further 200 men, to bring the total to 2000.[164]

221 The west front of the east range of the Queen Mary Building, drawn in 1777 to show the form of the pediment known as 'Ripley's Saddle' and the manner in which it was proposed to alter the building (Westminster City Archives).

By 1751 the Hospital was structurally complete: Wren's overall design, conceived over fifty years earlier, had been fulfilled at a cost of around £400,000. The new Chapel was in use, the temporary one removed, the apartments in the south pavilion of Queen Anne had been fitted up in 1748,[165] and the great geometrical stair in the south range of Queen Mary completed in 1749.[166] Ripley set the seal on his achievement by directing the building of the new west entrance gateway in 1751, dividing the Hospital from the town (see chapter 6). He failed in his attempt to persuade the governors of the need for a clock tower, but he did achieve a clock in 1754: over the Chapel, with two dials, one pointing west to King William and the other north to the river.[167] His had been a notable achievement. The inspirational designs of Wren and Hawksmoor had determined the overall layout of the site, and they had been responsible for those features which give the Hospital its singularity as a piece of great architecture. But Ripley had ensured that it was finished, and that it fulfilled its function. Certainly, the Queen Mary Building is the least dramatic of all the blocks of the Hospital, and his one external flourish, the pediment on the east range known as 'Ripley's Saddle', which caused the chimneys to smoke and had 'long been considered as a disgrace to the other parts of the Structure . . . , above which it is seen at a great distance', was removed in 1777 (fig. 221).[168] His Chapel also betrayed no trace of architectural or artistic grandeur; but by 1751 the magnificence intended by Queen Mary, which was to be criticised by Samuel Johnson, was no longer applicable. The pragmatic Ripley had completed the building in the less ostentatious spirit of his times, although in 1767 there were still those with a lingering desire for the fulfilment of the late queen's vision. When Stuart and the civil engineer John Smeaton investigated the construction of a new wharf at a cost of £7000, Smeaton noted that it would prove not only useful in cutting down the damp which afflicted the buildings next to the river, but would 'add greatly to the Grandeur and Magnificence of the Hospital'. The extension was deferred when the Clerk of Works, William

Robinson, reported that there had been no tidal flooding for over a year and, anyway, it was his view that the damp came from the drains rather than from the river. The work was to go ahead ten years later, in 1777, by which time Robert Mylne had succeeded Robinson as Clerk of Works.[169]

LATER WORKS: 1769–89 AND 1811–35

King Charles Building: south-west pavilion rebuilt; underground communication corridor to King William constructed; base block rebuilt.

Queen Mary Building: Chapel reconstructed after fire; steps built from courtyard to colonnade.

King William Building: Nelson pediment sculpture installed; steps built from courtyard to colonnade.

Although Ripley had left the building complete, he had not left it uniform. The Queen Mary and King William Buildings had been intended to be alike, but in Mary 'more regard has been paid to convenience than to ornament'. It was finished in Portland stone, leaving King William alone with brick exterior façades, although there was a continuing unrealised desire to case them in stone.[170] The south-west pavilion of King Charles was still the modest brick building erected by Wren in the first phase of work. Between 1769 and 1774, during the Surveyorship of James Stuart, Robinson supervised its rebuilding in stone, by the masons William Jelfe and John Bastard, to match its neighbour, at an estimated cost of £5664.[171] During this period, in response to the growth in the number of pensioners to over 2000, the dining accommodation was increased. The original dining hall in King Charles was refitted as such in 1772 to cater for a further 150 diners to add to the 640 capable of being accommodated in each of the colonnaded dining rooms beneath the Painted Hall and the Chapel (figs 222–4). Even with this extra provision, there was still insufficient space for one sitting at mealtimes, a situation

222   The dining room beneath the Chapel in the basement of the Queen Mary Building, from the west.

223 The central area of the former dining room in the King William Building, beneath the Painted Hall, subdivided in 1938 (see figs 224 and 265).

224 The basement dining room of the King William Building, in use by naval pensioners (*Illustrated London News*, 25 March 1865).

225   The west kitchen, beneath the Upper Hall of the King William Building (*Illustrated London News*, 25 March 1865).

comparable with Les Invalides, where 1500 could be accommodated in the refectories, necessitating two sittings.[172] An underground communication corridor was constructed between King Charles and King William to link the two dining areas and the associated kitchens in the basement of the south-west pavilion of King Charles and in the splendid, vaulted former guard room below the Upper Hall of King William (fig. 225).[173] The dining arrangements were described in 1787:

> We saw six hundred and forty sailors eating in the refectory in three naves. There are two the same, and one for the one hundred and fifty young boys. Four people attend each table. They serve a plate of broth with a large piece of good beef. Each has his ration of beer and bread. Each refectory has its own kitchen which is stone-flagged and vaulted. Here are lead water tanks, two fireplaces, cast-iron coppers for the broth, flour, soup and vegetables, and a cast-iron pastry oven.[174]

One provision deemed necessary at Les Invalides, but not at Greenwich, was a separate dining area for the blind so that they would not be cheated of their food by the sighted.[175]

A visitor in the previous year, 1786, provided an invaluable description of the wards and cabins occupied by the 'well-dressed, contented-looking old men' (figs 226 and 227):

> Their dormitories are very pleasant; large, light and lofty, with cubicles containing glass windows on the side, where each has his own bed, small table, chair, wardrobe, tea and smoking outfit which he can lock up. No humanitarian with a philosophical

turn of mind could be indifferent to the way in which they decorate their cubicles: a number of them have sea and land charts, with the voyages they have made marked out on them, or spots where storms have been overcome or battles fought, where they have lost an arm or a leg, or conquered an enemy ship, and so on; others have stuck figures of every nationality on cardboard, others of strange beasts in foreign lands, while a number have collected books in several languages with which they amuse themselves.

> The corridors are wide enough to admit of eight people walking abreast. It is all beautifully panelled and the floor is covered with rugs. In the centre of each passage there stands a large fireplace around which a crowd of men were sitting; two of them had a bench in the corridor, where they sat astride, leaning up against each other at play; and beneath it was a chamber (in good old English fashion) for their mutual use, so as they should not have to leave their labours.

> Everything is spotless. Each man has two white shirts weekly, and a hundred and four women are employed to do the laundry and keep the place clean.[176]

James Stuart was succeeded as Surveyor in February 1788 by Sir Robert Taylor, but he had no time to make any impact on the Hospital, as he died in September that year, when John Yenn took over. At this time the King Charles base wing, dwarfed between its two large pavilions, remained as built by Wren, but following demolition in 1811, it was rebuilt in stone by Yenn and the Clerk of Works Henry Hake Seward in 1812–15 in a rich neo-classical

226 (*above*)   Cabins in the Royal Charles ('show') Ward in the King Charles Building (*Pictorial Times*, 15 April 1843).

227   The interior of a cabin in the Royal Charles Ward (*Illustrated London News*, 22 April 1865).

style at a cost of around £75,000 (figs 228–30). Originally planned with a central spine wall, in the manner of Queen Anne, it was constructed with a central passage with wards to each side reached through large, arched openings.[177] A proposed attic storey was omitted on the grounds of appearance and in order to enable the freer circulation of air to the wards and apartments on the other sides of the internal court.[178]

Two weeks before Yenn's death in 1821, the General Court concurred that the post of Surveyor would at last be discontinued, since all architectural duties could by this time be carried out by a Clerk of Works, as they had been by Seward, since Yenn 'has been for many years incapable of any duties'.[179] The two posts were combined in the person of Seward, who held them for two years before retiring in 1823. He was succeeded as Clerk of Works by Joseph Kay, but the position changed once again in the 1830s when Kay usually was known as the Surveyor, assisted by Inspectors of Works.

REBUILDING THE CHAPEL

The fire which gutted Ripley's Chapel in the early morning of 2 January 1779 'began in the taylor's shop, wherein the men had been at work the preceding day, but had mingled holiday rejoicing too much with their labours'.[180] The fire raged for several hours since the tanks of water at the top of the building

228 The west, base wing of the King Charles Building, rebuilt in 1812–15.

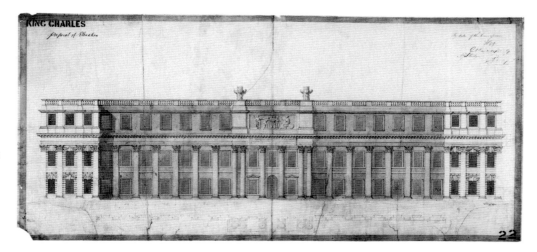

229 John Yenn, proposed elevation for the rebuilding of the base wing of the King Charles Building, showing the attic storey which subsequently was omitted (BAL E5/21(4)).

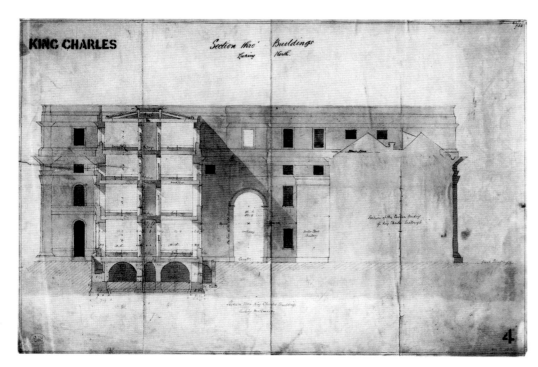

230 Cross-section through the new west wing of the King Charles Building, looking north, showing the central passages with wards to each side (BAL E5/22).

were almost empty and the line of pensioners handing buckets from the Thames was not adequate to the task. Fire engines arrived from London at about eleven o'clock and the fire was eventually put out by the evening.[181] It was reported to the directors that 'the Chappel with its Cupola and some of the adjoining Wards were destroyed and other damage done', and agreed that the damages should be made good as quickly as conveniently possible with the Chapel and wards put into their original state; that some apartments should be pressed into use as wards; that the Painted Hall should be used for worship; and, in a suspicious vein, prompted perhaps by Thomas Baillie's vigorous attack on the administration of the Hospital the year before (see chapter 6), that a £500 reward would be granted to any person who could show who had been guilty of wilfully starting the fire. They also promised rewards to those who had helped to put out the blaze.[182] After 'a most strict and diligent investigation . . . which lasted several days . . . nothing came out that could lead to a discovery'.[183]

The destruction was not total. The cupola still stood, although burned internally, with staining that is still visible, and the fire had been prevented from spreading along the wards as far as the central staircase in the east wing by the expedient of cutting away the roofs and floors. The repair of the damaged paving and of the tables and forms in the dining hall below the chapel and the reinstatement of the wards was completed by September 1779.[184] The stonework of the colonnade was made good and then coated within in 1780 with Liardet cement purchased from William Adam and Company.[185] The durability of this stucco had been attested in Chancery in 1778 by Stuart, Mylne and the mason John Devall, so its use here in finishing the ceiling of the east colonnade in a manner far simpler, and cheaper, than the west, is no surprise.[186]

John Devall began work on the dome in 1783, taking down the west pediment and carving replacement stones for those damaged.[187] Devall was one of the craftsmen who had been working on Somerset House, in a team recommended in its entirety by Stuart in 1781 and approved by the directors 'for reinstating the Chapel and Cupola in a Style of elegance equal at least to what they were in before the Fire'.[188]

It was agreed also that Samuel Green should be commissioned to supply a new organ and 'that a picture for the Altar piece (the subject to be approved of by the General Court and to be painted by one of the most eminent Masters) should be provided'. Four months later, in November 1781, the job was given to Benjamin West, who had put himself forward, the General Court having 'a high opinion of his abilities'.[189] West himself proposed four subjects, three of which are unrecorded: 'St Paul's Shipwreck, and subsequent reception on the Island of Malta, being best approved of, by himself and the Court, as the most emblematical and best adapted for the purpose, it was unanimously made choice of'.[190] The story, as told in the Acts of the Apostles (28: 1–6), describes how Paul, a prisoner of the Romans, was shipwrecked on the island of Malta. A fire having been lit to dry out the survivors, a viper was driven from the faggots by the heat and fastened itself onto Paul's hand. Miraculously he was able to cast it back into the flames (an image given additional resonance by the identification of the snake as the Christian symbol of Satan): 'Howbeit they looked when he should have swollen, or fallen down dead suddenly: but after they had looked a great while, and saw no harm come to him, they changed their minds, and said that he

was a god' (v. 6) (fig. 232). West was paid £1200 for his 25-foot high canvas, set into a carved and gilded frame made by Richard Lawrence. In the words of Cooke's and Maule's official guide to the Hospital, the scene could not fail 'of having a proper effect on the minds of sea-faring men, and of impressing them with a due sense of past preservation, and their present comfortable situation and support in this glorious asylum for naval misfortune and naval worth'.[191] In his sermon at the re-opening of the Chapel on Sunday 20 September 1789, the officiating chaplain, the Reverend John Cooke, co-author of the history of the Hospital, took as his theme the 'extraordinary dangers' and 'extraordinary deliverances' of the story depicted by West, the lesson of which was clear:

> You, venerable seamen! grown old, or otherwise disabled, in the service of your country . . . have been preserved amidst the tempest and the storm . . . God hath covered your heads in the day of battle. . . . Delivered, by his sovereign protection, from those hard services which ye have undergone; from those perils to which ye have been exposed, you, here, in the bounty of your country, find your reward; an exemption from future toils, and a security from future wants.[192]

The story had been well chosen. The narratives of the Acts of the Apostles had a considerable force for Anglicans in presenting the history of an undivided Church, with Paul, the zealous preacher, a particular hero.[193] Thornhill had already drawn on the Acts for his series of eight grisaille compositions in the dome of St Paul's Cathedral, completed in 1717. Both he and Benjamin West inevitably were indebted to the example of the Raphael Cartoons, which as exemplars of the art of history painting on the grand scale had a profound impact on painters in England as paradigms of Renaissance art. Acquired for the Royal Collection in 1623 by Charles I, when still Prince of Wales, the Cartoons were put on display by William III in 1699 at Hampton Court in the gallery designed by Wren. They were moved in 1763 to Buckingham House and then to Windsor Castle before returning to Hampton Court in 1804 when West was involved in their reinstallation.[194] Recently characterised as 'a benchmark of acceptable scriptural representation',[195] they greatly enriched the vocabulary of form and gesture available to painters. Late in his career, Thornhill painted three sets of copies of the Cartoons,[196] and West himself, as President of the Royal Academy from 1792 in succession to Sir Joshua Reynolds, was keen to keep Thornhill's copies on display at the Academy for purposes of instruction. He had himself made a small copy of *The Death of Ananias* in 1785, the subject of his last lecture to the Academy in 1817 (fig. 233).[197] In Sir Thomas Lawrence's full-length portrait of West, painted in 1818–21, the copy of the Raphael is shown on the easel next to the artist.[198] Henry Fuseli also used this painting as a model of pictorial order and classical composition in his lecture 'On Composition' to the Royal Academy.[199]

It was to this favoured composition that West turned when considering his altarpiece for Greenwich, basing the figure of Paul on the Pauline apostle who stands next to St Peter.[200] This is the only major painting by West to remain in the situation for which it was painted. Containing about fifty figures, the largest of which are 8 feet high, it is a painting of enormous ambition. Its great compositional strength, the powerful diagonal which leads the eye up to the figure of the apostle, enables it to communicate the full

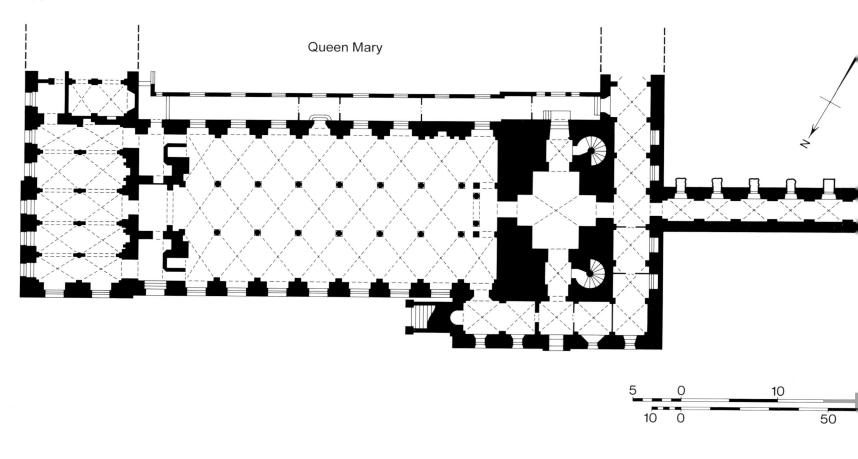

Queen Mary

231   Plan showing the underground corridors between the basements of Queen Mary and King William (1741) and between King William and King Charles (1772).

length of the Chapel. But, the number of figures and the lack of clarity in the depiction of the business in which they are engaged make it extremely difficult to read without the text which was probably provided by the artist himself for Cooke's and Maule's guidebook.[201] St Paul is shown shaking the viper from his hand into the fire, but the painting also includes the mariners salvaging goods from the wreck and the hospitable islanders lowering fuel for the relief of the shipwrecked. In addition, for further didactic purposes, West introduced a Roman matron carrying an urn containing the ashes of her husband, and an infirm old man carried in the arms of two robust young men. This over-staffing compromises the clarity and vivacity of design apparent in the original sketches, which presumably won West the commission.[202] He himself would not have countenanced any criticism. As a stranger to self-doubt, and firm in the perception of his own greatness, he regarded this picture as 'a little burst of genius'.[203] The absence of compositional clarity is compounded by the coarseness of the canvas, which tends to attract dirt and resist cleaning.

In rebuilding the Chapel, Stuart introduced a cove, with consequent alterations to the window-heads, to replace the original flat, compartmented ceiling. The hacked-back original cornice is still visible within the roof space. There were problems in obtaining the lengths of oak required for the new roof, since most of that which was available was needed for ships. Stuart was told on no account to accept the Navy Board's offer of Danzig fir; delays while appropriate oak was seasoned were preferable. Stuart's elevations and designs for the Chapel were approved in March 1782, together with his model of the roof, but the smooth progress of restitution was hampered by ill feeling. Two months later Stuart reported visiting 'to verify some measures . . . as might enable me to complete my design for restoring that Chaple'. He found masons working under the directions of Robert Mylne, the Clerk of Works, on mouldings, 'the designs for which had not been given by me, neither had they been communicated to me for my approbation; and were absolutely repugnant to the design which I had conceived and meant to execute'.[204] Mylne had already been

King William

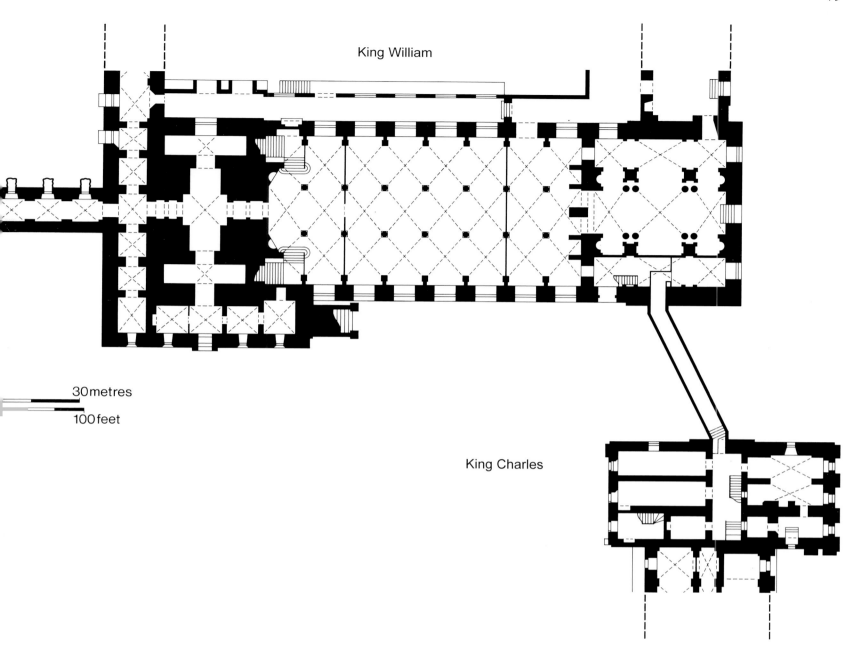

30 metres
100 feet

King Charles

responsible for some designs at the Hospital, in 1780 erecting the flight of steps from the courtyard of King William up to the colonnade,[205] which was to be mirrored in rather less grand form by Joseph Kay in 1835 in the courtyard of Queen Mary,[206] but by 1782 the directors reported irreconcilable differences between him and Stuart, possibly rooted in Mylne's perception of himself as an architect and of Stuart as a mere interior designer.[207] In September, according to the Surveyor, Mylne had attempted to ruin Stuart's reputation by falsifying drawings and 'his vindictive Temper had determined him to deform and spoil the Chapel'. Stuart followed up his charges by producing letters from officers and artificers complaining of the ill-treatment received from Mylne, a man described elsewhere as 'a rare jintleman, but as hot as pepper and as proud as Lucifer'.[208] He was accordingly dismissed, taking with him the three volumes of drawings of the Hospital in the compilation begun by Ripley, retrieved after litigation in 1793 and now in the National Maritime Museum.[209] He was replaced by Stuart's assistant William Newton, translator of an edition of Vitruvius

which was posthumously published in 1791.[210] The extent of the respective roles of Newton and Stuart in the design of the new Chapel, a neo-classical masterpiece, has been the subject of some speculation. Although there is nothing in the accounts to suggest that Newton was doing anything other than following Stuart's approved designs, the evidence brought forward by Lesley Lewis suggests a high degree of collaboration between the two in 'the production of a highly wrought casket of a chapel, which, as a pendant to the Painted Hall, has a brilliant element of both surprise and rightness and, however it may have been arrived at, can hardly be too highly praised' (figs 234–6).[211]

Before his dismissal, Mylne had produced a design for the Chapel roof, clearly modelled on that of the Painted Hall, which probably also had been the exemplar for the roof which was destroyed.[212] Newton adapted the design, omitting the subsidiary posts above the galleries and reinforcing the structure with wrought-iron king rods as well as cast-iron ties at the angles.[213] Although Stuart had been advised to use oak rather than fir, the

the ornamentation of the Chapel as a very fine example of plasterer's work done by hand, a skill which became extinct when it was superseded by cast work.[217]

Outside, the leading of the dome was completed and the scaffold struck in 1785.[218] Within, the scagliola pilasters and eight

233   Raphael, *The Death of Ananias* (The Royal Collection © 2000, HM Queen Elizabeth II).

large columns, carved in London by Jonathan Richter, were installed in the Chapel in 1788; Richter cleaned, oiled and repolished them before the re-opening the following year.[219] Other carving was carried out by Richard Lawrence: over the gallery doors; the leaves to the soffits of the windows; two marble statuary angels; eight candelabra (with dolphins, lions' heads, festoons of oak and laurel leaves) and 462 balusters for the galleries.[220] But one of the most significant contributions to the decoration of the new Chapel came from Eleanor Coade's artificial stone factory: thirty-two pilaster capitals and bases;[221] thirty-two cherubs' heads;[222] the Hospital arms; and six angels for the support of the communion table.[223] She also provided in 1789, from drawings by Benjamin West, four oval medallions of the prophets Daniel, Micah, Zechariah and Malachi as well as six circular medallions depicting scenes from the Acts of the Apostles: *The Conversion of St Paul, Paul Preaching at Athens, Paul Pleading before Felix* (the Roman procurator), *Peter Released from Prison, The Vision of Cornelius* (the Roman centurion baptised by Peter) and *The Blinding of Elymas* (the sorcerer punished by Paul).[224] These were all set into James Arrow's three-decker pulpit and reader's desk, together with a further medallion of Elymas.[225] The pulpit and desk were positioned originally in a commanding position at the head of the central aisle. Now, the desk is preserved in the dome and the pulpit is placed between the pews and the choir stalls on the south side (fig. 237).

In addition to the large *St Paul*, installed in the Chapel in 1789, West was responsible also for the design of four Coade stone statues, 6 feet high, of Charity, Faith, Meekness and Hope in the niches of the entrance vestibule beneath the dome (fig. 238)[226] and for the designs of the several paintings in grisaille by Biagio Rebecca in the Chapel, including the fourteen life-size figures of the apostles and evangelists.[227] Four other oval pictures

232   Benjamin West, *St Paul's Shipwreck on the Island of Malta*, altarpiece of the Chapel.

roof and its internal floor were constructed in a combination of both, the floorboards being laid on an insulating layer of lath and plaster.

By the end of 1784 the roof was completed (and floored in 1787), and the plasterer John Papworth produced estimates for the ceiling,[214] first showing an ornamental panel to illustrate the intended effect.[215] He submitted bills in 1787 and 1788 for the foliage, scallop shells, fifty-nine cherubim with wings and 'an exceedingly rich central ornament', all wrought by hand, with successive coats of oil and colour.[216] Papworth's work was praised by his grandson Wyatt Papworth, who recalled his father describing

234   The Chapel, looking east towards Benjamin West's altarpiece.

'in Chiara Oscuro' were painted by Charles Catton,[228] and four paintings on copper by Theodore de Bruyn: *The Nativity*, *The Annunciation to the Shepherds*, *The Adoration of the Magi* and *The Flight into Egypt*.[229]

Although we might have expected a more accomplished painting from Jacopo Amigoni for Ripley's Chapel than West was able to provide for Stuart's, the overall neo-classical ensemble provided by the architect, the painter and their collaborators is one of a richness unprecedented and unsurpassed in English art: a return to magnificence, with moreover an appropriate accompanying message of faith and salvation for the thousand seafaring men who could be accommodated at any one time. It was last restored in 1954–5, when the original colour scheme was reinstated, following years of discolouration by smoke: the plaster ceiling was stabilised following the loosening caused by war-time

bomb blasts, and a memorial chapel constructed in the space to the east formerly occupied by the sanctuary.[230] At its re-opening on 21 June 1955, the hitherto unnamed Chapel was dedicated to Sts Peter and Paul.[231]

THE NELSON PEDIMENT

Just as the Raphael Cartoons inspired emulation as paradigms of Renaissance painting, so did the Elgin Marbles as pre-eminent examples of the art of ancient Greece. These sculptures from the Parthenon were first put on display in London in 1807 to a limited but enthusiastic audience, including Benjamin West and the young Benjamin Robert Haydon. The latter was particularly moved by the experience: 'I felt as if a divine truth had blazed inwardly upon my mind, and I knew that they [the marbles] would at last rouse

235   The Chapel, view to the west.

236   The geometrical staircase in the south-west corner of the entrance hall of the Chapel.

the art of Europe from its slumber of darkness'.[232] West was to draw on their example in his final contribution to Greenwich Hospital: the Nelson pediment of the King William block. Following Nelson's death at the Battle of Trafalgar in October 1805, his body had lain in state in the Painted Hall from 4 to 7 January 1806 before being taken by funeral barge to Whitehall on the 8th and on to St Paul's Cathedral for the public funeral on the 9th. West, with considerable speed (and with Nelson's prior approval), in 1806 painted *The Death of Lord Nelson*,[233] comparable in its conception with his earlier *Death of General Wolfe*,[234] and in the next two years followed this with *The Death of Lord Nelson in the Cockpit of the Victory*,[235] the *Sketch for a Monument to Lord Nelson*[236] and, deriving from it, *The Immortality of Nelson*.[237] He returned to this image of Neptune delivering the immortal hero to Britannia for the huge pediment sculpture at Greenwich, 40 feet wide and 10 feet high at its apex, which he modelled in Coade's artificial stone with Joseph Panzetta in 1810–12.[238] This was intended as the first in a series of compositions commemorative of great naval actions, to be placed in the various vacant pediments around the Hospital. West also produced a drawing for a Lord Howe pediment, but the Nelson was the only one to be executed.[239]

The Nelson pediment, for which West was paid £1000, was considered by the Coade firm to be its finest achievement: 'The units of the composition are enormous, and leave one astonished, as always, at the huge masses of clay which the workmen were

able to handle, let alone fire' (figs 239 and 242).[240] Although it was recorded as having been erected in 1812,[241] the pediment is inscribed 1813. An undated commemorative pamphlet in praise of both the subject and the manufacturing process probably was published the same year, no doubt with West's collaboration.[242] We are left in no doubt as to the efficacy of the material and the benefits which it might have brought to the sculptors of the Parthenon. A work which would have taken ten years in marble was executed in two. And whereas stone or marble can be eroded by the atmosphere, the intense fires to which this 'Lithodipyra' (stone hardened by fire) is exposed give it a durability equal to jasper or porphyry:

> consequently it ever retains that sharpness given it by the genius and hands of the sculptor, every fine touch depicting the passions, and swelling the sinews, is not only preserved, but heightened; nothing is lost from passing through the chissels of inferior workmen. . . . [H]ad Phidias, that eminent Grecian sculptor, worked with a material like this, the touch of his graceful figures, would have been preserved to the latest period, in all its native elegance.[243]

West's allegorical depiction of *The Immortality of Nelson* was criticised in 1810 by one who saw in it 'an accumulation of incongruities' and expressed the hope that a time would come when 'such gross allegories' would be deemed repugnant.[244] West was not deterred: 'To represent the heroic Lives of men who have signalized themselves in the service of their Country, seems peculiarly calculated to excite universal admiration, and an ardent desire to emulate their example; and Allegory alone is the proper medium to do it justice'.[245] The hero is represented at the time of his death 'in the Arms of Victory', in a pose which recalls Michelangelo's *Pietà*, 'with some of those events of his life, in which the powers of the mind and intrepidity of conduct were most eminently conspicuous'. Here, as in the Chapel, West is delivering a message to sea-faring men. The central figure of Britannia, representing the British Empire, with her Trident 'in token of the dominion of the Seas', her face marked by 'the most pungent (though suppressed) grief', receives Nelson's body at the command of Neptune from a Triton, accompanied by Victory. Neptune, in his car drawn by marine horses, with his left hand gestures towards the dead hero, and with his right to the sinking of ships at Trafalgar. On the right-hand side of the pediment, three personifications of England, Scotland and Ireland, 'in most expressive though disconsolate attitudes', are 'affectionately reclining on each other, and reciprocally lamenting their individual and irreparable loss'. Between the disconsolate trio and Britannia, Nelson's victories at the Nile and Copenhagen are commemorated and the British Lion, 'an emblem of the whole nation', roars in exultation 'that Nelson has bled in One Hundred and Twenty-two Battles in the defence of his country', before falling in his 123rd, accompanied by 'the heart-broken British Seaman, in whose rough weather beaten countenance, sorrow and anguish are highly depicted'.[246]

The lessons to be drawn from this representation were not only imperial and martial, but also artistic: 'This model eminently conveys to the beholder the high state of the art of sculpture in this country, as keeping pace with our celebrity in arms'.[247] Not only would Coade stone sculpture last longer and remain sharper than the work of the Greeks, their artistry could be equalled: the Triton has 'perhaps the finest Torso ever executed since the days of Phidias' and the horses 'appear to have equal merit with those of that celebrated artist, lately brought from Athens by Lord Elgin'.[248] This is an almost explicit acknowledgement of West's debt to the recently arrived sculptures, not only in the general idea of a frieze-like arrangement, but also in direct borrowings from it. The wonderfully expressive head of the Horse of the Chariot of Selene (fig. 240) from the east pediment of the Parthenon is copied in the foremost sea-horse at Greenwich, and the pose and modelling of the Neptune owes much to the river god Ilissus (fig. 241), from the west pediment, a piece especially admired by William Hazlitt who, struck by 'the sway of the limbs and negligent grandeur' of the Elgin Marbles, particularly praised 'the distinction and union of all the parts [of the Ilissus] and the effect of action everywhere impressed on the external form, as if the very marble were a flexible substance'.[249] Comfortable in such elevated artistic company, West is depicted seated in front of this sculpture, with the head of the horse in front of him on the floor, in Archer's painting of *The Temporary Elgin Room in the British*

237 An engraving of the Chapel, showing the central placing of the originally three-decker pulpit (NMM).

238 (*right*) Benjamin West, figures of Faith and Charity flanking the west door into the entrance vestibule of the Chapel.

239   The Nelson pediment, installed in 1812 in the pediment of the colonnade facing the courtyard of the King William Building. The steps up to the colonnade were constructed under the direction of Robert Mylne in 1780.

240 (*facing page bottom left*)   Head of the Horse of the Chariot of Selene from the east pediment of the Parthenon (BM).

241 (*facing page bottom right*)   The river god Ilissus, from the west pediment of the Parthenon (BM).

242 (*above*)   The Nelson pediment: detail showing Britannia receiving the body of Nelson.

Museum in 1819.[250] As Hazlitt recollected, West 'lived long in the firm persuasion of being one of the elect among the sons of Fame, and went to his final rest in the arms of Immortality'.[251] At Greenwich, Benjamin West, tilting at eternity, confidently and consciously situated himself as heir to the great tradition of classical and Renaissance art running from Phidias to Raphael and Michelangelo.

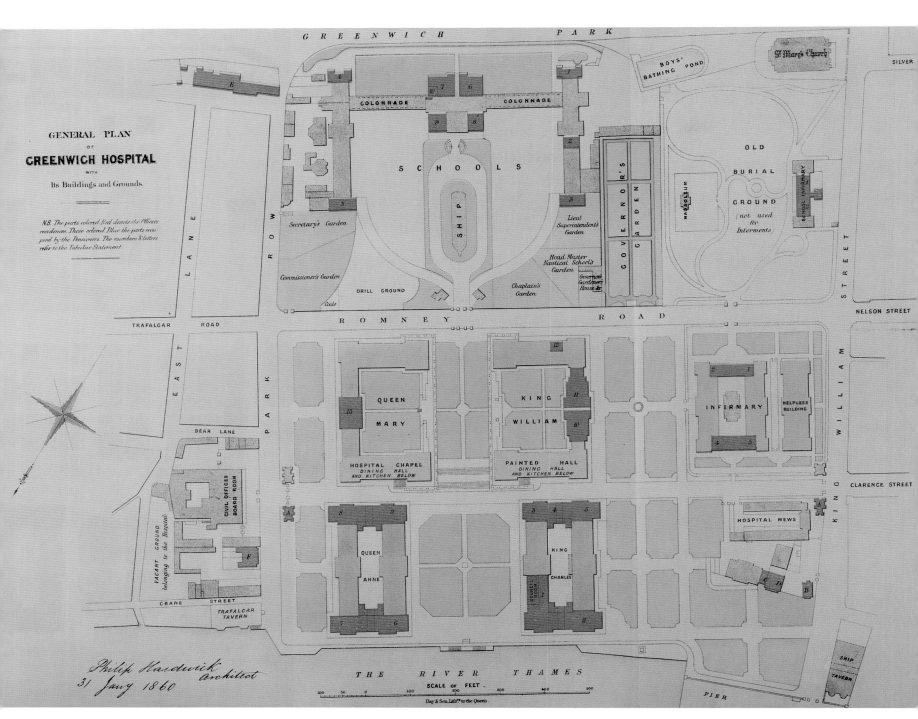

243   Philip Hardwick, *General Plan of Greenwich Hospital*, 1860 (Wellcome Institute Library, London).

Chapter 6

THE ROYAL HOSPITAL FOR SEAMEN:
USES, ABUSES, IMPROVEMENTS AND DEPARTURES

The plan prepared by Philip Hardwick in 1860 to accompany the *Report of the Commissioners Appointed to Inquire into Greenwich Hospital* provided eloquent testimony of an institution which had lost its way. Approximately two-thirds of the ground plan of the Hospital was coloured red to denote the residences of officers rather than wards for pensioners: the pavilions of King Charles and Queen Anne, the north end of the main range of King Charles, the west range of King William and the centre of the east range of Queen Mary (fig. 243). The *Report* had been prepared by Commissioners appointed 'to inquire into the internal Economy and Management of Greenwich Hospital, and of the Funds by which it is maintained . . . and also whether the Resources of the Hospital can be more advantageously applied for the Benefit of Seamen who have served in our Navy'.[1] This report was to begin the process which ended with the closure of the Hospital at Greenwich in 1869. Periodically, throughout its history, the directors had found it necessary to remind themselves of the overall purpose of the institution. Abuses within the Hospital administration had been the subject of concerned discussion almost from its inception, but it was not until the later eighteenth century that detailed accusations were formally presented. When they came, they were potentially the more damaging for coming from within.

In *The Case of the Royal Hospital for Seamen at Greenwich*, printed in March 1778 and given limited circulation, Captain Thomas Baillie, the Lieutenant-Governor since 1774, provided a highly critical, although highly partial view of its internal government, citing abuses, fraudulent contractors, wasted revenues and the conversion of wards into elegant apartments for clerks and their deputies.[2] He opened his attack with an appeal to history; to the days of the Hospital's foundation as 'one of the eldest born children of the Revolution', a time when 'the minds of men were elevated by that glorious event' and public business was conducted honourably.[3] He contrasted this with the present situation in which Commissioners and directors, many of whom had never been to sea, were inattentive and non-attending and many members of the Board had conflicting interests. The officers were, in Baillie's view, no better. The Auditor was paid £100 per year and given a suite of elegant apartments in return for very occasional attendance. The job of the Surveyor was a sinecure when no new building was going on: his sole task was to attend meetings in order 'to espouse the estimate'. The Clerk of Works, the 'too grand' and arrogant Mylne, who 'has assumed to himself the authority of the Governor', ensured the permanence of his office by sanctioning perpetual 'Necessary Works', some of which were solely for the benefit of officers who were given grand lodgings at the expense of both accommodation and convenience for pensioners. The Auditor and the Secretary had both appropriated passages in the Queen Anne Building for the domestic use of themselves and their families, which in Baillie's view not only compromised the grandeur of the building but also its healthiness and safety by reducing fire-escapes and by limiting the circulation areas necessary for ventilation and for exercise in wet weather. The Steward had even gone so far as to remove a urinal to a place near the gates in order to extend his apartment, to the great inconvenience of the feeble and diabetic men who were 'often obliged to wet their breeches before they [could] reach a proper place'.[4]

The colonisation of public spaces for private apartments was clear in the Queen Anne Building where many of the magnificent, formerly open, vaulted east-west passages, most notably in the north pavilions, continued to be used for domestic purposes until 1999 rather than for circulation and ventilation (fig. 244). The intention of the architects to utilise these passages as exercise and meeting places, in the absence of common rooms, is apparent in the second-floor passages of the pavilions which have window cills set at a 'leaning height'[5] to enable the men to look down into the internal courtyard (fig. 245).

Baillie, an architectural behaviourist ahead of his time, attributed the spatial imperialism of the officers of the Hospital to the grandeur of the architecture itself, which encouraged excess. Already living in the 'most magnificent palace in the kingdom', the officers appeared in his view to have been inspired by the possibility of achieving still greater splendour. Was it not time to acknowledge that the building was finished, since 'the new works which have been lately undertaken, show plainly that the active imagination of the Clerk of Works is almost exhausted'. These works included the demolition of 'Ripley's Saddle', and the removal of the iron gates at the ends of the gravel path along the Thames, thereby lengthening the walk and making the buildings look grander from the river. The opening up of the frontage had the disadvantage of exposing to view Wren's smaller-scale, brick,

244   The passage at the north end of the west range of the Queen Anne Building, appropriated for domestic use; reclaimed as a corridor during the restoration of the building in 1999.

245   The second-floor passage at the south end of the west range of the Queen Anne Building with window cills set at a 'leaning height'.

base wing of King Charles, leading to the need to rebuild it in stone.[6] Baillie's resounding, Johnsonian conclusion, that 'elegance has already encroached too much on propriety', points to the disjunction which he identified between form and content in the management of the Hospital, and to the unfulfilled expectations aroused by its magnificent architecture: 'the pensioners, for whose account this princely pile is said to be appropriated, are already sufficiently tantalized and insulted with the profusion of architectural beauties amidst which they live. Columns, colonnades, architraves and frizes, ill accord with bull-beef and sour small beer mixed with water'.[7]

Lord Sandwich, Lord Commissioner of the Admiralty, held by Baillie to be both directly and tacitly responsible for the abuses at the Hospital, suspended him from office and encouraged the Hospital officers to begin a libel action. Sandwich vigorously defended his position in the House of Lords in May 1779, taking credit for establishing the Infirmary and for extending the dining areas. He excused the extension of the Secretary's apartments in the manner common to all administrators for whom the institutional processes have taken precedence over its original purposes: 'the business of the Secretary has been so greatly augmented, that he had not room for his papers, or for the clerks to do their business'.[8] At the same time, in a publication which Sandwich must have approved, a refutation of Baillie's charges was attempted. The significance of the closing of passages was dismissed; the charges against Mylne were refuted; that pensioners were wetting their breeches was denied; and the opinion of James Adam was obtained in support of the removal of Ripley's pediment as an improvement which he would have recommended himself if he had been in the post.[9]

These defences followed the libel action against Baillie. Although he was cleared of the charge in November 1778, his naval career was over. He had succeeded in identifying serious problems, but had imputed to colleagues the worst possible motives, when mere institutional incompetence or complacency might have accounted for some of the abuses. Clearly unfitted for senior management, he remained unemployed for four years until Charles Lennox, 3rd Duke of Richmond, upon his appointment as Master-General of the Ordnance, gave him the lucrative post of Clerk of the Deliveries, a position he held until his death in 1802. The strength of his case and the feelings it aroused were attested not only by the dismissal of the charges against him, and his subsequent appointment, but also by the legacy of £500 which he received in 1784 from John Barnard, son of a former Lord Mayor, 'as a small token of my approbation of his worthy and disinterested, though ineffectual, endeavours to rescue that noble national charity [Greenwich Hospital] from the rapacious hands of the basest and most wicked of mankind'.[10]

Baillie was concerned only with drawing attention to organisational abuses. For a more dispassionate view of the Hospital at this time, the opinion of Dr Jacques Tenon is invaluable. One of the most celebrated surgeons of his time, Tenon was in 1785 appointed to a commission charged with drawing up proposals for improving the hospitals of Paris. The Hôtel-Dieu, once praised by English visitors, now gave great cause for alarm because of its very high mortality rate of one death in four patients, at a time when the hospital in Edinburgh lost one in twenty-five. Tenon and his colleagues saw the hospital not as a place of charity for housing those afflicted by God-given illness, the traditional French view, but as a vehicle for general social improvement. His visit to

England in 1787, made possible by the Treaty of Versailles of 1783, was undertaken in the general context of French admiration for British commercial, industrial and social advances, not least in the development of hospitals in which great strides had been made in both the quantity and quality of provision. It was the combination of the spatial, sanitary and administrative elements of these 'machines for curing' which engaged him in his visits to almost forty hospitals in southern England, as detailed in his *Observations*.[11]

At Greenwich, Tenon was a most unusual visitor, taking little note of the grandeur of the buildings and avoiding making sentimental remarks about the pensioners. He concentrated on functions, describing the service arrangements at length: the dining rooms; the stone troughs with lead taps in stone-flagged vestibules for washing the face and hands, each with another trough underneath to recycle the spilt water; the cabins, varying in size from one bed in the smallest to eight in the largest, all with partitions 8 feet high to allow for the circulation of air into the corridors. The four-bed cabins he saw measured 12 by 9 feet, and were 12 feet high. The beds themselves interested him to the extent that he sketched one of those in the Infirmary and described it in detail: made of iron, with a central support to prevent bowing, 5 feet 9 inches long, 2 feet 6 inches wide, with a canopy for curtains; the woollen mattress weighing 32 pounds, the feather bolster 6 pounds and the feather pillow 2 pounds; each with two sheets and two covers. He noted the distinction between the corridors of officers and men: the former lit by whale-oil lamps, the latter by common fish-oil. He gave particular attention to fire precautions, recording the use of iron doors, the alarm bell system, the pumps and hoses, and the arrangements for the storage of water in the principal tank in the brewery and in the five others elsewhere on the site.[12]

Tenon's purpose was to record. He eschewed value judgements in his *Observations*, but for the principles which he published in *Mémoires sur les hôpitaux de Paris* in 1788 concerning ventilation, the separation of maladies, abundant water, adequate sanitation, appropriate clothing and furniture, he was indebted to his visit to England where his notions of physical and cultural environmentalism crystallised. It was on the basis of this experience that he came to the optimistic and influential view of the hospital as 'a cumulative, collaborative, supranational effort of scientists, learned societies, governments, even peoples united by common aspirations of humanity and peace' – 'the hospital was the conscience of a civilisation'.[13] He was not alone in France in drawing attention to eighteenth-century advances in England: J.-N. Hallé, in the year of Tenon's visit, praised Greenwich, apparently without irony, for being 'as salubrious as a convent for women'.[14]

The Civil Offices (Trafalgar Quarters)

Notwithstanding these golden opinions from across the Channel, many of Baillie's criticisms of the administration of the Hospital for Seamen appear to have been soundly based, and steps were taken during the nineteenth century to improve both procedures and accommodation. The need for office space for the institution had been acknowledged as early as 1745 when 'a proper office for keeping the several Books, Papers, & Records of the Hospital' was made in the north-west corner of Queen Anne.[15] In 1783 it was noted that the increase in paperwork and administration had become such as to require a dedicated building, but no action was taken until 1813, when the design for the Civil Offices (now the Trafalgar Quarters) was approved.[16] Built between 1813 and 1816, these purpose-built offices and storerooms were designed to accommodate the civil (as opposed to the military) concerns of the institution: maintaining accounts and records; controlling, storing and issuing provisions, clothing and other goods; paying subsistence money to the pensioners; administering the expanding out-pensions department, established in 1763, and managing activities relating to funding. The number of men claiming out-pensions had risen from about 3000 in 1803 to 9000 in 1813; most of them were required to go quarterly to Greenwich to collect their payment, although those who lived too far away could receive payment from officers of the Customs and Excise. A further administrative burden was added in 1805 when the task of administering prize or bounty money, derived from the proceeds from captured enemy ships, was given to the Hospital, which since 1707 had benefited greatly from such unclaimed prizes, but had not hitherto been involved in the onerous distribution of money to late claimants.[17] The increased administrative workload within the Hospital resulted in the offices' becoming so crowded as to be 'injurious to the Health' of the clerks. The problem was compounded by the number of works which were taking place during this period – the building of the Helpless Ward in 1808–10, the restoration of the Infirmary in 1811–13 following a fire, and the rebuilding of the base block of King Charles in 1812–15. The directors first considered making additions to the existing accommodation but the Surveyor, John Yenn, reported in 1812 that this would not 'answer the purpose, or remedy the evils complained of' and a new building would be necessary.[18] The eventual, consequent removal of the Steward and his office from the main building had the incidental benefit of releasing space for the accommodation of ninety-six more pensioners.

The building designed by Yenn, for erection to the east of the Hospital on a site that had been a works yard throughout the building programme, was essentially utilitarian but since it was positioned directly opposite the gates, terminating the eastward vista, a degree of pomp was required. The west range had offices on two floors, with, in front, a loggia of paired Tuscan columns set in the middle of a projecting arcade, an embellishment which also served to provide a sheltered waiting area (fig. 246). There may originally have been as many as four entrances on this front, none of which appears to have occupied the position of the present one.[19] Above, the three central bays are adorned with a Coade-stone frieze comprising the Hospital arms supported by a Triton and Hippocampus, with sprays of palms and oak foliage to each side. This was the last order from Greenwich Hospital for stone from the Coade factory (fig. 247).[20] To the rear, single-storey ranges enclosing a courtyard contained storerooms and further offices. This is a handsome building, characterised by restraint and economy of ornament, comparable in its simplicity with such contemporary naval buildings as Edward Holl's office of 1808 at Chatham Dockyard and Henry Pilkington's Royal Naval Hospital of 1808–11 at Great Yarmouth.

Within fifteen years alterations were made to the Civil Offices following the removal of two of the functions which had prompted their building; a reform of procedures ensued. In 1825 the out-pensions department, which by 1820 was dealing with

246   Trafalgar Quarters, from the south-west.

247   The Coade stone frieze on the west front of Trafalgar Quarters.

30,000 claimants, was moved to central London, to be joined five years later by the Prize Office.[21] The discovery of financial deficits in the Hospital accounts in 1828 initially was attributed to loose accounting, but subsequently was shown to be the result of fraud. A review of the administrative systems followed and in 1829 the Board of Directors and the General Court were abolished, the civil affairs of the Hospital being entrusted to five Commissioners.[22] In 1830–31 the Prize Office on the ground floor of the Offices was refitted as a Commissioner's room and accommodation for the Secretary's department was moved to the first floor.[23] When the Hospital closed in 1869, the building was converted into accommodation for the servants of the Greenwich Hospital School and by the 1880s had become known as the Trafalgar Building or Quarters, a name perhaps acquired through its proximity to the Trafalgar Tavern to the north. In 1886 the building was drastically remodelled to provide accommodation for the boys of the school, a large dining room being constructed within the western part, and the first floor and the rear ranges being converted into dormitories.[24] Following the removal of the Royal Hospital Schools to Suffolk in 1933, the building was given to the Royal Naval College which continued to use it as accommodation but rebuilt the west range as a gymnasium in 1939.[25]

The Programme of Improvements

Although Baillie's criticisms had been refuted by the Hospital, accusations of mismanagement periodically resurfaced over the following decades. The directors and the General Court were able to deflect these attacks, but as the nineteenth century progressed, the pressure for change proved irresistible. The need to rationalise the Hospital's growing estate in Greenwich was a major factor in this process. The enclosing of the grounds in 1752 did not amount to completion of the Hospital, as the subsequent construction of the Infirmary, the School and Civil Offices testify. This incremental expansion, which also included the continuing acquisition of other adjoining properties, was given a major boost in 1821 by the incorporation into the Hospital grounds of those of the Naval Asylum. Coincidentally, proposed improvements to the Woolwich Road and Deptford Creek Bridge Road, which were under consideration at the time, allowed the directors to broaden the scope of their deliberations. Thought could be given to improving the road access to the Hospital and to revitalising the still unprofitable market. Outline planning for an ambitious scheme of improvements was granted formal approval by the General Court in 1824. Coeval with its implementation, there was a minor revolution in the administration, which was finally restructured in 1829–30 in the wake of a financial scandal involving the Treasurer. Always envisaged as a long-term project, the scheme of improvements took three decades to accomplish under the respective surveyorships of Joseph Kay and Philip Hardwick. Kay's efforts were concentrated initially on the rebuilding of the market, completed by 1831, then on improving the Hospital's outbuildings, and finally on the provision of a formal approach to the west gate. Although this represented the greater proportion of the work, several tasks fell to Hardwick: appointed in 1848, he was responsible for the clearance and re-enclosure of the Hospital's enlarged grounds between 1849 and 1856. The overarching purpose of all this work was to make manifest the ideals of order and discipline which, it

was hoped, characterised the institution, while providing a ceremonial approach to the Hospital and effecting a physical separation between the institution and the town. Such a separation had long been desired: a report of 1841 recalled that before the improvements, 'the space to the westwards in the vicinity of the Hospital, was occupied by Buildings, and by a Population of the lowest and worst description', while 'its avenues of approach were circuitous, narrow and unsightly', with slum dwellings, brothels and alehouses crowding up to the outer walls of the Hospital (fig. 143).[26] The lofty ambition, as expressed by one of the moving forces behind the plan, the Hospital Secretary, Edward Hawke Locker, who was appointed a Commissioner in 1829, was to fulfil 'the intentions of the first founders and Benefactors'. Wren's original design could at last be honoured by creating 'an open area laid out ornamentally in Walks and Plantations for the use of the Pensioners and for the appropriate completion of the architectural effect of the Building now debased and concealed by enclosures and Buildings applied to the meanest purposes'.[27] As a result, institutional decline was paralleled by continuing physical improvement. An awareness of the iconic status of Greenwich, made explicit through the use of the Painted Hall for the lying-in-state of Nelson in 1806, underpinned its growth into a bigger and visually more orderly complex.

From 1823 until his death in 1847, Kay also carried out a steady programme of maintenance and improvements to the Hospital buildings themselves, addressing some of the problems which Baillie had identified. The roofs of King Charles and Queen Anne, the paving of the courts and colonnades and the masonry of the west dome were all repaired, and the steps built from the east colonnade to the Queen Mary courtyard. The allegedly badly constructed wind dial on top of the cupola was replaced by one made 'on an improved principle' in 1830. He also reappropriated for the use of pensioners the apartments taken over by the steward's clerk.[28]

Captain Baillie had been particularly dismissive of the unimaginative use of the Painted Hall which he considered had not been used, for many years, 'for any other purpose than as a spectacle for strangers', each of whom contributed 3d for the privilege.[29] In 1795 Lieutenant-Governor William Locker suggested that it might be used as a national gallery of marine paintings, but the proposal was not acted upon until his son, Edward Hawke Locker, while Secretary to the Hospital, succeeded in establishing the gallery in 1823 for the display of naval portraits and other paintings 'commemorative of the distinguished services of the Royal Navy'. The lower windows of the Hall were covered temporarily and pictures arranged to see if there was sufficient light for viewing from the upper windows alone. The view of the three eminent representatives of the plastic arts, called in to advise, was positive. Sir Thomas Lawrence, Francis Chantrey and Robert Smirke (painter, sculptor and architect – all members of Locker's circle) recommended the masonry infilling of the lower windows of the Hall and the hanging of pictures between the pilasters from a rod below the entablature. This conversion work, together with the installation of a hot-water pipe heating system along the north and south walls (which never achieved more than 65 degrees Fahrenheit), was completed in 1824.[30] This was the first gallery dedicated to any aspect of national history, just pre-dating the opening of what was to become the National Gallery (fig. 248). It remained a picture gallery until 1936 when the paintings, by then numbering nearly

248   The Painted Hall in use as a picture gallery: the view towards the Upper Hall in 1929.

300, were removed to the National Maritime Museum which opened on the other side of Romney Road in 1937.[31]

The vestibule of the Hall, where those responsible for showing the collection awaited the arrival of visitors, was heated by a stove which was found to be highly unsatisfactory whenever the wind was from the south-east: the Hall filled with smoke and the stove had to be extinguished. By 1843 a thorough cleaning was necessary, all the paintings being taken down for the purpose. At the same time, new granite steps were built in the vestibule, part of Kay's programme of improving access to public areas, which had included the making of alterations to the entrances to the east and west dining halls in 1832. The smoke problem continued until 1851 when the flue was altered,[32] possibly utilising the 'Patent Chimney Pump' for securing an upward current and obtaining down draft, 'invented by Sir Henry Hart, Commissioner of Greenwich Hospital, where the invention has been in successful use for several months'.[33]

Kay returned to the questions of fire, illumination and sanitation which had exercised Tenon fifty years before. Although in the opinion of a consultant surveyor, the presence of dividing walls in the roofs made the Hospital better protected against fire than most other public buildings, Kay recognised that improvements were necessary. He saw that the extension of apartments beyond the main dividing walls of the buildings resulted in a significant fire risk, since as a result they were separated from the wards not by walls but by partitions. In 1841 William Baddeley of Islington and William Merryweather of Long Acre, engineers, were invited to report on the fire-fighting equipment at the Hospital. They found the wells, tanks, conduits, reservoirs, engines and pumps all in excellent condition, with abundant water and a judicious distribution of tanks. In their not disinterested view, improvements nevertheless could be made by the purchase of four, more powerful fire engines of the type made by Merryweather for the 'London Fire Establishment', and by the acquisition of Baddeley's hose reels, from which any length of hose could be run out for immediate action. Kay recommended the purchase of the reels and engines in 1842, but demonstrated that he was paying proper attention by limiting himself to three engines rather than four, and refurbishing two of the old ones. He further argued the need for 'an efficient set of men . . . in constant training'.[34]

Baddeley's and Merryweather's report notwithstanding, an improvement to the water supply was deemed necessary. A reservoir was constructed in the park in 1845 (see chapter 1) and 9 inch iron pipes were laid to carry water to the Hospital. Working by pressure alone, it was considered that this would be sufficient to allow the water 'to force its way through lengths of leathern hose sufficient to reach the highest part of the building'.[35]

The impression gained from Kay's regular 'Works Reports' is that the maintenance of cleanliness had not been a priority at the Hospital in recent years. In 1832 he introduced gas lighting, beginning in the dining halls as part of a general programme of cleaning and refurbishment. He extended this provision over the next ten years to all the public spaces, including the staircases, to replace the inefficient oil lamps, but costs initially prevented the extension of this improvement to the wards, although some at least were gas-lit by 1865.[36] Prompted by the complaints of the Surgeon-General, in 1834 Kay proposed a washroom for the pensioners next to the east kitchen; there they could clean their notoriously dirty legs and feet, which presumably gave rise to the 'territorial offences' that encroached upon the space of others living in close proximity.[37] There were already washing places within the buildings, but these were perhaps not accessible enough for the inflexible or infirm to reach unaided all the parts in need of water.

Kay sought also to replace the outside privies. Each of the four toilet blocks on the east and west sides of the Hospital were at least 100 feet away from the nearest building, and the pensioners on upper floors especially had to undertake long walks to reach them, to their 'inconvenience and occasional suffering'. Between 1835 and 1841 Kay introduced water-closets next to the staircases, at a cost of £300 per building, fed by the existing reservoirs and cisterns. Although welcome, these improvements were spread disproportionately between officers and men. In all, 140 new water-closets were installed for the use of the pensioners between 1835 and 1859 (one seat per eleven men), while a further 126 were installed for the ninety officers' apartments.[38]

THE BREWHOUSE

The first report of faulty beer at the Hospital, which resulted in compensation payments to the pensioners who were forced to drink water, had been made in 1708,[39] but it was not until 1716 that the directors gave their considered attention to a recurring problem. They began by checking with Chelsea the amount paid to the brewer (7s 6d per barrel), and whether the payment of excise was excused (it was not: the brewer paid it). Since the annual cost of beer at Greenwich was £900, and it was moreover 'frequently prejudicial to health', to the 'great discontent and Clamour of the men', they decided in 1717 that it would be preferable to brew their own beer on site at an annual cost of £763, with an initial outlay of £800 on the building of a brewhouse on the west side of the site, with a pipeline laid in 1718 to bring the beer to cellars underneath the kitchen. A master brewer was appointed at £60 per year.[40] The situation was reviewed in 1738, when the brewhouse was found to be old, decayed and too small. A new one was approved, to be built 'with all possible frugality' at a cost of £600 with a further £430 for utensils, on the basis that by brewing its own beer, the Hospital saved £800 per year.[41] This was substantially erected in 1739–40, and was ready for use by 1742, when a brewer was appointed at the reduced rate of

249 Joseph Kay's stable block to the west of the principal Hospital buildings, referred to as 'Hospital mews' on Hardwick's plan of 1860 (fig. 243).

£40 per year.[42] A large cistern was housed nearby in order to provide water in the event of fire, an action taken following a fire in the steward's manservant's room after he had become drunk and neglected to put out his candle.[43] Two pipes, 1½ inches in diameter, were laid from the brewhouse to the north-east corner of Queen Mary, one for beer to serve the two dining halls, the other for water.[44] The pipes were diverted to serve the Infirmary as well in 1768.[45]

In 1829 Kay reported that the brewhouse, bakehouse and stables, to the west of the main Hospital buildings, had become expensive to maintain.[46] As part of the continuing improvements, he succeeded in securing the agreement of the Commissioners to their complete rebuilding, to his design.[47] The stables and coach-house, erected in 1835–6, continued in this use after the closure of the Hospital, although the south range of the building was converted into quarters for the police (fig. 249). The adjacent brewery, a single-storey structure with a basement, of which a remnant survives, was described as 'recently erected' in 1834.[48] The Hospital had been brewing on or near this location since the early eighteenth century. The new building, which had to be extensively repaired in 1843 following a fire, ceased to be used as a brewery before the Hospital closed. It was used for a time as an engine house, with an engine below ground,[49] and subsequently has functioned as an electricity substation. Kay's post-fire cast-iron fireproofing survives.

★   ★   ★

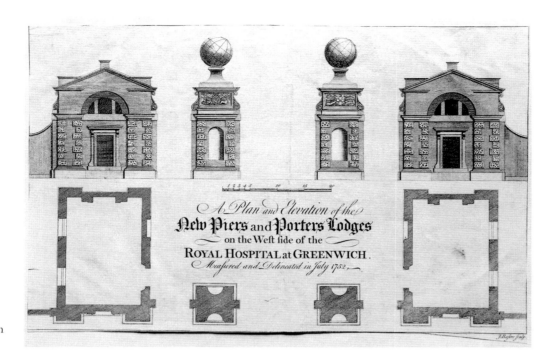

250 An engraving of the plan and elevation of the gatepiers and lodges on the west side of the Royal Hospital in 1752.

PENSIONERS' CONDITIONS

During this prolonged phase of improvements the Senior Medical Officer John Liddell made numerous proposals for ameliorating the pensioners' conditions. In 1846 he recommended better cooking and a more varied diet. He found that the meat was too rapidly cooked and 'converted into a hard mass, ill adapted to the toothless mouths and feeble digestions of the great body of our veterans'. He proposed roast meat and pork to vary the diet of beef and mutton (see Appendix 3) and recommended the

251 The east gate lodges of the Hospital.

reduction by half of the festival allowance of half a gallon of strong ale. This was 'sufficient to intoxicate any man, thus legalising debauchery' and encouraged the 'festival fits' which were well known to the nurses of the Infirmary.[50] Liddell also played a role of fundamental importance in the acquisition by the Hospital of the piece of land on the Isle of Dogs which was to become Island Gardens. There was good reason, he reported in 1848, to fear the coming there of 'a second Manchester with a series of manufactories' and consequent deleterious effects on the respiratory condition of the men. He pressed successfully for the purchase of Island Gardens by the Hospital, 'to prevent the total closure of its vista and to shut out the annoyances of gloomy unsightly and offensive buildings that are sure to be erected on the North side of the Thames'. Purchase followed in 1849 for £10,000. Island Gardens became a public amenity in 1895.[51]

RAILINGS, GATES AND LODGES

The programme of improvements to the sanitation, services and fabric of the Hospital was continued by Kay's successor, Philip Hardwick,[52] who removed the last of the external privies in 1849–50 and also supervised the completion of his predecessor's works in the town. His major contribution however lay in his regularisation of the setting of the Hospital, the iron railings, gates, lodges and grassed outer courts all being created between 1849 and 1856. The enclosing of the Hospital within regularised bounds had been first accomplished in 1752, when the outer areas, much less extensive on the west side than they are now, were enclosed within brick walls. Within and beyond was a jumble of outbuildings and cross-walls, later transformed through clearance and re-enclosure, and enlargement on the west side, as part of the wide-ranging plan of improvements in the nineteenth century. This was the last major phase of construction work to be carried out by the Royal Hospital in fulfilment at last of the intentions of the original founders and benefactors. The real beneficiary of the works was not the Royal Hospital, which was facing closure within a decade of their completion, but the Royal Naval College, which maintained the grounds and enclosures for over a century with only minor alterations and respectful additions.

The original grant of land for the Hospital had been neither as extensive nor as inclusive as the founders would have wished. Less ground was being supplied than was available at Chelsea, in order to accommodate a greater number of pensioners. The more or less fixed boundaries were the north, where the river frontage was given its present alignment in 1713, and the south, where the Romney Road was established in 1697–9. The east and west boundaries were rather more mutable and the directors until the mid-eighteenth century consistently sought to expand the Hospital holdings in both directions. These endeavours reached their first fruition with the erection of the east and west gates and the building of two pairs of lodges in 1751–4, with a roadway running between (fig. 250).[53] The lodges, of red brick with stone dressings, were all of the same design. Simple, heated, rectangular single-storey buildings with attics, they were intended for the use of the watch or guards, and in the case of the south-west lodge, one of the two nearest the town, for the use of the Hospital porter. All the lodges subsequently were rebuilt and in some cases moved under the direction of Hardwick in 1850–51, all except the south-west building being given a single-storey extension which in all cases was raised to two storeys in 1906 (fig. 251).[54] Since the 1960s the guard duties at Greenwich have been carried out by Ministry of Defence Police. They have continued to use the lodges but have been housed in the three-storey Police Section House next to the Pepys Building (see below), built by Lucas Brothers to the design of Hardwick in 1853–4 as the Steward's house.[55] By the 1880s this was in use as Infectious Sick Quarters;[56] as a result the interior has been heavily reworked although it retains an original, open-string, turned-baluster stair.

Both eighteenth-century entrances to the Hospital had large iron carriage gates flanked by small wicket gates for pedestrians. The great gates at the west entrance were moved to their present position in 1850, from their earlier location immediately to the west of the King Charles and King William Buildings, where they had been placed in 1751,[57] possibly replacing the gates proposed by Hawksmoor in 1713 to stand between the Painted Hall and the kitchen of King Charles (figs 252 and 253). The decorative stone panels on the gatepiers, displaying the Hospital arms and naval trophies, and the royal arms, with helmet, flag and cannon, are all now badly eroded.[58] Above, the remarkable monumental globes, each 6 feet in diameter, composed of six stones and weighing nearly 7 tons, represent the celestial and terrestrial spheres. They were 'placed in an oblique position, agreeable to the latitude of the place in which they stand'.[59] When new, the terrestrial globe to the south had inlaid in copper 'the parallels of latitude to every ten degrees in each hemisphere', while the celestial sphere to the north had inlays of the '24 meridians, the equinoxial, ecliptic, tropics, and circles', all delineated by Richard Oliver, former mathematics master at the Academy at Greenwich, who was paid 50 guineas in 1754 for his 'Trouble, Care and Skill'.[60] These inlays now stand proud of the eroded stonework. Originally, both of the globes had further detailing. There were a great number of stars on the celestial sphere, while the terrestrial had the route of Admiral Lord Anson's circumnavigation of the globe made in 1740–44 in HMS *Centurion*.

Responsibility for the design of the gates and lodges lies with the Surveyor Thomas Ripley and the Clerk of Works William Robinson, but the location of any drawings is unknown and there does not seem to have been any discussion of the design by the directors. First published in an engraving in 1751,[61] the rusticated lodges and piers are in the well-established Palladian style, but the ensemble is raised to the level of the extraordinary by the addition of the globes. By the eighteenth century these had become a rather syncretic symbol, combining ideas of both imperial and religious dominion, informed by speculative sixteenth-century reconstructions of the pillars of the Temple of Solomon (which bears on eighteenth-century freemasonry), and such Renaissance motifs as the pillars of Hercules.[62] Such allusions made them particularly apposite forms for institutional gateways where a message might be desirable.[63] At Greenwich, the broad meanings which might be attributed to the gates also bear more specific readings. In their detailed delineation of the mapped world, and their memorialising of Anson's voyage, they celebrate British naval supremacy, while in their scientific character they celebrate the educational role of the institution which they guard. Responsibility for the present disposition of the west gate and lodges lies with Joseph Kay, who replanned the approach road in the 1830s to provide a more ceremonial route to the Hospital, and Philip Hardwick, who oversaw their re-erection in 1850: 'On Monday, the anniversary of the battle of Trafalgar, the new west gates at Greenwich Hospital were opened by Admiral Sir James Gordon. . . . These gates, with the lodges and celestial and terrestrial globe-capped pillars, have been removed, in the course of the improvement in their immediate neighbourhood, to their present position'.[64]

The improvements to the grounds carried out by Kay and Hardwick, with the removal of the mid-eighteenth-century dividing walls, drying courts, washhouses and other ancillary structures, all followed Edward Hawke Locker's notably successful initiatives, first as Secretary, then as Commissioner, proposed in fulfilment of the Hospital's original design. He did not succeed in achieving all his aims, failing to have the Romney Road moved to the south of the Queen's House, a proposal put forward in 1824 to unite the grounds of the Hospital and the Asylum, which he then wished to have embellished by a Naval Column.[65] The clearance of the outer courts, suggested by Locker in 1824, was not fully achieved until after his death in 1849. He had retired five years earlier and some credit for maintaining the impetus of the programme of improvements must go to Sir Charles Adam, Governor from 1847 until 1853.[66] Locker hoped that the grounds might be turfed, set out as walks for the pensioners and 'adorned with appropriate embellishments corresponding with the designs of Sir Christopher Wren'.[67] Hardwick's Dolphin Fountains, surmounted by gas lamps, to the west of the King Charles and King William Buildings, were installed in 1850 (fig. 254),[68] and the railing of the site was completed soon afterwards.

Although the river terrace to the north and the southern boundary had stretches of railings from the eighteenth century onwards, none of these survives. The Infirmary railings were put up by Kay in 1836. These appear to have set the pattern for the standardised plain leaf-head design that Hardwick followed between 1849 and 1859, when the remainder of the site was railed, eventually enclosing all of the Hospital's property on both sides

252   The west gates in their original location, close to the King Charles and King William Buildings, photographed by Fox Talbot.

of Romney Road, including the old burial ground.[69] The orna-mental cast- and wrought-iron gates to each side also date from this last phase of improvements.[70] The late nineteenth-century east gate is configured differently from the other three, with spearheads on top of standards as high as the gatepiers, in an arrangement which echoes the railings and gates of the Trafalgar Quarters opposite. The north, south and west gates all closely follow the

same model as each other with only slight variations. All have double gates bearing the Hospital arms to the centre and a naval coronet above. The south gate was the first to be erected in 1851, 'to Mr Hardwick's design'.[71] When the west entrance was re-sited in 1850, its gates came with it, but in 1858 these were replaced[72] and the old ones appear to have been put on the market: 'How did it happen that the Government sold by auction, at less than

253 The west gates in 1997, looking towards College Approach.

their value as old iron, the wrought-iron gates from Greenwich Old Palace, as we are told they did? At any rate there are the gates at Mr. Pratt's, in Bond Street, in perfectly good order, and though not particularly handsome, certainly a dozen times more interesting than the cast-iron affairs put up in their stead'.[73]

The date of the north, river gate cannot be so clearly established but it is likely to have been erected during the same period, replacing the rather more modest gates of the eighteenth century (fig. 255). William Newton had produced several proposals for river gates of some grandeur in the 1780s, including one based on a Palladian motif.[74] Other ideas included re-siting the west gates here, where they would 'be seen to much greater advantage',[75] but the directors restricted themselves to rebuilding the river stairs and landing around 1790. An opportunity for reframing the great ceremonial space of the Grand Court and the magnificent vista to the park was lost.

★   ★   ★

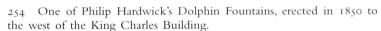

254 One of Philip Hardwick's Dolphin Fountains, erected in 1850 to the west of the King Charles Building.

255 The north, river gate of the Royal Hospital.

THE HOSPITAL BURIAL GROUNDS

During its lifetime, the Hospital had three consecutive burial grounds, the first of which was at the north-east corner of the park. At some time in the seventeenth century, following the walling-in of the park by James I in 1619–24, a large L-shaped plot at this point was enclosed as a dwarf orchard with a house in the corner, apparently all surrounded by a low wall.[76] It may be that this was done as part of Sir William Boreman's planting in the 1660s when so many other improvements were being made in the park (see chapter 1). The east (Maze Hill) arm of the orchard, an area of about 300 feet by 60 feet, was granted to Greenwich Hospital in January 1707 by Prince George of Denmark, Lord High Admiral, to become a burial ground.[77] It had become apparent that the parish could not be expected to cope with the burial of pensioners among whom, in the nature of things, the death rate was high. The Hospital had wanted a larger 2-acre ground, 660 feet by 132 feet, but had to settle for much less, the site granted being defined by the foundations of the orchard wall.[78] The ground was levelled and walled in under John James's supervision within the year.[79] The walls of this burial ground survive in large measure, though much repaired. The east side went with the widening of Maze Hill in 1823, but the other three sides endure with openings and blocked openings into the park to the west, all inserted save one near the south end which is flanked by stone-capped piers and appears to have been an original point of access.

When Benjamin Hoskins, Captain of the Hospital and a member of the governing council, died in 1712, his widow requested that a burial vault be made for him. In response, a vault for all Hospital officers and their families was built in 1713–14 at the south end of the burial ground, with a superstructure 'for the minister to stand dry under'.[80] This officers' mausoleum was built under the supervision of Nicholas Hawksmoor, with the brick-work probably executed by Richard Billinghurst. It is now in use as a shed in the garden of 40 Maze Hill (see chapter 8), albeit an

257 C. Raymond Smith, *Britannia*. The monument was erected in the burial ground next to Romney Road in 1892, 'In Memory of the Gallant Officers and Men of the Royal Navy and Marines to the number of about twenty thousand formerly inmates of the Royal Hospital Greenwich whose remains were interred in this cemetery between the years 1749 and 1869' (PRO ADM 195/47). (From 1857 interments had taken place at the new burial ground to the east of the Hospital; 1869 was the date of closure of the Hospital itself.)

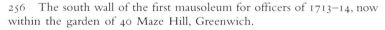

256   The south wall of the first mausoleum for officers of 1713–14, now within the garden of 40 Maze Hill, Greenwich.

unusually handsome one. It is a single-storey, three-by-one-bay pavilion over a vault, of about 25 feet by 18 feet, of brown stock brick with finely gauged rubbed red-brick arches (fig. 256). Its round-headed openings originally were wholly open to the north, the direction from which it was intended to be seen, and blind elsewhere. The three-bay north elevation now has a central door and flanking sash windows. In 1749 it was depicted with a triple roof on the north-south axis, with a taller central gable.[81] The upper parts appear to have been wholly rebuilt in the early nineteenth century with stone-coped gables to a slate roof on an east-west axis. Below, the three-bay, groined brick vault retains burials and evidence for entrances from the north and the west.

By the 1730s the burial ground was proving inadequate to the needs of the more populated Hospital. As it could not be enlarged, it was directed that burials should be stacked, a strategy which presumably involved exhumation.[82] By 1747 the ground had become such a nuisance to its neighbours that they requested its closure[83] and in 1749 a new burial ground was established south-west of the Hospital's main buildings. The first burial ground then appears to have lapsed into being part of the garden of the house at the north-east corner of the park.[84] The mausoleum was described as

258   The mausoleum for officers built in 1750 in the new burial ground to the south of Romney Road. In the foreground is the tomb of Sir James Alexander Gordon, Admiral of the Fleet and the last Governor of Greenwich Hospital, who died in 1869.

ruinous in 1786, and repairs were intended. Notwithstanding the closure of the burial ground, the officers' vault continued to be in use for burials until 1820.[85] The widening of the road in 1823 placed the east end of the mausoleum next to the pavement, permitting a change of use, first to coachhouse then to garage. The sealed vault was forgotten until it was accidentally rediscovered during repairs in 1952.[86]

The new burial ground was established in the 'Great Garden Ground' to the south of Romney Road, which, having been leased out since the 1720s, reverted to the Hospital in 1747. An area of $3\frac{1}{2}$ acres was set aside for use as a new 'Burying Ground', extended in 1783 to $4\frac{1}{2}$ acres (fig. 302).[87] A simple, single-storey, brick-built mausoleum for officers was erected in 1750, probably to the designs of Thomas Ripley, who had made drawings for it.[88] This is a neo-Palladian version of Hawksmoor's mausoleum (fig. 258). Above the three finely gauged round arches of its west front is an open pediment which carries a cartouche with an inscription

commemorating the first burial on the site, of pensioner John Meriton, on 5 July 1749. Entrance to the vault, which extends some 27 feet westwards, is by a stairway on the east side.[89] The coffins were lowered by a machine which was replaced in 1812.[90]

In 1777 it was noted that the burials were 'very frequent, and the Graves, from necessity being larger', were 'kept open longer, than is usually practised' – an average of three weeks.[91] This was a consequence of the Hospital's practice of placing eighteen coffins in each grave, arranged two abreast to a depth of 16 feet, with a minimum of 4 inches of earth between each layer.[92] Burials took place on Tuesdays and Fridays, the bodies being kept beforehand in the mortuary or dead house in the basement of the Infirmary. At ten o'clock the coffins were borne out through the Infirmary courtyard and across the road to the graveyard.

By the early nineteenth century the burial ground was becoming full just as the number of pensioners reached its peak. More space was made in 1817 by removing some of the wooden coffins,[93] but there was little opportunity for overall expansion since the grounds were hemmed in by other buildings. The Hospital's senior medical officer, Dr Liddell, in 1847 feared that 'the effluvia of a graveyard, crowded I believe, beyond a parallel . . . might endanger the health and safety of all'. Reporting three years later, Philip Hardwick was more sanguine, finding, as a result of the introduction of lead coffins, that the vault had 'no effluvium of any kind arising from it'.[94] In 1855, however, the Hospital acknowledged the inevitable and decided to close the burial ground, although interments continued until 1 September 1857, when its successor was opened to the east of the Hospital on a plot of land known as the 'East Greenwich Pleasaunce' (fig. 257).[95] The bodies were transported here from the mortuary in the Infirmary by hearse and were buried at a depth of 8 feet, one body per grave. The new burial ground continued to be used by the Royal Hospital School for some time after the Hospital's closure in 1869.[96] The area was partly built over in the 1920s, but a public garden and the lodges and gates fronting Woolwich Road survive.

Decline and Departures

In his evidence to the Commissioners inquiring into the Hospital, Hardwick (like Kay, called 'Architect', rather than 'Clerk of Works') agreed that 'the harmony which is so desirable in all establishments, does not prevail at Greenwich Hospital', but in the area for which he was responsible he was predictably more optimistic.[97] He reported the condition of the fabric as 'very good indeed; very solid'. He found the building well arranged, with better ventilation introduced in recent years, although bugs remained a serious problem. It was the view of others that the ventilation at the Hospital was excessive. The men often had to wait up to two hours in the unheated and unglazed central vestibule of the King Charles Building in order to see the Adjutant in the adjacent Council Room to the north, the present Stuart Room (fig. 259), and within the main buildings they were allowed at this time to smoke only in the Chalk Walk (under the Queen Mary colonnade), which was very cold, with a strong draught. Hardwick agreed that the vestibule could be glazed, using wrought iron for the framing, and that the cold stone paving of the wards could be replaced with timber, for the comfort of the men. He produced a drawing to show that it had been Wren's intention to ornament the openings in the vestibule with ironwork, and his experience at St Bartholomew's Hospital, where he had introduced glazed doors, was that this could easily be done without disfiguring the fabric. The glazing of the King Charles and, much later, the Queen Anne vestibules followed.

The superintendent of the dining halls, a Mr Allen, suggested that life would be still more agreeable for the men if common rooms could be provided, attached to each ward, since in order to smoke in company and keep warm, the only places to go were the local taverns. Hardwick demurred on the grounds that the provision of common rooms would reduce the accommodation available in the wards and besides, in the view of W. Sivell, the 'Inspector of Works' responsible for repairs, common rooms would encourage smoking, since sailors 'are very great smokers', and spitting inevitably would follow. Besides, a curving, wooden colonnade with a river view had been erected between 1854 and 1859 to the design of Hardwick for the benefit of smokers, to the west

259   The Stuart Room, with a magnificent early eighteenth-century chimneypiece, to the north of the central entrance vestibule of the King Charles Building.

260   Pensioners outside the King William Building next to Romney Road.

261   Philip Hardwick, smoking colonnade to the west of the King Charles Building.

of the King Charles Building (fig. 261).[98] It was shortened at its western end in 1883 to make space for a racquet court, now part of the Pepys Building.

Notwithstanding the opportunities for convivial alfresco smoking, life for the seamen was monastic and boring. A visitor in 1810, while acknowledging the Hospital as 'a most beautiful edifice', had found 'the old sailors who inhabit it . . . looking very tired and melancholy; they are seen warming themselves in the sun, or crawling languidly along the magnificent colonnades or porticoes [fig. 260], of which the elegance and beauty makes a sad contrast with their crippled, infirm, and dependent old age'.[99] This picturesque and somewhat zoological assessment did not however apply to all. The vitality of some of the men was extraordinary; among the 2400 pensioners in 1803, there were ninety-six over eighty, sixteen over ninety and one aged 102.[100] Some were fit enough for the occasional, bizarre game of cricket, the one-armed beating the one-legged at Blackheath in 1766, the latter belatedly gaining their revenge at Walworth in 1796, despite five wooden legs being broken and the carpenter much in demand.[101]

In 1814 the Hospital had been capable of accommodating 2710 pensioners. A number of factors contributed to the subsequent decline in occupation: the long period of relative peace following the end of the war with France in 1815; the growth in the demand for merchant seamen; the increase in settlement in the colonies; and the greater popularity of out-pensions, which allowed seamen to receive the small income of £7 per year without submitting themselves to the discipline and boredom of institutional life, an arrangement authorised by Parliament in 1763 which by 1820 was costing the Hospital over £200,000 per year, a burden which was taken on by the government in 1829.[102] The Commissioners recognised that the weekly shilling pocket money was inadequate for resident men, tending to exclude them 'from social intercourse with all but those of their own mono-tonous fraternity, thereby aggravating the evils which attend all monastic institutions'.[103] In 1860 there were 1518 pensioners resident at the Hospital; seven wards were closed. Despite the falling roll, there were twenty officers in charge (Governor, Lieutenant-Governor, four captains, four commanders, eight lieutenants and two masters) and a supernumerary body of police (Inspector, three sergeants, fourteen constables), more than enough to deal with the transgressions of men of considerably greater vigour than the pensioners, and fully capable of keeping out the dogs, 'beggars, vagrants, pedlars or other idle and disorderly persons of either sex' who might otherwise have slipped in. Only 'persons of decent appearance and behaviour', who were not smoking at the time, and 'the carriages of gentlemen' were permitted to pass through the gates. If a lady or gentleman was followed by dogs, however inadvertently, the parties would be 'civilly acquainted with the regulation'.[104]

Overspending was not confined to management and security. Even after the expenditure of £282,000 over a twenty-year period on the Hospital and school, which saw a major programme of improvements completed, there were still ninety-five artisans employed by the Hospital's works department.[105] In comparing expenditure between 1805 and 1859, the expense of an individual pensioner remained constant but the cost of the overall establishment had doubled even with a 30 per cent reduction in numbers. There was a disproportion between the money spent on pensioners and the sums absorbed in management, discipline and the maintenance of the fabric. With over twice as many pensioners, the overall costs of Les Invalides and its branch at Avignon (£112,342 in 1848 – £31 per pensioner, of which £5 was spent on administration and fabric) were slightly less than those incurred at Greenwich (£119,811 in 1859 – £58 per pensioner, of which £28 was spent on administration and fabric).[106]

Official reports which arrive at wholly damning conclusions and present radical proposals have the potential to be counterproductive in disturbing too many vested interests. They are therefore shelved. The Commissioners were perhaps alive to this possibility: notwithstanding their detailed criticisms, their proposals were mild and judiciously expressed. They recommended the continuation of the Hospital as an asylum for infirm, decrepit and imbecilic naval men and their wives and children, with amendments to the administration: the establishment of an executive council under Admiralty control; a reduction in the numbers of Commissioners and staff; cutting costs and increasing efficiency by, for example, buying in domestic service rather than employing a disproportionately large number of pensioners and their wives.[107] The *Report* was in effect an enabling device: discussions on the future of the Hospital and the implementation of improvements to its administration could begin in earnest. Those who agreed with the writer in 1859 who 'found that there had been apparently no amelioration of the pensioners' condition since Captain Baillie's immolation on the Sandwich altar' could now have their say. Those who were familiar only with the grand spaces – the Painted Hall, the Chapel, the dining halls and one 'show ward' (the Royal Charles on the first floor of the east wing of the King Charles Building) (figs 226 and 227) – would become more fully informed as the future of the Hospital became a matter of debate and report.[108] One positive result for the pensioners was an increase in their pocket money from 1s to between 3s and 5s per week, depending on rank.

The Greenwich Hospital Bill, passed in 1861 and taking effect on 1 January 1862, took the first steps in the amendment of the administration, dissolving the Commissioners and passing authority to the Paymaster General, the First Commissioner of Her Majesty's Works and Public Buildings and three Commissioners to be appointed by the Lords of the Admiralty: a Civil Commissioner, a Medical Commissioner and an Admiral Superintendent. The office of Governor would continue but the number of officers would be reduced to a captain, a commander and three lieutenants.[109]

Commissioner Sir Richard Bromley, appointed in 1863, lost no time in applying the administrative talents which he had deployed already in the Admiralty and as the accountant to the Burgoyne Commission on the Irish famine.[110] In 1864 he recommended further improvements to the management and constitution of the Hospital, which by this time housed only 1423 pensioners. He laid particular stress on the tedium of the lives of the men, noting that although there was a library (which had been established in 1824), old sailors are not great readers. He supported the Governor's proposal of a bowling alley (constructed in the Chalk Walk underneath the east colonnade) (fig. 262), and recommended lectures on 'homely and interesting subjects' to keep the men out of the local pubs. The First Lord of the Admiralty, Edward Seymour, 12th Duke of Somerset, concurred: the pensioners 'pass their Day in a state of listless Idleness and Mental Vacuity, until recalled at fixed Intervals to their Meals or their Beds. It is not surprising that old Sailors so circumstanced should resort to the Alehouse or to worse Places'. In his view, the Hospital should accommodate only the infirm since able-bodied pensioners could be admitted only if they sacrificed the freedom, comfort and social independence 'which

262   The bowling alley installed in the Chalk Walk towards the end of the occupation of the buildings by the Royal Hospital.

263   Able-bodied pensioners leaving the Hospital in 1865 (*Illustrated London News*, 21 October 1865).

no Englishman would willingly resign'.[111] The obdurate Jack Tars, those 'embodied symbols of the national imagination',[112] are here brought to centre-stage, but as pale shadows of the heroic figures celebrated by William Hazlitt forty years before: 'Stung with wounds, stunned with bruises, bleeding and mangled, an English sailor never finds himself so much alive as when he is flung half dead into the cockpit; for he then perceives the extreme consciousness of his existence in his conflict with external matter'.[113] These were the men who had prompted the flippant remark of Princess Caroline of Brunswick on her arrival in 1795: 'Do all Englishmen have only one arm or one leg?'.[114] Few of the pensioners of Somerset's day would have seen such action, but whether they had or not, watching the ships go by on the Thames and recalling or imagining past glories for the benefit of susceptible visitors could not have been other than tediously debilitating:

> Why, as for the matter o' that, sir, what else have we got to do? Here we are, snug moored in Greenwich, riding out the gale of life till death brings our anchors home, and then our service being worn through, and the cable stranded, we slip and run for the haven of eternal rest. Why, sir, if it warn't for our spinning a yarn now and then, we should spit and sputter at each other like a parcel of cats in a gutter.[115]

The pensioners as well as the visitors were, by the mid-nineteenth century, victims of the romantic dislocation of those who have missed the opportunity to participate, however remotely, in blood-stirring conflict. It was re-created for them in the works of such artists as Clarkson Stanfield (Honorary Curator of the Painted Hall) who continued the tradition of marine painting established in the seventeenth century by Willem van de Velde, father and son, but painted the scenes long after the battles were

over. The peg-legged pensioner telling his story, most famously depicted by Thomas Davidson in 1883, long after the Hospital at Greenwich had closed, had become a sanitised and rather fraudulent figure, far removed from Hazlitt's mangled hero.[116] Such paintings, populated by men with wooden legs rather than by those with more potentially shocking disabilities or scarring, presented the acceptable face of patriotism in showing men who had fought for their country, but who now, no longer vigorous or dangerous, were reliant upon such benefits as could be afforded by a grateful nation.[117] There were many who went to listen and to contribute, particularly after London's first suburban railway line reached Greenwich in 1838: 5785 visited the Painted Hall and 4476 the Chapel, at 3d each, on one day in 1843.[118]

By the Greenwich Hospital Act of 1865 the roles of the Commissioners, Governor and Lieutenant-Governor were all abolished, but the officers continued in residence at the Hospital.[119] With their families, they continued to live in comfort in the best parts, including the river frontage, occupying almost half the cubic space of the four main blocks.[120] Meanwhile, the number of pensioners in residence fell rapidly as they took the option encouraged by the Duke of Somerset of receiving out-pensions, rather than living in. The *Illustrated London News* recorded the departure of the able-bodied in October 1865, noting that almost 1000 had recently taken their leave, 'in search of the consolations which only social and domestic affection will bestow' (fig. 263).[121] This left a complement of only 450 infirm and crippled men,[122] a number which had fallen to 380 by March 1867, each costing £114 per year, at a time when the annual cost per patient per bed in civil hospitals was about £30. By this time, two of the four blocks were unused and the Seamen's Hospital Society, which cared for men of the merchant fleet on the *Dreadnought* hospital ship, moored off Greenwich, was petitioning for space. The Queen Anne Building was favoured by the Society since the removal of the wooden cabin partitions would restore its large, lofty wards to something very like St Bartholomew's, enabling the accommodation of 300 men, and the ventilation could readily be improved by cutting openings in the central dividing walls. Furthermore, the Thames frontage would enable the Society to advertise its presence to sailors on the river. Other buildings might be used as a hospital for the town of Greenwich, which had a population of 150,000 and no hospital at all to serve them. Such solutions were fantasies. The Seamen's Hospital Society was no match for the officers of the Hospital who successfully lobbied the Admiralty, or indeed for the entrenched opinions within the Admiralty itself. This was not a mercantile but a Royal Naval foundation and there were those who viewed such a takeover rather as the established Church has often viewed the use of its redundant buildings by other denominations. Even at this late stage in the life of the institution at Greenwich, despite all the criticism of unnecessary expense, one of the lieutenants was reported to be throwing two storeys into one 'to please this gallant officer', at a cost of twice his salary. The twelve officers who occupied the Queen Anne pavilions were not ready to give up their twelve halls, thirty sitting rooms, seventy-two bedrooms, twenty-two cellars and fifteen kitchens. The Admiralty stood by them and offered accommodation to the Seamen's Hospital Society in the Queen Mary Building, whose fire-proof cabins of brick and stone, poor ventilation and prevalence of vermin was wholly unconducive to the care of the sick and impossibly expensive to convert.[123] It was time for another *Report*.

The new *Report of the Committee Appointed to Look into the Management of Greenwich Hospital and Schools* was presented to the House of Commons in 1868.[124] The committee found that the management of the Hospital 'has so long been considered by outside opinion as synonymous with all that is costly and extravagant, and the building itself has of late come to be considered as so unsuited to the habits of seamen, that all further attempts [to improve it] . . . may . . . by many be regarded as hopeless'. Remarkably, refusing to acknowledge the logical consequences of their own conclusions, the committee members did not recommend closure. Rather, taking the position of God in his reply to Abraham on the fate of Sodom (Genesis 18: 22–33), they felt that even if some of the helpless and bedridden could be catered for at Haslar or Netley, there would still be 200 remaining who must be spared.[125] Furthermore, they deemed it of vital importance to maintain the capacity of the Hospital to fulfil its original purposes in the event of a sudden outbreak of naval warfare, and accordingly made detailed recommendations for the conversion of the buildings for the accommodation of 1200 men. *The Times* was sceptical: 'If external advice could make one wise, then would the Admiralty be of all departments the most effective. Unhappily it is only bad administrators who appeal to the advice of others. . . . [T]he whole Office is deranged'.[126] The Royal Hospital at Greenwich was now in its death throes. That which appears now to have been inevitable since the *Report* of 1860 could no longer be resisted; a great 'Imperial institution' was about to close.[127] The transfer of invalids to other naval hospitals continued during 1869 until there were only thirty-one men left, in the Helpless Ward of the Infirmary and then, following a final spasm of removal, only twenty who could not be moved. Although the Admiralty reserved the right to use the Hospital again for its original purpose in the event of war, on 1 October 1869, 'the walls of Greenwich Hos-

pital were closed against the pensioners of the Royal Navy. . . . [It is] impossible to contemplate without regret the dissolution of one of the noblest of our national institutions. The traditions of a profession are part of its strength, and Greenwich Hospital is entwined with the memories of well-nigh two centuries of the British Navy'.[128] The profession was then faced with the problem of what to do with its buildings. By the Greenwich Hospital Act of 1869, the Lords Commissioners of the Admiralty were permitted 'from time to time' to allow the Hospital to be occupied and used temporarily for the naval service, for any department of government, or for the benefit of 'persons engaged in seafaring pursuits', the payment of rent being discretionary.[129]

The Royal Naval College

By April 1870 the Infirmary was occupied by the Seamen's Hospital Society (see chapter 7), but the principal blocks of the Hospital were still 'unused and unoccupied' in 1871 when a local deputation to Prime Minister Gladstone urged the government to find an appropriate national use. He agreed the importance of the site but, in view of the 'vast extent and magnificent range of the building', did not wish to treat it sectionally. Ten months later, in June 1872, the King Charles Building was said to be being cleared of fittings for conversion into a Royal College for Naval Cadets.[130] In January 1873 the Admiralty, taking the opportunity to transfer its Naval College from Portsmouth (established in 1841), sanctioned the formation of the Royal Naval College at Greenwich – the 'University of the Navy' – for the education of officers of all ranks above midshipman in all branches of theoretical and scientific study bearing on their profession; its opening was planned for 1 February 1874, with arrangements for higher courses of study to be completed by October 1874. Professorships, under the overall guidance of a Director of Studies, were to be established in Mathematics, Physical Sciences, Chemistry, Applied Mechanics and Fortifications.[131] £10,000 had been voted by Parliament for its alteration and utilisation.[132] The Lords Commissioners, using their discretion, in 1873 determined that the buildings, excluding the Painted Hall and the Infirmary, would be occupied rent-free by the Royal Naval College. The Infirmary was leased to the Seamen's Hospital Society, which inherited the twenty helpless and six sick pensioners who could not be moved when the Hospital closed.[133] The Admiralty reserved the right to use the Painted Hall as a dining hall but expressed the hope that the public would still be able to visit.[134] Its maintenance was to remain the responsibility of Greenwich Hospital, a continuing institution administered by the Admiralty, which would pay for the three 'Yeomen' who would look after it and for the Metropolitan Police (reduced to two sergeants and eight constables) who continued to control access to the site. The Deputy Keeper of Public Records was to be invited to inspect the building accounts of the Hospital to consider their possible transfer to the Public Record Office.[135]

The works of conversion at Greenwich Hospital for the use of the Royal Naval College were overseen by Colonel Andrew Clarke, Director of Works for the Navy from 1864 to 1873, when he was knighted and appointed Governor of the Straits Settlements. An able administrator, rather than an architect, proud to recall his role as one of the framers of the first constitution of Victoria, where he had been Agent-General for the colony, this was his final task in the Works post.[136] Direct control of the oper-

264   The 'Jason' display outside the room in the King William Building which housed the nuclear reactor.

ation was exercised by the Clerk of Works, J. G. Loughborough, continuing in the post he had held at the Hospital in the 1860s, following the retirement of Hardwick in 1861 and succeeding Sivell, the Inspector of Works at the time of the 1860 *Report*.[137] As Clerk of Works in 1867 Loughborough had produced a plan of the Hospital for the 1868 *Report*. The building works were carried out by George Smith and Company of Westminster. Although described as extensive, the works were principally of conversion and renovation, involving the removal of partitions in the King Charles, Queen Anne and King William Buildings and the conversion of wards into classrooms, making it 'so fitly furnished as to satisfy any one but the veriest sybarite'.[138] The dining rooms under the Painted Hall and Chapel were redecorated as mess rooms by Cox and Sons of Southampton Street[139] and a two-storey lecture theatre was created at the east end of the south range of King William. This survives above the hall which was fitted out in steel and concrete in 1962–3 to house 'Jason', the water-cooled nuclear reactor designed as part of the Polaris missile programme to allow naval officers to gain operational experience before taking control of nuclear installations at sea (fig. 264).[140]

The plans of the Greenwich Hospital Estate made in 1879 and 1884[141] indicate the usage of the buildings after the conversion: in King Charles, the library and offices on the ground floor, class and examination rooms on the first and second floors, quarters for the President and officers in the north pavilions and quarters for officer students and the Director of Studies in the south pavilions;

in Queen Anne, quarters for senior officers and senior officer students in the north and south pavilions, with a Naval Museum occupying three floors of former wards in the east and west ranges. This contained a collection of naval models, together with relics of famous naval commanders, all moved to the National Maritime Museum in 1936, and models of ships' equipment used for purposes of instruction.[142] In King William, in addition to the lecture theatre and adjacent laboratories and demonstrators' rooms in the south wing, there were quarters for senior officer students on all four floors of the west wing. The junior and commissioned officer students were all housed in Queen Mary on the first, second and third floors of the east and south wings, with servants housed above on the fourth floor. Baths and storekeeper's rooms were in the ground-floor east wing; the bowling alley remained under the east colonnade; the former dining room beneath the Chapel was partitioned to create a billiard room and ante-room, with a smoking room to the east.[143] A second billiard room was provided for the use of engineer students on the third floor of the south range of Queen Mary and by 1910 a gymnasium had been installed on the first floor at the south-east corner.[144] The dining room subsequently was opened out to its original form and until 1998 served as the bar of the Officers' Mess.

It is clear that the broad pattern of accommodation established by the Hospital survived the conversion of 1873 and moreover continued until vacated by the Navy in 1998, with basic living accommodation in Queen Mary and the west range of King William (where members of the Women's Royal Naval Service were housed, following their reinstatement to the Service in 1938).[145] The grander apartments continued to be situated in the desirable pavilions of King Charles and Queen Anne, with the library and administration in King Charles where the College's administrative and teaching rooms replaced wards. The wards of Queen Anne, partitioned for cabins, were opened out in order to house the Naval Museum, with workshops on the top floor of the base wing. New openings were made at the ends of the spine walls in all but the ground floor of the west range, to adapt the circulation for the new function. By 1910 the Museum had contracted and was concentrated on the ground and first floors of the west range, and in the east range on the ground floor of the north end, with classrooms to the south. The two upper floors of the east block and the top floor of the west were partitioned to provide teaching rooms and accommodation for officers, with large openings in the spine walls in the centres as well as the ends.[146] Following the complete removal of the Museum, openings were made at the ends of the spine walls in the ground floor of the west range, and further partitioning was introduced to provide more accommodation. The original back-to-back chimneybreasts, providing one fireplace to each ward, survived the transition to museum use, but they have since been removed from all but the ground-floor south rooms of the west block and the north rooms of the east block. The most radical change has been the postwar installation of a two-storey lecture theatre at the north end of the west block, involving the demolition of part of the central dividing wall.

During the restoration of the Painted Hall in 1938, the former dining room below was subdivided by a partition to create a lower ground-floor vestibule, with two new flights of steps up to the Hall (fig. 265).[147] In the Hall itself, the lower windows were reinstated, and in the adjacent Nelson Room, a service lift installed

265 Part of the former dining room in the basement of the King William Building, subdivided in 1938 to create a vestibule with steps up to the Painted Hall (see fig. 223).

degree of ornamentation appears unnecessary, but the prominent location of the building, close to the former Hospital and visible from the river, evidently inspired a desire for show. The west racquet court, like the school gymnasium, is often assigned to Colonel Andrew Clarke, but he was more an administrator than an architect and besides he was succeeded in 1873 by Colonel Charles Pasley, RE, whose obituary notice gives him credit for the design.[151]

The racquet courts have continued in use, with some alterations, as squash courts but in deference to the increasingly technical nature of the College's training, the fives court was roofed over in 1905–6 in order to provide space for an engineering laboratory. A mezzanine was inserted against the north wall for a model room and research laboratory reached by a cast-iron spiral stair.[152] This middle section was for some years in use as a storeroom but the western squash courts were converted by the architects Timpson Manley in 1997 in order to provide a temporary Millennium Experience Visitors Centre. In 2000 the whole building became a Greenwich World Heritage Site Visitor Centre, a function well suited to its position between the town, the pier and the former Naval College.

THE 'FIVE FOOT WALK'

The riverside walk, a matter of concern to the Hospital, was established in 1731 and continued to be an object of discussion within

to bring food from the renovated kitchen. The restored Hall was opened as the Officers' Mess in 1939, shortly before the outbreak of the Second World War and sixty-six years after the proposal to convert it for this purpose was first mooted. The temporary mess accommodation, erected in the King William courtyard in 1917 to provide dining facilities for officers and servants, was removed at the same time.[148]

THE PEPYS BUILDING

The only substantial addition to the complex of buildings at Greenwich made by the Royal Naval College was the Pepys Building, built to the west of the main ranges of the former Hospital on the site of some of the outbuildings, including the brewhouse and bakehouse, which had been rebuilt by Joseph Kay. It was built in two phases, for sports, but subsequently was converted partly into an engineering laboratory. The single-storey building comprised a racquet court to the west, built in 1874–5 (fig. 266), with a second racquet court to the east, and an open fives court between the two, added in 1882–3.[149] The buff stucco exterior has Portland stone dressings and a giant order of Doric pilasters and paired Ionic columns which carry obelisk terminals; roundels (from east to west) contain the busts of national naval heroes: Anson, Drake, Cook, Howard, Blake, Benbow, Sandwich, Rodney, Duncan, Collingwood, Howe, Nelson and St Vincent (fig. 267). The boldly handled busts were the work of C. Raymond Smith, who worked at the Royal Observatory and at the Hospital School. The whole façade originally had channelled rustication throughout its lower storey, but in 1905–6 a doorway and windows were inserted into the central section.[150] In view of its function, such a

266 The west racquet court of the Pepys Building (PRO ADM 195/47).

267   The north front of the Pepys Building.

the Naval College, the priorities of the latter often coming into conflict with the interests of the local population (fig. 202). Since its foundation the Hospital had restricted itself to maintaining the stairs, landing and footpath. In 1898 the path was repaired at the cost of the Royal Navy, but within seven years Greenwich Borough Council was complaining about its condition.[153] This was an area of particular concern to the local authority since the path and the foreshore had become a public amenity both for locals and for day trippers: a 'favourite resort of children in the summer season'.[154] In 1908 the Greenwich Ratepayers Association approached the Admiralty with proposals for widening the path but the Admiral President John Fisher emphatically rejected these on the grounds that it would become 'the haunt of the "loafer" class and other undesirable persons', and that the noise would disturb the residents of the College.[155]

During the inter-war years many schemes were put forward unavailingly for widening the footpath, for providing an over-hanging promenade and for improving the siting of the Bellot memorial. Some of these were linked with proposals for slum clearance to the east and the building of a new Town Hall on the site of the Trafalgar Tavern, partly as a measure for the relief of the unemployed.[156] In 1930 George Lansbury, the Labour MP for Bow and Bromley, unsuccessfully attempted to allay Admiralty fears by the ingenious suggestion that 'instead of a narrow path likely to encourage seekers after darkness, there would be a broader footway with fewer opportunities for concealment'.[157] In 1961 Greenwich Council returned to the fray with a proposal for a 90 foot wide embankment in front of the College which was opposed by the Ministry of Works and the Royal Fine Art Commission on the grounds that it would have compromised a distinguishing feature of the original layout, the placing of build-ings close to the water's edge.[158] So the path remains narrow, and innocent visitors risk finding themselves jostling for space with the indigenous loafers.

★   ★   ★

MARITIME GREENWICH

The modern idea of 'Maritime Greenwich' is essentially a construction of the 1920s and 1930s, begun by Professor Geoffrey Callender, who was appointed the first Director of the National Maritime Museum in 1934. As both Secretary and Treasurer of the Society for Nautical Research (from 1930) and Professor of History and English at the Royal Naval College (from 1922), he fashioned Greenwich's history 'so that its naval associations were seen to go much further back in time, to the days of the Tudor Navy and to the Elizabethan sea-dogs and adventurers'.[159] The long-term success of Callender's myth-making has been demonstrated by the designation in 1997 of the 'Maritime Greenwich' World Heritage Site, but its short-term impact paled before an extraordinary initiative which took place at the Royal Naval College: the Greenwich pageants of June 1933, unveiled by the Admiral President Sir Barry Domvile. Scripted by Sir Arthur Bryant, the pageants were close to Fascist theatre. Complete with searchlights, military band and orchestra, male-voice choir and 2500 players, they were designed to tell the story of Greenwich and the Navy from the birth of Queen Elizabeth to the funeral of Nelson, in a performance of two hours, conducted at high speed, at night. A huge temporary grandstand for 12,000 people was erected, pioneering in its use of a tubular-steel scaffold frame. With its back to the river, it faced a stage which had a screen behind it, set between the colonnades of Queen Mary and King William, for the display of a backdrop. With performances on several nights, Domvile's pageant could be dedicated to a different distinguished personage or body on each occasion: a member of the royal family, members of the government and of the Board of Admiralty, the Lord Mayor of London and so on. The proceeds of the events were divided between naval and local charities.[160]

The usurpation by Bryant of Callender's role as 'unofficial remembrancer of Greenwich's naval history'[161] did not meet with the wholly uncritical reception that the organiser might have expected. One critic, perhaps mindful of the measured approach which the National Government was seeking to adopt in leading the country out of the Depression, deplored 'the transformation of patriotics from an emotion of innate and unconscious self-respect into one of exterior and artificially boosted vulgarity'. He concluded that 'the modern patriotic publicist is not so necessary to our national conscience as he thinks'.[162] A critic of the court masques of three centuries before might have said the same. Certainly the remark has some resonance in the context of political celebrations of the 1990s. The fine line between fantasy and reality appears to have become blurred for Domvile. One of the Royal Navy's brightest stars, he became an apologist for Nazism and was interned during the Second World War.[163]

THE SECOND WORLD WAR AND LATER RECONSTRUCTION

The threat from bombs in 1940, coupled with the fear of accidental damage which was rekindled by a domestic fire in the Vice-Admiral's quarters in King Charles in 1935, prompted the beginning of the photographic survey carried out by Helmut Gernsheim, 'as this might facilitate the preparation of working drawings if such important features were completely destroyed'.[164] The fears were well founded, but the College was extremely fortunate in escaping lightly in view of its proximity to the docks

268   The north end of the internal courtyard of the King Charles Building, photographed after bomb damage sustained in 1943.

and power stations which were prime targets for attack. Incendiary bombs in September 1940 damaged the roofs of King William and Queen Mary, and in 1943 there was bomb damage to the north front of Queen Anne. The most significant damage was sustained at the north-east end of King Charles, which received a direct hit in a daylight raid in 1943 (fig. 268). This resulted in the death of an officer and in serious damage to the north front, the Admiral President's residence and the south wall of the east front vestibule. Temporary repairs were put in hand, but it was not until 1957 that all the works of reconstruction were completed, including the re-roofing of the centre of the north pavilions and the replanning of the officers' apartments.[165] The early established institutional principle of survival on limited government funds was here repeated. The south end of John Webb's magisterial vestibule for ten years was screened merely by a temporary wall, awaiting its proper reinstatement as one of the finest rooms in the Hospital (fig. 167).

THE DEPARTURE OF THE NAVY

The Royal Naval College premises passed out of the control of the Navy on Monday 6 July 1998, two days after the last dance of the final summer ball, bringing to an end 300 years of naval occupation of the buildings at Greenwich.[166] Since 1983 the Royal Navy had to a small degree shared the accommodation, the buildings serving as the Joint Services Defence College. They could not, however, cater for all the officer-training needs of the Army and the Royal Air Force in addition to those of the Navy, so a new Joint Services Command and Staff College is to be developed at Shrivenham, near Swindon, which already is home to the Royal Military College of Science.

The location of a single 'Royal Defence College' has been the subject of periodic consideration for over thirty years. Denis Healey, the Labour Government's Secretary of State for Defence, in 1967 accepted the findings of the departmental report which he had commissioned, but disagreed with its conclusion, proposing that the joint college should be sited at Shrivenham, rather than at Greenwich, even though the latter had been recommended on both economic (£2 million as opposed to £3 million) and educational grounds. Greenwich, it was argued, would attract top-grade permanent staff and visiting lecturers. Furthermore, since academic and military establishments tend to become inward looking and hidebound, it was thought that 'exposure to the cultural atmosphere of the metropolis may be a valuable corrective'. If indeed the Naval College did move, then what would happen to the buildings?: 'It would be a tragedy if they were handed over by the Government to one of its innumerable colourless and prosaic agencies'.[167]

Such factors as institutional and political inertia, financial constraints and a vested interest within the Navy in remaining in one of the finest complexes of buildings in Europe encouraged discussions on the future of the College to go on for even longer than those which had characterised the final years of the Hospital. No discerning officer in the history of the buildings has willingly given up residence in the riverside apartments of King Charles and Queen Anne, at least not since their heating was sorted out.

In 1993 the decision to merge the three service colleges on one site was taken again, with a view to bringing together the Royal Navy, the Royal Air Force (from Bracknell) and the Army (from Camberley). The initial choice this time, Camberley, was rejected on grounds of cost, made higher by the presence in the existing buildings of asbestos, in favour of building a wholly new college at Shrivenham at an estimated cost of £500 million. Meanwhile, a temporary tri-service college would be established at Bracknell, even though, it was argued in the press, the cheapest option, at £11 million, would have been to upgrade the buildings at Greenwich whose future again became a matter for speculation.[168] A surreal episode in the life of the island race followed this decision.

In 1995 the Conservative Government's Secretary of State for Defence, Michael Portillo, in alliance with the Secretary of State for National Heritage, Virginia Bottomley, invited estate agents to seek 'expressions of interest from organisations able to propose appropriate uses' for 'An outstanding group of Listed Grade I Baroque Buildings adjoining the River Thames'. Prospective tenants were reminded that the buildings at Greenwich were held in trust by the Ministry of Defence for the benefit of Greenwich Hospital, whose interests needed to be taken into account. The Ministry undertook to 'address the removal of all specialist plant and equipment including a small research and training nuclear reactor'. Those who were 'able to demonstrate enduring long term proposals sympathetic to the character of the site' were required to put forward their ideas.[169]

The Member of Parliament for Greenwich, Nick Raynsford, was not impressed, referring in the House of Commons to 'the shocking and demeaning spectacle of a British Secretary of State for Defence hawking some of the country's finest buildings and one of its most historic sites around the world in search of a buyer'.[170] Caroline Elam, editor of the *Burlington Magazine*, in a piece appropriately entitled 'Greenwich Grotesquerie', referred to

'the wreckage of this public relations disaster', observing that 'Truth in Britain today becomes stranger and more risible than satire. . . . It is as though the government is now so enslaved to the dogma of privatisation that the only method it knows of initiating an enquiry into an issue of national importance is by launching a "marketing campaign"'. She went on to pose the rhetorical question: 'What is the point of having a Department of National Heritage if it cannot devise due processes of policy and consultation about one of the most important sites in the country?'.[171]

A 'predictable and proper clamour of concern' followed, until more moderate counsels eventually prevailed. Since 'few proposals of national significance' emerged, a panel, the Greenwich Advisory Group, which might usefully have been set up at an earlier stage, was established to advise the Secretary of State on the future use and management of the site. It recommended the setting-up of an independent trust, 'charged with preserving the architectural and historic integrity of the site, with the proper maintenance of the buildings, and ensuring public access'. Mr Portillo accepted the recommendation.[172]

Two years later, after long negotiations on the complex lease and future use, the buildings formally were handed over to the new trustees, the Greenwich Foundation for the Royal Naval College, which leases the site from Greenwich Hospital and will oversee its occupation by new tenants: the University of Greenwich will occupy the Queen Anne, King William and Queen Mary Buildings, as well as the adjoining Dreadnought Hospital and Devonport Nurses' Home; and Trinity College of Music will occupy King Charles.[173] The Foundation will ensure continued public access to the site, including the Painted Hall and Chapel, and will ensure that the buildings and their surroundings are properly maintained and appropriately used. As well as the considerable financial contributions of the government and the Heritage Lottery Fund for the conversion of the buildings, the government has undertaken to provide £1.5 million per year for seven years, as a contribution to running costs. If this does not fall into arrears as quickly as the £2000 per year promised by William III, the buildings of the Royal Hospital for Seamen at Greenwich might continue 'to play a living national role, symbolic of a powerful national history'.[174]

As the buildings enter a new phase of life, lessons from the past might be drawn. While the splendour and fitness for institutional purposes of the four main buildings of the Royal Hospital has played a large part in their long-term survival and adaptation, it has been the generally good husbandry required in circumstances in which the money supply is limited that has ensured their preservation. Notwithstanding the continuing problem of basement flooding, there has been enough money for maintenance, but not enough to effect major, irreversible changes. Although the management of the Hospital has been subject to detailed and occasionally trenchant attack, such criticism has tended to be procedural or occasioned by excessive spending on the fabric, particularly during the early nineteenth century, rather than by a failure to care for it. Despite the extended building campaign, the politics and vicissitudes of institutional life, and the change of use from Hospital to College, the Royal Hospital for Seamen is remarkably intact. It continues to proclaim the enduring power of great architecture to inspire and to delight. Wren and Hawksmoor would have no difficulty in recognising their extraordinary creation.

269 Charles White's view of Greenwich Hospital from the west, with James Stuart's Infirmary on the right and the King William Building beyond (NMM).

Chapter 7

THE BUILDINGS OF THE SEAMEN'S HOSPITAL SOCIETY

The Infirmary of the Royal Hospital for Seamen

The stuccoed courtyard building, self-contained within its own railed grounds in the south-west corner of the former Royal Naval College, has its beginnings in the 1760s. It was then that the core of the present structure was erected as an infirmary for the pensioners and staff of the Royal Hospital (fig. 269). In 1870, following the closure of the institution, the building was leased to the Seamen's Hospital Society to replace their hospital ship, the *Dreadnought*, moored offshore. Onshore the Dreadnought Seamen's Hospital, as the building then became, was in use as a specialist medical facility until 1986. Inevitably, as a consequence of changing medical practice, there have been alterations and additions to its fabric, but while it was in this use it had a continuity of function, unusual among the buildings at Greenwich, for over 200 years.

For an institution such as the Royal Hospital some form of infirmary may be considered to have been a prerequisite, but its achievement was long delayed. Providing 'reliefe and support' for seamen 'who by reason of Age, Wounds or other disabilities shall be uncapable of further Service at sea and be unable to maintain themselves', entailed making provision for the infirm or incapable.[1] The ideal, often cited as necessary for the completion of the Hospital[2] was, as noted in 1743, a separate building dedicated to the care of the 'Sick, Hurt & Helpless'.[3] However, while the principal buildings remained unfinished such proposals were unlikely to be realised and the result was an *ad hoc* arrangement within the main ranges during this period. The Hospital directors, although slow to provide a dedicated building, none the less took the medical welfare of the pensioners seriously. The first medical officers, a Physician and a Surgeon, were appointed before the arrival of the first pensioners in 1705,[4] followed by a Dispenser in 1713, the first recorded instance of this post in the Navy.[5] The status of these officers, along with the founding of a specialist medical library in the early eighteenth century, all indicate a genuine concern, although not all judgements were sound: the appointment of a 'rupture doctor', Dr Lee, in the 1750s proved a mistake when he was revealed as a quack.[6] Experimental treatments were also sanctioned, such as Dr William Adam's operation for cataracts performed on twenty pensioners in 1812.[7] Until the 1750s, when the Royal Naval Hospital at Haslar began operation, Greenwich Hospital was the pre-eminent medical establishment of the Navy,

albeit with a particularly specialised purpose.[8] Until the Infirmary was built, however, the facilities for actual research were limited; a 'laboratory' in use in the 1730s was in fact the Physician's back kitchen.[9]

By 1738, when the number of pensioners reached 1000, two wards of the Hospital were in use as an infirmary and at least one ward was given over to the pensioners classified as helpless.[10] This provision soon became inadequate so further wards were granted for the helpless in 1740 and for the Infirmary in 1743.[11] In the 1740s a campaign to advance the erection of a detached building was begun in earnest and in 1743 a strongly worded representation was made to the General Court by the Physician and Surgeon 'shewing the necessity of Building an Infirmary',[12] presumably with the support of the Governor, who had previously tried to get the Board of Directors to approach the General Court on the subject.[13] The medical officers argued that the adapted wards were too small and inconvenient, preventing the patients from being properly placed 'according to the nature of the Disease'. This had serious consequences when outbreaks of contagion occurred: the insufficient accommodation resulted in delays in removing the sick from the wards and, as it was reported in May 1743, occasioned 'the Death of many, of which we have had several melancholy instances, in this last epidemical Distemper'. This potentially endangered the entire institution. The officers also noted the inadequate facilities for preparing food, 'without which the cure must be much retarded, as in many cases the Diet is the only cure'. Other complaints included the lack of a proper laboratory and the difficulty of keeping the sick to the Infirmary wards and preventing spirits and liquors from being brought in.[14] For the directors and General Court, space was another consideration, since the medical department was taking over an increasing number of wards. Furthermore, as the Infirmary had by necessity to be put at ground level, this reduced the potential for expansion 'without putting a great many Old Men out of those wards who are incapable of moving higher'.[15]

Although the General Court had postponed making a decision in 1743, the subject was reintroduced four years later by the directors, convinced of the 'great use and benefit' of a detached Infirmary.[16] The Surveyor Thomas Ripley in 1747 was directed to provide plans and estimates for a new building as part of a wider scheme affecting the grounds to the west of the Hospital.[17] However, the proposals foundered when the General Court in the following year judged the estimate of £40,000 too high.[18] Ripley then produced new drawings of 'a more Plain, & less costly building' at half the amount of the previous estimate, but the General Court eventually decided to fit out part of the Queen Mary Building instead. In addition to the Infirmary and Surgery, an apartment for the Surgeon was made in the south-east corner of the building.[19] Yet more plans and estimates were requested from Ripley in 1755 but to little avail.[20] In 1760 James Stuart, who had succeeded Ripley as Surveyor two years earlier, was asked by the Board of Directors to 'consider of a proper plan for an Infirmary',[21] specifying a building for 200 sick men and their nurses with apartments for a Physician, Surgeon and Dispenser, requirements that had changed little since the early eighteenth century.[22] At last the times were propitious and within three years the General Court had reached the point of ordering construction to begin.[23]

Having accepted the necessity for the building some twenty years earlier, the catalyst for action appears to have been the availability of funds. At the conclusion of the Seven Years War in 1763 the Hospital found itself owed a considerable sum of money, in total almost £80,000, by the Treasury of the Navy. This represented several years' worth of unclaimed prize money and seamen's sixpences and was sufficient to finance the new Infirmary building, at an estimated cost of £18,489 6s 4d, without recourse to Parliament for extra funding.[24] While lack of funds may have been the principal impediment to building hitherto, there were other considerations. The original grant of land to the Hospital had been insufficient for any but the principal buildings and therefore any infirmary schemes were dependent on the acquisition of further ground. From the first, it had usually been envisaged that the proposed building would be on the west side of the Hospital facing the King William Building. In 1714 the directors, advised by Hawksmoor, agreed the acquisition of a plot of land in this position from a Mr Wise for £1800 – that is, £300 more than they hoped to pay and £200 less than he had wanted.[25] This purchase later provided most of the site for the Infirmary when it came to be built. When the new building was being considered in 1747 it was referred to as 'the Waste Ground, now in the Hospital's hand',[26] and by the time Stuart was directed to produce his designs in 1763, it had become the 'piece of Ground set apart for that purpose'.[27]

The earliest design for an infirmary was shown in the model, now lost, for which Hawksmoor was paid £15 in 1699.[28] This probably originally was attached to the model of the principal blocks, which survives in the National Maritime Museum.[29] There is no surviving plan from this period to show the proposed internal layout. Although the land was acquired in 1714, the first detailed, surviving plan is dated 1728. Earlier, undated block plans show two single ranges to the west of King Charles and King William[30] and Hawksmoor's dated drawing of 1723, now at Wilton House, depicts a single block to the west of King William, with detached pavilions at each end.[31] In the plan of 1728 the pavilions are lengthened into attached wings. A four-column portico on the east front is set in front of a colonnaded hall, with an apsed vestibule with flanking staircases on the west side. In the main block of the Infirmary a central corridor gives access to small rooms to either side, while in the wings the corridors run along the outer north and south walls. A separate building to the south

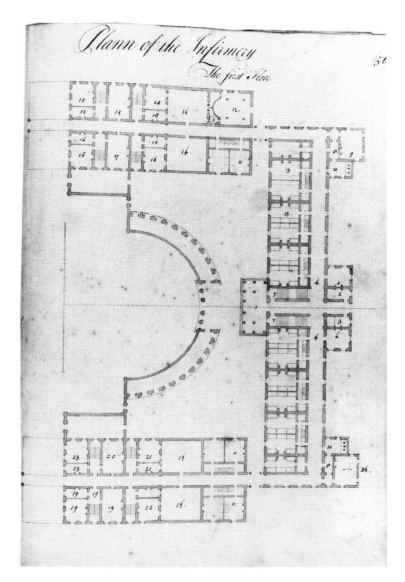

270 Nicholas Hawksmoor, ground plan of the proposed Infirmary (NMM ART 1/56).

was proposed for the accommodation of the medical staff (fig. 144).[32]

In a second plan of 1728, the Infirmary is shown by Hawksmoor in block form, with four ranges around an internal courtyard, the arrangement eventually used by Stuart. Here, Hawksmoor incorporated in one two-storey building accommodation for the sick and for the medical staff.[33] In his most fully worked-out proposal, however, presumably therefore his favoured option, he developed the single range with wings. The scheme is undated, but in representing a significant development from the dated drawing in both architectural grandeur and efficiency of planning, it probably also derives from the late 1720s, coming at the end of a period of prolonged consideration (fig. 270).[34] Although there is no accompanying elevation drawing, it is clear that this would have been a building fully in keeping with the magnificence of the principal buildings on the site. The Palladian inspiration has been transferred from the interior to the exterior, the colonnaded entrance hall giving way to a grand staircase hall, with a deep hexastyle portico facing an eastern forecourt enclosed by quadrant screen walls, arcaded on the inner face, with a central, columned entrance. Garrets for lodgings and stores at second-floor level, above the entrance and at the ends of the wings facing King William, would have reflected the attics of the pavilions of King Charles and Queen Anne.

The Infirmary was designed to house 200 men. The principal accommodation was disposed on the two floors of the main north-south range, each comprising fourteen small, heated wards with five beds in each, with a single corridor running along the west side. Six more wards and a two-storey, galleried chapel were placed at the west end of the wings. The plan is distinguished by its ample staircase provision, arranged on collegiate lines with each pair of wards served by a single stair, flanked by a nurse's room, 'stool room' and coal store. The departments of the Physician and the Apothecary were in the south wing and that of the Surgeon and Dispenser in the north. The sanitary arrangements were limited, but in view of the infirmity of most of the occupants, the provision of two sets of three-seat privies per floor was perhaps sufficient. Hawksmoor, ever thoughtful, also provided three smoking rooms, 'for such as are recovering', at the north-west and south-west corners, one of which was placed over 'the room for the dead'. The vaulted cellars housed the services, including the kitchen, scullery and larder, a drying room, an eating room for the nurses, storage areas for fuel and beer and cellars for the use of the Physician, Apothecary and Surgeon, each of whom had his own kitchen.

Hawksmoor's Infirmary would have been an ornament to the Royal Hospital, but compared with the utilitarian structure which eventually was built, it had an unrealistically high level of provision and grandeur of concept for an institution bent on cost-cutting. It is possible that Hawksmoor's drawings had some influence on Ripley's schemes, and perhaps also on those of Stuart, since the drawings remained on site, but since none of Ripley's proposals for the Infirmary survives, this remains in the realms of conjecture.

In designing the Infirmary at Greenwich, precedents for the architects were of little help. At Les Invalides, to the south-east of the main buildings, single-storey ranges were placed around court-yards in a cross formation with a central altar, following medieval precedents. The nursing was carried out by nuns. Accommodation was provided for 289 sick, with separate provision for 261 with 'contagious distempers'. The beds were arranged in pairs, with access between to close-stools, housed in niches, which were emptied from passages to the rear.[35] At Chelsea, a separate infirmary was intended but it was not provided until 1810 when Sir John Soane converted Walpole House to this use. Other possible influences could have been the two purpose-built, general naval hospitals nearing completion in 1760, but Haslar and Stonehouse were each designed to accommodate over 1000 patients in wards containing at least twenty beds.[36] These great institutions bore eloquent testimony to the commitment of the Admiralty to maintaining the health of the Navy as a whole.[37] The Infirmary at Greenwich, designed to fulfil a more specialised and localised requirement, was to be altogether more modest. The directors and General Court looked to their own judgement and experience in framing the requirements and approving the final form of the new building.

The architect James Stuart had gained his appointment as Surveyor in 1758 through his connections with Admiral George Anson, First Lord of the Admiralty in 1757–62. George and his brother Thomas were members of the Society of Dilettanti, to which Stuart also belonged and from which his most important patrons came. They also were both subscribers to Stuart's and Revett's *Antiquities of Athens*, the first volume of which was published in 1762. At this point in his career, 'Athenian' Stuart was an inexperienced architect. His training had been as a painter and in the three years since returning from his Mediterranean travels he had designed little and built less, interior decoration and garden buildings forming the bulk of his practice. Designing the Hospital's Infirmary presented the most ambitious architectural project he had faced.

How Stuart's ideas for the building evolved between 1760 and 1763 can be deduced from a series of drawings, which, although unsigned and undated, includes a version of the structure almost as built and may be attributed to him.[38] One drawing of an elevation, annotated 'A Design not proposed being a Study for the Plan to be founded on', is an unconfident composition, as might be expected from an inexperienced architect. The combination of a temple-front centrepiece with lateral half-pediments in the manner of a Palladian church, and end pavilions with heavy balustrades, make for an unintegrated and top-heavy effect.[39] Other versions, all clearly intended as a single range, between 233 feet and 250 feet in length, experiment with different window forms and architectural details (fig. 271).[40] A further scheme, illustrated by elevations of the north and south sides of a courtyard building 162 feet in length, retains the pedimented end pavilions with arched recesses and Diocletian and Venetian windows of the earlier designs.[41] This proposal marks the transition from the over-elaborate single range to the pared-down courtyard form of the final building (fig. 272).[42] For his inspiration Stuart seems to have turned to domestic Palladian models, to such houses as Wilton, Houghton, Holkham and Hagley, where he had built a Greek Doric temple. His eventual solution was austere and utilitarian, although recognisably Palladian in inspiration.

The building he designed was a brick-built courtyard structure, of two and three storeys, 196 feet (east and west) by 174 feet (north and south), with a one-storey toilet block in the central courtyard and vaulted basements throughout. Its grounds were enclosed by brick walls which had various outbuildings abutting to the west and into which a group of private houses encroached in the south-west corner. Greenwich market, re-established by the Hospital in 1737, was re-sited against the outer face of the west wall. Construction began in 1764, the principal contractors for the work being Mr Morehouse, mason, and Mr Richard Glode, bricklayer. The carpentry was done by Messrs Philips & Shakespeare and the smith's work by Mr Jackson. Within two years the joiners, plasterers and painters were at work.[43] In August 1768 the directors viewed the building and were informed by the Clerk of Works William Robinson, who had overseen its construction, that it would be ready for occupation by mid-September. There is evidence that the fitting-out was completed in a hurry since the contractors were called before the directors in August to give assurances as to when they would be finished and warned that 'they would certainly experience some mark of the Boards displeasure' if they failed to meet their deadline. The directors were keen to have back the wards and apartments within the Hospital for other uses, since the number of pensioners, inevitably increasing after a period of war, was by now approaching 2000.

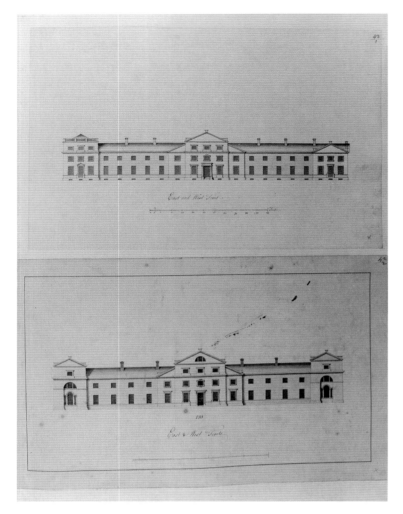

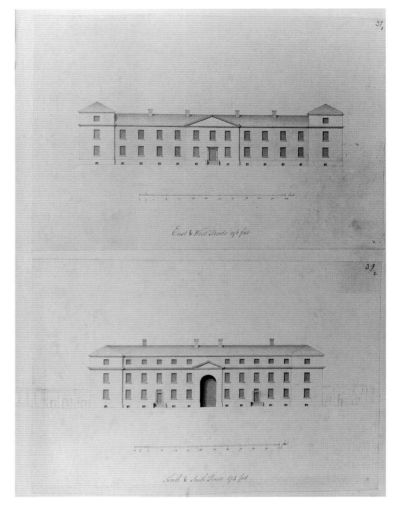

271   James Stuart, alternative elevations for the east and west fronts of the proposed Infirmary (NMM ART 2/42).

272   James Stuart, finalised elevations for the east and west, and north and south fronts of the Infirmary (NMM ART 2/39).

By April 1769 the former Infirmary wards had been refitted to accommodate a further 211 men.[44]

All the elevations as built retained the residual end pavilions with pyramidal roofs present in some of the earlier schemes. The identical three-storey façades to the north and south have tall, narrow carriageways at their centres with pediments above. The two doorways apparently had plain architraves with flat-headed windows above, the present surrounds to the north side and the porches to the south being additions of the 1840s. The east and west elevations were two storeys high between the end pavilions, the three centre bays being stepped forward and pedimented. The elevations were painted to suggest stone. The external appearance of the building was significantly changed by later refacing and other alterations and additions. Until recent demolitions, to convert the building as the Dreadnought Library of Greenwich University, the heavily compromised appearance of the east and west façades made difficult any appreciation of Stuart's modestly attractive elevations.

The adoption of a courtyard plan was logical for a building of this type, quadrangular or U-shaped arrangements having featured in earlier Infirmary schemes as well as being the form of the main blocks at Greenwich. It was also well suited to the functional needs of the Hospital since the Physician and the Surgeon had separate departments and therefore required duplicate facilities, which Stuart put into the east and west ranges (fig. 273).[45] The Physician's department was to the east, with wards on both floors, the upper ones being used for convalescents, and, on the ground floor, a central entrance hall appropriately faced the main Hospital (fig. 274). His house was at the south end of the building, while the equivalent space to the north housed the Dispenser and his assistant. To the west was the Surgeon's department, similarly arranged, with, on the ground floor, a central kitchen with a simple chapel on the floor above. This appears to have been little more than an open space. Attempts were made in the 1840s to improve it, dividing it from the adjoining rooms in which the insane patients were kept and giving it an ante-chapel of sorts, but this may have come to nothing.[46] The Surgeon's residence was at the south end, while his assistants and the Matron had apartments to the north. In the courtyard were the sanitary facilities, a position that had the advantage of being readily accessible to both ranges, to which they were linked by open-sided, colonnaded passages that were lit by fish- or whale-oil lamps. In 1787 the passage was described by Jacques Tenon as little more than a corridor, with washing places and conveniences off it. Possibly in order to keep it dry, the colonnade was raised above ground level, with stone steps down to the courtyard. When the building was completed, the surrounding land had drying grounds, walks for the patients, with a bench against the west wall for them to sit on, with the hot and cold baths and the nurses' washhouses abutting the same wall.[47]

The Infirmary was able to hold up to 256 patients, in sixty-four four-man wards. These were arranged to each side of a central corridor. They were heated by a fireplace in the party wall and had four iron-framed bedsteads with half-canopies from which were hung curtains in the winter. They were lit by sash windows, in addition to which there were shuttered openings above the door and two apertures high in the wall or in the ceiling near the fireplace for ventilation.[48] In these and other respects the Infirmary was a progressive building for its day. The other notable features included the provision of separate wards for medical and surgical patients, the provision of hot and cold baths, and having its principal staircases built of stone.[49] To modern eyes, perhaps the most striking aspect of the building was its small wards (17 feet by 11 feet 6 inches, by 10 feet 10 inches high). At Greenwich this arrangement appears to have been the established preference. Hawksmoor's scheme had five men per room, and Ripley in 1755 was asked to provide for the accommodation of 200 men at six per room.[50] Although this now appears small, there were in fact no fixed norms at this date. In 1789 John Howard noted the average hospital ward size as being between fifteen to thirty beds and varying in width from 17 feet to 24 feet,[51] although he himself advocated rooms holding no more than eight beds.[52] A large number of small wards allowed for the separation of the cases by condition, it being noted by Tenon that there were wards for

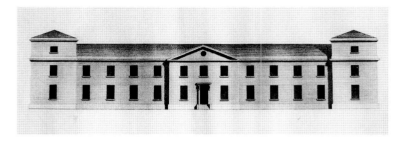

274 The east, entrance front of the Infirmary, engraved by J. Newton for publication in J. Cooke and J. Maule, *An Historical Account of the Royal Hospital for Seamen at Greenwich*, 1789.

fever, gout, dropsy, rheumatism, colds, smallpox and scabies in the late eighteenth century. A century later Greenwich's wards were described as having the advantages of 'isolation, quietude, an equable temperature, and a sense of comparative privacy'. They could 'after occupation by contagious cases, be cleaned, purified, and kept empty for some time, without detriment to the general working of the hospital'.[53]

Although following the same planning principle of small wards, Stuart's Infirmary was a far more modest building than the one envisaged by Hawksmoor, partly for reasons of cost. He was expressly directed by the General Court in 1763 to design a building 'to be as plain and as little expensive as the Nature of it will admit' (fig. 275).[54] Throughout its construction the directors were concerned to make savings, directing the re-use of the old kitchen coppers from the Hospital and suggesting that three stone chimneypieces from the Governor's Apartments 'may be applied

273 Ground plan of the Infirmary, oriented with north at the top. The entrance hall facing the King William Building is at the centre of the east (Physician's) wing, on the right of the plan. The equivalent space on the west (Surgeon's) wing housed the kitchen (NMM ART 2/37).

275 The south front of the Infirmary (the Dreadnought Seamen's Hospital) in 2000, following restoration by Dannatt, Johnson & Partners for use as the Dreadnought Library and Learning Centre of Greenwich University.

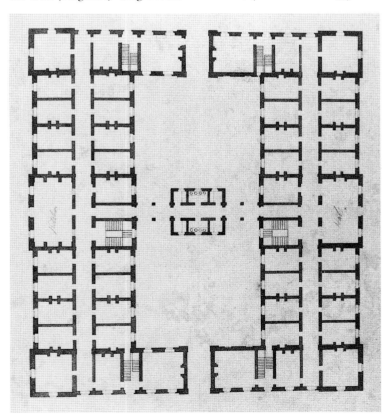

to uses in the New Infirmary'.[55] However, its modesty may not simply have been due to economy. The splendid isolation in which many of the earlier Infirmary schemes had been depicted did not match the cluttered reality of the Hospital's environs in the eighteenth century. The untidy group of outbuildings and the mews, brewery and bakehouse to the north militated against any grandeur or unnecessary architectural display and encouraged the directors' flight from external magnificence. Instead attention was given to the building's plan, which the General Court in 1763 approved as 'a very proper one for the purpose'.[56] The provision of smaller wards, although they would be more expensive to maintain, was prompted by concerns for the comfort of the sick pensioners. The building of the Infirmary clearly was considered to be a meritorious act by John Montagu, 4th Earl of Sandwich, one of whose intermittent spells in office as First Lord of the Admiralty coincided with its commencement. When his portrait was painted by Gainsborough in 1783 for presentation to the Hospital,[57] he took credit for the building by having himself depicted holding idealised plans.[58]

In the hierarchy of the Infirmary, the Physician held seniority and was paid the highest salary, although both he and the Surgeon alike were notionally equivalent in rank to a Captain.[59] The Navy had few Doctors of Medicine within its ranks in the eighteenth century, its medical needs being then more usually supplied by surgeons. In fact in the 1790s there were only three physicians in the Navy, including the one at Greenwich.[60] The first Physician to the Hospital, Dr Salisbury Cade, had been appointed in November 1703.[61] Exceptionally, he was not a naval man although he had been involved in promoting the building of the institution since the 1690s and was one of its first directors. His successors additionally held the post of Physician of the Fleet, the senior medical rank in the Navy, responsible for pharmaceutical supplies, through a process known as 'viewing the drugs', checking medical equipment in the 'Surgeon's Chests', and serving on medical boards.[62] Of the men who held the post perhaps the most eminent was Dr Robert Robertson, Physician from 1790 to 1807. He was a contributor to Dr James Lind's pioneering studies on tropical diseases and keenly advocated 'Peruvian bark' as a cure for fevers.[63] Another key figure, Sir John Liddell, held the post of Inspector General of Hospitals and Fleets, as it was then titled, from 1844 to 1854. He was a medical reformer of note and has been credited with finally clearing the Infirmary of pests, a common cause of complaint within the Hospital generally, and improving the overall conditions of the pensioners, recommending improved cooking and a more varied diet. He was influential also in the purchase in 1849 of Island Gardens (see chapter 6).[64]

The first surgeon to be appointed to the Hospital, James Christie, arrived in December 1704.[65] As holder of the lesser post, it was the Surgeon who was required to attend accidents 'out of the hours of dressing' and to visit his patients up to twice a day if need be, while the Physician was required to visit only as necessary. Neither was allowed to interfere with the other's patients.[66] The lowest ranked medical officer was the Dispenser, a post to which Henry Blakey was appointed in 1713, the first recorded Dispenser in the Navy; at Greenwich the post was upgraded to Apothecary in 1807.[67] The Dispenser/Apothecary was responsible mainly for the preparation of the drugs. The Infirmary Matron and the nurses, one for every sixteen patients, were paid slightly more than their equivalents in the Hospital, implying higher status if not greater competency since all nurses were required first and foremost to be the widows of seamen to comply with the intentions of the founding charter.

It was not just the pensioners who were treated in the Infirmary but the entire Hospital establishment, including the officers' families. The period for which most information about the patients survives is the early nineteenth century, thanks largely to Dr Robertson who kept meticulous records, published in 1807–10.[68] He stated that the simple criterion for admission to the Infirmary was 'the inability of a Pensioner to fetch his own victuals from the Kitchen'. The medical staff were informed of sick pensioners by the ward nurses, the ailing individuals then being visited by the Dispenser for an initial diagnosis. Once admitted to the Infirmary, carried across Friars Road which then separated the two sites, in a chair if necessary, they were issued blue gowns. This was intended to limit the spread of disease, by marking them out from the other pensioners and to prevent them from being served alcohol in the town.[69] Such precautions were necessary as, according to Dr Robertson, many of the patients admitted to the Infirmary were suffering from the effects of intoxication. This may partly explain why the numbers of beds in the Surgeon's department was considerably higher than in that of the Physician: a ratio of approximately 2 : 1 in 1819.[70] At a time when surgery was a developing science and surgeons were often restricted to treating wounds or injuries, this distribution of patients might seem unusual.[71] But Robertson himself noted that intemperance 'has occasioned innumerable accidents, chirurgical practice will bear ample record'.[72] Other common causes of complaint were ruptures, influenza, rheumatism and 'pulmonic affections', which alone accounted for one-sixth of the Physician's patients. Inevitably the mortality rate was high, put down by Robertson to the 'many sources of infections, disease arising from ships, hulks, dockyards . . . whence are often received infected Pensioners, Nurses and Boys'. Furthermore, the Hospital was 'beyond parallel, a receptacle for the dying' constantly refilling with the 'diseased and maimed'. Even the weather could prove fatal, some of the 'valetudinarians' being carried away by 'a sudden change from hot to cold, and vice versa'.[73]

During the period when building an infirmary was under discussion, it was often assumed that this would also accommodate the helpless pensioners. However, while under construction it was decided that the existing Helpless Wards would be sufficient.[74] This was never entirely satisfactory, and in 1777 the directors were complaining that the helpless men, then located in ground-floor wards in the Queen Anne Building, 'who made their appearance out of Doors for the Benefit of Air are the most miserable and shocking objects'.[75] It was thought that a separate building might serve their needs and this idea was resurrected in 1807 following complaints from the medical staff about the inadequacy of the existing arrangements.[76] The Surveyor John Yenn was asked to suggest improvements to the existing facilities, which by this date were in 'that part of the Hospital next Romney Road', or if this was not possible to draw up plans and estimates for a separate building.[77] Following much debate among the directors and the General Court, including the consideration of raising the two-storey ranges of the Infirmary, it was decided in 1808 that 'the health of the Helpless Pensioners would be better promoted by the erection of a separate Building for their reception, contiguous to the Infirmary'.[78]

Yenn designed a one-storey brick building to house 140 help-less pensioners at an estimated cost of £14,000.[79] Built on the site of the existing market house and some of the Infirmary's out-buildings, it extended for 'the whole length of the Infirmary wall',[80] which had recently been extended following the demoli-tion in 1803 of the private houses that had long stood in the south-west corner of the grounds.[81] Work on the Helpless Wing, as it was called, began in 1808, overseen by George Knight, who functioned as Clerk of Works, although never officially holding that title.[82] Completed in 1810, this was a simple brick structure, distinguished by a stone portico at its southern end, whose plan of small wards off a central corridor echoed the adjoining Infirmary.[83]

Unfortunately, work on the Helpless Ward had barely finished when, on the morning of 1 October 1811, the Infirmary suffered a fire so severe that 'nearly the whole of the north and west sides of the interior of that Building were consumed'. The fire appar-ently started in the Surgeon's second assistant's room, 'occasioned by some windage or defect in the side or bottom of the chimney'. Several wards, the surgery, the kitchen and the north-west apart-ments were destroyed or badly damaged. Reinstatement of the building was ordered immediately and it was decided to raise the Surgeon's department on the west side to three storeys at the same time, at an estimated total cost of £24,220.[84] Raising the east side also was considered but a decision was postponed. Requested to look into methods of future fire prevention, Yenn proposed the installation of cast-iron doors in the central passageways. Although this was unpopular with the Physician and Surgeon, who feared that doors would prevent a free current of air, they were swiftly installed, and inspected by the directors in June 1812;[85] two doors remain *in situ* at the north end of the west range. The new storey was ready for patients by the summer of 1813.[86]

In 1834–5 the Hospital's Surveyor Joseph Kay put forward pro-posals for external and internal improvements to the Infirmary, to improve the existing facilities and to remedy perceived shortcom-ings. His suggested alterations included the raising of the east side, the rebuilding of the courtyard building and shortening the Help-less Ward. This substantial reworking of the structure was accom-panied by proposals for the improvement of the building's exterior and its setting, part of the ambitious scheme of improvements to the Hospital estate in progress at that time. The first phase of work on the Infirmary was approved by the Commissioners in 1834,[87] but discussions continued into the following year, perhaps as a consequence of objections to aspects of the scheme from the medical officers. Work on the Helpless Wing and the courtyard building began in 1835.[88]

The work to the exterior consisted principally of the 'cement-ing' or stuccoing of the outer walls 'both for the improvement of the general temperature of the building and of the external appearance'.[89] This was carried out in stages, the eastern side not being completed until 1845.[90] The result was a transformation. The work included the addition of rusticated quoins to the archways and end pavilions along with the embellishment of the window architraves and the door surrounds on the north side.[91] The other significant alteration was the addition of porches on the south side, intended to alter 'the present mean appearance of the entrance doorways of the Houses of the Physician and Surgeon'.[92] These porches, which have anthemion and palmette panels above the doors, and rosette motifs on the jambs, were added in the 1840s,

276 The Infirmary (the Dreadnought Seamen's Hospital), with the Somerset Ward (formerly the Helpless Wing) to the west, photographed *c*.1900 after the transformation of the building in the 1840s (NMM).

probably contemporaneously with internal works in the resi-dences. The shortened Helpless Ward, brought into line with the main buildings by 1835, was given a similar external treatment. The existing portico was re-sited, but proposals for matching por-ticoes on the north and west elevations were rejected as being too costly. These elevations were given a simpler finish by the addi-tion of piers and blank recesses. Ornamental screen walls were then erected, linking the Helpless Ward with the main building to the north and south; this created a courtyard area to be used for drying grounds, a washhouse and other purposes 'unseemly for exposure' (fig. 276).[93]

The surrounding grounds, which had long been in use as drying courts and gardens for the Physician and the Surgeon, were then cleared of their cross-walls and laid out with walks for the pen-sioners, completed by 1839.[94] The brick walls that previously had enclosed the Infirmary were replaced with cast-iron railings in 1838–40, with iron double gates, wicket gates and stone gate piers, to the north and south sides. Those fronting Romney Road remain.[95]

Of the works carried out at the Infirmary, it was the external remodelling that was the most directly related to the broader improvements to the Hospital estate. The clearance of the western out-courts of their walls and buildings, and the consequent opening-up of the views, clearly affected the Infirmary and the Hospital's stables and outbuildings to the north. That their status was increased is evident from the work to the Infirmary's exte-rior and the related rebuilding of the other ancillary structures in the 1830s. Furthermore, these improvements were carried out before the decision to extend the grounds to include the out-buildings had been made officially in 1847. But there were other motives behind the changes to the setting of the Infirmary. By limiting admission to the north entrances and closing off the south

277 The internal courtyard of the Infirmary (the Dreadnought Seamen's Hospital), viewed from the north in 1993.

grounds to all but pensioners, it was hoped that much closer control could be established over access. With the entrances directly under the control of the medical officers, Kay in 1834 expressed the hope that outsiders could be prevented from gaining 'promiscuous intercourse with the wards'.[96]

The internal alterations to the Infirmary were intended primarily to remedy shortcomings in the cooking and sanitary facilities. Kay considered the courtyard block responsible for the 'constant accumulation of foul air', and further noted that the location of the kitchen in the west range was far from ideal and that the intended improvements to the grounds would necessitate the demolition of the hot and cold bathhouses. His solution, proposed in 1834, was a new two-storey courtyard building, housing a bathhouse on the ground floor and kitchens on the upper floor. Once again, the medical staff were concerned about the implications for the light and ventilation to the wards. As a result, the existing single-storey structure with basements was extended in 1835 to house the kitchen, baths and privies.[97] It retained the cross-passage to the east and west ranges, and an open-sided first-floor bridge was constructed at the same time.[98] The pair of flat-roofed blocks were of brick with stone plinths, impost bands and cornice. The north block, which remains little altered externally, has round-headed recesses with windows in the heads to the north side and round-headed windows in the return elevations (fig. 277). The passageway was lit by gas lamps, the numbers of which were increased after the medical officers complained about poor light.[99] The level of the courtyard was also raised at this time.[100] Other internal alterations relate to a rearrangement of the accommodation of the medical staff. Between 1840 and 1844 all of the residences were refurbished and, as a result, the Inspector of Fleets, formerly known as the Physician, was moved to the south-west house and the south-eastern house was given to his Deputy.[101] The staircase in the north-east apartment was taken down and moved to its present position at this date.[102]

One consequence of the alterations was a reduction in the number of wards, a particular cause of complaint for the medical

officers.[103] Kay's proposal to move the privies inside the building, as he did in the main Hospital buildings, into converted wards off the main stairs, was not carried out, perhaps because of this concern,[104] but it may be that the sanitary towers were added to the corners of the building at this time. The solution to the problem of ward space was the raising of a third storey to the Physician's Department on the east side, ready for occupation in December 1836.[105] The former kitchen in the west range and the entrance hall on the east side were also converted into wards. But the loss of four of the Helpless Wards continued to cause problems and in 1841 the Surgeon requested another free-standing wing, mirroring the existing building, to the east of the Infirmary.[106] This was under serious consideration in 1847 when it was a factor in the decision to move the western boundary of the Hospital, but ultimately accommodation had to be made within the main Hospital buildings, taking up six wards in 1855.[107] With these works completed, the Infirmary had a capacity of 324 sick and 84 helpless.[108]

Paradoxically, it was in the decades following Kay's improvements to Greenwich Hospital that the decline of the institution became apparent, most clearly demonstrated by the reduction in the number of pensioners from 2617 in 1850 to 1518 in 1860. The Infirmary was perhaps less affected by this diminution since the condition of the new pensioners was so poor that one-fifth required immediate medical attention upon admission.[109] Unsurprisingly, little new building work was carried out during this period, although by 1854 an open-sided shed with a galvanised iron roof had been put up between the Infirmary and the Helpless Ward as a smoking room.[110] In the *Report of the Commissioners Appointed to Inquire into Greenwich Hospital* (1860), the Infirmary and its medical officers were among the few parts of the Hospital establishment to escape censure, and it was even suggested that the whole institution could be converted into a medical hospital.[111] In 1867 the last works by the Hospital Estates were carried out: the first-floor bridge was covered over and the sides of the smoking shed walls were enclosed; this was overseen by the Clerk of Works J. G. Loughborough.[112] When the Hospital closed in 1869, six patients remained in the Infirmary and twenty pensioners in the Helpless Ward. The latter were still resident when the building reopened as the Dreadnought Seamen's Hospital the following year.[113]

The Dreadnought Seamen's Hospital

The new occupant of the Infirmary, the Seamen's Hospital Society, had its origins in early nineteenth-century initiatives for the relief of unemployed merchant seamen, whose numbers had swollen at the conclusion of the Napoleonic wars when some 125,000 seamen were laid off.[114] Many were unemployed and homeless, 'roaming the streets of London', facing an early death from disease, infirmity or poverty.[115] Along with the large numbers of military veterans in a similar position, they presented the capital with a social problem and were viewed by some sections of society as a potential source of unrest.[116] In 1818 a 'small band of philanthropists', including the noted anti-slavery campaigners William Wilberforce and Zachary Macaulay, formed a 'Committee of the association for the relief of distressed seamen' to launch a public appeal for their relief.[117] As a temporary measure six ships were moored along the Thames to act as reception centres. However, when the demand failed significantly to decrease, it became apparent that more permanent measures would be needed. An institution dedicated to the medical care and welfare of merchant seamen was proposed and the Seamen's Hospital Society was formed in 1821 to oversee its establishment. It was intended also that unemployed seamen would be assisted in finding new ships.[118] The new Society attracted royal patronage and the management committee included representatives of both the Navy and Trinity House.[119] The Admiralty provided further assistance by granting the use of a hospital ship that same year. This became the first of three ships, the *Grampus*, the *Dreadnought* and the *Caledonian* (renamed the *Dreadnought*) used successively by the Society from 1821 until 1870. They were moored at Greenwich, upstream from the Hospital, a site chosen as being the most convenient for taking sick men from passing ships.[120]

The use of ships as hospitals had been an established practice in the armed forces since the seventeenth century.[121] For the Seamen's Hospital Society this type of facility had certain advantages, not the least being that conversion was relatively cheap, the refitting of the *Dreadnought* in 1831 costing only £2393, a significant consideration for a voluntarily funded body.[122] A ship could also be an advertisement, the *Grampus* and its successors bearing the legend 'Hospital for sick seamen supported by voluntary subscription for seamen of all nations' painted on its sides, visible to all the passing river traffic. The *Dreadnought* hulk eventually became a well-known Thames-side landmark, attracting large numbers of visitors while it was being fitted out.[123] Since many of its patients arrived by boat, being offshore was no disadvantage. Ships also made effective isolation hospitals during epidemics, as happened during the outbreaks of cholera that swept London in 1832–5, when the Society used several other ships moored at Greenwich to accommodate the afflicted.[124]

There were, however, obvious shortcomings in using a ship as a hospital, notably the poor ventilation, lack of light, the noise of the open wards and the difficulties of maintaining hygiene.[125] By the mid-nineteenth century it was becoming clear that cleanliness was the crucial factor in improving the survival rates of patients. In 1848 the *Dreadnought* was treated with 'Sir William Burnett's fluid' to prevent the absorption of 'animal poisons' into the timbers.[126] The increasing industrialisation of the Thames and the consequent rise in the volume of river traffic compounded the already poor conditions, making life both less healthy and more hazardous aboard ship.[127] By the 1860s the medical staff of the Society were pressing for action. As a result, in 1865 it was resolved that 'the use of the hospital-ship Dreadnought shall be discontinued, and that a suitable site, with a river frontage, and accessible by boats, shall be procured'.[128]

The Society first approached the Treasury, requesting £20,000 towards a new building and, after this was rejected, £5000 for the purchase of land at East Greenwich owned by the Royal Hospital. They argued that money from the sale of dead seamen's effects, and unclaimed wages, could be used for this purpose.[129] Although the Treasury was unable to grant funds, officials suggested an approach to the Admiralty to request the use of part of the Royal Hospital, then in the process of closing.[130] The Society felt some justification in doing so as merchant seamen had contributed financially to its upkeep although unable to receive the benefits, paying sixpence a month into the Sixpenny Office until 1834.[131] The Admiralty was not well disposed to this idea, claim-

ing that all the buildings were needed for the intended Naval College.[132] However, a deputation from the Society to the Prime Minister, Edward Stanley, Lord Derby, in 1867 was successful in gaining an agreement to their using part of the site. This decision may have been influenced by a campaign in the press in support of the Seamen's Hospital.[133] Despite this, the negotiations were protracted, as the Admiralty offered, and then withdrew, part of the Queen Anne Building. The Queen Mary Building was then offered, but the Society was keen to have a river frontage in order to advertise itself. Furthermore, the type of accommodation in Queen Mary was deemed inappropriate, since disease would lodge itself in the 'retired fireproof safes' (as the cabins were described) and the cost of conversion would be prohibitive.[134] In 1868 the position of the Society was summed up in *The Lancet*:

> They have expended a large sum in the purchase of a site close to the water's edge, and they have petitioned Parliament for money or for a certain vacant wing of Greenwich Hospital. . . . It is currently reported that no subscriptions will be obtained from shipowners as long as the wards of Greenwich Hospital remain as now, a reproach and disgrace to the Board of Admiralty.[135]

It was only after the Society had ordered drawings for a new building on the East Greenwich site that the Admiralty acted. In November 1869 a formal application was made for the loan of the Infirmary and Somerset Ward, previously known as the Helpless Ward, 'in lieu of the Hospital Ship, Dreadnought' which was granted by the Lord Commissioners of the Admiralty in January 1870.[136]

The lease, with accompanying conditions, was for ninety-nine years at an annual rent of one shilling.[137] In the 1930s this was renegotiated to £200 per annum when the Hospital extended to the south. One condition was that the remaining twenty helpless pensioners were to be maintained on payment of 3s per person per day.[138] They were kept separately from the other patients and were allowed to continue to wear their distinguishing blue coats.[139] Other conditions were concerned with the maintenance of the building, requiring the exterior to be repainted every four years and any works to the exterior and the 'principal walls' to be approved by the Admiralty, a right which they fully exercised. They also retained the right to reclaim the buildings 'in consequence of existing or apprehended war or other national cause or requirement', with six months notice to quit and no compensation payable.[140] Access to the Hospital was not permitted through College grounds and the Society was obliged to put up railings matching the existing on the unenclosed sides to the north and east to separate the sites, with gates on Romney Road and King William Street (now Walk), which later became the principal entrance.[141] The Society requested a gate on the north side as well, since all deliveries had to be taken a considerable distance along the central corridor in order to reach the kitchen and storerooms, but this was not permitted.[142] The Admiralty was never entirely comfortable with having part of the former Hospital complex out of its immediate control and considered repossessing it on several occasions. Proposals for reclaiming the building as an overflow for the other naval hospitals were considered in 1917.[143] At the same time a scheme for its re-use as part of a War College was under consideration and the Society was actively encouraged to move the Dreadnought to a site outside the grounds. These ideas were resurrected in 1944–7 in a scheme for a Naval University, an inflated proposal that included replacing all the buildings on the east and west sides of the Royal Naval College with grandiose symmetrical blocks.[144]

The first patients were transferred from ship to shore on 13 April 1870. No significant alterations were necessary, the building being considered well suited for its new purposes. Even the allocation of medical cases to the eastern wing and surgical cases to the west initially was maintained,[145] and many of the fittings and furnishings of the old Infirmary were taken over.[146] The Somerset Ward was used as an out-patients and casualty department and continued the practice begun on the *Dreadnought* of treating local emergency cases, since medical provision in the Greenwich area was so poor at this time.[147] The south-western house, last occupied by the Inspector of the Fleet, was renovated as the residence of the Society's Secretary. Evidence of its various refurbishments remain in the several surviving nineteenth-century fittings, including chimneypieces and an attractive jib doorcase on the ground floor. The other main residence on the south side became the house of the Principal Medical Officer but, like the apartments to the north, this was later absorbed into the medical facilities, thus losing its original domestic character.

According to the Society's own publicity, the patients treated at the Dreadnought were 'seamen of every grade and nation, whatever their ailment'.[148] This was only a slight exaggeration. Although smallpox sufferers were excluded, the Hospital was unusual during a period of expansion in specialist provision in admitting patients with venereal and other infectious diseases.[149] Convalescing patients also had to be accommodated here since few had families available to care for them. This situation continued until 1918, when the Society was bequeathed a house in Cudham, Kent, for this use. Tubercular patients also were treated and in 1900 an open-sided wooden shelter was erected on the roof of the Dreadnought for an outdoor cure.[150] This remained in use until the opening of the Society's sanatorium in 1921.[151]

The diversity of diet, language and religious observance among the Dreadnought patients was probably unique and racial tensions were not unknown on the wards.[152] Admitting and releasing the men was a complex operation as it had to be co-ordinated with the shipping movements and required regular contact with foreign embassies, shipping agencies and, later, with immigration authorities.[153]

The Dreadnought was not just the principal medical facility but also the administrative headquarters of the Seamen's Hospital Society, whose broader activities included training, research and campaigning work. By the late nineteenth century the medical staff already had made notable contributions in the fight against scurvy and cholera, but perhaps their most important work came in the field of tropical medicine, an endeavour which later earned the Society the epithet 'the Foster Mother of Tropical Medicine in London'.[154] This was a comparatively recent field of research whose development may be interpreted primarily as a consequence of the drive to facilitate the exploitation of colonial resources.[155] For the Society it was an obvious specialisation, the Dreadnought Hospital providing unparalleled scope for the study of tropical cases in London at this time. While much of the pioneering work by Dr Patrick Monson was done at the Society's branch hospital at Albert Dock, opened in 1890,[156] some research was undertaken at Greenwich, particularly following the construction of the new Pathological Laboratory in 1929.[157] The

278   A plaque commemorating the endowment of the Silver Thimble Ward 'by the gifts of thousands of British and allied men and women throughout the world who gladly gave their trinkets and treasures as a thank-offering to the men of the mercantile marine to commemorate their service in the Great War 1914–1918'.

Society was influential also in medical training. The *Dreadnought* had been recognised as suitable for this as early as 1837[158] and in 1901 the London School of Clinical Medicine was established at Greenwich.[159] One result of moving ashore had been that women and children were admitted as casualties for the first time. This led to the Society's starting to employ female nurses and in 1877 to the establishment of the Dreadnought School for Nurses, one of the first to be set up on the lines prescribed by Florence Nightingale.[160] Their accommodation was crammed into the attic storey of the Dreadnought until the Devonport Nurses' Home was built in 1924–35.

As the Society was a voluntarily funded body, the maintenance of income was critical. When afloat, the *Dreadnought* had proved an effective advertisement, but once ashore, subscriptions decreased, for which the lack of a river frontage was blamed by some of the Board members. They also feared that by moving into the Infirmary they had given the impression that they were no longer a private charity, so made it clear in a public appeal in 1875 that they were not funded by the government.[161] Money was raised through the endowment of beds, and for £1000 or more a plaque or dedication was installed, some of which survive (fig. 278).[162] Other fund-raising tactics were introduced to publicise the Hospital, the press being invited to participate in Christmas celebrations, drawn by the exotic appeal of the patients (fig. 279).[163] In the 1930s attempts to alleviate the Society's financial difficulties included a proposal in 1934 for an illuminated beacon on the roof of the Dreadnought for publicity. This was firmly resisted by the Admiralty which, maintaining a fine sense of geographical propriety, commented that a similar light in Croydon 'might be quite inoffensive', but ' it would clash most violently with the buildings at Greenwich'.[164]

A new source of funding for hospitals, the Prince of Wales Hospital Fund for London (later renamed King Edward's Hospital Fund for London or more commonly the King's Fund), was established in 1897. The allocation of the annual grants was conditional on the maintenance of certain standards by the recipient

279 'Christmas with Poor Jack at the Seamen's Hospital' (*Illustrated London News*, 6 January 1877).

institutions.[165] The inclusion of the Dreadnought as one of the original thirteen chosen for assistance may have been due in part to its connection with the noted reformer Sir Henry C. Burdett, a moving force behind the creation of the Fund, who had begun his career at the Seamen's Hospital. The Dreadnought was eventually to receive a total of £154,944 in annual and one-off grants from the King's Fund between 1897 and 1948.[166]

Following the Society's take-over of the Hospital, the first significant works to the property that it carried out were prompted

by problems with the sewers. They had been treated but not cured in 1879, when they were 'ventilated and trapped'.[167] Proposals for the complete replacement of the drainage on the site were made in 1884. The Admiralty, not always unhelpful, contributed £1500 towards the overall cost, estimated at £2500. In view of the inevitable disruption the work would cause, it was decided to close the Hospital and combine it with other alterations. These, carried out under the direction of the architect Stephen Salter, included the construction of a new chapel over the central section of the

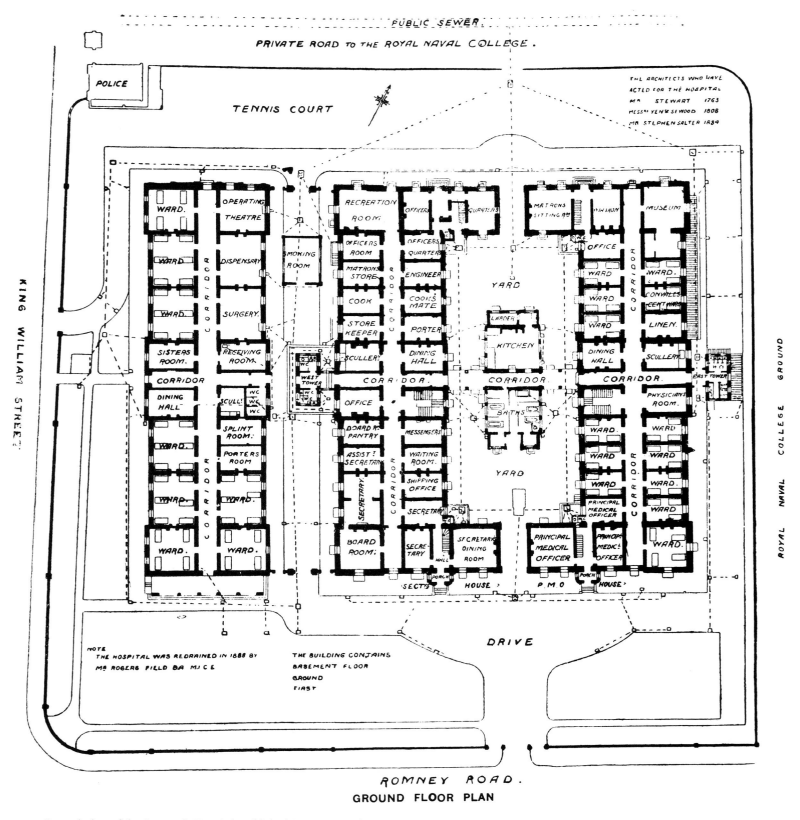

THE SEAMENS HOSPITAL GREENWICH

SCALE [scale bar] OF FEET

PUBLIC SEWER.

PRIVATE ROAD TO THE ROYAL NAVAL COLLEGE.

POLICE

TENNIS COURT

THE ARCHITECTS WHO HAVE
ACTED FOR THE HOSPITAL
MR STEWART 1763
MESS. YENN & SEWOOD 1808
MR STEPHEN SALTER 1884

KING WILLIAM STREET

ROYAL NAVAL COLLEGE GROUND

WARD. OPERATING THEATRE
WARD DISPENSARY
WARD SURGERY.
SISTERS ROOM. RECEIVING ROOM.
CORRIDOR
DINING HALL SCULL. WC WC WC
SPLINT ROOM.
WARD. PORTERS ROOM
WARD. WARD.
WARD. WARD.

CORRIDOR

SMOKING ROOM

WEST TOWER

RECREATION ROOM OFFICERS QUARTERS
OFFICERS ROOM OFFICERS QUARTERS
MATRONS STORE ENGINEER
COOK COOKS MATE
STORE KEEPER PORTER
SCULLERY DINING HALL
CORRIDOR
OFFICE
BOARD R. PANTRY MESSENGERS
ASSIST. SECRETARY WAITING ROOM.
SECRETARY SHIPPING OFFICE
SECRETARY
BOARD ROOM. SECRE- TARY SECRETARY DINING ROOM
SECT'S HOUSE

YARD

LARDER
KITCHEN
CORRIDOR
BATHS
YARD

PRINCIPAL MEDICAL OFFICER PRINCIPAL MEDICAL OFFICER
P.M.O HOUSE

MATRONS SITTING RM. MATRON MUSEUM
OFFICE
WARD CONVALES CENT WARD
WARD LINEN
WARD
DINING HALL SCULLERY
CORRIDOR EAST TOWER
PHYSICIANS ROOM.
WARD WARD
WARD WARD
WARD WARD
PRINCIPAL MEDICAL OFFICER WARD
WARD.

DRIVE

NOTE
THE HOSPITAL WAS REDRAINED IN 1888 BY
MR ROGERS FIELD BA M.I.C.E

THE BUILDING CONTAINS
BASEMENT FLOOR
GROUND
FIRST

ROMNEY ROAD.

GROUND FLOOR PLAN

280 Ground plan of the Seamen's Hospital, published in H. C. Burdett, *Hospitals and Asylums of the World*, 1891–3 (Wellcome Institute Library, London). Burdett shows Yenn's Helpless Ward and Kay's alterations, including the rebuilt courtyard block. The plan is oriented with north at the top.

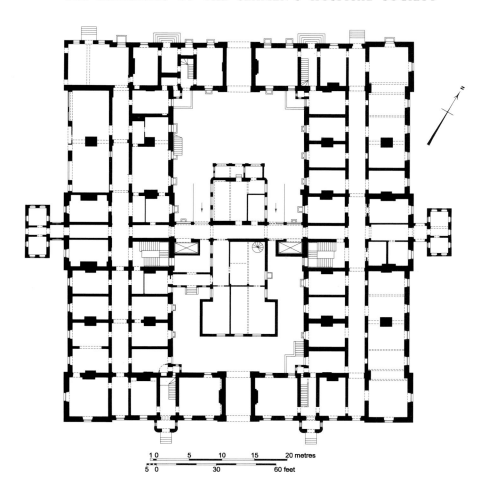

281 Ground plan of the Seamen's Hospital, taken from the survey made by Dannatt, Johnson & Partners, showing the layout at the time of closure in 1986.

Somerset Ward and the installation of three-storey sanitary towers, projecting from the centres of the east and west sides, which were removed in 1998. On the west side a bridge from the chapel to the sanitary block was made, presumably to save the expense and inconvenience of making a stair in the Somerset wing. This also made a continuous, although ill-lit, passageway through the entire Hospital from east to west at first-floor level.[168] The classically treated chapel was slightly more sophisticated than its predecessor in the west range, having two stained-glass windows and two rows of Doric columns which notionally divided the space into a nave and aisles. The windows commemorated John Lydekker, an important benefactor, and the Society employees who had died in its service.[169] The Hospital was closed from November 1884 for almost a year for all but emergencies as the works were carried out, re-opening in October 1885 (fig. 280).[170]

One aspect of the former Infirmary's planning, its small wards, was considered particularly noteworthy by the medical press. In 1859 the senior medical officer at the Royal Hospital, Dr John Wilson, had commented that the plan of the Infirmary was 'in some respects very different from many hospitals, that is to say, we have no large wards'.[171] Ideas on ward sizes had developed since John Howard's day, Florence Nightingale recommending wards for between twenty and thirty patients as being 'best suited for fulfilling all the requirements of ventilation, light, cheerfulness, recovery of health, and economy' — advantages that could never be provided by small wards.[172] But this view was not unchallenged. In 1870 an editorial in The Lancet described the old Greenwich Infirmary as 'the only small-ward hospital, pure and simple, in the

United Kingdom', seeing in the relocation of the Dreadnought an opportunity to judge the effectiveness of smaller wards.[173] Similarly, the British Medical Journal noted that 'An opportunity will thus be afforded to observe how far extreme subdivision of hospital patients is conducive to good sanitary results'.[174] However, more pragmatic voices noted that 'unless some structural changes are made, efficiency will be purchased at the cost of a very large nursing staff'.[175] This was evidently the view of some members of the Society's management and an answer of sorts was given in 1897, when an application was made to the Admiralty for funds to enlarge the wards as they were 'exceeding small and difficult of ventilation'.[176] An experiment was tried in that year, creating a larger ground-floor ward in the east range by throwing two rooms together. It was estimated that it would cost £1395 to carry out similar alterations throughout the Hospital.[177]

In December 1899 the Society's architect Keith D. Young produced a report recommending the enlargement of the wards, building an isolation ward and installing electric lighting, a lift for the patients and improving the kitchens.[178] This coincided with another report by the King's Fund that was critical not only of the small wards but also the out-patients' facilities and the nurses' accommodation. It even went so far as to say that 'Were wounded sailors after a great naval battle treated in the Hospital in its present state a great public outcry would inevitably arise'.[179] Such criticism from a significant source of funding could not be ignored and in 1901 a new out-patients' department was made at the same time as the conversion of the Principal Medical Officer's house to accommodate the London School of Clinical Medicine, which the

Society had founded that year.[180] However, it was clear that the only real solution to many of the weightier problems highlighted by the two reports was to extend the building. In 1906 the Society made an approach to the Admiralty for approval for extensions either to the north or east sides, but it was a further seventeen years before agreement to the expansion of the Dreadnought finally was reached.[181] Meanwhile, between 1907 and 1914 the King's Fund financed the removal of many of the partition walls in order to create the larger wards considered necessary (fig. 281).[182]

The 1906 proposals foundered on the objections of the Admiralty, which was only really prepared to consider an addition to the Somerset Ward, although it seems likely that the Society's funds were insufficient for so ambitious an undertaking. The initiative was not regained until 1916, credit for which belongs largely to Hudson Ewbanke Kearley, Lord Devonport. A forceful and energetic personality, he had made his fortune through his chain of International Stores, and his political reputation as Chairman of the Port of London Authority (1909–25). Following a visit to the building in 1916 he had suggested to the Society that they allow him to launch a public appeal to fund an extension. The Board agreed and made Devonport Vice-President of the Society so that he could attend committee meetings. But his involvement came at a price, since he insisted on forming his own special building committee, retaining control of the funds that were raised, and making his own choice of architect, Edwin Cooper. The Society had little option but to agree. They had 'either to accept Lord Devonport's offer or lose this opportunity, and they could not dictate to him'.[183]

The improvements cited as most pressing in the war-time appeal literature were lifts for patients, isolation wards and improved nurses' quarters, although 'every department is hampered in its work by lack of funds'.[184] Cooper's first proposal was ready in 1916: a three-storey 'front building' to Romney Road, in red brick with white stone facings, clearly inspired by Wren but reminiscent of Chelsea Hospital rather than Greenwich. While the war raged, no other action was taken, but in January 1918 the Society decided to approach the Admiralty with its proposals. The options presented were for either a large scheme of reconstruction on the present site or a new building elsewhere. However, any significant rebuilding was rejected by the Admiralty for fear of 'overshadowing or eclipsing' the main Hospital buildings. The Admiralty, consistent in its pursuit of due propriety in all its dealings with the Seamen's Hospital Society, preferred the option of new building and in June 1918 ordered the Greenwich Estate Office to prepare costings for three possible sites: the north-west corner of the College grounds, the Greenwich Market block and – the option promoted most forcefully to the Society – the site around and including the Trafalgar Quarters. This they considered the best option since it would sweep away the then derelict Trafalgar Hotel, and, seeking perhaps to hoist the Society with its own petard, 'so far as its subscriptions are concerned every craft passing up and down river would see it'. But the Society turned down the proposal, partly on grounds of cost but also because of the opposition of Lord Devonport. In November 1918 the Society resolved to stay in its present buildings and seek permission for adjacent lands for an extension.[185] Devonport in 1922 again promoted his preferred option to the Admiralty, an extension to the south. This was not unanimously supported by all members of the Society,

whose medical officers were concerned that it would block light and air to the existing building.[186]

Wishing to remain in Greenwich, rather than moving its operations to the Albert Dock Hospital,[187] but faced by apparently intractable problems, the Society was at a standstill. Arthur Smallwood, Director of the Greenwich Hospital Estate, in 1922 provided a solution to the impasse. He proposed a site then occupied by the Royal Hospital School's Infirmary building and the former Hospital burial ground for the new building, now conceived as a war memorial to the dead of the Merchant Marine. In 1923 the Society accepted the offer and, with £250,000 already raised from the appeal, designs for the new buildings and for the alterations to the existing facilities were started immediately.[188] Building work began first on the new nurses' accommodation and it was not until the first phase of the Devonport Nurses' Home had been completed that the alterations were made to the Dreadnought. The north and south ends of the Somerset Ward were raised to two storeys in 1931–3 in order to provide space for a new out-patients' department, operating theatres and surgical ward.[189] It was also intended to rebuild the old courtyard block, replacing it with a new three-storey building to house kitchens, a dining room and sleeping accommodation, but a financial crisis in 1932 brought work to a halt, and only the southern section of the existing building was extended.[190]

The new facilities had only a short period of use, an official at the Ministry of Works noting in 1944 that the Seamen's Hospital had been 'to a large extent destroyed' by enemy action.[191] The most serious damage was done in September 1940, when the north end of the Somerset Ward received a direct hit, destroying the new operating theatres and the chapel and necessitating the demolition of two-thirds of the wing.[192] Incendiary attacks in April and March 1941 caused further damage, destroying much of the roof of the main building. The Dreadnought was then closed for the remainder of the war, although a limited service for twenty-four patients operated until 1945 from the Devonport Nurses' Home.[193] The cost of rebuilding was then estimated as up to £500,000.[194]

War-time proposals for a new tropical diseases hospital in a reconstructed Dreadnought were overtaken by the creation of the National Health Service, ushered in by the National Health Act of 1946. Negotiations over the future of the buildings between the Society and the Ministry of Health recognised the unique character of the Seamen's Hospital and eventually it was allowed to retain its specialist function. From 1948, when responsibility (along with the Albert Dock Hospital and the Angus Convalescent Home) passed to the National Health Service, until 1974, the Dreadnought was run by the Seamen's Hospital Management Committee.[195] Before the changeover, a new out-patients' department was built at the north end of the west range and a casualty department sited in the surviving portion of the Somerset Ward. These alterations, designed by the firm of Collcutt and Hamp, included the infilling of Yenn's colonnade at the south end of the Somerset Ward. In the same year the operating theatres and an X-ray department on the ground and first floor in the north-west corner of the building were recommissioned.[196]

Other repairs to the building took much longer and some upper-floor wards were still awaiting restoration in 1957. The reluctance of the Regional Hospital Board to authorise the work may have been related to the consideration of further proposals to move the Hospital to the Albert Dock site.[197] Notwithstanding this delay, a new chapel, the building's third, was opened in 1952–3. Removed in 1998, it was placed in the south-east corner of the building on the third floor. Designed in a contemporary 1950s manner, it comprised a single undivided space, with a canted ceiling that rose to a steeply pitched apex, light-coloured wooden fittings and an etched glass memorial window, dedicated, as a window in the earlier chapel had been, to John Lydekker.[198]

Although the Hospital was eventually fully restored, its future under the NHS was always uncertain and it was finally closed in 1986, to be replaced by a 'Dreadnought Unit' at St Thomas's Hospital. Proposals for its re-use as offices for Greenwich University, to designs by Dannatt, Johnson & Partners, were first made in 1993.[199] In 1998–9 it was restored as the Dreadnought Library and Learning Centre, with a courtyard restaurant, for the same client, to the designs of the same architectural practice.

Devonport House

The origins of this dignified red-brick neo-Georgian building, built in two phases between 1925 and 1934 as a Nurses' Home, lay in the need of the Seamen's Hospital Society to extend beyond the bounds of the Greenwich Hospital Infirmary, which the Society had occupied since 1870 as the Dreadnought Seamen's Hospital (fig. 282). The offer of a site to the south of the Hospital was made in 1922 following several years of negotiations between the Society and the Admiralty. Funds for the new building had been raised by a public appeal, launched by Lord Devonport in 1916, which had eventually accrued some £250,000.[200] Devonport was the driving force behind the extension, although not always with the wholehearted support of the other members of the Society's board of management. From the first the Admiralty had refused to consider any substantial additions to the Dreadnought itself, wishing to avoid having a new building which might overshadow the former Hospital, and had encouraged the Society to consider another site outside the grounds of the Royal Naval College. Although the Society had voted to remain in the former Infirmary buildings and to pursue approval for an extension, they had nevertheless suggested to the Admiralty in 1918 the 'uncovered ground' of the Royal Hospital School as a possible site.[201] Although not acted upon at the time, when another approach was made in 1922, requesting permission for an extension to the Dreadnought, the Admiralty responded with the offer of the Infirmary of the Royal Hospital School and its grounds.[202] Initially, this was conditional upon the schoolboys being treated at the Dreadnought, saving the Admiralty an estimated £5000 per year, but this was soon overtaken by events: the school moved to Suffolk.[203] The site, separated from the Royal Naval College and the Dreadnought by Romney Road, was acceptable to the Admiralty in being suitably remote from the former Hospital and besides it was not possible to view both buildings at the same time. Notwithstanding Lord Devonport's apparent reluctance to accept the offer, the Society formally accepted it in March 1923. By April the following year the first designs were ready for consideration by the Office of Works in its capacity as architectural adviser to the Admiralty.[204]

Sir Edwin Cooper, appointed in 1916 to design the proposed extension to the Dreadnought, received the commission through Lord Devonport. Their association dated from at least 1912, when Cooper won the competition for the headquarters of the Port of London Authority, of which Devonport was Chairman. The architect had built up a reputation as a competent designer of institutional buildings. While working on the schemes at Greenwich he also was engaged in designing the Star and Garter Home for Incurable War Veterans in Richmond (1921) and an extension to the Royal College of Nursing in Henrietta Street (1922). The commission for Greenwich presented difficulties as the grounds contained a variety of existing structures that had to be retained, and any new building had to be acceptable to the sensibilities of the Office of Works and the Admiralty. But Cooper was, in the words of A. E. Richardson, an architect who 'remained loyal to the classical tradition'.[205] His stylistic discretion, his skills as a planner and his evident sympathy towards the surrounding architecture resulted in a building that was not only well received in the architectural press,[206] but was considered by the Office of Works in 1924 to be 'a very dignified design . . . which will in no way conflict with or discredit the very important buildings in the immediate vicinity'.[207]

In the new lease, drawn up in 1923–4, the Admiralty agreed to the construction of a nurses' home, with a motor-garage to the south reached by a covered way. A 'building of considerable architectural effect' was anticipated. The Society also proposed a wholesale reconsideration of the facilities of the Dreadnought. Ideas under consideration included a new kitchen and dining room on the new site, with food being delivered to the Hospital through a subterranean passage under the road. Aside from issues of cost this idea would have been rendered unviable by the presence of College Tunnel, a cut-and-cover railway tunnel running under the northern edge of the site to carry the original Greenwich line of 1836–8 east of the town in 1878.[208]

At the beginning of planning, the Nurses' Home was envisaged as a new quadrangular building, to the east of Newton's Hospital School of 1783–4 which was to be retained in its entirety. This

282 Devonport House (formerly Nurses' Home) from the north, with C. Raymond Smith's *Britannia* in front (see fig. 257).

proposal was soon modified to a Z-shaped arrangement when it was decided to rebuild the kitchen block in the courtyard of the Dreadnought, rather than building a new range on the new site. The layout was determined largely by the position of the school buildings and the burial vault and other surviving monuments of the Royal Hospital's burial ground. The original intention had been to move the eighteenth-century brick mausoleum at the east side of the site to the Hospital's last burial ground off Woolwich Road, but this was later rejected, possibly on grounds of cost, and the building was retained in its original position. The layout went through a number of modifications, not reaching its final form until after the construction of the first phase of building had begun in 1925. As late as 1928 an out-patients' department was proposed as a potential fourth side for the U-shaped school building.[209]

Work on the construction of the first phase of the Nurses' Home and the Pathological Laboratory had been due to start in June 1924 but was delayed until August 1925, following the belated discovery that a licence for the removal of human remains, issued in 1875 when the Royal Hospital School was proposing to build a new dining hall, had lapsed. The burial ground had not been cleared of remains after its closure in 1857, and when approval was granted, 1247 skulls and fifty-eight boxes of bones were reinterred at the Hospital cemetery in East Greenwich in August and September 1925.[210] The foundations were laid by November 1925 and building commenced.[211] The first phase had been completed by 1929,[212] leaving the western half of the principal range of the Nurses' Home to be completed: the break in the brickwork on the east side of the central carriageway is still visible on the south elevation. The building was formally opened by the Duke and Duchess of York on 15 July 1929. Both the Nurses' Home and the Pathological Laboratory were named after Devonport in recognition of the prominent part he had played in their funding and development.

The halt in the building programme in 1929 was necessary because the Society was obliged to wait until 1933 for the Royal Hospital School to vacate the eighteenth-century building, latterly the Infirmary.[213] During the interim, works on the Dreadnought Hospital were carried out. By the time work resumed on the new site, the Society was in financial crisis, precipitated both by the costs of the work, increased after storm damage at the Dreadnought, and the discovery that the branch hospital at Albert Dock would have to be rebuilt.[214] The difficulties were exacerbated by the realisation that the north range of the School Infirmary would have to be rebuilt rather than refaced, as had been the intention.[215] The generally inferior finish of the western part of the Nurses' Home, resumed in 1933 and completed by 1934, may have been a consequence of this crisis. The proposed western range to the School Infirmary had by now also fallen by the wayside. The financial problems may also have been behind the application made to the Admiralty in 1934 requesting permission to sublet part of the new Nurses' Home as 'high class offices'.[216]

Cooper, while designing a more modest building, clearly was indebted to Ralph Knott's influential County Hall, whose river

283   Devonport House, the entrance vestibule.

284   Devonport House, the staircase.

front, completed in 1922, changed the face of municipal and institutional architecture in England.[217] The principal elevation to the north side is strictly symmetrical. It has a rusticated ground floor and a high roof with dormer windows and tall stone-capped chimneys. The remorseless horizontality of the twenty-one bay elevation is relieved at the centre by a recessed section with a giant order of Doric columns above a low carriageway, and anchored at the ends by ornate pedimented window surrounds. One casualty of the extended building campaign was the central stone tower shown in several published drawings in 1926 but abandoned by 1929.[218] This, with its ship-shaped weathervane, would have given the façade a central accent, but in proportion to the overall length of the building it would, like the tower on County Hall, have represented a rather feeble conclusion to its architect's efforts.

Devonport House is built in red sand-faced bricks, with Portland stone dressings. Cooper had suggested red pantiles for the roof but the Admiralty preferred Westmorland slate.[219] The building now is covered in Roman tiles, following war-time bomb damage.[220] The style may be loosely characterised as being in the 'Wrenaissance' manner, vaguely described by *The Builder* as 'in the tradition associated with Greenwich'.[221] Its genesis lies in the earliest proposals for the Dreadnought extension, the first design for which was for a red-brick building with a large stone portico and dentilled cornice that showed a clear debt to Wren's Royal Hospital at Chelsea.[222] Learning from Wren, Cooper in the 1920s developed his own reproducible style of institutional architecture: red brick, high roofs and tall chimneys. The Star and Garter Home at Richmond, the School of Biochemistry in Cambridge and the South London Hospital for Women at Clapham Common all bear a clear family resemblance to the Devonport.[223]

The Nurses' Home was intended to provide accommodation of a high standard for a hundred sisters and nurses, as well as forty ward maids and kitchen staff. There were separate rooms for the nurses, as well as sitting rooms, writing rooms, classrooms and even a cookery demonstration room; in short, all the 'amenities of the Edith Cavell Home at the London Hospital or similar'.[224] The nurses' rooms on the upper three floors were placed off a central corridor, with bathrooms and kitchen facilities at the junctions of the ranges. This represented a significant improvement on the previous arrangement, when the accommodation was located on the top floors of the east and west ranges of the main Dreadnought building, with up to four nurses sharing a room.[225] Classrooms and reception rooms were distributed around the ground floors of the three ranges, a suite of rooms in the principal range being particularly richly finished. The marble-lined entrance vestibule still contains the foundation stone and the memorial inscription (fig. 283).[226] There is also a late seventeenth-century-style dogleg staircase (fig. 284) and a former reception room, later used as a boardroom, which has wooden panelling, a decorative plaster ceiling and marble chimneypiece.

The Devonport Nurses' Home escaped the severity of bomb damage suffered by the Dreadnought Seamen's Hospital, which was closed from 1941 until the end of the war. A limited emergency service of twenty-four beds was then operated from the Nurses' Home.[227] The building was handed over to the National Health Service in 1948, and remained in use until 1995. The possibility of its re-use as a health faculty for Greenwich University was proposed in 1993, in a scheme designed by Dannatt, Johnson & Partners[228] but in 1998–9 it was redeveloped by the University

in partnership with Hyde Housing to the designs of Spence Harris Hogan Associates as a residential conference centre, with a new wing on King William Walk as a residence for postgraduates.

Devonport Pathological Laboratory

The Pathological Laboratory was erected in 1924–9 as part of the expansion of the Dreadnought Seamen's Hospital. In Sir Edwin Cooper's initial scheme of 1923–4 the new Pathological and Bacteriological Departments were intended for the upper floors of the former School Infirmary.[229] At that time the only new building in the south-west corner of the site was to be a detached motor-garage (for six cars and six visiting doctors' cars), workshops, laundry and boiler house. The decision to place the Pathological Department in a new building, grouped with the services block, was apparently a late amendment made in mid-1924. Construction was delayed through problems over the licence to remove the human remains from the site and the foundations were not begun until August 1925.[230] By 1929 the Devonport Pathological School and the Nurses' Home, both constructed by Foster and Dicksee, were finished and in operation.

The Laboratory is composed of four blocks around an oblong courtyard. Both the east and west ranges are two storeys high, stepped down at the ends where they join the single-storey north and south ranges (fig. 285). The elevations are brick-faced with Portland stone dressings. The main elevation on the west side facing King William Walk has a Doric portico *in antis*, with stone architraves, cill band and parapet head. The other elevations have tile architraves to the windows and the east side has three large semicircular tile arches forming the garage openings. The

285 The west, entrance front of the Devonport Pathological Laboratory.

286   The hall and staircase of the Devonport Pathological Laboratory.

courtyard elevations are distinguished by a semicircular bay to the centre of the west range and a tall brick chimney stack extending from the middle of the east range.

The overall impression of the building is dignified and block-like, described at the time of completion as 'broad and unaffected'.[231] The handling of the details is less quirky than the Nurses' Home and the style more purely classical, in keeping with its southern neighbour, George Basevi's church of St Mary of 1823–4, which was demolished in 1936. Its design is also closely related to two other modest buildings that Cooper was working on at the same time: the South Dock Offices of the West India Docks (1926–7; demolished in the early 1980s)[232] and the Staff Offices for the King George v Dock (1933),[233] both for the Port of London Authority. All three were brick buildings with a blocky outline enlivened by central stone Doric porticoes. For Cooper, this was a design capable of repetition, bringing a degree of *gravitas* to otherwise prosaic buildings.

The west range of the Pathological Laboratory has several interiors of a richness befitting their function as the general offices of the Seamen's Hospital Society. On the ground floor there is a marble-lined hall and elegant apsidal open-well staircase, reproducing the detailing of the vestibule and staircase in the Nurses' Home (fig. 286).[234] A library and museum were placed in the large rooms at either end of the vaulted, axial corridor. The Pathology Laboratory was on the first floor, while the mortuary, post-mortem room and other facilities were in the single-storey side ranges. The back range housed the 'heating chamber' in the basement, whose steam boilers served the entire Hospital via pipe ducts that crossed beneath the road to reach the main buildings.[235] Above this was the garage and, at the first-floor level, a water treatment plant. The building underwent little alteration before the closure of the Dreadnought in the 1980s. After standing empty for several years it was restored in 1998–9 as the students' union for the University of Greenwich, and renamed the Cooper Building after its architect.

Chapter 8

BUILDINGS FOR EDUCATION

The origins of the majority of the buildings on the south side of the Romney Road, now principally occupied by the National Maritime Museum, lie in eighteenth-century naval initiatives in education. Greenwich Hospital initially placed boys in the Academy founded at Greenwich in 1715 by Thomas Weston. To accommodate greater numbers, the first substantial Greenwich Hospital School was built in 1783–4. This survives as part of Devonport House. The School remained there until 1821, when it merged with its neighbour, the Royal Naval Asylum. The Asylum, a school initiated in 1798, moved to Greenwich into the Queen's House and the new buildings to each side which were erected for the purpose in 1807–11. Following merger of the two educational institutions, the new school was known as the Greenwich Hospital Schools, and from 1892, the Royal Hospital School, Greenwich. The Infirmary of the Asylum, built in 1808–12 at the north end of Maze Hill on the site of the Hospital's early eighteenth-century burial ground, was moved in 1821, when the schools merged, into the Greenwich Hospital School building of 1783–4. The Maze Hill building then became residential. The Royal Hospital School left Greenwich in 1933 and its buildings were taken over by the newly created National Maritime Museum, which opened in 1937.

Old Greenwich Hospital School, King William Walk

Towards 1750, as the main buildings of Greenwich Hospital neared completion, attention turned to the improvement and completion of the institution through the provision of outlying and ancillary facilities, from lodges to a new burial ground. In efforts designed to remove secondary functions from the main buildings, to make more space available for pensioners, separate special-purpose buildings were provided in the form of the long-intended Infirmary in the 1760s and a residential boys' school in 1783–4. The provision of a school at an institution principally devoted to the care of the old and infirm calls for some explanation.

The Hospital's Royal Charter of 1694 referred to 'the Maintenance and Education of the Children of Seamen happening to be slaine or disabled' as one purpose of its foundation, albeit not a primary concern. In 1712 the Council of the Hospital additionally committed itself to the 'improvement of navigation'. It was

resolved that as soon as funding permitted the Hospital would accommodate 'orphans of the sea', that is feed, board and clothe the sons of dead or disabled seamen, teach them reading, writing, accounts, navigation and mathematics, and thus prepare them to be bound out to serve at sea. Three years later ten boys were selected and found places at a Greenwich school recently established by Thomas Weston, who had been trained in astronomical observation at the Royal Observatory by John Flamsteed and who was immortalised with his master in the south-east corner of Thornhill's Painted Hall (fig. 33).[1]

Leased from Greenwich Hospital, Weston's school was in a substantial house, perhaps Heyton Hall (previously Copped Hall, a courtier's house in the sixteenth century), which fronted onto what was then King Street (on the site of the Pathological Laboratory) on a site of 7 acres known as Goddard's Ground. This was bounded to the north by Romney Road, to the south by the road along the park wall to the Queen's House, and to the east by Friars' Road.[2] The Hospital charity boys, whose number rose to thirty by 1730, were educated at Weston's Academy alongside young gentlemen, many the sons of naval officers.[3] They were nominated by the directors, and were admitted, so long as they could read, when aged eleven to thirteen.[4] This was an age at which many boys already were at sea, the more usual place for the receipt of a rudimentary naval education: 'There was a lot to be learnt, and it had to be mastered before a boy had grown to manhood if youthful strength and quickness were to be matched by experience and confidence'.[5] In 1735 the number of Hospital boys was increased to a hundred and John Weston (brother of Thomas, who had died in 1728) put up a rectangular block north of the Academy's house in which to teach them separately.[6] In 1747 the lease fell in and the Hospital took possession of the Academy property in connection with the making of its new burial ground.[7] The Hospital boys continued to be educated at the Academy under the Westons' successors; in 1755 the Revd Francis Samuel Swinden altered the school building to accommodate twenty additional boys.[8] In 1758–9 the Hospital itself erected a modest new school building for the boys whom it was sponsoring, the work being carried out under the supervision of William Robinson, Clerk of Works, for £328.[9] This was within the burial ground, along its west side where it backed onto the Academy grounds. It was a rectangular block, about 50 feet long, with a canted bay on its south side.[10] An open-fronted 'playing place', nine bays long (80 feet by 15 feet), was built in 1759, after which the boys were enjoined to play only in the burial ground and were forbidden to play in the Hospital's colonnades.[11] A schoolmaster's house adjoining the school also was provided.[12] Following Swinden's retirement in 1763 the Hospital became wholly responsible for the education of its charity boys in this building, a purpose to which the institution had not previously given direct attention.[13] By 1779 there were 150 boys learning writing, arithmetic and navigation from the Hospital's own schoolmaster.[14]

As the number of boys had risen, their night-time accommodation had become ever more intrusive within the main buildings of the Hospital. Further, the rate at which pensioners died meant that the burial ground was rapidly filling up. In 1782 the Hospital decided to clear both its own inconveniently sited school buildings of 1758–9 and the now-empty Academy, to allow enlargement of the burial ground and the building of a new school building with dormitories, to provide space for 200 boys. One recommendation for the scheme was that the boys would 'have less communication with the pensioners', some of whom were regarded as a corrupting influence.[15] The decision to build the school might also have been influenced by the controversy generated by Captain Thomas Baillie in 1778 through the publication of his coruscating critique of the Hospital's departure from its original purposes, and in particular of the sacrifice of pensioners' ward space.[16] It may also have been a competitive reaction to the Marine Society's plans for a naval school and the establishment in 1782 of a naval academy in Chelsea.[17]

The new school building was designed to be 'more uniform and compact' than its predecessors, providing a schoolroom under dormitories, with 'Lodgings and Conveniences for the Guardian and his Mates, and for the Nurses'. An existing house (that of John Collins, the Hospital's joiner) on King Street was taken for the schoolmaster.[18] The first plans, with an estimate of £2928 17s 0d, were prepared in late 1782, apparently following the September dismissal of Robert Mylne. They were thus by William Newton, Mylne's successor as Clerk of Works, under whom 'the business of that department has been carried on with much greater vigour and alacrity'.[19] There is no evidence to suggest that James Stuart, then Surveyor to Greenwich Hospital, and preoccupied at that time with the reconstruction of the Hospital Chapel, had any involvement in the design of the building. Revised plans and estimates were approved in March 1783. By the end of that year £3238 had been spent, yet building work continued through 1784.[20]

A number of drawings survive for the building of 1783–4, so the evolution of its design can be traced. It was conceived as a nine-bay, two-storey range with a single dormitory over a ground floor which was divided longitudinally as a long schoolroom with long desks, alongside a play area in an open arcaded loggia. There were to be slightly projecting three-bay, two-storey-and-attic pedimented end pavilions for circulation, with ancillary rooms for warming, washing, staff and storage. This basic layout was clearly in an established tradition of institutional building for children (see below). The elevations were given round-headed openings and relieving arches, with numerous small blind oculi.[21] As in the Infirmary of two decades earlier, there was no attempt to echo the magnificence of the Hospital's main buildings. A more modest architectural style, in keeping with less exuberant times, accorded with the Hospital's funding as well as with its self-perception,

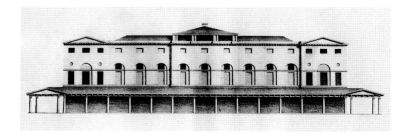

287 Elevation of the east front of the boys' school and dormitory, designed by William Newton, engraved for publication in J. Cooke and J. Maule, *An Historical Account of the Royal Hospital for Seamen at Greenwich*, 1789.

bruised by the criticisms of grandeur in excess of purpose made by Thomas Baillie.

This scheme was superseded, perhaps following a decision to provide space for 200 rather than 150 boys.[22] When Jacques Tenon visited in 1787 there were still only 150 boys; the number was not in fact increased to 200 until some time after 1789.[23] In the revised plans the whole of the ground floor was enclosed as a schoolroom of 100 feet by 25 feet, with an external stone Tuscan colonnade, 180 feet long, added onto the east side of the building, to provide a gravelled 'play place' and shelter within a walled forecourt (fig. 287). The main range was raised with a full attic to provide two dormitories of the same dimensions as the schoolroom below, the upper being lit through a central three-bay lantern. Heating in the large rooms was provided by a central cylindrical stack, a curiosity, with openings to either side. In the absence of a spine wall, structural support was supplied by two rows of timber posts which also served, in the dormitories, to provide fixings for hammocks (fig. 289). The latter were arranged in pairs, one above the other, in a manner no doubt designed to test the resolve of the children for a life at sea, and to save expenditure on beds. Each had only a mattress and a bolster with two woollen covers; there were no sheets.[24]

This building survives with surprisingly little alteration, though the north pavilion and one bay of the main range were demol-

288 William Newton's boys' school and dormitory of 1783–4, subsequently the Infirmary for Greenwich Hospital Schools, King William Walk.

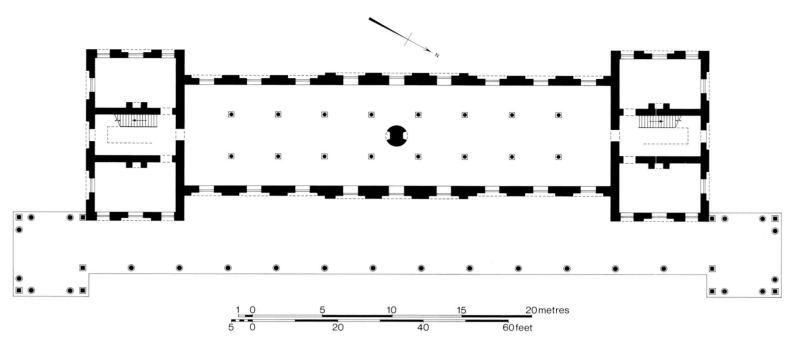

289   Reconstructed ground plan of the boys' school and dormitory, with its colonnaded 'play place' (based on drawings in BAL K9/16/6 and PRO ADM 79/81, no. 84).

ished in 1933 when Devonport House was built across the north end. Curiously, given one of the reasons cited for building the school, it stands close to the site of its predecessor of 1758–9, set well back from the road and thus formerly surrounded by the burial ground. It is of grey stock brick throughout, with Portland stone dressings (fig. 288). Exceptionally for its date there were iron window frames, made by Elizabeth Jackson, smith, as 'circular rebate' or 'swing' sashes, on horizontal pivots, which Tenon likened to the windows used in certain Dutch hospitals.[25] Introduced at Newton's request, to admit extra light, these must have had few and thin glazing bars. Perhaps their additional cost was also justified with the logic that was applied to the use of stone in the colonnade – in a school it would be 'cheaper in the end'.[26] The iron windows have been replaced with timber sashes and casements, in some places in enlarged openings, but the fenestration pattern remains largely as built. Internally many of the original timber posts remain, although the former schoolroom on the ground floor has been subdivided. Embedded within secondary partitions there are five tall timber columns, 13 inches in diameter with moulded caps and bases, on pedestals 3 feet high. It is likely that there were sixteen of these columns originally, in two rows.[27] They must have given the room a chapel-like aspect, with their bases appearing not above pews but above rows of desks. In the former dormitories on the upper floors the supports are square in section and, despite applied mouldings, much cruder, making for spaces more like a warehouse interior. The schoolroom was plastered, the upper storeys probably only limewashed.[28] On the first floor twelve original 8 inch square posts survive, in two rows on either side of the centre of the building. In the attic storey there are twelve more posts similarly arranged, rising centrally to support the pyramidally roofed lantern, with 'aisle ties' pegged into the outer posts. Additional structural strength may have been provided through the use of trussed floor beams,[29] evidence perhaps of Newton's interest in constructional innovation. The

south end has an open-well staircase, evidently remade, with crude wrought-iron balustrading fixed to the ends of re-used stone treads. The boundary wall along King William Walk immediately west of the school retains brickwork of an early character. It was rebuilt in 1784 with bricks from the demolished school of 1758–9.[30]

This building is a rare example of a large purpose-built eighteenth-century residential school. Such English schools as there were for large numbers of residential children tended to adapt earlier structures for their purposes. Few schools of any type were so big. In 1793 Eton had 477 boys, and in 1778 Winchester had 186. Ackworth, a Quaker school near Pontefract, Yorkshire, was a foundling hospital (orphanage) of 1758, built to resemble a country house, converted in 1779 to be a school for 309 children, not all residential.[31] Industrial and workhouse schools were only exceptionally big enough for 200 children, and they were not residential.[32] When Newton set about designing the school there were therefore only a few possible models, albeit well known. The first scheme with its arcaded loggia and pronounced end pavilions reflected precedent more closely than did the modified design.

The basic arrangement of a dormitory over an open ground floor can be traced to monastic medieval quadrangular origins. At Christ's Hospital, an orphanage school partly devoted to equipping boys for a life at sea, there were ranges around a quadrangle, largely rebuilt after 1666, but still reflecting the monastic origins of the site. Wren's and Hawksmoor's addition there of Sir John Moore's Writing School in 1692–3 was an upper-storey schoolroom, 96 feet long, for 300 or more boys over an arcaded loggia with projecting end pavilions.[33] At the Old Grammar School at Appleby, Leicestershire, also paid for by Sir John Moore, and built in 1693–7, Sir William Wilson altered Wren's first designs to provide an H-plan building of two storeys and attics with a first-floor schoolroom in the main range, stairs in the end wings, and an arcaded loggia across the front.[34] Lord Burlington's Scholars'

Dormitory at Wesminster School of 1722–9 is a fifteen-bay Palladian range. It originally had an open ground-floor arcade with a single huge dormitory above, but no end pavilions were needed since access to the dormitory was through adjoining buildings.[35]

These examples are not particularly close to the Greenwich building in formal terms, but they do provide precedent in terms of school architecture. A much closer model was to be found at the Foundling Hospital, though not strictly a school. Theodore Jacobsen's complex, designed after a study of continental orphanages, was built in 1742–5. It comprised separate boys' and girls' ranges to either side of a courtyard behind which stood a chapel. Each two-storey-and-attic side range had inner arcaded loggias and projecting corner pavilions. Internally the ground floors were divided longitudinally with dining rooms behind the arcades. There were open-well staircases at each end of both wings, and large open dormitories on the upper floors.[36] A further link comes via Jonas Hanway, an early Governor, Vice-President and Treasurer of the Foundling Hospital. Hanway was a reformer and philanthropist, largely responsible for legislation that provided for nurseries in workhouses, as well as an advocate of solitary confinement for the improving of prostitutes and prisoners: 'There is scarce any wickedness that solitude will not work on it'.[37] In another endeavour he founded the Marine Society in 1756, a charity that trained and sent to sea thousands of poor London boys.[38] In connection with this he promoted a project for a naval school. Donations to a building fund were made in 1779 and in 1783 Hanway published a scheme for a long three-storey range, housing a schoolroom and dormitories, with projecting end pavilions.[39] It may be that this scheme helped prompt Greenwich Hospital to put up its new building.

The large columnar schoolroom on the ground floor of the Greenwich school does not have any obvious precedent, nor is it clear how lessons were conducted. The beginnings of the application of educational theory to the layout of large schoolrooms and the 'classification' of ever-larger numbers of children within such rooms seem not to be earlier than about 1790.[40] While evidence as to the layout and use of the 1783–4 schoolroom is elusive, the use and derivation of the play area is rather more obvious. The grand colonnades of the King William and Queen Mary blocks at the Hospital, in which boys evidently had played before 1759, provide a link in the evolution of the covered walk derived from medieval cloisters to the creation of covered areas for play at the school of 1758–9. The Foundling Hospital also had long Tuscan colonnades extending along the sides of the grounds in front of the buildings, presumably for sheltered play. The Hospital School's colonnaded 'play place' and forecourt, a forerunner of the school playground, represented a continuation in this development, although they perhaps should be regarded as being the minimum necessary vent for juvenile exuberance rather than as an amenity. In 1804 the colonnade was said to have been 'destroyed by the Boys repeatedly breaking the slates'.[41] The attitude to play in the context of a late eighteenth-century Nonconformist school – 'neither do we allow any time for play on any day'[42] – may perhaps be contrasted with the more realistic naval experience of children at sea – 'a great part of our time was spent in play'.[43] It would not have been sensible for boys destined for a life at sea to have been confined indoors. In this and other respects the building of 1783–4 provided a model for the Royal Naval Asylum of 1807–11, a school on a much larger scale.

The building's life as a school was short. In 1821 Greenwich Hospital was obliged to take over the Royal Naval Asylum. This was merged with the Hospital's own much smaller school and the accommodation was re-organised to cater for a vast establishment of 1000 boys and girls. All the schoolrooms and dormitories were put into the former Naval Asylum buildings, and the school building of 1783–4 was converted to be the Infirmary for the amalgamated school, replacing the Naval Asylum's Infirmary on Maze Hill. One reason for this change was that the building of 1783–4 was conveniently close to the Hospital's Infirmary.[44] Plans for the 1821 conversion, at an estimated cost of £2082, were prepared by Henry Hake Seward, the Hospital's Clerk of Works, in consultation with the physician and surgeon. The works involved the addition of a full-height sanitary or washhouse annexe to the west, which still stands, some internal subdivision to provide twelve wards, the insertion of new windows and the removal of the east colonnade.[45]

The school extended its infirmary in 1881–2. A zymotic (infectious disease) ward was built, extending westwards from the north pavilion. This was a nine-bay, three-storey, polychrome-brick building designed by Colonel Charles Pasley.[46] In addition a single-storey range was added, extending westwards from the south pavilion to enclose a yard on the building's west side. The south wing survives in altered form. At its west end it had a dead-house or mortuary, latterly converted to be an electricity substation.[47]

From 1923 the acquisition of the school infirmary by the Seamen's Hospital Society to form a part of the Dreadnought Hospital complex was anticipated, in expectation of the departure of the Royal Hospital School from Greenwich.[48] This handover was not realised until 1933, when demolition of the north end of the building (including the zymotic ward) ensued. The rest of Newton's building of 1783–4 was converted for a range of hospital purposes, including consulting rooms and quarters for hospital staff.[49] Following closure of the Dreadnought Hospital it was vacated in 1995. The conversion of the overall complex for Greenwich University accommodation was undertaken in 1998–9.

The Royal Naval Asylum

The context of the Queen's House has twice changed significantly since it was built as a 'house of delight' next to a red-brick Tudor palace: first when it became the fulcrum of Wren's and Hawksmoor's Hospital, the distant centrepiece in Canaletto's view from over the river; and second when it became the central component of the group of buildings erected in successive phases through the nineteenth century to house a large school and which now are occupied by the National Maritime Museum.

The origins of these nineteenth-century buildings lie not within the history of Greenwich Hospital, but in the war-time foundation of a charity first known as the British National Endeavour. This was initiated by Andrew Thompson in 1798 and accommodated in Clarence House, Paddington Green, for the 'education, maintenance and apprenticing out' of orphans of war casualties. Stimuli for this may have been falling naval recruitment and the fleet mutinies of 1797, as much as popular sentiment in respect of casualties at sea after the Battle of the Nile. The charity attracted respectable support and large subscriptions, and Prince Augustus Frederick, Duke of Sussex, was appointed Chairman. However, as soon as December 1800 it required reformation when government plans to form a Military Asylum at Chelsea for soldiers' orphans caused it to devote itself solely to sailors' children. Further, it emerged that Thompson had pocketed about £1000 of the subscribers' money. Following his arrest the institution was renamed the Naval Asylum and given officers and rules.[50]

Leading protagonists at the time of this reformation were the Revd Dr Thomas Brooke Clarke and John Julius Angerstein. Clarke, the institution's Auditor from February 1801, had a non-residential living in Ireland, but no naval connections.[51] Angerstein, a prominent merchant and underwriter, was instrumental in establishing Lloyd's away from its coffee-house origins.[52] Admiral Sir John Colpoys joined the Naval Asylum's Committee in February 1801.[53] He had commanded ships from the 1770s until the 1797 mutiny in which he was a central figure. Thereafter he was knighted but kept ashore, also becoming a Director and Treasurer of Greenwich Hospital.[54] The support of City merchants was sought and Benjamin and Abraham Goldsmid were on the committee from July 1801. The institution depended heavily on the support of the Goldsmids, financiers who had extensive connections in the higher echelons of the Navy as well as in the City.[55] From February 1803 the Duke of Sussex, regularly abroad because asthmatic, was succeeded on the Naval Asylum's committee by his brother, Prince Ernest Augustus, Duke of Cumberland. Otherwise an Army man, Cumberland was titled President of the Naval Asylum from 1804.[56]

The Paddington house could hold only fifty-five children, so in 1802 a search for unoccupied Crown land began, in order to build new premises. This search was chiefly prosecuted by Clarke, who appears to have been the Asylum's most active officer and the only exception to a rule that staff must be linked to Naval service. In 1804 he framed an application for a Royal Charter and state funding on the basis of the precedents of the Foundling Hospital and the newly built Royal Military Asylum.[57] In June 1805 Parliament approved the application,[58] and George Rose, Vice-President of the Board of Trade, Joint Paymaster General and an intimate of Prime Minister William Pitt, was co-opted onto the committee.[59] With this impetus it was determined that a new building would be erected near Greenwich Hospital for 500 children, with £20,000 granted by Parliament.[60] Upon the issue of a Royal Warrant on 25 July 1805, the Royal Naval Asylum was established on a substantially sounder and larger footing than previously envisaged, with state funding of over £20,000 annually for the accommodation 'at or near Greenwich' of 700 boys and 300 girls.[61] Lloyd's coffee-house members on the committee secured a further £40,000 from Lloyd's Patriotic Fund, established in 1803 to support those wounded, widowed or orphaned in the war.[62] Such ample provision clearly reflects the Navy's high status and the popular esteem in which it was held at the time.

The move to Greenwich was still an aspiration rather than an achievement, as the search for a property continued. In July 1805 Clarke was corresponding with Thomas Martyn, architect, about designs 'for the Naval Asylum about to be built at Greenwich', and in August Rose told Clarke that he had 'found a piece of ground which is attainable'.[63] Some form of architectural competition had been devised, but by November only two plans had been submitted. By that time the architect Daniel Asher Alexander was in discussions with Clarke.[64]

At its Commissioners' first meeting on 7 November 1805, the day following the receipt of the news of the Battle of Trafalgar, the institution was refounded.[65] Cumberland remained President and Clarke retained his post as Auditor, while Angerstein and Rose were translated from the earlier committee to positions as Commissioners. In 1808 Captain Richard Dacres was appointed Governor.[66]

On 23 November 1805 Cumberland reported that he had with Commissioners (Samuel Viscount) Hood and (Sir Evan) Nepean inspected the Ranger's House at Greenwich (i.e. the Queen's House). Finding it most suitable for the purposes of the Naval Asylum, they had represented this view to Pitt, who had undertaken to speak to the king since 'there was a degree of delicacy due to His Majesty in the mode of proceeding'.[67] Only seven weeks earlier, on 4 October, the king's appointment of Caroline of Brunswick, Princess of Wales, to be 'Keeper of His Palace at Greenwich "commonly called the King's House or the Queen's House"' had been announced.[68] Separated from the Prince of Wales, Caroline had been living in Montague House adjoining Greenwich Park since 1798. The king, also estranged from his son, was fond of Caroline and had conceived the idea of giving her the Greenwich rangership himself.[69] In so doing, he may inadvertently have precipitated a crisis. Following years of widespread suspicion surrounding Caroline's unguarded conduct, on 5 November 1805 Lady Charlotte Douglas gave a false statement to the Prince of Wales and the Duke of Sussex alleging that the princess had an illegitimate son who was to be passed off as the prince's own, and thus as heir to the throne.[70] Sir John and Lady Douglas had been intimates of Caroline at Montague House, but had fallen out badly. They lived in a house at the foot of Maze Hill, within Greenwich Park. Upon her appointment as ranger, Caroline may have intended or may have been suspected of intending to take this from them, perhaps prompting Lady Douglas's allegations, from which there followed the so-called 'Delicate Investigation' into Caroline's sexual history.[71] It may be coincidence, but the timing of Cumberland's visit to consider use of the Queen's House for the Naval Asylum, within three weeks of Lady Douglas's allegation, may signify a desire on the part of the Prince of Wales and his camp to deprive the despised and now apparently dangerous Caroline of the symbolism of a building known as the Queen's House.

Pitt's death in January 1806 caused delay, but in March Lord Grenville, the new Prime Minister, advised Cumberland that the views of the Princess of Wales needed to be sought on the proposed appropriation of the Queen's House. Rose ascertained that she was 'entirely disposed to acquiesce', provided she received compensation to the value of the house.[72] Grenville thought this unreasonable and Cumberland proposed that the costs of fitting up Montague House should be the only compensation. In June 1806 Caroline accepted: 'I feel myself proud to be of any use to the Public by giving up the Ranger's House'.[73] The arrangement was put into effect through a Memorandum of Agreement between Caroline and Cumberland in October 1806.[74] An Act[75] was obtained in April 1807 to regularise the transaction whereby the Queen's House, which had 'not for many years past been appropriated to any useful purpose whatever',[76] with associated and outlying properties, including buildings on Park Place that had been occupied by the princess's steward and Sir John and Lady Douglas's house on Maze Hill, were transferred to the Naval Asylum which paid £7875 to Caroline.

290   Daniel Alexander's skilful disposal of well-proportioned play colonnades enabled him to bridge the gap between Jones's Queen's House and his new school buildings for the Royal Naval Asylum, while maintaining an appropriate distance between old and new (see fig. 120).

Earlier plans to advertise for architectural designs had been shelved. In November 1806 Alexander submitted a report with plans for the 'disposition and arrangement' of the buildings. These were approved and worked-up drawings were requested.[77] How it was that Daniel Asher Alexander came to be given the job is not transparent, although he had good connections with maritime institutions, holding surveyorships to the London Dock Company, the Fishmongers' Company and Trinity House; in 1793–1801 he built the Mote, near Maidstone, his only major country house, for Charles Marsham, Earl of Romney, one of the Commissioners.[78] Alexander reportedly later said that 'When the Naval Asylum was begun in 1807, I slipped a note into the Duke of Cumberland's hand . . . [t]hat the architect be directed to form his plan in strict accordance with the style of Inigo Jones; the Board at that sitting adopted it, and the building now tells the tale'.[79] The consequence of Alexander's persuasive note was the conversion of the Queen's House, to which were added long colonnades leading to substantial but distant neo-Palladian wings to east and west (which originally were shorter than they now are) (fig. 290).

Possession of the properties was taken in December 1806, and an estimate of £41,492 was presented for the building work.[80] Alexander set out to obtain tenders for the building contracts from those working with him at the London Docks. Robert Browne, an architect in the Office of Works, was brought in to judge these and other tenders and the main contracts were given on 2 January 1807. A Building Committee of Commissioners Angerstein,

291   J. M. W. Turner, *London from Greenwich Park*, 1809 (Tate Gallery, London).

Nepean and (George) Villiers was appointed and work on the adaptation and extension of the Queen's House to form the Naval Asylum began.[81]

The east wing was begun first, that to the west being left until late 1807.[82] The buildings being erected were big enough for only 600 children, despite the Parliamentary provision for 1000. In May 1808 Alexander presented a model with an estimate of additional expenditure of £12,982 for extending the wings to accommodate all 1000 children. This was approved, but set aside and the east wing was finished to the original plan.[83] It is depicted, still scaffolded, by J. M. W. Turner in *London from Greenwich Park* (exhibited in 1809), although the perspective is slightly distorted in order to show more of the Queen Mary Building (fig. 291). The composition was engraved for his *Liber Studiorum* and published in 1811.[84]

Approval to extend the wings northwards was given in January 1809, following the rejection of an alternative proposal to raise them, and by June work was well advanced.[85] Following a review of progress in February 1811, considerable expense was incurred to ensure that the buildings, including the extensions, were essen-

tially complete by the end of that year.[86] By the close of 1813 the final accounts had been settled, the overall cost of the whole building project being £175,357.[87] The number of children at the school rose from 520 at the end of 1810 to 834 by the end of 1815.[88]

The numinous presence of the iconic Queen's House caused the school to be split through the middle. Alexander's self-attested deference to Jones was manifested in the two colonnades extending along the line of the road which had run through the centre of the house. They were not replacing empty space, but the clutter of outbuildings and walls that had accumulated to either side of the building during the course of the seventeenth and eighteenth centuries. The colonnades not only reinstated the line astride which the Queen's House had been built, but did so by echoing Wren's Hospital colonnades. Alexander's sensitivity to the work of his two great predecessors helped him to preserve the sacrosanct vista from the house to the Thames and, by distancing the bulk of the new east and west wings away from the house, he effectively concealed them in the view south from the river. The shorter wings of the original project, moreover, would have ranged

292   A late nineteenth-century view of Daniel Alexander's east wing of the Royal Naval Asylum, now the National Maritime Museum (PRO ADM 195/47).

with the Queen's House symmetrically along both north-south and east-west axes. The elongation of the wings undermined this stasis.

Alexander closely followed the lead of the Queen's House in his elevations, eschewing his own characteristically more severe classicism, as employed in the site's remote Infirmary. The wings are two-storey stuccoed ranges with stone dressings and hipped slate roofs. The original wings were 155 feet long, eight-bay ranges with rustication to the lower storeys on vermiculated stone plinths. Single-bay projecting end pavilions carry Doric pilasters. At the south ends there are *distyle-in-antis* Doric porticoes. The east wing retains internal walling in the basement which indicates that the north end briefly mirrored the south, with a recess for columns *in antis*.[89] The 165 feet long, eleven-bay north extensions have rusticated basements with round-headed openings, channelled rustication on the principal storeys, and more emphatic single-bay north pavilions (fig. 292). The overall length of the

wings (320 feet) echoes the identical north-south length of the Queen Mary and King William blocks. In their shorter form, the original wings had two-bay deep central projections on their outer elevations. That to the west has been rebuilt and incorporated into later extensions, that to the east remodelled as an entrance (fig. 293). The entrances originally were at the south ends of the wings and from the colonnades.[90] The twenty-three-bay, 180-foot long Tuscan colonnades are of Portland stone with very shallow-pitched leaded roofs, formerly copper-covered.[91] Stone repair on the south columns shows where they were linked by dwarf walls and railings, removed in 1935–6.[92]

Of the original east and west wing interiors, virtually nothing survives. There were four spatially complex staircases, a predilection of Alexander, all top-lit, but each one different. There were stairs within an ellipse in the south-east pavilion, and in a circle to the south-west. Those to the centre-east rose in Imperial flights round another ellipse, and to the centre-west there was an open well with an apsidal back.[93] The upper storeys had timber floors and the roofs rested on queen-post timber trusses.[94]

The internal layout of the Royal Naval Asylum was utilitarian:

The lower part of each wing is to be appropriated to the school rooms for the children, male and female respectively; the upper parts as dormitories for them, and the servants of the institution. . . . The boys are taught reading, writing, and figures; and where their capacities display fitness, are to be instructed in navigation; and during the hours of relaxation, the elder boys are taught rope and sail making; and they are to be instructed in the rudiments of naval discipline, by regular veteran boatswains. The girls are taught to read and write, and are instructed in needlework, and household industry.[95]

Boys were admitted aged five to twelve, girls aged five to ten, provided they were 'children born in Wedlock of Warrant and Petty Officers and Seamen of the Royal Navy; and Non-Commissioned Officers and Privates of Your Majesty's Royal Marines'. Surprisingly, perhaps, the boys were sent to sea only with their own consent.[96]

The classrooms, each probably seating a hundred or more children at a time, were on the ground floor in the south ranges of the wings, with access from lobbies off the colonnade entrances. Each wing appears to have had three classrooms, one in each arm of the T formed by each south range. Four of the rooms measured about 30 feet by 40 feet and two about 25 feet by 45 feet. The classrooms in the west wing, and perhaps originally also those to the east, had two or three rows of desks in radiating horseshoes or extended semicircles (fig. 294).[97] This lecture-theatre-type arrangement is very different from the layout of the massive schoolrooms that were coming to dominate contemporary educational debate. In a reforming period during which the provision of education to the poor was becoming a widespread concern, there was a massive shift upwards in the scale of schools in the first years of the nineteenth century. From about 1800 large Sunday schools were being built, and Joseph Lancaster and Dr Andrew Bell were successfully promulgating systems for educating as many as 1000 children in one space through the use of child monitors. Lancaster was specific about physical arrangements, using his own school at Borough Road, Southwark, as a model. There the boys and girls each had large rectangular schoolrooms with row upon row of long desks all facing the front.[98]

The Royal Naval Asylum was one of the largest schools built at this time. In 1808, having advised the Naval Asylum's Board that Bell's system of monitorial instruction was in use at the Royal Military Asylum and that it 'was highly spoken of', George Rose was sent to confer with him.[99] Whether from this root or otherwise, responsibility for teaching and discipline in the Naval Asylum was assigned to a single Quarter Master of Instruction with Serjeant Assistants, one to every fifty children. Military order was maintained, the children being drummed awake, to meals, to prayers, to lessons and to bed.[100] Whether this comprised hierarchical social control through monitorial education as promoted by Bell and Lancaster is not clear. The multiple, relatively small classrooms with horseshoe seating rather suggests a lecturer-audience relationship, with the Serjeant Assistants commanding from the front, rather than delegating instruction to boys in control of smaller groups. They also imply classification of the children, perhaps by ability rather than by age. The Royal Naval Asylum

293 Part of Daniel Alexander's east wing of the Royal Naval Asylum, now remodelled as the entrance to the administrative wing of the National Maritime Museum. The doors on the west side give access directly into the colonnade in what has always been an entrance position. The marble statues of Admiral Sir Edward Pellew, 1st Baronet and 1st Viscount Exmouth, to the left, and Sir William Peel, to the right, are by Patrick Macdowell and William Theed respectively.

was unusually amply funded and may, therefore, have found no need for the application of industrial principles and economies of scale. It was also perhaps atypical in that building design appears to have been in the hands of military administrators and an architect, with no evidence save Rose's mention of Bell for any input from experienced educators. The military asylums were at this time a special case, being in effect the first large-scale state-funded schools, a generation before 1833 when public funding for schools in England properly began. The use of the term 'asylum' reflects the origins of these institutions as orphanages; places where education for the poor was an adjunct to refuge. But support for these institutions, particularly in war time, was not wholly charitable. The schools aimed to supply the forces with skilled and disciplined manpower. Their purpose therefore was very much in keeping with the wider social manipulation advocated by contemporary educational and penal reformers.

The colonnades immediately adjoining the classrooms were not simply an architectural device, but functional spaces providing covered areas for play, exercise and shelter. The narrow tunnel below the colonnades which links the wings may be one with the 'rope walk' that was also a 'publick cellar', set up for the boys to learn ropemaking.[101] Railed to the south, the colonnades opened onto playgrounds to the north. The provision of such spaces reflects the precedents set ahead of their time by Greenwich Hospital School and the Royal Military Asylum. Playgrounds were not generally adopted as worthwhile adjuncts to schools before the 1820s.[102] In addition, a ten-bay building fronted by a colonnade was put up in 1813 to the west of the west wing, facing an area

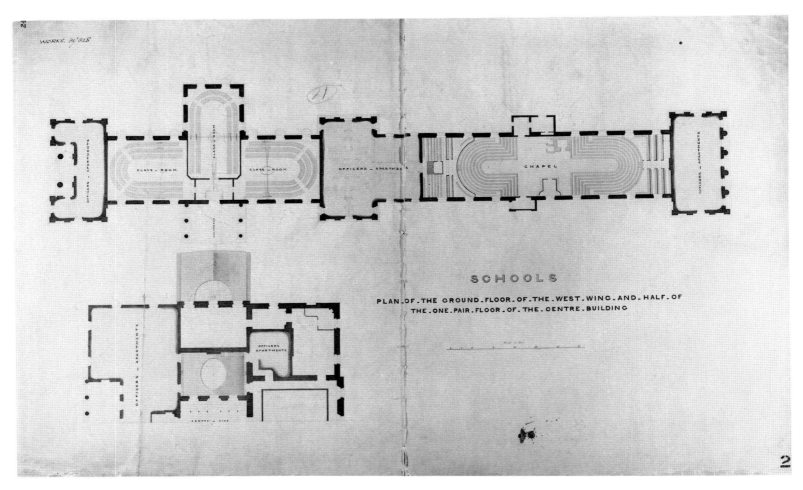

294   Plan of the ground floor of the west wing of the Royal Naval Asylum, *c.*1830 (PRO WORK 31/328).

that was termed both a playground and a gymnastic ground. This building was designated the 'evening playroom' in 1844.[103] However much these purpose-built play places may reflect the particular requirements of military education, they do seem also, or perhaps by the same measure, to be evidence of a pre-Victorian awareness of children's play as an end in itself.

The lower levels of the north extensions of the wings were for communal indoor spaces that the Greenwich Hospital boys shared with the pensioners, that is a dining hall and a chapel. The latter appears to have been an impressive and unusual space rising through the basement and ground floor of the west wing extension. It was about 115 feet long and 30 feet wide, with opposing semicircles of tiered concentric benches (apparently sufficient to accommodate the whole school) to north and south of a central area with a pulpit and reading desk to the west, and a railed communion table to the east. The double radial arrangement was used to separate the sexes. North and south galleries accommodated pews for the staff and, from 1821, an organ.[104]

The top storeys of the wings were dormitories throughout, three with hammocks in double tiers, one with beds, each accommodating around 200 children.[105] Some of the apartments for officers were in the end pavilions; others were in the Queen's House, where the girls also were eventually wholly accommodated.[106] The heating of all the interiors save in the Queen's House appears to have been by 'elliptical Rumford stoves',[107] although in February 1811 instructions had been given for the insertion of fireplaces

since many of the children had chilblains.[108] The three south bays of the basements of the wing extensions were arcades with iron gates and louvred windows, in part simply to allow circulation through rather than around the elongated wings.[109] The service buildings near Park Row on the eastern edge of the site, screened from view by the east wing, included a kitchen, an octagonal lavatory block and a laundry, all linked to the wing by covered ways.[110] To the north, a pair of diagonally set single-storey lodges flanked the central entrance to the site from Romney Road.[111]

It is important to register the exceptional scale of the Royal Naval Asylum. Greenwich Hospital had built an unusually large new residential school for 200 in 1783–4, but the Asylum was designed for five times that number and, unlike contemporary Sunday schools or Lancasterian schoolrooms in which similar numbers were educated, it was residential. Its closest functional parallel was with the Royal Military Asylum at Chelsea, built to designs by John Sanders in 1801–3, also for 700 boys and 300 girls. This comprised a central block with short arcaded links to dormitory wings which had colonnades along their outer elevations facing separate playgrounds for boys and girls.[112] The elements at Greenwich and Chelsea were thus much the same, though otherwise arranged. The layout of Chelsea was comparable with that of Ange-Jacques Gabriel's École Militaire in Paris (1751–73), an academy for training 500 poor young gentlemen, where colonnades extending behind the main block faced each other across a courtyard. The main elements of the Naval Asylum, particularly before it was extended, were more immediately echoes of Greenwich Hospital's school of 1783–4. In each case there were long ranges with teaching spaces below, dormitories above and play colonnades outside, set between end pavilions for staff accommodation and internal circulation. A telling difference between the two was the change from a single schoolroom to multiple classrooms.

There were other precedents for the overall architectural form of the Asylum complex. Theodore Jacobsen's Foundling Hospital of 1742–5 had boys' and girls' wings which extended forward from a central block to enclose a large forecourt. Similarly three sides of a courtyard were enclosed by arcaded ranges at the same architect's Naval Hospital at Haslar of 1746–61.[113] The adaptation of institutional models to the Palladian context of Greenwich was mediated also by reference to domestic design. The neo-Palladian formula adopted by John James at Wricklemarsh in 1723 and by Isaac Ware at Chesterfield House in 1747–9 – long colonnades to either side of a cubic villa that led to service ranges at right angles to the house – gained some currency later in the century, albeit in varied guises, as for example at Attingham, Shropshire (1783–5) by George Steuart, Heaton Hall, Lancashire (1772) and Castle Coole, Fermanagh (1790), both by James Wyatt. Perhaps more pertinent in this context was Ackworth, near Pontefract, built on these lines as a foundling hospital in 1758.[114] As influences, however, these buildings are suggestive rather than directly comparable. In the prominent severity of the Greenwich colonnades in particular there is something of French neo-classicism. The Royal Naval Asylum was one of the few grand institutional projects of this radical period to be built in England by an architect with a sense of drama and a sure classical touch. Despite the primacy given to context in its design, it holds on to the spirit of visionary classicism more fully realised across the English Channel.

Alexander lived up to the challenge of the site and the difficult task of extending the Queen's House tactfully. His solution respected the autonomy and architecture of Jones's building and, particularly before he was obliged to extend the wings, its scale. Further, he did this without compromising the function of the new complex, simply re-organising the elements of the school which Greenwich Hospital had built twenty-five years earlier. The layout is full of precedent and logic, both in terms of the site and in terms of the use of the buildings.[115] The re-orientation of the play colonnades to link the wings to the Queen's House was a masterstroke. Of Alexander, whose approach at Greenwich was praised by John Soane, it was later said: 'in his hands the architecture, whatever it was, was ever made to grow out of and to form an inherent necessity of the structure, and not something superadded as a vestment to exhibit a mere reprint or impression of some previously accredited combinations'.[116]

When the Napoleonic Wars ended in 1815, economies inevitably had to be made. The annual grant of money to the Naval Asylum no longer had full public support in peace time and there were imputations of extravagance.[117] Questions had earlier been asked about the accommodation given to the Asylum's officers and, in particular, about Clarke's living in Ireland.[118] The institution's annual running costs had risen to about £21,000 by 1816.[119] Having received Parliamentary grants of £431,906 in total, the Asylum was put onto a new footing in 1818, when it was determined that its costs would be met by the Admiralty. Cumberland stood down as President and in 1819 amalgamation

with Greenwich Hospital was suggested. The institutions had hitherto remained distinct, despite the similar purposes of their adjoining schools. As already noted, this merger was effected in 1821.[120]

Buildings at 32–40 Maze Hill
(formerly the Royal Naval Asylum Infirmary)

Towards the north-east corner of Greenwich Park, at the bottom of Maze Hill, there is a row of five houses with walled gardens (figs 295 and 296). The site is part of the park land that was enclosed to be a dwarf orchard in the seventeenth century. In 1707 this part was given up to be the first burial ground for Greenwich Hospital and enclosed by tall brick walls. Within, an officers' mausoleum of 1713–14 survives in altered form (see chapter 6). Disused from 1747, the burial ground was developed in 1808–12 with the building of a children's hospital, the Royal Naval Asylum Infirmary, designed by Daniel Asher Alexander. Since 1822 the hospital has been subdivided for residential use.

The Queen's House was granted to the Royal Naval Asylum by an Act of 1807[121] in order to provide the basis of the accommodation required for the maintenance and education of up to 1000 children of naval casualties. Outlying properties also were transferred to the new institution. Among these was the disused burial ground on Maze Hill.[122] The remote site had been appropriated in November 1806 for the school's Infirmary, for which Alexander prepared plans. A suggestion made in July 1807 that the site might be used for the Auditor's House, and the Infirmary moved into the existing group of buildings just east of the Asylum, was resisted by Alexander and John Doratt, the Asylum's surgeon. Alexander wanted 'a separate and proper tho' plain Infirmary' and agreed with Doratt that it needed to be distant from the school, on high ground 'according to ye best practise and principles throughout Europe'. Initially, it appears that although the 1807 Act specified up to 1000 children, accommodation was being provided for only 600 so Doratt specified that on the basis of 6 per cent illness (36 in 600), six wards were needed: one for each sex for accidents (on the ground floor), contagion and general disease. Also needed were two nurses' rooms, a dispensary and an operating room. He recommended that the wards should have brick walls without lath and plaster which 'would but be Nests to collect the Semina of disease': 'Brick walls, good elevation and good ventilation expedite cures, and restoration from disease, often as much, and sometimes more, than Medicine'.[123] The point was won and building work began in 1808, but since foundations had to be dug between graves, progress was halted until it had been established that the old burial ground had not been consecrated.[124] By 1809 the building had been erected as an eight-bay block at the centre of the burial ground.

By this time it had been decided that the Asylum as a whole would be enlarged to the capacity specified in the establishing Act, so the Infirmary, which had been designed to serve an institution of 600, was after all required to serve 1000.[125] Accordingly, in 1810–12 it was doubled in length, extended to the south with nine more bays to allow for over double the number of beds, from thirty-two to seventy.[126] The whole was made to seem unified in appearance, but straight joints in the front and rear walls and a slight change in brick colour do betray the change of plan. In a two storeys, seven for the ill among the school's 700 boys and two for its 300 girls, most wards being equipped with nurses' cabins.[127] As a late Georgian general hospital, this building is not atypical. Its overall domestic appearance and the opposed windows for cross-ventilation were standard in hospitals of the period. It is, however, a notably early example of a substantial purpose-built children's hospital (fig. 297).

The north end of the Infirmary had accommodation for the assistant surgeon, above a dispensary. The south end, since rebuilt, had a sky-lit operating room over small contagious wards, it being standard practice at the time to have small rooms in hospitals to isolate infection. The water closets, behind the south staircase, were unusual in being integrated into the main block. The building could be entered from either side. There was a large 'kitchen building' with recessed quadrant corners immediately west of the 1808–9 section. This also housed a scullery and bath, as well as small 'scald head' and 'itchy' (scabies) wards. There were separate boys' and girls' 'courts' or play areas to east and west, and a porter's lodge inside a gate in the burial ground wall to the east. The surgeon had the house and garden at the north-east corner of the park, formerly occupied by Sir John and Lady Douglas.[128]

The main Infirmary building survives, without its outbuildings and with its east side abutting the pavement to the widened road. It is a long two-storey structure with a main block of fifteen bays. It has plain stock-brick elevations, flat and minimally embellished, with twelve-pane sash windows under flat-arched gauged-brick heads. A simple timber modillioned cornice sets off a slate roof with pedimental panels in the end-wall brickwork. The austerity of its appearance is not simply in keeping with its original institutional use, but is also the architectural style with which Alexander appears to have been most comfortable. Here, away from the Queen's House, he did not need to defer to Inigo Jones. The main block has three entrances under projecting flat hoods, those to the centre and north with shaped brackets. The central entrance probably was inserted in 1822. The somewhat grander outer entrances are set in relieving arches. That to the north has steps up to a door that had a side light; that to the south has an opening side panel, perhaps to admit the sedan chairs that carried the sick from the Asylum.[129] As the building is set into a hill, the slightly later south door has steps down, cut back from a semicircular flight. The plainer rear elevation, to the west, has a relieving arch and stairs up to the former north section entrance. The single-bay dispensary block to the north is lower, with an awkwardly proportioned fanlight over its entrance, dentilled eaves and its own hipped roof. A low outshut addition on the three-bay north return wall conceals a simple double arch over an entrance leading to the basement. The lie of the land means that only the building of 1808–9 has a basement, in which there are substantial relieving arches.

Inside, the building has been much altered in successive subdivisions for residential use. No longer are there brick-lined wards, though some simply moulded early joinery and fireplaces with unmoulded surrounds survive. Notwithstanding its utilitarian qualities, Alexander gave the building two fine stairs, economically finished, yet beautifully designed, which have survived the later subdivision of the building. They are tightly wound and dramatically self-supporting open-well stone staircases with delicately finished wrought-iron balustrading, the thin square balusters subtly bowing out near their bases.[130] The stair compartments, the smaller

295   The former Royal Naval Asylum Infirmary, 32–40 (right to left) Maze Hill, Greenwich, viewed from the south.

296   The garden (park) side of 32–40 Maze Hill, Greenwich, viewed from the north, showing the walls of the Hospital's burial ground of 1707.

review of progress in February 1811 the Infirmary was found to be nearly complete, but Alexander was asked to rearrange its interiors to provide more ward space. In March he submitted plans that met this demand, providing twelve rather than nine wards on

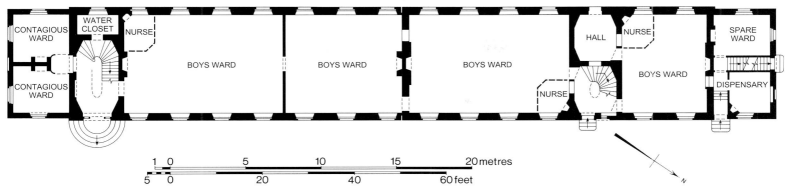

297 Ground plan of the Royal Naval Asylum Infirmary, as completed in 1812 to designs by Daniel Alexander (based on plans in PRO ADM 80/98).

one to the north retaining its stone flag floor, are octagonal, the walls rising to segmentally domed heads in an unusual, almost Soanian manner (figs 298 and 299). This treatment is repeated in the former nurses' room over the former entrance hall west of the north stair. The domical ceilings may allow flues from corner fireplaces to rise to an axial ridge stack. The cross-stair in the north block is much simpler, bifurcating to the two rooms that formed the assistant surgeon's apartment.

In 1821 the Royal Naval Asylum was amalgamated with Greenwich Hospital. The schools of the two institutions were merged and their accommodation rationalised. The smaller Greenwich Hospital school building was vacated and converted to be a larger

and more conveniently situated Infirmary for the whole school. The Maze Hill Infirmary was thus available for subdivision to house some of the Hospital's 'inferior officers'. Henry Hake Seward prepared plans for housing a Butler and his 1st and 2nd Mates, a Cook's Mate, a Master Shoemaker, a Master Taylor, an Assistant Laundress, a Store Labourer and a Messenger.[131] The works were carried out in 1822 by James Russell for £767.[132] Some of the joinery of this time, including a kitchen fireplace, dresser and two cupboards as drawn by Seward for the Cook's Mate, survives in No. 34. A simple dogleg staircase with stick balusters in No. 36 appears to be the one installed between the apartments for the Butler and the Butler's 2nd Mate.[133]

298 Staircase in 38 Maze Hill.

299 Staircase in 34 Maze Hill.

In 1823 Maze Hill, too narrow for two carriages to pass (as with car parking it is again), was widened. The eastern part of the old burial ground wall was demolished, along with the porter's lodge and the former surgeon's house to the north.[134] In 1832 the apartments in the former Infirmary were vacant and Greenwich Hospital was advertising leases for conversion into houses.[135] Privately occupied, they came to be known as Maze Hill Buildings. The south end bay, No. 40, was rebuilt and enlarged in 1864 by Greenwich Hospital, presumably to the designs of P. C. Hardwick for the lessee, W. P. Lethbridge.[136] It was made into a substantial two-storey and basement house, tactfully rising above the block of 1810–12 as if stepping Alexander's design up the hill. It has three bays to the road, blind save to the north where there is an entrance in a relieving arch. The two-bay south gable end has a cast-iron raised ground-floor balcony and margin-glazed windows retaining valances at their heads, all under a pedimental gable. A projecting two-storey block to the west has a bay window commanding a magnificent view of the park, and a three-bay tented veranda to the south on openwork cast-iron supports. The houses later reverted to being official residences,[137] then were again leased and sold off as five private houses.

Greenwich Royal Hospital Schools

The Royal Naval Asylum was taken over by Greenwich Hospital for amalgamation with its own school by a Royal Warrant of 31 January 1821. The rearrangements, which were intended to save money, were carried through by Edward Hawke Locker. Former Naval Asylum staff were discharged and the total number of children was reduced by eighty to 1000. Modestly adapted, the Naval Asylum buildings were re-organised as an Upper School (the old Greenwich Hospital boys) of 200 in the east wing, and a Lower School of 600 boys and 200 girls, the latter kept on despite doubts as to the usefulness of educating girls. A few months previously at Locker's suggestion the Hospital had adopted the National System of Education, that is the tenets of the National Society for Promoting the Education of the Poor in the Principles of the Established Church, which had been founded by Dr Andrew Bell in 1811. This introduced monitorial education to Greenwich, a system whereby older children instructed the younger. Such delegation was unavoidable in an institution where there were only nine teachers to 1000 children.[138] The Naval Asylum name continued to be used until 1825, when the establishment was designated the Upper and Lower Schools of the Royal Hospital, alternatively and more simply known as the Greenwich Hospital Schools. From 1892 the form Royal Hospital School, Greenwich, was adopted.[139]

In 1828 the boys' Lower School was reduced to 400 and the Upper School enlarged to 400 to meet a proposal from the Duke of Clarence, Lord High Admiral (later King William IV), that places at the latter should be reserved for the sons of officers.[140] This appears to have occasioned a remodelling of the east wing classrooms to a plan devised by Edward Riddle, Master of the Upper School. This provided a single schoolroom for all 400 boys of the Upper School in an essentially rectangular space with rows of desks and masters positioned at either end, an arrangement suited to monitorial instruction.[141]

From 1824 training in 'the art of swimming' was given to the trainee seamen.[142] As early as 1581 Richard Mulcaster had noted the desirability of being able to swim in the event of 'fightes by sea' and by the early seventeenth century it was considered a manly pursuit for a gentleman. Fynes Moryson, writing in 1617, while recognising the value of swimming, suggested that it was an accomplishment best kept secret, since 'many excellent swimmers . . . have sunke by the waight of their fearefull companions knowing their skill'.[143] But notwithstanding the obvious usefulness of swimming, only a small proportion of sailors could do so.[144] It was to correct this potentially fatal shortcoming in the trainee sailors that the decision was made in 1831 to build an outdoor swimming bath at Greenwich. Positioned south-west of the school, encroaching into the park towards St Mary's church, this early swimming pool, measuring 150 feet by 60 feet, was designed by Joseph Kay in 1832 and built in 1833 with its sides and bottom formed of mass concrete, a striking construction at this date. The brick lining that Kay had always intended was not added until 1839, once the concrete had suffered decay.[145] In 1874–5 the bath was covered with a sky-lit timber and wrought-iron superstructure designed by Colonel Charles Pasley.[146]

In 1840 about seventy boys ran away from the school complaining of 'ill usage and indifferent food', as well as 'apprehension of being made soldiers'.[147] Such deep disaffection and reports of poor educational standards prompted the Admiralty to initiate an inquiry into the school's conduct and attainments. An investigation by Seymour Tremenheere and Henry Moseley, inspectors for a government committee on education, damned the Lower School in particular and led to several reforms. In 1841 the girls' school was closed down since 'the propinquity of the sexes had led to many evils'.[148] The Upper School was divided with the formation of the Nautical School, for the further education under Edward Riddle of promising boys selected at the age of fourteen for a professional maritime training.[149] Those not so selected expressed their feelings about these changes and their lot in December 1841 by breaking 370 panes of window glass. Under Moseley's guidance staff numbers were increased and class sizes reduced; the pupils per master ratio in the Lower School decreased from seventy-eight to fifty-four in 1842–4. Discipline and standards improved,[150] but relations between the schools were still not always smooth. In 1848 Lower School boys reacted to favouritism towards the Upper School in precautions taken against scarlet fever by themselves breaking 168 panes of glass.[151]

To meet one of Tremenheere's recommendations a full-size replica frigate, *Fame*, was erected in 1843 in what had been the girls' playground immediately north of the Queen's House, for boys from both schools to practice 'nautical gymnastics' – rigging and gunnery.[152] This practical exemplar was noted favourably by Richard Ford when he visited the naval school in Seville and found the students being taught from a small model of a ship on a table. He referred to the ship at Greenwich as 'a floating frigate' but this mistake does not devalue his enthusiastic remarks about 'the school of young chips of old blocks, who every day behold in the veterans of Cape St. Vincent and Trafalgar living examples of [those who have] "done their duty". The evidence of former victories thus becomes a guarantee for the realisation of their young hopes, and the future is assured by the past'.[153] Replaced in 1862 and again in 1872, the *Fame* was a landmark in Greenwich until 1933, blocking for nearly a century the vista so carefully guarded before and since (fig. 300).[154]

300 A mid-nineteenth-century view of the model-frigate *Fame* in front of the Queen's House, showing the walls which had enclosed the girls' playground (NMM).

Edward Riddle and the Revd George Fisher, the School's Chaplain and Headmaster from 1834 to 1860, and Principal from 1860 until 1863, were both keen astronomers. Fisher, who had served as an astronomer on naval Arctic expeditions,[155] instigated the building of an observatory for the Nautical School in 1849–50, ostensibly under the supervision of the Hospital's Surveyor, Philip Hardwick, though it is likely that the work was actually carried out by his son, Philip Charles Hardwick (see chapter 6). This was a three-bay two-storey block with two observation domes, sited just east of the east wing south pavilion.[156] Other improvements during this period included the erection of cast-iron railings on stone plinths along Romney Road on the north perimeter of the school site in 1859–60, imitating those on the Hospital side and apparently replacing brick walls.[157] The grand gates on the central axis of the Queen's House also mirror those on the Hospital side of Romney Road: four openwork cast- and wrought-iron, ogee-capped piers ornamented with roses, thistles, trefoils and crowns support single side gates and central double gates carrying maritime symbols.

In the 1850s renewed disciplinary problems brought further government reports and led to further reform and building work. The 1860 Royal Commission appointed to look into Greenwich Hospital as a whole took on the findings of the previous year's committee and recommended that a smaller Upper School should be competitively selected from a larger Lower School, the boys no longer to be admitted by patronage, with greater emphasis on practical training. Rhode Hawkins, architect of the Committee of Council on Education, reported that the school had inadequate space for day rooms and industrial teaching. Further, in the dormitories each boy had only about 220 cubic feet, which compared unfavourably with prisons and barracks. He recommended substantial additions and other works to an estimated cost of £31,200. The Commission also recommended that bedsteads should replace hammocks in the Upper School; that additional lavatories and baths were required; that the Hospital staff residences should be removed from the school buildings; that the chapel should be converted into a hall; and that a gymnasium should be erected.[158] The Admiralty acted on the recommendations by making the establishment a single school with a Nautical Division of 110 boys and a Lower Division of 690 boys in three subdivisions.[159]

In response to the Commission's findings a scheme for new east and west wings to provide additional classroom and dormitory space was prepared in late 1860 by Philip Charles Hardwick. The new west wing was built for the Lower Divisions in 1861–2.[160] This was an L-shaped extension across the gymnastic ground and along the east side of the Hospital's former burial ground in what had been the Governor's garden, connected via an open archway under a first-floor link to the classroom projection on the west side of the 1807–11 west wing. At the other end the new building returned to the north as far forwards as the existing wings. It originally accommodated four large classrooms and a reading room on the raised ground floor. In the dormitories above, each boy was allocated 600 cubic feet of space. The building, of two storeys with a basement, with rendered brick elevations and ground-floor rustication, has fireproof flooring and hipped slate roofs with timber trusses and wrought-iron queen rods (fig. 301). At either end of the west range, there were open-well staircases with iron balustrades; the one to the north survives. A three-bay Doric frontispiece on the north front echoes the earlier wings.[161] Hardwick was following Alexander closely, though with somewhat heavier footsteps.[162]

The plans for a new east wing for the Nautical Division foundered in 1863 since the estimated costs of £60,000, which included buying property and diverting Park Row, were prohibitive.[163] As a fallback, the chapel in the 1807–11 west wing was converted to classrooms, the boys attending services in the Hospital chapel. Improved ventilation and nominally increased cubic footage in the east wing dormitories were provided by the removal of ceilings, opening up the roof spaces.[164]

Further reform followed the recommendations made by the Du Cane Committee which enquired into the management of the

301 Philip Charles Hardwick, south front of the west wing of Greenwich Hospital Schools, 1861–2.

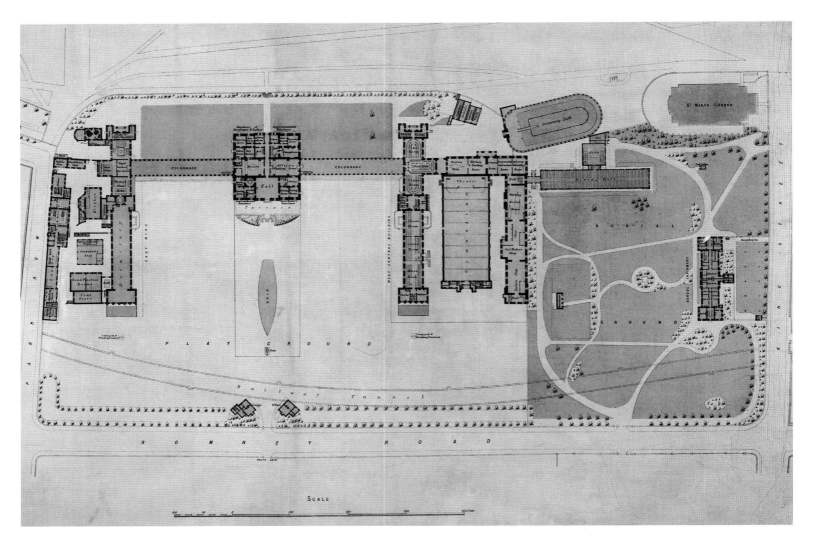

302 Ground plan of Greenwich Hospital Schools, 1875 (PRO ADM 79/77). This plan shows the dining hall in the long east wing, to the left, with its then projected use as a dormitory, with service rooms – laundry, washhouse etc. – in the outbuildings and narrow range to the east of that, on the edge of the site. The west wing of 1807–11 is divided into classrooms. Next to these is the gymnasium, with workshops in the embracing ranges to the south and west: the tailors', sailmakers' and shoe-makers' shops, and the working model room. The adjoining east-west range was the as yet unbuilt dining hall, with adjoining kitchen. The swimming bath is shown to the south with St Mary's church to the west. The school infirmary in the former school of 1783–4 is shown near to the western edge of the site. The Hospital burial ground fills the area east of the infirmary, up to Ripley's mausoleum. The Queen's House is shown divided for the accommodation of officers and masters. The training ship *Fame* is shown to the north.

winding down of Greenwich Hospital in 1867. The school's purpose as a feeder for the Navy was reaffirmed, and industrial training was given new emphasis to avoid educating the boys 'above their station'. Through E. Carleton Tufnell, a superinten-dent of schools for pauper children, industrial schools were referred to as a model. Tufnell took the robust view that 'A common seaman may have to consider whether he would not have been better off, if he had been taught to mend his own clothes instead of to solve quadratic equations'.[165]

Upon the closure of Greenwich Hospital in 1869, the Admi-ralty took control of the school. In the following year, yet another committee of inquiry was established. Chaired by Sir George O. Trevelyan and including Tufnell, it recommended admission of ten-year-old boys for discharge at thirteen to fourteen; with the Nautical Division reduced to eighty, the boys were bound at the age of fourteen to enter the Navy.[166] To meet a range of specific recommendations, works were carried out under Colonel Andrew Clarke, Director of Works for the Navy, who as an administrator would have delegated matters of design and construction (fig. 302). The classrooms in the 1861–2 ranges were divided to form indus-trial training rooms: a steering room, a hitching and bending room, a compass room, a seamanship instruction room, a splicing and knotting room, a working model room and shoemakers', sail-makers' and tailors' shops.[167]

The most significant work arising from the Trevelyan commit-tee's recommendations was the building of a roofed gymnasium in 1872–3.[168] By the 1840s there was a pole or model mast and other apparatus designated 'gymnasium' in the gymnastic ground near the swimming bath.[169] The apparatus was moved to the yard within the 1861–2 extension as soon as it was built. Additionally, fences and walls in the grounds north of the buildings were removed to open up a single large playground.[170] This was not suitable for all pursuits. With a degree of hyperbole incompre-hensible to the non-sporting, the report presented to the House

304 The Doric screen front of the gymnasium of the Royal Hospital School, now the entrance to the Neptune Court, National Maritime Museum.

303 (*left*) The entrance to the gymnasium, now the entrance to the Neptune Court.

of Commons after the investigation of 1867 into the management of the Hospital and Schools notes that 'the most striking defect is the absence of a turfed cricket-ground. The present gravel is not favourable to the enjoyment of that manly game; and is most destructive to the boots'.[171]

Indoor gymnasia were a novelty in England at this date. The first purpose-built gymnasium in any English public school was a modest room at Uppingham in 1859.[172] The German Gymnasium of 1864–5 at King's Cross is a notable and rare surviving example of the building type from this period.[173] The Royal Hospital School gymnasium of 1872–3, which soon became known as Neptune's Hall, was designed to be a single large space attached to the north side of the 1861–2 south range. The building contractors J. Weeks and Company, ironfounders and engineers, were specialists in the manufacture of horticultural glasshouses.[174] Drawings were evidently prepared within the Admiralty. The north end of the building had small ancillary spaces and an internal gallery behind a grandiose Portland stone Doric screen which reflects but does not slavishly follow Alexander's architecture. It forms a five-bay front with a rusticated basement, and an attic within a giant order of attached columns (fig. 304). Framing a central entrance, adorned with the royal arms, sculpted by C. Raymond Smith, paired columns project forward with V and R medallions in the frieze and model galleys above. Over an outer entrance arch with a Neptune keystone is a panel, formerly inscribed 'GYMNA-SIUM', and rising centrally in a balustraded parapet there is a stele with naval arms under a segmental pediment. A superb pair of wrought-iron gates, made by Bunnett and Company, with 'ER' (for

Edward VII) at the centre was installed at the entrance, presumably after his accession in 1901 (fig. 303). The hall, 76 feet by 186 feet, was roofed with elegant lattice-girder, wrought-iron trusses which formed shallow pointed arches in nine bays (fig. 305). There were ornamental ironwork spandrels and a lantern along the ridge. This roof form followed that of the German Gymnasium, although there the roof trusses were of laminated timber. These buildings needed large clear floors and tall clearances without tie-beams, for full-height climbing ropes. Such spaces could also accommodate other activities. At the south end of the hall at Greenwich, a stage 30 feet deep for dramatic productions was inserted in 1874 to designs by Pasley, who had succeeded Clarke in 1873. Flanking its proscenium arch there were roundels with Britannia and Neptune, reiterating for the benefit of new generations the long-established tradition of British maritime dominion.[175] Known as the Neptune Hall from 1972, following its internal re-organisation as a large exhibit gallery for the National Maritime Museum, the gymnasium was demolished in 1996–7. Its iron structure was transferred to Childe Beale Wildlife Park in Berkshire, where there are plans to incorporate it in a new building. Its commanding north front remains as the frontispiece of Neptune Court.

Plans for a substantial dining hall extension westwards into the former burial ground were being considered by Pasley and J. G. Loughborough, the school's Clerk of Works, by January 1875.[176] This scheme appears to anticipate the Admiralty's decision, taken that year, based on earlier recommendations, to increase the numbers at the school from 800 to 1000.[177] The extension meant

305   The gymnasium of the Royal Hospital School, viewed from the north in the late nineteenth century (PRO ADM 195/47).

that the former dining hall in the east wing could be made into a dormitory, with further new dormitory accommodation provided on the floor above the new dining hall. The new wing was built in 1876 by Hill, Higgs & Hill.[178] Its stuccoed elevations follow the Palladian precedents of the site, though in a loose and unscholarly manner; there are round-headed windows with Venetian tracery. There is channelled rustication to the basement as well as to the end bays and west return of the pilastered principal storey. The dormitory floor appears as an attic in fifteen-bay elevations under a hipped slate roof. There is a north entrance into a three-bay vestibule link to the east, above which a roundel is dated 1876. The south elevation has a central break forward, formerly an organ bay, with an attic oculus. From this point there is a projecting square block, formerly the kitchen, pyramidally roofed with a lantern. The principal, raised ground-floor storey was occupied by the long dining hall (182 feet by 33 feet) in which 1000 boys could eat at once (figs 306 and 307). There was an organ gallery on the south side and the walls and panelled ceiling were

painted with maritime scenes and figures. The dormitory had beds under a wrought-iron and timber trussed roof. The basement housed lavatories and a scullery.[179]

In the cause of more directly serving the Navy, the significant expansion and expenditure at the Hospital school between 1860 and 1876 had been carried out to the neglect of the fundamental requirements of a residential school – education and nutrition, both of which had become seriously compromised. By 1880 illness was rife and up to 40 per cent of the boys were being rejected for naval service as physically unfit.[180] Subsequent reforms directing the school's curriculum towards the training of skilled artisans led to a rise in the proportion of boys joining the Navy or Dockyards, from 28 per cent in 1885 to 76 per cent in 1906.[181]

In 1921 Gifford Sherman Reade, a wealthy planter, presented his estate at Holbrook, near Ipswich in Suffolk, to Greenwich Hospital, in gratitude that none of his fleet of tea ships had been sunk in the war of 1914–18. Under Arthur Smallwood, the Hospital's Director, this was taken as an opportunity to vacate the

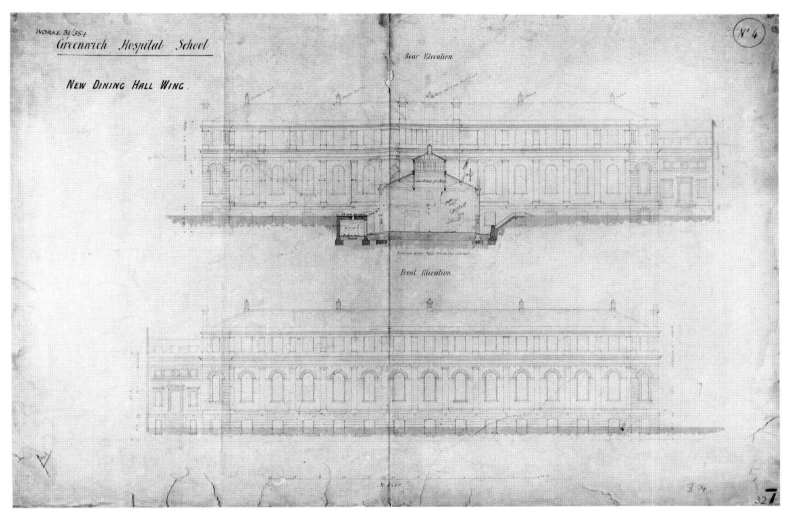

306 The south (top) and north (bottom) elevations of the west, dining-hall wing of the Greenwich Hospital Schools, designed by Colonel Charles Pasley, drawn in 1875 and erected the following year (PRO WORK 31/354).

school buildings which were regarded as dilapidated and unhealthy. The building of a new Royal Hospital School at Holbrook was begun in 1928 and preparations for the school's removal from Greenwich continued until its departure in 1933.[182]

The National Maritime Museum

The possible removal of the Hospital school from Greenwich and the need to find a new use for the Queen's House in particular were under discussion from 1924 when the Society for Nautical Research, founded in 1910, launched a campaign for a National Naval Museum.[183] This was spearheaded by Professor (Sir) Geoffrey Callender, Secretary and Treasurer of the Society for Nautical Research from 1920, and Professor of History at the Royal Naval College from 1922. He was the principal active force behind the establishment of the National Maritime Museum during the 1920s and 1930s and was knighted in 1938.

By 1927 the campaign had borne fruit. The Society's Chairman, Admiral Sir George Webley Hope, who was also then the officer in charge at Greenwich, persuaded the Admiralty that, despite the relative inaccessibility of Greenwich, there was 'a golden opportunity' to establish there a National Naval Museum based on the

Navy's own Royal Naval Museum at the Royal Naval College, largely comprising important ship models and memorabilia, to be combined with other available collections.[184] These included the entirely separate Greenwich Hospital collection of paintings and the Nelson and Franklin memorabilia largely shown in the Painted Hall's 'Naval Gallery'. The support of the Office of Works was enlisted, and the intention to adapt at least the Queen's House for use as a museum was made public in June 1927, when Hope announced plans for the National Naval and Nautical Museum.[185] Trustees were appointed in the same year with James, Lord Stanhope, Civil Lord of the Admiralty, as Chairman. Callender and Hope were also Trustees, along with Sir Lionel Earle, Permanent Secretary to the Office of Works, Dr Roger Charles Anderson, a collector and benefactor, and Sir James Caird, Bt.[186] Caird was a Scottish millionaire shipowner who had in large measure paid for the Society's restoration of HMS *Victory* in 1923. He was also at this time acquiring important private collections for the nation with the formation of the museum in mind.

In 1928 the intended establishment began to be called the National Maritime Museum, reportedly at the suggestion of Rudyard Kipling.[187] Callender envisaged a large establishment encompassing a picture gallery, a model collection and a library, in some measure educative, but to a greater degree conceived as

307   Aerial view of Greenwich and the Isle of Dogs, c.1925, showing the Schools at their fullest extent.

something of a shrine to what he regarded as hallowed reminders of national glory. By 1930 the need to use parts of the school beyond the Queen's House was accepted and negotiations were in train as to how much of it would be needed by the Royal Naval College.[188] There were difficulties, not least the general opposition which came from Admiral Sir Barry Domvile, President of the Royal Naval College in 1931–2, and organiser of the spectacular Greenwich Night Pageant of 1933 at which *son et lumière* techniques and tubular-steel construction were innovatively introduced in the service of historical patriotic propaganda (see chapter 6).[189] It is in the mythifying milieu of Callender's and Domvile's separate but parallel efforts to put Greenwich on the map through the glorification of naval history that the artificial notion of 'Maritime Greenwich' was invented.

In 1932 an Admiralty Committee decided to transfer virtually all of the school buildings for use as a state-funded museum.[190] An inter-departmental Admiralty, Treasury and Office of Works Committee was formed in April 1933 under the chairmanship of Sir Oswyn Murray, Permanent Secretary to the Admiralty, to manage the transition to the formation of a new national museum with

Callender as prime organiser. Progress was slow so Stanhope, a staunch supporter of the project, approached Caird who wrote to James Ramsay Macdonald, Prime Minister, in December 1933 offering to pay the estimated £29,000 cost of converting the school excepting the Queen's House, provided the museum could be inaugurated by 1935, remain in the control of its Trustees, and be thrown into Greenwich Park. As was intended, this had a galvanising effect. A scheme for the transfer of the whole school site of 11½ acres to the Office of Works was settled in early 1934.[191] The National Maritime Museum Act[192] was passed in July 1934, the 1927 Board of Trustees being supplemented with Stanhope as Chairman and Callender the Director-designate. In proposing the Bill in the Lords, Stanhope, whose family seat was Chevening, near Sevenoaks in Kent, explained:

Your Lordships may say that Greenwich is a long way off. I think I can take you there by car in probably not more than ten minutes longer than it would take you to get to South Kensington – and after all, not the whole of London lives in Mayfair and Belgravia. A great many live south of the river, and

I do not see why our museums should all be concentrated in one spot.[193]

The conversion of the buildings by the Office of Works was carried out under Sir Patrick Duff, Earle's successor as Permanent Secretary, and Sir Eric de Normann, one of his Principals. (Sir) James Grey West was Chief Architect at the time, and A. J. Pitcher was the Senior Architect responsible for the project, working with A. W. Heasman and Clifford E. Mee.[194] They worked closely with Callender, who devised his own plans, and behind the backs of the officials, involved trusted friends and assistants, Harold S. Rogers and Reginald Lowen.[195] The first plans were drawn up in 1933, with an estimate of £38,400. Inclusion of the former dining-hall wing of 1876 the following year took this up to £48,000. Building work began in early 1935 and was completed in time for a royal opening by George VI on 27 April 1937.[196]

Callender wished to spare no expense and accused the Office of Works, which inevitably was bent on economy, of 'cheese-paring'.[197] From the other side, de Normann summed up the project to a colleague in 1940:

My experience of the National Maritime Museum and of Sir Geoffrey Callender goes back to the beginning and I make you a present of it. Sir Geoffrey is a very able man and a redoubtable controversialist. He has made a practice of consulting technical officers unofficially and of extracting from them figures and dates, and he has thus always been able to skirmish against the Department with some adroitness.[198]

The conversion involved a general refitting of the buildings, which was far-reaching in its scope. A new east-west axis was created in anticipation of the arrival of visitors via Maze Hill railway station. A new entrance was formed to the east with elaborate iron piers and gates in the manner of those on Romney Road. The two-bay east projection from the east wing was given a grand entrance under a royal monogram, remade after the abdication of Edward VIII in December 1936. A public vestibule gave onto a passage along the colonnades and through the Queen's House into the west buildings, to what were named the Caird Galleries. In the 1807–11 west wing, in front of a new grand staircase, there was another vestibule, with rooms to either side for the display of Dutch paintings en grisaille (penschilderij). A library was formed in the north half of this wing on the ground floor. Most of the west wing and the Queen's House were refloored in concrete for purposes of fireproofing. The extensions of 1861–2 were redivided to form eight exhibition galleries on two levels, organised on chronological principles, with pre-eighteenth-century items being displayed in the Queen's House. The former dining hall of 1876 became the Navigation Room (for cases of astrolabes, globes, chronometers including Harrison's, sextants, etc.), with a Print Room and related Students' Room above. New staircases with metal balustrading were inserted at each end of this wing. Most of the work on the east wing was deferred.

Offices for the Museum's staff of fourteen were confined to the north pavilion of Alexander's west wing, where a new staircase was inserted and on the ground floor two marble chimneypieces were introduced into the Trustees' Room and the Director's Office. The Office of Works had salvaged these from buildings demolished 'some years' previously for the building of government offices.[199] The former kitchen block was adapted as a refreshment room, the

Mecca Café, with a terrace to the east and a second room added to the south in 1937–8 to allow for licensing regulations. The swimming bath had been demolished.

Works on the grounds for the sake of public access and ornament included the relaying to grass of the asphalt forecourt north of the Queen's House, the clearance of outbuildings along the site's east side for a car park, and perimeter railings along the north part of Park Row. As the plans were amended in 1935 and 1936 by the Office of Works, Caird repeatedly defrayed all additional costs in the building programme, to an eventual total of £77,430, in addition to a much larger sum given for the acquisition of objects for display. His benefactions to the National Maritime Museum eventually amounted to more than £1,000,000.[200]

The Society for Nautical Research determined to honour Caird with a bronze bust. In deference to his conservative tastes, Sir William Reid Dick was given the commission. He, in his turn, asked Sir Edwin Lutyens to design a pedestal and they visited the site together in December 1935.[201] When a month later Caird, Reid Dick and Callender visited Lutyens in Eaton Place to see his design, they found that – as one who seldom missed an opportunity – he had produced plans for entirely remodelling the library vestibule in which the bust was to be placed (formerly the central stair compartment of Alexander's west wing).[202] Caird liked the scheme, but Callender was ambivalent. It was accepted in March, principally, it seems, because Caird agreed to foot the additional costs, which eventually rose to £5760, of which a startling £2000 was Lutyens's fee. Variously and disparagingly referred to in the planning stage as the 'Caird Shrine', the 'temple' and the 'marble palace',[203] this space eventually came to be called the Rotunda. The final design proved 'much more elaborate and costly than we could have contemplated. That however is one of the results of employing Sir Edwin Lutyens'.[204] When Reid Dick produced the bronze bust, it was deprecated by Caird, Callender and the other Trustees as being too green and had to be remade in marble,[205] the material matching the Tivoli Travertine marble which lines the Rotunda itself.[206] Taking his cue from the semicircular stair that had occupied the space previously, Lutyens remodelled it as an ellipse. There is an intricate fluted frieze, using the 'Delhi' order that he had invented for the Viceroy's House in Delhi, with Caird's arms over the entrance to the library. Balustrading at first-floor level runs around a lightwell which was introduced in order to avoid giving the impression that the space was a mausoleum. The geometrical star-pattern floor is of Tivoli and Golden Travertine. This interior holds considerable interest as a late and relatively uncelebrated work by Lutyens. It gives a lift to the otherwise rather pedestrian interiors of the Museum (fig. 308).

The Grand, Great, Ship or Caird Staircase was built as a substantial open-well stair, top-lit with a square lantern in a coved ceiling. Most building anecdotes which refer to the re-use of old ships' timbers are apocryphal, but not here. The stair, which was thoroughly re-ordered in the 1990s, was made of teak salvaged from sailing ships then being broken up: the *Ganges, Defence, Defiance* and *Arethusa*. The robust balustrading incorporated a belfry for a bell reputedly from *Vanguard*, Nelson's flagship at the Battle of the Nile in 1798 (fig. 311).[207]

The library was 'very close to Callender's heart' and thus the subject of dispute before plans could be agreed in 1936.[208] The oak bookcases were designed by him with help from Frank Maggs of Maggs Brothers, and made by Messrs J. P. White of Pyghtle

308   The Rotunda in the west wing of the National Maritime Museum, designed by Sir Edwin Lutyens, with the bust of Sir James Caird by Sir William Reid Dick.

310   The central staircase of 1950–51 in the east wing of the National Maritime Museum.

309   The library in the west wing of the National Maritime Museum, viewed from the south.

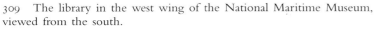

Works, Bedford, established Arts and Crafts suppliers. They are arranged in a collegiate manner and there are royal cyphers in open segmental pediments over the doors at either end of the room (fig. 309). Since the library originally was open to the public for the purpose of viewing exhibitions in desk cases, a reading room was provided on the upper floor, the full length of which also eventually included specialist curatorial areas for navigational material, ship plans and staff offices.[209]

The former Gymnasium was the scene of the royal opening in 1937. Thereafter, work was begun on converting this space into a display area which continued to be called Neptune's Hall, for figureheads and large ship models. It did not open to the public until October 1945, when the museum re-opened after war-time closure.[210]

The refitting of the east wing also was arranged to follow the 1937 opening. A scheme involving strengthening the floors with steel girders at an estimated cost of £28,230 was approved in October 1938, Caird again bearing the cost.[211] The building work, complete by July 1940, was carried through for the Office of Works by Mee. Rather than reinforcement, it involved the replacement of timber floors with concrete and the building of three new staircases, two of which were made of teak in the neo-Georgian manner adopted for the Caird Staircase (fig. 310).[212] Fitting-out was deferred as war intervened and the building was occupied by the Admiralty. Work started again in 1950 and the east wing was opened to the public on 3 July 1951 with exhibition galleries

311 The Caird Staircase in the west wing of the National Maritime Museum, as completed in 1936, before later alterations.

relating to post-1815 history, a Lecture Room and an Arctic Gallery.[213]

The primacy of the eastern approach was short-lived as a new main entrance from Romney Road to Neptune's Hall was formed in 1949.[214] Many other minor works occurred in the 1950s and 1960s, among which was the building in 1955 of a long and narrow sky-lit Barge House in the gap between Neptune's Hall and the 1861–2 west wing, to accommodate four barges, including a state barge of 1732.[215]

With Basil Greenhill as Director from 1967, the Maritime Museum undertook a thorough refitting and modernisation of its galleries to broaden its remit to cover all matters maritime, concentrating less on the strictly naval. In part this reflected the recent attachment of the former Royal Observatory to the Museum. Early work included the rearrangement of what became the New Neptune Hall, with the rebuilt steam-paddle tug *Reliant* at its centre from 1972. Mezzanine floors were inserted in the 1861–2 ranges in the mid-1970s and the Caird Staircase consequently altered. An archaeological gallery was added and the east wing displays were remade.[216]

The National Maritime Museum was substantially remodelled again in the 1990s, following re-roofing and services renewals during the 1980s. In 1992–4 the wings of 1807–62 were refurbished and refitted in phases, with the Building Design Partnership as architects. The east wing was now entirely given over to offices, as was most of the upper storey of the west wing of 1807–11, for which a new staircase and lift well was formed through all floors to the west of the Caird Rotunda. Following a benefaction from the Leopold Muller Foundation, the north end of the west wing of 1861–2 was converted to be an education centre, providing seminar rooms, new stairs and a lecture theatre below the 'All Hands' interactive gallery. Meanwhile a £37 million scheme for a new glass-roofed exhibition space at the heart of the west complex, together with excavated collections storage beneath the lawns north of the Queen's House was mooted in 1991, with the Building Design Partnership as appointed architects.[217] The excavation did not go ahead, but after revisions a £14 million scheme for the glass-roofed building was approved, with Rick Mather Architects working with BDP, with the support of the Heritage Lottery Fund.[218]

312   The interior of the Neptune Court, from the north-east, photographed by Dennis Gilbert.

In 1996–7 the Neptune Hall was demolished behind its north front to make way for Neptune Court, built in 1998–9, and opened by Queen Elizabeth II on 11 May 1999 (fig. 312). Of a new total projected building cost of £20 million, £11.8 million came from the Heritage Lottery Fund. Neptune Court makes the most of the opportunity to unify the space between the 1807–11 and 1861–2 west wings, to the point that the classical screen built to front the gymnasium of 1872–3 appears as if it had always been intended to be the main entrance to the complex. It is a dramatic piece of architecture which has greatly improved the circulation within the Museum. Behind the entrance screen a vast, light-weight, steel-framed glass roof hovers over the almost 3000 square yards of upper floor space. At the lower level, which is now at the same level as the 1807–62 basements, there are 'streets' around an exhibition podium. The rebuilt north block behind the entrance screen presents a cleanly modernist elevation to the upper part of Neptune Court, with high-level walkways linking the framing wings, the classical elevations of which have been carefully restored. To the south, the archway at the east end of the 1861–2 range has been re-opened and glazed to give views into Green-wich Park, and the Caird Staircase has been reconfigured to conform with the changed circulation requirements. In the view of the architecture critic of *The Guardian*, it is now clear from the moment of arrival that the National Maritime Museum has been imbued with 'a clarity and nobility lacking since its opening in 1937'. Visitors no longer enter through 'an obscure side entrance', but sail into BDP and Mather's 'magnificent new Neptune Court, bright and wide as the sea'.[219]

AMS	Ancient Monuments Society		NPG	National Portrait Gallery
BAL	British Architectural Library, RIBA		PRO	Public Record Office
BL	British Library		ADM	Admiralty Papers
BM	British Museum		AO	Audit Office
DNB	*Dictionary of National Biography*		CRES	Crown Estate Commissioners Papers
EH	English Heritage		E351	Exchequer, Pipe Office, Declared Accounts
GLHL	Greenwich Local History Library		MR	Map Room
HMC	Historical Manuscripts Commission		PROB	Probate Registers
LMA	London Metropolitan Archives		SP	State Papers
NLW	National Library of Wales		WORK	Office of Works Accounts, Drawings etc.
NMM	National Maritime Museum		RCHME	Royal Commission on the Historical Monuments of England
ART/1–3	Greenwich Hospital copies of prints, plans and other drawings, compiled 1793		RGO	Royal Greenwich Observatory
ART/4	Greenwich Hospital copies of drawings, and the Royal Warrant for granting the site for the building of the Hospital, 1696		RIBA	Royal Institute of British Architects
			RNC	Royal Naval College
NMR	National Monuments Record		SPAB	Society for the Protection of Ancient Buildings

Notes to the Text

Introduction

1 D. Defoe, *A Tour through the Whole Island of Great Britain, 1724–6*, ed. G. D. H. Cole, London 1974, I, 94.

2 K. Littlewood and B. Butler, *Of Ships and Stars*, London and New Brunswick 1998, 49 and 157; for the World Heritage Site, see J. Bold, C. Bradbeer and P. van der Merwe, *Maritime Greenwich*, London 1999.

3 H. M. Colvin, ed., *The History of the King's Works*, IV, *1485–1660* (Part II), London 1982; S. Thurley, *The Royal Palaces of Tudor England*, New Haven and London 1993.

4 D. Howse, *Greenwich Observatory*, III, *The Buildings and Instruments*, London 1975.

5 I. Roy, 'Greenwich and the Civil War', *Transactions of the Greenwich and Lewisham Antiquarian Society*, X/1, 1985, 13.

1   Greenwich Park: Landscape and Buildings

1 Survey of London, XLIV, *Poplar, Blackwall and The Isle of Dogs*, London 1994, 522.

2 P. Shepheard, *The Cultivated Wilderness*, Cambridge, Mass., and London 1997, 168–9.

3 G. Berto and L. Puppi, *L'opera completa del Canaletto*, Milan 1981, nos 275, 285, 286, 288 and 289.

4 NMM BHC1827; J. G. Links, *Canaletto*, Oxford 1982, 173–4; M. Liversidge and J. Farrington, eds, *Canaletto and England*, London 1993, 92. The earlier view, from approximately the same position, although taking a slightly higher viewpoint, is on loan to the Tate Gallery, London, from a private collection: L01926.

5 Survey of London, op. cit., 375–7.

6 See the sketch by J. W. Carmichael dated 1848, NMM. This was the viewpoint taken also by Jacques Rigaud in his painting *View of the Royal Hospital, Greenwich*, Sotheby's, *British Paintings 1500–1850*, London, 3 April 1996, no. 83. The close relationship between Rigaud's etching of

1736 and Canaletto's earlier view is discussed in J. Dacey, 'A Note on Canaletto's Views of Greenwich', *Burlington Magazine*, CXXIII, August 1981, 485–7.

7 C. Morris, ed., *The Journeys of Celia Fiennes*, London 1947, 131.

8 W. S. Lewis, ed., *The Yale Edition of Horace Walpole's Correspondence*, XXXV, London 1973, 234.

9 A. D. Webster, *Greenwich Park: Its History and Associations*, London 1902, 67–98; F. C. Elliston Erwood, 'Roman Remains from Greenwich Park', *Transactions of the Greenwich and Lewisham Antiquarian Society*, III/2, 1925, 62–75; J. E. G. de Montmorency, 'Excavations in Greenwich Park', *Transactions of the Greenwich and Lewisham Antiquarian Society*, III/3, 1927, 94–5; *The Victoria History of the County of Kent*, III, London 1932, 116; H. Sheldon and B. Yule, 'Excavations in Greenwich Park, 1978–9', *London Archaeologist*, III, 1979, 311–17; S. Greep, 'Two Roman Ivories from Greenwich Park, London', *Transactions of the London and Middlesex Archaeological Society*, XXXIV, 1983, 61–5.

10 *Illustrated London News*, 29 June 1844, 420.

11 J. Douglas, *Nenia Britannica*, London 1793, 89–91.

12 M. J. Swanton, *Corpus of Pagan Anglo-Saxon Spear Types*, British Archaeological Reports British Series 7, Oxford 1974, 54; for a full description and discussion of the burial mounds and the archaeology of the park, see P. Pattison and P. Struth, 'Greenwich Park: An Archaeological Survey', RCHME, unpublished report, 2 vols, Swindon 1994.

13 D. Lysons, *The Environs of London*, London 1796, 427.

14 H. H. Drake, ed., *Hasted's History of Kent, Hundred of Blackheath*, London 1886, 44; *Calendar of Patent Rolls, 1429–36*, 250.

15 P. Dixon, *Excavations at Greenwich Palace 1970–1971*, Greenwich 1972.

16 H. M. Colvin, ed., *The History of the King's Works*, II, *The Middle Ages*, London 1963, 949.

17 Dixon, op. cit., 8.

18 W. Howarth, *Greenwich Past and Present*, London 1886, 94.

19 NMM BHC1820.

20 Pattison and Struth, op. cit., I, fig. 1.

21 Webster, op. cit., 3.

22 D. Defoe, *A Tour through the Whole Island of Great Britain, 1724–6*, ed. G. D. H. Cole, London 1974, I, 94.

23 H. J. Fear, 'Westcombe', *Transactions of the Greenwich and Lewisham Antiquarian Society*, VII/1, 1964, 8–13.

24 PRO WORK 16/28/3; Webster, op. cit., 4.

25 Land Use Consultants, 'Greenwich Park Historical Survey', unpublished report, London 1986.

26 PRO WORK 16/1450.

27 The church was built to relieve the overcrowding of the parish church of St Alfege. It was closed in 1919 some time after the closure of the Hospital and the consequent loss of population in the town, and was demolished in 1936 (A. R. Martin, 'St Mary's Church, Greenwich, and its Architect', *Transactions of the Greenwich and Lewisham Antiquarian Society*, IV/1, 1936, 37–43). The parallel walls are also clearly depicted in a late seventeenth-century *View of London from Greenwich with the Queen's House in the Foreground*, from the circle of Hendrik Danckerts: Sotheby's, op. cit., no. 84.

28 Land Use Consultants, op. cit.

29 J. Bold, *John Webb*, Oxford 1989, 126–46.

30 R. Strong, *The Renaissance Garden in England*, London 1979, 191.

31 Plan of Greenwich Park c.1675–80, Pepys Library, Magdalene College, Cambridge.

32 PRO SP 29/56.39. According to Boreman, the planting was so successful that 'not one tree in 100 fails'. The total expenditure was £543 2s 6d (*Calendar of State Papers Domestic, 1661–62*, 403).

33 R. C. Latham and W. Matthews, eds, *The Diary of Samuel Pepys*, III, London 1995, 63.

34 Catalogue III/1 Prints and Drawings, Pepys Library, Magdalene College, Cambridge.

35 Pattison and Struth, op. cit., 2, 26.

36 D. Green, 'Planner of Royal Parks', *Country Life*, 1 March 1956, 372.

37 Bibliothèque de l'Institut de France, Paris, MS 1605; E. de Ganay, *André Le Nostre*, Paris 1962, 137–8.

38 Plan at Wilton House, Wiltshire; K. Downes, *Hawksmoor*, London 1979, no. 358.

39 C. Thacker, *The History of Gardens*, London 1979, pl. 19.

40 Bold, op. cit., 128–31; J. Bold, 'Greenwich: "The Grott & ascent by mr. Webb"', *Burlington Magazine*, CXXIX, March 1982, 149–50.

41 W. H. Adams, *The French Garden*, London 1979, 57–62.

42 PRO WORK 5/7; G. H. Chettle, *The Queen's House, Greenwich*, London 1937, 42–4.

43 PRO SP 29/56.39.

44 J. Dixon Hunt and E. de Jong, *The Anglo-Dutch Garden in the Age of William and Mary*, special issue of *Journal of Garden History*, VIII/2–3, 1988, 223–6.

45 *Calendar of State Papers Domestic*, 1670, 195 and 294.

46 Land Use Consultants, op. cit.

47 Webster, op. cit., 16–18.

48 S. Thurley, *The Royal Palaces of Tudor England*, New Haven and London 1993, 164.

49 GLHL, copy of a plan of *c.*1715, mis-annotated 'Commissioner's House (Vicarage), *c.*1780'; J. Kimbell, *An Account of the Legacies, Gifts, Rents, Fees etc. Appertaining to the Church and Poor of the Parish of St Alphege, Greenwich, etc.*, Greenwich 1816, 224; PRO ADM 67/254, 80/111, 67/70, 17 and 79, 68/873, 65/109, 67/80; PRO WORK 16/129; Church of England Record Centre, Files K6760, NB 37/115; EH, London Casework Files, 434; P. Newell, *Greenwich Hospital: A Royal Foundation 1692–1983*, Greenwich 1984, 123, 141–7, 156.

50 PRO E36/215, fo. 276v; Kimbell, op. cit., 221; PRO ADM 80/62.

51 NMM BHC1820.

52 NMM BHC1818.

53 EH, London Casework Files, 434.

54 Samuel Travers, 'Survey of the King's Lordship or Manor of East Greenwich', November 1695, PRO MR 253.

55 PRO ADM 67/3–4.

56 PRO ADM 68/682–3.

57 PRO ADM 68/685–6.

58 PRO ADM 68/688.

59 These are outlined in J. Watson, 'The Greenwich Conduits', *Subterranea Britannica*, IV, 1976, 9.

60 PRO WORK 16/132, 16/463.

61 PRO ADM 68/685–6.

62 Land Use Consultants, op. cit.

63 PRO ADM 79/74.

64 PRO ADM 68/683.

65 PRO WORK 16/132.

66 *Illustrated London News*, 22 June 1844, 398.

67 *Pictorial Times*, 6 September 1845.

68 PRO WORK 16/132–3.

69 D. Howse, *Greenwich Observatory*, III, *The Buildings and Instruments*, London 1975; D. Howse, *Greenwich Time and the Longitude*, London 1997.

70 M. Hunter, *Science and Society in Restoration England*, Cambridge 1981, 8–13.

71 J. Betts, *John Harrison*, Greenwich 1997, 2–3.

72 Hunter, op. cit., 79.

73 RGO, Cambridge 1/37.

74 Howse, *Greenwich Observatory*, 1–2.

75 Howse, *Greenwich Time*, 42.

76 Ibid., 44.

77 H. W. Robinson and W. Adams, eds, *The Diary of Robert Hooke*, London 1935, 171.

78 Howse, *Greenwich Observatory*, 4.

79 *Wren Society*, V, Oxford 1928, 21–2.

80 J. A. Bennett, *The Mathematical Science of Christopher Wren*, Cambridge 1982, 50–54.

81 Hunter, op. cit., 133.

82 W. H. Quarrell and M. Mare, eds, *London in 1710: From the Travels of Zacharias Conrad von Uffenbach*, London 1934, 21.

83 Howse, *Greenwich Time*, 51.

84 Flamsteed made this prediction also to his German visitors in 1710: 'In particular he said that in the year 1715 on the 22 April there would be a quite unprecedented eclipse; in fact, as he assured us: "totus Sol obscurabitur", the whole sun would be darkened' (Quarrell and Mare, op. cit., 23).

85 F. Baily, *An Account of the Reverend John Flamsteed*, London 1835, 340–51.

86 RGO, 7/58, 1894.

87 J. Conrad, *The Secret Agent*, London 1907, reprinted 1994, 65 and 210.

88 G. T. di Lampedusa, *The Leopard*, trans. A. Colquhoun, London 1960, 34.

89 G. Williams, *The Royal Parks of London*, London 1978, 144.

90 PRO ADM 67/5.

91 R. Longhurst, 'Greenwich Fair', *Transactions of the Greenwich and Lewisham Antiquarian Society*, VII/4, 1970, 198–210.

92 C. Dickens, *Sketches by Boz*, London 1839, reprinted 1995, 138.

93 Ibid., 144.

94 Longhurst, op. cit.

95 GLHL cuttings, Greenwich Park, 1846.

96 S. Inwood, *A History of London*, London 1998, 668.

97 'The Park Encroachments', *Kentish and Surrey Mercury*, 23 March and 1 June 1850.

98 H. M. Colvin, ed., *The History of the King's Works*, IV, *1485–1660* (Part II), London 1982, 114; J. Harris and G. Higgott, *Inigo Jones: Complete Architectural Drawings*, New York 1989, 137–9.

99 PRO WORK 16/136, 32/255.

100 PRO WORK 16/1640.

101 PRO WORK 16/463.

102 PRO WORK 16/129, 145 and 146.

103 Quarrell and Mare, op. cit., 21.

104 Williams, op. cit., 146. According to a

visitor in 1786 Captain Cook's goat also lived in the park: 'The rain deprived me of a visit to Greenwich Park and Captain Cook's goat, which after accompanying him on his voyage round the world and supplying him with fresh milk, had also earned the recognition of the marines and permission to spend the remainder of her days amongst the tars, where she may eat her fill without disturbance' (C. Williams, ed., *Sophie in London 1786 being the Diary of Sophie v. la Roche,* London 1933, 253).

105 J. Thorne, *Handbook to the Environs of London*, London 1876, reprinted Chichester 1983, 259.

106 *The Times*, 20 August 1872, 10.

107 PRO WORK 16/142B.

108 PRO WORK 16/642.

109 PRO WORK 38/360; Land Use Consultants, op. cit.

110 Webster, op. cit., 37.

111 PRO WORK 16/1643.

112 PRO WORK 16/1083.

113 PRO WORK 16/635.

114 Plan of Greenwich Park, *c.*1675–80, Pepys Library, Magdalene College, Cambridge; Samuel Travers, 'Survey of the King's Lordship or Manor of East Greenwich', November 1695, PRO MR 253.

115 *Illustrated London News*, 29 June 1844.

116 *Daily News*, 11 April 1899.

117 PRO WORK 16/28/3; PRO CRES 25/3–6.

118 PRO WORK 1/37–8, 5/156, 16/638 and 32/516.

119 P. Greenhalgh, *Ephemeral Vistas*, Manchester 1988, 93–4.

120 PRO ADM 195/47.

121 J. Physick, *Designs for English Sculpture 1680–1860*, London 1969, 40–41. In view of the later influence of the Elgin Marbles on Benjamin West's work at Greenwich (see chapter 6), it is worth noting that Flaxman's *Britannia* was in the monumental, figurative tradition established by Phidias with the *Athena Promachos* on the Athenian Acropolis, one of the most famous statues of antiquity.

122 Land Use Consultants, op. cit.

2 The Queen's House: Building and Function

1 J. A. Gotch, 'Inigo Jones's Principal Visit to Italy in 1614', *Journal of the Royal Institute of British Architects*, XLVI, 21 November 1938, 85; J. Harris, S. Orgel and R. Strong, *The King's Arcadia: Inigo Jones and the Stuart Court*, London 1973, 52–6, 63–4, 217–18; British Council, *Inigo Jones 1573–1652*, Milan 1973, 31–2.

2 M. Girouard, *Robert Smythson and the Elizabethan Country House*, New Haven and London 1983, 28.

3 Chamberlain to Sir Dudley Carleton,

Calendar of State Papers Domestic, 1617, 70; Girouard, op. cit., 18–28.

4   J. Howell, *Instructions for Forreine Travell*, London 1642, ed. E. Arber, London 1869, 73; quoted in D. Howarth, *Lord Arundel and his Circle*, New Haven and London 1985, 244.

5   H. Wotton, *The Elements of Architecture*, London 1624, reprinted Farnborough 1969, 1.

6   See especially G. H. Chettle, *The Queen's House, Greenwich*, London 1937; H. M. Colvin, ed., *The History of the Kings Works*, III, *1485–1660* (Part I), London 1975, and IV, *1485–1660* (Part II), London 1982; J. Summerson, *Inigo Jones*, Harmondsworth 1966; J. Harris and G. Higgott, *Inigo Jones: Complete Architectural Drawings*, New York 1989.

7   Harris and Higgott, op. cit., 56–7.

8   S. Thurley, *The Royal Palaces of Tudor England*, New Haven and London 1993, 48.

9   S. Foister, 'Foreigners at Court: Holbein, Van Dyck and the Painter-Stainers Company', in D. Howarth, ed., *Art and Patronage in the Caroline Courts*, Cambridge 1993, 35.

10 Ashmolean Museum, Lar. IV; reproduced in Colvin, ed., op. cit., IV, pls 4–5.

11 NMM, *Greenwich from the Park*, BHC 1820; Museum of London, Flemish School, *View of Greenwich*, 64.52; M. Galinou and J. Hayes, *London in Paint*, London 1996, no. 2.

12 W. Howarth, *Greenwich Past and Present*, London 1886, 94.

13 Travers Survey, 1695, PRO MR 253.

14 Colvin, ed., op. cit., IV, 101.

15 C. Williams, ed., *Thomas Platter's Travels in England 1599*, London 1937, 226.

16 Quoted in D. Howse, *Greenwich Time and the Discovery of the Longitude*, Oxford 1980, 31.

17 *DNB*; PRO PROB 11/123 55 Lawe.

18 L. Levy Peck, *Northampton: Patronage and Policy at the Court of James I*, London 1982, 40 and 73–4.

19 *Archaeologia*, XLII, 1869, 371; Howarth, *Lord Arundel and his Circle*, 57; *DNB*.

20 Levy Peck, op. cit.

21 *Archaeologia*, XLII, 1869, 369.

22 Ibid., 369–70.

23 *DNB*; PRO AO1/2422/48.

24 *Les Voyages du Sieur Albert de Mandelslo*, ed. P. Van der Aa, Amsterdam 1719, 754–6.

25 M. Exwood and H. L. Lehmann, eds, *The Journal of William Schellinks' Travels in England 1661–1663*, London 1993, 47.

26 *Calendar of State Papers Domestic*, 1675–6, 173.

27 PRO E351/3230.

28 R. Strong, *The Renaissance Garden in England*, London 1979, 46.

29 Quoted in Strong, op. cit., 48.

30 Strong, op. cit., 23.

31 HMC, *Calendar of Manuscripts of Hatfield*, XXI, 1970, 340.

32 Colvin, ed., op. cit., IV, 113.

33 S. Eiche, 'Prince Henry's Richmond', *Apollo*, CLXVIII, November 1998, 10–14.

34 *Calendar of State Papers Domestic*, 1612, 116.

35 PRO E351/3384.

36 A. Robey, 'A 17th Century Water Maze at Greenwich', *Caerdroia*, XXIX, 1998, 33.

37 PRO AO1 2427/631 and 2429/71; PRO E351/3249.

38 Sherburn to Carleton, PRO SP 14/86/95 and 87/40, quoted in C. Carlton, *Charles I: The Personal Monarch*, London and New York 1995, 24.

39 H. J. Louw, 'Some Royal and other Great Houses in England: Extracts from the Journal of Abram Booth', *Architectural History*, XXVII, 1984, 504.

40 Mandelslo, op. cit., 754–6 [my translation].

41 H. Wölfflin, *Renaissance and Baroque*, London 1964, 147.

42 F. Colonna, *Hypnerotomachia Poliphili*, Venice 1499; Eng. trans. by R. Dallington, London 1592; reissued with introduction by L. Gent, *Hypnerotomachia: The Strife of Love in a Dreame*, New York 1973. Colonna's authorship of the original has been questioned in L. Lefaivre, *Leon Battista Alberti's Hypnerotomachia Poliphili*, Cambridge, Mass., and London 1997. The first complete translation into English, made by Joscelyn Godwin, was published in an appropriately handsome edition by Thames and Hudson, London 1999.

43 H. K. Szépe, 'Desire in the Printed Dream of Poliphilo', *Art History*, XIX/3, 1996, 381.

44 Colonna, trans. Dallington, op. cit., London 1890, 41 and 172–5.

45 A. Blunt, *Artistic Theory in Italy 1450–1600*, Oxford 1973, 39–43; see also D. Rosand, 'Giorgione, Venice and the Pastoral Vision', in R. Cafritz, L. Gowing and D. Rosand, *Places of Delight: The Pastoral Landscape*, Washington 1988, 73–6.

46 Gent, introduction to Colonna, op. cit., vi–xvii.

47 For the Italian parallels and the influence on French gardens, see G. Polizzi, introduction to the reprint of Jean Martin's French edition of Colonna's text, *Le Songe de Poliphile*, Paris 1546, Paris 1994, xxii; for the English context, see Strong, op. cit., 16–17.

48 *Calendar of State Papers Domestic*, 1613, 212; J. Nichols, *The Progresses, Processions, and Magnificent Festivities, of King James the First*, II, London 1828, 671.

49 S. Heiberg, ed., *Christian IV and Europe*, Council of Europe exhibition, Denmark 1988, 463–4; see also J. A. Skovgaard, *A King's Architecture: Christian IV and his Buildings*, London 1973.

50 D. Howard, *Scottish Architecture from the Reformation to the Restoration 1560–1660*, Edinburgh 1995, 26–8.

51 PRO E351/3250.

52 PRO E351/3251.

53 Colvin, ed., op. cit., IV, 113–14.

54 J. Peacock, *The Stage Designs of Inigo Jones: The European Context*, Cambridge 1996, 23.

55 R. Strong, *Henry, Prince of Wales and England's Lost Renaissance*, London 1986, 16.

56 The Blickling Hall portrait has early over-painting in order to secure this effect.

57 Skovgaard, op. cit., 129.

58 Colvin, ed., op. cit., IV, 213–14.

59 R. Strong, *The English Icon*, London 1969, 26–7; O. Millar, *The Tudor, Stuart and Early Georgian Pictures in the Collection of Her Majesty the Queen*, London 1963, 81.

60 As described by Ben Jonson, quoted in J. Newman, 'Inigo Jones and the Politics of Architecture', in K. Sharpe and P. Lake, eds, *Culture and Politics in Early Stuart England*, Stanford, Calif., 1993, 254.

61 M. Whinney and O. Millar, *English Art 1625–1714*, Oxford 1957, 20.

62 Skovgaard, op. cit., 129; Howard, op. cit., 26–8.

63 PRO AO1 2487/356.

64 Harris and Higgott, op. cit., 66–7.

65 Ibid., 70–71.

66 PRO AO1 2487/356.

67 *Calendar of State Papers Domestic*, 1617, 473.

68 PRO AO1 2487/356.

69 PRO AO1 2422/50.

70 Galinou and Hayes, op. cit.

71 P. Palme, *Triumph of Peace*, London 1957, 66; J. Bold with J. Reeves, *Wilton House and English Palladianism*, London 1988, 84–5.

72 The investigation was carried out in 1999 by Julian Bowsher of the Museum of London Archaeology Service. The basement was rendered in 1999 as part of a scheme to improve access to the Queen's House carried out to the designs of Allies and Morrison. A ramped entry to the north front basement door was created to allow wheelchair access, a new pedestrian basement entrance was created on the west side and a lift and elegant secondary stair installed from the basement to the ground and first floors.

73 Harris and Higgott, op. cit., 304–5.

74 The openings survive, subsequently altered to become segmentally headed, and one was revealed in its entirety, immediately to the west of the door during the course of the restoration in the 1930s.

75 S. Marks, ed., 'The Queen's House, Greenwich: The Project', *Transactions of the Association for Studies in the Conservation of Historic Buildings*, XIV, 1989, 12.

76 PRO WORK 5/3.

77 See, for example, the original arrangement at Poggio a Caiano; the arrangement at the Villa Foscarini (illustrated in O. Bertotti Scamozzi, *Le fabbriche e i disegni di Andrea Palladio*, 1796, London 1968, bk 3, pl. 50); and the staircases at the Villa Foscari alla Malcontenta (L. Puppi, *Andrea Palladio: The Complete Works*, London 1989, 175–6).

78 Extraordinary ambassadors were welcomed at Greenwich; resident ambassadors at Tower Wharf.

79 A. J. Loomie, ed., *Ceremonies of Charles I: The Note Books of John Finet 1628–1641*, New York 1987, 27–8.

80 Ibid., 30.

81 Ibid., 108.

82 Ibid., 65.

83 Thurley, op. cit., plan 2.

84 cf. Strong, *Renaissance Garden*, 92; S. Orgel and R. Strong, *Inigo Jones: The Theatre of the Stuart Court*, I, London 1973, 41.

85 T. Campion, *The Caversham Entertainment*, in D. Lindley, ed., *Court Masques*, Oxford 1995, 92–101.

86 Loomie, op. cit., 219.

87 PRO AO1 2424/54.

88 PRO AOI 2425/58.

89 Webster, op. cit., 3.

90 PRO AO1 2424/54; Harris and Higgott, op. cit., 137–9.

91 Millar, op. cit., 111. The picture was sold at the Commonwealth sale for £5 but was recovered at the Restoration and is now in the Royal Collection: O. Millar, ed., *Abraham van der Doort's Catalogue of the Collections of Charles I*, Walpole Society, XXXVII, 1958–60, Oxford 1960, 195; O. Millar, ed., *The Inventories and Valuations of the King's Goods 1649–1651*, Walpole Society, XLIII, 1970–72, Oxford 1972, 66.

92 PRO E351/3263.

93 PRO WORK 5/2, 5/3, 5/4.

94 NLW, Wynnstay 175.

95 NLW, Wynnstay 176.

96 NLW, Wynnstay 178.

97 NLW, Wynnstay 179.

98 *Calendar of State Papers Venetian*, 1635, 386–7.

99 NLW, Wynnstay 183.

100 PRO AO1/2427/63–7.

101 PRO AO1/2428/69.

102 NLW, Wynnstay 181.

103 NLW, Wynnstay 182.

104 M. A. Everett Green, ed., *Letters of Queen Henrietta Maria, including her Private Correspondence with Charles I*, London 1857, 19.

105 J. Harris and A. A. Tait, *Catalogue of the Drawings by Inigo Jones, John Webb & Isaac de Caus at Worcester College, Oxford*, Oxford 1979, 38. The fountain does not survive but there is a reminiscence of Webb's river god in an artificial stone keystone in the park wall at 37 Park Vista, installed there in the 1970s by Raymond Smith, the architect responsible for the modern house.

106 Harris and Higgott, op. cit., 322–3.

107 PRO WORK 5/3.

108 PRO ADM 68/683.

109 Mandelslo, op. cit., 754–6; J. W. Neumayr von Ramssla, *Wahrhaftige Beschreibung der Reise*, Jena 1734, 310–12.

110 Newman, op. cit., 234–5.

111 Strong, *Renaissance Garden*, 80.

112 A. Blunt, *Philibert de l'Orme*, London 1958, 29–30 and pl. 29. For Caprarola, see W. Kennet and E. Young, *Northern Lazio: An Unknown Italy*, London 1990, 120–30; and J. Recupero, *The Farnese Palace at Caprarola*, Florence 1990. It should also be noted that the balusters of the Greenwich steps have the asymmetrical bulbous quality of the Vignolesque baluster; see R. Wittkower, 'The Renaissance Baluster and Palladio', in his *Palladio and English Palladianism*, London 1974, 43.

113 The archaeological investigations during the 1980s restoration of the house and again in 1999 revealed the original brick footings.

114 J. Harris, *The Palladians*, London 1981, 46.

115 Harris and Higgott, op. cit., 68–9.

116 There were windows on the inner wall which were removed in 1708. Although this vestibule below the first-floor loggia might have been intended at first to be left open, by the time of Hollar's view of 1637 it was closed.

117 B. Allsopp, ed., *Inigo Jones on Palladio*, I, Newcastle-upon-Tyne 1970, 13.

118 Colvin, ed., op. cit., IV, 159.

119 PRO WORK 5/3.

120 H. M. Colvin and J. Newman, eds, *Of Building: Roger North's Writings on Architecture*, Oxford 1981, 62 and 129–30.

121 PRO AO1/2428/69; 'House of Delight' is the term used by T. Phillipot in *Villare Cantianum: or Kent Surveyed and Illustrated*, London 1659.

122 P. Henderson, 'Secret Houses and Garden Lodges: The Queen's House, Greenwich, in Context', *Apollo*, CXLVI, July 1997, 33–5.

123 L. Hutchinson, *Memoirs of the Life of Colonel Hutchinson*, ed. J. Sutherland, London 1973, 46. Life outside court circles continued to be robust. Richard Brome's 'Facetious Comedy' *The Weeding of Covent Garden*, published in 1658 but written probably in the later 1630s, states that 'the times are much alter'd, and youth more corrupted now, they did not drink and wench in those dayes, but nay, o 'tis abominable in these' (Act II, scene i).

124 Orgel and Strong, op. cit., I, 55 and 67.

125 K. Sharpe, *The Personal Rule of Charles I*, New Haven and London 1992, 170.

126 Duchy of Cornwall, Roll 742. Swimming in the river was rare enough to be worthy of note, John Evelyn recording an 'aboundance of Ladys and others bathing in the River' in France in 1651 (E. S. de Beer, ed., *The Diary of John Evelyn*, London 1959, 304), so it is likely that this reference is to wild-fowling on the Thames rather than swimming in it.

127 R. Herrick, 'Corinna's going a Maying', in L. C. Martin, ed., *The Poems of Robert Herrick*, Oxford 1965, 67–9; see also Everett Green, ed., op. cit., 1857, 19; R. Ward Bissell, *Orazio Gentileschi and the Poetic Tradition in Caravaggesque Painting*, Pennsylvania 1981, 55. Such harmless follies of the 1630s came to be regarded with nostalgia during the following decade when Parliament began its attacks on maypoles and other frivolities. The republication of Herrick's poem in 1648 enabled the author to comment critically on the times while denying any such intent by claiming that it was part of just another backward-looking miscellany (C. Burrow, 'Then place my purboil'd Head upon a Stake', *London Review of Books*, XXI/1, January 1999, 26).

128 Loomie, op. cit., 157.

129 J. Howell, quoted in Carlton, op. cit., 13.

130 Orgel and Strong, op. cit., II, 602.

131 'Shackerley Marmion', in J. Maidment and W. H. Logan, eds, *Dramatists of the Restoration*, London 1875, xviii. Marmion's poem was dedicated to the king's nephew Charles Louis, son of Elizabeth of Bohemia, who was visiting England to seek aid in his efforts to reclaim the Palatinate. William Adlington's translation of *The Golden Ass* (1566) also enjoyed a wide currency: further editions appeared in 1571, 1582, 1596, 1600 and 1639.

132 G. Parry, *The Golden Age Restor'd: The Culture of the Stuart Court, 1603–42*, Manchester 1981, 141–2; G. Martin, 'Rubens and Buckingham's "Fayrie Ile"', *Burlington Magazine*, CVIII, December 1966, 613–18.

133 *The Golden Asse of Lucius Apuleius*, trans. W. Adlington, 1566, reprinted London n.d., 94.

134 Ibid., 94.

135 Orgel and Strong, op. cit., II, 604.

136 R. Strong, *Van Dyck: Charles I on Horseback*, London 1972, 70.

137 R. Cocke and P. de Vecchi, *The Complete Paintings of Raphael*, Harmondsworth 1987, no. 130.

138 W. Shakespeare, *The Winter's Tale* (1611), Act V, scene ii. This is Shakespeare's only reference to a major Renaissance artist and it is anachronistic. He referred to Giulio Romano as a sculptor who 'had he himself eternity and could put breath into his work, would beguile Nature of her custom, so perfectly he is her ape'. For the Palazzo Te, see G. Suitner and C. T. Perina, *Palazzo Te in Mantua*, Milan 1990, 61–77.

139 Although, as it has been noted in another context: 'Passage from a naked painted person to libidinous arousal is not an uncomplicated one, and there is room for interference along the route' (T. Screech, *Sex and the Floating World*, London 1999, 102).

140 J. Bold, *John Webb*, Oxford 1989, 16.

141 R. Lightbown, 'Charles I and the Tradition of European Princely Collecting' and F. Haskell, 'Charles I's Collection of Pictures', both in A. MacGregor, ed., *The Late King's Goods*, London and Oxford 1989, 64 and 212–14; D. Howarth, '"Mantua Peeces": Charles I and the Gonzaga Collections', in D. Chambers and J. Martineau, eds, *Splendours of the Gonzaga*, London 1981, 95–103.

142 cf. E. H. Gombrich, '"That Rare Italian Master . . ." Giulio Romano, Court Architect, Painter and Impresario', in Chambers and Martineau, eds, op. cit., 77–85. The inscription in the frieze of the Sala di Amore e Psiche refers to the Palazzo Te as a place for honest leisure, restoring strength after work.

143 Hutchinson, op. cit., 46.

144 S. Orgel, *The Illusion of Power*, Berkeley, Los Angeles and London 1975, 88.

3   The Queen's House: Decoration and Later History

1 C. Campbell, *Vitruvius Britannicus*, I, London 1715, introduction.

2 J. Harris, 'Inigo Jones and his French Sources', *Metropolitan Museum of Art Bulletin*, XIX, 1961, 254–7.

3 J. Harris and G. Higgott, *Inigo Jones: Complete Architectural Drawings*, New York 1989, 228–35.

4 J. Newman, 'Strayed from the Queen's House?', *Architectural History*, XXVII, 1984, 33–5. John Newman suggests that the chimneypiece might have been moved in 1662, when work was being carried out at Charlton House by Sir William Ducie. Although this attribution of the design to Inigo Jones is plausible, the proposed date of removal is less likely in view of the works of improvement being carried out at the Queen's House at that time. Nicholas Cooper has suggested that the room in which the chimneypiece at Charlton is housed was possibly an open loggia until the late eighteenth century: this would be a more likely time for the installation of a chimneypiece in a newly enclosed room (N. Cooper, *Houses of the Gentry 1480–1680*, New Haven and London 1999, 136–8).

5 O. Millar, *The Age of Charles I*, London 1972, cat. 1. Archaeological investigation by Julian Bowsher of the Museum of London Archaeology Service in 1999 suggests that originally the arched openings in the east and west walls of the ground floor of the Hall, unlike the openings at gallery level, did not have doors, thus allowing for freer ground-floor circulation than was possible later.

6 PRO AO1 2429/71.

7 PRO AO1 2428/69.

8 PRO AO1 2429/71.

9 BL, Harley 7352; O. Millar, ed., *The Inventories and Valuations of the King's Goods 1649–1651, Walpole Society*, XLIII, 1970–72, Oxford 1972, 138–9.

10 A. MacGregor, 'The King's Goods and the Commonwealth Sale, Materials and Context', in A. MacGregor, ed., *The Late King's Goods*, London and Oxford 1989, 25.

11 *The Non-Such Charles, his Character, Extracted out of Divers Original Transactions, Dispatches, and the Notes of Several Public Ministers, as well at Home as Abroad*, 1651.

12 The niche became a door in the early eighteenth century following the removal of the road and the construction of a room beneath the bridge room; plan by John James, Worcester College, Oxford.

13 R. Lightbown, 'The Journey of the Bernini Bust of Charles I to England', *Connoisseur*, CLXIX, 1968, 217–20; D. Howarth, 'Charles I, Sculpture and Sculptors', in MacGregor, ed., op. cit., 95–6; R. Wittkower, *Gian Lorenzo Bernini: The Sculptor of the Roman Baroque*, Oxford 1981, 14–15 and 207–8; C. Avery, *Bernini: Genius of the Baroque*, London 1997, 224–8; C. Brown, *Van Dyck*, Oxford 1982, 174–7.

14 R. Barthes, *Mythologies*, Paris 1957, Eng. trans. Annette Lavers, St Albans 1973, 92–3. Although the discussion is about electoral photography, the description is applicable independently of the medium.

15 S. Orgel and R. Strong, *Inigo Jones: The Theatre of the Stuart Court*, 2 vols, London 1973.

16 I. Bristow, 'Interior Paintwork', in M. Airs, ed., *The Seventeenth Century Great House*, Conference Proceedings, Oxford 1995, 109.

17 R. Ward Bissell, *Orazio Gentileschi and the Poetic Tradition in Caravaggesque Painting*, Pennsylvania 1981, 50–62 (56) and 195–8; G. Finaldi, ed., *Orazio Gentileschi at the Court of Charles I*, London 1999.

18 PRO E403/2807.

19 PRO E403/2808.

20 Ward Bissell, op. cit.

21 J. Schulz, *Venetian Painted Ceilings of the Renaissance*, Berkeley and Los Angeles 1968, 53; M. Muraro and P. Marton, *Venetian Villas*, Cologne 1986, 220–26; G. Piovene, *L'opera completa del Veronese*, Milan 1968, 102; R. Cocke, *Veronese*, London 1980, 33; D. Rosand, *Painting in Sixteenth-Century Venice*, Cambridge 1997, 133.

22 PRO E351/3267.

23 Ward Bissell, op. cit., 106 and 190–92; Finaldi, op. cit.

24 Millar, *Inventories and Valuations*, 137.

25 A. Weston-Lewis, 'Orazio Gentileschi's Two Versions of *The Finding of Moses* Reassessed', *Apollo*, CXLV, June 1997, 27–35.

26 Finaldi, op. cit.

27 O. Millar, *Abraham van der Doort's Catalogue of the Collections of Charles I, Walpole Society*, XXXVII, 1958–60, Oxford 1960, 194.

28 Weston-Lewis, op. cit.; Ward Bissell, op. cit., 188.

29 H. Maddicott, 'The Provenance of the "Castle Howard" Version of Orazio Gentileschi's "Finding of Moses"', *Burlington Magazine*, CXL, February 1998, 120–22.

30 Millar, *Inventories and Valuations*, 137.

31 M. Exwood and H. L. Lehmann, eds, *The Journal of William Schellinks' Travels in England 1661–1663*, London 1993, 47.

32 PRO WORK 5/3.

33 Ward Bissell, op. cit., 198; Finaldi, op. cit., 29–31.

34 Information from Roger Quarm, NMM.

35 E. Croft-Murray, *Decorative Painting in England 1537–1837*, I, London 1962, 243–5.

36 J. Charlton, *The Queen's House, Greenwich*, London 1976, 24. Cheron clearly was indebted to Poussin's *Time and Truth* for his composition; cf. P. Rosenberg, *Nicolas Poussin 1594–1665*, Paris 1994, cat. 99.

37 Sotheby's sale catalogue, London, 11 July 1990.

38 S. Marks, ed., 'The Queen's House, Greenwich: The Project', *Transactions of the Association for Studies in the Conservation of Historic Buildings*, XIV, 1989, 12.

39 S. A. Sykes, 'Henrietta Maria's "House of Delight": French Influence and Iconography in the Queen's House, Greenwich', *Apollo*, CXXXIII, May 1991, 332.

40 R. Pennington, *A Descriptive Catalogue of the Etched Work of Wenceslaus Hollar 1607–1677*, Cambridge 1982, cat. 977.

41 H. Yexley, 'The Renovation of the Queen's House', typescript, NMM, 1996.

42 Charlton, op. cit., 30.

43 S. Madocks, '"Trop de beautez decouvertes": New Light on Guido Reni's Late "Bacchus and Ariadne"', *Burlington Magazine*, CXXVI, September 1984, 544–7; M. Levey, *The Later Italian Pictures in the Collection of Her Majesty the Queen*, Cambridge 1991, 127–8; C. Garboli and E. Baccheschi, *L'opera completa di Guido Reni*, Milan 1971, no. 191.

44 Levey, op. cit., xxvi–xxvii and 155–6.

45 R. Spear, *The 'Divine' Guido*, New Haven and London 1997, 126–7 and 220. Spear quotes the contemporary comment that while painting the *Bacchus and Ariadne*, Guido's mind 'was dull and the work dragged' because 'he no longer had the heart to take on such large subjects'.

46 PRO E351/3265.

47 H. M. Colvin, ed., *The History of the Kings Works*, IV, *1485–1660* (Part II), London 1982, 121.

48 BL, Harley 7352; Millar, *Inventories and Valuations*, 137.

49 PRO WORK 5/3.

50 Levey, op. cit., 156.

51 G. H. Chettle, *The Queen's House, Greenwich*, London 1937, 54.

52 Charlton, op. cit., 30.

53 M. A. Everett Green, ed., *Letters of Queen Henrietta Maria, including her Private Correspondence with Charles I*, London 1857, 35.

54 Millar, ed., *Abraham van der Doort's Catalogue*, 194; J. Shearman, *The Early Italian Pictures in the Collection of Her Majesty the Queen*, Cambridge 1983, 123–6 and 242–4.

55 E. Chaney, 'Notes towards a Biography of Sir Balthazar Gerbier', in his *The Evolution of the Grand Tour*, London 1998, 215–25.

56 Further instructions from William Murrey, Groom of the Bedchamber; Chettle, op. cit., 93.

57 D. Schlugleit, 'L'Abbé de Scaglia, Jordaens et l' "Histoire de Psyche" de Greenwich-House (1639–1642)', *Revue belge d'archaeologie et d'histoire de l'art*, VII, 1937, 139–66.

58 Chettle, op. cit., 92–6.

59 Ibid., 93.

60 BL, Harley 7352; Millar, *Inventories and Valuations*, 137.

61 Schlugleit, op. cit.; R.-A.D'Hulst, *Jacob Jordaens*, London 1982, 26.

62 *The Golden Asse of Lucius Apuleius*, trans. W. Adlington, 1566, reprinted London, n.d., 106.

63 R.-A. D'Hulst, *Jacob Jordaens (1593–1678)*, II, *Drawings and Prints*, Antwerp 1993, cat. B41, 66.

64 R.-A. D'Hulst, N. de Poorter and M. Vandenven, *Jacob Jordaens (1593–1678): Tableaux et tapisseries*, Antwerp 1993, cat. A84–6, 258–67.

65 R.-A. D'Hulst, *Jacob Jordaens*, London 1982, 30.

66 H. Gerson and E. H. ter Kuile, *Art and Architecture in Belgium 1600–1800*, Harmondsworth 1960, 132.

67 *The Golden Asse*, op. cit., 119–20.

68 O. Millar, *Van Dyck in England*, London 1982, 97–8; C. Brown, op. cit., 186–8; A. K. Wheelock, S. J. Barnes and J. S. Held, *Anthony van Dyck*, Washington 1990, 316–19; C. Brown and H. Vlieghe, *Van Dyck 1599–1641*, New York 1999, 326–9.

69 M. Ashley, *The Stuarts in Love*, London 1963, 131.

70 T. Phillipot, *Villare Cantianum: or Kent Surveyed and Illustrated*, London 1659.

71 L. Gent, 'The Rash Gazer: Economics of Vision in Britain, 1550–1660', in L. Gent, ed., *Albion's Classicism: The Visual Arts in Britain, 1550–1660*, New Haven and London 1995.

72 The influence of the Queen's House within the extended royal family is worthy of note. Mary Stuart, wife of William of Orange, and one of Henrietta Maria's granddaughters, decorated a hunting lodge at Soestdijk in Utrecht, Holland, with similar themes, commissioning Gérard de Lairesse during the 1670s to paint *Odysseus and Calypso*, symbolising love and fidelity, and *Selene and Endymion*, symbolic of chaste love (both in the Rijksmuseum, Amsterdam). The garden of the lodge was extensive and filled with fruit, flowers and statues (D. Jacques and A. J. van der Horst, *The Gardens of William and Mary*, London 1988, 37–8).

73 J. Bold, *John Webb*, Oxford 1989, 3.

74 Millar, ed., *Inventories and Valuations*, xix.

75 E. S. de Beer, ed., *The Diary of John Evelyn*, London 1959, 319.

76 R. Spalding, ed., *The Diary of Bulstrode Whitelocke, 1605–1675*, Oxford 1990, 234.

77 MacGregor, op. cit., 16.

78 The decisive battle of the First Dutch War, which enabled the English fleet to blockade the Dutch coast, was fought on 2–3 June near the Gabbard shoal, 25 miles from Felixstowe. Deane was killed by almost the first shot fired.

79 Blake died of natural causes off Plymouth, not in action. J. R. Powell, *Robert Blake*, London 1972, 209 and 239; E. Razzell and P. Razzell, eds, *The English Civil War: A Contemporary Account*, IV, *1648–1656*, London 1996, 139. These lyings-in are of interest as precedents for Nelson's lying-in-state in the Painted Hall at the Naval Hospital in 1806.

80 R. Sherwood, *The Court of Oliver Cromwell*, Cambridge 1989, 18; *Calendar of State Papers Domestic, 1653–4*, 373. Inappropriate usage was again noted in 1661 when Zachary Plott petitioned the king for the place of Gardener at Greenwich and Keeper of the Queen Mother's Buildings, which are 'now employed to entertain rude and debauched persons to drink and revel on Sabbath days' (*Calendar of State Papers Domestic, 1661–2*, 77).

81 Razzell and Razzell, eds, op. cit., V, *1657–1675*, 202.

82 Bold, op. cit., 126.

83 M. Exwood and H. L. Lehmann, eds, *The Journal of William Schellinks' Travels in England 1661–1663*, London 1993, 47.

84 Ibid., 165. A warrant was issued to Hugh May in February 1662 for 'pulling down the old house at Greenwich'. In the same year William Ryley, Deputy Keeper of the Tower records, requested a grant of the 'old brick tower, some decayed wood, and two ruined houses, in the Tilt Yard, Greenwich'. He had served twenty-eight years in his post, following his father's forty-eight, and had received no remuneration for twelve years (*Calendar of State Papers Domestic, 1661–2*, 273, 275 and 628).

85 PRO WORK 5/3.

86 Chettle, op. cit., 109–10.

87 PRO AOI 2434/86 and 87.

88 PRO WORK 5/3.

89 PRO WORK 5/3.

90 Croft-Murray, op. cit., 226; Chettle, op. cit., 41.

91 PRO WORK 5/3.

92 PRO WORK 5/13.

93 S. Thurley, lecture to Greenwich Historical Society, November 1998.

94 Exwood and Lehmann, op. cit., 173.

95 Beer, de, ed., op. cit., 430.

96 Bold, op. cit., 126–7.

97 Beer, de, ed., op. cit., 441–2.

98 HMC, *Report of the Manuscripts of Allan George Finch Esq.*, I, London 1913, 205.

99 Razzell and Razzell, eds, op. cit., V, *1657–1675*, 299.

100 HMC, op. cit., 387.

101 J. Harris, *Catalogue of the Drawings Collection of the Royal Institute of British Architects: Inigo Jones and John Webb*, Farnborough 1972, cat. 166–9.

102 V. Hart and P. Hicks, trans., *Sebastiano Serlio on Architecture*, I, New Haven and London 1996, 240.

103 Bold, op. cit., 127–8; J. Bold, 'Greenwich: "The Grott & ascent by mr. Webb"', *Burlington Magazine*, CXXIX, March 1982, 149–50.

104 Bibliothèque de l'Institut de France, MS 1605, fo. 61.

105 Exwood and Lehmann, op. cit., 165.

106 Jacques and Van der Horst, op. cit., 20–21.

107 Spalding, ed., op. cit., 692.

108 Bold, *Webb*, 128–31.

109 Spalding, ed., op. cit., 692.

110 PRO WORK 5/10.

111 PRO WORK 5/13 and 8.

112 An edition of Vollenhove's diary is being prepared by Professor G. R. W. Dibbets of the Katholieke Universiteit Nijmegen. I am indebted to Roger Quarm, NMM, for this reference.

113 F. Baily, *An Account of the Reverend John Flamsteed*, London 1835, 42.

114 D. Howse, *Greenwich Time and the Longitude*, London 1997, 45.

115 Chettle, op. cit., 46.

116 PRO WORK 5/24.

117 D. C. A. Agnew, *Henri de Ruvigny, Earl of Galway: A Filial Memoir with a Prefatory Life of his Father Le Marquis de Ruvigny*, Edinburgh 1864; Beer, de, ed., op. cit., 852.

118 HMC, *MS of the Marquess of Downshire*, I (Part 1), 138. Ruvigny died in 1689.

119 *DNB*; Beer, de, ed., op. cit., 871.

120 Beer, de, ed., op. cit., 873.

121 Ibid., 864 and 869.

122 Chettle, op. cit., 111–13; EH Files, Queen's House, Greenwich, Extracts from Building Accounts 1689–95.

123 Chettle, op. cit., 48.

124 *Wren Society*, VI, Oxford 1929, 19–21.

125 PRO ADM 67/3.

126 PRO ADM 68/683 and 686. The upper-floor casements were removed for the installation of sashes in the late 1720s (information from Geoffrey Parnell), but at least one, on the roadway, survived until 1934–5 (see Appendix 8).

127 PRO ADM 67/4, 68/683.

128 PRO ADM 68/686 and 687.

129 PRO ADM 68/688.

130 PRO ADM 68/686.

131 PRO ADM 68/688.

132 Charnock view of the Queen's House from the north-east, NMM negative no. 6633.

133 PRO ADM 67/4, 66/28.

134 H. M. Colvin, *A Catalogue of Architectural Drawings of the 18th and 19th Centuries in the Library of Worcester College, Oxford*, Oxford 1964, cat. 209–10.

135 H. M. Colvin, *A Biographical Dictionary of British Architects 1600–1840*, revised 3rd edition, New Haven and London 1995, 536–7.

136 J. Brushe, 'Wricklemarsh and the Collections of Sir Gregory Page', *Apollo*, CXXII, November 1985, 364–71.

137 PRO ADM 67/6.

138 NMM negative nos 3121 and 6632.

139 *Wren Society*, VI, 59.

140 For a general discussion of Jones's roofs, see D. Yeomans, 'Inigo Jones's Roof Structures', *Architectural History*, XXIX, 1986, 85–101.

141 PRO ADM 67/7.

142 H. M. Colvin, ed., *The History of the King's Works*, V, *1660–1782*, London 1976, 152.

143 Cutting from GLHL.

144 H. S. Richardson, *Greenwich: Its History, Antiquities, Improvements and Public Buildings*, London 1834, 65.

145 PRO WORK 5/60.

146 PRO CRES 6/100, 279–80.

147 PRO CRES 6/100, 281.

148 PRO CRES 6/100, 300.

149 PRO CRES 6/100, 279.

150 F. Fraser, *The Unruly Queen: The Life of Queen Caroline*, London 1996.

151 Montague House was one of three villas built by Andrew Snape in the late seventeenth century outside the park wall. Caroline added two rooms, a greenhouse and a bathing room, both probably of light latticed-timber and glass construction, projecting from the house into the garden. The bathing room comprised a small ante-room and a plunge pool surrounded by seats, with doors opening into the garden (PRO CRES 6/100). It may have been plumbed with hot water. Internal bathrooms and detached garden bathhouses both featured in late Georgian aristocratic houses; this one is a variation falling midway between the two. The superstructure was demolished in 1890 and the bath itself was filled in 1983: its surround remains visible (Land Use Consultants, 'Greenwich Park Historical Survey', unpublished report, London 1986, 81). In creating the garden, Caroline desired 'to enclose so much from the Park, as it will be necessary for my comfort and pleasure . . . to be laid out and planted after my own direction' (PRO WORK 16/129). The work was planned and executed by James Meader, an influential gardener who had worked at the court of Catherine the Great in the 1780s (D. Shvidkovsky, *The Empress and the Architect: British Architecture and Gardens at the Court of Catherine the Great*, London 1996, 4). The garden was completed by 1808 (PRO WORK 16/28/3 and 16/129), survived the demolition of Montague House in 1815 and became attached to the neighbouring Chesterfield House (PRO WORK 16/28/3; PRO CRES 25/17 and 30/24), remaining as a private garden for the ranger until it was returned to the park in 1897 (PRO WORK 16/465).

152 PRO ADM 67/254.

153 *Gentleman's Magazine*, XXVI/2, August 1846, 212; G. Jones, *Sir Francis Chantrey,*

R.A.: Recollections of his Life, Practice and Opinions, London 1849, 7–8.

154 PRO ADM 65/107.

155 PRO ADM 67/71.

156 PRO ADM 68/866.

157 PRO ADM 67/17.

158 PRO WORK 31/258–61.

159 PRO WORK 31/328.

160 Chettle, op. cit., 77.

161 *Report of the Commissioners Appointed to Inquire into Greenwich Hospital*, London 1860, lxxv.

162 PRO WORK 14/2438.

163 K. Littlewood and B. Butler, *Of Ships and Stars*, London and New Brunswick 1998, 74.

164 PRO WORK 14/2438.

165 Ibid.

166 For a detailed description of the interior, see Chettle, op. cit., 63–77.

167 EH Files, schedule of works to be undertaken, October 1934; see Appendix 8.

168 This parallel is being explored by Dr Elizabeth McKellar, University of London.

169 Marks, op. cit., 15.

170 EH Files.

171 Survey of London, XIII, *Parish of St. Margaret, Westminster* (Part II), London 1930, 167–80, pl. 73; NMM Trustees' Minutes, 29 June 1936.

172 All Souls, Oxford.

173 EH Drawings.

174 EH Drawings and Files; Littlewood and Butler, op. cit., 103.

175 Littlewood and Butler, op. cit., 127–8.

176 Yexley, op. cit., 7.

177 EH, CB 023/001/B/00 Part 1.

178 Ibid.

179 C. England, 'The Queen's House', *Construction*, LXXVI, July 1990, 58–82.

180 Marks, op. cit., 8.

181 England, op. cit.

182 EH Files.

183 EH, CB 023/001/B/00 Part 2.

184 R. Ormond, *Restoration of the Queen's House*, NMM, n.d.

185 England, op. cit.

186 M. Girouard, *Life in the English Country House*, New Haven and London 1978, v.

187 J. Harris, 'Disneyland in Greenwich: The Restoration of the Queen's House', *Apollo*, CXXXII, October 1990, 256–60.

4   The Royal Hospital for Seamen: A Benevolent Foundation

1 J. Cooke and J. Maule, *An Historical Account of the Royal Hospital for Seamen at Greenwich*, London 1789.

2 HMC, *Report on the Mss. of the Marquis of Downshire*, I, London 1924, 280.

3 *Calendar of Treasury Books*, 1689–92, 1226.

4 *Calendar of State Papers Domestic*, 1691–2, 481.

5 H. M. Colvin, ed., *The History of the King's Works*, V, *1660–1782*, London 1976, 151.

6 *Calendar of Treasury Books*, 1693–6, 770.

7 Ibid., 794. It was removed to a large magazine built in 1694–6 on the Greenwich Peninsula. This remained the principal gunpowder store of the Board of Ordnance until the 1760s: M. Mills, *Greenwich Marsh: The 300 Years before the Dome*, London 1999, 24–9.

8 PRO ADM 67/4 and 67/20.

9 P. Newell, *Greenwich Hospital: A Royal Foundation 1692–1983*, Greenwich 1984, 8.

10 E. S. de Beer, ed., *The Diary of John Evelyn*, London 1959, 990.

11 *Calendar of Treasury Books*, 1693–6, 797; the avenue is 115 feet wide, the same width as the house.

12 See the late seventeenth-century *View of London from Greenwich with the Queen's House in the Foreground*, from the circle of Hendrik Danckerts: Sotheby's, *British Paintings 1500–1850*, London, 3 April 1996, no. 84.

13 PRO ADM 68/686.

14 PRO ADM 68/687.

15 Colvin, ed., op. cit., V, 152.

16 F. Saxl and R. Wittkower, *British Art and the Mediterranean*, Oxford 1948, 48.

17 A. Palladio, *The Four Books of Architecture*, Venice 1570, trans. R. Tavernor and R. Schofield, Cambridge, Mass., and London 1997, III/XIII, 188–9.

18 cf. R. Evans, *Translations from Drawing to Building and Other Essays*, London 1997, 271.

19 *Commission for Greenwich Hospital*, London 1695; see also *Calendar of Treasury Books*, 1693–6, 925–6 and 1189–90, and *Calendar of State Papers Domestic*, 1695, 346.

20 Newell, op. cit., 14–17.

21 *Calendar of Treasury Books*, 1703, 50.

22 PRO ADM 67/5.

23 C. Wren, *Parentalia*, London 1750, reprinted Farnborough 1965, 328.

24 K. Downes, *Sir John Vanbrugh*, London 1987, 481.

25 Ibid., 480.

26 E. Hatton, *A New View of London*, London 1708, II, 737.

27 Ibid., 746.

28 Beer, de, ed., op. cit., 58.

29 J. D. Alsop, 'Some Notes on Seventeenth Century Continental Hospitals, *British Library Journal*, VII, 1981, 70–74.

30 Beer, de, ed., op. cit., 163; see also E. Chaney, 'Philanthropy in Italy: English Observations on Italian Hospitals, 1545–1789', in his *The Evolution of the Grand Tour*, London 1998, 239–77.

31 C. Stevenson, 'Robert Hooke's Bethlem', *Journal of the Society of Architectural Historians*, LV/3, 1996, 254–75.

32 J. D. Thompson and G. Goldin, *The Hospital: A Social and Architectural History*, New Haven and London 1975, 41.

33 Chaney, op. cit., 261.

34 Ibid., 263.

35 J. G. Coad, *The Royal Dockyards 1690–1850*, Aldershot 1989, 293–302; H. Richardson, ed., *English Hospitals 1660–1948*, Swindon 1998, 76–81; C. Lloyd, 'Naval Hospitals', in

F. N. L. Poynter, ed., *The Evolution of Hospitals in Britain*, London 1964, 147–55.

36 L'Abbé Perau, *Description historique de l'Hôtel Royal des Invalides*, Paris 1756, i.

37 M. Whinney and O. Millar, *English Art 1625–1714*, Oxford 1957, 217.

38 *A Pattern of a Well-Constituted and Well-Governed Hospital*, London 1695, 17; this is an anonymous translation of Le Jeune de Boulencourt, *Description générale de l'Hostel Royal des Invalides*, Paris 1683.

39 Ibid., v.

40 Ibid., xiv.

41 NMM ART/1, fo. 40r.

42 M. Whinney, *Wren*, London 1971, 27.

43 M. L. T., *Réflexions sur le projet de suppression de l'Hôtel des Invalides*, Paris 1791, 5: 'plusieurs Peuples voisins, frappés d'un si grand exemple, se sont empressés de le suivre. Les Anglois ont bâti l'Hospice de Greenwich, qui ne le cede pas en magnificence a l'Hôtel, et celui de Chelsea destiné pour les Invalides de terre'.

44 NMM SOC 23/3.

45 F. Poche and J.-C. Rochette, *Le Dôme des Invalides*, Paris 1995, celebrates the dome and its recent restoration.

46 Alsop, op. cit.

47 *A Pattern*.

48 K. Downes, *English Baroque Architecture*, London 1966, 53; and K. Downes, *Hawksmoor*, London 1979, 89–97.

49 See, for example, Hawksmoor's drawing of *c.*1701, Courtauld Institute, Witt Collection.

50 *Wren Society*, VI, Oxford 1929, 16–27.

51 Ibid., 20.

52 All Souls, Oxford, IV, 19.

53 Sir John Soane's Museum, London, vol. 109, II, nos 5 and 6.

54 J. Bold, *John Webb*, Oxford 1989, 126–46.

55 *Wren Society*, VI, 83; plan in Lambeth Palace Library MS 933/99.

56 Sir John Soane's Museum, vol. 109, II, no. 12; Thompson and Goldin, op. cit., 149–50.

57 *Wren Society*, VI, pl. XLV.

58 Ibid., pl. XXVIII.

59 NMM BHC1827.

60 *St. James's Chronicle*, 14–17 July 1781; G. Milne, 'A Tudor Landing Stage at Greenwich', *London Archaeologist*, VIII/3, 1996, 70–74.

61 BAL, Burlington Devonshire Collection 5/12.

62 From Wren's Tract I; Wren, op. cit., 351; see also L. M. Soo, *Wren's 'Tracts' on Architecture and Other Writings*, Cambridge 1998, 153.

63 J. Boswell, *The Life of Samuel Johnson*, 1791, London 1906, I, 284.

64 Ibid., 480.

65 S. Johnson, *A Dictionary of the English Language*, London 1755.

66 *Wren Society*, VI, 19–20.

67 'The French Journal of William Mildmay', 1730, Essex County Record Office D/DMy15M50/1302.

68 Stevenson, op. cit., 268.

69 J. Gwynn, *London and Westminster Improved*, London 1766, 118–19.

70 NMM ART/4, 1.

71 NMM ART/4, 2 and 3.

72 Newell, op. cit., 41.

73 BAL E5/11.

74 Thompson and Goldin, op. cit., fig. 153.

75 P. D. G. Pugh, 'The Planning of Haslar', *Journal of the Royal Naval Medical Service*, LXII, 1976, 104.

76 BAL E5/2.

77 Elsewhere, a figure of 1980 is given at this time, including 200 in the infirmary (NMM ART/1, fo. 69r).

78 BAL E5/2.

79 Sir John Soane's Museum, vol. 109, I, nos 19–26; NMM ART/3, 5B.

80 PRO ADM 67/1.

81 This and other proposals are among 'Contract Prices for Building Greenwich Hospital 1696', BAL, Sir Christopher Wren Box 2.

82 PRO ADM 67/1.

83 PRO ADM 68/671.

84 PRO ADM 67/2.

85 Ibid.

86 PRO ADM 67/1.

87 Ibid.

88 PRO ADM 68/671 and 672.

89 NMM ART/1, fos 11v, 13v.

90 PRO ADM 68/670 and 671; NMM ART/4, fos 1–8.

91 PRO ADM 68/672 and 673.

92 PRO ADM 67/2 and 68/672.

93 PRO ADM 67/2.

94 PRO ADM 68/673.

95 Beer, de, ed., op. cit., 989.

96 Ibid., 1052; PRO ADM 67/2.

97 R. T. Gunther, *The Architecture of Sir Roger Pratt*, Oxford 1928, 22; H. Wotton, *The Elements of Architecture*, London 1624, reprinted Farnborough 1969, 65; J. Wilton-Ely, 'Wren, Hawksmoor and the Architectural Model', in J. Bold and E. Chaney, eds, *English Architecture Public and Private*, London and Rio Grande 1993, 151–5; Wren's Tract I; Soo, op. cit., 155.

98 PRO ADM 68/682.

99 PRO ADM 67/2.

100 Ibid.

101 Beer, de, ed., op. cit., 1016; PRO ADM 67/2 catalogues Sheppard's 'scandalous behaviour'.

102 PRO ADM 67/2.

103 Ibid.

104 PRO ADM 67/3.

105 PRO ADM 67/1.

106 PRO ADM 67/2.

107 Ibid.

108 Ibid.

109 PRO ADM 67/3.

110 PRO ADM 67/2.

111 J. Cooke and J. Maule, *A Concise Description of the Royal Hospital for Seamen at Greenwich*, London 1793, 8.

112 PRO ADM 68/674.

113 PRO ADM 68/678.

114 *Illustrated London News*, 26 January 1946, 107.

115 R. Gunnis, *Dictionary of British Sculptors 1660–1851*, London 1951, 221.

116 PRO ADM 68/675.

117 PRO ADM 68/681.

118 PRO ADM 68/674.

119 PRO ADM 80/113–14; RNC photographs.

120 EH 168D/139–40; A. Copeman, 'Maritime Match', *Building*, 21 January 1994, 14–15.

121 RCHME survey report on Beverley Minster, by P. S. Barnwell, 1999, NMR 96958; see also P. S. Barnwell, '"The Church of Beverley is Fully Repaired": The Roofs of Beverley Minster', *Transactions of the Ancient Monuments Society*, XLIV, 2000, 9–24.

122 BAL E5/25 (16); see also D. Yeomans, *The Architect and the Carpenter*, London 1992, 45. The Hall roof bears a strong similarity to Palladio's design for a wooden bridge: Palladio, op. cit., III/VIII, 176.

123 PRO WORK 14/938; EH 168C/8.

124 PRO ADM 67/2.

125 Ibid.

126 Ibid.

127 PRO ADM 68/674.

128 cf. the crypt of San Sebastiano, Mantua.

129 PRO ADM 68/675.

130 PRO ADM 67/2.

131 Beer, de, ed., op. cit., 1099.

132 Ibid., 965–6.

133 PRO ADM 67/3.

134 PRO ADM 67/2.

135 NMM REC/4.

136 PRO ADM 68/673.

137 PRO ADM 68/675.

138 PRO ADM 68/677.

139 PRO ADM 68/677 and 67/3.

140 PRO ADM 68/678.

141 Colvin, ed., op. cit., IV, 111.

142 NMM BHC1818.

143 NMM BHC1808.

144 NMM BHC1817.

145 PRO ADM 68/676.

146 Ibid.

147 PRO ADM 68/681.

148 PRO ADM 68/678.

149 PRO ADM 68/676.

150 PRO ADM 68/677.

151 Ibid.

152 PRO ADM 68/681.

153 PRO ADM 68/678.

154 PRO ADM 67/7.

155 PRO ADM 67/8.

156 cf. *Wren Society*, VI, pl. 21.

157 K. Downes, *The Architecture of Wren*, London 1982, 110.

158 BAL E5/5. There is a sectional model of the dome, together with the model of the Hospital, in the National Maritime Museum. The models are discussed by J. Wilton-Ely in H. A. Millon, ed., *The Triumph of the Baroque*, Milan 1999, 542–5.

159 Hawksmoor depicts oculi at upper and lower levels in each bay of the dome. As constructed, the dome has the lower in

each bay but the upper are in alternate bays. There are marks on certain timbers, visible when the lead was removed during restoration in 1999, which suggest that there may originally have been openings in every bay. Whether this represents a change of mind during or following construction is not known.

160 BAL E5/17 (5).

161 See also the more modest derivation at John James's St George, Hanover Square, of 1721–4.

162 PRO ADM 67/3.

163 Ibid.

164 PRO ADM 68/678 and 67/4. The officers' accommodation in 1710 included apparently the first use of a painted floorcloth in England, in imitation of black and white marble (I. Bristow, 'They will look very well: Painted Floorcloths in the 18th Century', *SPAB News*, XI/2, 1990, 11–13).

165 This was not a perfect solution. In 1717 Mr Burt, one of the pensioners who had been confined in Bethlem for lunacy and then discharged, was again 'seized with madness'. Bethlem refused to readmit him 'because he is uncapable, by Weaknesse, of going through their methods of cure'. Since he was now confined in a madhouse at a charge of 15s per week, the Hospital preferred to bring him back, accommodate him in a private room and take proper care of him (PRO ADM 67/5).

166 PRO ADM 67/3.

167 PRO ADM 68/684.

168 PRO ADM 67/8.

169 NMM ART/2, fo. 10r.

170 PRO ADM 67/19. The sewer house was probably the brick-lined cesspit which survives to the east of the Queen Mary Building. This is a large chamber 36 feet long, 10 feet wide and 7½ feet high, with canted sides and an apsidal end to the south. It narrows at the north, riverward end, to a recess which presumably once formed an opening to a sluice. An internal cesspit was discovered in 2000 in the basement of the east end of the south range of the King William Building.

171 P. van der Merwe, '*A Refuge for All*': *Greenwich Hospital 1694–1994*, London 1994.

172 *A Pattern*, v.

173 Ibid., 164.

174 PRO ADM 67/3.

175 PRO ADM 68/681.

176 *Wren Society*, VI, 25–6.

177 PRO ADM 68/681.

178 PRO ADM 67/2.

179 PRO ADM 68/681.

180 PRO ADM 67/3.

181 Ibid.

182 Ibid.

183 PRO ADM 68/682.

184 The floor above was not completed until 1731, when it was inserted and fitted up as an apartment for the nurses (PRO ADM 68/712).

185 PRO ADM 67/3 and 68/682.

186 PRO ADM 67/3. The death rate at the Hospital inevitably was high, given the age and infirmity of the men, even after the building of the Infirmary. This was exacerbated during such 'epidemical Distempers' as the one which struck London in 1743, causing 'upwards of twenty Hospital Men and Boys [to be] buried in a Night' (*Gentleman's Magazine*, May 1743).

187 Cooke and Maule, *An Historical Account*, 120.

188 PRO ADM 68/682.

189 PRO ADM 67/3.

190 Ibid.

191 PRO ADM 67/4.

192 PRO ADM 67/3.

193 Ibid.

194 Ibid.

195 PRO ADM 67/4.

196 PRO ADM 68/684.

197 PRO ADM 68/682.

198 Lane Fine Art.

199 J. H. V. Davies, 'The Dating of the Buildings at the Royal Hospital at Greenwich', *Archaeological Journal*, CXIII, 1956, 128–32; Downes, *Hawksmoor*, 85–8.

200 cf. N. MacGregor, *A Victim of Anonymity: The Master of the Saint Bartholomew Altarpiece*, London 1993.

201 PRO ADM 68/683.

202 M. G. Power, 'The Chronicles of Greenwich: An Informal Account of the History of Greenwich Hospital 1692–1986', typescript, RNC Library, supplies an authoritative discussion of the financing of the Hospital.

203 PRO ADM 67/3.

204 PRO ADM 67/4.

205 PRO ADM 68/684.

206 PRO ADM 67/4.

207 The needful repairs included the repair of the leading of the roofs. The use of thin, milled lead, which shrank and cracked in the sun, had resulted in leaks all over the Hospital (R. Neve, *The City and Country Purchaser, and Builder's Dictionary*, London 1726, reprinted Newton Abbot 1969, 188).

208 PRO ADM 67/4.

209 Ibid.

210 Ibid.

5 The Royal Hospital for Seamen: Building an Institution

1 John James was responsible for the carpentry of the roof, being given space in the mews on the west side of the Hospital in 1713 for framing, at a charge of £10 (PRO ADM 67/4).

2 Ibid.

3 Not all prizes were received: 'A Proposall was made by a french Gentleman called Mr. Wheelbarrow [in 1712], to discover some concealments made by a Captain of a man of War who had taken a prize

about three years ago, which he conceives ought to belong to the Hospitall' (ibid.).

4 PRO ADM 67/4 and 5.

5 PRO ADM 68/706.

6 PRO ADM 67/4.

7 PRO ADM 68/687.

8 PRO ADM 67/4.

9 PRO ADM 67/8.

10 PRO ADM 67/4.

11 PRO ADM 67/4 and 68/688.

12 PRO ADM 67/5.

13 PRO ADM 68/688.

14 PRO ADM 67/4. There was an established formula for this: 'These are to Certifie that the Workmanship contained in this Booke was done in Workmanlike manner, and that the Materialls were delivered and used as is mentioned in the foregoing account and were good and every way fitt for the Service they have been applyed to, and the rates and prices charged for both, as either according to Contracts Subsisting, or were (if not in Contract) the Reasonable Current prices at the times the particulars were furnished and the workmanship performed, amounting in the whole to the sume of . . .'. Hawksmoor and James also shared the less glamorous responsibility for directing the labourers clearing snow and Richard Wright the carter for carting hay, rubbish and for example in 1717 '15 Loads of Dung to Several parts of the Gardens by two Teams at 16d p. load – £1-00-00' (PRO ADM 68/694).

15 PRO ADM 67/5.

16 K. Downes, *Hawksmoor*, London 1979, 249.

17 PRO ADM 67/5.

18 PRO ADM 68/689.

19 PRO ADM 68/690.

20 Ibid.

21 PRO ADM 68/691.

22 F. Saxl and R. Wittkower, *British Art and the Mediterranean*, Oxford 1948, 48.

23 G. B. da Vignola, *Regola delli cinque ordini d'architettura*, Siena 1635, pl. 37.

24 J. Moxon, *Vignola: or, the Compleat Architect*, London 1694, 4th edition, pl. 38.

25 PRO ADM 67/4.

26 NMM ART/3, fo. 8r.

27 S. Jeffery, *English Baroque Architecture: The Work of John James*, PhD thesis, University of London 1986, 116.

28 NMM ART/1, fo. 23r. This is an attribution owed to the highly critical Batty Langley, who, reacting to James's criticism of his design for Westminster Bridge, alleged that the kitchen vaulting would have fallen down 'if the Props and Struts, placed to prevent it, were taken away: and which deterr'd the laying of the Floors, and render'd that part of the Building both dangerous and useless'; quoted in Jeffery, op. cit., 108.

29 BL MS 70046 865D, fo. 556; copy exhibited in the exhibition organised by John Brushe, 'John James c.1672–1746: An Architect of National Importance',

Orleans House Gallery, Twickenham, 1997.

30 PRO ADM 68/694.

31 PRO ADM 67/5.

32 PRO ADM 68/692.

33 PRO ADM 67/5; use as the Pensioners' Library is noted on NMM ART/3, fo. 42.

34 PRO ADM 67/5.

35 Ibid.

36 PRO ADM 67/4 and 68/690.

37 PRO ADM 67/5.

38 M. I. Webb, *Michael Rysbrack Sculptor*, London 1954, 162–3.

39 PRO ADM 67/5.

40 C. Campbell, *Vitruvius Britannicus*, III, London 1725, pls. 3–4.

41 Downes, op. cit., no. 241.

42 PRO ADM 67/4 and 5.

43 PRO ADM 67/5.

44 Ibid.

45 PRO ADM 67/6. No attempt has been made here to differentiate the contribution to Greenwich of the two Edward Strongs when they were working together. The careers of the elder (*c.*1652–1724) and the younger (1676–1741) are outlined in R. Gunnis, *Dictionary of British Sculptors 1660–1851*, 2nd edition, London 1964, 376–7.

46 PRO ADM 68/699. £151 was deducted from the total of £2961 as already paid by benefactors; this appears to have been an accounting error in Thornhill's favour, since in July 1717 it was stated that he had already received £635 (including an imprest of £300 in 1712) and in November, £651 (PRO ADM 67/5).

47 PRO ADM 67/5; J. Cooke and J. Maule, *An Historical Account of the Royal Hospital for Seamen at Greenwich*, London 1789.

48 PRO ADM 68/688.

49 PRO ADM 67/4.

50 PRO ADM 67/5 and 68/697.

51 G. Vertue, *Vertue Note Books*, III, *Walpole Society*, 22, 1933–4, Oxford 1934, 31.

52 PRO ADM 67/5.

53 PRO ADM 67/6.

54 PRO ADM 67/8.

55 R. Steele, *The Lover*, London 1715, 223–31.

56 Three quarters of the income was designated for charity; PRO ADM 67/6.

57 J. Schulz, *Venetian Painted Ceilings of the Renaissance*, Berkeley and Los Angeles 1968, 53; R. Wittkower, *Art and Architecture in Italy 1600–1750*, Harmondsworth 1973, 250–53; G. Knox, *Antonio Pellegrini 1675–1741*, Oxford 1995, 47 *et seq.*

58 L. Stainton and C. White, *Drawing in England from Hilliard to Hogarth*, London 1987, 232–5; see also E. de N. Mayhew, *Sketches by Thornhill in the Victoria and Albert Museum*, London 1967.

59 E. Croft-Murray, *Decorative Painting in England 1537–1837*, I, London 1962, 71.

60 Historic Royal Palaces Agency, *The Banqueting House*, London 1997.

61 S. Alpers and M. Baxandall, *Tiepolo and the Pictorial Intelligence*, New Haven and London 1994, 110–18.

62 Croft-Murray, op. cit., 76.

63 PRO ADM 68/699.

64 PRO ADM 68/696.

65 Stainton and White, op. cit., 41 and 234.

66 PRO ADM 67/6.

67 The compass is no longer *in situ* and the opening is covered with boards. The balustrade, which survives and once would have enabled vertiginous viewing, is now out of sight from below.

68 J. Thornhill, *An Explanation of the Painting in the Royal Hospital at Greenwich*, Greenwich *c.*1726/7, 4 and 8.

69 PRO ADM 67/6.

70 PRO ADM 67/5.

71 PRO ADM 67/7.

72 PRO ADM 68/706.

73 J. Cooke and J. Maule, *A Description of the Royal Hospital for Seamen at Greenwich*, London 1803, 27.

74 *Déscription de L'Hôpital Royal pour les marins, Greenwich*, London 1851.

75 *Gentleman's Magazine*, 13 May 1734, 274–5.

76 *Wren Society*, VI, Oxford 1929, 22. The quality of the Painted Hall, 'one of London's high points', was recognised by Ian Nairn: *Nairn's London*, London 1988, 161–2. In his depiction of Juno in the ceiling of the Upper Hall, Thornhill displayed an indebtedness to Pellegrini's painting of the goddess, now at Hampton Court (M. Levey, *The Later Italian Pictures in the Collection of Her Majesty the Queen*, Cambridge 1991, no. 562).

77 PRO ADM 67/10, 68/736 and 737.

78 PRO ADM 67/11.

79 W. Percival-Prescott, 'The Hand of the Restorer', typescript for the exhibition 'Idea and Illusion', Painted Hall 1960. For illustrations of work in progress, see *The Sphere*, 1 March 1958, 353; *Illustrated London News*, 20 December 1958, 1097, and 9 July 1960, 70–71.

80 PRO ADM 68/699. This was Christopher Fox, who offered to do the whole building for £35. He brought a reference from Clerkenwell workhouse, where he had destroyed vermin, and it was agreed that if successful he would be paid £10 per year to keep Greenwich bug-free (PRO ADM 67/6).

81 PRO ADM 68/700.

82 Hawksmoor and James occupied adjoining houses.

83 PRO ADM 67/6.

84 Ibid. This system was abused by a later porter who was found guilty of 'great frauds and abuses' in keeping the money collected for showing the Painted Hall which was intended to contribute to the maintenance of the charity boys (PRO ADM 67/10).

85 PRO ADM 68/711.

86 PRO ADM 67/10.

87 PRO ADM 67/6 and 7.

88 PRO ADM 67/7 and 68/702–4.

89 PRO ADM 67/20.

90 PRO ADM 67/10.

91 *The Builder*, XIV, 1856, 368–9.

92 PRO ADM 67/7 and 68/705.

93 PRO ADM 68/706.

94 NMM ART/1, fo. 67r.

95 PRO ADM 67/7.

96 Ibid.

97 PRO ADM 68/708 and 709.

98 PRO ADM 67/7.

99 Ibid.

100 PRO ADM 68/711.

101 PRO ADM 68/712.

102 PRO ADM 68/713 and 67/8.

103 PRO ADM 67/8.

104 Ibid.

105 PRO ADM 67/8 and 9.

106 PRO ADM 67/9.

107 PRO ADM 67/5.

108 PRO ADM 67/10. John Watts, a superannuated butler, abused this hospitality in 1731 and his £10 per year pension was stopped following a conviction for theft (PRO ADM 67/8).

109 PRO ADM 67/9.

110 PRO ADM 67/10.

111 G. Vigarello, *Concepts of Cleanliness*, Cambridge 1988, 59 and 149.

112 PRO ADM 67/10.

113 Ibid.

114 PRO ADM 67/3.

115 PRO ADM 67/7 and 8.

116 PRO ADM 67/8.

117 PRO ADM 67/9.

118 PRO ADM 67/10.

119 *Report of the Commissioners Appointed to Inquire into Greenwich Hospital*, London 1860, xiv–xv and 94.

120 PRO ADM 67/10.

121 PRO ADM 67/9.

122 Ibid.

123 PRO ADM 68/721.

124 PRO ADM 68/722.

125 The stalls were to be allocated following the drawing of lots: 34 butchers, 4 poulterers, 3 cheesemongers, 2 bacon men, 1 pork woman, 2 pork men, 1 baker, 1 baked ox cheek man, 2 corn chandlers, 2 herb women, 1 tanner, 2 fishmongers, 1 cook, 1 milk and butter man, 1 grocer and 1 hatter (PRO ADM 67/9).

126 NMM ART/1, fo. 45r.

127 NMM ART/3, fo. 4.

128 NMM ART/3, fo. 5B.

129 J. Cooke and J. Maule, *A Concise Description of the Royal Hospital for Seamen at Greenwich*, London 1793, 8.

130 *The Times*, 5 April 1867, 9; 11 April 1867, 10.

131 NMM ART/1, after fo. 69.

132 NMM ART/3, fo. 52.

133 PRO ADM 68/724. In the construction of standard 13 inch thick walls, 100 bricks = 1 square yard.

134 PRO ADM 67/9.

135 PRO ADM 67/10.

136   PRO ADM 68/728.

137   PRO ADM 68/729.

138   PRO ADM 68/713.

139   *Report of the Commissioners*, 1860, lxxiii.

140   PRO ADM 67/8.

141   This basement room was used as a smoking room from 1772, as an additional eating place for the charity boys (where they were too much subject to the influence of pensioners and in 1779 were accommodated in a room under the west colonnade, PRO ADM 67/11) and later as a skittles alley; part of it appears also to have been used for the confinement of 'Lunatick and Disorderly Pensioners' (PRO ADM 68/742).

142   PRO ADM 67/10.

143   PRO ADM 67/18.

144   PRO ADM 68/733.

145   PRO ADM 68/735.

146   PRO ADM 68/736.

147   PRO ADM 67/10.

148   PRO ADM 68/740.

149   His widow was paid £6 6s in July 1747 for '12 different elevations drawn by Mr James at 10/6 each' (PRO ADM 68/743).

150   PRO ADM 67/10.

151   PRO ADM 68/741.

152   NMM ART/3, fo. 33.

153   PRO ADM 67/10.

154   PRO ADM 68/743.

155   PRO ADM 68/745 and 746.

156   NMM ART/3, fo. 32.

157   PRO ADM 68/748.

158   PRO ADM 68/749.

159   J. Daniels, *Sebastiano Ricci*, Hove 1976, 54-5.

160   GLHL, cutting in Ephemera File.

161   Vertue, op. cit., 94.

162   PRO ADM 67/10.

163   Ibid.

164   PRO ADM 67/11.

165   PRO ADM 68/746.

166   PRO ADM 68/747.

167   PRO ADM 67/10.

168   Westminster Archives Box 58, no. 5B; PRO ADM 67/11.

169   PRO ADM 67/11.

170   Cooke and Maule, *A Concise Description*, 8.

171   PRO ADM 68/876 and 67/11; NMM ART/3, fo. 39.

172   L'Abbé Perau, *Description historique de l'Hôtel Royal des Invalides*, Paris 1756, 53-4.

173   PRO ADM 67/11.

174   J. Tenon, *Journal d'observations sur les principaux hôpitaux et sur quelques prisons d'Angleterre* (1787), ed. J. Carré, Clermont-Ferrand 1992, 67 [my translation].

175   *A Pattern of a Well-Constituted and Well-Governed Hospital*, London 1695, 51.

176   C. Williams, ed., *Sophie in London 1786, being the Diary of Sophie v. la Roche*, London 1933, 251.

177   PRO ADM 68/884; BAL E5/21-2. The openings were closed with glazed partitions during the tenure of the Royal Naval College.

178   PRO ADM 67/15.

179   PRO ADM 67/16.

180   *The Annual Register*, quoted in B. Watson, *A Short Guide to the Chapel of St Peter and St Paul*, Greenwich 1972, 5.

181   Watson, op. cit., 5.

182   PRO ADM 67/11.

183   Cooke and Maule, *An Historical Account*, 34.

184   PRO ADM 68/877.

185   PRO ADM 68/878.

186   F. Kelsall, 'Liardet versus Adam', *Architectural History*, XXVII, 1984, 119.

187   PRO ADM 68/881.

188   John Groves (bricklayer), John Devall (mason), Samuel Wyatt (carpenter), Samuel Palmer (smith), John Papworth (plasterer), Charles Catton (painter), George Holroyd and Jeremiah Deval (plumbers), William Bent (ironmonger), James Arrow (joiner) and Richard Lawrence (carver) (PRO ADM 67/12).

189   In a draft of a letter to 'My Lord –', on the verso of a compositional sketch for the painting, West expressed hopes that his wishes would be made known to the Board of the Hospital. The drawing was exhibited at the Bernard Black Gallery, New York, 1968; photograph in the Courtauld Institute, Witt Library, London.

190   PRO ADM 67/12.

191   Cooke and Maule, *A Description*, 1803 edition, 35-6.

192   J. Cooke, *A Sermon Preached at the Opening of the Chapel of the Royal Hospital for Seamen at Greenwich*, Greenwich 1789, 14-15.

193   A. Meyer, *Apostles in England: Sir James Thornhill and the Legacy of Raphael's Tapestry Cartoons*, New York 1996, 67-9.

194   J. Shearman, *Raphael's Cartoons in the Collection of Her Majesty the Queen*, London 1972, 154-5.

195   Meyer, op. cit., 72.

196   Ibid., 39.

197   Ibid., 78; H. von Erffa and A. Staley, *The Paintings of Benjamin West*, New Haven and London 1986, no. 513.

198   Erffa, von, and Staley, op. cit., frontispiece.

199   T. Puttfarken, 'Caravaggio's "Story of St Matthew": A Challenge to the Conventions of Painting', *Art History*, XXI/2, 1998, 163.

200   Although this figure is of the Paul type, he is not named as such in all commentaries on the Raphael Cartoons. S. Fermor (*The Raphael Tapestry Cartoons*, London 1996, 81) considers this to be Paul, but the apostle properly belongs to later events in the Acts rather than to this Petrine story of divinely inspired wrath.

201   Cooke and Maule, *A Description*, 34-5.

202   See particularly the two pen and wash drawings in the Boston Museum of Fine Arts.

203   W. Hazlitt, *The Plain Speaker* (1826), ed. P. P. Howe, London, n.d., 94-5.

204   PRO ADM 65/106.

205   NMM ART/3, fo. 16v.

206   PRO ADM 80/114.

207   Stuart was regarded as an interior designer rather than as an architect in his own lifetime (information from Kerry Bristol, who is working on his biography). Notwithstanding its overall grandeur, there is indeed a flatly decorative quality to Stuart's Chapel which lacks the architectonic articulation of the Hospital as a whole.

208   H. M. Colvin, *A Biographical Dictionary of British Architects 1600–1840*, revised 3rd edition, New Haven and London 1995, 681.

209   NMM ART/1-3.

210   PRO ADM 67/12.

211   L. Lewis, 'Greece and Rome at Greenwich', *Architectural Review*, CIX, 1951, 24; see also L. Lewis, 'The Architects of the Chapel at Greenwich Hospital', *Art Bulletin*, XXIX, 1947, 260-67.

212   BAL E5/25(16).

213   BAL E5/25(17) and E5/18.

214   PRO ADM 67/12.

215   PRO ADM 68/615.

216   PRO ADM 68/818 and 821. The sequence of coats in the colouring of the plasterwork was as follows: nut oil; nut oil and turpentine; parchment size and Nottingham white; parchment size and Nottingham white stained with blue verditure; parchment size and Nottingham white; the grounds coloured azure blue (PRO ADM 68/821).

217   *The Builder*, XVIII, 1860, 77-8.

218   PRO ADM 68/815.

219   PRO ADM 68/820 and 823.

220   PRO ADM 68/813, 816 and 818.

221   PRO ADM 68/813.

222   PRO ADM 68/815.

223   PRO ADM 68/821.

224   PRO ADM 68/823.

225   PRO ADM 68/823 and 824.

226   The figures representing Meekness (signed Coade, Lambeth 1790) and Hope flank the stairs leading to the entrance to the Chapel; they face Charity with her three children and Faith, which flank the main outside door.

227   On the north side: Mark, James the Less, Bartholomew, Andrew, Peter, Philip and Matthew; on the south side: Matthias, John, Thomas, Jude, Simon, James the Great and Luke.

228   PRO ADM 68/823.

229   PRO ADM 68/820.

230   This now houses various memorial plaques, removed during the restoration, and the large, low-relief monument to Sir John Franklin's lost Arctic expedition. This was originally installed in the blind doorway on the south side of the entrance vestibule of the Painted Hall.

231   Watson, op. cit., 1-3.

232   British Museum, *An Historical Guide to the Sculptures of the Parthenon*, London 1975, 13-14.

233   Walker Art Gallery, Liverpool.

234   National Gallery of Canada, Ottawa.

235   NMM BHC0566.

236 Yale Center for British Art, New Haven.

237 NMM BHC2905; Erffa, von, and Staley, op. cit., nos 108–11; C. Mitchell, 'Benjamin West's Death of Nelson', in D. Fraser, H. Hibbard and M. Lewine, *Essays in the History of Art Presented to Rudolf Wittkower*, London 1967, 265–73.

238 A. Kelly, *Mrs Coade's Stone*, Upton-upon-Severn 1990, 235–7; A. Kelly, 'A Camouflage Queen by the River: Mrs Coade at Greenwich', *Country Life*, CLXV, January 1979, 244–5.

239 Erffa, von, and Staley, op. cit., no. 110.

240 Kelly, *Mrs Coade's Stone*, 237.

241 *Gentleman's Magazine*, II, November 1812, 490.

242 *Description of the Grand Model of Neptune giving up the Body of Nelson, with the Dominion of the Sea into the Arms of Britannia, Executed from a Design of Benjamin West, Esq. for Greenwich Hospital, At Coade and Sealy's Ornamental Stone Manufactory, Lambeth* (National Library of Scotland, AP.1.82.46).

243 Ibid., 7.

244 Erffa, von, and Staley, op. cit., no. 111.

245 *Description of the Grand Model*, 3.

246 Ibid., 4–6.

247 Ibid., 4.

248 Ibid., 5.

249 T. Paulin, *The Day-Star of Liberty: William Hazlitt's Radical Style*, London 1998, 105 and 294.

250 British Museum, op. cit., frontispiece, figs 19 and 27; for comparable river gods – the Nile and the Tiber – see F. Haskell and N. Penny, *Taste and the Antique*, New Haven and London 1982, figs 9 and 164.

251 Hazlitt, op. cit., 95.

6 The Royal Hospital for Seamen: Uses, Abuses, Improvements and Departures

1 *Report of the Commissioners Appointed to Inquire into Greenwich Hospital*, London 1860; Wellcome Institute Library.

2 T. Baillie, *The Case of the Royal Hospital for Seamen at Greenwich*, London 1778 (copy at GLHL).

3 Ibid., 6.

4 Ibid., 24–39.

5 A phrase used by John Webb to describe the cill height of the windows at the Whitehall Banqueting House. During the restoration of the building in 1999, these privatised spaces were brought back into the public realm.

6 The east side 'alcove', a wall with niches, is clearly depicted in a view of 1835 by George Chambers senior (NMM BHC1823), and the difference in scale between the base block and its rebuilt pavilions, prior to John Yenn's rebuilding of the base block itself, is clearly, and possibly exaggeratedly, apparent in an engraving published in 1793. The 'alcoves' were depicted also by Canaletto.

7 Baillie, op. cit., 40–42; see also R. Ollard, 'Greenwich', *History Today*, V, November 1955, 780–82.

8 Documents relating to Baillie, op. cit., GLHL.

9 *State of Facts Relative to Greenwich Hospital*, 1779, GLHL.

10 *DNB*.

11 J. Tenon, *Journal d'observations sur les principaux hôpitaux et sur quelques prisons d'Angleterre* (1787), ed. J. Carré, Clermont-Ferrand 1992. The discussion of the context of Tenon's visit follows Carré's account.

12 Ibid., 65–71.

13 L. S. Greenbaum, 'Measure of Civilisation: The Hospital Thought of Jacques Tenon on the Eve of the French Revolution', *Bulletin of the History of Medicine*, XLIX, 1975, 43–56.

14 J.-N. Hallé, 'Air des hôpitaux de terre et de mer', *Encyclopédie Méthodique Médicine*, I, Paris 1787, 575.

15 PRO ADM 67/10.

16 PRO ADM 67/12 and 15.

17 J. Cooke and J. Maule, *A Description of the Royal Hospital for Seamen at Greenwich*, London 1813.

18 PRO ADM 67/61.

19 PRO ADM 79/76 2, block plan of *c*.1812–13; PRO WORK 31/605, ground-floor plan of *c*.1886.

20 PRO ADM 68/885; A. Kelly, *Mrs Coade's Stone*, Upton-upon-Severn 1990, 225.

21 P. van der Merwe, '*A Refuge for All*': Greenwich Hospital 1694–1994, London 1994; PRO ADM 80/114.

22 P. Newell, *Greenwich Hospital: A Royal Foundation 1692–1983*, Greenwich 1984, 141–5.

23 PRO ADM 80/114.

24 PRO WORK 31/605.

25 EH Drawings.

26 PRO ADM 80/113.

27 PRO ADM 80/114.

28 Ibid.

29 Baillie, op. cit., 10.

30 EH Greenwich Files.

31 C. Lloyd, *Greenwich: Palace, Hospital, College*, London 1960, 24.

32 PRO ADM 80/113.

33 *The Builder*, VII, 1849, 48.

34 PRO ADM 80/113.

35 *The Builder*, II, 1844, 209.

36 *Illustrated London News*, 22 April 1865, 375–7.

37 A. Corbin, *The Foul and the Fragrant*, London 1996, 163.

38 *Report of the Commissioners*, 1860, xxii.

39 PRO ADM 67/4.

40 PRO ADM 67/5 and 68/695.

41 PRO ADM 67/10.

42 Ibid.

43 PRO ADM 67/18.

44 PRO ADM 67/10.

45 NMM ART/2, fo. 33.

46 PRO ADM 80/114.

47 PRO ADM 67/87 and 76/25.

48 H. Richardson, *Greenwich: Its History, Antiquities, Improvements and Public Buildings*, London 1834, 62.

49 PRO WORK 31/405.

50 Newell, op. cit., 162.

51 Ibid., 165–6; Survey of London, XLIV, *Poplar, Blackwall and the Isle of Dogs*, London 1994, 518–23.

52 PRO ADM 65/109.

53 PRO ADM 68/752–3 and 755–7.

54 PRO ADM 65/109; RNC photographs 1906.

55 PRO ADM 65/109.

56 PRO WORK 31/405.

57 PRO ADM 68/752.

58 Ibid.

59 J. Cooke and J. Maule, *An Historical Account of the Royal Hospital for Seamen at Greenwich*, London 1789.

60 Ibid.; PRO ADM 67/20.

61 J. Barrow, *A New and Universal Dictionary of Arts and Sciences*, London 1751.

62 H. Rosenau, *Vision of the Temple*, London 1979, 101–2; J. Stevens Curl, *The Art and Architecture of Freemasonry*, London 1991, 28–32.

63 The form did not in itself preclude frivolity. Daniel Marot had incorporated Terrestrial and Celestial Sphere fountains, each showering water from tiny holes, in the gardens which he designed at Het Loo in Holland in the late seventeenth century for the future King William III and Queen Mary (M. Symmes, ed., *Fountains Splash and Spectacle*, New York 1998, 100).

64 *Illustrated London News*, 26 October 1850, 335.

65 PRO ADM 80/114.

66 Newell, op. cit., 165–6.

67 PRO ADM 80/114.

68 PRO ADM 65/109.

69 PRO ADM 65/110, 67/87 and 268.

70 In 1728 Hawksmoor had picturesquely named the outer gates after the British rivers Humber, Medway, Trent, Thames, Severn and Tyne, recalling the personifications in the Painted Hall.

71 PRO ADM 65/109.

72 PRO ADM 65/110.

73 *The Builder*, XVI, 1858, 621.

74 BAL K9/17(1).

75 Cooke and Maule, *An Historical Account*.

76 Plan of Greenwich Park, *c*.1675–80, Pepys Library, Magdalene College, Cambridge; Travers Survey, 1695, PRO MR 253; GLHL, Martin Collection 2532, 'Woodlands Plan', *c*.1704.

77 PRO ADM 67/254 and 169/539; EH, London Region Historian's Report, Greenwich/88, R. Bowdler, 1993.

78 Newell, op. cit., 33–4.

79 PRO ADM 67/3 and 68/682.

80 PRO ADM 169/539 and 68/688; EH, loc. cit.

81 GLHL, copy of engraved plan of Greenwich Park, *London Magazine*, XVIII, 1749.

82 Newell, op. cit., 73.

83   PRO ADM 67/19.

84   PRO WORK 16/129.

85   PRO ADM 65/106; GLHL, Greenwich Hospital Burial Ground Folder.

86   GLHL, Greenwich Hospital Burial Ground Folder; Newell, op. cit., 38. The rediscovery was made, to her great alarm, by the young Margaret (later Lady Jay), the daughter of James (later Lord) Callaghan (Prime Minister 1976–9), who was the Opposition spokesman for Transport and lived at 40 Maze Hill at that time; information from P. van der Merwe.

87   PRO ADM 67/10 and 19; site plan, BAL E5/8.

88   PRO ADM 67/10.

89   PRO ADM 79/81/4; undated plan.

90   PRO ADM 67/61.

91   PRO ADM 67/11.

92   PRO ADM 65/109.

93   PRO ADM 169/539.

94   PRO ADM 65/109.

95   PRO ADM 169/515.

96   PRO ADM 169/43.

97   *Report of the Commissioners*, 1860, 132.

98   Ibid., 93–7.

99   C. Hibbert, ed., *Louis Simond: An American in Regency England*, London 1968, 51–2.

100 Ollard, op. cit., 784.

101 GLHL, Pensioners File.

102 Van der Merwe, op. cit., 6; for a full discussion of funding at this period, see Newell, op. cit., 127–32.

103 *Report of the Commissioners*, 1860, xiii.

104 *Regulations Established by the Lords Commissioners of the Admiralty for the Government of Greenwich Hospital*, Greenwich 1853, 131–8.

105 *Report of the Commissioners*, 1860, xxxii.

106 Ibid., xlviii.

107 Ibid., xvii–xviii, xlviii–l.

108 'Greenwich Hospital as it is', *United Services Magazine*, June–August 1859, 195–203, 386–97, 556–62.

109 House of Lords, *Bills Public*, II, 1861, 433.

110 *DNB*.

111 House of Lords, *Accounts and Papers*, XXIII, 1864, 139 and 167.

112 T. Paulin, *The Day-Star of Liberty: William Hazlitt's Radical Style*, London 1998, 30.

113 Ibid.

114 F. Fraser, *The Unruly Queen*, London 1996, 53.

115 [Barker, M. H.], *Greenwich Hospital: A Series of Naval Sketches Descriptive of the Life of a Man-of-War's Man. By an Old Sailor* [Captain Matthew Henry Barker], London 1826.

116 NMM BHC1815.

117 cf. J. Hichberger, 'Old Soldiers', in R. Samuel, ed., *Patriotism: The Making and Unmaking of British National Identity*, III, London 1989, 50–63.

118 *Illustrated London News*, 22 April 1843.

119 House of Lords, *Bills Public*, II, 1865, 45.

120 *The Times*, 20 June 1865, 6.

121 *Illustrated London News*, 21 October 1865, 373–4.

122 *The Times*, 27 September 1865, 10.

123 *The Times*: 15 February 1867, 7; 1 March 1867, 5; 13 March 1867, 12; 5 April 1867, 9; 11 April 1867, 10; 16 April 1867, 7; 19 April 1867, 11; 22 May 1867, 9; and 11 June 1867, 9.

124 House of Lords, *Reports from Commissioners*, XVI, 1867–8, 393–1021.

125 Ibid., 415.

126 *The Times*, 15 April 1868, 9.

127 Ibid.

128 *The Times*, 2 October 1869, 6.

129 PRO ADM 169/43.

130 *The Times*: 22 April 1870, 4; 28 July 1871, 5; 11 August 1871, 12; 11 June 1872, 12.

131 House of Lords, *Accounts and Papers*, XLII, 1873, 601. Later expansion resulted in departments of Mathematics, Applied Mathematics, Physical and Electrical Engineering, Naval Architecture, Naval Engineering, History and English, Foreign Languages and Nuclear Science (C. Lloyd, op. cit., 35).

132 *The Builder*, XXX, 1872, 833.

133 PRO ADM 169/43.

134 *The Times*, 21 June 1873, 7.

135 PRO ADM 169/43.

136 Institution of Civil Engineers, *Minutes of Proceedings*, CXLIX, 1902, 342–5.

137 Hardwick had been ill for some time before his retirement but had retained responsibility for the Hospital and contributed to the 1860 *Report*. His son Philip Charles inherited most of his practice and certainly was the architect of the new west wing at the Hospital School built in 1861–2.

138 *The Builder*, XXXI, 1873, 80 and 305.

139 *The Builder*, XXXIII, 1875, 858.

140 *Port of London Authority Monthly*, March 1963, 82. Jason was removed in 1999. An interesting pedagogical aid survives in the fabric of the lecture theatre. Above a modern false ceiling, with a ceiling of *c.*1900 above that, there is a wooden sliding ceiling in two leaves. This was opened by a chain-driven mechanism, with interlocking horizontal and vertical shafts operated by the lecturer, presumably by turning a handle, in order to reveal the night sky above. This was visible probably through a large, glazed rooflight, which does not survive, canted to present a view northwards of the stars – a navigational aid. The lecturer also controlled a similar shaft-driven mechanism which operated a blind over the main east window in order to eliminate distracting light. Both vertical shafts survive behind panelling in the lecture room. The date 1873 is incised in the brickwork of the roof space.

141 NMM MS 84/118; PRO WORK 31/656–60.

142 W. R. Martin, 'The Royal Naval College at Greenwich', *Shipping World*, 1 November 1888, 203.

143 EH 168E/25.

144 NMM MS 84/118; EH 168/12A.

145 The auxiliary Women's Royal Naval Service had been disbanded at the close of the First World War, but was reinstated in 1938, continuing until 1993 when it was incorporated into the Royal Navy (S. J. Stark, *Female Tars*, London 1998, 2).

146 EH 168D/128.

147 EH 168C/52.

148 EH 1753.

149 PRO ADM 195/67.

150 PRO ADM 195/47.

151 Institution of Civil Engineers, *Minutes of Proceedings*, CIII, 1890–91, 388–91. Pasley, who died in 1890, was the son of another eminent military engineer, Sir Charles Pasley. The younger Pasley's most notable works were in dock construction, particularly at Chatham.

152 PRO WORK 31/650.

153 PRO ADM 169/480.

154 PRO WORK 14/2379.

155 PRO ADM 169/480.

156 PRO ADM 169/480; PRO WORK 14/2379.

157 PRO WORK 14/2379.

158 Newell, op. cit., 247.

159 K. Littlewood and B. Butler, *Of Ships and Stars*, London and New Brunswick 1998, 49.

160 *The Fleet*: February 1933, 27; June 1933, 86–7; and *The Engineer*, 23 June 1933.

161 Littlewood and Butler, op. cit., 61.

162 R. Byron, 'Greenwich Pageant', *Week End Review*, 1 July 1933.

163 Littlewood and Butler, op. cit., 60.

164 EH Drawings; *Illustrated London News*, 28 December 1935.

165 EH 168D/131–42.

166 *The Times*, 7 July 1998, 22.

167 John Grigg, *The Guardian*, 23 February 1967.

168 *Private Eye*, 19 September 1997, 15.

169 Sale Particulars, Knight Frank & Rutley International.

170 *Hansard*, 17 October 1995, 220.

171 *Burlington Magazine*, CXXXVII, November 1995, 719.

172 J. Musson, 'Greenwich: A Nation's Pride', *Country Life*, CXC, 6 June 1996, 83.

173 *The Times*, 7 July 1998, 22.

174 Musson, op. cit.

7   The Buildings of the Seamen's Hospital Society

1   Founding Charter of 1694 quoted in J. Cooke and J. Maule, *An Historical Account of the Royal Hospital for Seamen at Greenwich*, London 1789.

2   Minute Book of the Committee of the Fabrick, 18 June 1696; Abstract of the Estimate for finishing Greenwich Hospital, 27 April 1704; N. Hawksmoor, *Remarks on the Founding and Carrying on the Buildings of the Royal Hospital at Greenwich*, London 1728, reprinted in *Wren Society*, VI, Oxford 1929.

3   PRO ADM 67/10.

4   J. J. Keevil, *Medicine and the Navy*, II, Edinburgh and London 1958, 255–6, 264–5.

5   C. Lloyd and J. L. S. Coulter, *Medicine and the Navy*, III, Edinburgh and London 1961, 196–206.

6   Lloyd and Coulter, op. cit., 352–3.

7   *Official Papers Relating to Operations*, 1813.

8   Keevil, op. cit., 264–5.

9   Lloyd and Coulter, op. cit., 196–206.

10 The infirmary wards were in the King Charles and Queen Anne Buildings, the Helpless Ward was in Queen Anne (Lloyd and Coulter, op. cit., 196).

11 Council Ward in Queen Mary for the Helpless (PRO ADM 67/10); Royal William and Association in King William for the Infirmary (PRO ADM 67/18). In the nineteenth century Helpless Wards were established in both King William (Boyne and Nassau) and King Charles (Coronation and Nelson).

12 PRO ADM 67/10.

13 He asked the Board to apply to the General Court for an infirmary building but the paragraph was removed from the memo that was sent (PRO ADM 67/18).

14 PRO ADM 67/10.

15 PRO ADM 67/19.

16 PRO ADM 67/10.

17 PRO ADM 67/19.

18 PRO ADM 67/10.

19 PRO ADM 67/10 and 19.

20 PRO ADM 67/20.

21 Ibid.

22 PRO ADM 67/10.

23 Ibid.

24 Ibid.

25 *Wren Society*, VI, 69–70. This was possibly Henry Wise, gardener to Queen Anne and a big landowner around Deptford, or his brother Richard, a master caulker in Deptford Dockyard.

26 PRO ADM 67/19.

27 PRO ADM 67/10.

28 PRO ADM 68/673.

29 K. Downes, *Hawksmoor*, London 1979, 87.

30 Ibid., 90–92.

31 Ibid., 97.

32 BAL E5/11. See also a variant, and a part elevation of the Doctors' Pavilion, Sir John Soane's Museum, vol. 109, I, nos 50 and 58; no. 50 is reproduced in *Wren Society*, VI, pl. XLVIII.

33 NMM ART/1, fo. 64.

34 NMM ART/1, fos 6–7, 54–62.

35 *A Pattern of a Well-Constituted and Well-Governed Hospital*, London 1695, 51.

36 H. Richardson, ed., *English Hospitals 1660–1948*, Swindon 1998, 78–81.

37 N. A. M. Rodger, *The Wooden World*, London 1988, 110–12.

38 NMM ART/2, fos 39, 41–3, 45 and 49.

39 NMM ART/2, fo. 41r.

40 NMM ART/2, fos 41–3 and 45.

41 NMM ART/2, fo. 49.

42 NMM ART/2, fo. 39.

43 PRO ADM 67/21; contracts were issued in 1766 to John Chapman, painter, John Collins, joiner, and Thomas Clark, plasterer.

44 PRO ADM 67/22.

45 Cooke and Maule, op. cit.; J. Tenon, *Journal d'observations sur les principaux hôpitaux et sur quelques prisons d'Angleterre* (1787), ed. J. Carré, Clermont-Ferrand 1992, 69–71.

46 PRO ADM 65/109; letter from Joseph Kay, 3 September 1846.

47 PRO ADM 67/22; NMM ART/2, fo. 32.

48 Tenon, op. cit.; J. Cooke and J. Maule, *A Description of the Royal Hospital for Seamen at Greenwich*, London 1803.

49 These were all features recommended by John Howard, 'Hints on the Construction and Regulation of Hospitals', in *An Account of the Principal Lazarettos in Europe*, Warrington 1789, 141.

50 PRO ADM 67/20.

51 B. Abel-Smith, *The Hospital 1800–1948*, London 1964, 10.

52 Howard, op. cit.

53 *The Lancet*, II, 1870, 642.

54 PRO ADM 67/10.

55 PRO ADM 67/22 and 21.

56 PRO ADM 67/10.

57 NMM BHC3009.

58 Sandwich held office three times between 1748 and 1782. The portrait may have been intended partly as propaganda since one of the accusations made against Sandwich by the former Lieutenant-Governor Thomas Baillie in 1778 was his alleged indifference to the welfare of the pensioners, although he has also been described as hard-working and effective. The portrait was commissioned by Sir Hugh Palliser, whom Sandwich had appointed Governor.

59 Lloyd and Coulter, op. cit., 196–206. In the Navy generally, these often devoted men were 'no more ignorant than the run of doctors of the day', although their professional ability varied widely and in general 'their pretensions to gentility were insecure' (Rodger, op. cit., 20).

60 Lloyd and Coulter, op. cit., 46.

61 Keevil, op. cit., 255–6.

62 Ibid., 264–5.

63 Lloyd and Coulter, op. cit., 46–7.

64 P. Newell, *Greenwich Hospital: A Royal Foundation 1692–1983*, Greenwich 1984, 162–6.

65 Keevil, op. cit., 264–5.

66 *Bye Lawes, Rules, Orders and Directions, for the Better Government of His Majesty's Royal Hospital for Seamen at Greenwich*, London 1776.

67 Hawksmoor in 1728 optimistically had provided accommodation for both Apothecary and Dispenser.

68 R. Robertson, *Observations on the Disease incident to Seamen, Retired from Actual Service, by Reason of Accidents, Infirmities, or Old Age*, IV, London 1807; R. Robertson,

Synopsis Morborum, I, London 1810. Additionally, a review of the medical establishment was carried out in 1819: PRO ADM 105/24.

69 Lloyd and Coulter, op. cit., 196–206. When the helpless pensioners were admitted in 1810 they were allowed to continue to wear the blue coats.

70 PRO ADM 105/24.

71 Lloyd and Coulter, op. cit., 359.

72 Robertson, *Synopsis Morborum*.

73 Robertson, *Observations*.

74 *State of Facts relative to Greenwich Hospital*, London 1779.

75 PRO ADM 67/26.

76 PRO ADM 67/56.

77 PRO ADM 67/56 and 57.

78 PRO ADM 67/57.

79 PRO ADM 67/14.

80 PRO ADM 67/57.

81 PRO ADM 67/13.

82 The principal contractors were Thomas Suter, bricklayer; John Watson, mason; Richard Martyr, carpenter (PRO ADM 68/882).

83 PRO ADM 65/106.

84 PRO ADM 67/15.

85 PRO ADM 67/61.

86 PRO ADM 67/62.

87 PRO ADM 80/114.

88 PRO ADM 65/107.

89 PRO ADM 80/114.

90 PRO ADM 80/113.

91 An idea of how the exterior may once have looked can still be gained from the unadorned courtyard elevations.

92 PRO ADM 80/114.

93 Ibid.

94 PRO ADM 80/113.

95 The west side, whose boundary had been slightly moved to fully enclose the Helpless Ward was completed in 1838 (PRO ADM 80/113). The present railings on the north and east sides are of c.1870 although of an identical pattern.

96 PRO ADM 80/114.

97 Ibid.

98 PRO ADM 67/268.

99 PRO ADM 80/115.

100 PRO ADM 80/113.

101 PRO ADM 65/107.

102 PRO ADM 67/268.

103 PRO ADM 80/114.

104 Ibid.

105 PRO ADM 67/87.

106 PRO ADM 65/107.

107 Boyne and Nassau in King William; Council and Rodney in Queen Mary; Coronation and Nelson in King Charles (PRO ADM 65/110).

108 *Déscription de l'Hôpital Royal pour les marins*, Greenwich, London 1851.

109 *Report of the Commissioners Appointed to Inquire into Greenwich Hospital*, London 1860.

110 PRO ADM 67/269, and drawing dated 1851 (PRO ADM 79/82 8), on which it

is noted that pensioners were using the first-floor bridge as a smoking area.

111   PRO ADM 80/167.

112   PRO ADM 79/82 9.

113   PRO ADM 169/43.

114   J. Matthews, *Welcome Aboard: The Story of the Seamen's Hospital Society and the Dreadnought*, Buckingham 1992, 13.

115   A. G. McBride, *The History of the Dreadnought Seamen's Hospital at Greenwich*, London 1970, 7–8.

116   The attendance of large numbers of discharged sailors and soldiers at a radical meeting in Spa Fields in 1816 has been noted: J. Hichberger, 'Old Soldiers', in R. Samuel, ed., *Patriotism: The Making and Unmaking of British National Identity*, III, London 1989, 51.

117   Matthews, op. cit., 14.

118   Ibid., 15; McBride, op. cit., 8.

119   King George IV was its first patron, other royal patronage coming from Russia, Prussia, Denmark and Belgium. Vice-Admiral Young, who had links with the Marine Society, was also on the committee: Matthews, op. cit., 16–17; G. C. Cook, *From the Greenwich Hulks to Old St. Pancras: A History of Tropical Disease in London*, London 1992, 34.

120   McBride, op. cit., 9.

121   J. H. Plumridge, *Hospital Ships and Ambulance Trains*, London 1975, 13.

122   McBride, op. cit., 13.

123   Matthews, op. cit., 44. Its removal in 1872 was a well-attended occasion, marked by the press of the day.

124   Ibid., 35–6.

125   Ibid., 58.

126   Ibid., 43.

127   In 1863 the SS *Cossack* ran into the *Dreadnought*: ibid., 57.

128   Cook, op. cit., 48.

129   McBride, op. cit., 20.

130   Matthews, op. cit., 59.

131   Rodger, op. cit., 127.

132   Matthews, op. cit., 59.

133   *The Times*: 25 January 1867; 15 February 1867.

134   *The Times*: 16 April 1867; 22 May 1867.

135   *The Lancet*, II, 1868, 266.

136   Matthews, op. cit., 59; PRO ADM 169/10.

137   The original offer was for a twenty-one year lease but the Society successfully asked for its extension; the lease is dated 1 June 1870 (PRO ADM 169/10).

138   Provision of up to twenty-five beds for men entitled to Royal Hospital benefits was also negotiated (ibid.).

139   Until 1933 the more serious cases from the Royal Hospital School were also treated at the Dreadnought.

140   PRO ADM 169/10.

141   Contract awarded to Jukes, Coulson & Co. in 1870 (*The Builder*, XXVIII, 1870, 354). These railings were a reinstatement of Kay's railings of the 1830s which had been removed when the Royal Hospital grounds had been enlarged in 1849–50.

142   PRO ADM 169/10.

143   PRO ADM 169/446.

144   PRO WORK 14/1389.

145   *The Lancet*, I, 1870, 560–66.

146   PRO ADM 169/10.

147   *British Medical Journal*, 23 April 1870.

148   Cook, op. cit., 41.

149   Richardson, ed., op. cit., 118–20, 132–8.

150   PRO ADM 169/269.

151   McBride, op. cit., 23.

152   Matthews, op. cit., 49.

153   McBride, op. cit., 28.

154   P. Manson-Behr, *History of the School of Tropical Medicine in London*, London 1956. Sir James Michelli and Sir Patrick Nairne, Secretary and Chairman of the Society, were both knighted for their contributions in this field.

155   E.J. Hobsbawm, *The Age of Empire 1875–1914*, London 1994, 251; M. Worboys, 'The Spread of Western Medicine', in I. Loudon, ed., *Western Medicine*, Oxford 1997, 258–9.

156   Cook, op. cit., 101–46.

157   McBride, op. cit., 25.

158   Ibid., 15.

159   Matthews, op. cit., 88–9.

160   Cook, op. cit., 63.

161   Ibid., 60; *The Lancet*, I, 1876, 684.

162   Matthews, op. cit., 96. One such survival, in the first-floor ward at the south-east corner, reads: 'This bed is named by his mother in memory of Lieut. Gerald Leather RN who lost his life in HMS Pathfinder torpedoed by the enemy September 5th 1914'.

163   'Christmas with Poor Jack at the Seamen's Hospital', *Illustrated London News*, 6 January 1877; *The Graphic*, Christmas edition, 1879.

164   PRO WORK 14/940.

165   F. D. Long, *King Edward's Hospital Fund for London: The Story of its Foundation and Achievements, 1897–1942*, London 1942, 25–6.

166   F. K. Prochaska, *Philanthropy and the Hospitals of London: The Kings Fund 1897–1990*, Oxford 1992, 288.

167   *The Builder*, XXXVII, 1879, 83.

168   PRO ADM 169/127.

169   Matthews, op. cit., 77.

170   *Annual Report of the Seamen's Hospital Society*, 1915. The cost of the additional work, estimated as £1300, was borne by the Society alone (PRO ADM 169/127).

171   *Report of the Commissioners*, 1860.

172   'Sites and Construction of Hospitals', 'Construction of Hospitals: The Ground Plan', 'Hospital Construction-Wards', *The Builder*, XVI, 1858, 577–8, 609–10, 641–3.

173   *The Lancet*, II, 1870, 642.

174   'The "Dreadnought" on Land', *British Medical Journal*, 23 April 1870.

175   *The Lancet*, I, 1870, 560–61.

176   Cook, op. cit., 60; PRO ADM 169/259.

177   PRO ADM 169/259.

178   Ibid.

179   PRO ADM 169/254.

180   Matthews, op. cit., 88–9.

181   PRO ADM 169/446.

182   This was referred to as re-flooring in the Hospital accounts: Dreadnought Hospital File, LMA A/KE/246/12.

183   LMA, A/KE/515 (3). The Society used other eminent figures in their later appeals: James Lyle Mackay, Earl of Inchcape, Chairman of P & O, fronted that of 1919 and Noel Coward that of 1935.

184   Appeal notice: 'Merchant Service in War Time', 1916, GLHL, Dreadnought Ephemera Folder.

185   PRO ADM 169/446.

186   PRO ADM 169/515.

187   Matthews, op. cit., 91.

188   Ibid., 108; PRO ADM 169/515.

189   PRO WORK 14/940.

190   LMA A/KE/515 (3). The funds from Devonport's appeal and other bequests and grants from the King's Fund ensured that the new facilities for out-patients did not suffer a similar fate. The two lifts on the south side of the central passage probably were installed at this date.

191   PRO WORK 14/1389.

192   PRO ADM 169/770.

193   Matthews, op. cit., 120.

194   LMA A/KE/539 (3).

195   McBride, op. cit., 25.

196   LMA A/KE/539 (3).

197   LMA A/KE/735/45.

198   The chapel possibly was designed by Sir Robert Tasker & Partners who had submitted a scheme, not as built, in the previous year (letter in NMR Buildings Index File, 101280).

199   *Building Design*, 26 November 1993.

200   Matthews, op. cit., 108.

201   PRO ADM 169/446.

202   PRO ADM 169/515.

203   Ibid.

204   Ibid.

205   *DNB*.

206   *The Builder*: CXXXI, 1926, 126; CXXXVII, 1929, 96; and *Academy Architecture*, LXII, 1931, 122.

207   PRO ADM 169/515.

208   Ibid.; block plan 1924.

209   ADM 169/515.

210   Ibid.

211   The foundations were by Mowlems Ltd, and the building by Messrs Foster and Dicksee Ltd. The tenders had estimated the cost of the Nurses' Home at £86,929, with a further £33,045 for the Pathological Laboratory, although the actual cost for both was £135,000 (PRO ADM 169/515 and 901).

212   *The Builder*, CXXXVII, 1929, 96.

213   PRO WORK 14/2381.

214   Matthews, op. cit., 116.

215   PRO WORK 14/2381.

216   PRO WORK 14/940.

217   Survey of London, *County Hall*, London 1991.

218   *The Builder*: CXXXI, 1926, 126; CXXXVII, 1929, 96.

219   PRO ADM 169/515.

220 PRO ADM 169/895.

221 *The Builder*, CXXXI, 1926, 126.

222 PRO ADM 169/446.

223 A. Powers, 'Corinthian Epics: The Architecture of Sir Edwin Cooper', *Thirties Society Journal*, II, 1982, 13–17.

224 PRO ADM 169/515.

225 PRO ADM 169/259.

226 The inscription reads: 'The Devonport Pathological Laboratories and Nurses' Home, erected as a Memorial to the devotion of the men in the Mercantile Marine in the Great War from funds collected by the Right Honourable the Viscount Devonport P. C. from all parts of the British Empire, were declared open on 15 July 1929 by Their Royal Highnesses the Duke of York, the President of the Seamen's Hospital Society, and the Duchess of York'.

227 Matthews, op. cit., 120.

228 *Building Design*, 26 November 1993.

229 These had been small departments in the Dreadnought building (PRO ADM 169/515).

230 PRO ADM 169/515.

231 *The Builder*, CXXXVII, 1929, 96.

232 Survey of London, XLIII, *Poplar, Blackwall and the Isle of Dogs*, London 1994, 318–19.

233 *The Builder*, CXLIV, 1933, 59–60.

234 *Academy Architecture*, LXII, 1931, 122.

235 *The Builder*, CXXXVII, 1929, 96.

8 Buildings for Education

1 P. Newell, *Greenwich Hospital: A Royal Foundation 1692–1983*, Greenwich 1984, 38–44; PRO ADM 67/121 (cited in K. Sloan, 'Thomas Weston and the Academy at Greenwich', *Transactions of the Greenwich and Lewisham Antiquarian Society*, IX/6, 1984, 313–33).

2 Sloan, op. cit.; NMM ART/2, fos 7–10; G. H. Chettle, *The Queen's House, Greenwich*, London 1937, pl. 25.

3 Sloan, op. cit., 320, 324; Newell, op. cit., 44–51.

4 H. D. Turner, *The Cradle of the Navy: The Story of the Royal Hospital School at Greenwich and at Holbrook, 1694–1988*, York 1990, 23.

5 N. A. M. Rodger, *The Wooden World*, London 1988, 68–9.

6 PRO ADM 67/237, cited in Sloan, op. cit., 324–5.

7 PRO ADM 75/154.

8 Sloan, op. cit., 327.

9 PRO ADM 80/98: the bricklayer was John Rose, the carpenters Barnard and Phillips; Newell, op. cit., 76; Turner, op. cit., 25.

10 BAL L9/32, survey plan, 1782.

11 Newell, op. cit., 76.

12 BAL L9/32.

13 Sloan, op. cit., 327.

14 Turner, op. cit., 27.

15 PRO ADM 67/12.

16 T. Baillie, *The Case of the Royal Hospital for Seamen at Greenwich*, London 1778.

17 N. Hans, *New Trends in Education in the Eighteenth Century*, London 1966, 101–3.

18 PRO ADM 67/12.

19 Ibid.

20 PRO ADM 67/32–3, 68/811–13. John Taylor was the bricklayer, using bricks supplied by Benjamin Ricketts and the Trimmers of Brentford. Shepherd and Martyr were the carpenters, John Collins was the joiner, and John Brough the mason (PRO ADM 68/811–12).

21 BAL K9/16/5, 7–9.

22 PRO ADM 67/12.

23 J. Tenon, *Journal d'observations sur les principaux hôpitaux et sur quelques prisons d'Angleterre* (1787), ed. J. Carré, Clermont-Ferrand 1992, 68; J. Cooke and J. Maule, *An Historical Account of the Royal Hospital for Seamen at Greenwich*, London 1789; Newell, op. cit., 102 and 136.

24 Tenon, op. cit., 68; BAL K9/16/6; PRO ADM 67/32–3; J. Cooke and J. Maule, *A Description of the Royal Hospital for Seamen at Greenwich*, London 1805.

25 Tenon, op. cit., 68.

26 PRO ADM 67/32–3, 68/812–13.

27 A drawing of 1821 shows ten columns, asymmetrically disposed with a row of eight to the east of centre and only two to the west, perhaps reflecting alterations then intended (PRO ADM 79/81, no. 84).

28 PRO ADM 67/33.

29 BAL K9/16/6.

30 PRO ADM 67/33.

31 M. Seaborne, *The English School: Its Architecture and Organization, 1370–1870*, London 1971, 79–81, 113.

32 T. A. Markus, *Buildings and Power: Freedom and Control in the Origin of Modern Building Types*, London 1993, 42–4.

33 *Wren Society*, XI, Oxford 1934, pls xlviii–li.

34 N. Pevsner and E. Williamson, *The Buildings of England: Leicestershire and Rutland*, London 1984, 75–6; *Wren Society*, XI, pls liii–lvi.

35 The first plans for the building, by William Dickinson in 1713–14, were of a similar nature in terms of layout, with a central spine of ground-floor internal columns (P. D. Kingsbury, *Lord Burlington's Town Architecture*, London 1995, 21–8).

36 R. H. Nichols and F. A. Wray, *The History of the Foundling Hospital*, London 1935; *Country Life*, 16 and 23 October 1920, 502–9, 534–41; Markus, op. cit.

37 R. Evans, *The Fabrication of Virtue: English Prison Architecture, 1750–1840*, Cambridge 1982, 71–3; Nichols and Wray, op. cit. In reformist prisons of the late eighteenth century there are multiple examples of open ground-floor arcades under cell storeys (Evans, op. cit., 151).

38 Rodger, op. cit., 162.

39 Markus, op. cit., 44–5; G. L. Green, *The Royal Navy and Anglo-Jewry, 1740–1820*, London 1989, 79.

40 Ibid.; Seaborne, op. cit., 136.

41 NMM SOC 23/1.

42 Kingswood School, near Bristol, 1768, as quoted in Seaborne, op. cit., 96.

43 O. Equiano, *The Interesting Narrative of the Life of Olaudah Equiano or Gustavus Vassa the African*, London 1789, quoted in Rodger, op. cit., 68.

44 PRO ADM 67/16.

45 PRO ADM 67/70, 79/81, nos 84 and 86, plans of 1821.

46 PRO ADM 79/81, nos 59, 63, 65, 67, drawings of 1881; PRO ADM 195/47, photograph album, 38–9.

47 PRO WORK 31/607, basement plan, 1886.

48 PRO ADM 169/515.

49 PRO ADM 169/895; EH, copy of Office of Works drawing 168A/6.

50 PRO ADM 67/278; J. Kimbell, *An Account of the Legacies, Gifts, Rents, Fees etc. Appertaining to the Church and Poor of the Parish of St Alphege, Greenwich, etc.*, Greenwich 1816, 160; Green, op. cit., 78.

51 PRO ADM 67/278; BL, *Parliamentary Papers*, 1816 (521), xix.55, 'Paper Relating to the Royal Naval Asylum at Greenwich'; NMM CLA/1/B, Spencer Perceval to T. B. Clarke, 26 July 1810.

52 Angerstein (1735–1823) was also an art collector whose pictures from 1824 formed the nucleus of the National Gallery in London. He owned 'Woodlands', a house in Blackheath which is now occupied by the Greenwich Local History Library, and was buried at the church of St Alfege (*DNB*).

53 PRO ADM 67/278.

54 *DNB*.

55 PRO ADM 67/278; Green, op. cit., 79–87.

56 PRO ADM 67/278; H. S. Richardson, *Greenwich: Its History, Antiquities, Improvements and Public Buildings*, London 1834, 63–4; *DNB*.

57 PRO ADM 67/254 and 278, 80/99; BL, *Parliamentary Papers*, 1805 (174), III, 329, 'Petition of the Governors and Committee of the Naval Asylum'.

58 *Parliamentary Papers*, 1805, op. cit.; Turner, op. cit., 32.

59 *DNB*.

60 PRO ADM 67/278.

61 BL, 45 Geo III, cap.129, s.17.

62 A further donation from this Fund of the interest on £61,000 in 1806 3 per cent consols followed to provide a regular income. The Patriotic Fund Committee was thenceforth entitled to nominate a certain number of boys for places in the school (PRO ADM 67/254 and 278; *The Pictorial Guide to Greenwich*, 1844, 18–19).

63 NMM CLA/1/B.

64 PRO ADM 67/254.

65 PRO ADM 67/254 and 278, 169/652, typescript Admiralty history of the Naval Asylum, 1933.

66 Other Commissioners included Samuel, Viscount Hood, then Governor of Greenwich Hospital; Sir Evan Nepean, an

Admiralty Lord Commissioner and Secretary to the Admiralty from 1795 to 1804; Samuel Thornton, President of Guy's Hospital and a Director of the Bank of England; Lieutenant-General John Barclay of the Royal Marines; Charles Marsham, Earl of Romney, President of the Marine Society, Lord Lieutenant of Kent, and steward of the manor of East Greenwich; George Villiers, Paymaster of the Royal Marines; John Jervis, Lord St Vincent; and Charles Meadows, Viscount Newark (PRO ADM 67/278, 80/110 and 111; DNB; The Complete Peerage, XI, Gloucester 1982; Kimbell, op. cit., 220).

67 PRO ADM 169/652.
68 London Gazette, 15848, 1–5 October 1805, 1245.
69 F. Fraser, The Unruly Queen: The Life of Queen Caroline, London 1996, 131–2.
70 Ibid., 152.
71 Ibid., 135–9, 152, 158–9, 166–92.
72 PRO ADM 169/652.
73 PRO WORK 16/129; PRO ADM 67/254.
74 PRO CRES 6/100. The Earl of Romney and Viscount Newark were involved in drawing up the agreement. Prince Ernest Augustus, Duke of Cumberland defended Caroline against his brother in 1806 (Fraser, op. cit., 132, 174, 176.).
75 BL, 47 Geo III cap.52.
76 PRO WORK 16/129.
77 PRO ADM 67/254.
78 H. M. Colvin, A Biographical Dictionary of British Architects, 1600–1840, revised 3rd edition, New Haven and London 1995, 71–2. While working at Greenwich, Alexander was also engaged as the architect for Dartmoor Prison of War.
79 Gentleman's Magazine, XXVI/2, August 1846, 212. For his colonnades Alexander appears to have been indebted particularly to the portico of Inigo Jones's St Paul's, Covent Garden, which had been faithfully restored in 1795.
80 PRO ADM 67/254.
81 The principal building contractors were John and Henry Lee, bricklayers, James Browning, carpenter, and John Bacon, plasterer; mason's work was divided, one wing each, between Thomas and George Marshall, and John Watson (PRO ADM 67/254, 80/110 and 111). Among others paid for works were Charles Randall for marble chimneypieces, Oswald and Nicholls for furniture and John Bramah as engine maker (PRO ADM 67/255, 80/110 and 111).
82 PRO ADM 67/254.
83 PRO ADM 67/254, 80/98 and 112.
84 Tate Gallery N 00483; Tate Gallery, Turner 1775–1851, London 1974, no.152.
85 The extensions necessitated the acquisition from Greenwich Hospital of some ground from Viscount Hood's garden on the west side of the site (PRO ADM 67/254 and 80/111). By this time, Alexander was

reporting to a reformed Building Committee which included Lieutenant-General John Barclay and two new Commissioners, Sir Andrew Snape Hamond, retired Comptroller of the Navy, and Admiral Bentinck (PRO ADM 80/98, 111 and 112; DNB).
86 PRO ADM 67/254, 80/98 and 112.
87 PRO ADM 80/112; BL, Parliamentary Papers, 1816 (521), XIX, 55, 'Paper Relating to the Royal Naval Asylum at Greenwich', 25 June 1816.
88 Parliamentary Papers, 1816, op. cit.
89 PRO WORK 31/342, east wing plan, 1863; Building Design Partnership, survey drawing, L7844/(0-)D48, 1992.
90 PRO WORK 31/328.
91 PRO ADM 67/256.
92 Illustrated London News, 19 February 1848, 99; PRO ADM 195/47, Photograph Album, 31–2; NMM Board of Trustees Minutes, I, 27 January 1936.
93 PRO ADM 65/110 and 80/111; PRO WORK 31/328, 340, 342, 344, 375. The southern staircases were removed in the later nineteenth century, though their wells survive at basement level. The central staircases came out in the 1930s.
94 PRO WORK 17/185, photographs.
95 Naval Chronicles, XVIII, 1807, 199.
96 Newell, op. cit., 110–11.
97 PRO WORK 31/348; Illustrated London News, 19 February 1848, 98.
98 Seaborne, op. cit., 136–42; Markus, op. cit., 44–61; D. Upton, 'Lancasterian Schools, Republican Citizenship, and the Spatial Imagination in Early Nineteenth-Century America', Journal of the Society of Architectural Historians, LV/3, 1996, 238–51.
99 PRO ADM 67/254. A huge classroom at the Royal Military Asylum was illustrated by Rowlandson for W. H. Pyne and W. Combe, The Microcosm of London, 3 vols, London 1808–11. It shows hundreds of boys sitting in rows, and others in semicircles reciting to monitors, as Lancaster prescribed.
100 Newell, op. cit., 111.
101 PRO ADM 67/254 and 80/112.
102 S. Wilderspin, On the Importance of Educating the Infant Children of the Poor, London 1823.
103 PRO WORK 31/255; PRO ADM 67/70; NMM MCK/1, Naval Asylum Papers, December 1826.
104 PRO WORK 31/328, plan; Illustrated London News, 19 February 1848, 99; Turner, op. cit., 39; NMM MCK/1, Naval Asylum Papers, December 1826.
105 PRO ADM 80/112; Illustrated London News, 19 February 1848, 100.
106 PRO WORK 31/328; PRO ADM 80/111 and 67/16.
107 PRO ADM 80/111.
108 PRO ADM 80/98.
109 PRO WORK 31/257, 348, 607, 609. Internal rustication survived in the former arcade in the west wing in 1997.

110 PRO ADM 80/112.
111 PRO ADM 79/76; PRO WORK 31/255 and 406, plans.
112 G. Richardson, New Vitruvius Britannicus, II, London 1808, pls 39–42.
113 H. Richardson, ed., The English Hospital 1660–1948, Swindon 1998, 78–9.
114 Seaborne, op. cit., pls 103–4.
115 Sixty years later the arrangement of a new school as a centre block with arcaded links to outer blocks was echoed by Charles Barry junior in his New Buildings for Dulwich College, 1866–70.
116 Gentleman's Magazine, XXVI/2, August 1846, 211.
117 PRO ADM 169/652.
118 NMM CLA/1/B.
119 BL, Parliamentary Papers, 1816, op. cit.
120 PRO ADM 169/652; Report of the Commissioners Appointed to Inquire into Greenwich Hospital, 1860, xciv.
121 BL, 47 Geo III cap.52.
122 PRO ADM 67/254.
123 Ibid.
124 PRO ADM 67/254 and 80/111–12. John and Henry Lee were the bricklayers, Thomas and George Marshall the masons.
125 GLHL, 'Plan of Royal Naval Asylum Hospital (for 600) with Offices for 1000 Children', 1809.
126 PRO ADM 67/254 and 80/112.
127 PRO ADM 80/98.
128 GLHL, 1809, op. cit.; PRO ADM 80/98.
129 PRO ADM 67/255.
130 The Asylum paid John Hanson for 'fine wrought iron for a winding staircase' in 1809 (PRO ADM 80/111).
131 PRO ADM 67/70; GLHL, 'Plan for Dividing the Late Infirmary of the Naval Asylum into Apartments', H. H. Seward, 1821.
132 ADM 67/70.
133 GLHL, 1821, op. cit.
134 PRO ADM 67/70–71; PRO CRES 25/26 and 28; GLHL, 'General Plan of the Infirmary at the Naval Asylum', undated; PRO WORK 32/254.
135 PRO WORK 16/129.
136 PRO ADM 65/110; GLHL, drainage plan, 1857; Ordnance Survey, 1867.
137 EH, copy of Greenwich Hospital Plan, 1884.
138 PRO ADM 67/16; BL, 6 Geo. IV, cap.26; PRO ADM 67/70; Newell, op. cit., 135–7.
139 Turner, op. cit., 41.
140 Turner, op. cit., 43–4; NMM MCK/1, Naval Asylum Papers, March 1828.
141 PRO ADM 65/107.
142 PRO ADM 67/73.
143 M. Vale, The Gentleman's Recreations, Cambridge 1977, 122.
144 Rodger, op. cit., 53. Some have argued that an ability to swim was not desirable since it merely prolonged the agony of life, delaying the inevitable end, for a sailor who may have lost his ship hundreds of

miles from land. It may be noted, however, that the shipwrecked Lemuel Gulliver, fortified by half a pint of brandy, reached the shore of Lilliput by swimming as Fortune directed him, 'pushed forward by wind and tide' (J. Swift, *Gulliver's Travels* (1726), London 1985, 55).

145 PRO WORK 16/129; PRO ADM 80/113–14.

146 PRO WORK 31/349.

147 GLHL, cutting in GH School File, 'Revolt in the Greenwich Asylum', 1840.

148 *Report of the Commissioners*, 1860, op. cit., xxxvi; Turner, op. cit., 44–7; Newell, op. cit., 169–73.

149 C. Lloyd, *A History of the Royal Hospital School*, Holbrook 1962 [unpaginated]; *Illustrated London News*, 19 February 1848, 97.

150 Newell, op. cit., 173; Turner, op. cit., 56–8.

151 Turner, op. cit., 60.

152 *Illustrated London News*, 19 August 1843, 117; Newell, op. cit., 171.

153 R. Ford, *Gatherings from Spain*, 1846, London 1906, 239.

154 The last vessel was built for the school by Messrs R. H. Green and Silley Weir (Turner, op. cit., 26–7, 51–4; PRO ADM 76/22).

155 *DNB*.

156 PRO ADM 80/113; Turner, op. cit., 68–9.

157 PRO ADM 65/110.

158 *Report of the Commissioners*, 1860, op. cit., xxxvi–lxxxv; Newell, op. cit., 179–81.

159 PRO ADM 169/843, N. McLeod, typescript history of Greenwich Hospital School, 1945; GLHL, Regulations for the Admission of Boys to the Royal Hospital School at Greenwich, 1861; PRO ADM 76/22, P. C. Hardwick's Report, 30 November 1860.

160 The contractor was a Mr Smith, probably George Smith and Company of Westminster, who carried out the work for £21,255 (PRO ADM 76/22 and 65/110; PRO WORK 31/327).

161 PRO ADM 76/22; PRO WORK 31/329–40.

162 The fireproof flooring derived from the Fox and Barrett system, the patent of which had expired in 1859. Thick layers of concrete are supported on iron joists and girders, all between lath and plaster ceilings and timber floorboards (PRO WORK 31/609 and 341; B. L. Hurst, 'Concrete and the Structural Use of Cements in England before 1890', *Proceedings of the Institution of Civil Engineers: Historic Concrete*, August–November 1996, 286; information kindly supplied by Ian Fisher of the Building Design Partnership.

163 PRO ADM 76/22; GLHL, cutting in GH School File, 'The Nautical School at Greenwich', August 1863.

164 *The Builder*, XXI, 1863, 581; PRO WORK 31/342–7.

165 PRO ADM 169/843.

166 Ibid.

167 PRO ADM 169/4, Report of the Committee Appointed to Inquire into the Present Condition, Cost, and Utility of Greenwich Hospital School, 15 June 1870.

168 Ibid.

169 *Illustrated London News*, 19 February 1848, 98; PRO ADM 79/42.

170 PRO ADM 76/22; Ordnance Survey, 1867.

171 House of Commons, *Reports from Commissioners*, XVI, 1867–8, 463.

172 Seaborne, op. cit., 270.

173 M. Hunter and R. Thorne, *Change at King's Cross*, London 1990, 26–7.

174 *Post Office Directory*, 1872.

175 PRO WORK 31/379–97; PRO ADM 195/47.

176 PRO ADM 169/515.

177 PRO ADM 169/843.

178 *The Builder*, XXXIII, 1875, 896.

179 PRO WORK 31/327; Turner, op. cit., 75.

180 PRO ADM 169/843 and 76/22; Newell, op. cit., 181–3; Turner, op. cit., 75–6.

181 Turner, op. cit., 87.

182 Turner, op. cit., 126–30; Newell, op. cit., 208–10.

183 PRO ADM 169/652; G. Callender, 'The National Maritime Museum, Greenwich', *Museums Journal*, XXXVI/2, May 1937, 45–56. For a full story of the establishment of the National Maritime Museum, see K. Littlewood and B. Butler, *Of Ships and Stars*, London and New Brunswick 1998.

184 PRO WORK 14/2380.

185 *Daily Telegraph*, 9 June 1927.

186 PRO WORK 17/139.

187 Littlewood and Butler, op. cit., 52.

188 PRO ADM 169/652.

189 Littlewood and Butler, op. cit., 60.

190 PRO ADM 169/631; PRO WORK 14/2381.

191 PRO ADM 169/667; PRO WORK 17/139.

192 BL, 24–5 Geo. v, cap.43.

193 *Hansard*, House of Lords, 18 July 1937, 692, quoted in Littlewood and Butler, op. cit., 72.

194 *Whitaker's Almanack*, London 1933–7.

195 PRO WORK 17/142; NMM, Caird Library Report, typescript by G. Charles, 1996.

196 The building contractors were Messrs Thomas and Edge Ltd, of Woolwich, tendering at £16,202 (NMM Board of Trustees Minutes, I, 18 February 1935; PRO WORK 17/185).

197 Littlewood and Butler, op. cit.

198 PRO WORK 17/246.

199 PRO WORK 17/185.

200 NMM Board of Trustees Minutes, I, 1934–8; PRO WORK 17/185; NMM, Photographs, negatives 558, 560, 809–12, 1503–8, 1513, 1693, 1923–4; G. Callender,

op. cit.; G. Callender, 'The National Maritime Museum', *Mariner's Mirror*, XXIII, 1937, 255–76; *Illustrated London News*, 1 May 1937, 734–5; NMM, Caird Library Report, op. cit.; Littlewood and Butler, op. cit.

201 As members of the Royal Fine Arts Commission both men had already had occasion to comment on the plans for the museum (PRO WORK 17/185; NMM, Caird Library Report, op. cit.; Littlewood and Butler, op. cit.).

202 NMM, Board of Trustees Minutes, I, 27 January 1936; NMM MSS 5, Callender Correspondence, letter to Reid Dick, 18 February 1936.

203 NMM, Board of Trustees Minutes, I, 29 June 1936; NMM MSS 5, Callender Correspondence, letters to Stanhope, 31 January and 12 February 1936; PRO WORK 17/142–3.

204 PRO WORK 17/143.

205 NMM, Caird Library Report, op. cit.; Littlewood and Butler, op. cit., 77. The bronze bust survives in Caird's daughter's family.

206 Supplied by Messrs Walter W. Jenkins and Company Ltd of Torquay (PRO WORK 17/143).

207 Callender, *Mariner's Mirror*, op. cit.; NMM, Caird Library Report, op. cit., 18.

208 De Normann, as quoted in NMM, Caird Library Report, op. cit.

209 Littlewood and Butler, op. cit.; NMM, Caird Library Report, op. cit.

210 PRO WORK 14/2381; NMM, Board of Trustees Minutes, I, 11 October 1937; NMM MS NOT/11, R. Lowen, 'A Review for the Period 1937–1966', 1966; NMM Photographs, negatives 2893–4.

211 NMM, Board of Trustees Minutes, I, 10 October 1938; PRO WORK 17/187.

212 PRO WORK 17/246.

213 *A Concise Guide to the National Maritime Museum, Greenwich*, London 1954; 'East Wing of the National Maritime Museum', *Trident*, July 1951; NMM MS NOT/11, R. Lowen, op. cit.

214 Littlewood and Butler, op. cit.

215 NMM MS NOT/11, R. Lowen, op. cit.; PRO WORK 17/370.

216 B. Greenhill, 'The Last Fifteen Years at the National Maritime Museum', *Museums Journal*, LXXXII/4, March 1983, 213–16.

217 *The Independent*, 12 November 1991; *Building Design*, 17 April 1992, 1.

218 *Building Design*, 16 February 1996, 1.

219 J. Glancey, 'The ship of things to come', *The Guardian*, 31 May 1999; see also D. Stonham and J. Green, 'The Neptune Hall Decant', *Maritime Heritage*, I/1, December 1996, 42–5; NMM leaflet, *A New Era*, 1998; *Building Design*, 23 April 1999, 14–19; NMM, *Souvenir Guide*, London 1999.

1 The Wards and the Numbers of Beds in the Hospital

The names of wards and the number of beds were subject to change during the life of the Hospital. Some names remained the same, others changed according to commemorative requirements or to political circumstances. The changing of Ormonde to Orford, for example, followed the impeachment of James Butler, 2nd Duke of Ormonde, as a Jacobite in 1715. The ward in the King Charles Building, which was named after him, was retitled Orford after the more politically acceptable Edward Russell, Earl of Orford, who had been first Lord of the Admiralty. This was a particularly economical substitution of only two letters, a significant consideration in view of the fact that all chests and stools were painted with ward names as well as the inscriptions over the ward doors.[1]

No attempt has been made here to chart the individual changes at the Hospital precisely. The names given at three dates are listed: as proposed around 1701 and as existing in 1793 and 1864.

1a The Wards Proposed c.1701

From an undated drawing by Nicholas Hawksmoor, BAL E5/2.

KING CHARLES

East wing: Neptune, Royal Prince, Royal Charles, Rupert, Gloucester, Cambridge, Chester, Happy Return, Montague, Monk, Restoration, Crown

West wing: Osprey, Grafton, Sandwich, Somers

Total: 304

PRINCESS ANNE

East wing: Mayflower, Hanson, Rose, Basle, Foresight, Resolution, Hope, Victory, Revenge, Barfleur

West wing: Princess Anne, St George, Constant Warwick, Royal Princess, Assurance, Bonaventure, Assistance, Reserve, Dreadnought, Expedition, London, Defiance

Total: 460

KING WILLIAM

Nassau, Crown, Royal William, Sovereign, Torbay, Exeter, La Hogue, Boyne

Total: 640

QUEEN MARY

Britannia, Queen, Mary, Phoenix, Nonsuch, Advice, Relieve, Coronation

Total: 640

Overall total: 2044 (men, women and children, excluding officers and staff)

1b The Wards and the Number of Beds in the Hospital in 1793

From J. Cooke and J. Maule, *A Concise Description of the Royal Hospital for Seamen at Greenwich*, 1793.

KING CHARLES

		Floors			
		Grd	1st	2nd	3rd
Monk	west	11			
Prince	west	12			
Restoration	east	8			
Orford[2]	east	14			
Coronation[3]	west		43		
Success	west		11		
Neptune	east		12		
London	east		12		
Royal Charles	east		37		
Royal Escape and Greyhound	east			18	
Soldado	east			12	
North Crown	east			35	
South Crown	east			26	
Palliser	south				50

Total number of beds: 301

KING WILLIAM

	Floors			
	Grd	1st	2nd	3rd
Boyne	48			
Nassau	59			
Association and Kent Hall		62		
Royal William			55	
Sandwich Hall		21		
Ramillies			50	
Barfleur			58	
Union			46	
Marlborough				56
Namur				50
Britannia				46

Total number of beds: 551

QUEEN ANNE

		Floors			
		Grd	1st	2nd	3rd
Jennings	west	16			
Wager	west	16			
Edinburgh	west	19			
Le Barrington	west	19			
Augusta	east	13			
Hawke	east	14			
Weasel	east	14			
Windsor Castle	east	16			
Royal George	west		40		
Vanguard	west		23		
Victory	west		23		
West Norris	east		17		
Prince of Orange	east		17		
Princess of Orange	east		15		
East Norris	east		15		
Louisa Hall	west			10	
Torrington	west			26	
Cumberland	west			24	
Royal Oak	west			23	
Shrewsbury	west			17	
Princess Amelia	east			15	
Caroline	east			15	
Hamilton	east			15	
Princess Mary	east			15	

Total number of beds: 437

QUEEN MARY

	Floors				
	Grd	1st	2nd	3rd	4th
Sandwich	20				
Hardy	24				
Council	30				
Rodney	74				
Royal Charlotte		211			
Prince of Wales		82			
Anson			76		
Duke			134		
Townsend			82		
Queen				210	
King				82	

	Floors				
	Grd	1st	2nd	3rd	4th
New Ward[4]					24
Duke of York					43

Total number of beds: 1092

Overall total: 2381

Plus 140 nurses (the widows of seamen, under the age of forty-five at the time of admission); 150 boys (the sons of seamen); and the Establishment as below.

1c   *The Wards and the Numbers of Beds in the Hospital in* 1864

House of Lords Accounts and Papers, XXIII, 1864, 160–61.

KING CHARLES

East wing

	Present no.	No. before reduction
Restoration	8	8
Royal Charles	27	27
London	11	11
Neptune	11	11
North Crown	–	38
Saumarez	–	24
Sandwich	14	14
Hardy	11	11

West wing

Coronation	–	38 (Helpless Ward)
Nelson	–	24 (Helpless Ward)
Melville	52	52
Lord Hood	27	47
Prince	32	56
Monk	28	52
Keats	–	19
Association	–	19
Palliser	–	36
Total:	**221**	**487**

KING WILLIAM

Boyne	37	37 (Helpless Ward)
Nassau	43	43 (Helpless Ward)
Adelaide	36	38
Royal William	39	39
Ramillies	40	43
Barfleur	45	52
Marlborough	55	55
Namur	50	50
Total:	**345**	**357**

QUEEN ANNE

East wing

Windsor Castle	13	13
Augusta	13	13
Howe	13	13
Hawke	13	13

	Present no.	No. before reduction
Prince of Orange	9	17
Princess of Orange	14	15
East Norris	15	15
Duncan	14	15
Princess Amelia	8	15
Princess Caroline	14	15
Princess Mary	–	15
Hamilton	14	15

West wing

Wager	16	16
Anson	16	16
Barrington	19	19
Edinburgh	19	19
Victory	17	17
Vanguard	16	17
Royal George	22	22
St Vincent	22	22
Royal Oak	17	19
Torrington	20	33
Cumberland	18	31
Shrewsbury	17	19
Total	**359**	**424**

QUEEN MARY

Rodney	51	51
Council	36	36
Royal Charlotte	100	200
Prince of Wales	40	82
Jennings	33	65
Duke	64	128
Townsend	38	78
Queen	64	128
Exmouth	36	72
Clarence	–	96
King William	36	72
Duke of York	–	34
Total:	**498**	**1042**
Overall total:	**1423**	**2310**

NOTES

1 ADM 68/692. A similarly minimalist approach to name changing for political reasons occurred more recently with the renaming of Lubetkin's postwar Lenin Court, Finsbury, as Bevin Court.
2 Originally named Ormonde.
3 A new ward, Lord Hood, was fitted up next to Coronation Ward between 1793 and 1803.
4 Named Duke of Clarence by 1803.

2 *Establishment of the Hospital*

From J. Cooke and J. Maule, *A Description of the Royal Hospital for Seamen at Greenwich*, 1797.

Master and Governor	Surgeon
Lieutenant Governor	Clerk of the Cheque
Four Captains	Surveyor
Eight Lieutenants	Clerk of Works
Treasurer and Receiver General	Dispenser
Secretary	Three Matrons
Auditor	Schoolmaster
Two Chaplains	Organist
Physician	Butler
Steward	Several Clerks and Under Officers

(The Governor and Treasurer were appointed by Royal Patent; the rest of the officers by the Board of the Admiralty, except the Surveyor and Clerk of Works, appointed by the General Court of Commissioners, and the Schoolmaster appointed by the Board of Directors.)

3 *Admission, Diet, Clothes etc.*

From J. Cooke and J. Maule, *A Description of the Royal Hospital for Seamen at Greenwich*, 1797; see also C. M. Dawson, *The Story of Greenwich: Palace, Hospital, College*, 1977; P. van der Merwe, *'A Refuge for All': Greenwich Hospital, 1694–1994*, 1994.

ADMISSION

Prospective pensioners applied at the Admiralty office at least ten days before the date of examination (the first Thursdays in January, April, July and October). If service in the Navy was confirmed by the Admiralty, those who were 'found to be proper objects' were minuted to be sent to the hospital as vacancies occurred. Admissions were fortnightly. Upon arrival, pensioners were shaved, bathed and clothed and their old clothes, if unfit or lousy, were destroyed.

DIET

16 oz loaf of bread and 2 quarts of beer per day
1 lb mutton – Sunday and Tuesday
1 lb beef – Monday, Thursday and Saturday
Pease soup (half-pint), cheese and butter – Wednesday and Friday

CLOTHES ('in the space of two years')

Blue suit of clothes – uniform coat, sleeved waistcoat and breeches
Cocked hat
Three pairs of blue yarn hose
Three pairs of buckled shoes
Four shirts
Also neckcloths, nightcaps and bedding, changed when worn out; greatcoats for the old and infirm and watch-coats for those on guard

POCKET MONEY (per week)

Boatswains	3s 6d
Mates	2s 6d
Private men	1s

An indefinite number of out-pensioners, appointed as above, were paid £7 per year in quarterly instalments.

4 Surveyors and Clerks of Works of the Hospital

From H. M. Colvin, *A Biographical Dictionary of British Architects 1600–1840*, 1995.

The distinction between Surveyor and Clerk of Works became blurred in 1821 when the posts were combined, but Kay and Hardwick continued to be regarded as Surveyors and addressed as such. They were assisted by Inspectors of Works.

SURVEYORS

Sir Christopher Wren	1696–1716
Sir John Vanbrugh	1716–26
Colen Campbell	1726–9
Thomas Ripley	1729–58
James Stuart	1758–88
Sir Robert Taylor	Feb–Sept 1788
John Yenn	1788–1821
Henry Hake Seward	1821–3
Joseph Kay	1823–47
Philip Hardwick	1848–61

CLERKS OF THE WORKS

John Scarborough	May–Nov 1696
Henry Symmonds	1696–8
Nicholas Hawksmoor	1698–1735
John James	1718–46
William Robinson	1746–75
Robert Mylne	1775–82
William Newton	1782–90
George Knight	1790–1810
Henry Hake Seward	1810–23

5 Complement of the Hospital

Principally from the *Report of the Commissioners Appointed to Inquire into Greenwich Hospital*, 1860, x.

1705	100	1799	2410
1706	200	1803	2447
1707	300	1806	2460
1709	350	1813	2510
1728	450	1814	2710
1731	900	(the maximum, subsequently reduced	
1738	1000	to 2642, including 290 in the	
1751	1300	Infirmary)	
1755	1550	1860	1518
1763	1720	1864	1423
1764	1783	1865	450
1770	2000	1867	380
1782	2356	1869	31 (at time of closure: 26)
1793	2381		

6 The Building Phases and Completion Dates of the Principal Buildings at Greenwich: Summary

THE QUEEN'S HOUSE

Phase 1, 1617–19: two separate buildings – basement and ground-floor north building; south building with ground floor only

Phase 2, 1629–30: platform and arch of linking, central bridge

Phase 3, 1632–8: first floor, north and south sides and central bridge; terrace and steps; interior decoration

Phase 4, 1661–3: east and west Bridge Rooms; interior re-organisation

Phase 5, 1708–13: installation of sash windows, ground floor; creation of room under central Bridge Room following removal of road (1697–9); cutting back and remaking of steps to form horseshoe shape

ROYAL HOSPITAL

See also J. H. V. Davies, 'The Dating of the Buildings of the Royal Hospital at Greenwich', *Archaeological Journal*, CXIII, 1956, 126–36.

Phases: 1696–1710; 1712–21; 1725–33; 1735–51; 1769–89; 1811–35
All foundations of the four principal buildings: 1696–1701

KING CHARLES BUILDING

East block (wing of proposed royal palace): 1664–72; remodelled 1696–1701, with work on the south front 1706 and on the staircases 1704 and 1707
West (base) block: 1696–9, with interior work until 1704; north-west pavilion rebuilt 1712–15, interior completed 1718; turret on pavilion removed 1733; south-west pavilion rebuilt 1769–74; base block rebuilt 1812–15

QUEEN ANNE BUILDING

West block, without pavilions, incorporating the undercroft of the earlier palace: exterior, brick front, 1699–1704; stone west front 1725–6; interior floored 1703, completed 1731 (although one ward occupied from 1713)
East (base) block, without pavilions: exterior, stone east front, 1699–1705; interior floored 1703, completed 1731
North pavilions: exterior 1716–20; interior 1725–7, completed 1730
South pavilions: exterior 1725–31; interior 1735–42, completed 1748
Temporary Chapel between east and west blocks: built 1707, demolished 1751

KING WILLIAM BUILDING

North (Hall) block: exterior 1698–1701; dome 1704; interior 1707; decorative painting of Painted Hall 1708–12 and 1718–25
South block: exterior 1698–1704, with later work 1713; interior 1708, with later work on the south-west stair 1719–21; completed 1728
West block: exterior 1701–8; interior 1708, with later work on the upper dormitories 1714; completed 1728
West colonnade 1698–1707, roofed 1714–17; steps from courtyard to colonnade 1780; Nelson pediment carving 1812
Steps between King William and Queen Mary 1713–14
Basement corridors: King William to Queen Mary 1741; King William to King Charles 1772

QUEEN MARY BUILDING

North (Chapel) block: exterior 1735–9; dome 1742; interior 1746–51; refitted after fire 1779–89

South block: exterior 1735–9; interior 1743, with later work on the south-west stair 1749 and minor works until 1751

East block: exterior 1735–9; interior 1743, with minor works until 1751; pediment removed 1777

East colonnade 1738–41; steps from courtyard to colonnade 1835

DREADNOUGHT HOSPITAL

Built as Greenwich Hospital Infirmary 1764–8; detached wing to the west added 1808–10; main building partly rebuilt after a fire and west side raised by one storey 1811–13; extensive alterations began with courtyard block, built 1835; east side raised one storey 1836; further works until 1845; taken over by Seamen's Hospital Society 1870; west wing partly raised for a chapel and sanitary towers added to east and west 1884–5; wards enlarged by removal of partition walls 1907–14; courtyard block extended (to the south) and north and south ends of west wing raised 1931–3; new out-patients' department added to west side 1946; sanitary tower and southern part of courtyard block demolished 1998

DEVONPORT NURSES' HOME

Phase 1, 1925–9; phase 2, incorporating the School Infirmary, 1933–4

OLD GREENWICH HOSPITAL SCHOOL, KING WILLIAM WALK

Built by Greenwich Hospital as a schoolroom and dormitories 1783–4; converted into Infirmary for Greenwich Royal Hospital Schools 1821; north pavilion demolished and remainder incorporated into Devonport Nurses' Home 1933–4

NATIONAL MARITIME MUSEUM (excluding the Queen's House)

Colonnades and east and west wings to form the Royal Naval Asylum residential school 1807–11; taken over by Greenwich Hospital 1821; extended with L-plan classroom and dormitory wing to west 1861–2; gymnasium added between west wings 1872–3 (demolished 1996–7 and replaced by Neptune Court 1998–9); dining hall wing added to west 1876; all converted to be National Maritime Museum 1933–7

32–40 MAZE HILL

Site of Greenwich Hospital burial ground of 1707, with officers' mausoleum of 1713–14; developed as Royal Naval Asylum Infirmary 1808–12; converted to be apartments for Greenwich Hospital's 'inferior officers' 1822; No. 40 rebuilt 1864; later divided and sold as five private houses

7   Instructions to Jacob Jordaens for Painting the Queen's House

The following is John Webb's contemporary transcript of the instructions to Jacob Jordaens, sent to Balthazar Gerbier, the agent in Brussels, which is inserted at the end of Webb's copy of Palladio's *I quattro libri dell'architettura*, Venice 1601 (Worcester College, Oxford):

Instructions for ye payntings in ye seeling of ye Queenes room with glases at Greenwich 1639

All the peeces of paynting are to bee made of the story of Cupid and Psyche, the neerest figures of such bignesse as the distance requires for ye seeling is but 19:fo:high:

The greatest peece in ye middle of the ceeling to bee of Cupid and Psyche in Heaven, and Jove setting presenting a Cupp of Nectar unto her, about them as many of the Gods as may bee without confusion as being Juno Pallas Hebe Bacchus Apollo & other Robustious Gods as Mars Hermees Neptune Pluto Vulcane and of these to choose such as ye paynter shall like best

ffor the other two square peeces in ye seeling hee is to choose such parts of ye story as will doe best over head and in shortening.

In ye lesser squares of ye ceeling because they are but narrow there may be only children like Loves flying & strewing of fflowers.

The peeces on ye sydes about ye roome must bee all of the same story of Cupid & Psyche & ye bignesse of ye neerest figures answerable to those in ye seeling.

The placing of the wyndowes in ye severall uprights show which way the lights doe come to strike on ye paintings, so as the shadowes may bee given accordingly.

All these peeces are to bee made of strong new Cloth & yt great care bee taken in ye measures for heretofore for want of yt care hath caused much trouble either in cutting or peecing them.

The English foote is putt on ye platt of ye ceeling marked A: The little foote by which ye designes were made is likewise putt on ye same platt marked B:

That ye peeces of paynting bee sent away as they are finished & not to stay untill they bee all done & yt those of ye ceeling bee furst made & yt they bee well rowled upp in Cases & so defended as they may not take salt water.

The measures sett on ye squares shows how much of ye paynting wil be seene besydes ye bredth of ye streyning frames which are hidden under ye Cornicement

That Sr Balthasar Gerbier doe bespeake these peeces as for himselfe & make the bargayne of ye prise & tyme they are to bee finished wch is desired to bee so soone as may bee so as they bee well done & studied the Queene mother hath heere a large peece sett up in her oratory at St. James wherein is 80: figures at the least and cost her 80li: Sterling shee sayth it is of ye hand of Jordains.

8 *Works at the Queen's House 1934–1935*

From English Heritage Files: the rooms are denoted by letters on the accompanying plan; the same letters are used for the ground and first floors (fig. 71).

SCHEDULE OF WORK TO BE UNDERTAKEN IMMEDIATELY [1934]

Pull down

Remove partition between room S and T on ground floor, and partition between T and passage on north.

Remove brick filling of doorways between T and U and between U and V.

Remove chimney breast at east end of U.

Remove brick filling of doorways between L and M and L and S.

Strip the two recesses at east end of north wall of U to expose the original openings, as has been done at the west end of this wall.

Remove studding on north wall of W, and modern brickwork (flue) at west corner of chimneybreast.

Remove stairs to first floor from N: floor at landing level over passage; and upper flights of stairs to first floor and attics.

Remove plaster vaulting and timber cradling from ceiling of roadway.

Remove wooden bridge across north end of east court, first-floor level.

Remove floors, including all beams, joists, etc. from rooms A, H, K and U first floor in preparation for new reinforced concrete floors.

GROUND FLOOR

Room A

Take up floor and remove decayed joists.

Clean out filling on top of brick vault.

Renew joists and floorboards, building up honeycomb sleeper walls on vault-top to carry joists.

Remove brick arch on south wall and build up new chimneybreast in brick, opening out original fireplace and making good.

Make good to brickwork of west wall.

Block door to circular stairs with brickwork, and present door to B.

Open original doorway to B and re-form east splayed jamb. Make good to segmental head.

After the reinforced concrete floor has been finished in room A first floor

Plaster west wall on brickwork.

Make good to battened surface of north wall, and to all plaster.

New ceiling.

Reinstate head of north-west window.

Make good to existing architraves.

Provide new cornice, dado rail and skirting to detail.

Treatment of door to hall to be settled later.

Room B

New floor, as for A.

Block up doorway to circular stairs in brick, and recess and fireplace above. Make good to brickwork all round, including wall by basement stairs.

Seal off basement stairs.

Open up original fireplace.

Replaster all walls with the exception of the south wall, for which instructions will be given later.

Make good to ceiling.

Remove window linings and make good to plaster jambs and head.

Doorway in north wall (see room A) will show splayed jambs and segmental head with no linings or architrave.

Circular stairs C

No work at present.

Hall D

Remove remainder of ply-wood panelling.

Continue work of stripping paint now being carried out.

Room E

New floor as for A.

Block up doorway to F in brickwork.

Make good to original fireplace opening, including relieving arch above.

Make good cornice, dado rail and skirting.

Remove picture-rail.

Treatment of door to Hall to be settled later.

Room F

Seal off basement stairs, building up in brickwork where the wall has been cut through.

Make good to partition between F and G.

Make good to floor.

Leave plasterwork etc. for further consideration.

Room G

New floor as for A.

Open up original fireplace and make good.

Reinstate lining in head of window in west wall and make good to shutters, etc.

Leave plasterwork for further consideration.

Roadway

Expose granite plinth under middle bridge on south as far as possible. Expose original windows to ground floor rooms as far as possible without removing brick vaulting.

Room L

Seal off basement stairs and make good in brickwork to north wall as high as old mezzanine floor. Fill up window to basement stairs in brick, and mezzanine fireplace. Make good to brickwork of walls where flues have been cut out.

Open out old fireplace, doorway to S and doorway to M and make good in all cases.

Make good to floor.

Remove existing casements and replace with sashes and frames similar to eighteenth-century ground-floor windows.

Make good to all plaster on walls and ceiling, window reveals, door jambs, etc. excepting the north wall, which is to be left for further consideration.

Rooms M, N, O, P, Q, R

No work at present.

Room S–T

Take out existing fireplace and open up original.

Open up doorway to L and make good to stone jamb.

Open up doorway to U and make good to brickwork.

Make good to floor.

Make good to lath and plaster of walls and ceiling.

Room U

No work at present except demolition as already specified.

Room V–W

Remove existing fireplace and open up original.

Investigate for original positions of doorways in north wall.

No further work can be done until the treatment of rooms Q and R is settled.

FIRST FLOOR

Rooms A, H, K and Loggia U

New reinforced concrete floors. See Engineer's instructions [not attached to this document].

Rooms A, B, C, D, E, and F

No work at present.

Room G

Remove ceiling and floor of attic above. Insert new joists at original level and lath and plaster.

Form partition as shown on E side. Lath and plaster.

Open up original fireplace.

Make good to plaster where necessary.

Fix new cornice, dado rail and skirting to detail, and architraves to window and door.

Door to K to show plaster jambs and head.

Room H

Build up doorway in west wall in brickwork.

Build up present doorway to L and open original doorway, making good in brick to splayed jamb and head.

Remove present chimneypiece.

Room J

Build up doorway in east wall in brickwork.

Repair stone lintel of south doorway, making good to brickwork above. Make good to mouldings of architrave in artificial stone.

Make good to floor joists and boards.

Room K

Build up doorway in south-east corner in brickwork.

Strip lath and plaster, and make good to earlier plaster face of walls.

Make good to mouldings of architraves of north and south doors in artificial stone.

Remove present chimneypiece.

Room L

Repair floor. Block present doorway to S and open up original doorway. Reform original doorway to M. Remove C.I. [cast-iron] interior from fireplace.

Make good to existing panelling, rearranging it to suit altered positions of doors, according to detail drawing.

Rooms M, N

No work at present, except making good of floors and floorboards.

Passage south of N

Form floor in place of stairs.

Open up doorway to O and make good to jambs and head.

Passage O

Repair floor.

Investigate for traces of original ceiling.

Open original doorways to N and to passage on south of N.

Form recess in west wall for false door.

Provide and fix stone architraves to doorway to N and to recess opposite, corresponding to existing architraves at south end of passage.

Rooms P, Q, R, S–T

No work at present.

Loggia U

Relay black and white paving after reinforced concrete floor is finished.

Set stone balustrade between columns to detail drawings.

Room V–W

Repair all decayed floor beams and joists.

Build up splayed brick jambs of doorway to U.

All further work here to be postponed.

Exterior

Start on repairs to roof-timbers.

Repair external stucco.

Colour a portion of the external wall where indicated with petromite as a sample.

Lower the ground in front of the north terrace to its original level, approximately 1'9″ below present level. [This sentence is crossed out].

QUEEN'S HOUSE. RECONSTRUCTION. NEW WORKS
[TO FEBRUARY 1935]

Expenditure to date: £3887

GROUND FLOOR

Room A

Ceiling plastered. All walls other than S.W. corner plastered. Square panel linings made and fixed to door from Hall. Walls under windows rendered.

Room B

Doorway to road bricked up, cupboard in south wall removed and opening bricked up. Reinforced concrete lintel cast over window, sleeper walls built, plates bedded and floor joists fixed, hearth concreted.

Hall D

Work proceeding with removal of paint from trusses and balusters of Balcony.

Room E

Walls under windows rendered, windows overhauled and sashes rehung, square panel linings fixed to doorway to Hall.

Roadway

Ceiling plastered west end and moulding run on east wall, ceiling plastered east end.

Room L

Casement frame removed from window and new box frame fixed and sashes hung. Door to roadway bricked up. New floor joists fixed where stairs have been removed.

Room M

Partition between M & N removed and new stud partition fixed. Flooring removed and decayed joists and plates removed. Window to roadway opened up and splayed jamb rebuilt.

Rooms Q & R

New reinforced concrete floor cast over both floors. Angle fireplaces and 18 inch. wall built 7 feet high.

Rooms S & T

Brickwork over door leading to orangery cut away and consolidated, including arch over. Floor joists repaired and trimmed round fireplace and new hearth arch turned.

Orangery U

Reinforced concrete floor cast. Four openings to north wall bricked up including forming splayed windows cills.

Rooms V & W

Floor joists repaired and trimmed around, fireplace and new hearth arch turned.

FIRST FLOOR

Room B

Decayed floor joists removed and new floor fixed and trimmed round fireplace and new hearth arch turned.

Room F

Mezzanine floor removed and partition between F & G removed.

Room G

Decayed timber under partition spliced and picked up with rolled steel channel. New reinforced concrete floor cast and mezzanine floor over removed.

Room K

Brickwork cut away and reinforced concrete bonding blocks built in north-west angle, including bonding brickwork between. Decayed bond timbers cut out of east and west walls and brickwork consolidated. Raking shore removed from angle.

Room M

Doorway to passage south of M removed and new doorway rebuilt in original position.

Rooms Q & R

Stud partition removed, sash and frame removed from window to roadway.

Rooms S & T

Ironwork fixed to all main floor timbers and wall under consolidated. New floor joists fixed, plaster and timber studding removed. Old doorway to L removed and new doorway built in original position.

Rooms V & W

Ironwork fixed to all main floor timbers and walls under consolidated new floor joists fixed, plaster and timber studding removed from north wall, doors and linings to R removed exposing original stone door frame.

East area

Work proceeding with the repairs to stucco and cornice.

West area

Area scaffold up to cornice level.

Roof

Temporary roof fixed over B room, lead and roof boarding removed, roof space cleaned out, decayed joists removed and timber picked up with ironwork, boarding and lead relayed and temporary roof removed. Temporary roof fixed over H room. Decayed end of main roof timber removed in south-east corner and picked up with two 10 by $3\frac{1}{2}$ inch rolled steel channels, ceiling joists picked up with hangers. Roof timber on south side, decayed end removed and picked up with 12 inch flitch plate. Wall over S room south side rebuilt.

BASEMENT, GROUND & 1ST FLOOR

Cutting away as required by engineers for heating installation and lighting.

No. of men employed:

1 Chargehand
6 Bricklayers
10 Carpenters
1 Plumber
2 Painters
3 Scaffolders
17 Labourers
4 Plasterers
44 Total.
[sd] W. McIntosh for Supt. of Works, 5th February 1935.

Bibliography

This bibliography comprises the principal published sources used in researching this book. It excludes Parliamentary Papers and Reports, fiction and unsigned periodical and newspaper articles in *The Builder*, the *Illustrated London News*, *The Times*, etc., which are acknowledged in the notes.

Abel-Smith, B., *The Hospital 1800–1948*, London 1964.

Ackermann, R., see Pyne and Combe, 1808–11.

Adams, W. H., *The French Garden*, London 1979.

Agnew, D. C. A., *Henri de Ruvigny, Earl of Galway: A Filial Memoir with a Prefaratory Life of his Father Le Marquis de Ruvigny*, Edinburgh 1864.

Airs, M., ed., *The Seventeenth Century Great House*, Conference Proceedings, Oxford 1995.

Alister, C., 'Montague House, Blackheath and "The Delicate Investigation"', *Transactions of the Greenwich and Lewisham Antiquarian Society*, VIII/6, 1977.

Allsopp, B., ed., *Inigo Jones on Palladio*, 2 vols, Newcastle-upon-Tyne 1970.

Alpers, S., and M. Baxandall, *Tiepolo and the Pictorial Intelligence*, New Haven and London 1994.

Alsop, J. D., 'Some Notes on Seventeenth Century Continental Hospitals', *British Library Journal*, VII, 1981.

Ashley, M., *The Stuarts in Love*, London 1963.

Avery, C., *Bernini: Genius of the Baroque*, London 1997.

Baillie, T., *The Case of the Royal Hospital for Seamen at Greenwich*, London 1778.

Baily, F., *An Account of the Reverend John Flamsteed*, London 1835.

[Barker, M. H.], *Greenwich Hospital: A Series of Naval Sketches Descriptive of the Life of a Man-of-War's Man. By an Old Sailor*, London 1826.

Barrow, J., *A New and Universal Dictionary of Arts and Sciences*, London 1751.

Barthes, R., *Mythologies*, Paris 1957, Eng. trans. Annette Lavers, St Albans 1973.

Beer, E. S. de, ed., *The Diary of John Evelyn*, London 1959.

Bennett, J. A., *The Mathematical Science of Christopher Wren*, Cambridge 1982.

Berto, G., and L. Puppi, *L'opera completa del Canaletto*, Milan 1981.

Bertotti Scamozzi, O., *Le fabbriche e i disegni di Andrea Palladio*, Vicenza 1796, ed. J. Quentin Hughes, London 1968.

Betts, J., *John Harrison*, Greenwich 1997.

Black, J., and J. Gregory, eds, *Culture, Politics and Society in Britain, 1660–1800*, Manchester 1991.

Blondel, J. F., *L'architecture françoise*, 4 vols, Paris 1752–3.

Blunt, A., *Philibert de l'Orme*, London 1958.

Blunt, A., *Artistic Theory in Italy 1450–1600*, Oxford 1973.

Bold, J., 'Greenwich: "The Grott & ascent by mr. Webb"', *Burlington Magazine*, CXXIX, March 1982.

Bold, J., *John Webb*, Oxford 1989.

Bold, J., with J. Reeves, *Wilton House and English Palladianism*, London 1988.

Bold, J., and E. Chaney, eds, *English Architecture Public and Private*, London and Rio Grande 1993.

Bold, J., C. Bradbeer and P. van der Merwe, *Maritime Greenwich*, London 1999.

Booth, A., see Louw, 1984.

Boswell, J., *The Life of Samuel Johnson*, 1791, 2 vols, London 1906.

Boulencourt, Le Jeune de, *Description générale de l'Hostel Royal des Invalides*, Paris 1683; trans., anon., as *A Pattern of a Well-Constituted and Well-Governed Hospital*, London 1695.

Bristow, I., 'They will look very well: Painted Floorcloths in the 18th Century', *SPAB News*, XI/2, 1990.

Bristow, I., 'Interior Paintwork', in Airs, ed., 1995.

British Council, *Inigo Jones 1573–1652*, Milan 1973.

British Museum, *An Historical Guide to the Sculptures of the Parthenon*, London 1975.

Brown, C., *Van Dyck*, Oxford 1982.

Brown, C., and H. Vlieghe, *Van Dyck 1599–1641*, New York 1999.

Brushe, J., 'Wricklemarsh and the Collections of Sir Gregory Page', *Apollo*, CXXII, November 1985.

Burdett, H. C., *Hospitals and Asylums of the World*, IV, London 1893.

Bye-laws, Rules, Orders and Directions for the Better Government of His Majesty's Royal Hospital for Seamen at Greenwich, London 1776.

Byron, R., 'Greenwich Pageant', *Week End Review*, 1 July 1933.

Cafritz, R., L. Gowing and D. Rosand, *Places of Delight: The Pastoral Landscape*, Washington 1988.

Callender, G., *The Queen's House, Greenwich: A Short History, 1617–1937*, London 1937.

Callender, G., 'The National Maritime Museum, Greenwich', *Museums Journal*, XXXVI/2, May 1937.

Callender, G., 'The National Maritime Museum', *Mariner's Mirror*, XXIII, 1937.

Campbell, C., *Vitruvius Britannicus*, 3 vols, London 1715–25.

Carlton, C., *Charles I: The Personal Monarch*, London and New York 1995.

Caus, S. de, *Les Raisons des forces mouvantes*, Paris 1624.

Chambers, D., and J. Martineau, eds, *Splendours of the Gonzaga*, London 1981.

Chaney, E., *The Evolution of the Grand Tour*, London 1998.

Chaney, E., 'Notes towards a Biography of Sir Balthazar Gerbier'; 'Philanthropy in Italy: English Observations on Italian Hospitals, 1545–1789', both in Chaney, 1998.

Charlton, J., *The Queen's House, Greenwich*, London 1976.

Cherry, B., and N. Pevsner, *The Buildings of England: London 2: South*, Harmondsworth 1983.

Chettle, G. H., *The Queen's House, Greenwich*, London 1937.

Coad, J. G., *The Royal Dockyards 1690–1850*, Aldershot 1989.

Cocke, R., *Veronese*, London 1980.

Cocke, R., and P. de Vecchi, *The Complete Paintings of Raphael*, Harmondsworth 1987.

Colonna, F., *Hypnerotomachia Poliphili*, Venice 1499; trans. by R. Dallington, *The Strife of Love in a Dreame*, London 1592, reissued with introduction by L. Gent, *Hypnerotomachia: The Strife of Love in a Dreame*, New York 1973; trans. by J. Godwin, *Hypnerotomachia Poliphili*, London 1999; French edition, J. Martin, *Le Songe de Poliphile*, Paris 1546, reprinted with introduction by G. Polizzi, Paris 1994.

Colvin, H. M., ed., *The History of the King's Works*, II, *The Middle Ages*, London 1963; III, *1485–1660* (Part I), London 1975; IV, *1485–1660* (Part II), London 1982; V, *1660–1782*, London 1976.

Colvin, H. M., *A Catalogue of Architectural Drawings of the 18th and 19th Centuries in the Library of Worcester College, Oxford*, Oxford 1964.

Colvin, H. M., *A Biographical Dictionary of British Architects 1600–1840*, revised 3rd edition, New Haven and London 1995.

Colvin, H. M., and J. Newman, eds, *Of Building: Roger North's Writings on Architecture*, Oxford 1981.

Commission for Greenwich Hospital, London 1695.

The Complete Peerage, XI, Gloucester 1982.

Cook, G. C., *From the Greenwich Hulks to Old St Pancras: A History of Tropical Disease in London*, London 1992.

Cooke, J., *A Sermon Preached at the Opening of the Chapel of the Royal Hospital for Seamen at Greenwich*, Greenwich 1789.

Cooke, J., and J. Maule, *An Historical Account of the Royal Hospital for Seamen at Greenwich*, London 1789; *A Concise Description of the Royal Hospital for Seamen at Greenwich*, London 1793 and later editions; *A Description of the Royal Hospital for Seamen at Greenwich*, London 1797 and later editions.

Cooper, N., *Houses of the Gentry 1480–1680*, New Haven and London 1999.

Copeman, A., 'Maritime Match', *Building*, 21 January 1994.

Corbin, A., *The Foul and the Fragrant*, London 1996.

Croft-Murray, E., *Decorative Painting in England 1537–1837*, 2 vols, London 1962–70.

Dacey, J., 'A Note on Canaletto's Views of Greenwich', *Burlington Magazine*, CXXIII, August 1981.

Daniels, J., *Sebastiano Ricci*, Hove 1976.

Davies, J. H. V., 'The Dating of the Buildings at the Royal Hospital at Greenwich', *Archaeological Journal*, CXIII, 1956.

Dawson, C. M., *The Story of Greenwich: Palace, Hospital, College*, London 1977.

Defoe, D., *A Tour through the Whole Island of Great Britain, 1724–6*, ed. G. D. H. Cole, London 1974.

Description de l'Hôpital Royal pour les marins, Greenwich, London 1851.

D'Hulst, R.-A., *Jacob Jordaens*, London 1982.

D'Hulst, R.-A., *Jacob Jordaens (1593–1678)*, II, *Drawings and Prints*, Antwerp 1993.

D'Hulst, R.-A., N. de Poorter and M. Vandenven, *Jacob Jordaens (1593–1678): Tableaux et tapisseries*, Antwerp 1993.

Dixon, P., *Excavations at Greenwich Palace 1970–1971*, Greenwich 1972.

Dixon Hunt, J., and E. de Jong, *The Anglo-Dutch Garden in the Age of William and Mary*, special issue of *Journal of Garden History*, VIII/2–3, 1988.

Douglas, J., *Nenia Britannica*, London 1793.

Downes, K., *English Baroque Architecture*, London 1966.

Downes, K., *Hawksmoor*, London 1979.

Downes, K., *The Architecture of Wren*, London 1982.

Downes, K., *Sir John Vanbrugh*, London 1987.

Drake, H. H., ed., *Hasted's History of Kent, Hundred of Blackheath*, London 1886.

Eiche, S., 'Prince Henry's Richmond', *Apollo*, CLXVIII, November 1998.

Elam, C., 'Greenwich Grotesquerie', *Burlington Magazine*, CXXXVII, November 1995.

Elliston Erwood, F. C., 'Roman Remains from Greenwich Park', *Transactions of the Greenwich and Lewisham Antiquarian Society*, III/2, 1925.

England, C., 'The Queen's House', *Construction*, LXXVI, 1990.

Equiano, O., *The Interesting Narrative of the Life of Olaudah Equiano or Gustavus Vassa the African*, London 1789.

Erffa, H. von, and A. Staley, *The Paintings of Benjamin West*, New Haven and London 1986.

Evans, R., *The Fabrication of Virtue: English Prison Architecture, 1750–1840*, Cambridge 1982.

Evans, R., *Translations from Drawing to Building and Other Essays*, London 1997.

Evelyn, J., see Beer, de, ed., 1959.

Everett Green, M. A., ed., *Letters of Queen Henrietta Maria, including her Private Correspondence with Charles I*, London 1857.

Exwood, M., and H. L. Lehmann, eds, *The Journal of William Schellinks' Travels in England 1661–1663*, London 1993.

Fear, H. J., 'Westcombe', *Transactions of the Greenwich and Lewisham Antiquarian Society*, VII/1, 1964.

Fermor, S., *The Raphael Tapestry Cartoons*, London 1996.

Fiennes, C., see Morris, ed., 1947.

Finaldi, G., ed., *Orazio Gentileschi at the Court of Charles I*, London 1999.

Finet, J., see Loomie, ed., 1987.

Foister, S., 'Foreigners at Court: Holbein, Van Dyck and the Painter-Stainers Company', in Howarth, ed., 1993.

Ford, R., *Gatherings from Spain*, 1846, London 1906.

Fraser, D., H. Hibbard and M. Lewine, *Essays in the History of Art Presented to Rudolf Wittkower*, London 1967.

Fraser, E., *Greenwich Royal Hospital and the Royal United Service Museum*, London 1910.

Fraser, F., *The Unruly Queen: The Life of Queen Caroline*, London 1996.

Galinou, M., and J. Hayes, *London in Paint*, London 1996.

Ganay, E. de, *André Le Nostre*, Paris 1962.

Garboli, C., and E. Baccheschi, *L'opera completa di Guido Reni*, Milan 1971.

Gent, L., ed., *Albion's Classicism: The Visual Arts in Britain, 1550–1660*, New Haven and London 1995.

Gent, L., 'The Rash Gazer: Economics of Vision in Britain, 1550–1660', in Gent, ed., 1995.

Gerson, H., and E. H. ter Kuile, *Art and Architecture in Belgium 1600–1800*, Harmondsworth 1960.

Girouard, M., *Life in the English Country House*, New Haven and London, 1978.

Girouard, M., *Robert Smythson and the Elizabethan Country House*, New Haven and London 1983.

Glancey, J., 'The ship of things to come', *The Guardian*, 31 May 1999.

Gombrich, E. H., '"That Rare Italian Master . . ." Giulio Romano, Court Architect, Painter and Impresario', in Chambers and Martineau, eds, 1981.

Gotch, J. A., *Inigo Jones*, London 1928.

Gotch, J. A., 'Inigo Jones's Principal Visit to Italy in 1614', *Journal of the Royal Institute of British Architects*, XLVI, November 1938.

Green, D., 'Planner of Royal Parks', *Country Life*, 1 March 1956.

Green, G. L., *The Royal Navy and Anglo-Jewry, 1740–1820*, London 1989.

Greenbaum, L. S., 'Measure of Civilisation: The Hospital Thought of Jacques Tenon on the Eve of the French Revolution', *Bulletin of the History of Medicine*, XLIX, 1975.

Greenhalgh, P., *Ephemeral Vistas*, Manchester 1988.

Greenhill, B., 'The Last Fifteen Years at the National Maritime Museum', *Museums Journal*, LXXXII/4, March 1983.

Greep, S., 'Two Roman Ivories from Greenwich Park, London', *Transactions of the London and Middlesex Archaeological Society*, XXXIV, 1983.

Gunnis, R., *Dictionary of British Sculptors 1660–1851*, London 1951, 2nd edition, London 1964.

Gunther, R. T., *The Architecture of Sir Roger Pratt*, Oxford 1928.

Gwynn, J., *London and Westminster Improved*, London 1766.

Hallé, J.-N., 'Air des hôpitaux de terre et de mer', *Encyclopédie méthodique médicine*, I, Paris 1787.

Hans, N., *New Trends in Education in the Eighteenth Century*, London 1966.

Harris, J., *Catalogue of the Drawings Collection of the Royal Institute of British Architects: Inigo Jones and John Webb*, Farnborough 1972.

Harris, J., 'Inigo Jones and his French Sources', *Metropolitan Museum of Art Bulletin*, XIX, 1961.

Harris, J., 'The Inigo Jones Exhibition', *Burlington Magazine*, CXV, December 1973. [letter]

Harris, J., *The Palladians*, London 1981.

Harris, J., 'Disneyland in Greenwich: The Restoration of the Queen's House', *Apollo*, CXXXII, October 1990.

Harris, J., and G. Higgott, *Inigo Jones: Complete Architectural Drawings*, New York 1989.

Harris, J., S. Orgel and R. Strong, *The King's Arcadia: Inigo Jones and the Stuart Court*, London 1973.

Harris, J., and A. A. Tait, *Catalogue of the Drawings by Inigo Jones, John Webb & Isaac de Caus at Worcester College, Oxford*, Oxford 1979.

Hart, V., *Art and Magic in the Court of the Stuarts*, London and New York 1994.

Hart, V., and P. Hicks, trans., *Sebastiano Serlio on Architecture*, I, New Haven and London 1996.

Haskell, F., 'Charles I's Collection of Pictures', in MacGregor, ed., 1989.

Haskell, F., and N. Penny, *Taste and the Antique*, New Haven and London 1982.

Hatton, E., *A New View of London*, 2 vols, London 1708.

Hawksmoor, N., *Remarks on the Founding and Carrying on the Buildings of the Royal Hospital at Greenwich*, London 1728, reprinted in *Wren Society*, VI, Oxford 1929.

Hazlitt, W., *The Plain Speaker*, 1826, ed. P. P. Howe, London n.d.

Heiberg, S., ed., *Christian IV and Europe*, Council of Europe exhibition, Denmark 1988.

Henderson, P., 'Secret Houses and Garden Lodges: The Queen's House, Greenwich, in Context', *Apollo*, CLXVI, July 1997.

Heydenreich, L. H., and W. Lotz, *Architecture in Italy 1400–1600*, Harmondsworth 1974.

Hibbert, C., ed., *Louis Simond: An American in Regency England*, London 1968.

Hichberger, J., 'Old Soldiers', in Samuel, ed., 1989.

Historic Royal Palaces Agency, *The Banqueting House*, London 1997.

Hobhouse, H., 'Philip and Philip Charles Hardwick: An Architectural Dynasty', in *Seven Victorian Architects*, London 1977.

Hobsbawm, E. J., *The Age of Empire 1875–1914*, London 1994.

Hooke, R., see Robinson and Adams, eds, 1935.

Howard, D., *Scottish Architecture from the Reformation to the Restoration 1560–1660*, Edinburgh 1995.

Howard, J., *An Account of the Principal Lazarettos in Europe*, Warrington 1789.

Howarth, D., '"Mantua Peeces": Charles I and the Gonzaga Collections', in Chambers and Martineau, eds, 1981.

Howarth, D., *Lord Arundel and his Circle*, New Haven and London 1985.

Howarth, D., 'Charles I, Sculpture and Sculptors', in MacGregor, ed., 1989.

Howarth, D., ed., *Art and Patronage in the Caroline Courts*, Cambridge 1993.

Howarth, W., *Greenwich Past and Present*, London 1886.

Howell, J., *Instructions for Forreine Travell*, London 1642, ed. E. Arber, London 1869.

Howse, D., *Greenwich Observatory*, III, *The Buildings and Instruments*, London 1975.

Howse, D., *Greenwich Time and the Discovery of the Longitude*, Oxford 1980.

Howse, D., *Greenwich Time and the Longitude*, London 1997.

Hunter, M., *Science and Society in Restoration England*, Cambridge 1981.

Hunter, M., and R. Thorne, *Change at King's Cross*, London 1990.

Hurst, B. L., 'Concrete and the Structural Use of Cements in England before 1890', *Proceedings of the Institution of Civil Engineers: Historic Concrete*, August–November 1996.

Hutchinson, L., *Memoirs of the Life of Colonel Hutchinson*, ed. J. Sutherland, London 1973.

Inwood, S., *A History of London*, London 1998.

Jacob, M. C., *The Radical Enlightenment: Pantheists, Freemasons and Republicans*, London 1981.

Jacques, D., and A. J. van der Horst, *The Gardens of William and Mary*, London 1988.

Jeffery, S., *English Baroque Architecture: The Work of John James*, PhD thesis, University of London 1986.

Jestaz, B., *L'Hôtel et l'église des Invalides*, Paris 1990.

Johnson, S., *A Dictionary of the English Language*, London 1755.

Jones, G., *Sir Francis Chantrey, R. A.: Recollections of his Life, Practice and Opinions*, London 1849.

Jones, I., see Allsopp, ed., 1970.

Keevil, J. J., *Medicine and the Navy*, II, Edinburgh and London 1958.

Kelly, A., 'A Camouflage Queen by the River: Mrs Coade at Greenwich', *Country Life*, CLXV, January 1979.

Kelly, A., *Mrs Coade's Stone*, Upton-upon-Severn 1990.

Kelsall, F., 'Liardet versus Adam', *Architectural History*, XXVII, 1984.

Kennet, W., and E. Young, *Northern Lazio: An Unknown Italy*, London 1990.

Kimbell, J., *An Account of the Legacies, Gifts, Rents, Fees etc. Appertaining to the Church and Poor of the Parish of St Alphege, Greenwich, etc.*, Greenwich 1816.

Kingsbury, P. D., *Lord Burlington's Town Architecture*, London 1995.

Knox, G., *Antonio Pellegrini 1675–1741*, Oxford 1995.

Land Use Consultants, 'Greenwich Park Historical Survey', unpublished report, London 1986.

Latham, R. C., and W. Matthews, eds, *The Diary of Samuel Pepys*, 11 vols, London 1995.

Lefaivre, L., *Leon Battista Alberti's Hypnerotomachia Poliphili*, Cambridge, Mass., and London 1997.

Levey, M., *The Later Italian Pictures in the Collection of Her Majesty the Queen*, Cambridge 1991.

Levy Peck, L., *Northampton: Patronage and Policy at the Court of James I*, London 1982.

Lewis, L., 'The Architects of the Chapel at Greenwich Hospital', *Art Bulletin*, XXIX, 1947.

Lewis, L., 'Greece and Rome at Greenwich', *Architectural Review*, CIX, 1951.

Lewis, W. S., ed., *The Yale Edition of Horace Walpole's Correspondence*, London 1973.

Lightbown, R., 'The Journey of the Bernini Bust of Charles I to England', *Connoisseur*, CLXIX, 1968.

Lightbown, R., 'Charles I and the Tradition of European Princely Collecting', in MacGregor, ed., 1989.

Lindley, D., ed., *Court Masques*, Oxford 1995.

Links, J. G., *Canaletto*, Oxford 1982.

Lipman, V., 'Greenwich: Palace, Park and Town', *Transactions of the Ancient Monuments Society*, XX, 1975.

Lippincott, K., *A Guide to the Old Royal Observatory: The Story of Time and Space*, London n.d.

Littlewood, K., and B. Butler, *Of Ships and Stars*, London and New Brunswick 1998.

Liversidge, M., and J. Farrington, eds, *Canaletto and England*, London 1993.

Lloyd, C., *Greenwich: Palace, Hospital, College*, London 1960.

Lloyd, C., *A History of the Royal Hospital School*, Holbrook 1962.

Lloyd, C., 'Naval Hospitals', in Poynter, ed., 1964.

Lloyd, C., and J. L. S. Coulter, *Medicine and the Navy*, III–IV, Edinburgh and London 1961–3.

Long, F. D., *King Edward's Hospital Fund for London: The Story of its Foundation and Achievements, 1897–1942*, London 1942.

Longhurst, R., 'Greenwich Fair', *Transactions of the Greenwich and Lewisham Antiquarian Society*, VII/4, 1970.

Loomie, A. J., ed., *Ceremonies of Charles I: The Note Books of John Finet 1628–1641*, New York 1987.

Loudon, I., ed., *Western Medicine*, Oxford 1997.

Louw, H. J., 'Some Royal and other Great Houses in England: Extracts from the Journal of Abram Booth', *Architectural History*, XXVII, 1984.

Lysons, D., *The Environs of London*, London 1796.

MacGregor, A., ed., *The Late King's Goods*, London and Oxford 1989.

MacGregor, A., 'The King's Goods and the Commonwealth Sale, Materials and Context', in MacGregor, ed., 1989.

MacGregor, N., *A Victim of Anonymity: The Master of the Saint Bartholomew Altarpiece*, London 1993.

Maddicott, H., 'The Provenance of the "Castle Howard" Version of Orazio Gentileschi's "Finding of Moses"', *Burlington Magazine*, CXL, February 1998.

Madocks, S., '"Trop de beautez decouvertes": New Light on Guido Reni's Late "Bacchus and Ariadne"', *Burlington Magazine*, CXXVI, September 1984.

Maidment, J., and W. H. Logan, eds, *Dramatists of the Restoration*, London 1875.

[Mandelslo, A. de], *Les Voyages du Sieur Albert de Mandelslo*, ed. P. Van der Aa, Amsterdam 1719.

Mansbridge, M., *John Nash: A Complete Catalogue*, London 1991.

Manson-Behr, P., *History of the School of Tropical Medicine in London*, London 1956.

Marks, S., ed., 'The Queen's House, Greenwich: The Project', *Transactions of the Association for Studies in the Conservation of Historic Buildings*, XIV, 1989.

Markus, T. A., *Buildings and Power: Freedom and Control in the Origin of Modern Building Types*, London 1993.

Martin, A. R., 'St Mary's Church, Greenwich, and its Architect', *Transactions of the Greenwich and Lewisham Antiquarian Society*, IV/1, 1936.

Martin, G., 'Rubens and Buckingham's "Fayrie Ile"', *Burlington Magazine*, CVIII, December 1966.

Martin, W. R., 'The Royal Naval College at Greenwich', *Shipping World*, November 1888.

Matthews, J., *Welcome Aboard: The Story of the Seamen's Hospital Society and the Dreadnought*, Buckingham 1992.

Mayhew, E. de N., *Sketches by Thornhill in the Victoria and Albert Museum*, London 1967.

McBride, A. G., *The History of the Dreadnought Seamen's Hospital at Greenwich*, London 1970.

Meyer, A., *Apostles in England: Sir James Thornhill and the Legacy of Raphael's Tapestry Cartoons*, New York 1996.

Mildmay, W., 'The French Journal of William Mildmay', 1730, Essex County Record Office D/DMy15M50/1302.

Millar, O., ed., *Abraham van der Doort's Catalogue of the Collections of Charles I*, Walpole Society, XXXVII, 1958–60, Oxford 1960.

Millar, O., *The Tudor, Stuart, and Early Georgian Pictures in the Collection of Her Majesty the Queen*, London 1963.

Millar, O., *The Age of Charles I*, London 1972.

Millar, O., ed., *The Inventories and Valuations of the King's Goods 1649–1651*, Walpole Society, XLIII, 1970–72, Oxford 1972.

Millar, O., *Van Dyck in England*, London 1982.

Millon, H. A., ed., *The Triumph of the Baroque: Architecture in Europe 1600–1750*, Milan 1999.

Millon, H. A., and V. M. Lampugnani, eds, *The Renaissance from Brunelleschi to Michelangelo: The Representation of Architecture*, Milan 1994.

Mills, M., *Greenwich Marsh: The 300 Years before the Dome*, London 1999.

Milne, G., 'A Tudor Landing Stage at Greenwich', *London Archaeologist*, VIII/3, 1996.

Mitchell, C., 'Benjamin West's Death of Nelson', in Fraser, Hibbard and Lewine, 1967.

M. L. T., *Réflexions sur le projet de suppression de l'Hôtel des Invalides*, Paris 1791.

Montmorency, J. E. G. de, 'Excavations in Greenwich Park', *Transactions of the Greenwich and Lewisham Antiquarian Society*, III/3, 1927.

Morris, C., ed., *The Journeys of Celia Fiennes*, London 1947.

Moxon, J., *Vignola: or the Compleat Architect*, London 1694, 4th edition.

Muraro, M., and P. Marton, *Venetian Villas*, Cologne 1986.

Musson, J., 'Greenwich: A Nation's Pride', *Country Life*, CXC, 6 June 1996.

Nairn, I., *Nairn's London*, London 1988.

National Maritime Museum, *A Concise Guide to the National Maritime Museum, Greenwich*, London 1954.

National Maritime Museum, *Concise Catalogue of Oil Paintings in the National Maritime Museum*, Woodbridge 1988.

National Maritime Museum, *Souvenir Guide*, London 1999.

National Maritime Museum, *The Queen's House: A Royal Palace by the Thames*, London n.d.

Neumayr von Ramssla, J. W., *Wahrhaftige Beschreibung der Reise*, Jena 1734.

Neve, R., *The City and Country Purchaser, and Builder's Dictionary*, London 1726, reprinted Newton Abbot 1969.

Newell, P., *Greenwich Hospital: A Royal Foundation 1692–1983*, Greenwich 1984.

Newman, J., 'The Inigo Jones Centenary', *Burlington Magazine*, CXV, August 1973.

Newman, J., 'Strayed from the Queen's House', *Architectural History*, XXVII, 1984.

Newman, J., 'Inigo Jones and the Politics of Architecture', in Sharpe and Lake, eds, 1993.

Nichols, J., *The Progresses, Processions, and Magnificent Festivities, of King James the First*, 4 vols, London 1828.

Nichols, R. H., and F. A. Wray, *The History of the Foundling Hospital*, London 1935.

Niedermeier, M., '"Strolling under Palm Trees": Gardens – Love – Sexuality', *Journal of Garden History*, XVII/3, 1997.

The Non-Such Charles, his Character, Extracted out of Divers Original Transactions, Dispatches, and the Notes of Several Public Ministers, as well at Home as Abroad, London 1651.

North, R., see Colvin and Newman, eds, 1981.

Ollard, R., 'Greenwich', *History Today*, V, November 1955.

Orgel, S., *The Illusion of Power*, Berkeley, Los Angeles and London 1975.

Orgel, S., and R. Strong, *Inigo Jones: The Theatre of the Stuart Court*, 2 vols, London 1973.

Ormond, R., *Restoration of the Queen's House*, NMM, n.d.

Oxford Archaeological Unit, 'Greenwich Royal Naval College: Historical Appraisal Report', unpublished report, Oxford 1995.

Palladio, A., *I quattro libri dell'architettura*, Venice 1601 [John Webb's copy, Worcester College, Oxford].

Palladio, A., *The Four Books of Architecture*, Venice 1570, trans. R. Tavernor and R. Schofield, Cambridge, Mass., and London 1997.

Palme, P., *Triumph of Peace*, London 1957.

Parry, G., *The Golden Age Restor'd: The Culture of the Stuart Court, 1603–42*, Manchester 1981.

A Pattern of a Well-Constituted and Well-Governed Hospital, London 1695; trans. of Boulencourt.

Pattison, P., and P. Struth, 'Greenwich Park: An Archaeological Survey', RCHME, unpublished report, 2 vols, Swindon 1994.

Paulin, T., *The Day-Star of Liberty: William Hazlitt's Radical Style*, London 1998.

Peacock, J., *The Stage Designs of Inigo Jones: The European Context*, Cambridge 1996.

Pennington, R., *A Descriptive Catalogue of the Etched Work of Wenceslaus Hollar 1607–1677*, Cambridge 1982.

Pepys, S., see Latham and Matthews, eds, 1995.

Perau, L'Abbé, *Description historique de l'Hôtel Royal des Invalides*, Paris 1756.

Pevsner, N., and E. Williamson, *The Buildings of England: Leicestershire and Rutland*, London 1984.

Phillipot, T., *Villare Cantianum: or Kent Surveyed and Illustrated*, London 1659.

Phillips, *Maritime Auction*, London, 26 January 2000.

Physick, J., *Designs for English Sculpture 1680–1860*, London 1969.

Piovene, G., *L'opera completa del Veronese*, Milan 1968.

Platter, T., see Williams, ed., 1937.

Plumridge, J. H., *Hospital Ships and Ambulance Trains*, London 1975.

Poche, F., and J.-C. Rochette, *Le Dôme des Invalides*, Paris 1995.

Powell, J. R., *Robert Blake*, London 1972.

Power, M. G., 'The Chronicles of Greenwich: An Informal Account of the History of Greenwich Hospital 1692–1986', typescript, RNC Library.

Powers, A., 'Corinthian Epics: The Architecture of Sir Edwin Cooper', *Thirties Society Journal*, II, 1982.

Poynter, F. N. L., ed., *The Evolution of Hospitals in Britain*, London 1964.

Prochaska, F. K., *Philanthropy and the Hospitals of London: The King's Fund 1897–1990*, Oxford 1992.

Pugh, P. D. G., 'The Planning of Haslar', *Journal of the Royal Naval Medical Service*, LXII, 1976.

Puppi, L., *Andrea Palladio: The Complete Works*, London 1989.

Puttfarken, T., 'Caravaggio's "Story of St Matthew": A Challenge to the Conventions of Painting', *Art History*, XXI/2, 1998.

Pyne, W. H., and W. Combe, *The Microcosm of London*, 3 vols, London 1904, reprint of R. Ackermann, *London*, 3 vols, London 1808–11.

Quarrell, W. H., and M. Mare, eds, *London in 1710: From the Travels of Zacharias Conrad von Uffenbach*, London 1934.

Razzell, E., and P. Razzell, eds, *The English Civil War: A Contemporary Account*, IV, *1648–1656*, V, *1657–1675*, London 1996.

RCHM, *An Inventory of the Historical Monuments in London*, V, *East London*, London 1930.

Recupero, J., *The Farnese Palace at Caprarola*, Florence 1990.

Regulations Established by the Lords Commissioners of the Admiralty for the Government of Greenwich Hospital, Greenwich 1853.

Report of the Commissioners Appointed to Inquire into Greenwich Hospital, London 1860.

Rhind, N., 'Joseph Kay: An Architect for Greenwich', *Journal of the Greenwich Historical Society*, 1/6, 1997.

Richardson, G., *New Vitruvius Britannicus*, II, London 1808.

Richardson, H., ed., *English Hospitals 1660–1948*, Swindon 1998.

Richardson, H. S., *Greenwich: Its History, Antiquities, Improvements and Public Buildings*, London 1834.

Robertson, R., *Observations on the Disease incident to Seamen, Retired from actual Service, by Reason of Accidents, Infirmitives, or Old Age*, IV, London 1807.

Robertson, R., *Synopsis Morborum: A Summary View of Observations on the Principal Diseases incident to Seamen or Soldiers, whether . . . in Actual Service or Retired from it . . .* , I, London 1810.

Robey, A., 'A 17th Century Water Maze at Greenwich', *Caerdroia*, XXIX, 1998.

Robinson, H. W., and W. Adams, eds, *The Diary of Robert Hooke*, London 1935.

Roche, S. von la, see Williams, ed., 1933.

Rodger, N. A. M., *The Admiralty*, Lavenham 1979.

Rodger, N. A. M., *The Wooden World*, London 1988.

Rogers, M., *William Dobson 1611–46*, London 1983.

Ronan, C. A., ed., *Greenwich Observatory: 300 Years of Astronomy*, London 1975.

Rosand, D., 'Giorgione, Venice and the Pastoral Vision', in Cafritz, Gowing and Rosand, 1988.

Rosand, D., *Painting in Sixteenth-Century Venice*, Cambridge 1997.

Rosenau, H., *Vision of the Temple*, London 1979.

Rosenberg, P., *Nicolas Poussin 1594–1665*, Paris 1994.

Roy, I., 'Greenwich and the Civil War', *Transactions of the Greenwich and Lewisham Antiquarian Society*, X/1, 1985.

Ruvigny, H. de, see Agnew, 1864.

Samuel, R., ed., *Patriotism: The Making and Unmaking of British National Identity*, III, London 1989.

Saxl, F., and R. Wittkower, *British Art and the Mediterranean*, Oxford 1948.

Schellinks, W., see Exwood and Lehmann, eds., 1993.

Schlugleit, D., 'L'Abbé de Scaglia, Jordaens et l' "Histoire de Psyche" de Greenwich-House (1639–1642)', *Revue belge d'archaeologie et d'histoire de l'art*, VII, 1937.

Schulz, J., *Venetian Painted Ceilings of the Renaissance*, Berkeley and Los Angeles 1968.

Screech, T., *Sex and the Floating World*, London 1999.

Scull, C., *The Soane Hogarths*, London 1991.

Seaborne, M., *The English School: Its Architecture and Organisation, 1370–1870*, London 1971.

Serlio, S., see Hart and Hicks, trans., 1996.

Sharpe, K., *The Personal Rule of Charles I*, New Haven and London 1992.

Sharpe, K., and P. Lake, eds, *Culture and Politics in Early Stuart England*, Stanford, Calif., 1993.

Shearman, J., *Raphael's Cartoons in the Collection of Her Majesty the Queen*, London 1972.

Shearman, J., *The Early Italian Pictures in the Collection of Her Majesty the Queen*, Cambridge 1983.

Sheldon, H., and B. Yule, 'Excavations in Greenwich Park, 1978–9', *London Archaeologist*, III, 1979.

Shepheard, P., *The Cultivated Wilderness*, Cambridge, Mass., and London 1997.

Sherwood, R., *The Court of Oliver Cromwell*, Cambridge 1989.

Shvidkovsky, D., *The Empress and the Architect: British Architecture and Gardens at the Court of Catherine the Great*, London 1996.

Skovgaard, J. A., *A King's Architecture: Christian IV and his Buildings*, London 1973.

Sloan, K., 'Thomas Weston and the Academy at Greenwich', *Transactions of the Greenwich and Lewisham Antiquarian Society*, IX/6, 1984.

Soo, L. M., *Wren's 'Tracts' on Architecture and Other Writings*, Cambridge 1998.

Sotheby's, *British Paintings 1500–1850*, London, 3 April 1996.

Spalding, R., ed., *The Diary of Bulstrode Whitelocke, 1605–1675*, Oxford 1990.

Spear, R., *The 'Divine' Guido*, New Haven and London 1997.

Spurgeon, D., *Discover Greenwich and Charlton*, London 1991.

Stainton, L., and C. White, *Drawing in England from Hilliard to Hogarth*, London 1987.

Stark, S. J., *Female Tars*, London 1998.

Starkey, D., ed., *Henry VIII: A European Court in England*, London 1991.

State of Facts Relative to Greenwich Hospital, London 1779.

Steele, R., *The Lover*, London 1715.

Stevens Curl, J., *The Art and Architecture of Freemasonry*, London 1991.

Stevenson, C., 'Robert Hooke's Bethlem', *Journal of the Society of Architectural Historians*, LV/3, 1996.

Stone, J. M., *The Underground Passages, Caverns, etc., of Greenwich and Blackheath*, London 1914.

Stow, J., *Survey of the Cities of London and Westminster*, London 1754.

Strong, R., *The English Icon*, London 1969.

Strong, R., *Van Dyck: Charles I on Horseback*, London 1972.

Strong, R., *The Renaissance Garden in England*, London 1979.

Strong, R., *Henry, Prince of Wales and England's Lost Renaissance*, London 1986.

Stonham, D., and J. Green, 'The Neptune Hall Decant', *Maritime Heritage*, I/1, December 1996.

Suitner, G., and C. T. Perina, *Palazzo Te in Mantua*, Milan 1990.

Summerson, J., *Inigo Jones*, Harmondsworth 1966.

Summerson, J., *The Life and Work of John Nash, Architect*, London 1980.

Summerson, J., *Architecture in Britain 1530–1830*, Harmondsworth 1983.

Survey of London, XI, *The Parish of Chelsea* (Part IV), *The Royal Hospital, Chelsea*, London 1927; XIII, *The Parish of St. Margaret, Westminster* (Part II), London 1930; XLIII and XLIV, *Poplar, Blackwall and the Isle of Dogs*, London 1994.

Survey of London, *County Hall*, London 1991.

Swanton, M. J., *Corpus of Pagan Anglo-Saxon Spear Types*, British Archaeological Reports British Series 7, Oxford 1974.

Sykes, S. A., 'Henrietta Maria's "House of Delight": French Influence and Iconography in the Queen's House, Greenwich', *Apollo*, CXXXIII, May 1991.

Symmes, M., ed., *Fountains Splash and Spectacle*, New York 1998.

Szépe, H. K., 'Desire in the Printed Dream of Poliphilo', *Art History*, XIX/3, 1996.

Tate Gallery, *Turner 1775–1851*, London 1974.

Tenon, J., *Journal d'observations sur les principaux hôpitaux et sur quelques prisons d'Angleterre* (1787), ed. J. Carré, Clermont-Ferrand 1992.

Thacker, C., *The History of Gardens*, London 1979.

Thompson, J. D., and G. Goldin, *The Hospital: A Social and Architectural History*, New Haven and London 1975.

Thorne, J., *Handbook to the Environs of London*, London 1876, reprinted Chichester 1983.

Thornhill, J., *An Explanation of the Painting in the Royal Hospital at Greenwich*, Greenwich c.1726/7.

Thurley, S., *The Royal Palaces of Tudor England*, New Haven and London 1993.

Turner, H. D., *The Cradle of the Navy: The Story of the Royal Hospital School at Greenwich and at Holbrook, 1694–1988*, York 1990.

Upton, D., 'Lancasterian Schools, Republican Citizenship, and the Spatial Imagination in Early Nineteenth-Century America', *Journal of the Society of Architectural Historians*, LV/3, 1996.

Vale, M., *The Gentleman's Recreations*, Cambridge 1977.

Van der Merwe, P., '*A Refuge for All': Greenwich Hospital 1694–1994*, London 1994.

Veevers, E., *Images of Love and Religion: Queen Henrietta Maria and Court Entertainments*, Cambridge 1989.

Vertue, G., *Vertue Note Books*, III, *Walpole Society*, XXII, 1933–4, Oxford 1934.

The Victoria History of the County of Kent, III, London 1932.

Vigarello, G., *Concepts of Cleanliness*, Cambridge 1988.

Vignola, G. B. da, *Regola delli cinque ordini d'architettura*, Siena 1635.

Walpole, H., see Lewis, ed., 1973.

Ward Bissell, R., *Orazio Gentileschi and the Poetic Tradition in Caravaggesque Painting*, Pennsylvania 1981.

Watkin, D., *Athenian Stuart: Pioneer of the Greek Revival*, London 1982.

Watson, B., *A Short Guide to the Chapel of St Peter and St Paul*, Greenwich 1972.

Watson, J., 'The Greenwich Conduits', *Subterranea Britannica*, IV, 1976.

Webb, M. I., *Michael Rysbrack Sculptor*, London 1954.

Webster, A. D., *Greenwich Park: Its History and Associations*, London 1902.

[West, B.], *Description of the Grand Model of Neptune giving up the Body of Nelson*, London n.d. [copy in the National Library of Scotland, Edinburgh].

Weston-Lewis, A., 'Orazio Gentileschi's Two Versions of *The Finding of Moses* Reassessed', *Apollo*, CLXV, June 1997.

Wheelock, A. K., S. J. Barnes and J. S. Held, *Anthony van Dyck*, Washington 1990.

Whinney, M., *Wren*, London 1971.

Whinney, M., and O. Millar, *English Art 1625–1714*, Oxford 1957.

Whitaker's Almanack, London 1933–7.

Whitelocke, B., see Spalding, ed., 1990.

Wilderspin, S., *On the Importance of Educating the Infant Children of the Poor*, London 1823.

Williams, C., ed., *Sophie in London 1786 being the Diary of Sophie v. la Roche*, London 1933.

Williams, C., ed., *Thomas Platter's Travels in England 1599*, London 1937.

Williams, G., *The Royal Parks of London*, London 1978.

Wilton-Ely, J., 'Wren, Hawksmoor and the Architectural Model', in Bold and Chaney, eds, 1993.

Wittkower, R., *Art and Architecture in Italy 1600–1750*, Harmondsworth 1973.

Wittkower, R., *Palladio and English Palladianism*, London 1974.

Wittkower, R., *Gian Lorenzo Bernini: The Sculptor of the Roman Baroque*, Oxford 1981.

Wölfflin, H., *Renaissance and Baroque*, London 1964.

Worboys, M., 'The Spread of Western Medicine', in Loudon, ed., 1997.

Wotton, H., *The Elements of Architecture*, London 1624, reprinted Farnborough 1969.

Wren, C., *Parentalia*, London 1750, reprinted Farnborough 1965.

Wren Society, V, Oxford 1928; VI, Oxford 1929; XI, Oxford 1934.

Yeomans, D., 'Inigo Jones's Roof Structures', *Architectural History*, XXIX, 1986.

Yeomans, D., *The Architect and the Carpenter*, London 1992.

Yexley, H., 'The Renovation of the Queen's House', typescript, NMM 1996.

Illustration Acknowledgements

The new photography for this book has been carried out princi-pally by Derek Kendall. Photographs from the National Monu-ments Record archive have also been used. These include work by Paul Barkshire (figs 47, 51, 78, 108, 120 and 267), and pho-tographs from the collection of the former Property Services Agency (figs 33, 97, 113, 122, 127, 177, 178, 191, 197, 200 and 268). The negatives for the photographs of the Marlborough House ceiling and for the photographs of images which are the copy-right of the Greenwich Local History Library, the Hertford Museum and the Warburg Institute are held by the National Mon-uments Record. All of the survey and reconstruction drawings were carried out by Andrew Donald, with the exception of those by Paul Pattison (fig. 7), Robin Evans (fig. 20) and Nancy Sut-cliffe (fig. 111).

All of the illustrations are the copyright of the National Mon-uments Record, with the exception of those which are reproduced by courtesy of: The Museum of London: 57 and 68; National Portrait Gallery, London: 148 and 149; Phillips International Fine Art Auctioneers: 151; and those which are reproduced by kind permission of the following: The Warden and Fellows of All Souls College, Oxford: 137 and 150; The Ashmolean Museum, Oxford: 55 and 56; J. Austin: 142; Bibliothèque de l'Institut de France, Paris: 19; John Bold: 3, 20, 29, 36, 65, 66, 69, 111, 115, 220 and 232; The British Architectural Library, RIBA, London: 37, 63, 75, 79, 80, 86–9, 144, 146, 163, 168, 172, 186, 229 and 230; The British Library, London: 59–61; The British Museum, London: 8, 103, 240 and 241; The Conway Library, Courtauld Institute of Art, London: 37, 54, 63, 64, 74, 76, 80, 86–9, 101, 118, 131, 133, 136, 142, 171, 240 and 241; Kerry Downes: 150; English Heritage Photographic Library: 70, 114, 277, 278, 283, 284 and 286; Thomas Ford and Partners: 77; Greenwich Local History Library: 10, 24, 28, 44, 218, 219, 224–7, 250, 260, 263, 274 and 287; Hertford Museum: 30; A. F. Kersting: 129; Lambeth Palace Library: 140; Lane Fine Art: 179; London Metropolitan Archives: 23; Benjamin Mouton: 135; Museo de Bellas Artes, Bilbao: 96; National Maritime Museum, London: 4, 5, 11, 12, 15, 25, 34, 35, 52, 104, 116, 117, 143, 152–5, 176, 188, 207, 208, 237, 269–73, 276, 300, 311 and 312; Pepys Library, Magdalene College, Cambridge: 14 and 17; The Public Record Office: 16, 22, 43, 58, 121, 128, 130, 257, 266, 292, 294, 302, 305 and 306; Pyms Gallery, London: 95; The Royal Collection © 2000, Her Majesty Queen Elizabeth II: 62, 73, 84, 91–4, 106 and 233; The Trustees of Sir John Soane's Museum: 138 and 139; St Bartholomew's Hospital Archives and Museum: 134; Stedelijk Prentenkabinet, Antwerp: 107; The Tate Gallery, London: 291; The Board of Trustees of the Victoria and Albert Museum: 233; The Warburg Institute, London: 173; The Wellcome Institute Library, London: 243 and 280; Westminster City Archives: 221; The Provost and Fellows of Worcester College, Oxford: 64, 74 and 118.

Index